PART 6: THE MACROECONOMICS OF OPEN ECONOMIES

Chapter 12 Open-Economy Macroeconomics: Basic Concepts — *A nation's economic interactions with other nations are described by its trade balance, net foreign investment, and exchange rate.*

Chapter 13 A Macroeconomic Theory of the Small Open Economy — *A long-run model of the small open economy explains the determinants of the trade balance, the real exchange rate, and other variables.*

PART 7: SHORT-RUN ECONOMIC FLUCTUATIONS

Chapter 14 Aggregate Demand and Aggregate Supply

Chapter 15 The Influence of Monetary and Fiscal Policy on Aggregate Demand

Chapter 16 The Short-Run Tradeoff between Inflation and Unemployment

The model of aggregate demand and aggregate supply explains short-run economic fluctuations, the short-run effects of monetary and fiscal policy, and the short-run linkage between real and nominal variables.

PART 8: FINAL THOUGHTS

Chapter 17 Five Debates over Macroeconomic Policy — *A capstone chapter presents both sides of five major debates over economic policy.*

Seventh Canadian Edition

PRINCIPLES OF macro ECONOMICS

N. Gregory Mankiw
HARVARD UNIVERSITY

Ronald D. Kneebone
UNIVERSITY OF CALGARY

Kenneth J. McKenzie
UNIVERSITY OF CALGARY

Principles of Macroeconomics, Seventh Canadian Edition
by N. Gregory Mankiw, Ronald D. Kneebone, and Kenneth J. McKenzie

VP, Product and Partnership Solutions:
Anne Williams

Publisher, Digital and Print Content:
Anne-Marie Taylor

Marketing Manager:
Christina Koop

Technical Reviewer:
Norman Smith

Content Development Manager:
Katherine Goodes, My Editor Inc.

Photo and Permissions Researcher:
Julie Pratt

Production Project Manager:
Jennifer Hare

Production Service:
MPS Limited

Copy Editor:
Kelli Howey

Proofreader:
MPS Limited

Indexer:
Edwin Durbin

Design Director:
Ken Phipps

Managing Designer:
Franca Amore

Cover Design:
Courtney Hellam

Cover Image:
Peter Mather/Getty Images

Compositor:
MPS Limited

Printed and bound in Canada
1 2 3 4 19 18 17 16

For more information contact Nelson Education Ltd., 1120 Birchmount Road, Toronto, Ontario, M1K 5G4. Or you can visit our Internet site at http://www.nelson.com

Library and Archives Canada Cataloguing in Publication Data

Mankiw, N. Gregory, author
Principles of macroeconomics / N. Gregory Mankiw, Harvard University, Ronald D. Kneebone, University of Calgary, Kenneth J. McKenzie, University of Calgary. — Seventh Canadian edition.

Includes bibliographical references and index.
Issued in print and electronic formats.
ISBN 978-0-17-659199-1 (paperback).—
ISBN 978-0-17-676777-8 (pdf)

1. Macroeconomics—Textbooks. 2. Macroeconomics—Canada—Textbooks. I. Kneebone, Ronald D. (Ronald David), 1955–, author II. McKenzie, Kenneth J. (Kenneth James), 1959–, author III. Title.

HB172.5.P744 2016 339
C2016-903262-0
C2016-903263-9

ISBN-13: 978-0-17-659199-1
ISBN-10: 0-17-659199-0

To Catherine, Nicholas, and Peter, my other contributions to the next generation

To our parents and Cindy, Kathleen, and Janetta—thanks for your support and patience

ABOUT THE AUTHORS

Kevin LeBlanc

N. Gregory Mankiw is Professor of Economics at Harvard University. As a student, he studied economics at Princeton University and MIT. As a teacher, he has taught macroeconomics, microeconomics, statistics, and principles of economics. He even spent one summer long ago as a sailing instructor on Long Beach Island.

Professor Mankiw is a prolific writer and a regular participant in academic and policy debates. His work has been published in scholarly journals such as the *American Economic Review*, *Journal of Political Economy*, and *Quarterly Journal of Economics*, and in more popular forums such as *The New York Times*, *The Financial Times*, *The Wall Street Journal*, and *Fortune*. He is also author of the best-selling intermediate-level textbook *Macroeconomics* (Worth Publishing). In addition to his teaching, research, and writing, Professor Mankiw has been a research associate of the National Bureau of Economic Research, an adviser to the Federal Reserve Bank of Boston and the Congressional Budget Office, and a member of the Educational Testing Service (ETS) test development committee for the advanced placement exam in economics. From 2003 to 2005, he served as Chairman of the President's Council of Economic Advisers.

Ronald D. Kneebone is Professor in the Department of Economics and the School of Public Policy at the University of Calgary. He received his Ph.D. from McMaster University. Professor Kneebone has taught courses in public finance and in macroeconomics from principles through to the Ph.D. level, and he is a two-time winner of the Faculty of Social Sciences Distinguished Teacher Award at the University of Calgary. His research interests are primarily in the areas of public-sector finances and fiscal federalism, but he has recently worked on the problems of homelessness and poverty reduction. He shared with Ken McKenzie the Douglas Purvis Memorial Prize for the best published work in Canadian public policy in 1999. Since 2008, he has been Director of Economic and Social Policy Research in The School of Public Policy at the University of Calgary.

Kenneth J. McKenzie is Professor in the Department of Economics and The School of Public Policy at the University of Calgary. He received his Ph.D. from Queen's University. Specializing in public economics with an emphasis on taxation and political economy, Professor McKenzie has published extensively in these areas. He is the winner of the 1996 Harry Johnson Prize (with University of Calgary colleague Herb Emery) for the best article in the *Canadian Journal of Economics*, a two-time winner of the Douglas Purvis Memorial Prize for a published work relating to Canadian public policy (1999 with Ron Kneebone and 2011 with Natalia Sershun), and a Faculty of Social Sciences Distinguished Researcher Award winner at the University of Calgary. Professor McKenzie has taught microeconomics and public economics from the principles to the graduate level, and has received several departmental teaching awards.

BRIEF CONTENTS

CONTENTS

© Lavinia Moldovan

CHAPTER 3

Interdependence and the Gains from Trade 46

© Lavinia Moldovan

PART 2 SUPPLY AND DEMAND: HOW MARKETS WORK

CHAPTER 4

The Market Forces of Supply and Demand 62

Lilyana Vynogradova/Shutterstock.com

PART 3 THE DATA OF MACROECONOMICS

CHAPTER 5

Measuring a Nation's Income 90

© IGphotography/iStockphoto.com

© Masterfile

Thinkstock

iStockphoto.com/Devonyu

THE CANADIAN PRESS/POOL-Fred Thornhill

PART 8 FINAL THOUGHTS

CHAPTER 17

PREFACE

As soon as we got our hands on the first U.S. edition of *Principles of Macroeconomics*, it was clear to us that "this one is different." If other first-year economics textbooks are encyclopedias, Gregory Mankiw's was, and still is, a handbook.

Between us, we have many years of experience teaching first-year economics. Like many instructors, we found it harder and harder to teach with each new edition of the thick, standard texts. It was simply impossible to cover all of the material. Of course, we could have skipped sections, features, or whole chapters, but then, apart from the sheer hassle of telling students which bits to read and not to read, and worries about the consistencies and completeness of the remaining material, we ran the risk of leaving students with the philosophy that what matters is only what's on the exam.

We do not believe that the writers of these other books set out with the intention of cramming so much material into them. It is a difficult task to put together the perfect textbook—one that all instructors would approve of and that all students would enjoy using. Therefore, to please all potential users, most of the books end up covering a wide range of topics. And so the books grow and grow.

Professor Mankiw made a fresh start in the first U.S. edition. He included all the important topics and presented them in order of importance. And in the seventh U.S. edition, he has resisted the temptation to add more and more material. We have, in adapting the text for Canadian students, taken a minimalist approach: "If it isn't broken, don't fix it!" While the book is easily recognizable as Mankiw's, we have made changes that increase its relevance to Canadian students. Some of these changes reflect important differences between the Canadian and U.S. economies. For example, the Canadian economy is much smaller and more open than the U.S. economy, and this fact is explicitly recognized in this edition. Other changes reflect important institutional differences between the two countries, including the structure of the tax system and the nature of competition policy. Finally, the Canadian edition focuses on issues and includes examples that are more familiar and relevant to a Canadian audience.

We would not have agreed to participate in the Canadian edition if we were not extremely impressed with the U.S. edition. Professor Mankiw has done an outstanding job of identifying the key concepts and principles that every first-year student should learn.

It was truly a pleasure to work with such a well-thought-out and well-written book. We have enjoyed teaching from the earlier Canadian editions and we look forward to using the seventh Canadian edition. We hope you do, too.

How the Book Is Organized

To write a brief and student-friendly book, Mankiw considered new ways to organize familiar material. What follows is a whirlwind tour of this text. This tour, we hope, will give you a sense of how the pieces fit together.

Introductory Material

Chapter 1, "Ten Principles of Economics," introduces students to the economist's view of the world. It previews some of the big ideas that recur throughout economics, such as opportunity costs, marginal decision making, the role of incentives, the gain from trade, and the efficiency of market allocations. Throughout the text an effort is made to relate the discussion back to the ten principles of economics introduced in Chapter 1. The interconnections of the material with the ten principles are clearly identified throughout the text.

Chapter 2, "Thinking Like an Economist," examines how economists approach their field of study, discussing the role of assumptions in developing a theory and introducing the concepts of an economic model. It also discusses the role of economists in making policy. The appendix to this chapter offers a brief refresher course on how graphs are used and how they can be abused.

Chapter 3, "Interdependence and the Gains from Trade," presents the theory of comparative advantage. This theory explains why individuals trade with their neighbours, as well as why nations trade with other nations. Much of economics is about how market forces coordinate many individual production and consumption decisions. As a starting point for this analysis, students see in this chapter why specialization, interdependence, and trade can benefit everyone.

The Fundamental Tools of Supply and Demand

The next chapter introduces the basic tools of supply and demand. Chapter 4, "The Market Forces of Supply and Demand," develops the supply curve, the demand curve, and the notion of market equilibrium.

More Macroeconomics

Our overall approach to teaching macroeconomics is to examine the economy in the long run (when prices are flexible) before examining the economy in the short run (when prices are sticky). We believe that this organization simplifies learning macroeconomics for several reasons. First, the classical assumption of price flexibility is more closely linked to the basic lessons of supply and demand, which students have already mastered. Second, the classical dichotomy allows the study of the long run to be broken up into several more easily digested pieces. Third, because the business cycle represents a transitory deviation from the economy's long-run growth path, studying the transitory deviations is more natural after the long-run equilibrium is understood. Fourth, the macroeconomic theory of the short run is more controversial among economists than the macroeconomic theory of the long run. For these reasons, most upper-level courses in macroeconomics now follow this long-run-before-short-run approach; our goal is to offer introductory students the same advantage.

Returning to the detailed organization, we start the coverage of macroeconomics with issues of measurement. Chapter 5, "Measuring a Nation's Income," discusses the meaning of gross domestic product and related statistics from the national income accounts. Chapter 6, "Measuring the Cost of Living," discusses the measurement and use of the consumer price index.

The next three chapters describe the behaviour of the real economy in the long run. Chapter 7, "Production and Growth," examines the determinants of the large variation in living standards over time and across countries. Chapter 8, "Saving, Investment, and the Financial System," discusses the types of financial institutions in our economy and examines their role in allocating resources. Chapter 9, "Unemployment and Its Natural Rate," considers the long-run determinants of the unemployment rate, including job search, minimum-wage laws, the market power of unions, and efficiency wages.

Having described the long-run behaviour of the real economy, the book then turns to the long-run behaviour of money and prices. Chapter 10, "The Monetary System," introduces the economist's concept of money and the role of the central bank in controlling the quantity of money. Chapter 11, "Money Growth and Inflation," develops the classical theory of inflation and discusses the costs that inflation imposes on a society.

The next two chapters present the macroeconomics of open economies, maintaining the long-run assumptions of price flexibility and full employment. Chapter 12, "Open-Economy Macroeconomics: Basic Concepts," explains the relationship among saving, investment, and the trade balance; the distinction between the nominal and real exchange rate; and the theory of purchasing-power parity. Chapter 13, "A Macroeconomic Theory of the Small Open Economy," presents a classical model of the international flow of goods and capital. The model sheds light on various issues, including the link between budget deficits and trade deficits and the macroeconomic effects of trade policies. Because instructors differ their emphasis on this material, these chapters are written so that they can be used in different ways. Some may choose to cover Chapter 12 but not Chapter 13, others may skip both chapters, and still others may choose to defer the analysis of open-economy macroeconomics until the end of their courses.

After fully developing the long-run theory of the economy in Chapters 5 through 13, the book turns to explaining short-run fluctuations around the long-run trend. This organization simplifies teaching the theory of short-run fluctuations because, at this point in the course, students have a good grounding in many basic macroeconomic concepts. Chapter 14, "Aggregate Demand and Aggregate Supply," begins with some facts about the business cycle and then introduces the model of aggregate demand and aggregate supply. Chapter 15, "The Influence of Monetary and Fiscal Policy on Aggregate Demand," explains how policymakers can use the tools at their disposal to shift the aggregate-demand curve. Chapter 16, "The Short-Run Tradeoff between Inflation and Unemployment," explains why policymakers who control aggregate demand face a tradeoff between inflation and unemployment. It examines why this tradeoff exists in the short run, why it shifts over time, and why it does not exist in the long run.

The book concludes with Chapter 17, "Five Debates over Macroeconomic Policy." This capstone chapter considers controversial issues facing policymakers: the proper degree of policy activism in response to the business cycle, the choice between rules and discretion in the conduct of monetary policy, the desirability of reaching zero inflation, the importance of reducing the government's debt, and the need for tax reform to encourage saving. For each issue, the chapter presents both sides of the debate and encourages students to make their own judgments.

walk-through

The purpose of this text is to help students learn the fundamental lessons of economics and to show how such lessons can be applied to the world in which they live. Toward that end, various learning tools recur throughout the book.

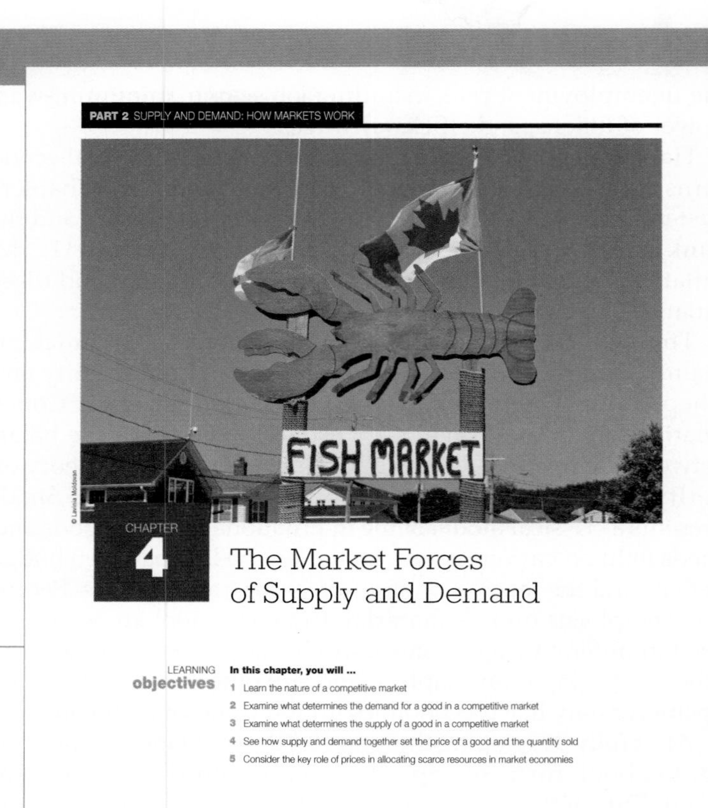

PART 2 SUPPLY AND DEMAND: HOW MARKETS WORK

© Lavinia Moldovan

CHAPTER 4

The Market Forces of Supply and Demand

LEARNING objectives

In this chapter, you will ...

1 Learn the nature of a competitive market
2 Examine what determines the demand for a good in a competitive market
3 Examine what determines the supply of a good in a competitive market
4 See how supply and demand together set the price of a good and the quantity sold
5 Consider the key role of prices in allocating scarce resources in market economies

62 NEL

Chapter Openers Well-designed chapter openers act as previews that summarize the major concepts to be learned in each chapter.

CHAPTER 8 SAVING, INVESTMENT, AND THE FINANCIAL SYSTEM **171**

virtuous circle in the late 1990s and early 2000s. This enabled federal election campaigns during the early to mid-2000s to be fought over the choices that a virtuous circle provides: tax cuts versus spending increases versus debt reduction.

By 2008, the effects of a financial crisis that significantly slowed economic growth around the world began to be felt in Canadian government budgets. After 12 straight years of surpluses, the federal budget fell into deficit in 2009. At the time, most analysts believed the economy would require only a few years before it improved enough to return the budget to surplus. Early in 2016, however, a new government announced its intention to run large deficits in the hope of stimulating economic activity. The return to balanced federal budgets now seems unlikely for some years to come.

case study **The Accumulation of Government Debt in Canada**

Budget deficits became a chronic problem in Canada only in the mid-1970s. From 1950 to 1974, the federal government ran budget surpluses as often as it ran budget deficits. These budget imbalances were generally small. In 1975, the federal government posted a large deficit and did so in every year until 1997. Between 1975 and 1997, the federal government accumulated about $550 billion in debt. In 1997, the string of deficits was broken and the federal government reported a budget surplus of $3.0 billion—the first time in 28 years that the federal government has actually paid down a portion of its debt. Between 1997 and 2008, the federal government ran a string of surpluses that enabled it to reduce its debt by over $90 billion. After 2008, however, the federal government returned to budget deficits. Between 2008 and 2014, the federal government added $166 billion to its net debt.

Figure 8.5 shows the net debt of the federal government and the combined net debts of the provinces and territories as a percentage of GDP. **Government net debt** is the difference between the value of the financial liabilities and the value of the financial assets it owns. Throughout the 1950s and until 1975, the federal government's debt-to-GDP ratio declined. Although the federal government ran budget deficits during many of these years, the deficits were small enough that the government's debt grew less rapidly than the overall economy. Because GDP is a rough measure of the government's ability to raise tax revenue, a declining debt-to-GDP ratio indicates that the economy is, in some sense, living within its means. By contrast, in the years following 1975 when the federal government's budget deficit ballooned, the debt started rising more rapidly than the overall economy. As a result, the debt-to-GDP ratio quickly increased. On three occasions—1982, 1989, and 1996—the federal government managed to halt the rise in its debt-to-GDP ratio. The first two efforts managed to halt the rise only temporarily. On both occasions, an economic slowdown caused government spending to increase and tax revenues to fall so that debt began to accumulate again. The effort initiated in 1996 proved more successful, and the federal government actually managed to reduce its debt-to-GDP ratio from its high of 73 percent in 1996 to 32 percent in 2009. Unfortunately, as a result of an economic slowdown that began in 2007, the federal budget returned to deficit in 2009. This pushed the federal debt-to-GDP ratio up to 37 percent by 2010 (from 32 percent in 2009). By 2014, the debt-to-GDP ratio had stabilized at 36 percent. In 2016, the federal government announced its intention to introduce significantly larger deficits than planned previously. Most analysts believe that despite this, so long as at least modest economic growth can be maintained, the debt-to-GDP ratio is not likely to rise significantly beyond what it was in 2014.

government net debt the difference between the value of government financial liabilities and financial assets

NEL

Case Studies Economic theory is useful and interesting only if it can be applied to understanding actual events and policies. Updated or replaced with more current Canadian examples, the numerous case studies apply the theory that has just been developed.

Figures and Tables Colourful and eye-catching visuals are used to make important economic points and to clarify Canadian and other key economic concepts. They have also proved to be valuable and memorable teaching aids.

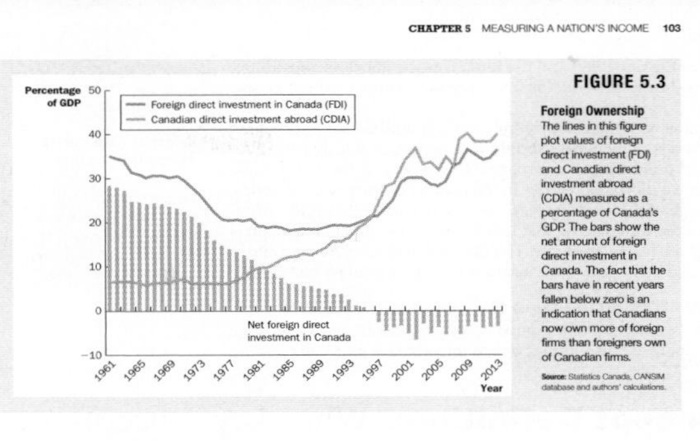
CHAPTER 5 MEASURING A NATION'S INCOME 103

FIGURE 5.3

Foreign Ownership
The lines in this figure plot values of foreign direct investment (FDI) and Canadian direct investment abroad (CDIA) measured as a percentage of Canada's GDP. The bars show the net amount of foreign direct investment in Canada. The fact that the bars have in recent years fallen below zero is an indication that Canadians now own more of foreign firms than foreigners own of Canadian firms.

Source: Statistics Canada, CANSIM database and authors' calculations.

CHAPTER 1 TEN PRINCIPLES OF ECONOMICS 15

TABLE 1.1

Ten Principles of Economics

How People Make Decisions
#1: People face tradeoffs.
#2: The cost of something is what you give up to get it.
#3: Rational people think at the margin.
#4: People respond to incentives.

How People Interact
#5: Trade can make everyone better off.
#6: Markets are usually a good way to organize economic activity.
#7: Governments can sometimes improve market outcomes.

How the Economy as a Whole Works
#8: A country's standard of living depends on its ability to produce goods and services.
#9: Prices rise when the government prints too much money.
#10: Society faces a short-run tradeoff between inflation and unemployment.

"In the News" Features One benefit that students gain from studying economics is a new perspective and greater understanding about news from Canada and around the world. To highlight this benefit, excerpts from many Canadian news articles, including opinion columns written by prominent economists, show how basic economic theory can be applied.

8 PART 1 INTRODUCTION

IN THE **news** Even Criminals Respond to Incentives

Principle #4, people respond to incentives, is at the core of the study of economics. As the following article explains, this principle applies to all sorts of activities, even of the criminal kind.

Risk, Reward and the Economics of the Criminal Mind

By Todd Hirsch

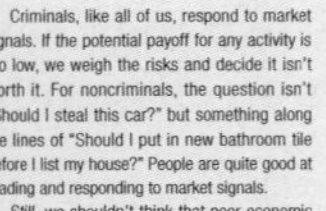

Last week's *Economist* magazine carried a headline reading, "The Curious Case of the Fall in Crime." It seems that all around the industrialized world—including Canada—all kinds of criminal activity are on the decline. Contrary to the belief that evil thugs lurk around every corner, we are actually safer than we have been in decades. In today's underground economy, identity theft makes better economic sense than stealing a flat-screen television.

The magazine's editorial offers only guesses as to why crime rates are falling. Aging demographics may play a role, along with better theft-prevention technologies. Stiffer punishment and "get tough on crime" policies might make for good political posturing, but they seem to have little impact: Crime rates are falling in countries where sentencing has become tougher as well as where it has been loosened.

The Economist failed to mention the most obvious reason for the change: economic incentives. Thieves are simply doing what most of us do every day: They are responding to market signals.

This is particularly true of property crimes such as residential break-and-enter, car theft and armed robbery. The possible payoff for stealing from a home is dwindling. What is there worth taking? Electronics are increasingly less valuable—a computer or a television in the 1980s would have been worth thousands of dollars on the street; now they would fetch a few hundred bucks. Why buy a stolen iPod dock out of the back of some guy's truck when you can get a new one for less than $100?

Car theft is down dramatically, too. According to Statistics Canada, car theft in Ontario plunged to 141 per 100,000 people last year, down from 443 in 1998. Better technology, car alarm systems and anti-theft devices have deterred most would-be thieves. And lower-priced cars without car alarms probably are not worth stealing anyway. The bad guys aren't less bad, they're just good economists.

Muggings and purse snatchings are increasingly less common as well. But let's not overthink the reasons why fewer thieves are snatching purses. It has nothing to do with the culprit's age or job situation. Whether there was a father present in the thief's childhood or whether he or she played violent video games are irrelevant. The reason is that there's just not much of value inside purses or wallets anymore. Cash has been largely replaced by debit and credit cards, and as long as the PIN is secure, the thief gets away with nothing more than plastic cards and chewing gum. Cellphones are more costly, but stolen ones are difficult to wipe and resell.

Criminals, like all of us, respond to market signals. If the potential payoff for any activity is too low, we weigh the risks and decide it isn't worth it. For noncriminals, the question isn't "Should I steal this car?" but something along the lines of "Should I put in new bathroom tile before I list my house?" People are quite good at reading and responding to market signals.

Still, we shouldn't think that poor economic incentives are making crime go away. Crime is simply morphing. Traditional crime statistics tend to focus on activities such as robbery, property theft and murder. Fewer long-term trend statistics are available for crimes that are doubtless increasing, such as identity theft and cyber-crime. Not only are they potentially more lucrative, they are global in scope and much more difficult to track.

Thieves are also getting smarter, using technology for evil deeds. Internet scams abound, and bank-card skimming and credit-card fraud is a serious problem. Banks have had to fight back with their own technology and it has been costly.

Economic incentives play a huge role motivating us in almost everything we do. Certain actions are no doubt spurred by altruism and generosity, such as helping our neighbour shovel snow or donating to charity (although we still want the tax receipt). Weighing the financial incentives against the potential risks is the basis of our economy. Criminals may not know they're doing it, but they're just responding to market signals—and doing a good job of it.

Source: "Risk, Reward and the Economics of the Criminal Mind," by Todd Hirsch, August 1, 2013, *The Globe and Mail*. Reproduced by permission of the author.

FYI The Employment Rate

How does one evaluate the health of an economy? There are many answers to this question, but a simple and reasonably comprehensive measure of success is the employment ratio. The employment ratio measures the fraction of those of working age (aged 15–64 years) who have found employment and so are able to support themselves or their families. It also provides insight into whether the community is able to fund social programs, a quality health care system, effective policing and courts, and more without unduly high tax rates. In short, a high employment ratio is a good indicator of a successful economy along many dimensions.

Alberta has typically had the highest employment rate amongst Canadian provinces. The employment rate in Alberta peaked at 80 percent in 2008. In that year, then, 80 percent of those aged 15–64 years in Alberta were employed.

Figure 9.4 shows the employment rate for Saskatchewan, Ontario, and Newfoundland and Labrador from 1976 to 2014. At the beginning of this period, Saskatchewan and Ontario had virtually the same employment rates but over time the rates have diverged. Whereas in Saskatchewan the employment rate has increased more or less steadily from 66 percent to 77 percent, in Ontario the employment rate has grown much less quickly and in 2014 was noticeably below that in Saskatchewan. But the biggest story is Newfoundland and Labrador. Starting from a woefully low level in 1976, when fewer than half of the working-age population were employed, the economy of Newfoundland and Labrador has undergone a remarkable transformation. In 2014, 65 percent of working-aged people had found employment, a level not far below the Canadian average of 72 percent. This transformation of the Newfoundland and Labrador economy has taken place just in the period since 1996; a period that corresponds to the development of off-shore oil fields and which has occurred despite the collapse of the cod fishery in 1992.

FIGURE 9.4

The Employment Rate in Three Provinces since 1976
This figure shows the percentage of the working-age population that is employed in Saskatchewan, Ontario, and Newfoundland and Labrador. It shows that since 1976 the employment rate has grown steadily in Saskatchewan, less quickly in Ontario, and, since 1996, remarkably quickly in Newfoundland and Labrador.

Source: Statistics Canada, CANSIM database and authors' calculations.

"FYI" Features These features provide additional material "for your information." Some of them offer a glimpse into the history of economic thought. Others clarify technical issues. Still others discuss supplementary topics that instructors might choose either to discuss or skip in their lectures.

interest rate. As long as the Canadian and the foreign assets are close substitutes, the difference in interest rates provides an arbitrage opportunity for either borrowers or savers.

The logic by which the real interest rates in Canada should adjust to equal the real interest rate in the rest of the world should remind you of our discussion of the law of one price and purchasing-power parity. This is because the concepts are closely related. Just as we discussed earlier in the context of the prices of goods, people taking advantage of arbitrage opportunities will ensure that price differentials disappear. The only difference is that here the price we are talking about is the price of borrowing: the real interest rate. The theory that the real interest rate in Canada should equal that in the rest of the world is known as **interest rate parity**.

interest rate parity a theory of interest rate determination whereby the real interest rate on comparable financial assets should be the same in all economies with full access to world financial markets

12-4c Limitations to Interest Rate Parity

Just as there are limitations to purchasing-power parity explaining how exchange rates are determined, there are also limitations to interest rate parity explaining

Key Concept Definitions When key concepts are introduced in the chapter, they are presented in **bold** typeface. In addition, their definitions are placed in the margin and in the Glossary at the back of the book. This treatment helps students learn and review the material.

QUICK **Quiz** *Why is a country better off not isolating itself from all other countries? • Why do we have markets and, according to economists, what roles should government play in them?*

QuickQuizzes After each major section, students are offered a quick quiz to check their comprehension of what they have just learned. If students cannot readily answer these quizzes, they should stop and reread the material before continuing.

Chapter Summaries Each chapter ends with a brief summary that reminds students of the most important lessons that they have just learned. Later in their study, it offers an efficient way to review for exams.

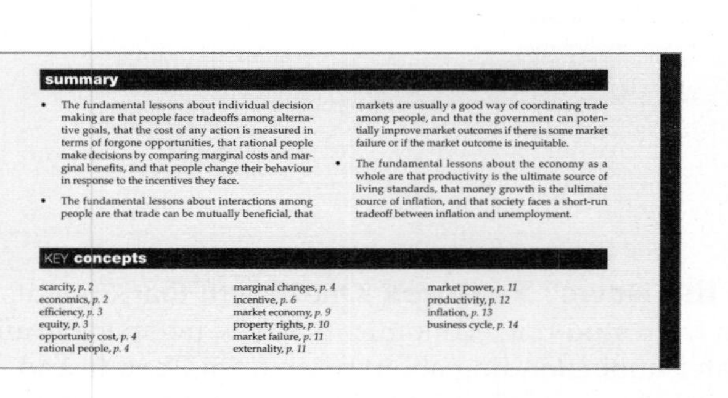
summary

- The fundamental lessons about individual decision making are that people face tradeoffs among alternative goals, that the cost of any action is measured in terms of forgone opportunities, that rational people make decisions by comparing marginal costs and marginal benefits, and that people change their behaviour in response to the incentives they face.
- The fundamental lessons about interactions among people are that trade can be mutually beneficial, that markets are usually a good way of coordinating trade among people, and that the government can potentially improve market outcomes if there is some market failure or if the market outcome is inequitable.
- The fundamental lessons about the economy as a whole are that productivity is the ultimate source of living standards, that money growth is the ultimate source of inflation, and that society faces a short-run tradeoff between inflation and unemployment.

KEY **concepts**

scarcity, *p. 2*
economics, *p. 2*
efficiency, *p. 3*
equity, *p. 3*
opportunity cost, *p. 4*
rational people, *p. 4*
marginal changes, *p. 4*
incentive, *p. 6*
market economy, *p. 9*
property rights, *p. 10*
market failure, *p. 11*
externality, *p. 11*
market power, *p. 11*
productivity, *p. 12*
inflation, *p. 13*
business cycle, *p. 14*

126 **PART 3** THE DATA OF MACROECONOMICS

QUESTIONS FOR **review**

1. Which do you think has a greater effect on the consumer price index: a 10 percent increase in the price of chicken or a 10 percent increase in the price of caviar? Why?
2. Describe the three problems that make the consumer price index an imperfect measure of the cost of living.
3. If the price of a military aircraft rises, is the consumer price index or the GDP deflator affected more? Why?
4. Over a long period of time, the price of a candy bar rose from $0.10 to $0.60. Over the same period, the consumer price index rose from 150 to 300. Adjusted for overall inflation, how much did the price of the candy bar change?
5. Explain the meaning of *nominal interest rate* and *real interest rate*. How are they related?

QUICK CHECK **multiple choice**

1. The consumer price index measures approximately the same economic phenomenon as which of the following?
   a. nominal GDP
   b. real GDP
   c. the GDP deflator
   d. the unemployment rate
2. What is the largest component in the basket of goods and services used to compute the CPI?
   a. food and beverages
   b. housing
   c. transportation
   d. apparel
3. If a Manitoba gun manufacturer raises the price of rifles it sells to the Canadian Army, which of the following will be increased by the price hikes?
   a. both the CPI and the GDP deflator
   b. neither the CPI nor the GDP deflator
   c. the CPI but not the GDP deflator
   d. the GDP deflator but not the CPI
4. Which of the following occurs because consumers can sometimes substitute cheaper goods for those that have risen in price?
   a. the CPI overstates inflation
   b. the CPI understates inflation
   c. the GDP deflator overstates inflation
   d. the GDP deflator understates inflation
5. If the consumer price index was 200 in 1980 and 300 today, then $600 in 1980 has the same purchasing power as what amount today?
   a. $400
   b. $500
   c. $700
   d. $900
6. You deposit $2000 in a savings account, and a year later you have $2100. Meanwhile, the consumer price index rises from 200 to 204. In this case, what are the nominal interest rate and the real interest rate, respectively?
   a. 1 percent; 5 percent
   b. 3 percent; 5 percent
   c. 5 percent; 1 percent
   d. 5 percent; 3 percent

PROBLEMS AND **applications**

1. Suppose that people consume only three goods, as shown in this table:

	Tennis Balls	Tennis Racquets	Gatorade
2014 price	$2	$40	$1
2014 quantity	100	10	200
2015 price	$2	$60	$2
2015 quantity	100	10	200

   a. What is the percentage change in the price of each of the three goods? What is the percentage change in the overall price level?
   b. Do tennis racquets become more or less expensive relative to Gatorade? Does the well-being of some people change relative to the well-being of others? Explain.
2. Suppose that the residents of Vegopia spend all of their income on cauliflower, broccoli, and carrots. In 2014 they buy 100 heads of cauliflower for $200, 50 bunches

NEL

List of Key Concepts A list of key concepts at the end of each chapter offers students a way to test their understanding of the new terms that have been introduced. Page references are included so that students can review terms they do not understand in the original context.

Questions for Review At the end of each chapter questions for review cover the chapter's primary lessons. Students can use these questions to check their comprehension and to prepare for exams.

Quick Check Multiple Choice New in this edition, these end-of-chapter questions provide a quick check of the student's understanding of the material in a multiple-choice format.

Problems and Applications Each chapter also contains a variety of problems and applications that ask students to apply the material they have learned. Some instructors may use these questions for homework assignments. Others may introduce them as a starting point for classroom discussion.

New in This Seventh Canadian Edition

The seventh Canadian edition of *Principles of Macroeconomics* has been carefully revised to ensure its contents are current and its examples reflect the interests and concerns of the student market. In the sixth edition, responding to reviewer requests for more emphasis on math, we added a new appendix "The Mathematics of Market Equilibrium" at the end of Chapter 4. With this new edition we have built on this foundation by including technical questions in the chapters 2 and 4 end-of-appendix assignments to raise the difficulty level. New topics discussed in this edition include the employment ratio and Statistics Canada's new definitions of the income components in national income accounting. Sections have been updated to include more analyses of the implications of the financial challenges experienced in 2008–09. Case Studies have been revised and updated to reflect current world trends. New FYI and In the News boxes address such issues as core inflation and why gold has been used as money throughout history. Examples, key figures, and graphs have been updated throughout the text. Most photos have been replaced and many new photos are added throughout the new edition. As well, the text's interior has a fresh new design.

Here is a chapter-by-chapter list of significant changes:

Chapter 1 A new FYI feature on the opportunity cost of gasoline has been provided.

Chapter 2 A new Graphing Functions section has been included in the appendix.

Chapter 4 The appendix "The Mathematics of Market Equilibrium," which guides the student through the process of solving market equilibrium for linear demand and supply curves, has been simplified using a strictly numerical approach.

Chapter 5 With this edition we adopt Statistics Canada's new categories of total income for deriving GDP and include data on the UN's Human Development Index in our case study of international differences in the quality of life.

Chapter 8 The existing case study "The Accumulation of Government Debt in Canada" has been adjusted to discuss the reversal of movements toward lower levels of government debt caused by the slowing of the Canadian economy in 2015.

Chapter 9 A new FYI feature discusses the employment rate as a measure of the health of an economy and reports on the remarkable transformation of the economy of Newfoundland and Labrador since 1996. Our discussion of frictional unemployment has been supplemented with a new Table 9.4 that reports rates of job creation and destruction in periods of recession and expansion. Finally, the existing FYI feature on the minimum wage now includes a discussion of how taking taxes into consideration affects the ranking of provinces according to which offers the highest minimum wage.

Chapter 10 A new In the News feature explains why throughout history it has made sense for societies to use gold as money. Our discussion of the tools available to the Bank of Canada to control the money supply now includes Figure 10.2, showing how the central bank's overnight rate responded to the onset of recession in 2008 and the halting recovery since that time. Finally, another new In the News feature discusses research being done at the Bank of Canada that seeks to learn lessons from the 2008–09 financial crisis and to understand how monetary policy might need to change to accommodate innovations such as Bitcoin.

Chapter 11 A new FYI feature defines, discusses, and shows data on the Bank of Canada's measure of "core CPI inflation" and how it compares to the rate of inflation measured using the total CPI. The distinction is important for understanding the Bank's monetary policy choices.

Chapter 13 In this edition we clarify our discussion of supply and demand in the market for foreign-currency exchange.

Chapter 14 Our existing Case Study on the recession of 2008–09 now includes a long quote from Bank of Canada Governor Stephen Poloz in which he emphasizes that one of the lessons to be drawn from that recession is the need for the Bank to be ever vigilant to excessive risk taking.

Chapter 15 With this edition we include in the opening paragraphs an explanation of why it is important to treat all cases of aggregate demand policy—fiscal and monetary policy in both open and closed economies—in a single chapter.

Instructor Resources

The **Nelson Education Teaching Advantage (NETA)** program delivers research-based instructor resources that promote student engagement and higher-order thinking to enable the success of Canadian students and educators. Visit Nelson Education's **Inspired Instruction** website at http://www.nelson.com/inspired/ to find out more about NETA.

The following instructor resources have been created for Mankiw, *Principles of Macroeconomics*, Seventh Canadian Edition. Access these ultimate tools for customizing lectures and presentations at www.nelson.com/instructor.

NETA Test Bank

This resource was written by Judith Street, Mount Royal University. It includes over 2800 multiple choice questions written according to NETA guidelines for effective construction and development of higher-order questions. The technical check was performed by Norm Smith, Georgian College. Also included are approximately 340 true/false and 170 short-answer questions, as well as 120 problems.

cognero® Full-Circle Assessment®

The NETA Test Bank is available in a new, cloud-based platform. **Nelson Testing Powered by Cognero®** is a secure online testing system that allows instructors to author, edit, and manage test bank content from anywhere Internet access is available. No special installations or downloads are needed, and the desktop-inspired interface, with its drop-down menus and familiar, intuitive tools, allows instructors to create and manage tests with ease. Multiple test versions can be created in an instant, and content can be imported or exported into other systems. Tests can be delivered from a learning management system, the classroom, or wherever an instructor chooses. Nelson Testing Powered by Cognero for Mankiw, *Principles of Macroeconomics*, Seventh Canadian Edition, can be accessed through www.nelson.com/instructor.

NETA PowerPoint

Microsoft® PowerPoint® lecture slides for every chapter have been created by Marc Prud'Homme, University of Ottawa. There is an average of 35–45 slides per chapter, many featuring key figures, tables, and photographs from Mankiw, *Principles of Macroeconomics*, Seventh Canadian Edition. These slides also include instructor notes of suggested classroom activities and links to videos and news articles for classroom discussion. NETA principles of clear design and engaging content have been incorporated throughout, making it simple for instructors to customize the deck for their courses.

Image Library

This resource consists of digital copies of figures, short tables, and photographs used in the book. Instructors may use these jpegs to customize the NETA PowerPoint or create their own PowerPoint presentations.

TurningPoint® Slides

TurningPoint® classroom response software has been customized for Mankiw, *Principles of Macroeconomics*, Seventh Canadian Edition. Instructors can author, deliver, show, access, and grade, all in PowerPoint, with no toggling back and forth between screens. With JoinIn instructors are no longer tied to their computers. Instead, instructors can walk about the classroom and lecture at the same time, showing slides and collecting and displaying responses with ease. Anyone who can use PowerPoint can also use JoinIn on TurningPoint.

NETA Instructor's Manual

The Instructor's Manual to accompany Mankiw, *Principles of Macroeconomics*, Seventh Canadian Edition, has been prepared by Phil Ghayad and Michel Mayer at Dawson College. This manual contains sample lesson plans, learning objectives, suggested classroom activities, and a resource integration guide to give instructors the support they need to engage their students within the classroom.

Instructor's Solutions Manual

This manual, prepared by the text authors Ron Kneebone and Ken McKenzie at University of Calgary, has been independently checked for accuracy by Norm Smith, Georgian College. It contains complete solutions to the text's QuickQuizzes, Questions for Review, Quick Check Multiple Choice questions, and Problems.

MindTap

MindTap®

Offering personalized paths of dynamic assignments and applications, **MindTap** is a digital learning solution that turns cookie-cutter into cutting-edge, apathy into engagement, and memorizers into higher-level thinkers. MindTap enables students to analyze and apply chapter concepts within relevant assignments, and allows instructors to measure skills and promote better outcomes with ease. A fully online learning solution, MindTap combines all student learning tools—readings, multimedia, activities, and assessments—into a single Learning Path that guides the student through the curriculum. Instructors personalize the experience by customizing the presentation of these learning tools to their students, even seamlessly introducing their own content into the Learning Path.

Aplia

Aplia™ is a Cengage Learning online homework system dedicated to improving learning by increasing student effort and engagement. **Aplia** makes it easy for instructors to assign frequent online homework assignments. **Aplia** provides students with prompt and detailed feedback to help them learn as they work through the questions, and features interactive tutorials to fully engage them in learning course concepts. Automatic grading and powerful assessment tools give instructors real-time reports of student progress, participation, and performance, while **Aplia**'s easy-to-use course management features let instructors flexibly administer course announcements and materials online. With **Aplia**, students will show up to class fully engaged and prepared, and instructors will have more time to do what they do best... teach.

Student Ancillaries

Study Guide

Revised by Peter Fortura, Algonquin College, and Shahram Manouchehri, MacEwan University, this Study Guide was prepared to enhance student success. Each chapter includes learning objectives, a description of the chapter's context and purpose, a chapter review, key terms and definitions, advanced critical thinking questions, and helpful hints for understanding difficult concepts. Students can develop their understanding by doing practical problems and short-answer questions and then assess theory mastery of the key concepts with the self-test, which includes true/false and multiple choice questions prepared and edited under the NETA program for effective question construction. Solutions to all problems are included in the study guide ISBN: 0-17-674541-6).

Student PowerPoint Slides

Microsoft® PowerPoint® lecture slides for every chapter average 35–45 slides per chapter, many featuring key figures, tables, and photographs from Mankiw, *Principles of Macroeconomics*, Seventh Canadian Edition. These slides will help to develop students' understanding and enhance their success.

MindTap

Stay organized and efficient with **MindTap**—a single destination with all the course material and study aids you need to succeed. Built-in apps leverage social media and the latest learning technology. For example:

- ReadSpeaker will read the text to you.
- Flashcards are pre-populated to provide you with a jump start for review—or you can create your own.
- You can highlight text and make notes in your MindTap Reader. Your notes will flow into Evernote, the electronic notebook app that you can access anywhere when it's time to study for the exam.
- Self-quizzing allows you to assess your understanding.

Visit http://www.nelson.com/student to start using **MindTap**. Enter the Online Access Code from the card included with your text. If a code card is not provided, you can purchase instant access at NELSONbrain.com.

Aplia

Founded in 2000 by economist and Stanford professor Paul Romer, **Aplia**™ is an educational technology company dedicated to improving learning by increasing student effort and engagement. Currently, **Aplia** products have been used by more than a million students at over 1300 institutions. **Aplia** offers a way for you to stay on top of your coursework with regularly scheduled homework assignments that increase your time on task and give you prompt feedback. Interactive tools and additional content are provided to further increase your engagement and understanding. See http://www.aplia.com for more information. If **Aplia** isn't bundled with your copy of Mankiw, *Principles of Macroeconomics*, Canadian seventh edition, you can purchase access separately at NELSONbrain.com. Be better prepared for class with **Aplia!**

ACKNOWLEDGMENTS

The success of each Canadian edition of *Principles of Macroeconomics* and *Principles of Microeconomics* has been due, in part, to the reviewers who helped us shape this text, edition after edition. We have benefited enormously from their advice and suggestions.

Ather H. Akbari, Saint Mary's University

Iris Au, University of Toronto

Collins Ayoo, Carleton University

Rauf Azhar, University of Guelph

Keith Baxter, Bishop's University

Ugurhan G. Berkok, Queen's University

Aurelia Best, Centennial College

Menouar Boulahfa, Dawson College

Bogdan Buduru, Concordia University

Bruce Cater, Trent University

Jyh-Yaw Joseph Chen, Kwantlen Polytechnic University

Saud Choudhry, Trent University

Nancy Churchman, Carleton University

Kevin Clinton, Bank of Canada

Daria Crisan, Mount Royal University

Weili Ding, Queen's University

Wendy Doell, University of Saskatchewan

Martin Dooley, McMaster University

Peter Dungan, University of Toronto

Byron Eastman, Laurentian University

Herb Emery, University of Calgary

Pierre Fortin, University of Quebec at Montreal

Michael Francis, Carleton University

Alexander Gainer, University of Alberta

Samuel Gamtessa, University of Regina

Pierre-Pascal Gendron, Humber College

David Gray, University of Ottawa

Michael Hare, University of Toronto

Ibrahim Hayania, Seneca College

Paul Hobson, Acadia University

Hannah Holmes, McMaster University

Ernie Jacobson, Northern Alberta Institute of Technology

Troy Joseph, Carleton University

Eric Kam, Ryerson University

Steven Lehrer, Queen's University

Colin Mang, Nipissing University

Peter McCabe, McMaster University

Chris McDonnell, Malaspina University-College

Stan Miles, Thompson Rivers University

Lavinia Moldovan, Mount Royal University

Robin Neill, University of Prince Edward Island and Carleton University

Costas Nicolau, University of Manitoba

Umut Oguzoglu, University of Manitoba

Amy Peng, Ryerson University

Julien Picault, University of British Columbia Okanagan

Stephen Rakocsy, Humber College

Ashantha Ranasinghe, University of Manitoba

Neil Roberts, Kwantlen Polytechnic University

Christos Shiamptanis, Wilfrid Laurier University

Scott Skjei, Acadia University

Gregor Smith, Queen's University

Xueda Song, York University

Kien Tran, University of Lethbridge

Mike Tucker, Fanshawe College

Maurice Tugwell, Acadia University

James Wishart, College of the Rockies

Canadianizing this book has been a team effort from the very start. We would like to acknowledge the editorial, production, and marketing teams at Nelson for their professionalism, advice, and encouragement throughout the process. Deserving special attention are publisher Amie Plourde and developmental editor Katherine Goodes for helping to ensure the timely completion of our work.

Special thanks go to Bill Scarth of McMaster University, who offered invaluable advice regarding the structure and emphasis of the Canadian editions. Dr. Scarth is an award-winning teacher and author, and to ignore his advice would have been perilous indeed. His extensive comments were instrumental in helping us formulate our approach to the Canadian editions.

Our thanks to Norm Smith, Georgian College, for the technical check to ensure the accuracy of content throughout this seventh Canadian edition and the relevant supplements.

We would also like to thank our colleagues at the University of Calgary who provided invaluable informal input and useful examples and applications. We, of course, bear full responsibility for any misinterpretations and errors.

The student and instructor ancillaries are a key component of this book and we gratefully acknowledge the work of the authors:

Peter Fortura, Algonquin College
Phil Ghayad, Dawson College
Michel Mayer, Dawson College
Eric Moon, University of Toronto
Shahram Manouchehri, MacEwan University
Marc Prud'Homme, University of Ottawa
Judith Street, Mount Royal University

Finally, we are grateful to our families for their indulgence and encouragement throughout the research and writing process. Their patience and understanding are greatly appreciated.

Ronald D. Kneebone

Kenneth J. McKenzie

August 2016

© Lavinia Moldovan

Ten Principles of Economics

LEARNING **objectives**

In this chapter, you will ...

1. Learn that economics is about the allocation of scarce resources
2. Examine some of the tradeoffs that people face
3. Learn the meaning of *opportunity cost*
4. See how to use marginal reasoning when making decisions
5. Discuss how incentives affect people's behaviour
6. Consider why trade among people or nations can be good for everyone
7. Discuss why markets are a good, but not perfect, way to allocate resources
8. Learn what determines some trends in the overall economy

The word *economy* comes from the Greek word for "one who manages a household." At first, this origin might seem peculiar. But, in fact, households and economies have much in common.

A household faces many decisions. It must decide which members of the household do which tasks and what each member gets in return: Who cooks the meals? Who does the laundry? Who gets the extra dessert at dinner? Who gets to choose what TV show to watch? In short, the household must allocate its scarce resources among its various members, taking into account each member's abilities, efforts, and desires.

Like a household, a society faces many decisions. A society must decide what jobs will be done and who will do them. It needs some people to grow food, other people to make clothing, and still others to design computer software. Once society has allocated people (as well as land, buildings, and machines) to various jobs, it must also allocate the output of goods and services that they produce. It must decide who will eat caviar and who will eat potatoes. It must decide who will drive a Ferrari and who will take the bus.

scarcity
the limited nature of society's resources

economics
the study of how society manages its scarce resources

The management of society's resources is important because resources are scarce. **Scarcity** means that society has limited resources and therefore cannot produce all the goods and services people wish to have. Just as each member of a household cannot get everything he or she wants, each individual in a society cannot attain the highest standard of living to which he or she might aspire.

Economics is the study of how society manages its scarce resources. In most societies, resources are allocated not by a single central planner but through the combined actions of millions of households and firms. Economists, therefore, study how people make decisions: how much they work, what they buy, how much they save, and how they invest their savings. Economists also study how people interact with one another. For instance, they examine how the multitude of buyers and sellers of a good together determine the price at which the good is sold and the quantity that is sold. Finally, economists analyze forces and trends that affect the economy as a whole, including the growth in average income, the fraction of the population that cannot find work, and the rate at which prices are rising.

The study of economics has many facets but it is unified by several central ideas. In this chapter, we look at ten principles of economics. Don't worry if you don't understand them all at first or if you aren't completely convinced. We explore these ideas more fully in later chapters. The ten principles are introduced here just to give you an overview of what economics is all about. Consider this chapter a "preview of coming attractions."

1-1 How People Make Decisions

There is no mystery to what an economy is. Whether we are talking about the economy of Vancouver, of Canada, or of the whole world, an economy is just a group of people interacting with one another as they go about their lives. Because the behaviour of an economy reflects the behaviour of the individuals who make up the economy, we start our study of economics with four principles of individual decision making.

1-1a Principle #1: People Face Tradeoffs

You may have heard the old saying, "There ain't no such thing as a free lunch." Grammar aside, there is much truth to this adage. To get one thing that we like, we usually have to give up another thing that we like. Making decisions requires trading off one goal against another.

Consider a student who must decide how to allocate her most valuable resource—her time. She can spend all of her time studying economics, spend all of it studying psychology, or divide it between the two fields. For every hour she studies one subject, she gives up an hour she could have used studying the other. And for every hour she spends studying, she gives up an hour that she could have spent napping, bike riding, watching TV, or working at her part-time job for some extra spending money.

Or consider parents deciding how to spend their family income. They can buy food, clothing, or a family vacation. Or they can save some of the family income for retirement or the children's college or university education. When they choose to spend an extra dollar on one of these goods, they have one less dollar to spend on some other good.

When people are grouped into societies, they face different kinds of tradeoffs. One classic tradeoff is between "guns and butter." The more society spends on national defence and security (guns) to protect its shores from foreign aggressors, the less it can spend on consumer goods (butter) to raise the standard of living at home. Also important in modern society is the tradeoff between a clean environment and a high level of income. Laws that require firms to reduce pollution raise the cost of producing goods and services. Because of the higher costs, these firms end up earning smaller profits, paying lower wages, charging higher prices, or some combination of these three. Thus, while pollution regulations give us the benefit of a cleaner environment and the improved health that comes with it, they have the cost of reducing the incomes of the regulated firms' owners, workers, and customers.

Another tradeoff society faces is between efficiency and equity. **Efficiency** means that society is getting the maximum benefits from its scarce resources. **Equity** means that the benefits of those resources are distributed fairly among society's members. In other words, efficiency refers to the size of the economic pie, and equity refers to how the pie is divided into individual slices.

efficiency
the property of society getting the most it can from its scarce resources

equity
the property of distributing economic prosperity fairly among the members of society

When government policies are designed, these two goals often conflict. Consider, for instance, policies aimed at achieving a more equal distribution of economic well-being. Some of these policies, such as the welfare system or Employment Insurance, try to help those members of society who are most in need. Others, such as the individual income tax, ask the financially successful to contribute more than others to support the government. Although these policies have the benefit of achieving greater equity, they have a cost in terms of reduced efficiency. When the government redistributes income from the rich to the poor, it reduces the reward for working hard; as a result, people work less and produce fewer goods and services. In other words, when the government tries to cut the economic pie into more equal slices, the pie gets smaller.

Recognizing that people face tradeoffs does not by itself tell us what decisions they will or should make. A student should not abandon the study of psychology just because doing so would increase the time available for the study of economics. Society should not stop protecting the environment just because environmental regulations reduce our material standard of living. The poor should not be ignored just because helping them distorts work incentives. Nonetheless, people are likely to make good decisions only if they understand the options that they have available. Our study of economics, therefore, starts by acknowledging life's tradeoffs.

1-1b Principle #2: The Cost of Something Is What You Give Up to Get It

Because people face tradeoffs, making decisions requires comparing the costs and benefits of alternative courses of action. In many cases, however, the cost of an action is not as obvious as it might first appear.

Consider the decision whether to go to college or university. The main benefits are intellectual enrichment and a lifetime of better job opportunities. But what are the costs? To answer this question, you might be tempted to add up the money you spend on tuition, books, and room and board. Yet this total does not truly represent what you give up to spend a year in college or university.

There are two problems with the calculation. First, it includes some things that are not really costs of going to college or university. Even if you quit school, you would need a place to sleep and food to eat. Room and board are costs of going to college or university only to the extent that they are more expensive there than elsewhere. Second, this calculation ignores the largest cost of going to college or university—your time. When you spend a year listening to lectures, reading textbooks, and writing papers, you cannot spend that time working at a job. For most students, the wages given up to attend school are the largest single cost of their education.

opportunity cost
whatever must be given up to obtain some item

The **opportunity cost** of an item is what you give up to get that item. When making any decision, decision makers should be aware of the opportunity costs that accompany each possible action. In fact, they usually are. College or university-age athletes who can earn millions if they drop out of school and play professional sports are well aware that their opportunity cost of a postsecondary education is very high. It is not surprising that they often decide that the benefit of this education is not worth the cost. Remember, an opportunity cost is an opportunity lost.

1-1c Principle #3: Rational People Think at the Margin

rational people
those who systematically and purposefully do the best they can to achieve their objectives

Economists normally assume that people are rational. For the most part the assumption that people are rational serves us very well. **Rational people** systematically and purposefully do the best they can to achieve their objectives, given the opportunities they have. As you study economics, you will encounter firms that decide how many workers to hire and how much of their product to manufacture and sell to maximize profits. You will also encounter individuals who decide how much time to spend working and what goods and services to buy with the resulting income to achieve the highest possible level of satisfaction.

Rational people know that decisions in life are rarely black and white, but usually involve shades of grey. At dinnertime, the decision you face is not "Should I fast or eat like a glutton?" More likely, you will be asking yourself "Should I take that extra spoonful of mashed potatoes?" When exams roll around, your decision is not between blowing them off or studying 24 hours a day, but whether to spend an extra hour reviewing your notes instead of watching TV. Economists use the term **marginal changes** to describe small incremental adjustments to an existing plan of action. Keep in mind that "margin" means "edge," so marginal changes are adjustments around the edges of what you are doing. Rational people often make decisions by comparing *marginal benefits* and *marginal costs.*

marginal changes
small incremental adjustments to a plan of action

For example, suppose you are considering calling a friend on your cell phone. You decide that talking with her for 10 minutes would give you a benefit that you value at about $7. Your cell phone service costs you $40 per month plus $0.50 per minute for whatever calls you make. You usually talk for 100 minutes a month,

FYI The Opportunity Cost of Gasoline

The opportunity cost of an item is what you give up to get it. As discussed earlier, out of pocket monetary costs can be a misleading indicator of opportunity cost. For example, consider the opportunity cost of gasoline. The price of gasoline has increased quite significantly over the years. For example, the average price of gasoline in Ontario rose from about 56 cents per litre in 1997 to over $1.28 in 2014, with several ups and downs in between. This represents an increase of almost 130 percent over this 17-year period.

However, this is misleading. Gasoline is not something that is consumed directly, but rather is used to drive your car. It is better to think of the price of gasoline in terms of how much it costs per kilometre driven. To do this we need to take account of how the fuel efficiency of cars has changed over this period. In 1997 the fuel efficiency of the average North American car was about 8.5 kilometres per litre (KPL). By 2014 this had increased to 10.3 KPL. So it took about 17.5 percent less gasoline to drive a car in 2014 than it did in 1997.

But this is not all. In order to buy the gasoline you need money. To earn that money you need to work. A useful way to think about the opportunity cost of gasoline, or any good for that matter, is in terms of the amount of time you have to work in order to pay for it. In this regard, consider the number of minutes you need to work in order to pay for gasoline on a per-kilometre basis. Let's call this minutes worked per kilometre driven (MWPKD). The average hourly wage in Ontario in 1997 was about $15.60 per hour; in 2014 it was $24.50, an increase of 57 percent. To calculate MWPKD, take the price of gasoline and divide it by the product of the wage rate (measured in dollars per minute, so $15.60 per hour is 26 cents per minute in 1997) and average fuel economy. For 1997 this gives MWPKD $= .56/(.26 \times 8.5) = .2533$. So, in 1997, in order to pay for the gasoline required to drive a car one kilometre, an average individual in Ontario had to work .2533 minutes, or 15.2 seconds. In 2014 the MWPKD was .3043, or 18 seconds. So, the opportunity cost of gasoline in 2014 measured in terms of the number of seconds of work needed to drive one kilometre was 18 seconds compared to 15 seconds in 1997! While the price of gasoline at the pump has indeed increased significantly since 1997, fuel economy has increased as well, as have wages, keeping the opportunity cost of gasoline relatively constant. Figure 1.1 shows MWPKD for Ontario for every year from 1997 to 2014.

The above calculations are based on fleet averages for cars in North America. Of course if you drive a more fuel-efficient car, or earn a higher than average wage, you have to work less to pay for the gasoline required to drive your car. For example, the hybrid Toyota Prius gets about 21 KPL, compared to the 2014 fleet average of 10.3. If you drive a Prius you have to work just under nine seconds per kilometre driven to pay for the gasoline. On the other hand, if you drive a Ford F150 truck (9.4 KPL), you have to work almost 20 seconds.

On his blog, Ed Dolan has undertaken similar calculations for the United States. Fuel economy is the same in the two countries, as we drive basically the same vehicles. However, gasoline prices are lower in the United States (due largely to lower taxes) and average wages are higher. For 2014 Dolan calculates that, on average, it costs a little under 7 seconds of work in the United States to pay for a kilometre of driving, significantly less than the 18 seconds in Canada.

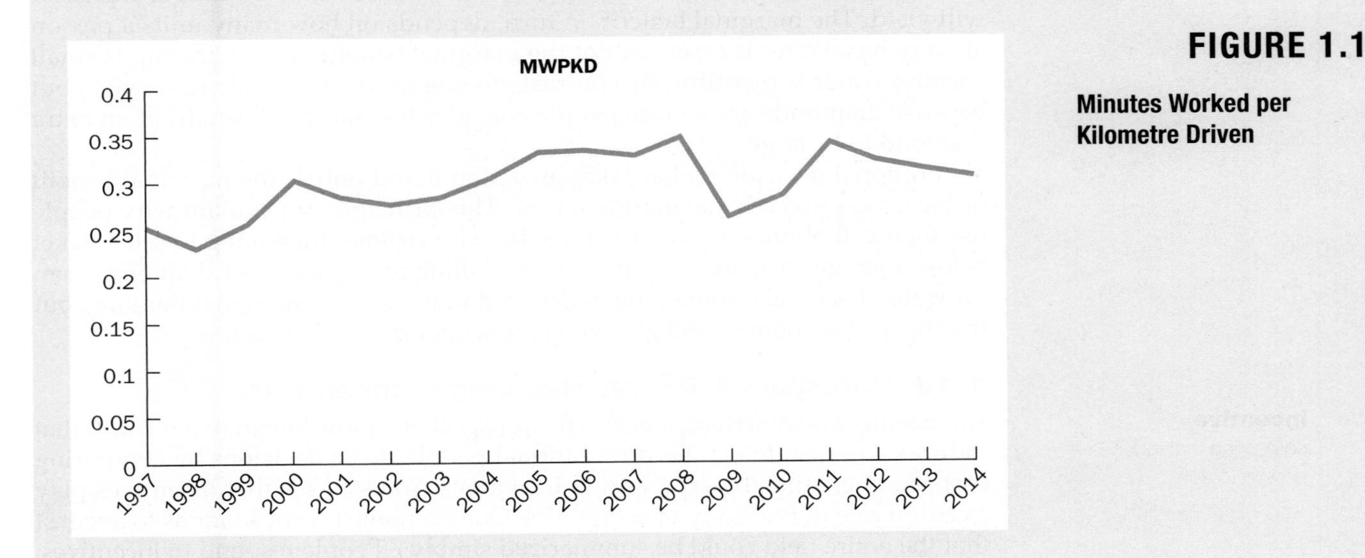

FIGURE 1.1

Minutes Worked per Kilometre Driven

so your total monthly bill is $90 ($0.50 per minute times 100 minutes, plus the $40 fixed fee). Under these circumstances, should you make the call? You might be tempted to reason as follows: "Because I pay $90 for 100 minutes of calling each month, the average minute on the phone costs me $0.90. So a 10-minute call costs $9. Because that $9 cost is greater than the $7 benefit, I am going to skip the call." That conclusion is wrong, however. Although the *average* cost of a 10-minute call is $9, the *marginal* cost—the amount your bill increases if you make the extra call—is only $5. You will make the right decision only by comparing the marginal benefit and the marginal cost. Because the marginal benefit of $7 is greater than the marginal cost of $5 (.50 × 10 = $5), you should make the call. This is a principle that people innately understand: Cell phone users with unlimited minutes (that is, minutes that are free at the margin) are often prone to make long and frivolous calls.

Thinking at the margin works for business decisions as well. Consider an airline deciding how much to charge passengers who fly standby. Suppose that flying a 200-seat plane across Canada costs the airline $100 000. In this case, the average cost of each seat is $100 000/200, which is $500. One might be tempted to conclude that the airline should never sell a ticket for less than $500. Actually, a rational airline can often find ways to raise its profits by thinking at the margin. Imagine that a plane is about to take off with 10 empty seats, and a standby passenger is waiting at the gate willing to pay $300 for a seat. Should the airline sell the ticket? Of course it should. If the plane has empty seats, the cost of adding one more passenger is tiny. Although the *average* cost of flying a passenger is $500, the *marginal* cost is merely the cost of the bag of peanuts and can of soda that the extra passenger will consume. As long as the standby passenger pays more than the marginal cost, selling him a ticket is profitable.

Marginal decision making can help explain some otherwise puzzling economic phenomena. Here is a classic question: Why is water so cheap, while diamonds are so expensive? Humans need water to survive, while diamonds are unnecessary; but, for some reason, people are willing to pay much more for a diamond than for a cup of water. The reason is that a person's willingness to pay for a good is based on the marginal benefit that an extra unit of the good will yield. The marginal benefit, in turn, depends on how many units a person already has. Water is essential but the marginal benefit of an extra cup is small because water is plentiful. By contrast, no one needs diamonds to survive, but because diamonds are so rare people consider the marginal benefit of an extra diamond to be large.

A rational decision maker takes an action if and only if the marginal benefit of the action exceeds the marginal cost. This principle can explain why people use their cell phones as much as they do, why airlines are willing to sell a ticket below average cost, and why people are willing to pay more for diamonds than for water. It can take some time to get used to the logic of marginal thinking, but the study of economics will give you ample opportunity to practise.

1-1d Principle #4: People Respond to Incentives

incentive
something that induces a person to act

An **incentive** is something (such as the prospect of a punishment or a reward) that induces a person to act. Because rational people make decisions by comparing costs and benefits, they respond to incentives. You will see that incentives play a central role in the study of economics. One economist went so far as to suggest that the entire field could be summarized simply: "People respond to incentives. The rest is commentary."

Incentives are crucial to analyzing how markets work. For example, when the price of an apple rises, people decide to eat fewer apples. At the same time, apple orchards decide to hire more workers and harvest more apples. In other words, a higher price in a market provides an incentive for buyers to consume less and an incentive for sellers to produce more. As we will see, the influence of prices on the behaviour of consumers and producers is crucial for how a market economy allocates scarce resources.

Public policymakers should never forget about incentives. Many policies change the costs or benefits that people face and, as a result, alter their behaviour. A tax on gasoline, for instance, encourages people to drive smaller, more fuel-efficient cars. That is one reason why people drive smaller cars in Europe, where gasoline taxes are high, than in Canada, where gasoline taxes are lower. A gasoline tax also encourages people to carpool, take public transportation, and live closer to where they work. If the tax were larger, more people would drive hybrid cars, and if it were large enough, they would switch to electric cars.

When policymakers fail to consider how their policies affect incentives, they often end up with unintended consequences. For example, consider public policy regarding auto safety. Today all cars have seat belts, but that was not true 50 years ago. In the 1960s, Ralph Nader's book *Unsafe at Any Speed* generated much public concern over auto safety. Parliament responded with laws requiring seat belts as standard equipment on new cars.

How does a seat belt law affect auto safety? The direct effect is obvious: When a person wears a seat belt, the probability of surviving an auto accident rises. But that's not the end of the story, because the law also affects behaviour by altering incentives. The relevant behaviour here is the speed and care with which drivers operate their cars. Driving slowly and carefully is costly because it uses the driver's time and energy. When deciding how safely to drive, rational people compare the marginal benefit from safer driving to the marginal cost. As a result, they drive more slowly and carefully when the benefit of increased safety is high. For example, when road conditions are icy, people drive more attentively and at lower speeds than they do when road conditions are clear.

Consider how a seat belt law alters a driver's cost–benefit calculation. Seat belts make accidents less costly because they reduce the likelihood of injury or death. In other words, seat belts reduce the benefits to slow and careful driving. People respond to seat belts as they would to an improvement in road conditions—by driving faster and less carefully. The result of a seat belt law, therefore, is a larger number of accidents. The decline in safe driving has a clear, adverse impact on pedestrians, who are more likely to find themselves in an accident but (unlike the drivers) don't have the benefit of added protection.

At first, this discussion of incentives and seat belts might seem like idle speculation. Yet in a classic 1975 study, economist Sam Peltzman argued that auto-safety laws have had many of these effects. According to Peltzman's evidence, these laws produce both fewer deaths per accident and more accidents. He concluded that the net result is little change in the number of driver deaths and an increase in the number of pedestrian deaths.

Peltzman's analysis of auto safety is an offbeat and controversial example of the general principle that people respond to incentives. When analyzing any policy, we must consider not only the direct effects but also the indirect effects that work through incentives. If the policy changes incentives, it will cause people to alter their behaviour.

IN THE **news**

Even Criminals Respond to Incentives

Principle #4, people respond to incentives, is at the core of the study of economics. As the following article explains, this principle applies to all sorts of activities, even of the criminal kind.

Risk, Reward and the Economics of the Criminal Mind

By Todd Hirsch

Last week's *Economist* magazine carried a headline reading, "The Curious Case of the Fall in Crime." It seems that all around the industrialized world—including Canada—all kinds of criminal activity are on the decline. Contrary to the belief that evil thugs lurk around every corner, we are actually safer than we have been in decades. In today's underground economy, identity theft makes better economic sense than stealing a flat-screen television.

The magazine's editorial offers only guesses as to why crime rates are falling. Aging demographics may play a role, along with better theft-prevention technologies. Stiffer punishment and "get tough on crime" policies might make for good political posturing, but they seem to have little impact: Crime rates are falling in countries where sentencing has become tougher as well as where it has been loosened.

The Economist failed to mention the most obvious reason for the change: economic incentives. Thieves are simply doing what most of us do every day: They are responding to market signals.

This is particularly true of property crimes such as residential break-and-enter, car theft and armed robbery. The possible payoff for stealing from a home is dwindling. What is there worth taking? Electronics are increasingly less valuable—a computer or a television in the 1980s would have been worth thousands of dollars on the street; now they would fetch a few hundred bucks. Why buy a stolen iPod dock out of the back of some guy's truck when you can get a new one for less than $100?

scyther5/Shutterstock.com

Car theft is down dramatically, too. According to Statistics Canada, car theft in Ontario plunged to 141 per 100,000 people last year, down from 443 in 1998. Better technology, car alarm systems and anti-theft devices have deterred most would-be thieves. And lower-priced cars without car alarms probably are not worth stealing anyway. The bad guys aren't less bad, they're just good economists.

Muggings and purse snatchings are increasingly less common as well. But let's not overthink the reasons why fewer thieves are snatching purses. It has nothing to do with the culprit's age or job situation. Whether there was a father present in the thief's childhood or whether he or she played violent video games are irrelevant. The reason is that there's just not much of value inside purses or wallets anymore. Cash has been largely replaced by debit and credit cards, and as long as the PIN is secure, the thief gets away with nothing more than plastic cards and chewing gum. Cellphones are more costly, but stolen ones are difficult to wipe and resell.

Criminals, like all of us, respond to market signals. If the potential payoff for any activity is too low, we weigh the risks and decide it isn't worth it. For noncriminals, the question isn't "Should I steal this car?" but something along the lines of "Should I put in new bathroom tile before I list my house?" People are quite good at reading and responding to market signals.

Still, we shouldn't think that poor economic incentives are making crime go away. Crime is simply morphing. Traditional crime statistics tend to focus on activities such as robbery, property theft and murder. Fewer long-term trend statistics are available for crimes that are doubtless increasing, such as identity theft and cyber-crime. Not only are they potentially more lucrative, they are global in scope and much more difficult to track.

Thieves are also getting smarter, using technology for evil deeds. Internet scams abound, and bank-card skimming and credit-card fraud is a serious problem. Banks have had to fight back with their own technology and it has been costly.

Economic incentives play a huge role motivating us in almost everything we do. Certain actions are no doubt spurred by altruism and generosity, such as helping our neighbour shovel snow or donating to charity (although we still want the tax receipt). Weighing the financial incentives against the potential risks is the basis of our economy. Criminals may not know they're doing it, but they're just responding to market signals—and doing a good job of it.

Source: "Risk, Reward and the Economics of the Criminal Mind," by Todd Hirsch, August 1, 2013, *The Globe and Mail.* Reproduced by permission of the author.

Describe an important tradeoff you recently faced. • Give an example of some action that has both a monetary and nonmonetary opportunity cost. • Describe an incentive your parents and/or guardians offered to you in an effort to influence your behaviour.

1-2 How People Interact

The first four principles discussed how individuals make decisions. As we go about our lives, many of our decisions affect not only ourselves but other people as well. The next three principles concern how people interact with one another.

1-2a Principle #5: Trade Can Make Everyone Better Off

You may have heard on the news that the Americans are our competitors in the world economy. In some ways this is true, for Canadian and U.S. firms do produce many of the same goods. BlackBerry and Apple compete for the same customers in the market for smart phones. Inniskillin and Gallo compete for the same customers in the market for wine.

Yet it is easy to be misled when thinking about competition among countries. Trade between Canada and the United States is not like a sports contest, where one side wins and the other side loses. In fact, the opposite is true: Trade between two countries can make each country better off.

To see why, consider how trade affects your family. When a member of your family looks for a job, he or she competes against members of other families who are looking for jobs. Families also compete against one another when they go shopping because each family wants to buy the best goods at the lowest prices. In a sense, each family in an economy competes with all other families.

Despite this competition, your family would not be better off isolating itself from all other families. If it did, your family would need to grow its own food, make its own clothes, and build its own home. Clearly, your family gains much from its ability to trade with others. Trade allows each person to specialize in the activities he or she does best, whether it is farming, sewing, or home building. By trading with others, people can buy a greater variety of goods and services at lower cost.

Countries as well as families benefit from the ability to trade with one another. Trade allows countries to specialize in what they do best and to enjoy a greater variety of goods and services. The Americans, as well as the French and the Egyptians and the Brazilians, are as much our partners in the world economy as they are our competitors.

1-2b Principle #6: Markets Are Usually a Good Way to Organize Economic Activity

The collapse of communism in the Soviet Union and Eastern Europe in the 1980s was one of the last century's most important changes. Communist countries operated on the premise that government officials were in the best position to allocate the economy's scarce resources. These central planners decided what goods and services were produced, how much was produced, and who produced and consumed these goods and services. The theory behind central planning was that only the government could organize economic activity in a way that promoted economic well-being for the country as a whole.

Most countries that once had centrally planned economies have abandoned this system and are trying to develop market economies. In a **market economy**, the decisions of a central planner are replaced by the decisions of millions of firms and households. Firms decide whom to hire and what to make. Households decide which firms to work for and what to buy with their incomes. These firms and households interact in the marketplace, where prices and self-interest guide their decisions.

market economy
an economy that allocates resources through the decentralized decisions of many firms and households as they interact in markets for goods and services

At first glance, the success of market economies is puzzling. In a market economy, no one is looking out for the economic well-being of society as a whole. Free markets contain many buyers and sellers of numerous goods and services, and all of them are interested primarily in their own well-being. Yet, despite decentralized decision making and self-interested decision makers, market economies have proven remarkably successful in organizing economic activity to promote overall economic well-being.

In his 1776 book *An Inquiry into the Nature and Causes of the Wealth of Nations*, economist Adam Smith made the most famous observation in all of economics: Households and firms interacting in markets act as if they are guided by an "invisible hand" that leads them to desirable market outcomes. One of our goals in this book is to understand how this invisible hand works its magic.

As you study economics, you will learn that prices are the instrument with which the invisible hand directs economic activity. In any market, buyers look at the price when determining how much to demand, and sellers look at the price when deciding how much to supply. As a result of the decisions that buyers and sellers make, market prices reflect both the value of a good to society and the cost to society of making the good. Smith's great insight was that prices adjust to guide these individual buyers and sellers to reach outcomes that, in many cases, maximize the well-being of society as a whole.

Smith's insight has an important corollary: When the government prevents prices from adjusting naturally to supply and demand, it impedes the invisible hand's ability to coordinate the millions of households and firms that make up the economy. This corollary explains why taxes adversely affect the allocation of resources: They distort prices and thus the decisions of households and firms. It also explains the harm that can be caused by policies that directly control prices, such as rent control. And it explains the failure of communism. In communist countries, prices were not determined in the marketplace but were dictated by central planners. These planners lacked the necessary information about consumers' tastes and producers' costs, which in a market economy is reflected in prices. Central planners failed because they tried to run the economy with one hand tied behind their backs—the invisible hand of the marketplace.

1-2c Principle #7: Governments Can Sometimes Improve Market Outcomes

If the invisible hand of the market is so great, why do we need government? One purpose of studying economics is to refine your view about the proper role and scope of government policy.

One reason we need government is that the invisible hand can work its magic only if the government enforces the rules and maintains the institutions that are key to a market economy. Most important, market economies need institutions to enforce **property rights** so individuals can own and control scarce resources. A farmer won't grow food if she expects her crop to be stolen, a restaurant won't serve meals unless it is assured that customers will pay before they leave, and an entertainment company won't make their movie available for streaming if too many potential customers avoid paying by making illegal copies. We all rely on government-provided police and courts to enforce our rights over the things we produce—and the invisible hand counts on our ability to enforce our rights.

property rights
the ability of an individual to own and exercise control over scarce resources

Yet there is another reason we need government: The invisible hand is powerful, but it is not omnipotent. There are two broad reasons for a government to intervene

FYI Adam Smith and the Invisible Hand

It may be only a coincidence that Adam Smith's great book *The Wealth of Nations* was published in 1776, the exact year in which American revolutionaries signed the Declaration of Independence. But the two documents share a point of view that was prevalent at the time: Individuals are usually best left to their own devices, without the heavy hand of government guiding their actions. This political philosophy provides the intellectual basis for the market economy and for free society more generally.

Why do decentralized market economies work so well? Is it because people can be counted on to treat one another with love and kindness? Not at all. Here is Adam Smith's description of how people interact in a market economy:

Adam Smith

> *Man has almost constant occasion for the help of his brethren, and it is in vain for him to expect it from their benevolence only. He will be more likely to prevail if he can interest their self-love in his favour, and show them that it is for their own advantage to do for him what he requires of them.... Give me that which I want, and you shall have this which you want, is the meaning of every such offer; and it is in this manner that we obtain from one another the far greater part of those good offices which we stand in need of.*
>
> *It is not from the benevolence of the butcher, the brewer, or the baker that we expect our dinner, but from their regard to their own interest. We address ourselves, not to their humanity but to their self-love, and never talk to them of our own necessities but of their advantages. Nobody but a beggar chooses to depend chiefly upon the benevolence of his fellow-citizens....*
>
> *Every individual ... neither intends to promote the public interest, nor knows how much he is promoting it.... He intends only his own gain, and he is in this, as in many other cases, led by an invisible hand to promote an end which was no part of his intention. Nor is it always the worse for the society that it was no part of it. By pursuing his own interest he frequently promotes that of the society more effectually than when he really intends to promote it.*

Smith is saying that participants in the economy are motivated by self-interest and that the "invisible hand" of the marketplace guides this self-interest into promoting general economic well-being.

Many of Smith's insights remain at the centre of modern economics. Our analysis in the coming chapters will allow us to express Smith's conclusions more precisely and to analyze more fully the strengths and weaknesses of the market's invisible hand.

in the economy and change the allocation of resources that people would choose on their own: to promote efficiency and to promote equity. That is, most policies aim either to enlarge the economic pie or to change how the pie is divided.

Consider first the goal of efficiency. Although the invisible hand usually leads markets to allocate resources to maximize the size of the economic pie, this is not always the case. As discussed above, when resources are allocated so that the size of the economic pie is maximized, economists refer to this as an efficient allocation of resources. Economists then use the term **market failure** to refer to a situation in which the market on its own fails to produce an efficient allocation of resources. As we will see, one possible cause of market failure is an **externality**, which is the impact of one person's actions on the well-being of a bystander. The classic example of an externality is pollution. When the production of a good pollutes the air and creates health problem for those who live near the factories, the market left to its own devices may fail to take this cost into account. Another possible cause of market failure is **market power**, which refers to the ability of a single person or firm (or a small group) to unduly influence market prices. For example, if everyone in town needs water but there is only one well, the owner of the well is not subject to the rigorous competition with which the invisible hand normally keeps self-interest in check; she may take advantage of this opportunity by restricting the output of water so she can charge a higher price. In the presence of externalities or market power, well-designed public policy can enhance economic efficiency.

market failure
a situation in which a market left on its own fails to allocate resources efficiently

externality
the impact of one person's actions on the well-being of a bystander

market power
the ability of a single economic actor (or small group of actors) to have a substantial influence on market prices

Now consider the goal of equity. Even when the invisible hand is yielding efficient outcomes, it can nonetheless leave sizable disparities in economic well-being. A market economy rewards people according to their ability to produce things that other people are willing to pay for. The world's best basketball player earns more than the world's best chess player simply because people are willing to pay more to watch basketball than chess. The invisible hand does not ensure that everyone has sufficient food, decent clothing, and adequate health care. This inequality may, depending on one's political philosophy, call for government intervention. In practice, many public policies, such as the income tax and welfare systems, aim to achieve a more equitable distribution of economic well-being.

To say that the government *can* improve on market outcomes at times does not mean that it always *will*. Public policy is made not by angels but by a political process that is far from perfect. Sometimes policies are designed simply to reward the politically powerful. Sometimes they are made by well-intentioned leaders who are not fully informed. As you study economics you will become a better judge of when a government policy is justifiable because it promotes efficiency or equity, and when it is not.

Why is a country better off not isolating itself from all other countries? • Why do we have markets and, according to economists, what roles should government play in them?

1-3 How the Economy as a Whole Works

We started by discussing how individuals make decisions and then looked at how people interact with one another. All these decisions and interactions together make up "the economy." The last three principles concern the workings of the economy as a whole.

1-3a Principle #8: A Country's Standard of Living Depends on Its Ability to Produce Goods and Services

The differences in living standards around the world are staggering. In 2014, the average Canadian had an income of about $49 000. In the same year, the average Mexican earned about $10 000, and the average Nigerian earned only $1400. Not surprisingly, this large variation in average income is reflected in various measures of the quality of life. Citizens of high-income countries have more TV sets, more cars, better nutrition, better health care, and longer life expectancy than citizens of low-income countries.

Changes in living standards over time are also large. In Canada, individuals' incomes have historically grown about 2 percent per year (after adjusting for changes in the cost of living). At this rate, average income doubles every 35 years. Over the past century, average Canadian income has risen about eightfold.

What explains these large differences in living standards among countries and over time? The answer is surprisingly simple. Almost all variation in living standards is attributable to differences in countries' **productivity**—that is, the amount of goods and services produced from each unit of labour input. In nations where workers can produce a large quantity of goods and services per hour, most people enjoy a high standard of living; in nations where workers are less productive, most people endure a more meagre existence. Similarly, the growth rate of a nation's productivity determines the growth rate of its average income.

productivity
the quantity of goods and services produced from each hour of a worker's time

The fundamental relationship between productivity and living standards is simple, but its implications are far-reaching. If productivity is the primary determinant of living standards, other explanations must be of secondary importance. For example, it might be tempting to credit labour unions or minimum-wage laws for the rise in living standards of Canadian workers over the past century. Yet the real hero of Canadian workers is their rising productivity. As another example, some commentators have claimed that increased competition from Japan and other countries explained the slow growth in Canadian incomes during the 1970s and 1980s. Yet the real villain was not competition from abroad but flagging productivity growth in Canada.

The relationship between productivity and living standards also has profound implications for public policy. When thinking about how any policy will affect living standards, the key question is how it will affect our ability to produce goods and services. To boost living standards, policymakers need to raise productivity by ensuring that workers are well educated, have the tools needed to produce goods and services, and have access to the best available technology.

1-3b Principle #9: Prices Rise When the Government Prints Too Much Money

In January 1921, a daily newspaper in Germany cost 0.30 marks. Less than two years later, in November 1922, the same newspaper cost 70 000 000 marks. All other prices in the economy rose by similar amounts. This episode is one of history's most spectacular examples of **inflation**, an increase in the overall level of prices in the economy. This particular example highlights the problem of hyperinflation when prices are increasing at a rate of more than 50% a month.

inflation
an increase in the overall level of prices in the economy

Although Canada has never experienced inflation even close to that in Germany in the 1920s, inflation has at times been an economic problem. During the 1970s, for instance, average inflation was 8 percent per year and the overall level of prices more than doubled. By contrast, inflation in the 1990s was about 2 percent per year; at this rate it would take 35 years for prices to double. Because high inflation imposes various costs on society, keeping inflation at a low level is a goal of economic policymakers around the world.

What causes inflation? In almost all cases of large or persistent inflation, the culprit is growth in the quantity of money. When a government creates large quantities of the nation's money, the value of the money falls. In Germany in the early 1920s, when prices were on average tripling every month, the quantity of money was also tripling every month. Although less dramatic, the economic history of Canada points to a similar conclusion: The high inflation of the 1970s was associated with rapid growth in the quantity of money, and the low inflation of the 1990s was associated with slow growth in the quantity of money.

1-3c Principle #10: Society Faces a Short-Run Tradeoff between Inflation and Unemployment

Although a higher level of prices is, in the long run, the primary effect of increasing the quantity of money, the short-run story is more complex and more controversial. Most economists describe the short-run effects of monetary injections as follows:

- Increasing the amount of money in the economy stimulates the overall level of spending and thus the demand for goods and services.

- Higher demand may, over time, cause firms to raise their prices, but in the meantime, it also encourages them to increase the quantity of goods and services they produce and to hire more workers to produce those goods and services.
- More hiring means lower unemployment.

This line of reasoning leads to one final economy-wide tradeoff: a short-run tradeoff between inflation and unemployment.

Although some economists still question these ideas, most accept that society faces a short-run tradeoff between inflation and unemployment. This simply means that, over a period of a year or two, many economic policies push inflation and unemployment in opposite directions. Policymakers face this tradeoff regardless of whether inflation and unemployment both start out at high levels (as they did in the early 1980s), at low levels (as they did in the late 1990s), or somewhere in between. This short-run tradeoff plays a key role in the analysis of the **business cycle**—the irregular and largely unpredictable fluctuations in economic activity, as measured by the production of goods and services or the number of people employed.

business cycle
fluctuations in economic activity, such as employment and production

Policymakers can exploit the short-run tradeoff between inflation and unemployment using various policy instruments. By changing the amount that the government spends, the amount it taxes, and the amount of money it prints, policymakers can influence the combination of inflation and unemployment that the economy experiences. Because these instruments of monetary and fiscal policy are potentially so powerful, how policymakers should use these instruments to control the economy, if at all, is a subject of continuing debate.

This debate heated up in 2008. In 2008 and 2009, the Canadian economy, as well as many other economies around the world, experienced a deep economic downturn. Problems in the financial system spilled over to the rest of the economy, causing incomes to fall and unemployment to soar. Policymakers responded in various ways to increase the overall demand for goods and services. The Canadian government introduced a major stimulus package of increased government spending. At the same time, the Bank of Canada increased the supply of money. The goal of these policies was to reduce unemployment. Some feared, however, that these policies might over time lead to an excessive level of inflation. This has not happened yet, but some argue that pent up inflationary pressures may emerge in time.

List and briefly explain the three principles that describe how the economy as a whole works.

1-4 Conclusion

You now have a taste of what economics is all about. In the coming chapters we develop many specific insights about people, markets, and economies. Mastering these insights will take some effort, but it is not an overwhelming task. The field of economics is based on a few basic ideas that can be applied in many different situations.

Throughout this book we will refer back to the *Ten Principles of Economics* highlighted in this chapter and summarized in Table 1.1. Keep these building blocks in mind: Even the most sophisticated economic analysis is founded on the ten principles introduced here.

TABLE 1.1

Ten Principles of Economics

How People Make Decisions

#1: People face tradeoffs.
#2: The cost of something is what you give up to get it.
#3: Rational people think at the margin.
#4: People respond to incentives.

How People Interact

#5: Trade can make everyone better off.
#6: Markets are usually a good way to organize economic activity.
#7: Governments can sometimes improve market outcomes.

How the Economy as a Whole Works

#8: A country's standard of living depends on its ability to produce goods and services.
#9: Prices rise when the government prints too much money.
#10: Society faces a short-run tradeoff between inflation and unemployment.

summary

- The fundamental lessons about individual decision making are that people face tradeoffs among alternative goals, that the cost of any action is measured in terms of forgone opportunities, that rational people make decisions by comparing marginal costs and marginal benefits, and that people change their behaviour in response to the incentives they face.
- The fundamental lessons about interactions among people are that trade can be mutually beneficial, that markets are usually a good way of coordinating trade among people, and that the government can potentially improve market outcomes if there is some market failure or if the market outcome is inequitable.
- The fundamental lessons about the economy as a whole are that productivity is the ultimate source of living standards, that money growth is the ultimate source of inflation, and that society faces a short-run tradeoff between inflation and unemployment.

KEY concepts

scarcity, *p. 2*
economics, *p. 2*
efficiency, *p. 3*
equity, *p. 3*
opportunity cost, *p. 4*
rational people, *p. 4*
marginal changes, *p. 4*
incentive, *p. 6*
market economy, *p. 9*
property rights, *p. 10*
market failure, *p. 11*
externality, *p. 11*
market power, *p. 11*
productivity, *p. 12*
inflation, *p. 13*
business cycle, *p. 14*

QUESTIONS FOR review

1. What is a tradeoff? Give three examples of tradeoffs involved in undertaking postsecondary studies.
2. What is the opportunity cost of seeing a movie?
3. Water is necessary for life. Is the marginal benefit of a glass of water large or small?
4. Why should policymakers think about incentives?

5. Why isn't trade among countries like a game, with some winners and some losers?
6. What does the "invisible hand" of the marketplace do?
7. Explain the two main causes of market failure and give an example of each.
8. Why is productivity important?
9. What is inflation, and what causes it?
10. How are inflation and unemployment related in the short run?

QUICK CHECK **multiple choice**

1. Economics is best defined as the study of which of the following?
   a. how society manages its scarce resources
   b. how to run a business most profitably
   c. how to predict inflation, unemployment, and stock prices
   d. how the government can stop the harm from unchecked self-interest
2. What is your opportunity cost of going to a movie?
   a. the price of the ticket
   b. the price of the ticket plus the cost of any soda and popcorn you buy at the theatre
   c. the total cash expenditure needed to go to the movie plus the value of your time
   d. zero, as long as you enjoy the movie and consider it a worthwhile use of time and money
3. Which of the following describes a marginal change?
   a. one that is NOT important for public policy
   b. one that incrementally alters an existing plan
   c. one that makes an outcome inefficient
   d. one that does NOT influence incentives
4. What is Adam Smith's "invisible hand"?
   a. the subtle and often hidden methods that businesses use to profit at consumers' expense
   b. the ability of free markets to reach desirable outcomes despite the self-interest of market participants
   c. the ability of government regulation to benefit consumers even if the consumers are unaware of the regulations
   d. the way in which producers or consumers in unregulated markets impose costs on innocent bystanders
5. When policymakers make policies that change the costs and benefits that people face, what is the result for society?
   a. people's behaviours are altered
   b. people ignore incentives
   c. inflation occurs
   d. government revenue is reduced
6. If a nation has high and persistent inflation, what is the most likely explanation?
   a. the central bank is creating excessive amounts of money
   b. unions are bargaining for excessively high wages
   c. the government is imposing excessive levels of taxation
   d. firms are using their monopoly power to enforce excessive price hikes

PROBLEMS AND **applications**

1. Describe some of the tradeoffs faced by each of the following.
   a. a family deciding whether to buy a new car
   b. a member of Parliament deciding how much to spend on national parks
   c. a company president deciding whether to open a new factory
   d. a professor deciding how much to prepare for class
2. You are trying to decide whether to take a vacation. Most of the costs of the vacation (airfare, hotel, forgone wages) are measured in dollars, but the benefits of the vacation are psychological. How can you compare the benefits to the costs?
3. You were planning to spend Saturday working at your part-time job, but a friend asks you to go skiing. What is the true cost of going skiing? Now suppose that you had been planning to spend the day studying at the library. What is the cost of going skiing in this case? Explain.
4. You win $100 in a hockey pool. You have a choice between spending the money now or putting it away for a year in a bank account that pays 5 percent interest. What is the opportunity cost of spending the $100 now?
5. The company that you manage has invested $5 million in developing a new product, but the development is not quite finished. At a recent meeting, your salespeople report that the introduction of competing products has reduced the expected sales of your new product to $3 million. If it would cost $1 million to finish development and make the product, should you

go ahead and do so? What is the most that you should pay to complete development?

6. The welfare system provides income for people who are very poor, with low incomes and few assets. If a recipient of welfare payments decides to work and earn some money, the amount he or she receives in welfare payments is reduced.
   a. How does the existence of the welfare system affect people's incentive to save money for the future?
   b. How does the reduction in welfare payments associated with higher earnings affect welfare recipients' incentive to work?
7. In 1997, the Government of Ontario reformed that province's welfare system. The reform reduced the amount of welfare payments to a person with no income, but also allowed welfare recipients to keep a larger part of their welfare payments if they did earn some income.
   a. How does this reform affect the incentive to work?
   b. How might this reform represent a tradeoff between equity and efficiency?
8. Your roommate is a better cook than you are, but you can clean more quickly than your roommate can. If your roommate did all of the cooking and you did all of the cleaning, would your chores take you more or less time than if you divided each task evenly? Give a similar example of how specialization and trade can make two countries both better off.
9. Nations with corrupt police and court systems typically have lower standards of living than nations with less corruption. Why might that be the case?
10. Explain whether each of the following government activities is motivated by a concern about equity or a concern about efficiency. In the case of efficiency, discuss the type of market failure involved.
    a. regulating cable TV prices
    b. providing some poor people with free prescription drugs
    c. prohibiting smoking in public places
    d. preventing mergers between major banks
    e. imposing higher personal income tax rates on people with higher incomes
    f. instituting laws against driving while intoxicated
11. Discuss each of the following statements from the standpoints of equity and efficiency.
    a. "Everyone in society should be guaranteed the best health care possible."
    b. "When workers are laid off, they should be able to collect unemployment benefits until they find a new job."
12. In what ways is your standard of living different from that of your parents or grandparents when they were your age? Why have these changes occurred?
13. Suppose Canadians decide to save more of their incomes. If banks lend this extra saving to businesses, which use the funds to build new factories, how might this lead to faster growth in productivity? Who do you suppose benefits from the higher productivity? Is society getting a free lunch?

© Lavinia Moldovan

CHAPTER 2 Thinking Like an Economist

LEARNING **objectives**

In this chapter, you will ...

1. See how economists apply the methods of science
2. Consider how assumptions and models can shed light on the world
3. Learn two simple models—the circular flow and the production possibilities frontier
4. Distinguish between microeconomics and macroeconomics
5. Learn the difference between positive and normative statements
6. Examine the role of economists in making policy
7. Consider why economists sometimes disagree with one another

Every field of study has its own language and its own way of thinking. Mathematicians talk about axioms, integrals, and vector spaces. Psychologists talk about ego, id, and cognitive dissonance. Lawyers talk about venue, torts, and promissory estoppel.

Economics is no different. Supply, demand, elasticity, comparative advantage, consumer surplus, deadweight loss—these terms are part of the economist's language. In the coming chapters, you will encounter many new terms and some familiar words that economists use in specialized ways. At first, this new language may seem needlessly arcane. But, as you will see, its value lies in its ability to provide you with a new and useful way of thinking about the world in which you live.

The purpose of this book is to help you learn the economist's way of thinking. Just as you cannot become a mathematician, psychologist, or lawyer overnight, learning to think like an economist will take some time. Yet with a combination of theory, case studies, and examples of economics in the news, this book will give you ample opportunity to develop and practise this skill.

Before delving into the substance and details of economics, it is helpful to have an overview of how economists approach the world. This chapter, therefore, discusses the field's methodology. What does it mean to think like an economist?

2-1 The Economist as Scientist

Economists try to address their subject with a scientist's objectivity. They approach the study of the economy in much the same way as a physicist approaches the study of matter and a biologist approaches the study of life: They devise theories, collect data, and then analyze these data in an attempt to verify or refute their theories.

To beginners, it can seem odd to claim that economics is a science. After all, economists do not work with test tubes or telescopes. The essence of science, however, is the *scientific method*—the dispassionate development and testing of theories about how the world works. This method of inquiry is as applicable to studying a nation's economy as it is to studying the earth's gravity or a species' evolution. As Albert Einstein once put it, "The whole of science is nothing more than a refinement of everyday thinking."

Although Einstein's comment is as true for social sciences such as economics as it is for natural sciences such as physics, most people are not accustomed to looking at society through a scientific lens. Let's discuss some of the ways in which economists apply the logic of science to examine how an economy works.

2-1a The Scientific Method: Observation, Theory, and More Observation

Isaac Newton, the famous 17th-century scientist and mathematician, allegedly became intrigued one day when he saw an apple fall from a tree. This observation motivated Newton to develop a theory of gravity that applies not only to an apple falling to the earth but to any two objects in the universe. Subsequent testing of Newton's theory has shown that it works well in many circumstances (although, as Einstein would later emphasize, not in all circumstances). Because Newton's theory has been so successful at explaining observation, it is still taught today in undergraduate physics courses around the world.

This interplay between theory and observation also occurs in economics. An economist might live in a country experiencing rapidly increasing prices and be moved by this observation to develop a theory of inflation. The theory might assert that high inflation arises when the government prints too much money. To test this theory, the economist could collect and analyze data on prices and money from many different countries. If growth in the quantity of money were not at all related to the rate at which prices are rising, the economist would start to doubt the validity of his theory of inflation. If money growth and inflation were strongly correlated in international data, as in fact they are, the economist would become more confident in his theory.

Although economists use theory and observation like other scientists, they do face an obstacle that makes their task especially challenging: In economics, conducting experiments is often impractical. Physicists studying gravity can drop many objects in their laboratories to generate data to test their theories. By contrast, economists studying inflation are not allowed to manipulate a nation's monetary policy simply to generate useful data. Economists, like astronomers and evolutionary biologists, usually have to make do with whatever data the world happens to give them.

To find a substitute for laboratory experiments, economists pay close attention to the natural experiments offered by history. When a war in the Middle East interrupts the flow of crude oil, for instance, oil prices skyrocket around the world. For consumers of oil and oil products, such an event depresses living standards. For economic policymakers, it poses a difficult choice about how best to respond. But for economic scientists, it provides an opportunity to study the effects of a key natural resource on the world's economies, and this opportunity persists long after the wartime increase in oil prices is over. Throughout this book, therefore, we consider many historical episodes. These episodes are valuable to study because they give us insight into the economy of the past and, more important, because they allow us to illustrate and evaluate economic theories of the present.

2-1b The Role of Assumptions

If you ask a physicist how long it would take for a marble to fall from the top of a ten-storey building, she will answer the question by assuming that the marble falls in a vacuum. Of course, this assumption is false. In fact, the building is surrounded by air, which exerts friction on the falling marble and slows it down. Yet the physicist will point out that friction on the marble is so small that its effect is negligible. Assuming the marble falls in a vacuum simplifies the problem without substantially affecting the answer.

Economists make assumptions for the same reason: Assumptions can simplify the complex world and make it easier to understand. To study the effects of international trade, for example, we might assume that the world consists of only two countries and that each country produces only two goods. In reality, there are numerous countries, each of which produces thousands of different types of goods. But by considering a world with only two countries and two goods, we can focus our thinking on the essence of the problem. Once we understand international trade in this simplified imaginary world, we are in a better position to understand international trade in the more complex world in which we live.

The art in scientific thinking—whether in physics, biology, or economics—is deciding which assumptions to make. Suppose, for instance, that when we were dropping a marble from the top of the building, we were also dropping a beach ball of the same weight. Our physicist would realize that the assumption of no friction is less accurate in this case: Friction exerts a greater force on a beach ball than on a marble because a beach ball is much larger. The assumption that gravity works in a vacuum is reasonable for studying a falling marble but not for studying a falling beach ball.

Similarly, economists use different assumptions to answer different questions. Suppose that we want to study what happens to the economy when the government changes the number of dollars in circulation. An important piece of this analysis, it turns out, is how prices respond. Many prices in the economy change infrequently; the newsstand prices of magazines, for instance, are changed only every few years. Knowing this fact may lead us to make different assumptions when studying the effects of the policy change over different time horizons. For studying the short-run effects of the policy, we may assume that prices do not change much. We may even make the extreme and artificial assumption that all prices are completely fixed. For studying the long-run effects of the policy, however, we may assume that all prices are completely flexible. Just as a physicist uses different assumptions when studying falling marbles and falling beach balls, economists use different assumptions when studying the short-run and long-run effects of a change in the quantity of money.

2-1c Economic Models

High-school biology teachers teach basic anatomy with plastic replicas of the human body. These models have all the major organs—the heart, the liver, the kidneys, and so on. The models allow teachers to show their students in a simple way how the important parts of the body fit together. Because these plastic models are stylized and omit many details, no one could mistake them for real people. Despite this lack of realism—indeed, because of this lack of realism—studying these models is useful for learning how the human body works.

Economists also use models to learn about the world, but unlike plastic manikins, they are most often composed of diagrams and equations. Like a biology teacher's plastic model, economic models omit many details to allow us to see what is truly important. Just as the biology teacher's model does not include all of the body's muscles and capillaries, an economist's model does not include every feature of the economy.

As we use models to examine various economic issues throughout this book, you will see that all the models are built with assumptions. Just as a physicist begins the analysis of a falling marble by assuming away the existence of friction, economists assume away many of the details of the economy that are irrelevant for studying the question at hand. All models—in physics, biology, or economics—simplify reality in order to improve our understanding of it.

2-1d Our First Model: The Circular-Flow Diagram

The economy consists of millions of people engaged in many activities—buying, selling, working, hiring, manufacturing, and so on. To understand how the economy works, we must find some way to simplify our thinking about all these activities. In other words, we need a model that explains, in general terms, how the economy is organized and how participants in the economy interact with one another.

Figure 2.1 presents a visual model of the economy, called a **circular-flow diagram**. In this model, the economy is simplified to include only two types of decision makers—households and firms. Firms produce goods and services using inputs such as labour, land, and capital (buildings and machines). These inputs

circular-flow diagram
a visual model of the economy that shows how dollars flow through markets among households and firms

FIGURE 2.1

The Circular Flow
This diagram is a schematic representation of the organization of the economy. Decisions are made by households and firms. Households and firms interact in the markets for goods and services (where households are buyers and firms are sellers) and in the markets for the factors of production (where firms are buyers and households are sellers). The outer set of arrows shows the flow of dollars, and the inner set of arrows shows the corresponding flow of inputs and outputs.

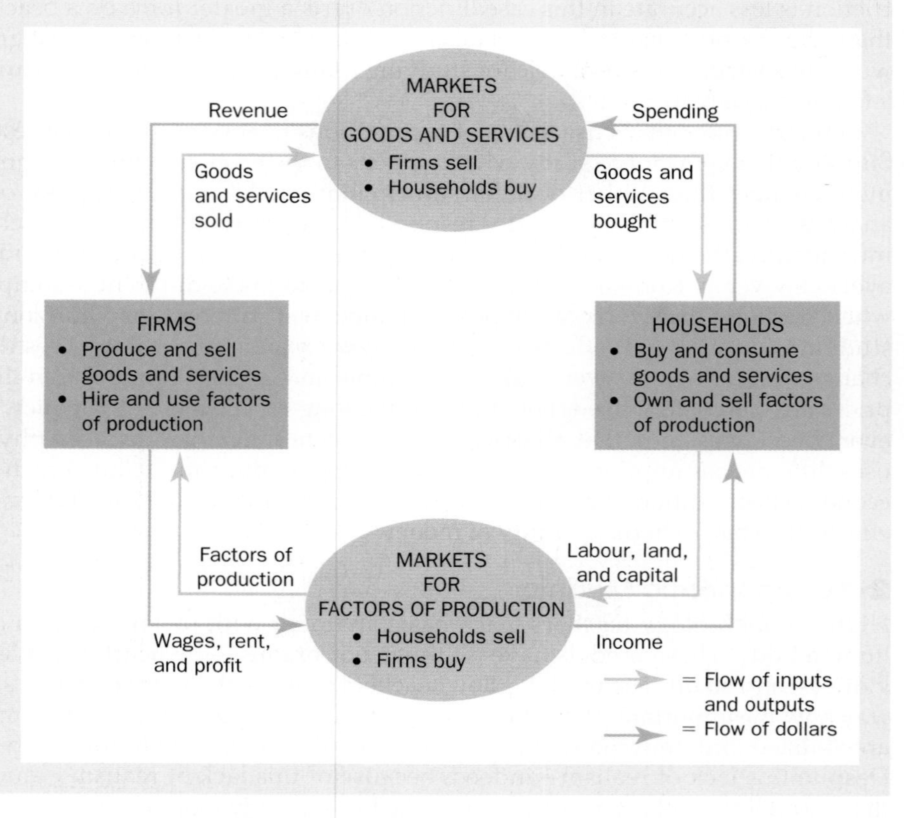

are called the *factors of production*. Households own the factors of production and consume all the goods and services that the firms produce.

Households and firms interact in two types of markets. In the *markets for goods and services*, households are buyers and firms are sellers. In particular, households buy the output of goods and services that firms produce. In the *markets for the factors of production*, households are sellers and firms are buyers. In these markets, households provide the inputs that the firms use to produce goods and services. The circular-flow diagram offers a simple way of organizing the economic transactions that occur between households and firms in the economy.

The two loops of the circular-flow diagram are distinct but related. The inner loop represents the flows of inputs and outputs. The households sell the use of their labour, land, and capital to the firms in the markets for the factors of production. The firms then use these factors to produce goods and services, which in turn are sold to households in the markets for goods and services. The outer loop of the diagram represents the corresponding flow of dollars. The households spend money to buy goods and services from the firms. The firms use some of the revenue from these sales to pay for the factors of production, such as the wages of their workers. What's left is the profit of the firm owners, who themselves are members of households.

Let's take a tour of the circular flow by following a dollar coin as it makes its way from person to person through the economy. Imagine that the dollar begins at a household, say, in your wallet. If you want to buy a cup of coffee, you take the dollar to one of the economy's markets for goods and services, such as your local Tim Hortons coffee shop. There you spend it on your favourite drink. When the dollar moves into the Tim Hortons cash register, it becomes revenue for the firm. The dollar doesn't stay at Tim Hortons for long, however, because the firm uses it to buy inputs in the markets for the factors of production. Tim Hortons might use the dollar to pay rent to its landlord for the space it occupies or to pay the wages of its workers. In either case, the dollar enters the income of some household and, once again, is back in someone's wallet. At that point, the story of the economy's circular flow starts once again.

The circular-flow diagram in Figure 2.1 is a very simple model of the economy. It dispenses with details that, for some purposes, are significant. A more complex and realistic circular-flow model would include, for instance, the roles of government and international trade. (Some of that dollar you gave to Tim Hortons might be used to pay taxes and/or to buy coffee beans from a farmer in Brazil.) Yet these details are not crucial for a basic understanding of how the economy is organized. Because of its simplicity, this circular-flow diagram is useful to keep in mind when thinking about how the pieces of the economy fit together.

2-1e Our Second Model: The Production Possibilities Frontier

Most economic models, unlike the circular-flow diagram, are built using the tools of mathematics. Here we consider one of the simplest such models, called the *production possibilities frontier,* and see how this model illustrates some basic economic ideas.

Although real economies produce thousands of goods and services, let's consider an economy that produces only two goods—cars and computers. Together the car industry and the computer industry use all of the economy's factors of production. The **production possibilities frontier** is a graph that shows the various combinations of output—in this case, cars and computers—that the economy can possibly produce given the available factors of production and the available production technology that firms use to turn these factors into output.

production possibilities frontier
a graph that shows the combinations of output that the economy can possibly produce given the available factors of production and the available production technology

Figure 2.2 shows this economy's production possibilities frontier. If the economy uses all of its resources in the car industry, it produces 1000 cars and

FIGURE 2.2

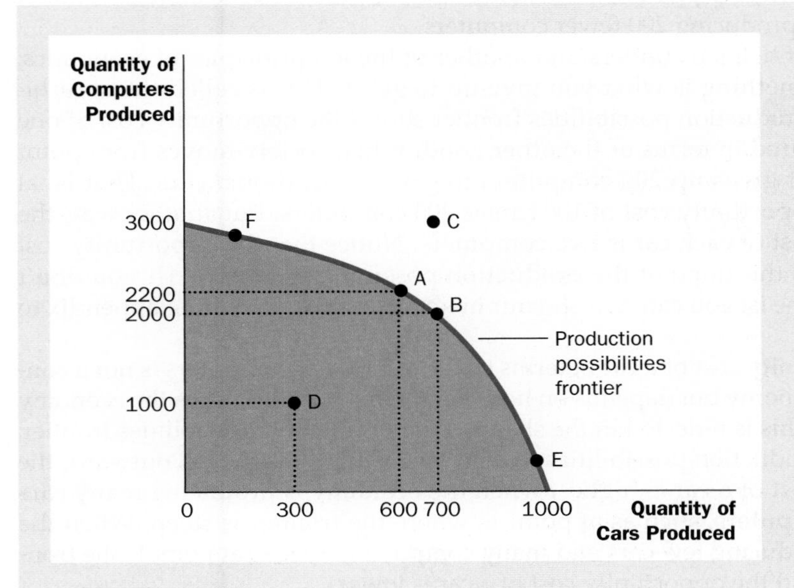

The Production Possibilities Frontier
The production possibilities frontier shows the combinations of output—in this case, cars and computers—that the economy can possibly produce. The economy can produce any combination on or inside the frontier. Points outside the frontier are not feasible given the economy's resources.

no computers. If it uses all of its resources in the computer industry, it produces 3000 computers and no cars. The two endpoints of the production possibilities frontier represent these extreme possibilities.

More likely, the economy divides its resources between the two industries, producing some cars and some computers. For example, it can produce 600 cars and 2200 computers, shown in the figure by point A. Or by moving some of the factors of production to the car industry from the computer industry, the economy can produce 700 cars and 2000 computers, represented by point B.

Because resources are scarce, not every conceivable outcome is feasible. For example, no matter how resources are allocated between the two industries, the economy cannot produce the number of cars and computers represented by point C. Given the technology available for manufacturing cars and computers, the economy does not have enough of the factors of production to support that level of output. With the resources it has, the economy can produce at any point on or inside the production possibilities frontier, but it cannot produce at points outside the frontier.

An outcome is said to be *efficient* if the economy is getting all it can from the scarce resources it has available. Points on (rather than inside) the production possibilities frontier represent efficient levels of production. When the economy is producing at such a point, say point A, there is no way to produce more of one good without producing less of the other. Point D represents an *inefficient* outcome. For some reason, perhaps widespread unemployment, the economy is producing less than it could from the resources it has available: It is producing only 300 cars and 1000 computers. If the source of the inefficiency is eliminated, the economy can increase its production of both goods. For example, if the economy moves from point D to point A, its production of cars increases from 300 to 600, and its production of computers increases from 1000 to 2200.

One of the ten principles of economics discussed in Chapter 1 is that people face tradeoffs. The production possibilities frontier shows one tradeoff that society faces. Once we have reached an efficient point on the frontier, the only way of producing more of one good is to produce less of the other. When the economy moves from point A to point B, for instance, society produces 100 more cars but at the expense of producing 200 fewer computers.

This tradeoff helps us understand another of the ten principles of economics: The cost of something is what you give up to get it. This is called the *opportunity cost.* The production possibilities frontier shows the opportunity cost of one good as measured in terms of the other good. When society moves from point A to point B, it gives up 200 computers to get 100 additional cars. That is, at point A, the opportunity cost of 100 cars is 200 computers. Put another way, the opportunity cost of each car is two computers. Notice that the opportunity cost of a car equals the slope of the production possibilities frontier. (If you don't recall what slope is, you can refresh your memory with the graphing appendix to this chapter.)

The opportunity cost of a car in terms of the number of computers is not a constant in this economy but depends on how many cars and computers the economy is producing. This is reflected in the shape of the production possibilities frontier. Because the production possibilities frontier in Figure 2.2 is bowed outward, the opportunity cost of a car is highest when the economy is producing many cars and fewer computers, such as at point E, where the frontier is steep. When the economy is producing few cars and many computers, such as at point F, the frontier is flatter, and the opportunity cost of a car is lower.

Economists believe that production possibilities frontiers often have this bowed shape. When the economy is using most of its resources to make computers, such as at point F, the resources best suited to car production, such as skilled autoworkers, are being used in the computer industry. Because these workers probably aren't very good at making computers, increasing car production by one unit will cause only a slight reduction in the number of computers produced. At point F, the opportunity cost of a car in terms of computers is small, and the frontier is relatively flat. By contrast, when the economy is using most of its resources to make cars, such as at point E, the resources best suited to making cars are already at use in the car industry. Producing an additional car means moving some of the best computer technicians out of the computer industry and making them autoworkers. As a result, producing an additional car will mean a substantial loss of computer output. The opportunity cost of a car is high, and the frontier is steep.

The production possibilities frontier shows the tradeoff between the outputs of different goods at a given time, but the tradeoff can change over time. For example, suppose a technological advance in the computer industry raises the number of computers that a worker can produce per week. This advance expands society's set of opportunities. For any given number of cars, the economy can now make more computers. If the economy does not produce any computers, it can still produce 1000 cars, so one endpoint of the frontier stays the same. But if the economy devotes some of its resources to the computer industry, it will produce more computers from those resources. As a result, the production possibilities frontier shifts outward, as in Figure 2.3.

This figure illustrates what happens when an economy grows. Society can move production from a point on the old frontier to a point on the new frontier. Which point it chooses depends on its preferences for the two goods. In this example, society moves from point A to point G, enjoying more computers (2300 instead of 2200) and more cars (650 instead of 600).

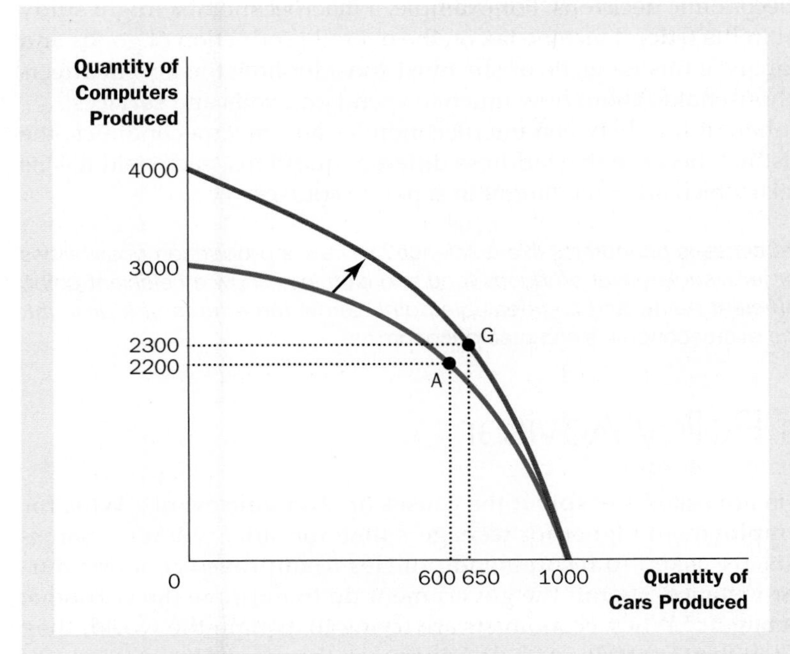

FIGURE 2.3

A Shift in the Production Possibilities Frontier
A technological advance in the computer industry enables the economy to produce more computers for any given number of cars. As a result, the production possibilities frontier shifts outward. If the economy moves from point A to point G, then the production of both cars and computers increases.

The production possibilities frontier simplifies a complex economy to highlight some basic but powerful ideas: scarcity, efficiency, tradeoffs, opportunity cost, and economic growth. As you study economics, these ideas will recur in various forms. The production possibilities frontier offers one simple way of thinking about them.

2-1f Microeconomics and Macroeconomics

Many subjects are studied on various levels. Consider biology, for example. Molecular biologists study the chemical compounds that make up living things. Cellular biologists study cells, which are made up of many chemical compounds and, at the same time, are themselves the building blocks of living organisms. Evolutionary biologists study the many varieties of animals and plants and how species change gradually over the centuries.

Economics is also studied on various levels. We can study the decisions of individual households and firms. Or we can study the interaction of households and firms in markets for specific goods and services. Or we can study the operation of the economy as a whole, which is the sum of the activities of all these decision makers in all these markets.

The field of economics is traditionally divided into two broad subfields. **Microeconomics** is the study of how households and firms make decisions and how they interact in specific markets. **Macroeconomics** is the study of economy-wide phenomena. A microeconomist might study the effects of rent control on housing in Toronto, the impact of foreign competition on the Canadian auto industry, or the effects of compulsory school attendance on workers' earnings. A macroeconomist might study the effects of borrowing by the federal government, the changes over time in the economy's rate of unemployment, or alternative policies to raise growth in national living standards.

microeconomics
the study of how households and firms make decisions and how they interact in markets

macroeconomics
the study of economy-wide phenomena, including inflation, unemployment, and economic growth

Microeconomics and macroeconomics are closely intertwined. Because changes in the overall economy arise from the decisions of millions of individuals, it is impossible to understand macroeconomic developments without considering the associated microeconomic decisions. For example, a macroeconomist might study the effect of a cut in the federal income tax on the overall production of goods and services. But to analyze this issue, he or she must consider how the tax cut affects the decisions of households about how much to spend on goods and services.

Despite the inherent link between microeconomics and macroeconomics, the two fields are distinct. Because they address different questions, each field has its own set of models, which are often taught in separate courses.

In what sense is economics like a science? • Draw a production possibilities frontier for a society that produces food and clothing. Show an efficient point, an inefficient point, and an infeasible point. Show the effects of a drought. • Define microeconomics *and* macroeconomics.

2-2 The Economist as Policy Adviser

Often economists are asked to explain the causes of economic events. Why, for example, is unemployment higher for teenagers than for older workers? Sometimes economists are asked to recommend policies to improve economic outcomes. What, for instance, should the government do to improve the economic well-being of teenagers? When economists are trying to explain the world, they are scientists. When they are trying to help improve it, they are policy advisers.

2-2a Positive versus Normative Analysis

To help clarify the two roles that economists play, we begin by examining the use of language. Because scientists and policy advisers have different goals, they use language in different ways.

For example, suppose that two people are discussing minimum-wage laws. Here are two statements you might hear:

> POLLY: Minimum-wage laws cause unemployment.
> NORM: The government should raise the minimum wage.

Ignoring for now whether you agree with these statements, notice that Polly and Norm differ in what they are trying to do. Polly is speaking like a scientist: She is making a claim about how the world works. Norm is speaking like a policy adviser: He is making a claim about how he would like to change the world.

In general, statements about the world are of two types. One type, such as Polly's, is positive. **Positive statements** are descriptive. They make a claim about how the world *is*. A second type of statement, such as Norm's, is normative. **Normative statements** are prescriptive. They make a claim about how the world *ought to be*.

positive statements
claims that attempt to describe the world as it is

normative statements
claims that attempt to prescribe how the world should be

A key difference between positive and normative statements is how we judge their validity. We can, in principle, confirm or refute positive statements by examining evidence. An economist might evaluate Polly's statement by analyzing data on changes in minimum wages and changes in unemployment over time. By contrast, evaluating normative statements involves values as well as facts. Norm's statement cannot be judged using data alone. Deciding what is good or bad policy is not merely a matter of science. It also involves our views on ethics, religion, and political philosophy.

Positive and normative statements are fundamentally different, but they are often intertwined in a person's set of beliefs. In particular, positive views about how the world works affect normative views about what policies are desirable. Polly's claim that the minimum wage causes unemployment, if true, might lead her to reject Norm's conclusion that the government should raise the minimum wage. Yet normative conclusions cannot come from positive analysis alone; they involve value judgments as well.

As you study economics, keep in mind the distinction between positive and normative statements because it will help you stay focused on the task at hand. Much of economics is positive. It just tries to explain how the economy works. Yet those who use economics often have normative goals: They want to learn how to improve the economy. When you hear economists making normative statements, you know they are speaking not as scientists but as policy advisers.

2-2b Economists in Ottawa

U.S. President Harry Truman once said that he wanted to find a one-armed economist. When he asked his economists for advice, they always answered, "On the one hand, … On the other hand, …."

Truman was right in realizing that economists' advice is not always straightforward. This tendency is rooted in one of the ten principles of economics: People face tradeoffs. Economists are aware that tradeoffs are involved in most policy decisions. A policy might increase efficiency at the cost of equity. It might help future generations but hurt current generations. An economist who says that all policy decisions are easy or clear-cut is an economist not to be trusted.

The Government of Canada, like other governments, relies on the advice of economists. Economists at Finance Canada help design tax policy. Economists at

TABLE 2.1

Websites of Some Major Economic Organizations

Here are the websites for two key government agencies that are responsible for collecting economic data and making economic policy. They are followed by the websites for just a few of the better-known organizations that employ economists and that are often thought to have an influence on government policy.

Department of Finance Canada	www.fin.gc.ca
Bank of Canada	www.bankofcanada.ca
C.D. Howe Institute	www.cdhowe.org
Institute for Research on Public Policy	www.irpp.org
Canadian Centre for Policy Alternatives	www.policyalternatives.ca

Industry Canada help design and enforce Canada's competition laws. Economists at Global Affairs Canada help negotiate trade agreements with other countries; the agency also employs economists, both on staff and as consultants, to give advice on overseas development projects. Economists at Employment and Social Development Canada analyze data on workers and on those looking for work to help formulate labour-market policies. Economists at Environment Canada help design environmental regulations. Statistics Canada employs economists to collect the data analyzed by other economists and then give policy advice. The Bank of Canada, the quasi-independent institution that sets Canada's monetary policy, employs more than 200 economists to analyze financial markets and macroeconomic developments.

Economists outside the government also give policy advice. The C.D. Howe Institute, the Fraser Institute, the Institute for Research on Public Policy, the Canadian Centre for Policy Alternatives, and other independent organizations publish reports by economists that analyze current issues such as poverty, unemployment, and the deficit. These reports try to influence public opinion and give advice on government policies. Table 2.1 provides the URLs for the websites of some of these organizations.

The influence of economists on policy goes beyond their role as advisers: Their research and writings often affect policy indirectly. Economist John Maynard Keynes offered this observation:

> The ideas of economists and political philosophers, both when they are right and when they are wrong, are more powerful than is commonly understood. Indeed, the world is ruled by little else. Practical men, who believe themselves to be quite exempt from intellectual influences, are usually the slaves of some defunct economist. Madmen in authority, who hear voices in the air, are distilling their frenzy from some academic scribbler of a few years back.

These words were written in 1935, but they remain true today. Indeed, the "academic scribbler" now influencing public policy is often Keynes himself.

2-2c Why Economists' Advice Is Not Always Followed

Any economist who advises government knows that his or her recommendations are not always heeded. Frustrating as this can be, it is easy to understand. The process by which economic policy is actually made differs in many ways from the idealized policy process assumed in economics textbooks.

Throughout this text, whenever we discuss economic policy, we often focus on one question: What is the best policy for the government to pursue? We act as if policy were set by a benevolent king. Once the king figures out the right policy, he has no trouble putting his ideas into action.

In the real world, figuring out the right policy is only part of the job for the government, sometimes the easiest part. For example, consider a political party that forms the government receiving advice from its economic advisers about what policy is best from their perspective. This is just the beginning of the process. Communication advisers will then assess how best to explain the proposed policy to the public, and they will try to anticipate any misunderstandings that might make the challenge more difficult. Press advisers will anticipate how the news media will report on the proposal and what opinions will likely be expressed on the nation's editorial pages. Political advisers will weigh in to discuss which groups will organize to support or oppose the proposed policy, how this proposal will affect party standing among different groups in the electorate, and whether it will affect support for other policy initiatives. After hearing and weighing all of this advice, a decision will be made on how to proceed.

Making economic policy in a representative democracy is a messy affair—and there are often good reasons why politicians do not advance the policies that economists advocate. Economists offer crucial input into the policy process, but their advice is only one ingredient of a complex recipe.

Give an example of a positive statement and an example of a normative statement. • Name three parts of government that regularly rely on advice from economists.

2-3 Why Economists Disagree

"If all economists were laid end to end, they would not reach to a conclusion." This quip by George Bernard Shaw is revealing. Economists as a group are often criticized for giving conflicting advice to policymakers.

Why do economists so often appear to give conflicting advice to policymakers? There are two basic reasons:

- Economists may disagree about the validity of alternative positive theories about how the world works.
- Economists may have different values and, therefore, different normative views about what a policy should try to accomplish.

Let's discuss each of these reasons.

2-3a Differences in Scientific Judgments

Several centuries ago, astronomers debated whether the earth or the sun was at the centre of the solar system. More recently, meteorologists have debated whether the earth is experiencing global warming and, if so, why. Science is a search for understanding about the world around us. It is not surprising that as the search continues, scientists can disagree about the direction in which truth lies.

Economists often disagree for the same reason. Economics is a young science, and there is still much to be learned. Economists sometimes disagree because they have different hunches about the validity of alternative theories or about the size of important parameters that measure how economic variables are related.

For example, economists disagree about whether the government should tax a household's income or its consumption (spending). Advocates of a switch from the current income tax to a consumption tax believe that the change would encourage households to save more because income that is saved would not be taxed. Higher saving, in turn, would free resources for capital accumulation, leading to more rapid growth in productivity and living standards. Advocates of the current income tax system believe that household saving would not respond much to a change in the tax laws. These two groups of economists hold different normative views about the tax system because they have different positive views about the responsiveness of saving to tax incentives.

2-3b Differences in Values

Suppose that Peter and Paula both take the same amount of water from the town well. To pay for maintaining the well, the town taxes its residents. Peter has income of $100 000 and is taxed $10 000, or 10 percent of his income. Paula has income of $20 000 and is taxed $4000, or 20 percent of her income.

Is this policy fair? If not, who pays too much and who pays too little? Does it matter whether Paula's low income is due to a medical disability or to her decision to pursue an acting career? Does it matter whether Peter's high income is due to a large inheritance or to his willingness to work long hours at a dreary job?

These are difficult questions on which people are likely to disagree. If the town hired two experts to study how the town should tax its residents to pay for the well, we would not be surprised if they offered conflicting advice.

This simple example shows why economists sometimes disagree about public policy. As we know from our discussion of normative and positive analysis, policies cannot be judged on scientific grounds alone. Sometimes, economists give conflicting advice because they have different values. Perfecting the science of economics will not tell us whether it is Peter or Paula who pays too much.

2-3c Perception versus Reality

Because of differences in scientific judgments and differences in values, some disagreement among economists is inevitable. Yet one should not overstate the amount of disagreement. Economists agree with one another to a much greater extent than is sometimes understood.

Table 2.2 contains 17 propositions about economic policy. In surveys of professional economists, these propositions were endorsed by an overwhelming majority of respondents. Most of these propositions would fail to command a similar consensus among the general public.

The first proposition in the table is about rent control, a policy that sets a legal maximum on the amount landlords can charge for their apartments. Almost all economists believe that rent control adversely affects the availability and quality of housing and is a costly way of helping the neediest members of society. Nonetheless, some provincial governments choose to ignore the advice of economists and place ceilings on the rents that landlords may charge their tenants.

The second proposition in the table concerns tariffs and import quotas, two policies that restrict trade among nations. For reasons we discuss more fully later in this text, almost all economists oppose such barriers to free trade. Nonetheless, over the years, Parliament has often chosen to restrict the import of certain goods.

TABLE 2.2

Propositions about Which Most Economists Agree

Proposition (and percentage of economists who agree)

1. A ceiling on rents reduces the quantity and quality of housing available. (93%)
2. Tariffs and import quotas usually reduce general economic welfare. (93%)
3. Flexible and floating exchange rates offer an effective international monetary arrangement. (90%)
4. Fiscal policy (e.g., tax cut and/or government expenditure increase) has a significant stimulative impact on a less than fully employed economy. (90%)
5. The government should not restrict employers from outsourcing work to foreign countries. (90%)
6. Economic growth in developed countries like Canada leads to greater levels of well-being. (88%)
7. Agricultural subsidies should be eliminated. (85%)
8. An appropriately designed fiscal policy can increase the long-run rate of capital formation. (85%)
9. Local and state governments should eliminate subsidies to professional sports franchises. (85%)
10. If the federal budget is to be balanced, it should be done over the business cycle rather than yearly. (85%)
11. Cash payments increase the welfare of recipients to a greater degree than do transfers-in-kind of equal cash value. (84%)
12. A large federal budget deficit has an adverse effect on the economy. (83%)
13. The redistribution of income is a legitimate role for the government. (83%)
14. Inflation is caused primarily by too much growth in the money supply. (83%)
15. A minimum wage increases unemployment among young and unskilled workers. (79%)
16. The government should restructure the welfare system along the lines of a "negative income tax." (79%)
17. Effluent taxes and marketable pollution permits represent a better approach to pollution control than imposition of pollution ceilings. (78%)

Source: Richard M. Alston, J. R. Kearl, and Michael B. Vaughn, "Is There Consensus among Economists in the 1990s?," *American Economic Review* (May 1992): 203–209; Dan Fuller and Doris Geide-Stevenson, "Consensus among Economists Revisited," *Journal of Economics Education* (Fall 2003): 369–387; Robert Whaples, "Do Economists Agree on Anything? Yes!" *Economists' Voice* (November 2006): 1–6; Robert Whaples, "The Policy Views of American Economic Association Members: The Results of a New Survey," *Econ Journal Watch* (September 2009): 337–348.

Why do policies such as rent control and trade barriers persist if the experts are united in their opposition? It may be that the realities of the political process stand as immovable obstacles. But it also may be that economists have not yet convinced the general public that these policies are undesirable. One purpose of this book is to help you understand the economist's view of these and other subjects and, perhaps, to persuade you that it is the right one.

Why might economic advisers to the Prime Minister disagree about a question of policy?

2-4 Let's Get Going

The first two chapters of this book have introduced you to the ideas and methods of economics. We are now ready to get to work. In the next chapter we start learning in more detail about the principles of economic behaviour and economic policy.

As you proceed through this book, you will be asked to draw on many of your intellectual skills. You might find it helpful to keep in mind some advice from the great economist John Maynard Keynes in *Essays in Biography* (1933):

> The study of economics does not seem to require any specialized gifts of an unusually high order. Is it not … a very easy subject compared with the higher branches of philosophy or pure science? An easy subject, at which very few excel! The paradox finds its explanation, perhaps, in that the master-economist must possess a rare *combination* of gifts. He must be mathematician, historian, statesman, or philosopher—in some degree. He must understand symbols and speak in words. He must contemplate the particular in terms of the general, and touch abstract and concrete in the same flight of thought. He must study the present in the light of the past for the purposes of the future. No part of man's nature or his institutions must lie entirely outside his regard. He must be purposeful and disinterested in a simultaneous mood; as aloof and incorruptible as an artist, yet sometimes as near the earth as a politician.

This is a tall order. But with practice, you will become more and more accustomed to thinking like an economist.

summary

- Economists try to address their subject with a scientist's objectivity. Like all scientists, they make appropriate assumptions and build simplified models in order to understand the world around them. Two simple economic models are the circular-flow diagram and the production possibilities frontier.
- The field of economics is divided into two subfields: microeconomics and macroeconomics. Microeconomists study decision making by households and firms and the interaction among households and firms in the marketplace. Macroeconomists study the forces and trends that affect the economy as a whole.
- A positive statement is an assertion about how the world *is*. A normative statement is an assertion about how the world *ought to be*. When economists make normative statements, they are acting more as policy advisers than scientists.
- Economists who advise policymakers sometimes offer conflicting advice either because of differences in scientific judgments or because of differences in values. At other times, economists are united in the advice they offer, but policymakers may choose to ignore the advice because of the many forces and constraints imposed by the political process.

KEY concepts

QUESTIONS FOR review

1. How is economics like a science?
2. Why do economists make assumptions?
3. Should an economic model describe reality exactly?
4. Name a way that your family interacts in the factor market and a way that it interacts in the product market.
5. Name one economic interaction that isn't covered by the simplified circular-flow diagram.
6. Draw and explain a production possibilities frontier for an economy that produces milk and cookies. What happens to this frontier if disease kills half of the economy's cow population?

7. Use a production possibilities frontier to describe the idea of "efficiency."
8. What are the two subfields into which economics is divided? Explain what each subfield studies.
9. What is the difference between a positive and a normative statement? Give an example of each.

QUICK CHECK **multiple choice**

1. What is an economic model?
   a. a mechanical machine that replicates the functioning of the economy
   b. a fully detailed, realistic description of the economy
   c. a simplified representation of some aspect of the economy
   d. a computer program that predicts the future of the economy
2. What does the circular-flow diagram illustrate in terms of markets for the factors of production?
   a. households are sellers and firms are buyers
   b. households are buyers and firms are sellers
   c. households and firms are both buyers
   d. households and firms are both sellers
3. Is a point inside the production possibilities frontier efficient and feasible?
   a. efficient but not feasible
   b. feasible but not efficient
   c. both efficient and feasible
   d. neither efficient nor feasible
4. An economy produces hot dogs and hamburgers. If a discovery of the remarkable health benefits of hot dogs were to change consumers' preferences, what would happen?
   a. it would expand the production possibilities frontier
   b. it would contract the production possibilities frontier
   c. it would move the economy along the production possibilities frontier
   d. it would move the economy inside the production possibilities frontier
5. Which of the following topics does NOT fall within the study of microeconomics?
   a. the impact of cigarette taxes on the smoking behaviour of teenagers
   b. the role of Microsoft's market power in the pricing of software
   c. the effectiveness of antipoverty programs in reducing homelessness
   d. the influence of the government budget deficit on economic growth
6. Which of the following is a positive, rather than a normative, statement?
   a. Law X will reduce national income.
   b. Law X is a good piece of legislation.
   c. Parliament ought to pass Law X.
   d. Law X will change the distribution of income unfairly.

PROBLEMS AND **applications**

1. Draw a circular-flow diagram. Identify the parts of the model that correspond to the flow of goods and services and the flow of dollars for each of the following activities.
   a. Selena pays a storekeeper $1 for a litre of milk.
   b. Stuart earns $7 per hour working at a fast-food restaurant.
   c. Shanna spends $30 to get a haircut.
   d. Salma earns $10 000 from her 10 percent ownership of Acme Industrial.
2. Imagine a society that produces military goods and consumer goods, which we'll call "guns" and "butter."
   a. Draw a production possibilities frontier for guns and butter. Explain why it most likely has a bowed-out shape.
   b. Show a point that is impossible for the economy to achieve. Show a point that is feasible but inefficient.
   c. Imagine that the society has two political parties, called the Hawks (who want a strong military) and the Doves (who want a smaller military). Show a point on your production possibilities frontier that the Hawks might choose and a point the Doves might choose.
   d. Imagine that an aggressive neighbouring country reduces the size of its military. As a result, both the Hawks and the Doves reduce their desired production of guns by the same amount. Which party would get the bigger "peace dividend," measured by the increase in butter production? Explain.
3. The first principle of economics discussed in Chapter 1 is that people face tradeoffs. Use a production possibilities frontier to illustrate society's tradeoff between a clean environment and the quantity of industrial

output. What do you suppose determines the shape and position of the frontier? Show what happens to the frontier if engineers develop an automobile engine with almost no emissions.

4. Classify the following topics as relating to microeconomics or macroeconomics.
   a. a family's decision about how much income to save
   b. the effect of government regulations on auto emissions
   c. the impact of higher national saving on economic growth
   d. a firm's decision about how many workers to hire
   e. the relationship between the inflation rate and changes in the quantity of money
5. Classify each of the following statements as positive or normative. Explain.
   a. Society faces a short-run tradeoff between inflation and unemployment.
   b. A reduction in the rate of growth of money will reduce the rate of inflation.
   c. The Bank of Canada should reduce the rate of growth of money.
   d. Society ought to require welfare recipients to look for jobs.
   e. Lower tax rates encourage more work and more saving.
6. If you were Prime Minister, would you be more interested in your economic advisers' positive views or their normative views? Why?
7. An economy consists of three workers: Larry, Moe, and Curly. Each works for ten hours per day and can produce two services: mowing lawns and washing cars. In an hour, Larry can either mow one lawn or wash one car, Moe can either mow one lawn or wash two cars, and Curly can either mow two lawns or wash one car.
   a. Calculate how much of each service is produced under the following circumstances, which we label A, B, C, and D:
      - All three spend all their time mowing lawns. (A)
      - All three spend all their time washing cars. (B)
      - All three spend half their time on each activity. (C)
      - Larry spends half his time on each activity, while Moe only washes cars and Curly only mows lawns. (D)
   b. Graph the production possibilities frontier for this economy. Using your answers to part (a), identify points A, B, C, and D on your graph.
   c. Explain why the production possibilities frontier has the shape it does.
   d. Are any of the allocations calculated in part (a) inefficient? Explain.

APPENDIX

Graphing: A Brief Review

Many of the concepts that economists study can be expressed with numbers—the price of bananas, the quantity of bananas sold, the cost of growing bananas, and so on. Often these economic variables are related to one another: When the price of bananas rises, people buy fewer bananas. One way of expressing the relationships among variables is with graphs.

Graphs serve two purposes. First, when developing economic theories, graphs offer a way to visually express ideas that might be less clear if described with equations or words. Second, when analyzing economic data, graphs provide a powerful way of finding and interpreting patterns. Whether we are working with theory or with data, graphs provide a lens through which a recognizable forest emerges from a multitude of trees.

Numerical information can be expressed graphically in many ways, just as there are many ways to express a thought in words. A good writer chooses words that will make an argument clear, a description pleasing, or a scene dramatic. An effective economist chooses the type of graph that best suits the purpose.

In this appendix we discuss how economists use graphs to study the mathematical relationships among variables. We also discuss some of the pitfalls that can arise in the use of graphical methods.

Graphs of a Single Variable

Three common types of graphs are shown in Figure 2A.1. The *pie chart* in panel (a) shows how total income in Canada is divided among the sources of income, including wages and salaries, corporation profits, and so on. A slice of the

FIGURE 2A.1

Types of Graphs

The pie chart in panel (a) shows how national income is derived from various sources. The bar graph in panel (b) compares the average income in three countries. The time-series graph in panel (c) shows the unemployment rate in Canada from January 2000 to December 2012.

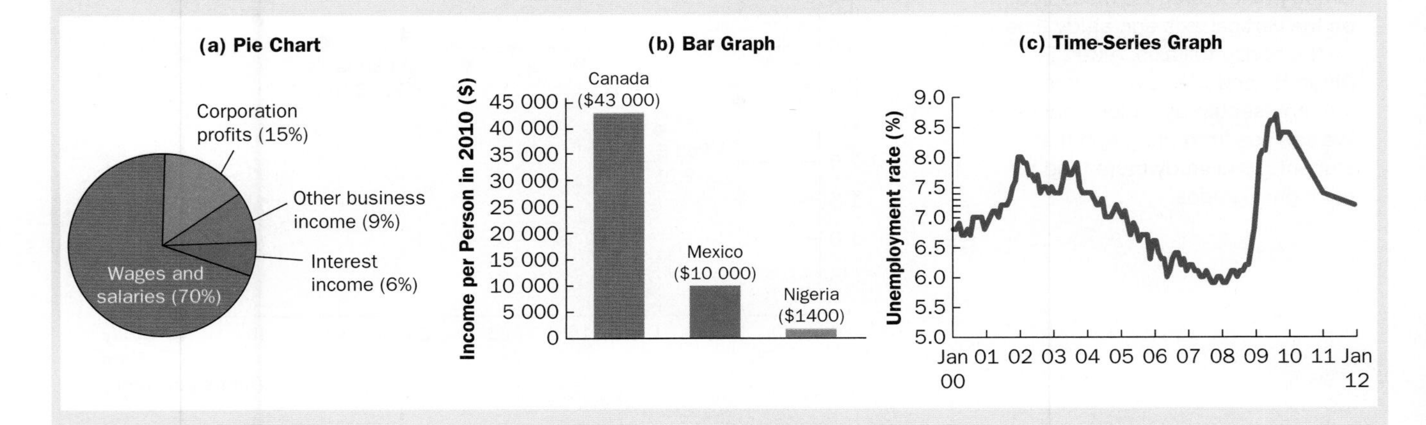

pie represents each source's share of the total. The *bar graph* in panel (b) compares income for three countries. The height of each bar represents the average income in each country. The *time-series graph* in panel (c) traces the Canadian unemployment rate over time. The height of the line shows the unemployment rate in each month. You have probably seen similar graphs in newspapers and magazines.

Graphs of Two Variables: The Coordinate System

The three graphs in Figure 2A.1 are useful in showing how a variable changes over time or across individuals, but they are limited in how much they can tell us. These graphs display information only on a single variable. Economists are often concerned with the relationships between variables. Thus, they need to display two variables on a single graph. The *coordinate system* makes this possible.

Suppose you want to examine the relationship between study time and grade point average. For each student in your class, you could record a pair of numbers: hours per week spent studying and grade point average. These numbers could then be placed in parentheses as an *ordered pair* and appear as a single point on the graph. Albert E., for instance, is represented by the ordered pair (25 hours/week, 3.5 GPA), while his "what-me-worry?" classmate Alfred E. is represented by the ordered pair (5 hours/week, 2.0 GPA).

We can graph these ordered pairs on a two-dimensional grid. The first number in each ordered pair, called the *x-coordinate,* tells us the horizontal location of the point. The second number, called the *y-coordinate,* tells us the vertical location of the point. The point with both an x-coordinate and a y-coordinate of zero is known as the *origin.* The two coordinates in the ordered pair tell us where the point is located in relation to the origin: x units to the right of the origin and y units above it.

Figure 2A.2 graphs grade point average against study time for Albert E., Alfred E., and their classmates. This type of graph is called a *scatterplot* because it plots scattered points. Looking at this graph, we immediately notice that points farther to the right (indicating more study time) also tend to be higher (indicating

FIGURE 2A.2

Using the Coordinate System

Grade point average is measured on the vertical axis and study time on the horizontal axis. Albert E., Alfred E., and their classmates are represented by various points. We can see from the graph that students who study more tend to get higher grades.

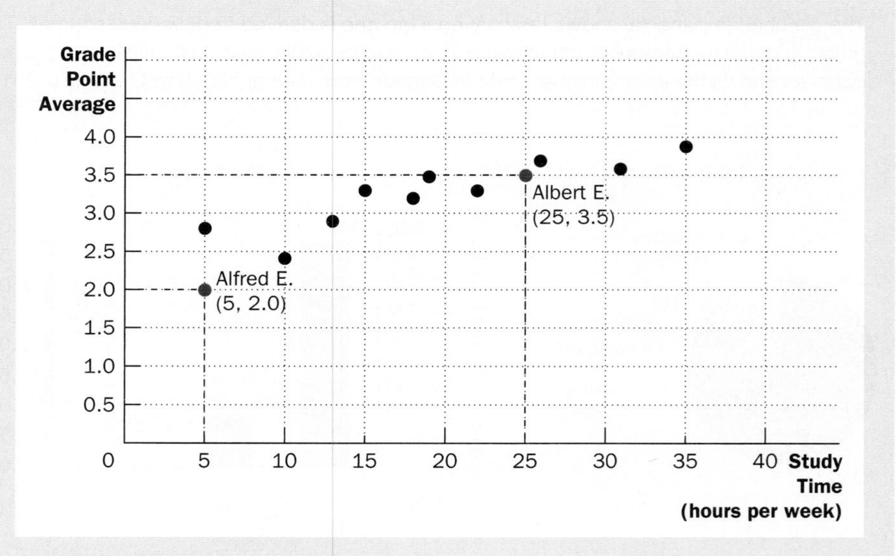

a better grade point average). Because study time and grade point average typically move in the same direction, we say that these two variables have a *positive correlation*. By contrast, if we were to graph party time and grades, we would likely find that higher party time is associated with lower grades; because these variables typically move in opposite directions, we would call this a *negative correlation*. In either case, the coordinate system makes the correlation between the two variables easy to see.

Curves in the Coordinate System

Students who study more do tend to get higher grades, but other factors also influence a student's grade. Previous preparation is an important factor, for instance, as are talent, attention from teachers, and even eating a good breakfast. A scatterplot like Figure 2A.2 does not attempt to isolate the effect that studying has on grades from the effects of other variables. Often, however, economists prefer looking at how one variable affects another, holding everything else constant.

To see how this is done, let's consider one of the most important graphs in economics—the *demand curve*. The demand curve traces the effect of a good's price on the quantity of the good consumers want to buy. Before showing a demand curve, however, consider Table 2A.1, which shows how the number of novels that Emma buys depends on her income and on the price of novels. When novels are cheap, Emma buys them in large quantities. As they become more expensive, she instead borrows books from the library or chooses to go to the movies instead of reading. Similarly, at any given price, Emma buys more novels when she has a higher income. That is, when her income increases, she spends part of the additional income on novels and part on other goods.

We now have three variables—the price of novels, income, and the number of novels purchased—which are more than we can represent in two dimensions. To put the information from Table 2A.1 in graphical form, we need to hold one of the three variables constant and trace the relationship between the other two. Because the demand curve represents the relationship between price and quantity demanded, we hold Emma's income constant and show how the number of novels she buys varies with the price of novels.

Suppose that Emma's income is $30 000 per year. If we place the number of novels Emma purchases on the x-axis and the price of novels on the y-axis, we can graphically represent the middle column of Table 2A.1. When the points that

TABLE 2A.1

Novels Purchased by Emma

This table shows the number of novels Emma buys at various incomes and prices. For any given level of income, the data on price and quantity demanded can be graphed to produce Emma's demand curve for novels, as shown in Figures 2A.3 and 2A.4.

	Income		
Price	$20 000	$30 000	$40 000
$10	2 novels	5 novels	8 novels
9	6	9	12
8	10	13	16
7	14	17	20
6	18	21	24
5	22	25	28
	Demand curve D_3	Demand curve D_1	Demand curve D_2

FIGURE 2A.3

Demand Curve
The line D_1 shows how Emma's purchases of novels depend on the price of novels when her income is held constant. Because the price and the quantity demanded are negatively related, the demand curve slopes downward.

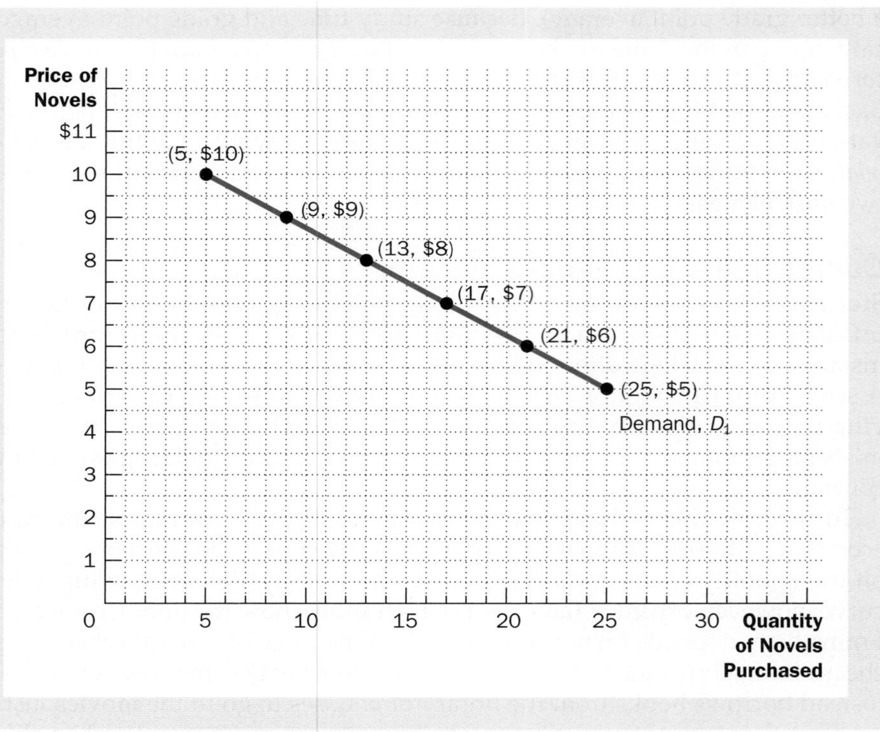

represent these entries from the table—(5 novels, $10), (9 novels, $9), and so on—are connected, they form a line. This line, pictured in Figure 2A.3, is known as Emma's demand curve for novels; it tells us how many novels Emma purchases at any given price. The demand curve is downward sloping, indicating that a higher price reduces the quantity of novels demanded. Because the quantity of novels demanded and the price move in opposite directions, we say that the two variables are *negatively related.* (Conversely, when two variables move in the same direction, the curve relating them is upward sloping, and we say the variables are *positively related.*)

Now suppose that Emma's income rises to $40 000 per year. At any given price, Emma will purchase more novels than she did at her previous level of income. Just as earlier we drew Emma's demand curve for novels using the entries from the middle column of Table 2A.1, we now draw a new demand curve using the entries from the right column of the table. This new demand curve (curve D_2) is pictured alongside the old one (curve D_1) in Figure 2A.4; the new curve is a similar line drawn farther to the right. We therefore say that Emma's demand curve for novels *shifts* to the right when her income increases. Likewise, if Emma's income were to fall to $20 000 per year, she would buy fewer novels at any given price and her demand curve would shift to the left (to curve D_3).

In economics, it is important to distinguish between *movements along a curve* and *shifts of a curve.* As we can see from Figure 2A.3, if Emma earns $30 000 per year and novels cost $8 apiece, she will purchase 13 novels per year. If the price of novels falls to $7, Emma will increase her purchases of novels to 17 per year. The demand curve, however, stays fixed in the same place. Emma still buys the same

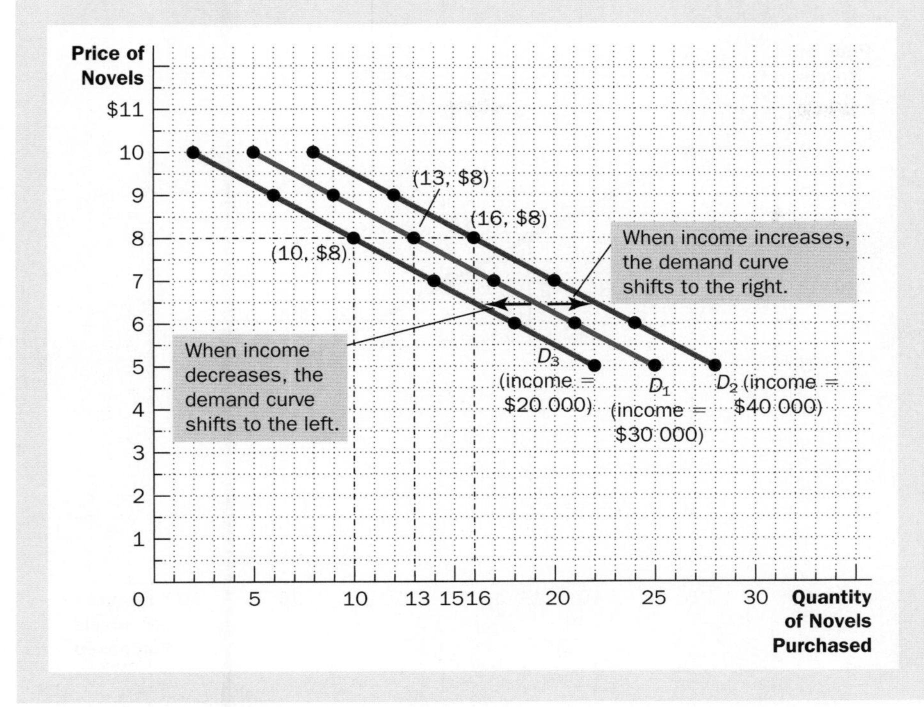

FIGURE 2A.4

Shifting Demand Curves
The location of Emma's demand curve for novels depends on how much income she earns. The more she earns, the more novels she will purchase at any given price, and the farther to the right her demand curve will lie. Curve D_1 represents Emma's original demand curve when her income is $30 000 per year. If her income rises to $40 000 per year, her demand curve shifts to D_2. If her income falls to $20 000 per year, her demand curve shifts to D_3.

number of novels *at each price,* but as the price falls she moves along her demand curve from left to right. By contrast, if the price of novels remains fixed at $8 but her income rises to $40 000, Emma increases her purchases of novels from 13 to 16 per year. Because Emma buys more novels *at each price,* her demand curve shifts out, as shown in Figure 2A.4.

There is a simple way to tell when it is necessary to shift a curve: When a relevant variable that is not named on either axis changes, the curve shifts. Income is on neither the *x*-axis nor the *y*-axis of the graph, so when Emma's income changes, her demand curve must shift. The same is true for any change that affects Emma's purchasing habits, with the sole exception of a change in the price of novels. If, for instance, the public library closes and Emma must buy all the books she wants to read, she will demand more novels at each price, and her demand curve will shift to the right. Or, if the price of movies falls and Emma spends more time at the movies and less time reading, she will demand fewer novels at each price, and her demand curve will shift to the left. By contrast, when a variable on an axis of the graph changes, the curve does not shift. We read the change as a movement along the curve.

Slope

One question we might want to ask about Emma is how much her purchasing habits respond to price. Look at the demand curve pictured in Figure 2A.5. If this curve is very steep, Emma purchases nearly the same number of novels regardless of whether they are cheap or expensive. If this curve is much flatter, the number of novels Emma purchases is more sensitive to changes in the price. To answer questions about how much one variable responds to changes in another variable, we can use the concept of *slope.*

FIGURE 2A.5

Calculating the Slope of a Line

To calculate the slope of the demand curve, we can look at the changes in the x- and y-coordinates as we move from the point (21 novels, $6) to the point (13 novels, $8). The slope of the line is the ratio of the change in the y-coordinate (−2) to the change in the x-coordinate (+8), which equals −1/4.

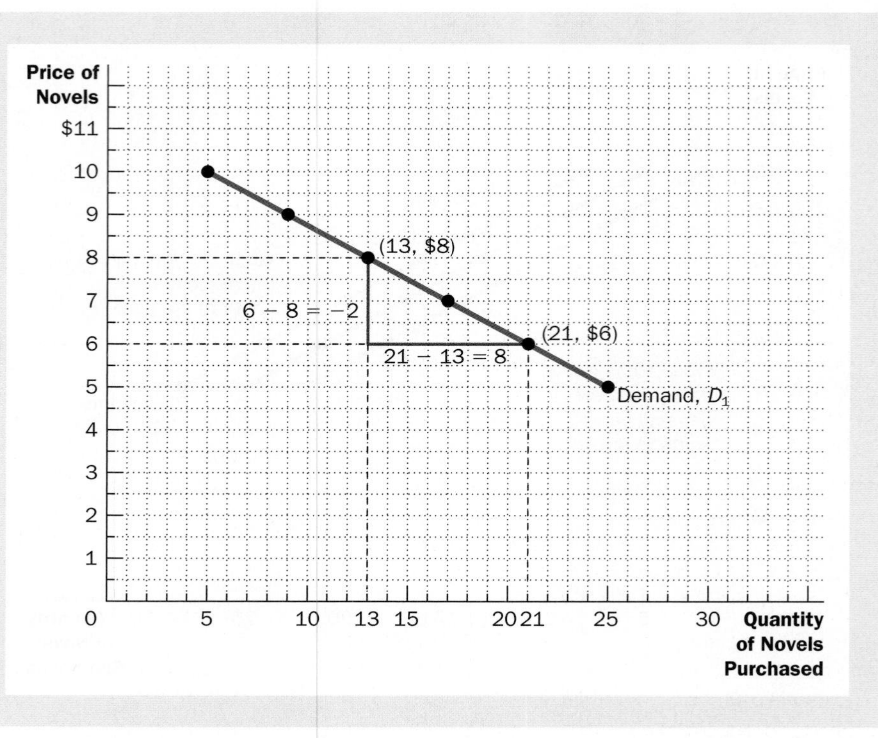

The slope of a line is the ratio of the vertical distance covered to the horizontal distance covered as we move along the line. This definition is usually written out in mathematical symbols as follows:

$$\text{Slope} = \frac{\Delta y}{\Delta x}$$

where the Greek letter Δ (delta) stands for the change in a variable. In other words, the slope of a line is equal to the "rise" (change in y) divided by the "run" (change in x). The slope will be a small positive number for a fairly flat upward-sloping line, a large positive number for a steep upward-sloping line, and a negative number for a downward-sloping line. A horizontal line has a slope of zero because in this case the y-variable never changes; a vertical line is said to have an infinite slope because the y-variable can take any value without the x-variable changing at all.

What is the slope of Emma's demand curve for novels? First of all, because the curve slopes down, we know the slope will be negative. To calculate a numerical value for the slope, we must choose two points on the line. With Emma's income at $30 000, she will purchase 21 novels at a price of $6 or 13 novels at a price of $8. When we apply the slope formula, we are concerned with the change between these two points; in other words, we are concerned with the difference between them, which lets us know that we will have to subtract one set of values from the other, as follows:

$$\text{Slope} = \frac{\Delta y}{\Delta x} = \frac{\text{First } y\text{-coordinate} - \text{Second } y\text{-coordinate}}{\text{First } x\text{-coordinate} - \text{Second } x\text{-coordinate}} = \frac{6 - 8}{21 - 13} = -\frac{2}{8} = -\frac{1}{4}$$

Figure 2A.5 shows graphically how this calculation works. Try computing the slope of Emma's demand curve using two different points. You should get exactly the same result, $-1/4$. One of the properties of a straight line is that it has the same slope everywhere. This is not true of other types of curves, which are steeper in some places than in others.

The slope of Emma's demand curve tells us something about how responsive her purchases are to changes in the price. A small slope (a number close to zero) means that Emma's demand curve is relatively flat; in this case, she adjusts the number of novels she buys substantially in response to a price change. A larger slope (a number farther from zero) means that Emma's demand curve is relatively steep; in this case, she adjusts the number of novels she buys only slightly in response to a price change.

Graphing Functions

In the previous section the notion of a demand curve was introduced. Table 2A.1 presents data indicating the number of novels that Emma buys at various prices, and for different levels of income. Figure 2A.3 plots these data to depict Emma's demand curve for novels when her income is $30 000. We saw that Emma's demand for novels depends upon the price, and indeed as the price of novels increases Emma purchases fewer novels, which is to say that Emma's quantity demanded for novels depends negatively on the price. Another way of saying this is that Emma's demand for novels is a *function* of their price—in this case a negative function, where "function of" means "depends upon."

We can express the idea that Emma's demand for novels is a function of (depends upon) the price mathematically, in general terms, by writing $Q^D = f(P)$, where P is the price of a novel and Q^D is Emma's quantity demanded at that price. The term $f(P)$ means simply that Emma's quantity demanded (Q^D) is a function of (depends upon) the price (P). The specific way in which her quantity demanded depends on the price of novels depends upon the *functional form* of $f(P)$. As is evident in Figure 2A.3, and as described above, the relationship between quantity demanded and price in Emma's case is a linear one—her demand curve for novels is a straight line. This is evident visually in the graph, and more precisely because the slope of the demand curve is constant (has the same slope everywhere).

The general functional form for a linear demand curve is:

$$Q^D = f(P) = a - bP$$

where a and b are called the parameters of the function, and represent positive numbers. The negative sign in front of bP therefore indicates that a negative relationship exists between the price of novels and Emma's quantity demanded—as the price goes up, her quantity demanded goes down. The precise values of a and b determine the exact placement and slope of the demand curve. Once we know the values of a and b, we can plug any price into this linear function and determine Emma's demand for novels. For Emma's demand curve depicted in Figure 2A.3, which remember assumes that her income is $30 000, the values for a and b are 45 and 4, respectively, and the precise functional form of her demand curve is:

$$Q^D = 45 - 4P$$

Plug any value for P into this linear demand curve and you will get the quantity of novels demanded by Emma when her income is $30 000. For example, at $P = 10$, $Q^D = 45 - 4(10) = 45 - 40 = 5$; at $P = 9$, $Q^D = 45 - 4(9) = 45 - 36 = 9$; and so on, which coincides exactly with Table 2A.1 and Figure 2A.3.

There are two points on Emma's demand curve that are particularly useful. These are the points where the demand curve intersects the x- and the y-axes (the quantity and price axis, respectively). The point where her demand curve intersects the x-axis, called the x-intercept, coincides with her demand for novels when the price of novels is zero. To determine this, simply plug $P = 0$ into the function depicting Emma's demand curve, giving $Q^D = 45 - 4(0) = 45 - 0 = 45$. The point where her demand curve intersects the y-axis, the y-intercept, coincides with the price at which her quantity demanded is zero. To determine this, plug $Q^D = 0$ into her demand curve and solve for P:

$$\begin{aligned} 0 &= 45 - 4P \\ 4P &= 45 \\ P &= 45/4 \\ P &= 11.25 \end{aligned}$$

So when the price of novels is $11.25 Emma will buy zero novels.

The graph of Emma's demand curve for novels with the x- and y-intercepts identified is shown in Figure 2A.6.

As discussed earlier, we can determine the slope of Emma's demand curve by calculating the "rise" over the "run." To do this, we look at the changes in the x- and y-coordinates as we move from one point on the demand curve to another. Because her demand curve is a straight line the slope is constant, and we can use any two points on the curve to determine its slope. Previously we used the points (21 novels, $6) and (13 novels, $8). Using these two points on her demand curve gave us a change in the y-coordinate, the "rise," of $(6 - 8 = -2)$, and a change in the x-coordinate, the "run," of $(21 - 13 = 8)$. Taking the ratio of the "rise" over the "run" gave us a slope of $-2/8 = -1/4$. Since we can use any two points on a linear demand curve to determine its slope, we can also use the x- and y-intercepts. The y-intercept is associated with the coordinate (0 novels, $11.25), and the x-intercept with the coordinate (45 novels, $0), which gives us a "rise" equal to $0 - 11.25 = -11.25$, which is the negative of the y-intercept, and a "run" equal to $45 - 0 = 45$, which is the x-intercept. Taking the ratio of the "rise" over the "run," which is just the negative of the ratio of the y-intercept over the x-intercept, gives us $-11.25/45 = -.25 = -1/4$, just as above. So calculating the x- and y-intercepts of a linear demand curve gives us an easy way to determine its slope.

FIGURE 2A.6

Emma's Demand Curve with Income of $30 000

This is Emma's demand curve for novels when her income is $30 000. In this case her demand curve is given by the linear equation $Q^D = 45 - 4P$, which gives an x-intercept of 4, a y-intercept of 11.25, and a slope of $-1/4$.

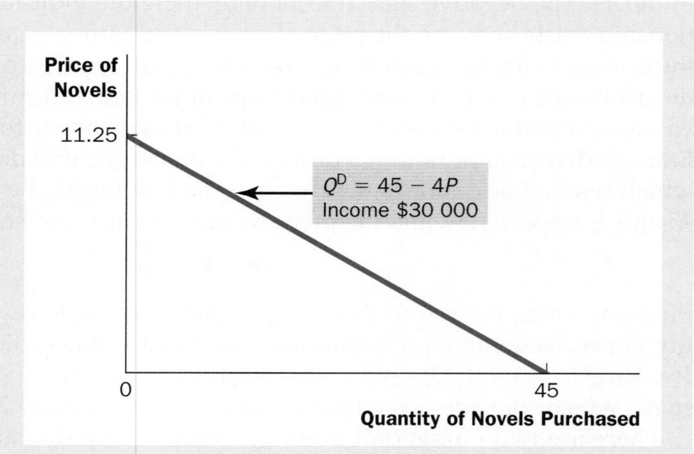

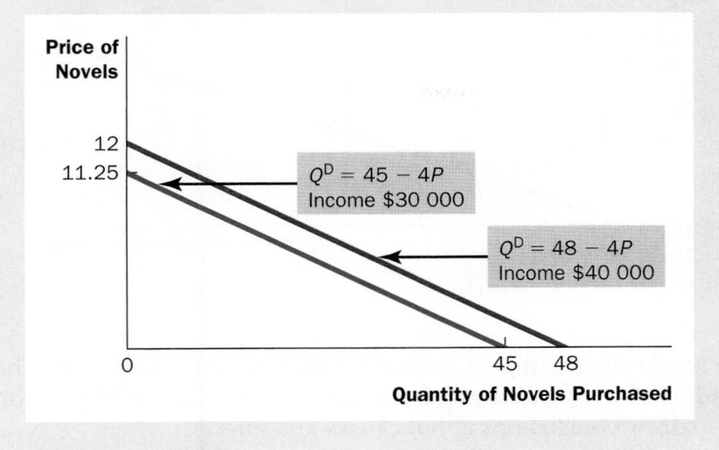

FIGURE 2A.7

Emma's Demand Curve with Different Incomes

This figure shows Emma's demand curves and the associated *x*- and *y*-intercepts when her income is $30 000 and $40 000. An increase in her income shifts her demand curve up in a parallel manner, increasing both intercepts but maintaining the slope.

By writing Emma's quantity of novels demanded as a function of the price of novels alone, we are holding everything else that might affect her demand for novels constant. For example, the demand curve given by $Q^D = 45 - 4P$ assumes that her income is $30 000. If her income increases to $40 000, we saw in Table 2A.1 and Figure 2A.4 that her demand curve shifts to the right and she demands more novels at every price. It turns out that her demand curve when her income is $40 000 is:

$$Q^D = 48 - 4P$$

Using the same approach as above we see that when her income is $40 000 the *x*-intercept of the associated demand curve is 48 and the *y*-intercept is 12. The slope of this demand curve is then $-12/48 = -1/4$, which is exactly the same as the demand curve associated with income of $30 000. So we see that in this case a change in income shifts Emma's demand curve for novels in a parallel manner to the right—that is, both the *x*- and *y*-intercepts increase by the same proportion but the slope does not change. The demand curve associated with income of $40 000 is shown in Figure 2A.7, along with her demand curve when her income is $30 000.

Cause and Effect

Economists often use graphs to advance an argument about how the economy works. In other words, they use graphs to argue about how one set of events *causes* another set of events. With a graph like the demand curve, no doubt exists about cause and effect. Because we are varying price and holding all other variables constant, we know that changes in the price of novels cause changes in the quantity Emma demands. Remember, however, that our demand curve came from a hypothetical example. When graphing data from the real world, it is often more difficult to establish how one variable affects another.

The first problem is that it is difficult to hold everything else constant when measuring how one variable affects another. If we are not able to hold variables constant, we might decide that one variable on our graph is causing changes in the other variable, when those changes are actually being caused by a third *omitted variable* not pictured on the graph. Even if we have identified the correct two variables to look at, we might run into a second problem—*reverse causality.*

FIGURE 2A.8

Graph with an Omitted Variable

The upward-sloping curve shows that members of households with more cigarette lighters are more likely to develop cancer. Yet we should not conclude that ownership of lighters causes cancer, because the graph does not take into account the number of cigarettes smoked.

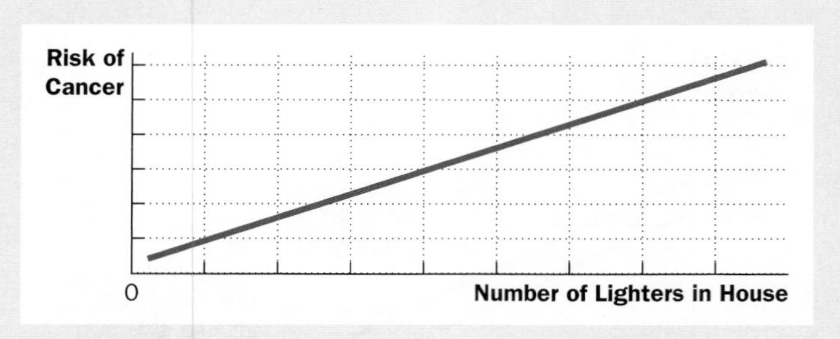

In other words, we might decide that A causes B when in fact B causes A. The omitted-variable and reverse-causality traps require us to proceed with caution when using graphs to draw conclusions about causes and effects.

Omitted Variables To see how omitting a variable can lead to a deceptive graph, let's consider an example. Imagine that the government, spurred by public concern about the large number of deaths from cancer, commissions an exhaustive study from Big Brother Statistical Services Inc. Big Brother examines many of the items found in people's homes to see which of them are associated with the risk of cancer. Big Brother reports a strong relationship between two variables: the number of cigarette lighters that a household owns and the probability that someone in the household will develop cancer. Figure 2A.8 shows this relationship.

What should we make of this result? Big Brother advises a quick policy response. It recommends that the government discourage the ownership of cigarette lighters by taxing their sale. It also recommends that the government require warning labels: "Big Brother has determined that this lighter is dangerous to your health."

In judging the validity of Big Brother's analysis, one question is key: Has Big Brother held constant every relevant variable except the one under consideration? If the answer is no, the results are suspect. An easy explanation for Figure 2A.8 is that people who own more cigarette lighters are more likely to smoke cigarettes and that cigarettes, not lighters, cause cancer. If Figure 2A.8 does not hold constant the amount of smoking, it does not tell us the true effect of owning a cigarette lighter.

This story illustrates an important principle: When you see a graph used to support an argument about cause and effect, it is important to ask whether the movements of an omitted variable could explain the results you see.

Reverse Causality Economists can also make mistakes about causality by misreading its direction. To see how this is possible, suppose the Association of Canadian Anarchists commissions a study of crime in Canada and arrives at Figure 2A.9, which plots the number of violent crimes per thousand people in major cities against the number of police officers per thousand people. The anarchists note the curve's upward slope and argue that because police increase rather than decrease the amount of urban violence, law enforcement should be abolished.

If we could run a controlled experiment, we would avoid the danger of reverse causality. To run an experiment, we would randomly assign different numbers

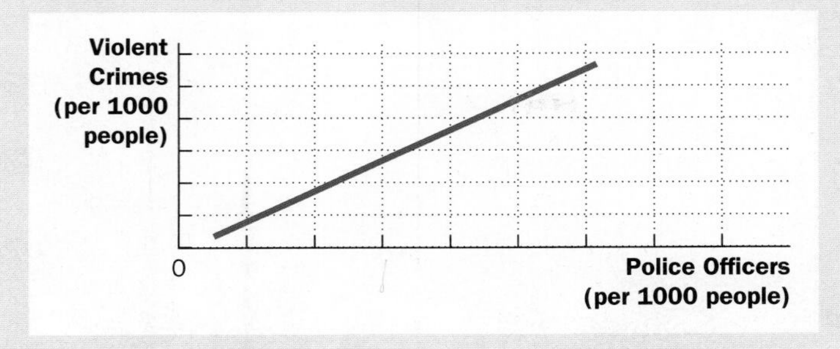

FIGURE 2A.9

Graph Suggesting Reverse Causality

The upward-sloping curve shows that cities with a higher concentration of police are more dangerous. Yet the graph does not tell us whether police cause crime or crime-plagued cities hire more police.

of police to different cities and then examine the correlation between police and crime. Figure 2A.9, however, is not based on such an experiment. We simply observe that more dangerous cities have more police officers. The explanation for this may be that more dangerous cities hire more police. In other words, rather than police causing crime, crime may cause an increase in police. Nothing in the graph itself allows us to establish the direction of causality.

It might seem that an easy way to determine the direction of causality is to examine which variable moves first. If we see crime increase and then the police force expand, we reach one conclusion. If we see the police force expand and then crime increase, we reach the other. Yet there is also a flaw with this approach: Often people change their behaviour not in response to a change in their present conditions but in response to a change in their *expectations* of future conditions. A city that expects a major crime wave in the future, for instance, might hire more police now. This problem is even easier to see in the case of babies and minivans. Couples often buy a minivan in anticipation of the birth of a child. The minivan comes before the baby, but we wouldn't want to conclude that the sale of minivans causes the population to grow!

There is no complete set of rules that says when it is appropriate to draw causal conclusions from graphs. Yet just keeping in mind that cigarette lighters don't cause cancer (omitted variable) and minivans don't cause larger families (reverse causality) will keep you from falling for many faulty economic arguments.

PROBLEMS AND **applications**

A1. Consider the linear demand curve:

$$Q^D = 56 - 4P$$

a. Determine the x- and y-intercepts of this demand curve.
b. Determine the slope of this demand curve.

A2. Using the general functional form for a linear demand curve, $Q^D = a - bP$, and the data in Table 2A.1,
a. Determine the values for a and b for Emma when her income is $20 000.
b. Determine the x- and y-intercepts of this demand curve.
c. Determine the slope of this demand curve.
d. Draw it on a diagram along with the demand curves when her income is $30 000 and $40 000, identifying the x- and y-intercepts in each case.

The Asahi Shimbun/Getty Images

CHAPTER 3

Interdependence and the Gains from Trade

LEARNING **objectives**

In this chapter, you will ...

1. Consider how everyone can benefit when people trade with one another
2. Learn the meaning of *absolute advantage* and *comparative advantage*
3. See how comparative advantage explains the gains from trade
4. Apply the theory of comparative advantage to everyday life and national policy

Consider your typical day. You wake up in the morning, and you pour yourself juice from oranges grown in Florida and coffee from beans grown in Brazil. Over breakfast, you watch a news program broadcast from Toronto on your television set made in China. You get dressed in clothes made of cotton grown in Georgia and sewn in factories in Thailand. You drive to class in a car made of parts manufactured in more than a dozen countries around the world. Then you open up your economics textbook written by authors living in Massachusetts and Alberta, published by a company located in Ontario, and printed on paper made from trees grown in New Brunswick.

Every day, you rely on many people, most of whom you have never met, to provide you with the goods and services that you enjoy. Such interdependence is possible because people trade with one another. Those people providing you with goods and services are not acting out of generosity. Nor is some government agency directing them to satisfy your desires. Instead, people provide you and other consumers with the goods and services they produce because they get something in return.

In subsequent chapters, we examine how our economy coordinates the activities of millions of people with varying tastes and abilities. As a starting point for this analysis, in this chapter we consider the reasons for economic interdependence. One of the ten principles of economics highlighted in Chapter 1 is that trade can make everyone better off. We now examine this principle more closely. What exactly do people gain when they trade with one another? Why do people choose to become interdependent?

The answers to these questions are key to understanding the modern global economy. Most countries today import from abroad many of the goods and services they consume, and they export to foreign customers many of the goods and services they produce. The analysis in this chapter explains interdependence not only among individuals but also among nations. As we will see, the gains from trade are much the same whether you are buying a haircut from your local barber or a T-shirt made by a worker on the other side of the globe.

3-1 A Parable for the Modern Economy

To understand why people choose to depend on others for goods and services and how this choice improves their lives, let's look at a simple economy. Imagine that there are two goods in the world: meat and potatoes. And there are two people in the world—a cattle rancher named Rose and a potato farmer named Frank—each of whom would like to eat both meat and potatoes.

The gains from trade are most obvious if Rose can produce only meat and Frank can produce only potatoes. In one scenario, Frank and Rose could choose to have nothing to do with each other. But after several months of eating beef roasted, boiled, broiled, and grilled, Rose might decide that self-sufficiency is not all it's cracked up to be. Frank, who has been eating potatoes mashed, fried, baked, and scalloped, would likely agree. It is easy to see that trade would allow them to enjoy greater variety: Each could then have a steak with a baked potato or a burger with fries.

Although this scene illustrates most simply how everyone can benefit from trade, the gains would be similar if Frank and Rose were each capable of producing the other good, but only at great cost. Suppose, for example, that Rose is able to grow potatoes but her land is not very well suited for it. Similarly, suppose that Frank is able to raise cattle and produce meat but he is not very good at it. In this case, Frank and Rose can each benefit by specializing in what he or she does best and then trading with the other person.

The gains from trade are less obvious, however, when one person is better at producing *every* good. For example, suppose that Rose is better at raising cattle *and* better at growing potatoes than Frank. In this case, should Rose choose to remain self-sufficient? Or is there still reason for her to trade with Frank? To answer this question, we need to look more closely at the factors that affect such a decision.

3-1a Production Possibilities

Suppose that Frank and Rose each work 8 hours a day and can devote this time to growing potatoes, raising cattle, or a combination of the two. The table in Figure 3.1 shows the amount of time each person requires to produce 1 kg of each good. Frank can produce a kilogram of potatoes in 15 minutes and a kilogram of meat in 60 minutes. Rose, who is more productive in both activities, can produce a kilogram of potatoes in 10 minutes and a kilogram of meat in 20 minutes. The last two columns in the table show the amounts of meat or potatoes Frank and Rose can produce if they devote 8 hours to producing only that good.

Panel (b) of Figure 3.1 illustrates the amounts of meat and potatoes that Frank can produce. If Frank devotes all 8 hours of his time to potatoes, he produces 32 kg of potatoes (measured on the horizontal axis) and no meat. If he devotes all his time to meat, he produces 8 kg of meat (measured on the vertical axis) and no potatoes. If Frank divides his time equally between the two activities, spending 4 hours on each, he produces 16 kg of potatoes and 4 kg of meat. The figure shows these three possible outcomes and all others in between.

This graph is Frank's production possibilities frontier. As we discussed in Chapter 2, a production possibilities frontier shows the various mixes of output that an economy can produce. It illustrates one of the ten principles of economics in Chapter 1: People face tradeoffs. Here Frank faces a tradeoff between producing meat and producing potatoes.

You may recall that the production possibilities frontier in Chapter 2 was drawn bowed out. In that case, the rate at which society could trade one good for the other depended on the amounts being produced. Here, however, Frank's technology for producing meat and potatoes (as summarized in Figure 3.1) allows him to switch between one good and the other at a constant rate. Whenever Frank spends 1 hour less producing meat and 1 hour more producing potatoes, he reduces his output of meat by 1 kg and raises his output of potatoes by 4 kg—and this is true regardless of how much he is already producing. As a result, the production possibilities frontier is a straight line.

Panel (c) of Figure 3.1 shows the production possibilities frontier for Rose. If Rose devotes all 8 hours of her time to potatoes, she produces 48 kg of potatoes and no meat. If she devotes all her time to meat, she produces 24 kg of meat and no potatoes. If she divides her time equally, spending 4 hours on each activity, she produces 24 kg of potatoes and 12 kg of meat. Once again, the production possibilities frontier shows all the possible outcomes.

If Frank and Rose choose to be self-sufficient rather than trade with each other, then each consumes exactly what he or she produces. In this case, the production possibilities frontier is also the consumption possibilities frontier. That is, without trade, Figure 3.1 shows the possible combinations of meat and potatoes that the farmer and rancher can each consume.

(a) The Production Opportunities

	Minutes Needed to Produce 1 kg of:		Amount of Meat or Potatoes Produced in 8 Hours	
	Meat	**Potatoes**	**Meat**	**Potatoes**
Frank	60 min/kg	15 min/kg	8 kg	32 kg
Rose	20 min/kg	10 min/kg	24 kg	48 kg

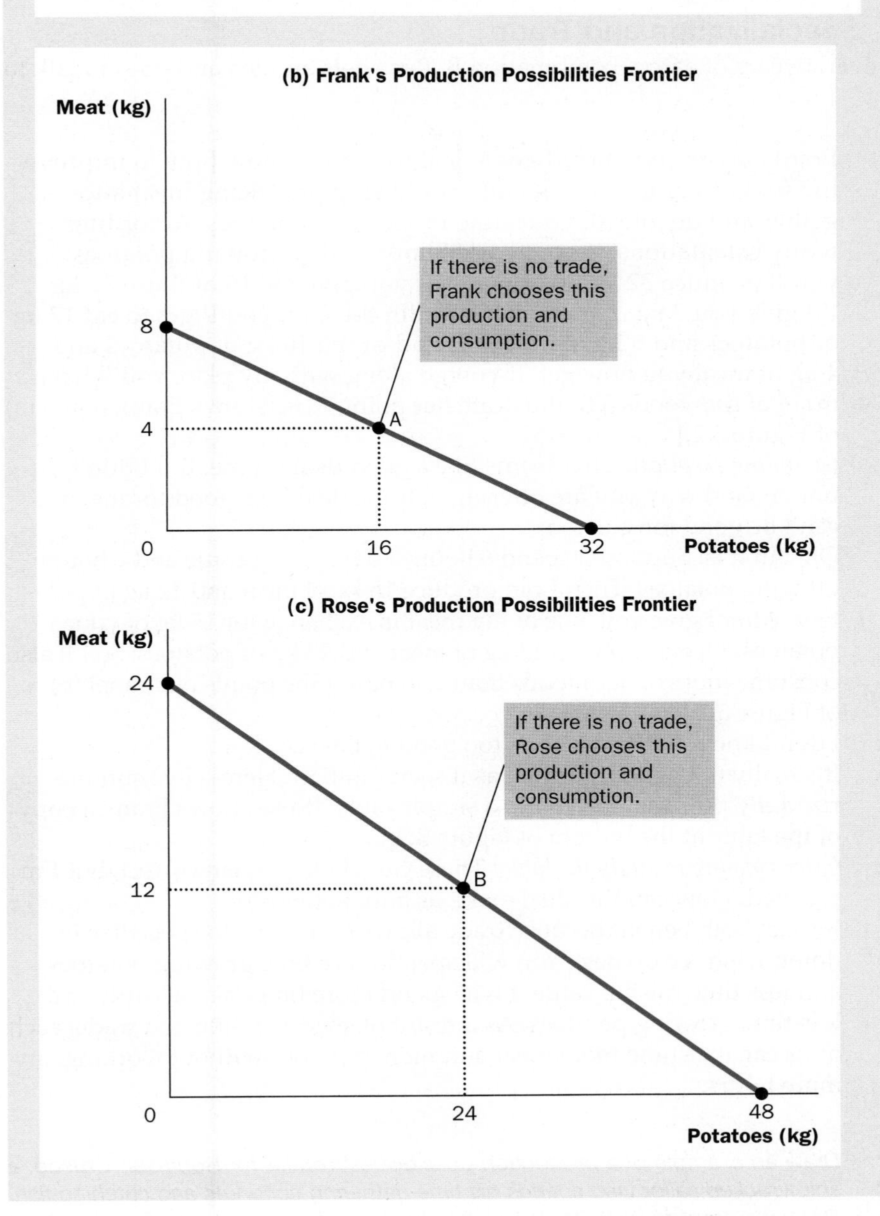

FIGURE 3.1

The Production Possibilities Frontier

Panel (a) shows the production opportunities available to Frank the farmer and Rose the rancher. Panel (b) shows the combinations of meat and potatoes that Frank can produce. Panel (c) shows the combinations of meat and potatoes that Rose can produce. Both production possibilities frontiers are derived assuming that Frank and Rose each work 8 hours a day. If there is no trade, each person's production possibilities frontier is also his or her consumption possibilities frontier.

These production possibilities frontiers are useful in showing the tradeoffs that Frank and Rose face, but they do not tell us what Frank and Rose will actually choose to do. To determine their choices, we need to know the tastes of Frank and Rose. Let's suppose they choose the combinations identified by points A and B in Figure 3.1. Based on his production opportunities and food preferences, Frank decides to produce and consume 16 kg of potatoes and 4 kg of meat, while Rose decides to produce and consume 24 kg of potatoes and 12 kg of meat.

3-1b Specialization and Trade

After several years of eating combination B, Rose gets an idea and goes to talk to Frank:

ROSE: Frank, my friend, have I got a deal for you! I know how to improve life for both of us. I think you should stop producing meat altogether and devote all your time to growing potatoes. According to my calculations, if you work 8 hours a day growing potatoes, you'll produce 32 kg of potatoes. If you give me 15 of those 32 kg, I'll give you 5 kg of meat in return. In the end, you'll get to eat 17 kg of potatoes and 5 kg of meat, instead of the 16 kg of potatoes and 4 kg of meat you now get. If you go along with my plan, you'll have more of *both* foods. [To illustrate her point, Rose shows Frank panel (a) of Figure 3.2.]

FRANK: *(sounding skeptical)* That seems like a good deal for me. But I don't understand why you are offering it. If the deal is so good for me, it can't be good for you too.

ROSE: Oh, but it is! Suppose I spend 6 hours a day raising cattle and 2 hours growing potatoes. Then I can produce 18 kg of meat and 12 kg of potatoes. After I give you 5 kg of my meat in exchange for 15 kg of your potatoes, I'll end up with 13 kg of meat and 27 kg of potatoes. So I'll also consume more of both foods than I do now. [She points out panel (b) of Figure 3.2.]

FRANK: I don't know.... This sounds too good to be true.

ROSE: It's really not as complicated as it seems at first. Here—I've summarized my proposal for you in a simple table. [Rose shows Frank a copy of the table at the bottom of Figure 3.2.]

FRANK: *(after pausing to study the table)* These calculations seem correct, but I'm puzzled. How can this deal make us both better off?

ROSE: We can both benefit because trade allows each of us to specialize in doing what we do best. You will spend more time growing potatoes and less time raising cattle. I will spend more time raising cattle and less time growing potatoes. As a result of specialization and trade, each of us can consume more meat and more potatoes without working any more hours.

Draw an example of a production possibilities frontier for Robinson Crusoe, a shipwrecked sailor who spends his time gathering coconuts and catching fish. Does this frontier limit Crusoe's consumption of coconuts and fish if he lives by himself? Does he face the same limits if he can trade with natives on the island?

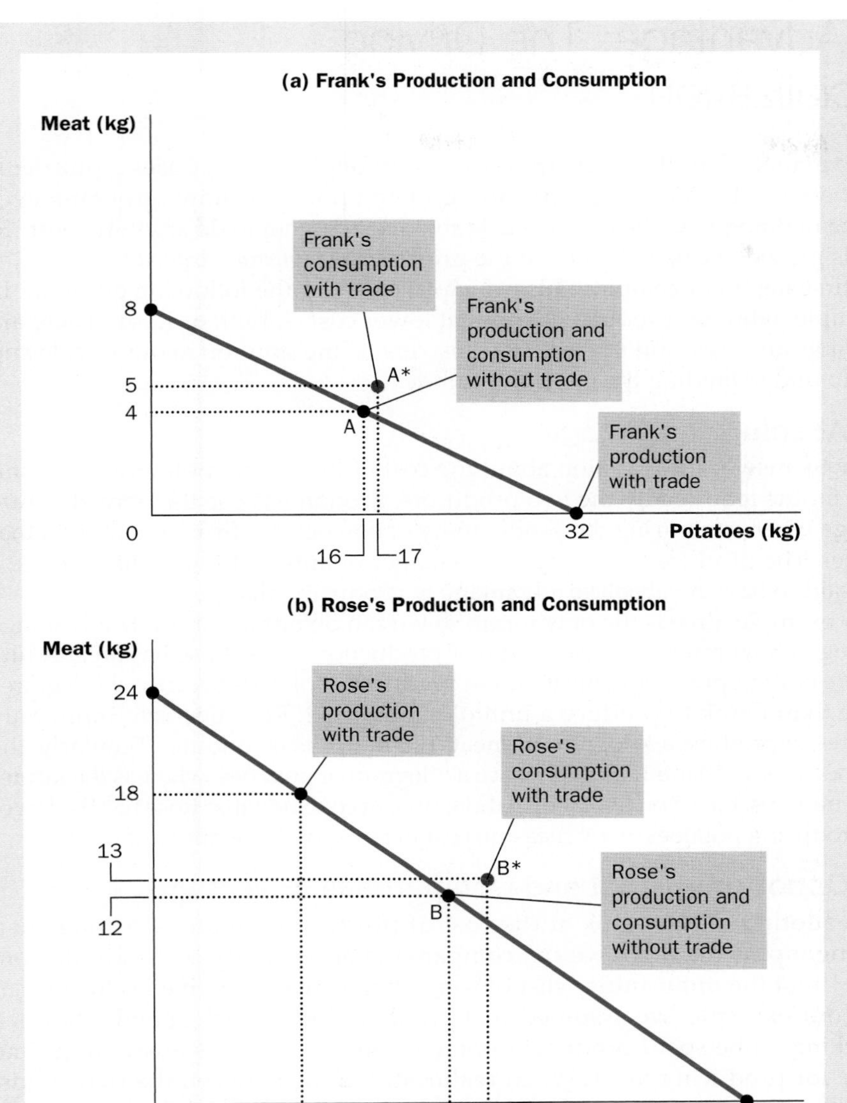

FIGURE 3.2

How Trade Expands the Set of Consumption Opportunities

The proposed trade between Frank the farmer and Rose the rancher offers each of them a combination of meat and potatoes that would be impossible in the absence of trade. In panel (a), Frank gets to consume at point A* rather than point A. In panel (b), Rose gets to consume at point B* rather than point B. Trade allows each to consume more meat and more potatoes.

(c) The Gains from Trade: A Summary

	Frank		Rose	
	Meat	**Potatoes**	**Meat**	**Potatoes**
Without Trade:				
Production and Consumption	4 kg	16 kg	12 kg	24 kg
With Trade:				
Production	0 kg	32 kg	18 kg	12 kg
Trade	Gets 5 kg	Gives 15 kg	Gives 5 kg	Gets 15 kg
Consumption	5 kg	17 kg	13 kg	27 kg
Gains from Trade:				
Increase in Consumption	+1 kg	+1 kg	+1 kg	+3 kg

3-2 Comparative Advantage: The Driving Force of Specialization

Rose's explanation of the gains from trade, although correct, poses a puzzle: If Rose is better at both raising cattle and growing potatoes, how can Frank ever specialize in doing what he does best? Frank doesn't seem to do anything best. To solve this puzzle, we need to look at the principle of *comparative advantage*.

As a first step in developing this principle, consider the following question: In our example, who can produce potatoes at lower cost—Frank or Rose? There are two possible answers, and in these two answers lie the solution to our puzzle and the key to understanding the gains from trade.

3-2a Absolute Advantage

absolute advantage
the comparison among producers of a good according to their productivity

One way to answer the question about the cost of producing potatoes is to compare the inputs required by the two producers. Economists use the term **absolute advantage** when comparing the productivity of one person, firm, or nation to that of another. The producer that requires a smaller quantity of inputs to produce a good is said to have an absolute advantage in producing that good.

In our example, time is the only input, so we can determine absolute advantage by looking at how much time each type of production takes. Rose has an absolute advantage both in producing meat and in producing potatoes because she requires less time than Frank to produce a unit of either good. Rose needs to input only 20 minutes to produce a kilogram of meat; Frank needs 60 minutes. Similarly, the rancher needs only 10 minutes to produce a kilogram of potatoes, whereas the farmer needs 15 minutes. Based on this information, we can conclude that Rose has the lower cost of producing potatoes, if we measure cost in terms of the quantity of inputs.

3-2b Opportunity Cost and Comparative Advantage

opportunity cost
whatever must be given up to obtain some item

There is another way to look at the cost of producing potatoes. Rather than comparing inputs required, we can compare the opportunity costs. Recall from Chapter 1 that the **opportunity cost** of some item is what we give up to get that item. In our example, we assumed that Frank and Rose each spend 8 hours a day working. Time spent producing potatoes, therefore, takes away from time available for producing meat. When reallocating time between the two goods, Rose and Frank give up units of one good to produce units of the other, thereby moving along the production possibilities frontier. The opportunity cost measures the tradeoff between the two goods that each producer faces.

Let's first consider Rose's opportunity cost. According to the table in panel (a) of Figure 3.1, producing 1 kg of potatoes takes her 10 minutes of work. When Rose spends those 10 minutes producing potatoes, she spends 10 minutes less producing meat. Because Rose needs 20 minutes to produce 1 kg of meat, 10 minutes of work would yield 0.5 kg of meat. Hence, Rose's opportunity cost of producing 1 kg of potatoes is 0.5 kg of meat.

Now consider Frank's opportunity cost. Producing 1 kg of potatoes takes him 15 minutes. Because he needs 60 minutes to produce 1 kg of meat, 15 minutes of work would yield 0.25 kg of meat. Hence, Frank's opportunity cost of 1 kg of potatoes is 0.25 kg of meat.

Table 3.1 shows the opportunity costs of meat and potatoes for the two producers. Notice that the opportunity cost of meat is the inverse of the opportunity cost of potatoes. Because 1 kg of potatoes costs Rose 0.5 kg of meat,

	Opportunity Cost of:	
	1 kg of Meat	**1 kg of Potatoes**
Frank the farmer	4 kg potatoes	0.25 kg meat
Rose the rancher	2 kg potatoes	0.50 kg meat

TABLE 3.1

The Opportunity Cost of Meat and Potatoes

1 kg of meat costs Rose 2 kg of potatoes. Similarly, because 1 kg of potatoes costs Frank 0.25 kg of meat, 1 kg of meat costs Frank 4 kg of potatoes.

Economists use the term **comparative advantage** when describing the opportunity cost faced by two producers. The producer who gives up less of other goods to produce Good X has the smaller opportunity cost of producing Good X and is said to have a comparative advantage in producing it. In our example, Frank has a lower opportunity cost of producing potatoes than Rose: A kilogram of potatoes costs Frank only 0.25 kg of meat, while it costs Rose 0.50 kg of meat. Conversely, Rose has a lower opportunity cost of producing meat than Frank: A kilogram of meat costs Rose 2 kg of potatoes, while it costs Frank 4 kg of potatoes. Thus, Frank has a comparative advantage in growing potatoes, and Rose has a comparative advantage in producing meat.

comparative advantage
the comparison among producers of a good according to their opportunity cost

Although it is possible for one person to have an absolute advantage in both goods (as Rose does in our example), it is impossible for one person to have a comparative advantage in both goods. Because the opportunity cost of one good is the inverse of the opportunity cost of the other, if a person's opportunity cost of one good is relatively high, the opportunity cost of the other good must be relatively low. Comparative advantage reflects the relative opportunity cost. Unless two people have exactly the same opportunity cost, one person will have a comparative advantage in one good, and the other person will have a comparative advantage in the other good.

3-2c Comparative Advantage and Trade

The gains from specialization and trade are based not on absolute advantage but rather on comparative advantage. When each person specializes in producing the good for which he or she has a comparative advantage, total production in the economy rises. This increase in the size of the economic pie can be used to make everyone better off.

In our example, Frank spends more time growing potatoes, and Rose spends more time producing meat. As a result, the total production of potatoes rises from 40 to 44 kg, and the total production of meat rises from 16 to 18 kg. Frank and Rose share the benefits of this increased production.

We can also look at the gains from trade in terms of the price that each party pays the other. Because Frank and Rose have different opportunity costs, they can both get a bargain. That is, each of them benefits from trade by obtaining a good at a price that is lower than his or her opportunity cost of that good.

Consider the proposed deal from Frank's viewpoint. Frank receives 5 kg of meat in exchange for 15 kg of potatoes. In other words, Frank buys each kilogram of meat for a price of 3 kg of potatoes. This price of meat is lower than his opportunity cost for 1 kg of meat, which is 4 kg of potatoes. Thus, Frank benefits from the deal because he gets to buy meat at a good price.

FYI The Legacy of Adam Smith and David Ricardo

Economists have long understood the principle of comparative advantage. Here is how the great economist Adam Smith put the argument:

> *It is a maxim of every prudent master of a family, never to attempt to make at home what it will cost him more to make than to buy. The tailor does not attempt to make his own shoes, but buys them of the shoemaker. The shoemaker does not attempt to make his own clothes but employs a tailor. The farmer attempts to make neither the one nor the other, but employs those different artificers. All of them find it for their interest to employ their whole industry in a way in which they have some advantage over their neighbors, and to purchase with a part of its produce, or what is the same thing, with the price of part of it, whatever else they have occasion for.*

This quotation is from Smith's 1776 book *An Inquiry into the Nature and Causes of the Wealth of Nations*, which was a landmark in the analysis of trade and economic interdependence.

Smith's book inspired David Ricardo, a millionaire stockbroker, to become an economist. In his 1817 book *Principles of Political Economy and Taxation*, Ricardo developed the principle of comparative advantage as we know it today. His defence of free trade was not a mere academic exercise. Ricardo put his economic beliefs to work as a member of the British Parliament, where he opposed the Corn Laws, which restricted the import of grain.

The conclusions of Adam Smith and David Ricardo on the gains from trade have held up well over time. Although economists often disagree on questions of policy, they are united in their support of free trade. Moreover, the central argument for free trade has not changed much in the past two centuries. Even though the field of economics has broadened its scope and refined its theories since the time of Smith and Ricardo, economists' opposition to trade restrictions is still based largely on the principle of comparative advantage.

© Bettmann/Corbis

Now consider the deal from Rose's viewpoint. Rose buys 15 kg of potatoes for a price of 5 kg of meat. That is, the price of potatoes is one-third of a kilogram of meat. This price of potatoes is lower than her opportunity cost of 1 kg of potatoes, which is 0.5 kg of meat. Rose benefits because she can buy potatoes at a good price.

The story of Rose the rancher and Frank the farmer has a simple moral, which should now be clear: Trade can benefit everyone in society because it allows people to specialize in activities in which they have a comparative advantage.

3-2d The Price of Trade

The principle of comparative advantage establishes that there are gains from specialization and trade, but it raises a couple of related questions: What determines the price at which trade takes place? How are the gains from trade shared between the trading parties? The precise answer to these questions is beyond the scope of this chapter, but we can state one general rule: *For both parties to gain from trade, the price at which they trade must lie between the two opportunity costs.*

In our example, Rose and Frank agreed to trade at a rate of 3 kg of potatoes for each 1 kg of meat. This price is between Rose's opportunity cost (2 kg of potatoes per 1 kg of meat) and Frank's opportunity cost (4 kg of potatoes per 1 kg of meat). The price need not be exactly in the middle for both parties to gain, but it must be somewhere between 2 and 4.

To see why the price has to be in this range, consider what would happen if it were not. If the price of 1 kg of meat was below 2 kg of potatoes, both Frank and Rose would want to buy meat because the price would be below their

IN THE **news**

Does Free Trade Create Jobs?

Canada has been involved in many free trade agreements over the years—the most important are with our NAFTA partners, the United States and Mexico—and we are currently involved in talks that may lead to new agreements. While politicians talk about the benefits of these agreements in terms of jobs, columnist William Watson (who teaches economics at McGill University) points out that comparative advantage isn't necessarily about more jobs but about better jobs.

Free-Trade Deals Don't Create Jobs, But They're Still Good for Canada

By William Watson

How many Canadians are currently unemployed because we don't have a free-trade deal with Japan? Not many, I bet. I also bet that if we do get such a deal, and I hope we do, the new Japanese demand for our goods does very little for overall employment. It's therefore unfortunate that in announcing free-trade talks with the Japanese the prime minister focused on jobs. "This is a truly historic step," the prime minister said in announcing the beginning of negotiations, "that will help create jobs and growth for both countries."

Politicians always say trade deals are about jobs. Brian Mulroney said Canada–U.S. free trade was about "Jobs, jobs, jobs." It wasn't about jobs. Free-trade deals generally aren't about jobs.

Think about it. Suppose we stopped trading altogether. Would the unemployment rate therefore be 32 per cent (exports equalling 32 per cent of our GDP)?

If we did outlaw trade tomorrow, there would be a huge spike in unemployment. We couldn't possibly eat all the wheat prairie farmers produce. They'd have to find something else to do. But of course outlawing trade also means outlawing imports. So there would be lots of new jobs producing goods and services we had been importing.

Zavatskiy Aleksandr/Shutterstock.com

Nothing against wheat farmers but, to begin with at least, they might not be so good at producing iPods. The new CanPods we'd all have to get used to might not function very well, not to mention they'd weigh three pounds and cost $2,000 apiece. But, assuming we'd want to keep consuming in the manner to which international trade had accustomed us, with imports illegal there would be lots of jobs in this kind of "import substitution."

Though most of us would therefore be employed, we'd also be poorer. Instead of doing what we're good at, we'd be trying to do what foreigners are good at. With trade we specialize in activities where we have a "comparative advantage." We are more productive in them than in alternative activities.

We don't get more jobs by trading. We get better jobs—jobs that pay more because we're better at them. Most politicians aren't economists so they can be forgiven for saying trade deals create jobs. The prime minister* is an economist and must know this. Maybe he believes jobs talk is the only language voters will understand.

Although economists have a professional predisposition toward free trade, it doesn't automatically follow that binational or regional free-trade deals are a good idea. While they create trade, which is good, they also divert trade, which is bad.

Suppose we do get a free-trade deal with Japan. Japanese cars that currently face a six-percent tariff will come in tariff free. That will create trade because some of us will decide to buy a now-cheaper Japanese car (imported from Japan) rather than a Canadian-made car, whether made here by a North American car company or by Honda, Toyota or Suzuki. That's good. If we Canadian consumers decide that under equal tax treatment the pure imports are what we prefer, more power to us. Canadian car manufacturers will have to either up their game or find something else to do.

But Canada–Japan free trade may also cause "trade diversion." Suppose Korea makes the best cars of all. After our deal with Japan, made-in-Japan cars won't face a tariff coming into Canada. But Korean cars will (unless we also finally get a free-trade deal with Korea after 17 years of negotiation but never mind that for the moment). Some Canadian car-buyers will respond by switching from made-in-Korea cars to made-in-Japan cars and that's not good: we end up diverting some of our trade away from the world's best producer, Korea, to our new best friend, Japan.

To figure out whether a given free-trade deal is good or bad, you have to look across all industries and calculate whether the deal creates more trade than it diverts, which is not actually an easy calculation to do.

The obvious solution is to go for the truly level playing field and try to get a free-trade deal with everybody—which is exactly what the WTO is for. Seen as a steppingstone to global free trade, free trade with special friends does make sense, even if that's a hard message to get across in Question Period.

*Stephen Harper was Prime Minister at the time this article was published.

Source: "Free-Trade Deals Don't Create Jobs, But They're Still Good for Canada," by William Watson, *Ottawa Citizen*, March 27, 2012. Material reprinted with the express permission of: *The Ottawa Citizen*, a division of Postmedia Network Inc.

opportunity costs. Similarly, if the price of meat were above 4 kg of potatoes, both would want to sell meat, because the price would be above their opportunity costs. But there are only two members of this economy. They cannot both be buyers of meat, nor can they both be sellers. Someone has to take the other side of the deal.

A mutually advantageous trade can be struck at a price between 2 and 4. In this price range, Rose wants to sell meat to buy potatoes, and Frank wants to sell potatoes to buy meat. Each party can buy a good at a price that is lower than his or her opportunity cost. In the end, both of them specialize in the good for which he or she has a comparative advantage and is, as a result, better off.

Robinson Crusoe can gather 10 coconuts or catch 1 fish per hour. His friend Friday can gather 30 coconuts or catch 2 fish per hour. What is Crusoe's opportunity cost of catching one fish? What is Friday's? Who has an absolute advantage in catching fish? Who has a comparative advantage in catching fish?

3-3 Applications of Comparative Advantage

The principle of comparative advantage explains interdependence and the gains from trade. Because interdependence is so prevalent in the modern world, the principle of comparative advantage has many applications. Here are two examples, one fanciful and one of great practical importance.

3-3a Should Sidney Crosby Shovel His Own Sidewalk?

Sidney Crosby spends a lot of time on the ice. One of the most talented hockey players in the world, he can shoot a puck with a speed and accuracy that most recreational hockey players can only dream of doing. Most likely, he is talented at other physical activities as well. For example, let's imagine that Crosby can shovel his sidewalk faster than anyone else. But just because he *can* shovel his walk quickly, does this mean he *should*?

Sidney Crosby

To answer this question, we can use the concepts of opportunity cost and comparative advantage. Let's say that Crosby can shovel his walk in one hour. In that same hour, he could film a television commercial and earn $20 000. By contrast, Forrest Gump, the boy next door, can shovel Crosby's walk in two hours. In that same two hours, he could work at McDonald's and earn $20.

In this example, Crosby has an absolute advantage in shovelling sidewalks because he can do the work with a lower input of time. Yet because Crosby's opportunity cost of shovelling the sidewalk is $20 000 and Gump's opportunity cost is only $20, Gump has a comparative advantage in shovelling sidewalks.

The gains from trade in this example are tremendous. Rather than shovelling his own sidewalk, Crosby should make the commercial and hire Gump to shovel the walk. As long as Crosby pays Gump more than $20 and less than $20 000, both of them are better off.

3-3b Should Canada Trade with Other Countries?

Just as individuals can benefit from specialization and trade with one another, as Frank and Rose did, so can populations of people in different countries. Many of the goods and services that Canadians enjoy are produced abroad, and many of the goods and services produced in Canada are sold abroad. Goods and services produced abroad and sold domestically are called **imports**. Goods and services produced domestically and sold abroad are called **exports**.

imports
goods and services produced abroad and sold domestically

exports
goods and services produced domestically and sold abroad

An interesting question concerns the sources of comparative advantage. For individuals, some of their comparative advantage is "natural"—Sidney Crosby clearly has an innate talent for hockey that most of us do not. This is also true at the country level. Canada has a clear comparative advantage in the provision of natural resources. We are a leading provider of oil, forest products, and agriculture goods to the world market because of our natural geographic, geological, and topological advantages. For example, Canada is a large exporter of pulp and paper products to the United States. This is due both to our large forest areas and to our access to cheap hydroelectricity, which provides the power required to process pulp.

However, hard work, training, education, and experience can create, or enhance, comparative advantage. Raw talent is only part of the reason that some individuals rise to the top of their professions. This is also true at the country level. The Canadian workforce is highly educated, healthy, and productive relative to many countries. This gives Canada a comparative advantage in the production of high-value-added goods that require a skilled labour force.

To see how countries can benefit from trade, suppose there are two countries, Canada and Japan, and two goods, food and cars. Imagine that the two countries produce cars equally well: A Canadian worker and a Japanese worker can each produce 1 car per month. By contrast, because Canada has more and better land, it is better at producing food: A Canadian worker can produce 2 tonnes of food per month, whereas a Japanese worker can produce only 1 tonne of food per month.

The principle of comparative advantage states that each good should be produced by the country that has the smaller opportunity cost of producing that good. Because the opportunity cost of a car is 2 tonnes of food in Canada but only 1 tonne of food in Japan, Japan has a comparative advantage in producing cars. Japan should produce more cars than it wants for its own use and export some of them to Canada. Similarly, because the opportunity cost of a tonne of food is 1 car in Japan but only 1/2 car in Canada, Canada has a comparative advantage in producing food. Canada should produce more food than it wants to consume and export some of it to Japan. Through specialization and trade, both countries can have more food and more cars.

In reality, of course, the issues involved in trade among nations are more complex than this example suggests. The most important among these issues is that each country has many citizens with different interests. International trade can make some individuals worse off, even as it makes the country as a whole better off. When Canada exports food and imports cars, the impact on a Canadian farmer is not the same as the impact on a Canadian autoworker. Yet, contrary to the opinions sometimes voiced by politicians and political commentators, international trade is not like war, in which some countries win and others lose. Trade allows all countries to achieve greater prosperity.

Suppose that a skilled brain surgeon also happens to be the world's fastest typist. Should he do his own typing or hire a secretary? Explain.

3-4 Conclusion

You should now understand more fully the benefits of living in an interdependent economy. When Canadians buy tube socks from China, when residents of Manitoba drink apple juice from British Columbia, and when a homeowner hires the kid next door to shovel the sidewalk, the same economic forces are at work. The principle of comparative advantage shows that trade can make everyone better off.

Having seen why interdependence is desirable, you might naturally ask how it is possible. How do free societies coordinate the diverse activities of all the people involved in their economies? What ensures that goods and services will get from those who should be producing them to those who should be consuming them? In a world with only two people, such as Rose the rancher and Frank the farmer, the answer is simple: These two people can bargain and allocate resources between themselves. In the real world with billions of people, the answer is less obvious. We take up this issue in the next chapter, where we see that free societies allocate resources through the market forces of supply and demand.

summary

- Each person consumes goods and services produced by many other people, both in Canada and around the world. Interdependence and trade are desirable because they allow everyone to enjoy a greater quantity and variety of goods and services.
- There are two ways to compare the ability of two people in producing a good. The person who can produce the good with the smaller quantity of inputs is said to have an *absolute advantage* in producing the good. The person who has the smaller opportunity cost of producing the good is said to have a *comparative advantage.* The gains from trade are based on comparative advantage, not absolute advantage.
- Trade makes everyone better off because it allows people to specialize in those activities in which they have a comparative advantage.
- The principle of comparative advantage applies to countries as well as to people. Economists use the principle of comparative advantage to advocate free trade among countries.

KEY concepts

absolute advantage, *p. 52*
opportunity cost, *p. 52*
comparative advantage, *p. 53*
imports, *p. 57*
exports, *p. 57*

QUESTIONS FOR review

1. Under what conditions is the production possibilities frontier linear rather than bowed out?
2. Explain how absolute advantage and comparative advantage differ.
3. Give an example in which one person has an absolute advantage in doing something but another person has a comparative advantage.
4. Is absolute advantage or comparative advantage more important for trade? Explain your reasoning using the example in your answer to question 3.
5. If two parties trade based on comparative advantage and both gain, in what range must the price of the trade lie?
6. Why do economists tend to oppose policies that restrict trade among nations?

QUICK CHECK **multiple choice**

1. In an hour, Ken can wash 2 cars or mow 1 lawn, and Ron can wash 3 cars or mow 1 lawn. Who has the absolute advantage in car washing, and who has the absolute advantage in lawn mowing?
   a. Ken in washing, Ron in mowing
   b. Ron in washing, Ken in mowing
   c. Ken in washing, neither in mowing
   d. Ron in washing, neither in mowing
2. Once again, in an hour, Ken can wash 2 cars or mow 1 lawn, and Ron can wash 3 cars or mow 1 lawn. Who has the comparative advantage in car washing, and who has the comparative advantage in lawn mowing?
   a. Ken in washing, Ron in mowing
   b. Ron in washing, Ken in mowing
   c. Ken in washing, neither in mowing
   d. Ron in washing, neither in mowing
3. What results when two individuals produce efficiently and then make a mutually beneficial trade based on comparative advantage?
   a. they both obtain consumption outside their production possibilities frontier
   b. they both obtain consumption inside their production possibilities frontier
   c. one individual consumes inside her production possibilities frontier, while the other consumes outside hers
   d. each individual consumes a point on her own production possibilities frontier
4. Which goods will a nation typically import?
   a. those goods in which the nation has an absolute advantage
   b. those goods in which the nation has a comparative advantage
   c. those goods in which other nations have an absolute advantage
   d. those goods in which other nations have a comparative advantage
5. Suppose that in Canada, producing an aircraft takes 10 000 hours of labour and producing a shirt takes 2 hours of labour. In China, producing an aircraft takes 40 000 hours of labour and producing a shirt takes 4 hours of labour. What will these nations trade?
   a. China will export aircraft, and Canada will export shirts.
   b. China will export shirts, and Canada will export aircraft.
   c. Both nations will export shirts.
   d. There are no gains from trade in this situation.
6. Mark can cook dinner in 30 minutes and wash the laundry in 20 minutes. His roommate takes half as long to do each task. How should the roommates allocate the work?
   a. Mark should do more of the cooking based on his comparative advantage.
   b. Mark should do more of the washing based on his comparative advantage.
   c. Mark should do more of the washing based on his absolute advantage.
   d. There are no gains from trade in this situation.

PROBLEMS AND **applications**

1. Maria can read 20 pages of economics in an hour. She can also read 50 pages of sociology in an hour. She spends 5 hours per day studying.
   a. Draw Maria's production possibilities frontier for reading economics and sociology.
   b. What is Maria's opportunity cost of reading 100 pages of sociology?
2. Canadian and Japanese workers can each produce 4 cars per year. A Canadian worker can produce 10 tonnes of grain per year, whereas a Japanese worker can produce 5 tonnes of grain per year. To keep things simple, assume that each country has 100 million workers.
   a. For this situation, construct a table analogous to panel (a) in Figure 3.1.
   b. Graph the production possibilities frontier of the Canadian and Japanese economies.
   c. For Canada, what is the opportunity cost of a car? Of grain? For Japan, what is the opportunity cost of a car? Of grain? Put this information in a table analogous to Table 3.1.
   d. Which country has an absolute advantage in producing cars? In producing grain?
   e. Which country has a comparative advantage in producing cars? In producing grain?
   f. Without trade, half of each country's workers produce cars and half produce grain. What quantities of cars and grain does each country produce?
   g. Starting from a position without trade, give an example in which trade makes each country better off.
3. Pat and Kris are roommates. They spend most of their time studying (of course), but they leave some time for their favourite activities: making pizza and brewing

root beer. Pat takes 4 hours to brew 5 L of root beer and 2 hours to make a pizza. Kris takes 6 hours to brew 5 L of root beer and 4 hours to make a pizza.

a. What is each roommate's opportunity cost of making a pizza? Who has the absolute advantage in making pizza? Who has the comparative advantage in making pizza?
b. If Pat and Kris trade products with each other, who will trade away pizza in exchange for root beer?
c. The price of pizza can be expressed in terms of litres of root beer. What is the highest price at which pizza can be traded that would make both roommates better off? What is the lowest price? Explain.

4. Suppose that there are 10 million workers in Canada, and that each of these workers can produce either 2 cars or 30 tonnes of wheat in a year.
   a. What is the opportunity cost of producing a car in Canada? What is the opportunity cost of producing a tonne of wheat in Canada? Explain the relationship between the opportunity costs of the two goods.
   b. Draw Canada's production possibilities frontier. If Canada chooses to consume 10 million cars, how much wheat can it consume without trade? Label this point on the production possibilities frontier.
   c. Now suppose that the United States offers to buy 10 million cars from Canada in exchange for 20 tonnes of wheat per car. If Canada continues to consume 10 million cars, how much wheat does this deal allow Canada to consume? Label this point on your diagram. Should Canada accept the deal?
5. England and Scotland both produce scones and sweaters. Suppose that an English worker can produce 50 scones per hour or 1 sweater per hour. Suppose that a Scottish worker can produce 40 scones per hour or 2 sweaters per hour.
   a. Which country has the absolute advantage in the production of each good? Which country has the comparative advantage?
   b. If England and Scotland decide to trade, which commodity will Scotland trade to England? Explain.
   c. If a Scottish worker could produce only 1 sweater per hour, would Scotland still gain from trade? Would England still gain from trade? Explain.
6. The following table describes the production possibilities of two cities:

	Red Sweaters per Worker per Hour	Blue Sweaters per Worker per Hour
Montreal	3	3
Toronto	2	1

   a. Without trade, what is the price of blue sweaters (in terms of red sweaters) in Montreal? What is the price in Toronto?
   b. Which city has an absolute advantage in the production of each colour of sweater? Which city has a comparative advantage in the production of each colour of sweater?
   c. If the cities trade with each other, which colour of sweater will each export?
   d. What is the range of prices at which trade can occur?
7. Are the following statements true or false? Explain in each case.
   a. "Two countries can achieve gains from trade even if one of the countries has an absolute advantage in the production of all goods."
   b. "Certain very talented people have a comparative advantage in everything they do."
   c. "If a certain trade is good for one person, it can't be good for the other one."
   d. "If a certain trade is good for one person, it is always good for the other one."
   e. "If trade is good for a country, it must be good for everyone in the country."
8. Canada exports oil and pulp and paper to the rest of the world, and it imports computers and clothing from the rest of the world. Do you think this pattern of trade is consistent with the principle of comparative advantage? Why or why not?
9. Conrad and Barbara produce food and clothing. In an hour, Conrad can produce 1 unit of food or 1 unit of clothing, while Barbara can produce 2 units of food or 3 units of clothing. They each work 10 hours a day.
   a. Who has an absolute advantage in producing food? Who has an absolute advantage in producing clothing? Explain.
   b. Who has a comparative advantage in producing food? Who has a comparative advantage in producing clothing? Explain.
   c. Draw the production possibilities frontier for the household (that is, Conrad and Barbara together) assuming that each spends the same number of hours each day as the other producing food and clothing.
   d. Barbara suggests that, instead, she specialize in making clothing. That is, she will do all of the clothing production, unless her time is fully devoted to clothing, and then Conrad will chip in. What does the household production possibilities frontier look like now?
   e. Conrad suggests that Barbara specialize in producing food. That is, Barbara will do all the food production, unless her time is fully devoted to food, and then Conrad will chip in. What does the

household production possibilities frontier look like under Conrad's proposal?

f. Comparing your answers to parts (c), (d), and (e), which allocation of time makes the most sense? Relate your answer to the theory of comparative advantage.

10. Suppose that in a year a Canadian worker can produce 100 shirts or 20 computers, while a Chinese worker can produce 100 shirts or 10 computers.
    a. Graph the production possibilities curve for the two countries. Suppose that without trade the workers in each country spend half their time producing each good. Identify this point in your graph.
    b. If these countries were open to trade, which country would export shirts? Give a specific numerical example and show it on your graph. Which country would benefit from trade? Explain.
    c. Explain at what price of computers (in terms of shirts) the two countries might trade.
    d. Suppose that China catches up with Canadian productivity so that a Chinese worker can produce 100 shirts or 20 computers. What pattern of trade would you predict now? How does this advance in Chinese productivity affect the economic well-being of the citizens of the two countries?

11. An average worker in Brazil can produce 30 mL of soy milk in 20 minutes and 30 mL of coffee in 60 minutes, while an average worker in Peru can produce 30 mL of soy milk in 50 minutes and 30 mL of coffee in 75 minutes.
    a. Who has the absolute advantage in coffee? Explain.
    b. Who has the comparative advantage in coffee? Explain.
    c. If the two countries specialize and trade with each other, who will import coffee? Explain.
    d. Assume that the two countries trade and that the country importing coffee trades 60 mL of soy milk for 30 mL of coffee. Explain why both countries will benefit from this trade.

12. A German worker takes 400 hours to produce a car and 2 hours to produce a case of wine. A French worker takes 600 hours to produce a car and X hours to produce a case of wine.
    a. For what values of X will gains from trade be possible? Explain.
    b. For what values of X will Germany export cars and import wine? Explain.

© Lavinia Moldovan

The Market Forces of Supply and Demand

LEARNING **objectives**

In this chapter, you will ...

1. Learn the nature of a competitive market
2. Examine what determines the demand for a good in a competitive market
3. Examine what determines the supply of a good in a competitive market
4. See how supply and demand together set the price of a good and the quantity sold
5. Consider the key role of prices in allocating scarce resources in market economies

When a cold snap hits Florida, the price of orange juice rises in supermarkets throughout Canada. When the weather turns warm in Quebec every summer, the price of hotel rooms in Cuba plummets. When a war breaks out in the Middle East, the price of gasoline in Canada rises and the price of a used SUV falls. What do these events have in common? They all show the workings of supply and demand.

Supply and *demand* are the two words that economists use most often—and for good reason. Supply and demand are the forces that make market economies work. They determine the quantity of each good produced and the price at which it is sold. If you want to know how any event or policy will affect the economy, you must think first about how it will affect supply and demand.

This chapter introduces the theory of supply and demand. It considers how buyers and sellers behave and how they interact with one another. It shows how supply and demand determine prices in a market economy and how prices, in turn, allocate the economy's scarce resources.

4-1 Markets and Competition

The terms *supply* and *demand* refer to the behaviour of people as they interact with one another in competitive markets. Before discussing how buyers and sellers behave, let's first consider more fully what we mean by a "market" and "competition."

4-1a What Is a Market?

A **market** is a group of buyers and sellers of a particular good or service. The buyers as a group determine the demand for the product, and the sellers as a group determine the supply of the product.

market
a group of buyers and sellers of a particular good or service

Markets take many forms. Some markets are highly organized, such as the markets for many agricultural commodities. In these markets, buyers and sellers meet at a specific time and place, where an auctioneer helps set prices and arrange sales.

More often, markets are less organized. For example, consider the market for ice cream in a particular town. Buyers of ice cream do not meet together at any one time. The sellers of ice cream are in different locations and offer somewhat different products. There is no auctioneer calling out the price of ice cream. Each seller posts a price for an ice-cream cone, and each buyer decides how much ice cream to buy at each store. Nonetheless, these consumers and producers of ice cream are closely connected. The ice-cream buyers are choosing from the various ice-cream sellers to satisfy their craving, and the ice-cream sellers are all trying to appeal to the same ice-cream buyers to make their businesses successful. Even though it is not as organized, the group of ice-cream buyers and ice-cream sellers forms a market.

4-1b What Is Competition?

The market for ice cream, like most markets in the economy, is highly competitive. Each buyer knows that there are several sellers from which to choose, and each seller is aware that his product is similar to that offered by other sellers. As a result, the price and quantity of ice cream sold are not determined by any single buyer or seller. Rather, price and quantity are determined by all buyers and sellers as they interact in the marketplace.

competitive market
a market in which there are many buyers and many sellers so that each has a negligible impact on the market price

Economists use the term **competitive market** to describe a market in which there are so many buyers and so many sellers that each has a negligible impact on the market price. Each seller of ice cream has limited control over the price because other sellers are offering similar products. A seller has little reason to charge less than the going price, and if he charges more, buyers will make their purchases elsewhere. Similarly, no single buyer of ice cream can influence the price of ice cream because each buyer purchases only a small amount.

In this chapter, we assume that markets are *perfectly competitive.* To reach this highest form of competition, a market must have two characteristics: (1) the goods offered for sale are all exactly the same, and (2) the buyers and sellers are so numerous that no single buyer or seller has any influence over the market price. Because buyers and sellers in perfectly competitive markets must accept the price the market determines, they are said to be *price takers.* At the market price, buyers can buy all they want, and sellers can sell all they want.

There are some markets in which the assumption of perfect competition applies perfectly. In the wheat market, for example, there are thousands of farmers who sell wheat and millions of consumers who use wheat and wheat products. Because no single buyer or seller can influence the price of wheat, each takes the price as given.

Not all goods and services, however, are sold in perfectly competitive markets. Some markets have only one seller, and this seller sets the price. Such a seller is called a *monopoly.* Your local cable television company, for instance, may be a monopoly. Residents of your small town probably have only one cable company from which to buy this service. Still other markets fall between the extremes of perfect competition and monopoly.

Despite the diversity of market types we find in the world, assuming perfect competition is a useful simplification and, therefore, a natural place to start. Perfectly competitive markets are the easiest to analyze because everyone participating in the market takes the price as given by market conditions. Moreover, because some degree of competition is present in most markets, many of the lessons that we learn by studying supply and demand under perfect competition apply in more complicated markets as well.

What is a market? • What are the characteristics of a competitive market?

4-2 Demand

We begin our study of markets by examining the behaviour of buyers. To focus our thinking, let's keep in mind a particular good—ice cream.

4-2a The Demand Curve: The Relationship between Price and Quantity Demanded

quantity demanded
the amount of a good that buyers are willing and able to purchase

The **quantity demanded** of any good is the amount of the good that buyers are willing and able to purchase. As we will see, many things determine the quantity demanded of any good, but in our analysis of how markets work, one determinant plays a central role—the price of the good. If the price of ice cream

FIGURE 4.1

Catherine's Demand Schedule and Demand Curve

The demand schedule shows the quantity demanded at each price. The demand curve, which graphs the demand schedule, shows how the quantity demanded of the good changes as its price varies. Because a lower price increases the quantity demanded, the demand curve slopes downward.

Price of Ice-Cream Cone	Quantity of Cones Demanded
$0.00	12
0.50	10
1.00	8
1.50	6
2.00	4
2.50	2
3.00	0

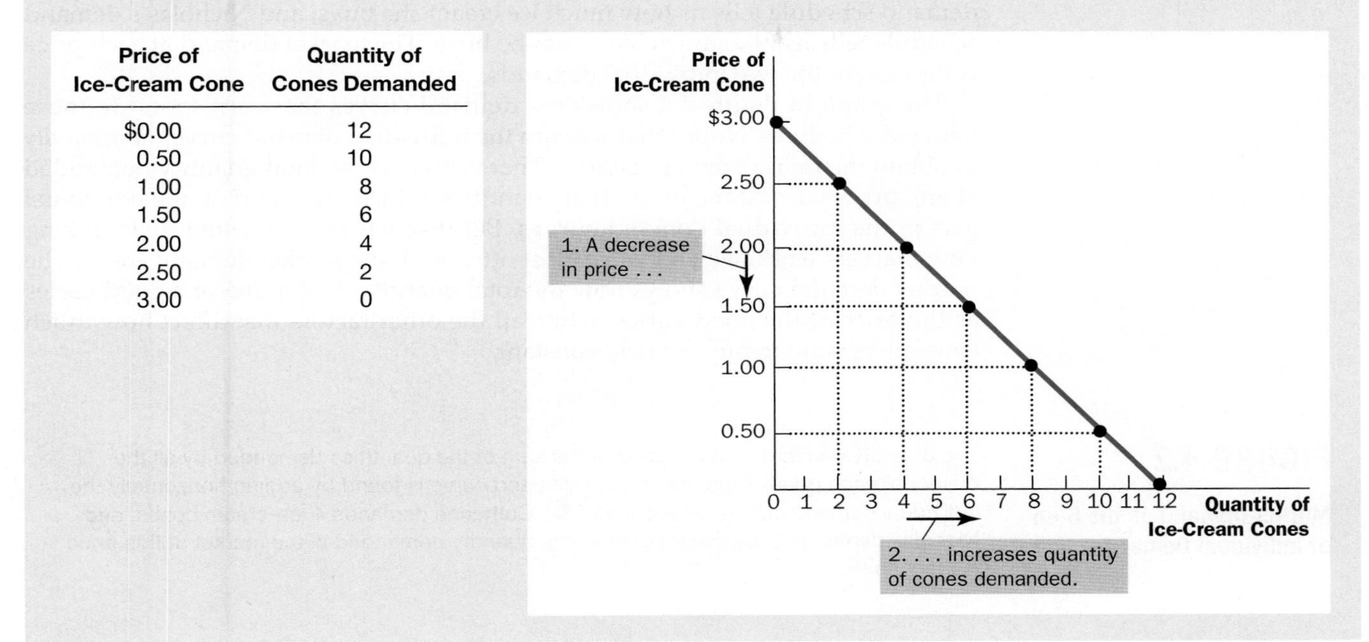

rose to $20 per scoop, you would buy less ice cream. You might buy frozen yogurt instead. If the price of ice cream fell to $0.20 per scoop, you would buy more. This relationship between price and quantity demanded is true for most goods in the economy and, in fact, is so pervasive that economists call it the **law of demand**: Other things equal, when the price of a good rises, the quantity demanded of the good falls, and when the price falls, the quantity demanded rises.

law of demand
the claim that, other things equal, the quantity demanded of a good falls when the price of the good rises

The table in Figure 4.1 shows how many ice-cream cones Catherine buys each month at different prices of ice cream. If ice cream is free, Catherine eats 12 cones. At $0.50 per cone, Catherine buys 10 cones each month. As the price rises further, she buys fewer and fewer cones. When the price reaches $3.00, Catherine doesn't buy any ice cream at all. This table is a **demand schedule**, a table that shows the relationship between the price of a good and the quantity demanded, holding constant everything else that influences how much of the good consumers want to buy.

demand schedule
a table that shows the relationship between the price of a good and the quantity demanded

The graph in Figure 4.1 uses the numbers from the table to illustrate the law of demand. By convention, the price of ice cream is on the vertical axis, and the quantity of ice cream demanded is on the horizontal axis. The line relating price and quantity demanded is called the **demand curve**. The demand curve slopes downward because, other things being equal, a lower price means a greater quantity demanded.

demand curve
a graph of the relationship between the price of a good and the quantity demanded

4-2b Market Demand versus Individual Demand

The demand curve in Figure 4.1 shows an individual's demand for a product. To analyze how markets work, we need to determine the *market demand,* which is the sum of all the individual demands for a particular good or service.

The table in Figure 4.2 shows the demand schedules for ice cream of the two individuals in this market—Catherine and Nicholas. At any price, Catherine's demand schedule tells us how much ice cream she buys, and Nicholas's demand schedule tells us how much ice cream he buys. The market demand at each price is the sum of the two individual demands.

The graph in Figure 4.2 shows the demand curves that correspond to these demand schedules. Notice that we sum the individual demand curves *horizontally* to obtain the market demand curve. That is, to find the total quantity demanded at any price, we add the individual quantities, which are found on the horizontal axis of the individual demand curves. Because we are interested in analyzing how markets work, we will work most often with the market demand curve. The market demand curve shows how the total quantity demanded of a good varies as the price of the good varies, while all the other factors that affect how much consumers want to buy are held constant.

FIGURE 4.2

Market Demand as the Sum of Individual Demands

The quantity demanded in a market is the sum of the quantities demanded by all the buyers at each price. Thus, the market demand curve is found by adding horizontally the individual demand curves. At a price of $2, Catherine demands 4 ice-cream cones, and Nicholas demands 3 ice-cream cones. The quantity demanded in the market at this price is 7 cones.

Price of Ice-Cream Cone	Catherine		Nicholas		Market
$0.00	12	+	7	=	19
0.50	10		6		16
1.00	8		5		13
1.50	6		4		10
2.00	4		3		7
2.50	2		2		4
3.00	0		1		1

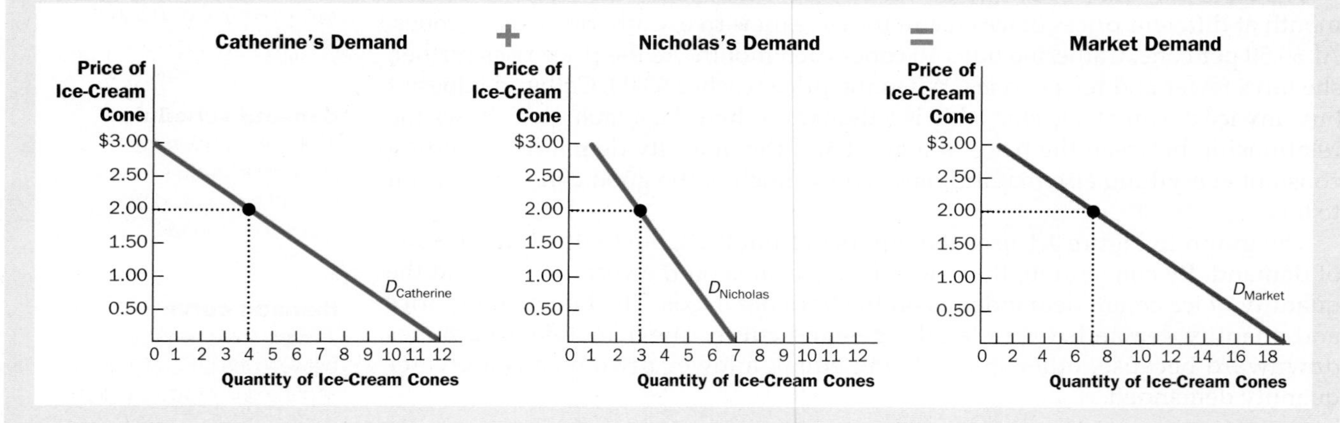

4-2c Shifts in the Demand Curve

Because the market demand curve holds other things constant, it need not be stable over time. If something happens to alter the quantity demanded at any given price, the demand curve shifts. For example, suppose the Canadian Medical Association discovered that people who regularly eat ice cream live longer, healthier lives. The discovery would raise the demand for ice cream. At any given price, buyers would now want to purchase a larger quantity of ice cream, and the demand curve for ice cream would shift.

Figure 4.3 illustrates shifts in demand. Any change that increases the quantity demanded at every price, such as our imaginary discovery by the Canadian Medical Association, shifts the demand curve to the right and is called *an increase in demand.* Any change that reduces the quantity demanded at every price shifts the demand curve to the left and is called *a decrease in demand.*

Many variables can shift the demand curve. Here are the most important:

Income What would happen to your demand for ice cream if you lost your job one summer? Most likely, it would fall. A lower income means that you have less to spend in total, so you would have to spend less on some—and probably most—goods. If the demand for a good falls when income falls, the good is called a **normal good**.

normal good
a good for which, other things equal, an increase in income leads to an increase in demand

Not all goods are normal goods. If the demand for a good rises when income falls, the good is called an **inferior good**. An example of an inferior good might be bus rides. As your income falls, you are less likely to buy a car or take a cab and more likely to ride a bus.

inferior good
a good for which, other things equal, an increase in income leads to a decrease in demand

Prices of Related Goods Suppose that the price of frozen yogurt falls. The law of demand says that you will buy more frozen yogurt. At the same time, you will probably buy less ice cream. Because ice cream and frozen yogurt are

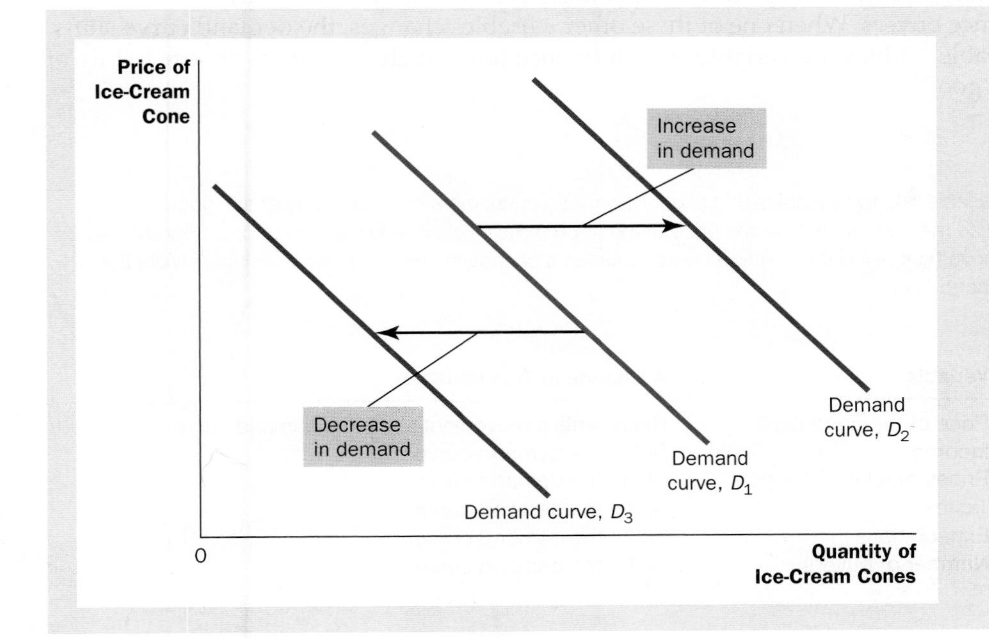

FIGURE 4.3

Shifts in the Demand Curve
Any change that raises the quantity that buyers wish to purchase at a given price shifts the demand curve to the right. Any change that lowers the quantity that buyers wish to purchase at a given price shifts the demand curve to the left.

Would this be your lunch if you had a higher income?

both cold, sweet, creamy desserts, they satisfy similar desires. When a fall in the price of one good reduces the demand for another good, the two goods are called **substitutes**. Substitutes are often pairs of goods that are used in place of each other, such as hot dogs and hamburgers, sweaters and sweatshirts, and movie tickets and streaming services.

Now suppose that the price of hot fudge falls. According to the law of demand, you will buy more hot fudge. Yet, in this case, you will buy more ice cream as well because ice cream and hot fudge are often used together. When a fall in the price of one good raises the demand for another good, the two goods are called **complements**. Complements are often pairs of goods that are used together, such as gasoline and automobiles, computers and software, and peanut butter and jelly.

substitutes
two goods for which an increase in the price of one leads to an increase in the demand for the other

complements
two goods for which an increase in the price of one leads to a decrease in the demand for the other

Tastes The most obvious determinant of your demand is your tastes. If you like ice cream, you buy more of it. Economists normally do not try to explain people's tastes because tastes are based on historical and psychological forces that are beyond the realm of economics. Economists do, however, examine what happens when tastes change.

Expectations Your expectations about the future may affect your demand for a good or service today. If you expect to earn a higher income next month, you may be more willing to spend some of your current savings buying ice cream. If you expect the price of ice cream to fall tomorrow, you may be less willing to buy an ice-cream cone at today's price.

Number of Buyers In addition to the preceding factors, which influence the behaviour of individual buyers, market demand depends on the number of these buyers. If Peter were to join Catherine and Nicholas as another consumer of ice cream, the quantity demanded in the market would be higher at every price and market demand would increase.

Summary The demand curve shows what happens to the quantity demanded of a good when its price varies, holding constant all the other variables that influence buyers. When one of these other variables changes, the demand curve shifts. Table 4.1 lists the variables that influence how much consumers choose to buy of a good.

TABLE 4.1

Variables That Influence Buyers

This table lists the variables that affect how much consumers choose to buy of any good. Notice the special role that the price of the good plays: A change in the good's price represents a movement along the demand curve, whereas a change in one of the other variables shifts the demand curve.

Variable	A Change in This Variable ...
Price of the good itself	Represents a movement along the demand curve
Income	Shifts the demand curve
Prices of related goods	Shifts the demand curve
Tastes	Shifts the demand curve
Expectations	Shifts the demand curve
Number of buyers	Shifts the demand curve

If you have trouble remembering whether you need to shift or move along the demand curve, it helps to recall a lesson from the appendix to Chapter 2. A curve shifts when there is a change in a relevant variable that is not measured on either axis. Because the price is on the vertical axis, a change in price represents a movement along the demand curve. By contrast, income, the prices of related goods, tastes, expectations, and the number of buyers are not measured on either axis, so a change in one of these variables shifts the demand curve.

What is the best way to stop this?

case study

Two Ways to Reduce the Quantity of Smoking Demanded

Public policymakers often want to reduce the amount that people smoke because of smoking's adverse health effects. There are two ways that policy can attempt to achieve this goal.

One way to reduce smoking is to shift the demand curve for cigarettes and other tobacco products. Public service announcements, mandatory health warnings on cigarette packages, and the prohibition of cigarette advertising on television are all policies aimed at reducing the quantity of cigarettes demanded at any given price. If successful, these policies shift the demand curve for cigarettes to the left, as in panel (a) of Figure 4.4.

Alternatively, policymakers can try to raise the price of cigarettes. If the government taxes the manufacture of cigarettes, for example, cigarette companies

FIGURE 4.4

Shifts in the Demand Curve versus Movements along the Demand Curve

If warnings on cigarette packages convince smokers to smoke less, the demand curve for cigarettes shifts to the left. In panel (a), the demand curve shifts from D_1 to D_2. At a price of $10.00 per pack, the quantity demanded falls from 20 to 10 cigarettes per day, as reflected by the shift from point A to point B. By contrast, if a tax raises the price of cigarettes, the demand curve does not shift. Instead, we observe a movement to a different point on the demand curve. In panel (b), when the price rises from $10.00 to $20.00, the quantity demanded falls from 20 to 12 cigarettes per day, as reflected by the movement from point A to point C.

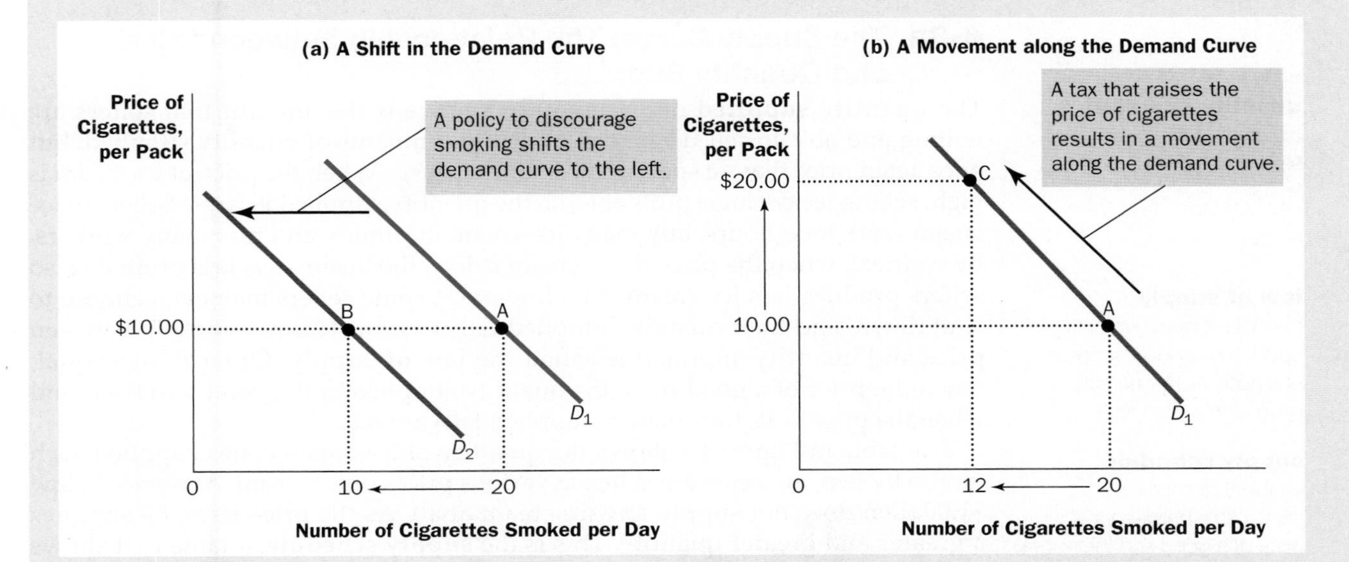

pass much of this tax on to consumers in the form of higher prices. A higher price encourages smokers to reduce the number of cigarettes they smoke. In this case, the reduced amount of smoking does not represent a shift in the demand curve. Instead, it represents a movement along the same demand curve to a point with a higher price and lower quantity, as in panel (b) of Figure 4.4.

How much does the amount of smoking respond to changes in the price of cigarettes? Economists have attempted to answer this question by studying what happens when the tax on cigarettes changes. They have found that a 10-percent increase in the price causes a 4-percent reduction in the quantity demanded. Teenagers are especially sensitive to the price of cigarettes: A 10-percent increase in the price causes a 12-percent drop in teenage smoking.

A related question is how the price of cigarettes affects the demand for illicit drugs, such as marijuana. Opponents of cigarette taxes often argue that tobacco and marijuana are substitutes, so that high cigarette prices encourage marijuana use. By contrast, many experts on substance abuse view tobacco as a "gateway drug" leading the young to experiment with other harmful substances. Most studies of the data are consistent with this view: They find that lower cigarette prices are associated with greater use of marijuana. In other words, tobacco and marijuana appear to be complements rather than substitutes. ■

Make up an example of a monthly demand schedule for pizza, and graph the implied demand curve. • Give an example of something that would shift this demand curve. • Would a change in the price of pizza shift this demand curve?

4-3 Supply

We now turn to the other side of the market and examine the behaviour of sellers. Once again, to focus our thinking, let's consider the market for ice cream.

4-3a The Supply Curve: The Relationship between Price and Quantity Supplied

quantity supplied
the amount of a good that sellers are willing and able to sell

law of supply
the claim that, other things equal, the quantity supplied of a good rises when the price of the good rises

supply schedule
a table that shows the relationship between the price of a good and the quantity supplied

The **quantity supplied** of any good or service is the amount that sellers are willing and able to sell. There are many determinants of quantity supplied, but once again price plays a special role in our analysis. When the price of ice cream is high, selling ice cream is profitable, so the quantity supplied is large. Sellers of ice cream work long hours, buy many ice-cream machines, and hire many workers. By contrast, when the price of ice cream is low, the business is less profitable, so sellers produce less ice cream. At a low price, some sellers may even choose to shut down, and their quantity supplied falls to zero. This relationship between price and quantity supplied is called the **law of supply**: Other things equal, when the price of a good rises, the quantity supplied of the good also rises, and when the price falls, the quantity supplied falls as well.

The table in Figure 4.5 shows the quantity of ice-cream cones supplied each month by Ben, an ice-cream seller, at various prices of ice cream. At a price below $1.00, Ben does not supply any ice cream at all. As the price rises, he supplies a greater and greater quantity. This is the **supply schedule**, a table that shows the relationship between the price of a good and the quantity supplied, holding

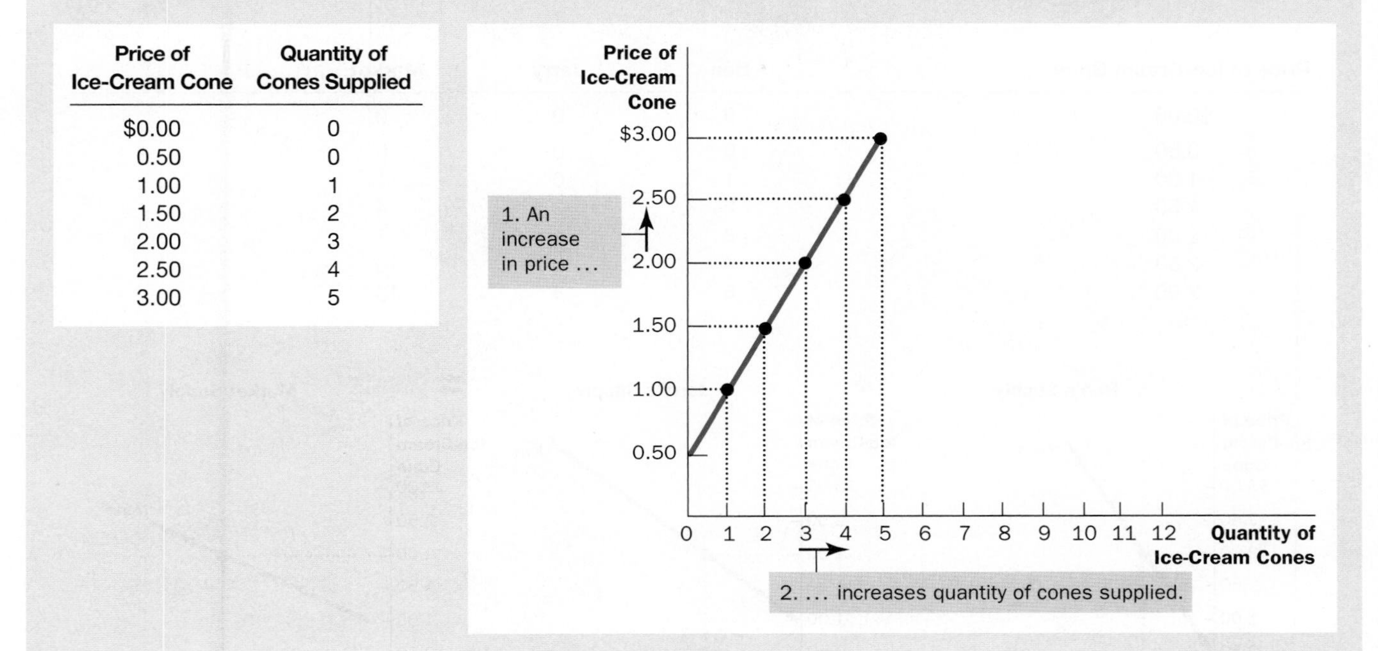

Price of Ice-Cream Cone	Quantity of Cones Supplied
$0.00	0
0.50	0
1.00	1
1.50	2
2.00	3
2.50	4
3.00	5

FIGURE 4.5

Ben's Supply Schedule and Supply Curve

The supply schedule shows the quantity supplied at each price. This supply curve, which graphs the supply schedule, shows how the quantity supplied of the good changes as its price varies. Because a higher price increases the quantity supplied, the supply curve slopes upward.

constant everything else that influences how much producers of the good want to sell.

The graph in Figure 4.5 uses the numbers from the table to illustrate the law of supply. The curve relating price and quantity supplied is called the **supply curve**. The supply curve slopes upward because, other things equal, a higher price means a greater quantity supplied.

supply curve
a graph of the relationship between the price of a good and the quantity supplied

4-3b Market Supply versus Individual Supply

Just as market demand is the sum of the demands of all buyers, market supply is the sum of the supplies of all sellers. The table in Figure 4.6 shows the supply schedules for two ice-cream producers—Ben and Jerry. At any price, Ben's supply schedule tells us the quantity of ice cream Ben supplies, and Jerry's supply schedule tells us the quantity of ice cream Jerry supplies. The market supply is the sum of the two individual supplies.

The graph in Figure 4.6 shows the supply curves that correspond to the supply schedules. As with demand curves, we sum the individual supply curves *horizontally* to obtain the market supply curve. That is, to find the total quantity supplied at any price, we add the individual quantities, which are found on the horizontal axis of the individual supply curves. The market supply curve shows how the total quantity supplied varies as the price of the good varies, holding constant all of the other factors beyond price that influence producers' decisions about how much to sell.

FIGURE 4.6

Market Supply as the Sum of Individual Supplies

The quantity supplied in a market is the sum of the quantities supplied by all the sellers at each price. Thus, the market supply curve is found by adding horizontally the individual supply curves. At a price of $2, Ben supplies 3 ice-cream cones, and Jerry supplies 4 ice-cream cones. The quantity supplied in the market at this price is 7 cones.

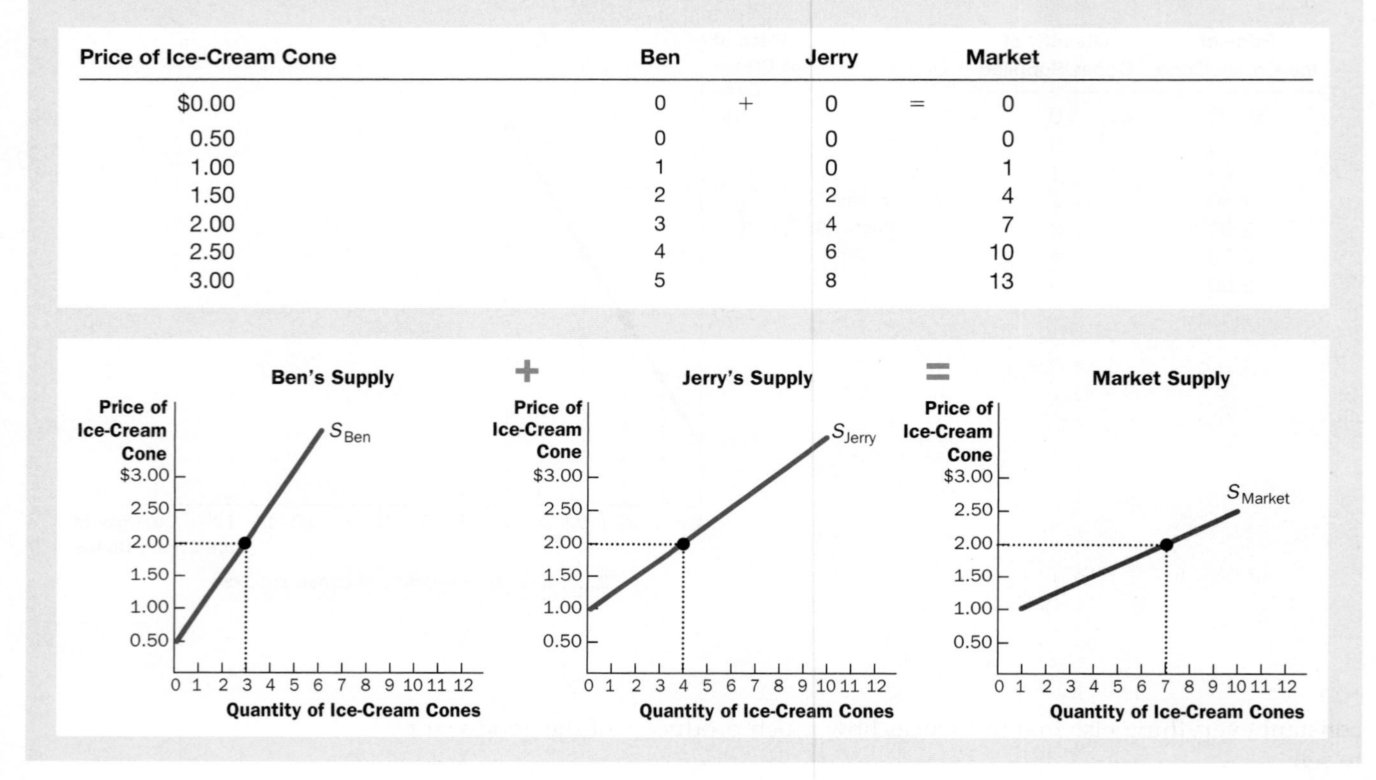

Price of Ice-Cream Cone	Ben		Jerry		Market
$0.00	0	+	0	=	0
0.50	0		0		0
1.00	1		0		1
1.50	2		2		4
2.00	3		4		7
2.50	4		6		10
3.00	5		8		13

4-3c Shifts in the Supply Curve

Because the market supply curve is drawn holding other things constant, when one of these factors changes, the supply curve shifts. For example, suppose the price of sugar falls. Sugar is an input into the production of ice cream, so the fall in the price of sugar makes selling ice cream more profitable. This raises the supply of ice cream: At any given price, sellers are now willing to produce a larger quantity. The supply curve for ice cream shifts to the right.

Figure 4.7 illustrates shifts in supply. Any change that raises quantity supplied at every price, such as a fall in the price of sugar, shifts the supply curve to the right and is called *an increase in supply.* Similarly, any change that reduces the quantity supplied at every price shifts the supply curve to the left and is called *a decrease in supply.*

Many variables can shift the supply curve. Here are some of the most important variables:

Input Prices To produce their output of ice cream, sellers use various inputs: cream, sugar, flavouring, ice-cream machines, the buildings in which the ice

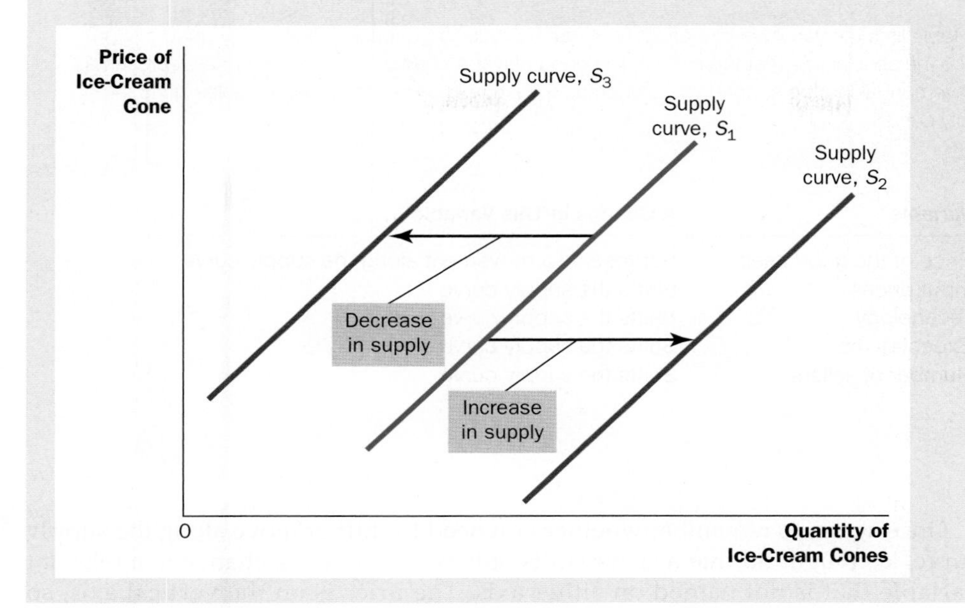

FIGURE 4.7

Shifts in the Supply Curve

Any change that raises the quantity that sellers wish to produce at a given price shifts the supply curve to the right. Any change that lowers the quantity that sellers wish to produce at a given price shifts the supply curve to the left.

cream is made, and the labour of workers to mix the ingredients and operate the machines. When the price of one or more of these inputs rises, producing ice cream is less profitable, and firms supply less ice cream. If input prices rise substantially, a firm might shut down and supply no ice cream at all. Thus, the supply of a good is negatively related to the price of the inputs used to make the good.

Technology The technology for turning inputs into ice cream is another determinant of supply. The invention of the mechanized ice-cream machine, for example, reduced the amount of labour necessary to make ice cream. By reducing firms' costs, the advance in technology raised the supply of ice cream.

Expectations The amount of ice cream a firm supplies today may depend on its expectations of the future. For example, if a firm expects the price of ice cream to rise in the future, it will put some of its current production into storage and supply less to the market today.

Number of Sellers In addition to the preceding factors, which influence the behaviour of individual sellers, market supply depends on the number of sellers. If Ben or Jerry were to retire from the ice-cream business, the supply in the market would fall.

Summary The supply curve shows what happens to the quantity supplied of a good when its price varies, holding constant all the other variables that influence sellers. When one of these other variables changes, the supply curve shifts. Table 4.2 lists the variables that influence how much producers choose to sell of a good.

TABLE 4.2

Variables That Influence Sellers

This table lists the variables that affect how much producers choose to sell of any good. Notice the special role that the price of the good plays: A change in the good's price represents a movement along the supply curve, whereas a change in one of the other variables shifts the supply curve.

Variable	A Change in This Variable ...
Price of the good itself	Represents a movement along the supply curve
Input prices	Shifts the supply curve
Technology	Shifts the supply curve
Expectations	Shifts the supply curve
Number of sellers	Shifts the supply curve

Once again, to remember whether you need to shift or move along the supply curve, keep in mind that a curve shifts only when there is a change in a relevant variable that is not named on either axis. The price is on the vertical axis, so a change in price represents a movement along the supply curve. By contrast, because input prices, technology, expectations, and the number of sellers are not measured on either axis, a change in one of these variables shifts the supply curve.

4-4 Supply and Demand Together

Having analyzed supply and demand separately, we now combine them to see how they determine the price and quantity of a good sold in the market.

4-4a Equilibrium

equilibrium
a situation in which the price has reached the level where quantity supplied equals quantity demanded

equilibrium price
the price that balances quantity supplied and quantity demanded

equilibrium quantity
the quantity supplied and the quantity demanded at the equilibrium price

Figure 4.8 shows the market supply curve and market demand curve together. Notice that there is one point at which the supply and demand curves intersect. This point is called the market's **equilibrium**. The price at this intersection is called the **equilibrium price**, and the quantity is called the **equilibrium quantity**. Here the equilibrium price is $2.00 per cone, and the equilibrium quantity is 7 ice-cream cones.

The dictionary defines the word *equilibrium* as a situation in which various forces are in balance—and this also describes a market's equilibrium. *At the equilibrium price, the quantity of the good that buyers are willing and able to buy exactly balances the quantity that sellers are willing to sell.* The equilibrium price is sometimes called the *market-clearing price* because, at this price, everyone in the market has been satisfied: Buyers have bought all they want to buy, and sellers have sold all they want to sell.

The actions of buyers and sellers naturally move markets toward the equilibrium of supply and demand. To see why, consider what happens when the market price is not equal to the equilibrium price.

Suppose first that the market price is above the equilibrium price, as in panel (a) of Figure 4.9. At a price of $2.50 per cone, the quantity of the good supplied

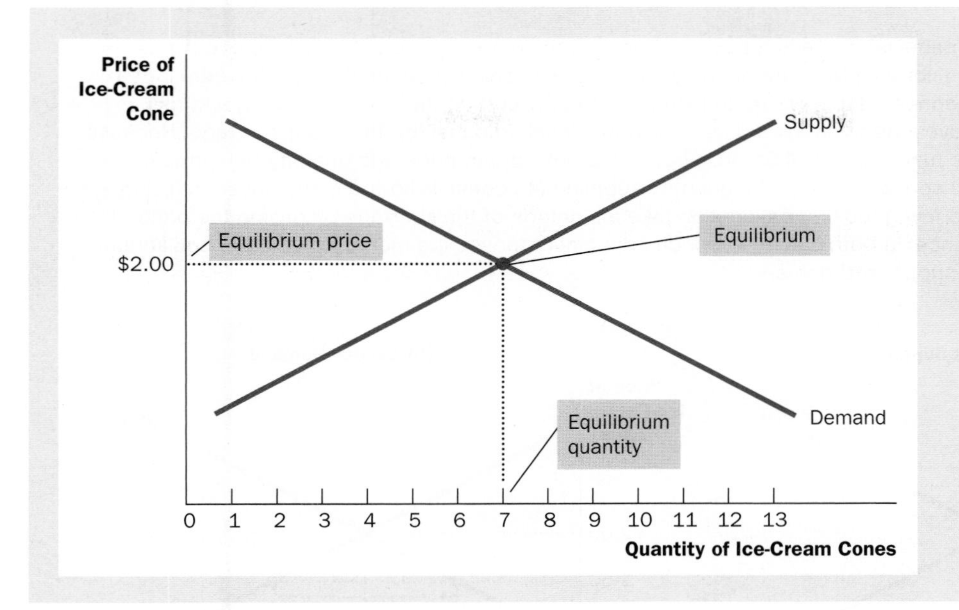

FIGURE 4.8

The Equilibrium of Supply and Demand

The equilibrium is found where the supply and demand curves intersect. At the equilibrium price, the quantity supplied equals the quantity demanded. Here the equilibrium price is $2: At this price, 7 ice-cream cones are supplied, and 7 ice-cream cones are demanded.

(10 cones) exceeds the quantity demanded (4 cones). There is a **surplus** of the good: Suppliers are unable to sell all they want at the going price. A surplus is sometimes called a situation of *excess supply*. When there is a surplus in the ice-cream market, sellers of ice cream find their freezers increasingly full of ice cream they would like to sell but cannot. They respond to the surplus by cutting their prices. Falling prices, in turn, increase the quantity demanded and decrease the quantity supplied. These changes represent movement along the supply and demand curves (not shifts in the curves). Prices continue to fall until the market reaches the equilibrium.

surplus
a situation in which quantity supplied is greater than quantity demanded

Suppose now that the market price is below the equilibrium price, as in panel (b) of Figure 4.9. In this case, the price is $1.50 per cone, and the quantity of the good demanded exceeds the quantity supplied. There is a **shortage** of the good: Demanders are unable to buy all they want at the going price. A shortage is sometimes called a situation of *excess demand*. When a shortage occurs in the ice-cream market, buyers have to wait in long lines for a chance to buy one of the few cones that are available. With too many buyers chasing too few goods, sellers can respond to the shortage by raising their prices without losing sales. These price increases cause the quantity demanded to fall and the quantity supplied to rise. Once again, these changes represent movements *along* the supply and demand curves, and they move the market toward the equilibrium.

shortage
a situation in which quantity demanded is greater than quantity supplied

Thus, regardless of whether the price starts off too high or too low, the activities of the many buyers and sellers automatically push the market price toward the equilibrium price. Once the market reaches its equilibrium, all buyers and sellers are satisfied, and there is no upward or downward pressure on the price. How quickly equilibrium is reached varies from market to market, depending on how quickly prices adjust. In most free markets, surpluses and shortages are only temporary because prices eventually move toward their equilibrium

FIGURE 4.9

Markets Not in Equilibrium

In panel (a), there is a surplus. Because the market price of $2.50 is above the equilibrium price, the quantity supplied (10 cones) exceeds the quantity demanded (4 cones). Suppliers try to increase sales by cutting the price of a cone, and this moves the price toward its equilibrium level. In panel (b), there is a shortage. Because the market price of $1.50 is below the equilibrium price, the quantity demanded (10 cones) exceeds the quantity supplied (4 cones). With too many buyers chasing too few goods, suppliers can take advantage of the shortage by raising the price. Hence, in both cases, the price adjustment moves the market toward the equilibrium of supply and demand.

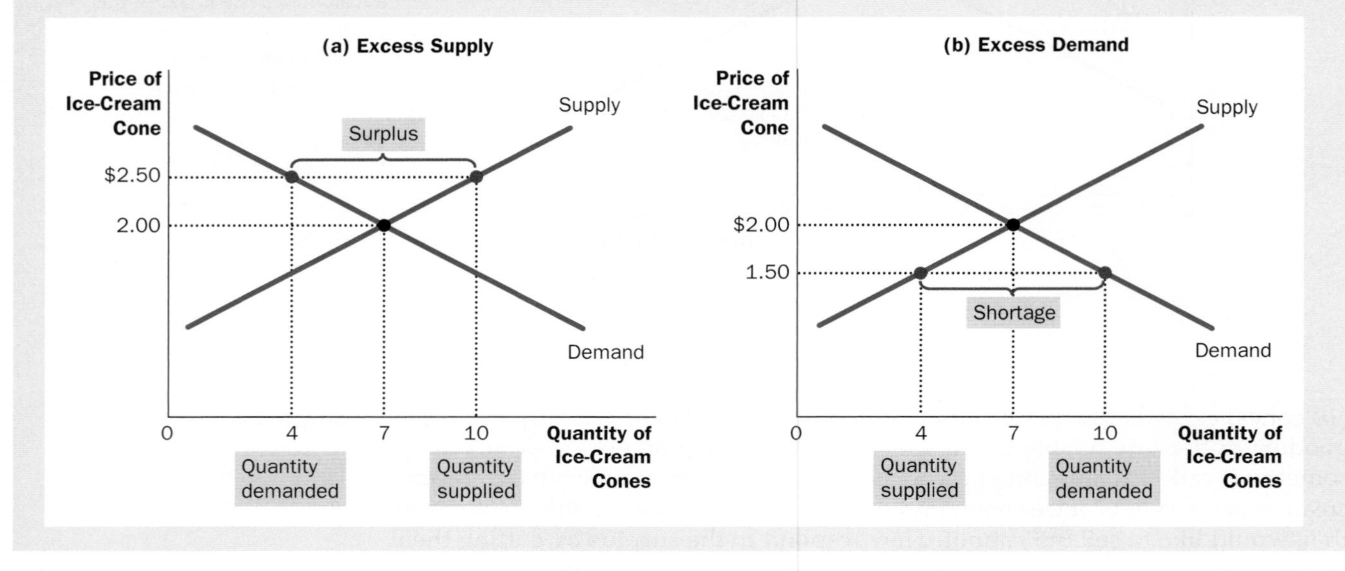

law of supply and demand
the claim that the price of any good adjusts to bring the quantity supplied and the quantity demanded for that good into balance

levels. Indeed, this phenomenon is so pervasive that it is called the **law of supply and demand**: The price of any good adjusts to bring the quantity supplied and quantity demanded for that good into balance.

4-4b Three Steps to Analyzing Changes in Equilibrium

So far we have seen how supply and demand together determine a market's equilibrium, which in turn determines the price and quantity of the good that buyers purchase and sellers produce. The equilibrium price and quantity depend on the position of the supply and demand curves. When some event shifts one of these curves, the equilibrium in the market changes, resulting in a new price and a new quantity exchanged between buyers and sellers.

When analyzing how some event affects the equilibrium in a market, we proceed in three steps. First, we decide whether the event shifts the supply curve, the demand curve, or in some cases, both curves. Second, we decide whether the curve shifts to the right or to the left. Third, we use the supply-and-demand diagram to compare the initial and the new equilibrium, which shows how the shift affects the equilibrium price and quantity. Table 4.3 summarizes these

1. Decide whether the event shifts the supply or demand curve (or perhaps both).
2. Decide in which direction the curve shifts.
3. Use the supply-and-demand diagram to see how the shift changes the equilibrium price and quantity.

TABLE 4.3

A Three-Step Program for Analyzing Changes in Equilibrium

three steps. To see how this recipe is used, let's consider various events that might affect the market for ice cream.

Example: A Change in Market Equilibrium Due to a Shift in Demand
Suppose that one summer the weather is very hot. How does this event affect the market for ice cream? To answer this question, let's follow our three steps.

1. The hot weather affects the demand curve by changing people's taste for ice cream. That is, the weather changes the amount of ice cream that people want to buy at any given price. The supply curve is unchanged because the weather does not directly affect the firms that sell ice cream.
2. Because hot weather makes people want to eat more ice cream, the demand curve shifts to the right. Figure 4.10 shows this increase in demand as the shift in the demand curve from D_1 to D_2. This shift indicates that the quantity of ice cream demanded is higher at every price.

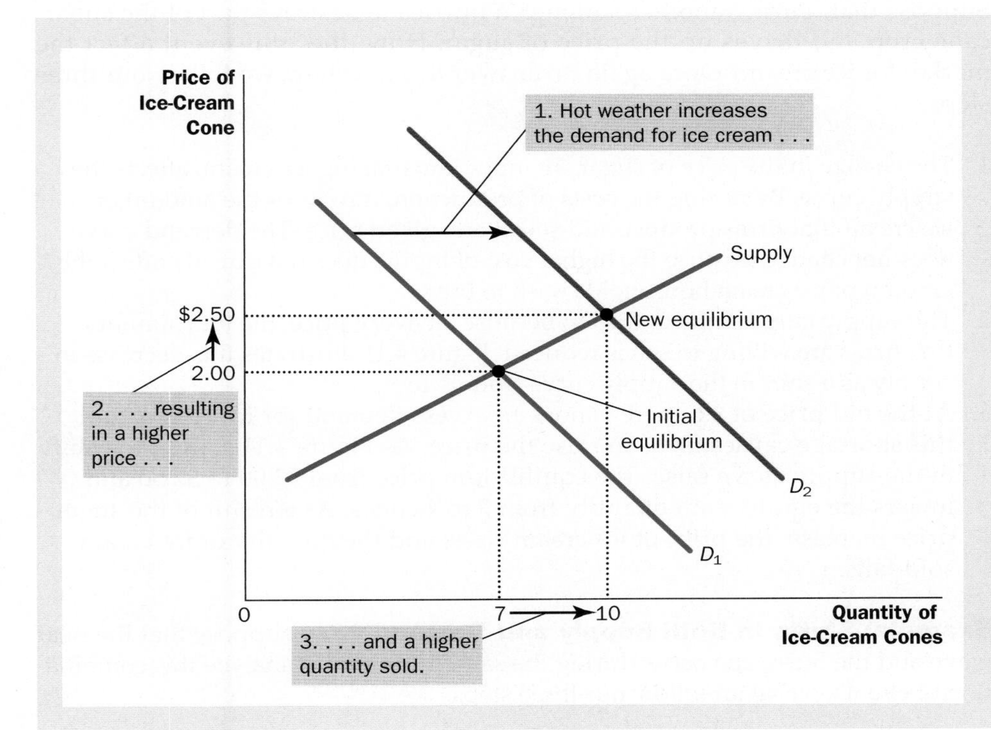

FIGURE 4.10

How an Increase in Demand Affects the Equilibrium
An event that raises quantity demanded at any given price shifts the demand curve to the right. The equilibrium price and the equilibrium quantity both rise. Here, an abnormally hot summer causes buyers to demand more ice cream. The demand curve shifts from D_1 to D_2, which causes the equilibrium price to rise from $2.00 to $2.50 and the equilibrium quantity to rise from 7 to 10 cones.

3. At the old price of $2, there is now an excess demand for ice cream, and this shortage induces firms to raise the price. As Figure 4.10 shows, the increase in demand raises the equilibrium price from $2.00 to $2.50 and the equilibrium quantity from 7 to 10 cones. In other words, the hot weather increases the price of ice cream and the quantity of ice cream sold.

Shifts in Curves versus Movements along Curves Notice that when hot weather increases the demand for ice cream and drives up the price, the quantity of ice cream that firms supply rises, even though the supply curve remains the same. In this case, economists say there has been an increase in "quantity supplied" but no change in "supply."

"Supply" refers to the position of the supply curve, whereas the "quantity supplied" refers to the amount suppliers wish to sell. In this example, supply does not change because the weather does not alter firms' desire to sell at any given price. Instead, the hot weather alters consumers' desire to buy at any given price and thereby shifts the demand curve to the right. The increase in demand causes the equilibrium price to rise. When the price rises, the quantity supplied rises. This increase in quantity supplied is represented by the movement along the supply curve.

To summarize, a shift *in* the supply curve is called a "change in supply," and a shift *in* the demand curve is called a "change in demand." A movement *along* a fixed supply curve is called a "change in the quantity supplied," and a movement *along* a fixed demand curve is called a "change in the quantity demanded."

Example: A Change in Market Equilibrium Due to a Shift in Supply Suppose that, during another summer, a hurricane destroys part of the sugarcane crop and drives up the price of sugar. How does this event affect the market for ice cream? Once again, to answer this question, we follow our three steps.

1. The change in the price of sugar, an input into making ice cream, affects the supply curve. By raising the costs of production, it reduces the amount of ice cream that firms produce and sell at any given price. The demand curve does not change because the higher cost of inputs does not directly affect the amount of ice cream households wish to buy.
2. The supply curve shifts to the left because, at every price, the total amount that firms are willing to sell is reduced. Figure 4.11 illustrates this decrease in supply as a shift in the supply curve from S_1 to S_2.
3. At the old price of $2, there is now an excess demand for ice cream, and this shortage causes firms to raise the price. As Figure 4.11 shows, the shift in the supply curve raises the equilibrium price from $2.00 to $2.50 and lowers the equilibrium quantity from 7 to 4 cones. As a result of the sugar price increase, the price of ice cream rises, and the quantity of ice cream sold falls.

Example: Shifts in Both Supply and Demand Now suppose that the heat wave and the hurricane occur during the same summer. To analyze this combination of events, we again follow our three steps.

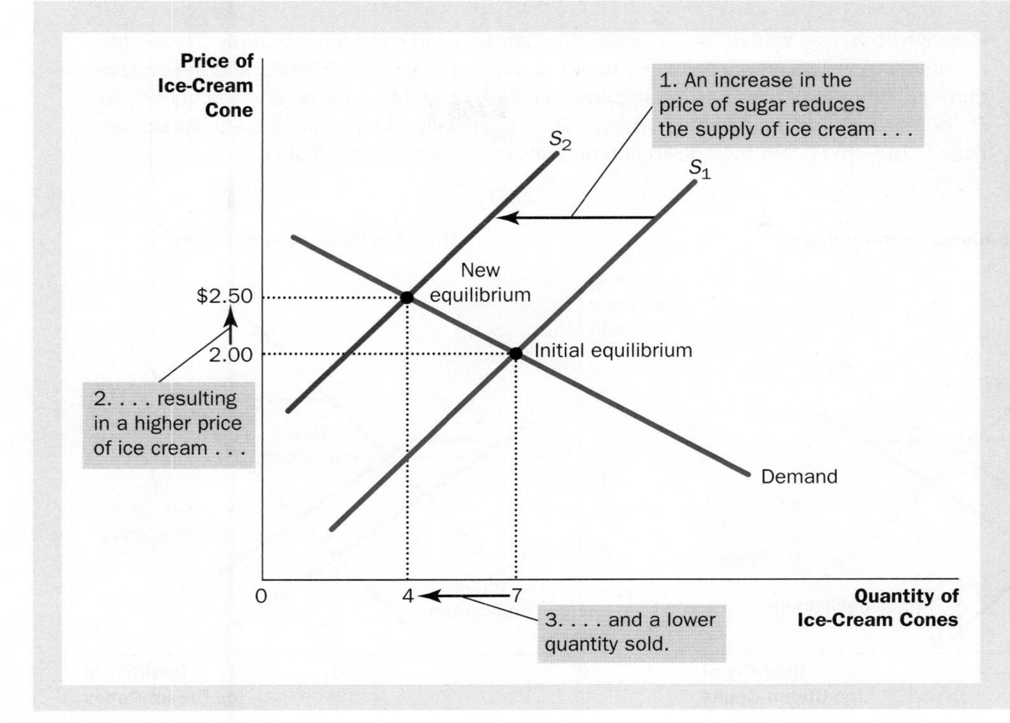

FIGURE 4.11

How a Decrease in Supply Affects the Equilibrium
An event that reduces quantity supplied at any given price shifts the supply curve to the left. The equilibrium price rises, and the equilibrium quantity falls. Here, an increase in the price of sugar (an input) causes sellers to supply less ice cream. The supply curve shifts from S_1 to S_2, which causes the equilibrium price of ice cream to rise from $2.00 to $2.50 and the equilibrium quantity to fall from 7 to 4 cones.

1. We determine that both curves must shift. The hot weather affects the demand curve because it alters the amount of ice cream that households want to buy at any given price. At the same time, when the hurricane drives up sugar prices, it alters the supply curve for ice cream because it changes the amount of ice cream that firms want to sell at any given price.
2. The curves shift in the same directions as they did in our previous analysis: The demand curve shifts to the right, and the supply curve shifts to the left. Figure 4.12 illustrates these shifts.
3. As Figure 4.12 shows, there are three possible outcomes that might result, depending on the relative size of the demand and supply shifts. In all cases, the equilibrium price rises. In panel (a), where demand increases substantially while supply falls just a little, the equilibrium quantity also rises. By contrast, in panel (b), where supply falls substantially while demand rises just a little, the equilibrium quantity falls. In panel (c), supply and demand both change by the same magnitude such that the equilibrium quantity stays the same but the price rises. Thus, these events certainly raise the price of ice cream, but their impact on the amount of ice cream sold is ambiguous (that is, it could go either way).

Summary We have just seen three examples of how to use supply and demand curves to analyze a change in equilibrium. Whenever an event shifts the supply curve, the demand curve, or perhaps both curves, you can use these tools to predict how the event will alter the price and quantity sold in equilibrium. Table 4.4 shows the predicted outcome for any combination of shifts in the two

FIGURE 4.12

A Shift in Both Supply and Demand

Here we observe a simultaneous increase in demand and decrease in supply. Three outcomes are possible. In panel (a), the equilibrium price rises from P_1 to P_2, and the equilibrium quantity rises from Q_1 to Q_2. In panel (b), the equilibrium price again rises from P_1 to P_2, but the equilibrium quantity falls from Q_1 to Q_2. Finally, in panel (c), the equilibrium price rises from P_1 to P_2, but the equilibrium quantity remains unchanged at Q_1.

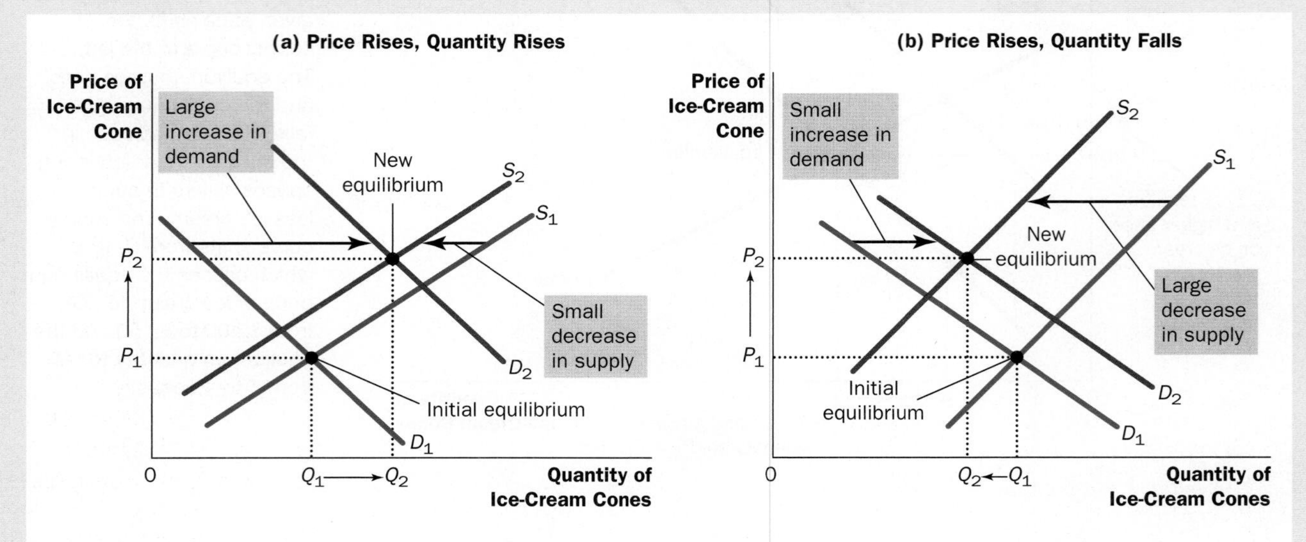

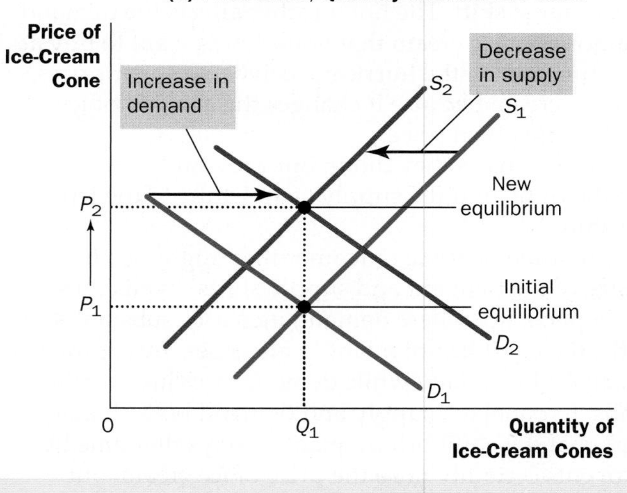

curves. To make sure you understand how to use the tools of supply and demand, pick a few entries in this table and make sure you can explain to yourself why the table contains the prediction it does.

On the appropriate diagram, show what happens to the market for pizza if the price of tomatoes rises. • On a separate diagram, show what happens to the market for pizza if the price of hamburgers falls.

IN THE **news**

Supply, Demand, and Technology

This article discusses how technology (a supply shifter) and changes in tastes and preferences (a demand shifter) can have a big impact on the market for traditional goods, such as pulp and paper.

Analysts Say Pulp Mill Closure Signals Tougher Times Ahead

FREDERICTON (CP)—Forestry officials are warning of tough times ahead as technology and the rise of the Internet swing through the pulp and paper industry like an axe.

The axe fell earlier this month on the small town of Nackawic in western New Brunswick, where 400 jobs were lost and hundreds of other people were affected by the abrupt closure of the St. Anne-Nackawic pulp mill.

Tupungato/Shutterstock.com

The New York–based owners of the mill blamed the rising cost of wood and the rising value of the loonie as major reasons for the closure.

Industry observers say it didn't help that the mill produced bleached hardwood pulp for use in products like photographic paper. David Chaundy, senior economist with the Atlantic Provinces Economic Council, said digital photography and the Internet are depressing demand for items like photographic paper and newsprint.

He said the Maritimes could see more closures in its all-important forestry sector. "There are definitely concerns that some of our mills are on the higher end of the cost curve and therefore are more vulnerable to reductions in commodity prices, or, if they're part of a multinational operation, to the closure of plants," Chaundy said. "That risk remains."

Analysts expect the demand for pulp, lumber and newsprint to be weaker over the next two to three years. Competition from countries in the southern hemisphere is hurting Canadian pulp and paper production. The strong Canadian dollar is also a factor in declining profits, since forest products such as lumber, pulp, and paper trade on world markets in U.S. dollars. It's estimated that each one-cent rise in the Canadian dollar drains about $500 million Cdn in revenues from the country's forest industry.

Yvon Poitras of the New Brunswick Forest Products Association said industries in New Brunswick feel the impact of volatile world markets more acutely because the province is so small. He said there are no other forestry closures in New Brunswick's immediate future. But he said all bets are off looking ahead to the next two or three years.

Source: *Canadian Press*, "Tough times seen for forestry industry," September 27, 2004. Copyright by The Canadian Press.

TABLE 4.4

What Happens to Price and Quantity When Supply or Demand Shifts?

As a quick quiz, make sure you can explain each of the entries in this table using a supply-and-demand diagram.

	No Change in Supply	**An Increase in Supply**	**A Decrease in Supply**
No Change in Demand	*P* same *Q* same	*P* down *Q* up	*P* up *Q* down
An Increase in Demand	*P* up *Q* up	*P* ambiguous *Q* up	*P* up *Q* ambiguous
A Decrease in Demand	*P* down *Q* down	*P* down *Q* ambiguous	*P* ambiguous *Q* down

4-5 Conclusion: How Prices Allocate Resources

This chapter has analyzed supply and demand in a single market. Although our discussion has centred around the market for ice cream, the lessons learned here apply in most other markets as well. Whenever you go to a store to buy something, you are contributing to the demand for that item. Whenever you look for a job, you are contributing to the supply of labour services. Because supply and demand are such pervasive economic phenomena, the model of supply and demand is a powerful tool for analysis. We will be using this model repeatedly in the following chapters.

One of the ten principles of economics discussed in Chapter 1 is that markets are usually a good way to organize economic activity. Although it is still too early to judge whether market outcomes are good or bad, in this chapter we have begun to see how markets work. In any economic system, scarce resources have to be allocated among competing uses. Market economies harness the forces of supply and demand to serve that end. Supply and demand together determine the prices of the economy's many different goods and services; prices in turn are the signals that guide the allocation of resources.

For example, consider the allocation of beachfront land. Because the amount of this land is limited, not everyone can enjoy the luxury of living by the beach. Who gets this resource? The answer is whoever is willing and able to pay the price. The price of beachfront land adjusts until the quantity of land demanded exactly balances the quantity supplied. Thus, in market economies, prices are the mechanism for rationing scarce resources.

Similarly, prices determine who produces each good and how much is produced. For instance, consider farming. Because we need food to survive, it is crucial that some people work on farms. What determines who is a farmer and who is not? In a free society, there is no government planning agency making this decision and ensuring an adequate supply of food. Instead, the allocation of workers to farms is based on the job decisions of millions of workers. This decentralized system works well because these decisions depend on prices. The prices of food and the wages of farm workers (the price of their labour) adjust to ensure that enough people choose to be farmers.

If a person had never seen a market economy in action, the whole idea might seem preposterous. Economies are enormous groups of people engaged in a multitude of independent activities. What prevents decentralized decision making from degenerating into chaos? What coordinates the actions of the millions of people with their varying abilities and desires? What ensures that what needs to be done does, in fact, get done? The answer, in a word, is *prices.* If an invisible hand guides market economies, as Adam Smith famously suggested, then the price system is the baton that the invisible hand uses to conduct the economic orchestra.

summary

- Economists use the model of supply and demand to analyze competitive markets. In a competitive market, there are many buyers and sellers, each of whom has little or no influence on the market price.
- The demand curve shows how the quantity of a good demanded depends on the price. According to the law of demand, as the price of a good falls, the quantity demanded rises. Therefore, the demand curve slopes downward.
- In addition to price, other determinants of how much consumers want to buy include income, the prices of substitutes and complements, tastes, expectations, and the number of buyers. If one of these factors changes, the demand curve shifts.

- The supply curve shows how the quantity of a good supplied depends on the price. According to the law of supply, as the price of a good rises, the quantity supplied rises. Therefore, the supply curve slopes upward.
- In addition to price, other determinants of how much producers want to sell include input prices, technology, expectations, and the number of sellers. If one of these factors changes, the supply curve shifts.
- The intersection of the supply and demand curves determines the market equilibrium. At the equilibrium price, the quantity demanded equals the quantity supplied.
- The behaviour of buyers and sellers naturally drives markets toward their equilibrium. When the market price is above the equilibrium price, there is a surplus of the good, which causes the market price to fall. When the market price is below the equilibrium price, there is a shortage, which causes the market price to rise.
- To analyze how any event influences a market, we use the supply-and-demand diagram to examine how the event affects the equilibrium price and quantity. To do this we follow three steps. First, we decide whether the event shifts the supply curve or the demand curve (or both). Second, we decide which direction the curve shifts. Third, we compare the new equilibrium with the initial equilibrium.
- In market economies, prices are the signals that guide economic decisions and thereby allocate scarce resources. For every good in the economy, the price ensures that supply and demand are in balance. The equilibrium price then determines how much of the good buyers choose to purchase and how much sellers choose to produce.

KEY **concepts**

market, *p.* 63
competitive market, *p.* 64
quantity demanded, *p.* 64
law of demand, *p.* 65
demand schedule, *p.* 65
demand curve, *p.* 65
normal good, *p.* 67
inferior good, *p.* 67
substitutes, *p.* 68
complements, *p.* 68
quantity supplied, *p.* 70
law of supply, *p.* 70
supply schedule, *p.* 70
supply curve, *p.* 71
equilibrium, *p.* 74
equilibrium price, *p.* 74
equilibrium quantity, *p.* 74
surplus, *p.* 75
shortage, *p.* 75
law of supply and demand, *p.* 76

QUESTIONS FOR **review**

1. What is a competitive market? Briefly describe the types of markets other than perfectly competitive markets.
2. What are the demand schedule and the demand curve, and how are they related? Why does the demand curve slope downward?
3. Does a change in consumers' tastes lead to a movement along the demand curve or a shift in the demand curve? Does a change in price lead to a movement along the demand curve or a shift in the demand curve?
4. Popeye's income declines and, as a result, he buys more spinach. Is spinach an inferior or a normal good? What happens to Popeye's demand curve for spinach?
5. What are the supply schedule and the supply curve, and how are they related? Why does the supply curve slope upward?
6. Does a change in producers' technology lead to a movement along the supply curve or a shift in the supply curve? Does a change in price lead to a movement along the supply curve or a shift in the supply curve?
7. Define the equilibrium of a market. Describe the forces that move a market toward its equilibrium.
8. Beer and pizza are complements because they are often enjoyed together. When the price of beer rises, what happens to the supply, demand, quantity supplied, quantity demanded, and the price in the market for pizza?
9. Describe the role of prices in market economies.

QUICK CHECK multiple choice

1. A change in which of the following will NOT shift the demand curve for hamburgers?
   a. the price of hot dogs
   b. the price of hamburgers
   c. the price of hamburger buns
   d. the income of hamburger consumers
2. An increase in ________ will cause a movement along a given demand curve, which is called a change in ________.
   a. supply, demand
   b. supply, quantity demanded
   c. demand, supply
   d. demand, quantity supplied
3. Movie tickets and DVDs are substitutes. If the price of DVDs increases, what happens in the market for movie tickets?
   a. The supply curve shifts to the left.
   b. The supply curve shifts to the right.
   c. The demand curve shifts to the left.
   d. The demand curve shifts to the right.
4. The discovery of a large new reserve of crude oil will shift the ________ curve for gasoline, leading to a ________ equilibrium price.
   a. supply, higher
   b. supply, lower
   c. demand, higher
   d. demand, lower
5. If the economy goes into a recession and incomes fall, what happens in the markets for inferior goods?
   a. prices and quantities both rise
   b. prices and quantities both fall
   c. prices rise, quantities fall
   d. prices fall, quantities rise
6. Which of the following might lead to an increase in the equilibrium price of jelly and a decrease in the equilibrium quantity of jelly sold?
   a. an increase in the price of peanut better, a complement to jelly
   b. an increase in the price of Marshmallow Fluff, a substitute for jelly
   c. an increase in the price of grapes, an input into jelly
   d. an increase in consumers' incomes, as long as jelly is a normal good

PROBLEMS AND applications

1. Explain each of the following statements using supply-and-demand diagrams.
   a. When a cold snap hits Florida, the price of orange juice rises in supermarkets throughout Canada.
   b. When the weather turns warm in Quebec every summer, the prices of hotel rooms in Caribbean resorts plummet.
   c. When a war breaks out in the Middle East, the price of gasoline rises, while the price of a used SUV falls.
2. "An increase in the demand for notebooks raises the quantity of notebooks demanded, but not the quantity supplied." Is this statement true or false? Explain.
3. Consider the market for minivans. For each of the events listed below, identify which of the determinants of demand or supply are affected. Also indicate whether demand or supply is increased or decreased. Then show the effect on the price and quantity of minivans.
   a. People decide to have more children.
   b. A strike by steelworkers raises steel prices.
   c. Engineers develop new automated machinery for the production of minivans.
   d. The price of SUVs rises.
   e. A stock market crash lowers people's wealth.
4. Over the past 30 years, technological advances have reduced the cost of computer chips. How do you think this has affected the market for computers? For computer software? For typewriters?
5. Using supply-and-demand diagrams, show the effect of the following events on the market for sweatshirts.
   a. A hurricane in South Carolina damages the cotton crop.
   b. The price of leather jackets falls.
   c. All universities require morning calisthenics in appropriate attire.
   d. New knitting machines are invented.
6. Suppose that in the year 2010, the number of births was temporarily high. How will this baby boom affect the price of baby-sitting services in 2015 and 2025? (*Hint:* Five-year-olds need baby-sitters, whereas fifteen-year-olds can *be* baby-sitters.)
7. Ketchup is a complement (as well as a condiment) for hot dogs. If the price of hot dogs rises, what happens to the market for ketchup? For tomatoes? For tomato juice? For orange juice?

8. The market for pizza has the following demand and supply schedules:

Price	Quantity Demanded	Quantity Supplied
$4	135	26
5	104	53
6	81	81
7	68	98
8	53	110
9	39	121

Graph the demand and supply curves. What is the equilibrium price and quantity in this market? If the actual price in this market was *above* the equilibrium price, what would drive the market toward the equilibrium? If the actual price in this market was *below* the equilibrium price, what would drive the market toward the equilibrium?

9. Because bagels and cream cheese are often eaten together, they are complements.
   a. We observe that both the equilibrium price of cream cheese and the equilibrium quantity of bagels have risen. What could be responsible for this pattern—a fall in the price of flour or a fall in the price of milk? Illustrate and explain your answer.
   b. Suppose instead that the equilibrium price of cream cheese has risen but the equilibrium quantity of bagels has fallen. What could be responsible for this pattern—a rise in the price of flour or a rise in the price of milk? Illustrate and explain your answer.

10. Suppose that the price of hockey tickets at your school is determined by market forces. Currently, the demand and supply schedules are as follows:

Price	Quantity Demanded	Quantity Supplied
$4	10 000	8000
8	8 000	8000
12	6 000	8000
16	4 000	8000
20	2 000	8000

   a. Draw the demand and supply curves. What is unusual about this supply curve? Why might this be true?
   b. What are the equilibrium price and quantity of tickets?
   c. Your school plans to increase total enrollment next year by 5000 students. The additional students will have the following demand schedule:

Price	Quantity Demanded
$4	4000
8	3000
12	2000
16	1000
20	0

   Now add the old demand schedule and the demand schedule for the new students to calculate the new demand schedule for the entire school. What will be the new equilibrium price and quantity?

11. Consider the markets for DVD movies, TV screens, and tickets to movie theatres.
   a. For each pair, identify whether they are complements or substitutes:
      —DVDs and TV screens
      —DVDs and movie tickets
      —TV screens and movie tickets
   b. Suppose a technological advance reduces the cost of manufacturing TV screens. Draw a diagram to show what happens to the market for TV screens.
   c. Draw two more diagrams to show how the change in the market for TV screens affects the markets for DVDs and movie tickets.

12. A survey shows an increase in drug use by young people. In the ensuing debate, two hypotheses are proposed:
   —Reduced police efforts have increased the availability of drugs on the street.
   —Cutbacks in educational efforts have decreased awareness of the dangers of drug addiction.
   a. Use supply-and-demand diagrams to show how each of these hypotheses could lead to an increase in the quantity of drugs consumed.
   b. How could information on what has happened to the price of drugs help us to distinguish between these explanations?

13. Consider the following events: Scientists reveal that consumption of oranges decreases the risk of diabetes and, at the same time, farmers use a new fertilizer that makes orange trees more productive. Illustrate and explain what effect these changes have on the equilibrium price and quantity of oranges.

APPENDIX

The Mathematics of Market Equilibrium

The appendix to Chapter 2 presented a discussion of how economists use graphs to help explain mathematical relationships among variables. We have already seen that these are very valuable tools to help us understand economic relationships. In this appendix, we illustrate how simple mathematical methods can help us solve algebraically for a market's equilibrium price and quantity using supply and demand curves.

In Figure 4.8, we saw how the equilibrium price and quantity for a good are determined by the intersection of the supply and demand curves. Although they don't have to be, for simplicity, we often draw these curves as linear (so our "curves" are actually straight lines!).

Consider the following example of a linear demand curve:

$$Q^D = 56 - 4P$$

where Q^D is the quantity demanded and P is the price of the good.

As we saw in the appendix to Chapter 2, for a linear demand curve we can determine its intercept with the price axis (the y-intercept), where quantity demanded is zero, by setting $Q^D = 0$ and solving the demand equation for P. For our demand curve the y-intercept is therefore determined by $0 = 56 - 4P$; solving for P gives $4P = 56$, $P = 56/4 = 14$. Similarly, the intercept with the quantity axis (the x-intercept), where price is equal to zero, is determined by setting $P = 0$ and solving for Q^D, which simply gives $Q^D = 56$. Figure 4A.1 plots the demand curve given by the equation $Q^D = 56 - 4P$, identifying the x- and y-intercepts determined above.

We also saw in the appendix to Chapter 2 that the slope of a linear demand curve is equal to the "rise over the run" as we move from one point on the demand curve to another. The "rise" is the change in price measured along the y-axis (Δy, where

FIGURE 4A.1

Linear Demand Curve

The demand curve $Q^D = 56 - 4P$ is plotted here, with the y-intercept (14) and x-intercept (56) identified. The slope of the demand curve is determined by taking the ratio of the negative of the y-intercept to the x-intercept, $\Delta y/\Delta x = -14/56 = -1/4$.

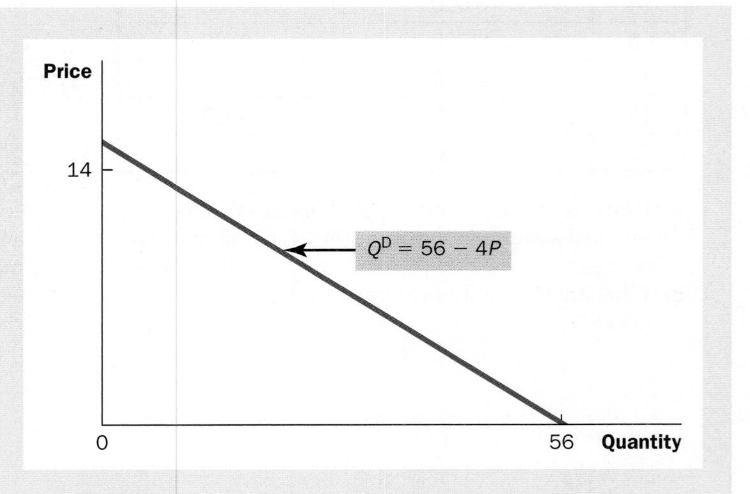

you'll recall that Δ is the Greek letter delta, which stands for "change in") as we move from one point on the demand curve to another; the "run" is the change in quantity demanded measured along the x-axis (Δx). So the slope of the demand curve is measured as $\Delta y/\Delta x$, as we move from one point on the demand curve to another.

Since the slope of a line is constant all along the line (that is what makes it a line!), we can use any two points on the demand curve to determine its slope. As discussed in the appendix to Chapter 2, two particularly useful points on the demand curve are the x- and y-intercepts determined above. We can use these points to determine the "rise over the run" from moving from the point on the demand curve that intersects the x-axis to the point on the demand curve that intersects the y-axis. In this case, the "rise" is just the y-intercept and the "run" is the negative of the x-intercept. So for this demand curve $\Delta y = 14$ and $\Delta x = -56$, and the slope is the negative of the ratio of the y-intercept and x-intercept, $\Delta y/\Delta x = -14/56 = -1/4$.

An example of a linear supply curve is:

$$Q^S = -4 + 2P$$

where Q^S is quantity supplied and P is again the price of the good.

As with the demand curve, we can determine the intercept of the linear supply curve with the price axis (the y-intercept), where quantity supplied is zero, by setting $Q^S = 0$ and solving the supply equation for P. The y-intercept is therefore determined by $0 = -4 + 2P$ and solving for P: $2P = 4$, $P = 4/2$, $P = 2$. Similarly, the intercept with the quantity axis (the x-intercept), where the price is zero, is determined by setting $P = 0$ and solving for Q^S, which gives $Q^S = -4$.

Note that because supply curves are upward sloping, in general they can intersect the x- or y-axis at either a positive or negative number. In our example the intersection with the x-axis is negative and with the y-axis is positive, which is often the case. Figure 4A.2 plots our supply curve given the intercepts calculated above. Because the intersection with the x-axis is negative, which corresponds to a negative supply and is clearly not possible, we show the "projection" of the curve into the negative quadrant with a dashed line.

As with the demand curve we can use any two points on the supply curve to determine its slope. Again, it is convenient to use the x- and y-intercepts of the

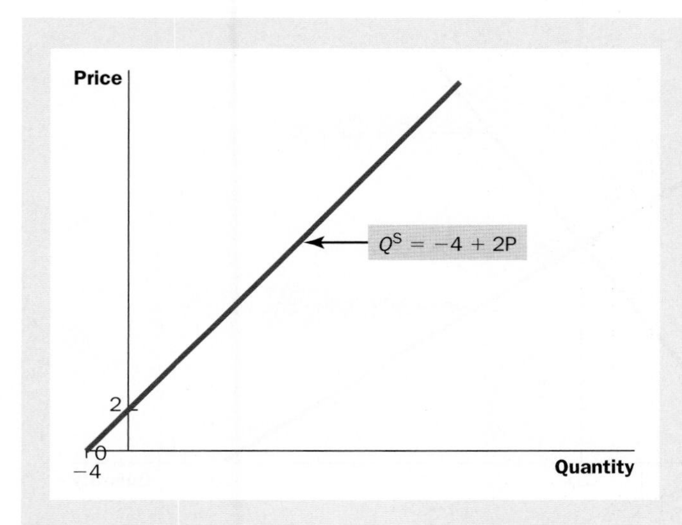

FIGURE 4A.2

Linear Supply Curve

The supply curve $Q^S = -4 + 2P$ is plotted here, with the y-intercept (2) and the x-intercept (-4) identified. The slope of the supply curve is determined by taking the negative of the ratio of the y-intercept and the x-intercept, $\Delta y/\Delta x = 2/4 = 1/2$.

supply curve determined above. In this case the "rise" is the y-intercept, giving $\Delta y = 2$, and the "run" is the negative of the x-intercept, so $\Delta x = 4$. The slope of the supply curve is the negative of the negative of the ratio of the y-intercept and the x-intercept, $\Delta y/\Delta x = 2/4 = 1/2$.

We have seen that the market equilibrium price and quantity are determined by the intersection of the demand and supply curves. In other words, the equilibrium price is such that the quantity demanded exactly equals the quantity supplied. To determine the equilibrium price, we start by using our linear demand and supply curves and set quantity demanded equal to quantity supplied ($Q^D = Q^S$):

$$56 - 4P = -4 + 2P$$

We now solve this equation for P. To do this, we use algebra to gather terms with P on the left-hand side and the other terms on the right-hand side and then solve for P as follows:

$$\begin{aligned} -2P - 4P &= -4 - 56 \\ -6P &= -60 \\ 6P &= 60 \\ P &= 60/6 \\ P &= 10 \end{aligned}$$

Therefore, for our example, the equilibrium price that clears the market and results in the quantity demanded equal to the quantity supplied is $P = 10$.

To determine the equilibrium quantity demanded in the market, substitute the equilibrium price into the equation for quantity demanded to get:

$$Q^D = 56 - 4P = 56 - 4(10) = 56 - 40 = 16$$

And to determine the equilibrium quantity supplied, use the supply curve to get:

$$Q^S = -4 + 2P = -4 + 2(10) = -4 + 20 = 16$$

As we would expect, at the equilibrium price the quantity demanded equals quantity supplied.

Figure 4A.3 plots the demand and supply curves for this example and shows the equilibrium price and quantity.

FIGURE 4A.3

Equilibrium with Linear Demand and Supply Curves

This diagram illustrates a linear demand curve given by $Q^D = 56 - 4P$ and a linear supply curve given by $Q^S = -4 + 2P$. The equilibrium price is determined by setting $Q^D = Q^S$ and solving for $P = 10$. The equilibrium quantity is determined by substituting the equilibrium price into either the demand or supply curve and solving for $Q = 16$.

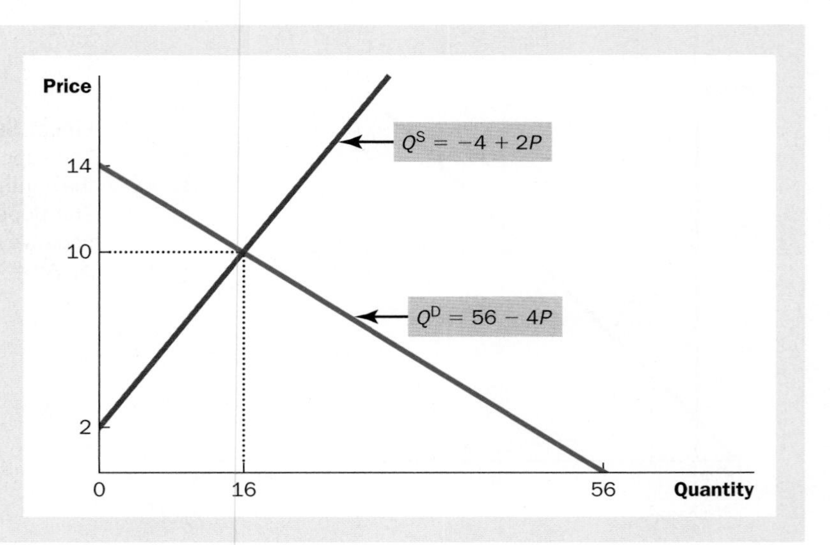

PROBLEMS AND **applications**

A1. Say that the demand schedule for a good is given by $Q^D = 20 - 2P$ and the supply schedule is given by $Q^S = -10 + 4P$.

a. Graph the demand and supply curves, showing the x- and y-intercepts for each.

b. Determine the equilibrium price and quantity.

A2. The demand and supply functions for hockey sticks are given by

$$Q^D = 286 - 20P$$
$$Q^S = 88 + 40P$$

a. Graph the supply and the demand curves, clearly showing the intercepts and indicating the slopes of the two curves.

b. Determine the equilibrium price and quantity of hockey sticks.

c. Suppose that both the men's and the women's teams win Olympic gold medals, causing an increase in the demand for hockey sticks across the country to $Q^D = 328 - 20P$. What impact does this have on the price of hockey sticks and the quantity sold?

A3. Suppose that the demand curve for concert tickets is linear. When the price of a ticket is $5.00, the number of tickets purchased is 1000; when the price of a ticket is $15.00, the number of tickets purchased is 200. Find the slope of the demand curve.

A4. At a price of $320 per tonne, the supply of wheat in Canada is 25 million tonnes and the demand is 26 million tonnes. When the price increases to $340 per tonne, the supply increases to 27 million tonnes and the demand decreases to 22 million tonnes. Assume that both the demand and supply curves are linear.

a. What is the equation for the demand curve for wheat?

b. What is the equation for the supply curve for wheat?

c. Using these equations, what is the equilibrium price and quantity of wheat?

A5. Market research has revealed the following information about the market for chocolate bars: The demand schedule can be represented by the equation $Q^D = 1600 - 300P$, where Q^D is the quantity demanded and P is the price. The supply schedule can be represented by the equation $Q^S = 1400 + 700P$, where Q^S is the quantity supplied.

a. Calculate the equilibrium price and quantity in the market for chocolate bars.

b. Say that in response to a major industry ad campaign, the demand schedule for chocolate bars shifted to the right, as represented by the equation $Q^D = 1800 - 300P$. What happens to the equilibrium price and quantity of chocolate bars in this case?

c. Returning to the original demand schedule, say that the price of cocoa beans, a major ingredient in the production of chocolate bars, increased because of a drought in sub-Saharan Africa, a major producer of cocoa, changing the supply schedule to $Q^S = 1100 + 700P$. What happens to the equilibrium price and quantity in this case?

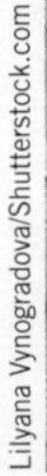
Lilyana Vynogradova/Shutterstock.com

CHAPTER 5

Measuring a Nation's Income

LEARNING **objectives**

In this chapter, you will ...

1. Consider why an economy's total income equals its total expenditure
2. Learn how gross domestic product (GDP) is defined and calculated
3. See the breakdown of GDP into its four major components
4. Learn the distinction between real GDP and nominal GDP

When you finish school and start looking for a full-time job, your experience will, to a large extent, be shaped by the prevailing economic conditions. In some years, firms throughout the economy are expanding their production of goods and services, employment is rising, and jobs are easy to find. In other years, firms are cutting back on production, employment is declining, and finding a good job takes a long time. Not surprisingly, any college or university graduate would rather enter the labour force in a year of economic expansion than in a year of economic contraction.

Because the condition of the overall economy profoundly affects all of us, changes in economic conditions are widely reported by the media. Indeed, it is hard to pick up a newspaper without seeing some newly reported statistic about the economy. The statistic might measure the total income of everyone in the economy (GDP), the rate at which average prices are rising or falling (inflation/deflation), the percentage of the labour force that is out of work (unemployment), total spending at stores (retail sales), or the imbalance of trade between Canada and the rest of the world (the trade deficit). All of these statistics are *macroeconomic.* Rather than telling us about a particular household or firm, they tell us something about the entire economy.

As you may recall from Chapter 2, economics is divided into two branches: microeconomics and macroeconomics. **Microeconomics** is the study of how individual households and firms make decisions and how they interact with one another in markets. **Macroeconomics** is the study of the economy as a whole. The goal of macroeconomics is to explain the economic changes that affect many households, firms, and markets simultaneously. Macroeconomists address diverse questions: Why is average income high in some countries while it is low in others? Why do prices rise rapidly in some periods of time while they are more stable in other periods? Why do production and employment expand in some years and contract in others? What, if anything, can the government do to promote rapid growth in incomes, low inflation, and stable employment? These questions are all macroeconomic in nature because they concern the workings of the entire economy.

microeconomics
the study of how households and firms make decisions and how they interact in markets

macroeconomics
the study of economy-wide phenomena, including inflation, unemployment, and economic growth

Because the economy as a whole is just a collection of many households and many firms interacting in many markets, microeconomics and macroeconomics are closely linked. The basic tools of supply and demand, for instance, are as central to macroeconomic analysis as they are to microeconomic analysis. Yet studying the economy in its entirety raises some new and intriguing challenges.

In this chapter and the next one, we discuss some of the data that economists and policymakers use to monitor the performance of the overall economy. These data reflect the economic changes that macroeconomists try to explain. This chapter considers *gross domestic product*, or simply GDP, which measures the total income of a nation. GDP is the most closely watched economic statistic because it is thought to be the best single measure of a society's economic well-being.

5-1 The Economy's Income and Expenditure

If you were to judge how a person is doing economically, you might first look at that person's income. A person with a high income can more easily afford life's necessities and luxuries. It is no surprise that people with higher incomes enjoy higher standards of living—better housing, better food, fancier cars, more opulent vacations, and so on.

The same logic applies to a nation's overall economy. When judging whether the economy is doing well or poorly, it is natural to look at the total income that everyone in the economy is earning. That is the task of GDP.

GDP measures two things at once: the total income of everyone in the economy and the total expenditure on the economy's output of goods and services. The reason that GDP can perform the trick of measuring both total income and total expenditure is that these two things are really the same. *For an economy as a whole, income must equal expenditure.*

Why is this true? An economy's income is the same as its expenditure because every transaction has two parties: a buyer and a seller. Every dollar of spending by some buyer is a dollar of income for some seller. Suppose, for instance, that Karen pays Doug $100 to mow her lawn. In this case, Doug is a seller of a service, and Karen is a buyer. Doug earns $100, and Karen spends $100. Thus, the transaction contributes equally to the economy's income and to its expenditure. GDP, whether measured as total income or total expenditure, rises by $100.

Another way to see the equality of income and expenditure is with the circular-flow diagram in Figure 5.1. (You may recall this circular-flow diagram from Chapter 2.) The diagram describes all the transactions between households and firms in a simple economy. In this economy, households buy goods and services from firms; these expenditures flow through the markets for goods and services. The firms in turn use the money they receive from sales to pay workers' wages, landowners' rent, and firm owners' profit; this income flows through the markets for the factors of production. In this economy, money flows from households to firms and then back to households.

FIGURE 5.1

The Circular-Flow Diagram

Households buy goods and services from firms, and firms use their revenue from sales to pay wages to workers, rent to landowners, and profit to firm owners. GDP equals the total amount spent by households in the market for goods and services. It also equals the total wages, rent, and profit paid by firms in the markets for the factors of production.

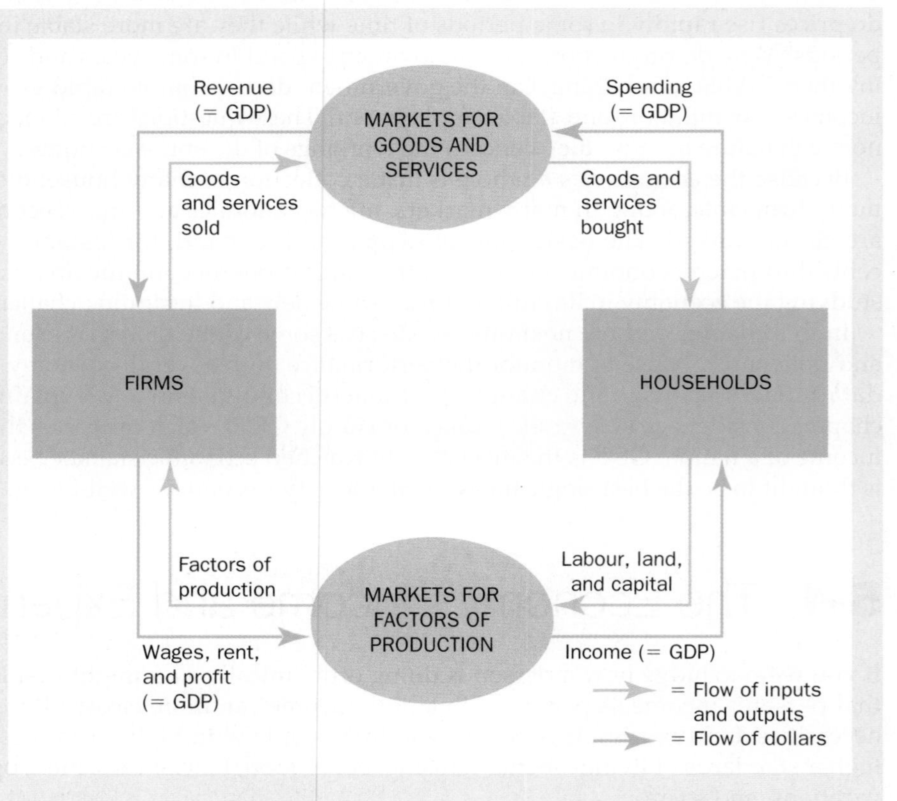

We can compute GDP for this economy in one of two ways: by adding up the total expenditure by households or by adding up the total income (wages, rent, and profit) paid by firms. Because all expenditure in the economy ends up as someone's income, GDP is the same regardless of how we compute it.

The actual economy is, of course, more complicated than the one illustrated in Figure 5.1. In particular, households do not spend all of their income. They pay some of it to the government in taxes, and they save some for use in the future. In addition, households do not buy all goods and services produced in the economy. Some goods and services are bought by governments, and some are bought by firms that plan to use them in the future to produce their own output. Yet, regardless of whether a household, government, or firm buys a good or service, the transaction has a buyer and seller. Thus, for the economy as a whole, expenditure and income are always the same.

What two things does gross domestic product measure? How can it measure two things at once?

5-2 The Measurement of Gross Domestic Product

Now that we have discussed the meaning of gross domestic product in general terms, let's be more precise about how this statistic is measured. Here is a definition of GDP:

- **Gross domestic product (GDP)** is the market value of all final goods and services produced within a country in a given period of time.

gross domestic product (GDP)
the market value of all final goods and services produced within a country in a given period of time

This definition might seem simple enough. But, in fact, many subtle issues arise when computing an economy's GDP. Let's therefore consider each phrase in this definition with some care.

5-2a "GDP Is the Market Value ..."

You have probably heard the adage "You can't compare apples and oranges." Yet GDP does exactly that. GDP adds together many different kinds of products into a single measure of the value of economic activity. To do this, it uses market prices. Because market prices measure the amount people are willing to pay for different goods, they reflect the value of those goods. If the price of an apple is twice the price of an orange, then an apple contributes twice as much to GDP as does an orange.

5-2b "... Of All ..."

GDP tries to be comprehensive. It includes all items produced in the economy and sold legally in markets. GDP measures the market value of not just apples and oranges, but also pears and grapefruit, books and movies, haircuts and health care, and on and on.

GDP also includes the market value of the housing services provided by the economy's stock of housing. For rental housing, this value is easy to calculate—the rent equals both the tenant's expenditure and the landlord's income. Yet many people own the place where they live and, therefore, do not pay rent.

The government includes this owner-occupied housing in GDP by estimating its rental value. That is, GDP is based on the assumption that the owner, in effect, pays rent to himself, so the rent is included both in his expenditure and in his income.

There are some products, however, that GDP excludes because measuring them is so difficult. GDP excludes most items produced and sold illicitly, such as illegal drugs. It also excludes most items that are produced and consumed at home and, therefore, never enter the marketplace. Vegetables you buy at the grocery store are part of GDP; vegetables you grow in your garden are not.

These exclusions from GDP can at times lead to paradoxical results. For example, when Karen pays Doug to mow her lawn, that transaction is part of GDP. If Karen were to marry Doug, the situation would change. Even though Doug may continue to mow Karen's lawn, the value of the mowing is now left out of GDP because Doug's service is no longer sold in a market. Thus, when Karen and Doug marry, GDP falls.

The way in which Doug and Karen's marriage affects GDP is an example of how measures of GDP can underestimate the true amount of productive activity taking place in the economy.

5-2c "... Final ..."

When Domtar Corporation makes paper, which Carlton Cards then uses to make a greeting card, the paper is called an *intermediate good,* and the card is called a *final good.* GDP includes only the value of final goods. The reason is that the value of intermediate goods is already included in the prices of the final goods. Adding the market value of the paper to the market value of the card would be double counting. That is, it would (incorrectly) count the paper twice.

An important exception to this principle arises when an intermediate good is produced and, rather than being used, is added to a firm's inventory of goods to be used or sold at a later date. In this case, the intermediate good is taken to be "final" for the moment, and its value as inventory investment is added to GDP. When the inventory of the intermediate good is later used or sold, the firm's inventory investment is negative, and GDP for the later period is reduced accordingly.

5-2d "... Goods and Services ..."

GDP includes both tangible goods (food, clothing, cars) and intangible services (haircuts, housecleaning, dentist visits). When you buy a CD by your favourite band, you are buying a good, and the purchase price is part of GDP. When you pay to hear a concert by the same band, you are buying a service, and the ticket price is also part of GDP.

5-2e "... Produced ..."

GDP includes goods and services currently produced. It does not include transactions involving items produced in the past. When Ford produces and sells a new car, the value of the car is included in GDP. When one person sells a used car to another person, the value of the used car is not included in GDP.

5-2f "... Within a Country ..."

GDP measures the value of production within the geographic confines of a country. When a British citizen works temporarily in Canada, his production is part of Canadian GDP. When a Canadian citizen owns a factory in Haiti, the production at her factory is not part of Canadian GDP. (It is part of Haiti's GDP.)

Thus, items are included in a nation's GDP if they are produced domestically, regardless of the nationality of the producer.

5-2g "... In a Given Period of Time"

GDP measures the value of production that takes place within a specific interval of time. Usually that interval is a year or a quarter (three months). GDP measures the economy's flow of income and expenditure during that interval.

When the government reports the GDP for a quarter, it usually presents GDP "at an annual rate." This means that the figure reported for quarterly GDP is the amount of income and expenditure during the quarter multiplied by 4. The government uses this convention so that quarterly and annual figures on GDP can be compared more easily.

In addition, when the government reports quarterly GDP, it presents the data after they have been modified by a statistical procedure called *seasonal adjustment*. The unadjusted data show clearly that the economy produces more goods and services during some times of the year than during others. (As you might guess, December's holiday shopping season is a high point.) When monitoring the condition of the economy, economists and policymakers often want to look beyond these regular seasonal changes. Therefore, government statisticians adjust the quarterly data to take out the seasonal cycle. The GDP data reported in the news are always seasonally adjusted.

Now let's repeat the definition of GDP:

- Gross domestic product (GDP) is the market value of all final goods and services produced within a country in a given period of time.

This definition focuses on GDP as total expenditure in the economy. But don't forget that every dollar spent by a buyer of a good or service becomes a dollar of income to the seller of that good or service. Therefore, in addition to applying this definition, the government adds up total income in the economy. The two ways of calculating GDP give almost exactly the same answer. (Why "almost"? The two measures should be precisely the same, but data sources are not perfect. The difference between the two calculations of GDP is called the *statistical discrepancy*.)

It should be apparent that GDP is a sophisticated measure of the value of economic activity. In advanced courses in macroeconomics, you will learn more about the subtleties that arise in its calculation. But even now you can see that each phrase in this definition is packed with meaning.

QUICK **Quiz** *Which contributes more to GDP—the production of a kilogram of hamburger or the production of a kilogram of caviar? Why?*

5-3 The Components of GDP

Spending in the economy takes many forms. At any moment, the Smith family may be having breakfast at Tim Hortons; Ford may be building a car factory; the Royal Canadian Navy may be repairing a submarine; and British Airways may be buying an airplane from Bombardier. GDP includes all of these various forms of spending on domestically produced goods and services.

To understand how the economy is using its scarce resources, economists are often interested in studying the composition of GDP among various types of spending. To do this, GDP (which we denote as Y) is divided into four components: consumption (C), investment (I), government purchases (G), and net exports (NX):

$$Y = C + I + G + NX$$

This equation is an *identity*—an equation that must be true by the way the variables in the equation are defined. In this case, because each dollar of expenditure included in GDP is placed into one of the four components of GDP, the total of the four components must be equal to GDP. Let's look at each of these four components more closely.

5-3a Consumption

consumption
spending by households on goods and services, with the exception of purchases of new housing

Consumption is spending by households on goods and services. "Goods" include household spending on durable goods, such as automobiles and appliances, and nondurable goods, such as food and clothing. "Services" include such intangible items as haircuts and dental care. Household spending on postsecondary education is also included in consumption of services (although one might argue that it would fit better in the next component—investment).

5-3b Investment

investment
spending on capital equipment, inventories, and structures, including household purchases of new housing

Investment is the purchase of goods that will be used in the future to produce more goods and services. It is the sum of purchases of capital equipment, inventories, and structures. Investment in structures includes expenditure on new housing. By convention, the purchase of a new house is the one form of household spending categorized as investment rather than consumption.

As mentioned earlier in this chapter, the treatment of inventory accumulation is noteworthy. When Apple produces a computer and, instead of selling it, adds it to its inventory, Apple is assumed to have "purchased" the computer for itself. That is, the national income accountants treat the computer as part of Apple's investment spending. (If Apple later sells the computer out of inventory, Apple's inventory investment will then be negative, offsetting the positive expenditure of the buyer.) Inventories are treated this way because one aim of GDP is to measure the value of the economy's production, and goods added to inventory are part of that period's production.

Notice that GDP accounting uses the word *investment* differently from how the term might be used in everyday conversation. When you hear the word *investment*, you might think of financial investments, such as stocks, bonds, and mutual funds—topics that we study later in the book. By contrast, because GDP measures expenditures on goods and services, here the word *investment* means purchases of goods (such as capital equipment, structures, and inventories) used to produce other goods.

5-3c Government Purchases

government purchases
spending on goods and services by local, territorial, provincial, and federal governments

Government purchases include spending on goods and services by local, territorial, provincial, and federal governments. It includes the salaries of government workers and spending on public works.

The meaning of *government purchases* requires a bit of clarification. When the government pays the salary of a Canadian Forces general, that salary is part of government purchases. But what happens when the government pays a Canada Pension Plan benefit to one of the elderly? Such government spending is called a *transfer payment* because it is not made in exchange for a currently produced good or service. Transfer payments alter household income, but they do not reflect the economy's production. (From a macroeconomic standpoint, transfer payments are like negative taxes.) Because GDP is intended to measure income from, and expenditure on, the production of goods and services, transfer payments are not counted as part of government purchases.

5-3d Net Exports

Net exports equal the purchases of domestically produced goods by foreigners (exports) minus the domestic purchases of foreign goods (imports). A domestic firm's sale to a buyer in another country, such as the Bombardier sale to British Airways, increases net exports.

net exports
the value of a nation's exports minus the value of its imports; also called the *trade balance*

The "net" in "net exports" refers to the fact that imports are subtracted from exports. This subtraction is made because imports of goods and services are included in other components of GDP. For example, suppose that a household buys a $30 000 car from Volkswagen, the German carmaker. That transaction increases consumption by $30 000 because car purchases are part of consumer spending. It also reduces net exports by $30 000 because the car is an import. In other words, net exports include goods and services produced abroad (with a minus sign) because these goods and services are included in consumption, investment, and government purchases (with a plus sign). Thus, when a domestic household, firm, or government buys a good or service from abroad, the purchase reduces net exports—but because it also raises consumption, investment, or government purchases, it does not affect GDP.

case study

The Components of Canadian GDP

Tables 5.1 and 5.2 both show the composition of Canadian GDP in 2014. Because there are two ways to calculate GDP, Table 5.1 shows the composition of GDP by category of expenditure, while Table 5.2 shows the composition of GDP by category of income.

The annual GDP of Canada was $1973 billion in 2014. If we divide this number by the 2014 Canadian population of approximately 35.3 million, we find that GDP per person—the amount of expenditure for the average Canadian—was about $55 822 in that year.

From Table 5.1 we see that in 2014, consumption made up 56 percent of GDP, or $31 311 per person. Investment averaged $13 530 per person and government purchases averaged $11 496 per person. Net exports averaged −$527 per person. This is a negative number because it is a measure of the difference between exports ($17 671 per person) and imports ($18 198 per person). Because in 2014 the value of imports exceeded the value of exports, net exports turned out to be a negative value. Note that although "net exports" is a relatively small amount, it reflects the difference between two very large amounts. International trade is therefore very important to the Canadian economy.

From Table 5.2 we see that in 2014, the compensation paid to employees (wages, salaries, and benefits) made up 51 percent of GDP, or $28 253 per person.

TABLE 5.1

GDP: Total Expenditure and Its Components
This table shows total GDP for the Canadian economy in 2014 and the breakdown of GDP between different categories of expenditure. When reading the table, recall the identity $Y = C + I + G + NX$.

	Total ($billions/year)	Per Person ($/year)	% of Total
Gross domestic product, *Y*	$1973	$55 822	100%
Consumption, *C*	1107	31 311	56
Investment, *I*	478	13 530	24
Government purchases, *G*	406	11 496	21
Net exports, *NX*	−19	−527	−1
(equals exports	= ($625	= ($17 671	= (32%
minus imports)	– $643)	– $18 198)	– 33%)

Source: Statistics Canada, updated with authors' calculations.

TABLE 5.2

GDP: Total Income and Its Components
This table shows total GDP for the Canadian economy in 2014 and the breakdown of GDP between different categories of income.

	Total ($billions/year)	Per Person ($/year)	% of Total
Gross domestic product, *Y*	$1973	$55 822	100%
Compensation of employees	999	28 253	51
Gross operating surplus	543	15 364	28
Gross mixed income	222	6 288	11
Taxes less subsidies	210	5 929	11
Statistical discrepancy	0	−11	0

Source: Statistics Canada and authors' calculations.

Gross operating surplus defines the income of corporations and government business enterprises. In 2014, this source of income made up 28% of GDP, or $15 364 per person. Gross mixed income defines the income paid to unincorporated businesses. This source of income explained 11% of GDP in 2014, or $6288 per person. The amount of taxes, less subsidies, paid by producers of goods and services accounted for 11% of GDP, or $5929 per person. Finally, the statistical discrepancy that closes the gap between the sum of all expenditures and the sum of all sources of income in the economy amounted to a very small amount in 2014; an amount equal to only $11 per person. ■

List the four components of expenditure. • What does it mean when net exports have a negative value?

5-4 Real versus Nominal GDP

As we have seen, GDP measures the total spending on goods and services in all markets in the economy. If total spending rises from one year to the next, one of two things must be true: (1) The economy is producing a larger output of goods and services, or (2) goods and services are being sold at higher prices. When studying changes in the economy over time, economists want to separate these two effects. In particular, they want a measure of the total quantity of goods and services the economy is producing that is not affected by changes in the prices of those goods and services.

To do this, economists use a measure called *real GDP*. Real GDP answers a hypothetical question: What would be the value of the goods and services produced this year if we valued these goods and services at the prices that prevailed in some specific year in the past? By evaluating current production using prices that are fixed at past levels, real GDP shows how the economy's overall production of goods and services changes over time.

To see more precisely how real GDP is constructed, let's consider an example.

5-4a A Numerical Example

Table 5.3 shows some data for an economy that produces only two goods—hot dogs and hamburgers. The table shows the quantities of the two goods produced and their prices in the years 2013, 2014, and 2015.

To compute total spending in this economy, we would multiply the quantities of hot dogs and hamburgers by their prices. In the year 2013, 100 hot dogs are sold at a price of $1 per hot dog, so expenditure on hot dogs equals $100. In the same year, 50 hamburgers are sold for $2 per hamburger, so expenditure on hamburgers also equals $100. Total expenditure in the economy—the sum of expenditure on

TABLE 5.3

Real and Nominal GDP

This table shows how to calculate real GDP, nominal GDP, and the GDP deflator for a hypothetical economy that produces only hot dogs and hamburgers.

	Prices and Quantities			
Year	Price of Hot Dog	Quantity of Hot Dogs	Price of Hamburger	Quantity of Hamburgers
2013	$1	100	$2	50
2014	2	150	3	100
2015	3	200	4	150

Year	Calculating Nominal GDP
2013	($1 per hot dog × 100 hot dogs) + ($2 per hamburger × 50 hamburgers) = $200
2014	($2 per hot dog × 150 hot dogs) + ($3 per hamburger × 100 hamburgers) = $600
2015	($3 per hot dog × 200 hot dogs) + ($4 per hamburger × 150 hamburgers) = $1200

Year	Calculating Real GDP (base year 2013)
2013	($1 per hot dog × 100 hot dogs) + ($2 per hamburger × 50 hamburgers) = $200
2014	($1 per hot dog × 150 hot dogs) + ($2 per hamburger × 100 hamburgers) = $350
2015	($1 per hot dog × 200 hot dogs) + ($2 per hamburger × 150 hamburgers) = $500

Year	Calculating the GDP Deflator
2013	($200/$200) × 100 = 100
2014	($600/$350) × 100 = 171
2015	($1200/$500) × 100 = 240

hot dogs and expenditure on hamburgers—is $200. This amount, the production of goods and services valued at current prices, is called **nominal GDP**.

nominal GDP
the production of goods and services valued at current prices

The table shows the calculation of nominal GDP for these three years. Total spending rises from $200 in 2013 to $600 in 2014 and then to $1200 in 2015. Part of this rise is attributable to the increase in the quantities of hot dogs and hamburgers, and part is attributable to the increase in the prices of hot dogs and hamburgers.

To obtain a measure of the amount produced that is not affected by changes in prices, we use **real GDP**, which is the production of goods and services valued at constant prices. We calculate real GDP by first choosing one year as a *base year.* We then use the prices of hot dogs and hamburgers in the base year to compute the value of goods and services in all of the years. In other words, the prices in the base year provide the basis for comparing quantities in different years.

real GDP
the production of goods and services valued at constant prices

Suppose that we choose 2013 to be the base year in our example. We can then use the prices of hot dogs and hamburgers in 2013 to compute the value of goods and services produced in 2013, 2014, and 2015. Table 5.3 shows these calculations. To compute real GDP for 2013, we use the prices of hot dogs and hamburgers in 2013 (the base year) and the quantities of hot dogs and hamburgers produced in 2013. (Thus, for the base year, real GDP always equals nominal GDP.) To compute real GDP for 2014, we use the prices of hot dogs and hamburgers in 2013 (the base year) and the quantities of hot dogs and hamburgers produced in 2014. Similarly, to compute real GDP for 2015, we use the prices in 2013 and the quantities in 2015. When we find that real GDP has risen from $200 in 2013 to $350 in 2014 and then to $500 in 2015, we know that the increase is attributable to an increase in the quantities produced because the prices are being held fixed at base-year levels.

To sum up: *Nominal GDP uses current prices to place a value on the economy's production of goods and services. Real GDP uses constant base-year prices to place a value on the economy's production of goods and services.* Because real GDP is not affected by changes in prices, changes in real GDP reflect only changes in the amounts being produced. Thus, real GDP is a measure of the economy's production of goods and services.

Our goal in computing GDP is to gauge how well the overall economy is performing. Because real GDP measures the economy's production of goods and services, it reflects the economy's ability to satisfy people's needs and desires. Thus, real GDP is a better gauge of economic well-being than is nominal GDP. When economists talk about the economy's GDP, they usually mean real GDP rather than nominal GDP. And when they talk about growth in the economy, they measure that growth as the percentage change in real GDP from one period to another.

5-4b The GDP Deflator

As we have just seen, nominal GDP reflects both the prices of goods and services and the quantities of goods and services the economy is producing. By contrast, by holding prices constant at base-year levels, real GDP reflects only the quantities produced. From these two statistics, we can compute a third, called the GDP deflator, which reflects the prices of goods and services but not the quantities produced.

GDP deflator
a measure of the price level calculated as the ratio of nominal GDP to real GDP times 100

The **GDP deflator** is calculated as follows:

$$\text{GDP deflator} = \frac{\text{Nominal GDP}}{\text{Real GDP}} \times 100$$

Because nominal GDP and real GDP must be the same in the base year, the GDP deflator for the base year always equals 100. The GDP deflator for subsequent years measures the change in nominal GDP from the base year that cannot be attributable to a change in real GDP.

The GDP deflator measures the current level of prices relative to the level of prices in the base year. To see why this is true, consider a couple of simple examples. First, imagine that the quantities produced in the economy rise over time but prices remain the same. In this case, both nominal and real GDP rise together, so the GDP deflator is constant. Now suppose, instead, that prices rise over time but the quantities produced stay the same. In this second case, nominal GDP rises but real GDP remains the same, so the GDP deflator rises as well. Notice that, in both cases, the GDP deflator reflects what's happening to prices, not quantities.

Let's now return to our numerical example in Table 5.3. The GDP deflator is computed at the bottom of the table. For the year 2013, nominal GDP is $200, and real GDP is $200, so the GDP deflator is 100. For the year 2014, nominal GDP is $600, and real GDP is $350, so the GDP deflator is 171.

Economists use the term *inflation* to describe a situation in which the economy's overall price level is rising. The *inflation rate* is the percentage change in some measure of the price level from one period to the next. Using the GDP deflator, the inflation rate between two consecutive years is computed as follows:

$$\text{Inflation rate in year 2} = \frac{\text{GDP deflator in year 2} - \text{GDP deflator in year 1}}{\text{GDP deflator in year 1}} \times 100$$

Because the GDP deflator rose from 100 in year 2013 to 171 in year 2014, the inflation rate is $100 \times (171 - 100)/100$, or 71 percent in 2014. In 2015, the GDP deflator rose to 240 from 171 the previous year, so the rate of inflation is $100 \times (240 - 171)/171$, or 40 percent in 2015.

The GDP deflator is one measure that economists use to monitor the average level of prices in the economy. We examine another—the consumer price index—in the next chapter, where we also describe the differences between the two measures.

case study

Real GDP over Recent History

Now that we know how real GDP is defined and measured, let's look at what this macroeconomic variable tells us about the recent history of Canada. Figure 5.2 shows quarterly data on real GDP for the Canadian economy since 1970.

The most obvious feature of these data is that real GDP grows over time. The real GDP of the Canadian economy in 2014 was nearly three and a half times its 1970 level. Put differently, the output of goods and services produced in Canada has grown on average about 2.7 percent per year since 1970. This continued growth in real GDP enables the typical Canadian to enjoy greater economic prosperity than his or her parents and grandparents did.

The second feature of the GDP data is that growth is not steady. The upward climb of real GDP is occasionally interrupted by periods during which GDP declines, called *recessions.* Figure 5.2 marks recessions with shaded vertical bars. (There is no ironclad rule for when we say that a recession has occurred, but a good rule of thumb is two consecutive quarters of falling real GDP.) Figure 5.2 shows that after nearly 20 years of continuous economic growth, Canada experienced a serious recession beginning late in 2008 and lasting until halfway through

FIGURE 5.2

GDP since 1970
This figure shows seasonally adjusted quarterly data on real GDP for the Canadian economy since 1970. Recessions, defined as two or more consecutive quarters of falling real GDP, are marked with the shaded vertical bars.

Source: Statistics Canada, CANSIM database.

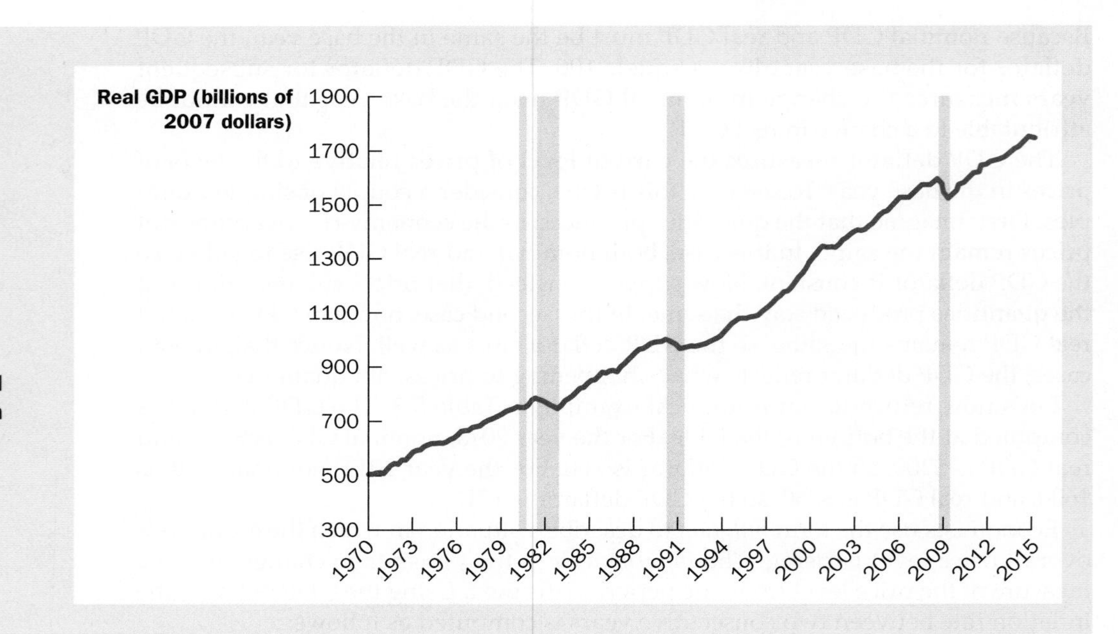

2009. As shown in Figure 5.2, economic growth returned at that time and continued to 2014. The 2008–09 recession saw real GDP fall by over 3 percent in less than one year—a loss of output greater than that suffered in the recession of 1990 but less than the loss of over 4 percent of GDP suffered in the more prolonged recession of the early 1980s.

Much of macroeconomics is aimed at explaining the long-run growth and short-run fluctuations in real GDP. As we will see in the coming chapters, we need different models for these two purposes. Because the short-run fluctuations represent deviations from the long-run trend, we first examine the behaviour of key macroeconomic variables, including real GDP, in the long run. Then in later chapters we build on this analysis to explain short-run fluctuations. ■

Define real and nominal GDP. Which is a better measure of economic well-being? Why?

Foreign Ownership

During the 1970s, many people in Canada became concerned over the amount of Canadian productive capacity owned by foreigners. The concern was that as foreigners increased their ownership of Canada's productive capacity decisions about employment and investment might be made that were not necessarily in the best interests of Canadians. Concerns like these prompted the federal government to impose controls on foreign ownership. The Foreign Investment Review Act (FIRA), passed in 1974, was designed to monitor and regulate the purchase of Canada's productive capacity by foreigners. The act was repealed in 1985 but even so concerns about foreign ownership sometimes make the news and prompt a response from government. Examples include a debate in 2008 over the proposed sale of the Canadian firm famous

Percentage of GDP
Foreign direct investment in Canada (FDI)
Canadian direct investment abroad (CDIA)
Net foreign direct investment in Canada
50, 40, 30, 20, 10, 0, −10
1961, 1965, 1969, 1973, 1977, 1981, 1985, 1989, 1993, 1997, 2001, 2005, 2009, 2013
Year

FIGURE 5.3

Foreign Ownership

The lines in this figure plot values of foreign direct investment (FDI) and Canadian direct investment abroad (CDIA) measured as a percentage of Canada's GDP. The bars show the net amount of foreign direct investment in Canada. The fact that the bars have in recent years fallen below zero is an indication that Canadians now own more of foreign firms than foreigners own of Canadian firms.

Source: Statistics Canada, CANSIM database and authors' calculations.

for designing and building the *Canadarm* used on U.S. space shuttle missions and used at the International Space Station, and the debate in 2010 over the attempted purchase of Potash Corporation of Saskatchewan by Australian firm BHP Billiton. More recently, in 2013, a good deal of concern was expressed over the sale of Nexen, a large Canadian oil and gas company, to the China National Offshore Oil Corporation (CNOOC).

How concerned should Canadians be about foreign ownership? There are a lot of factors to consider in answering that question and there is certainly no way we can do the debate justice in this case study. What we will do instead is simply offer some facts. Figure 5.3 shows values of what is known as *foreign direct investment* (FDI). This is a measure of how much of Canadian industry is owned by non-Canadians. The reference to "direct" investment means we are limiting our attention to ownership that is sufficient to have a significant influence on the management of the firm. The figure also shows values of Canadian direct investment abroad (CDIA). These values show how much Canadians own and control of industry in the rest of the world. Finally, the bars in the figure show the difference in these two values (FDI – CDIA). All of these variables are measured as a percentage of Canada's GDP.

Figure 5.3 tells an interesting story. The amount of Canadian industry owned and controlled by foreigners (FDI) fell during the period from 1961 to about 1990 but has since increased back to levels last seen in the early 1960s. On the other hand, the amount of foreign industry owned and controlled by Canadians has grown more or less steadily since the mid-1970s. This growth has been so rapid that today (and indeed since the mid-1990s) Canadians control more foreign industry than foreigners control Canadian industry.

GDP reflects the factory's production, but not the harm that it inflicts on the environment.

The trends in FDI and CDIA both reflect the increased integration of world financial markets and trading partnerships. Some people have pointed to the growth in FDI as evidence that globalization is resulting in a "selling of Canada" to foreign interests. It is interesting to evaluate and discuss those claims in light of the rapid growth in CDIA and the fact that today Canadians own and control more foreign firms than vice versa. ■

5-5 GDP and Economic Well-Being

Earlier in this chapter, GDP was called the best single measure of the economic well-being of a society. Now that we know what GDP is, we can evaluate this claim.

As we have seen, GDP measures both the economy's total income and the economy's total expenditure on goods and services. Thus, GDP per person tells us the income and expenditure of the average person in the economy. Because most people would prefer to receive higher income and enjoy higher expenditure, GDP per person seems a natural measure of the economic well-being of the average individual.

Yet some people dispute the validity of GDP as a measure of well-being. When U.S. senator Robert Kennedy was running for president of the United States in 1968, he gave a moving critique of such economic measures:

> [Gross domestic product] does not allow for the health of our children, the quality of their education, or the joy of their play. It does not include the beauty of our poetry or the strength of our marriages, the intelligence of our public debate or the integrity of our public officials. It measures neither our courage, nor our wisdom, nor our devotion to our country. It measures everything, in short, except that which makes life worthwhile, and it can tell us everything about America except why we are proud that we are Americans.

Much of what Robert Kennedy said is correct. Why then do we care about GDP?

The answer is that a large GDP does in fact help us to lead a good life. GDP does not measure the health of our children, but nations with larger GDP can afford better health care for their children. GDP does not measure the quality of their education, but nations with larger GDP can afford better educational systems. GDP does not measure the beauty of our poetry, but nations with larger GDP can afford to teach more of their citizens to read and to enjoy poetry. GDP does not take account of our intelligence, integrity, courage, wisdom, or devotion to our country, but all of these laudable attributes are easier to foster when people are less concerned about being able to afford the material necessities of life. In short, GDP does not directly measure those things that make life worthwhile, but it does measure our ability to obtain the inputs into a worthwhile life.

GDP is not, however, a perfect measure of well-being. Some things that contribute to a good life are left out of GDP. One is leisure. Suppose, for instance, that everyone in the economy suddenly started working every day of the week, rather than enjoying leisure on weekends. More goods and services would be produced, and GDP would rise. Yet, despite the increase in GDP, we should not conclude that everyone would be better off. The loss from reduced leisure would offset the gain from producing and consuming a greater quantity of goods and services.

Because GDP uses market prices to value goods and services, it excludes the value of almost all activity that takes place outside of markets. In particular, GDP omits the value of goods and services produced at home. When a chef prepares a delicious meal and sells it at his restaurant, the value of that meal is part of GDP. But if the chef prepares the same meal for his spouse, the value he has added to the raw ingredients is left out of GDP. Similarly, child care provided in day-care centres is part of GDP, whereas child care by parents at home is not. Volunteer work also contributes to the well-being of those in society, but GDP does not reflect these contributions.

Another thing that GDP excludes is the quality of the environment. Imagine that the government eliminated all environmental regulations. Firms could then produce goods and services without considering the pollution they create, and GDP might rise. Yet well-being would most likely fall. The deterioration in the quality of air and water would more than offset the gains from greater production.

GDP also says nothing about the distribution of income. A society in which 100 people have annual incomes of $50 000 has GDP of $5 million and, not surprisingly, GDP per person of $50 000. So does a society in which 10 people earn $500 000 and 90 suffer with nothing at all. Few people would look at those two situations and call them equivalent. GDP per person tells us what happens to the average person, but behind the average lies a large variety of personal experiences. The "In the News" feature that appears later in this chapter addresses the question of whether the distribution of income has become too skewed toward the rich. The suggestion is that a focus on GDP has caused society to fail to appreciate the importance of how aggregate income is distributed across society.

In the end, we can conclude that GDP is a good measure of economic well-being for most—but not all—purposes. It is important to keep in mind what GDP includes and what it leaves out.

case study

Measuring Economic Well-Being in Canada

Researchers Lars Osberg and Andrew Sharpe of the Centre for the Study of Living Standards have taken account of the criticisms of GDP as a measure of well-being to produce what they consider to be a preferred measure. Their index identifies the measure of GDP as just one of a long list of indicators of well-being. Also included in their index are measures of poverty, human capital, income inequality, natural resource consumption, and environmental degradation, in addition to other factors.

Figure 5.4 presents values of their index of well-being for Canada and each of the provinces for two years: 1981 and 2013. A higher value for the index indicates that the average person in that jurisdiction enjoyed a higher level of well-being.

By these estimates, in both 1981 and 2013, people in Alberta experienced the highest level of well-being. Over this period, the economic well-being of Canadians increased and this is true regardless of province of residence. Interestingly, over the course of 32 years, some changes in relative position have occurred. People in Newfoundland and Labrador have enjoyed a substantial increase in economic well-being and have moved from ranking last in terms of well-being in 1981 to ranking third in 2013. The general pattern of the estimates suggests that provincial differences in economic well-being have narrowed quite considerably since 1981. ■

FIGURE 5.4

Economic Well-Being in Canada

This figure shows values of an index of economic well-being for Canada and each of the provinces for 1981 and 2013.

Source: Centre for the Study of Living Standards. Modified from Beyond GDP: Measuring Economic Well-Being in Canada and the Provinces, 1981–2010, September 2011; 2013 data from Database of the Index of Economic Well-Being in Canada and the Provinces, 1981–2013 (www.csls.ca/iwb/prov.asp). Reprinted with permission.

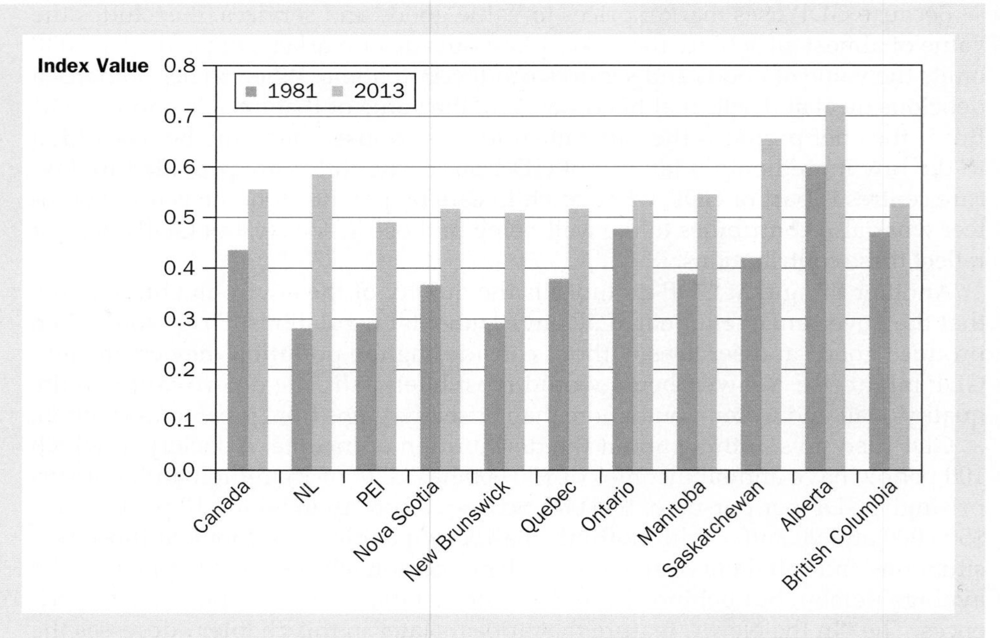

case study International Differences in GDP and the Quality of Life

One way to gauge the usefulness of GDP as a measure of economic well-being is to examine international data. Rich and poor countries have vastly different levels of GDP per person. If a large GDP leads to a higher standard of living, then we should observe GDP to be strongly correlated with measures of the quality of life. And, in fact, we do.

Table 5.4 shows Canada and 12 other countries ranked in order of GDP per person. The table also shows life expectancy (the expected life span at birth) and a measure of "human development" developed by researchers at the United Nations. The Human Development Index (HDI) provides a summary measure of the quality of life enjoyed by people living in each country. The HDI ranking depends on measures of years of education, inequality of income, gender equality, employment levels, measures of poverty, and many more. The HDI emphasizes that there is more to human development than simply GDP; that a country with high GDP may nonetheless be "poor" if, for example, life expectancy is short and the distribution of income is very uneven.

These data show a clear pattern. In rich countries, such as Norway, the United States, Canada, and Japan, people can expect to live into, or nearly into, their eighties, and citizens enjoy the benefits summarized by high values of the HDI. In poor countries, such as Kenya, Ethiopia, and The Congo, people typically live only until their sixties, and the United Nation's measure of human development is low. Although data on other aspects of the quality of life are less complete, they tell a similar story. Countries with low GDP per person tend to have more infants with low birth weight, higher rates of infant mortality, higher rates of maternal mortality, higher rates of child malnutrition, and less common access to safe drinking water. In countries with low GDP per person, fewer school-aged children are actually in school, and those who are in school must learn with fewer teachers per student. These countries also tend to have fewer televisions, fewer

TABLE 5.4

GDP, Life Expectancy, and the Human Development Index
This table shows GDP per person and two measures of the quality of life for 13 countries.

Country	Real GDP per Person	Life Expectancy at Birth	HDI
Norway	$62 448	81.6 years	0.944
United States	51 340	79.1	0.915
Canada	41 894	82.0	0.913
Japan	35 614	83.5	0.891
Russian Federation	23 564	70.1	0.798
Mexico	16 291	76.8	0.756
China	11 525	75.8	0.727
Indonesia	9 254	68.9	0.684
Philippines	6 326	68.2	0.668
India	5 238	68.0	0.609
Kenya	2 705	61.6	0.548
Ethiopia	1 336	64.1	0.442
Congo	783	58.7	0.433

Note: Data on GDP per person represent 2013 values. Real GDP per person is in 2011 dollars measured at purchasing power parity. Data on life expectancy at birth and the HDI represent 2014 values.

Source: Adapted from The Human Development Report 2015, http://hdr.undp.org/en/data. Reprinted with permission from the United Nations Human Development Report Office.

telephones, fewer paved roads, and fewer households with electricity. Taking into consideration all 187 countries for which the UN provides data, the correlation between real GDP per person and the HDI is very high at 73 percent. This means that differences in the HDI across countries are very closely related to differences in real GDP per person. International data therefore leave no doubt that a nation's GDP is closely associated with its citizens' standard of living. ■

QUICK **Quiz** *Why should policymakers care about GDP?*

5-6 Conclusion

This chapter has discussed how economists measure the total income of a nation. Measurement is, of course, only a starting point. Much of macroeconomics is aimed at revealing the long-run and short-run determinants of a nation's gross domestic product. Why, for example, is GDP higher in Canada, the United States, and Japan than in India and Nigeria? What can the governments of the poorest countries do to promote more rapid growth in GDP? Why does GDP in Canada rise rapidly in some years and fall in others? What can Canadian policymakers do to reduce the severity of these fluctuations in GDP? These are the questions we will address shortly.

At this point, it is important to acknowledge the importance of just measuring GDP. We all get some sense of how the economy is doing as we go about our lives. But the economists who study changes in the economy and the policymakers who formulate economic policies need more than this vague sense—they need concrete data on which to base their judgments. Quantifying the behaviour of the economy with statistics such as GDP is, therefore, the first step to developing a science of macroeconomics.

IN THE **news**

Identifying the 1 Percent

In September 2011, extensive media coverage was given to an "Occupy Wall Street" protest in New York City. By October, "Occupy" movements had spread around the world, including Canada. Although it is difficult to identify a single issue with the movement, concern about the concentration of wealth in the hands of a few—the richest 1 percent of people—was a common refrain of those involved in the protests.

The following newspaper article reports on research by economists that looks at the characteristics of the richest 1 percent. It includes a graph (Figure 5.5) showing how the share of total Canadian income received by the richest 1 percent has varied since 1920.

Who Are the 1%? They're Not Just CEOs

By Tavia Grant

For all the hue and cry over Canada's richest 1 per cent, little is known about just who they are. Until now. A new picture of that rarified club shows they are overwhelmingly men, older men in particular. They tend to have university degrees, and half of them work more than 50 hours a week. They're not, by any stretch, all bankers: they are also doctors, dentists, managers and veterinarians, who earn at least $230,000 a year to qualify.

A paper released last week by University of British Columbia economics professors sheds new light on income inequality trends in Canada, who the top earners are and what policies might best address the country's growing income gap.

They find, broadly speaking, that income distribution has not been this uneven in Canada since "the dark days of the Great Depression."

ckchiu/Shutterstock.com

"The ratcheting-up of inequality in Canada is real," the 43-page paper says. "Whatever else it achieved, the Occupy movement shone a light on our growing inequality."

Income inequality has been hotly debated in the past year, and a raft of recent studies has shown it is widening in most advanced economies. Growing income disparity has been linked with deteriorating outcomes for health-care, crime and long-term economic growth.

In Canada, about 8 per cent of the country's total income was concentrated in the hands of 1 per cent of the population back in the late 1970s. In recent years, that almost doubled to 14 per cent, the UBC paper said, which is based in part on details from the 2006 long-form census.

Reasons for the growing chasm vary. The wage gap between those with a university degree and those with just high school is widening. Younger workers are facing worse earnings prospects than a generation ago. Outsourcing, declining unionization rates and technological change may also be playing a role.

Policies that could narrow the gap include closing tax loopholes, hiking taxes on the richest 1 per cent and increasing refundable tax credits to lower-income Canadians, the authors say. Making the education system more flexible and reducing high school dropout rates could help support the middle class.

Here are some more of the findings from the study, entitled *Canadian Inequality: Recent Development and Policy Options:*

- The top 1 per cent of earners amount to 275,000 individuals.

summary

- Every transaction has a buyer and a seller, so the total expenditure in the economy must equal the total income in the economy.
- Gross domestic product (GDP) measures an economy's total expenditure on newly produced goods and services and the total income earned from the production of these goods and services. More precisely, GDP is the market value of all final goods and services produced within a country in a given period of time.
- GDP is divided among four components of expenditure: consumption, investment, government purchases, and net exports. Consumption includes spending on goods and services by households, with the exception of purchases of new housing. Investment includes spending on new equipment and structures, including households' purchases of new housing. Government purchases include spending on goods and services by local, territorial, provincial, and federal governments.

This figure shows the share of total Canadian income received by the richest 1 percent since 1920.

FIGURE 5.5

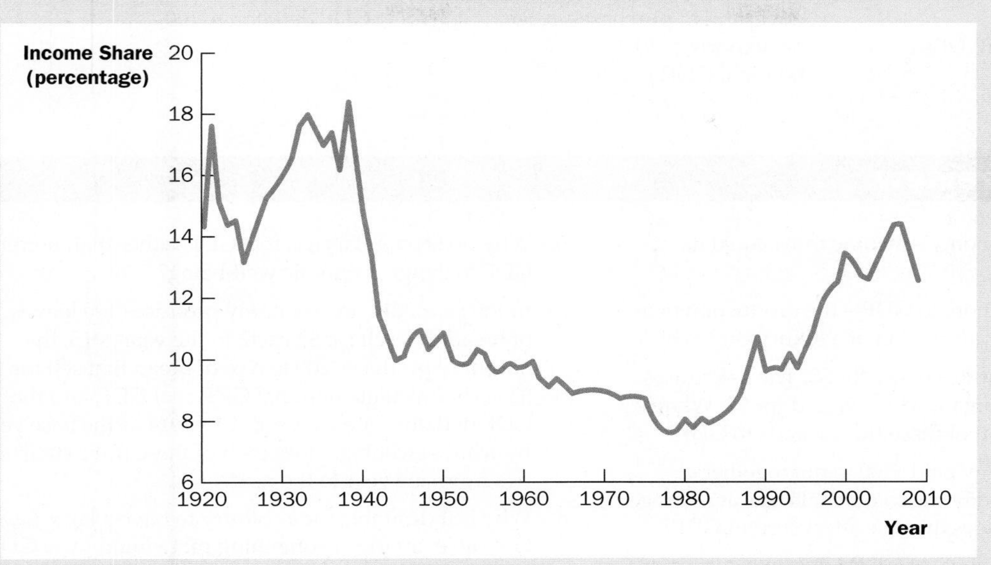

Share of Income Received by the 1 Percent since 1920

Source: Veall, M.R. (2012), "Top Income Shares in Canada: Recent Trends and Policy Implications," *Canadian Journal of Economics/ Revue canadienne d'économique*, 45:1247–1272. doi: 10.1111/j.1540-5982.2012.01744.x. Reproduced by permission of the author.

- Fifty-two percent of people in the top 1 per cent work at least 50 hours a week, compared to less than 20 per cent for the overall population.
- One needs an annual income of at least $230,000 to be part of the top 1 per cent. The average income in this group is $450,000, compared to only $36,000 for the whole Canadian population.
- One could safely call this a brotherhood—83 per cent of those in the top 1 per cent are men. "So despite the significant gains realized by women over the last few decades, they remain dramatically underrepresented at the very top of the income distribution." Young people (under age 35) are also underrepresented in the top income group, though this may just be transitory as most haven't yet reached their peak life-cycle earnings.
- Fifty-eight percent of individuals at the top have at least a bachelor's degree, a greater proportion than the broader population, where 19 per cent of the adult population are university graduates.
- Top earners hail from a variety of sectors. Just 10 per cent of people in the top 1 per cent work in the finance and insurance industry (despite garnering most of the public's wrath). Senior managers and CEOs are overrepresented in the top group, but still only account for 14 per cent of top earners. The only other large group of top income earners? Physicians, dentists and veterinarians who comprise almost 10 per cent of top earners, despite representing less than 1 per cent of the workforce.

The paper was jointly written by the University of British Columbia's Nicole Fortin, David Green, Thomas Lemieux, Kevin Milligan, and Craig Riddell for the Canadian Labour Market and Skills Researcher Network.

Source: "Who Are the Richest 1% in Canada? They're Not Just CEOs," by Tavia Grant, *Globe and Mail,* June 5, 2012.

Net exports equal the value of goods and services produced domestically and sold abroad (exports) minus the value of goods and services produced abroad and sold domestically (imports).

- Nominal GDP uses current prices to value the economy's production of goods and services. Real GDP uses constant base-year prices to value the economy's production of goods and services. The GDP deflator—calculated from the ratio of nominal to real GDP—measures the level of prices in the economy.
- GDP is a good measure of economic well-being because people prefer higher to lower incomes. But it is not a perfect measure of well-being. For example, GDP excludes the value of leisure and the value of a clean environment.

KEY concepts

microeconomics, *p. 91*
macroeconomics, *p. 91*
gross domestic product (GDP), *p. 93*
consumption, *p. 96*
investment, *p. 96*
government purchases, *p. 96*
net exports, *p. 97*
nominal GDP, *p. 100*
real GDP, *p. 100*
GDP deflator, *p. 100*

QUESTIONS FOR review

1. Explain why an economy's income must equal its expenditure.
2. Which contributes more to GDP—the production of an economy car or the production of a luxury car? Why?
3. A farmer sells wheat to a baker for $2. The baker uses the wheat to make bread, which is sold for $3. What is the total contribution of these transactions to GDP?
4. Many years ago Peggy paid $500 to put together a record collection. Today she sold her albums at a garage sale for $100. How does this sale affect current GDP?
5. List the four components of GDP. Give an example of each.
6. Why do economists use real GDP rather than nominal GDP to gauge economic well-being?
7. In the year 2014, the economy produces 100 loaves of bread that sell for $2 each. In the year 2015, the economy produces 200 loaves of bread that sell for $3 each. Calculate nominal GDP, real GDP, and the GDP deflator for each year. (Use 2014 as the base year.) By what percentage does each of these three statistics rise from one year to the next?
8. Why is it desirable for a country to have a large GDP? Give an example of something that would raise GDP and yet be undesirable.

QUICK CHECK multiple choice

1. If the price of a hot dog is $2 and the price of a hamburger is $4, then 30 hot dogs contribute as much to GDP as what number of hamburgers?
   a. 5
   b. 15
   c. 30
   d. 60
2. Angus the sheep farmer sells wool to Barnaby the knitter for $20. Barnaby makes two sweaters, each of which has a market price of $40. Collette buys one of them, while the other remains on the shelf of Barnaby's store to be sold later. What is the GDP here?
   a. $40
   b. $60
   c. $80
   d. $100
3. Which of the following does NOT add to Canada's GDP?
   a. Air France buys a plane from Bombardier, the Canadian aircraft manufacturer.
   b. PotashCorp develops a new mine in Saskatchewan.
   c. The city of Toronto pays a salary to a police officer.
   d. The federal government sends a Canada Pension Plan cheque to your grandmother.
4. A Canadian buys a pair of shoes manufactured in Italy. How is the transaction treated in Canada's national income accounts?
   a. net exports and GDP both rise
   b. net exports and GDP both fall
   c. net exports fall, while GDP is unchanged
   d. net exports are unchanged, while GDP rises
5. What is the largest component of GDP?
   a. consumption
   b. investment
   c. government purchases
   d. net exports
6. If all quantities produced rise by 10 percent and all prices fall by 10 percent, which of the following occurs?
   a. Real GDP rises by 10 percent, while nominal GDP falls by 10 percent.
   b. Real GDP rises by 10 percent, while nominal GDP is unchanged.
   c. Real GDP is unchanged, while nominal GDP rises by 10 percent.
   d. Real GDP is unchanged, while nominal GDP falls by 10 percent.

PROBLEMS AND **applications**

1. What components of GDP (if any) would each of the following transactions affect? Explain.
   a. A family buys a new refrigerator.
   b. Aunt Jane buys a new house.
   c. Ford sells a Thunderbird from its inventory.
   d. You buy a pizza.
   e. Quebec repaves Highway 50.
   f. Your parents buy a bottle of French wine.
   g. Honda expands its factory in Alliston, Ontario.
2. The "government purchases" component of GDP does not include spending on transfer payments such as Employment Insurance. Thinking about the definition of GDP, explain why transfer payments are excluded.
3. Why do you think households' purchases of new housing are included in the investment component of GDP rather than the consumption component? Can you think of a reason why households' purchases of new cars should also be included in investment rather than in consumption? To what other consumption goods might this logic apply?
4. As the chapter states, GDP does not include the value of used goods that are resold. Why would including such transactions make GDP a less informative measure of economic well-being?
5. Below are some data from the land of milk and honey.

Year	Price of Milk	Quantity of Milk (litres)	Price of Honey	Quantity of Honey (litres)
2013	$1	100	$2	50
2014	1	200	2	100
2015	2	200	4	100

   a. Compute nominal GDP, real GDP, and the GDP deflator for each year, using 2013 as the base year.
   b. Compute the percentage change in nominal GDP, real GDP, and the GDP deflator in 2014 and 2015 from the preceding year. For each year, identify the variable that does not change. Explain in words why your answer makes sense.
   c. Did economic well-being rise more in 2014 or 2015? Explain.
6. Consider an economy that produces only chocolate bars. In year 1, the quantity produced is 3 bars and the price is $4. In year 2, the quantity produced is 4 bars and the price is $5. In year 3, the quantity produced is 5 bars and the price is $6. Year 1 is the base year.
   a. What is nominal GDP for each of these three years?
   b. What is real GDP for each of these years?
   c. What is the GDP deflator for each of these years?
   d. What is the percentage growth rate of real GDP from year 2 to year 3?
   e. What is the inflation rate as measured by the GDP deflator from year 2 to year 3?
   f. In this one-good economy, how might you have answered parts (d) and (e) without first answering parts (b) and (c)?
7. Consider the following data on Canadian GDP:

Year	Nominal GDP (in billions)	GDP Deflator (base year 2007)
2013	$1893	111
2014	$1975	113

   a. What was the growth rate of nominal GDP between 2013 and 2014? (*Note:* The growth rate is the percentage change from one period to the next.)
   b. What was the growth rate of the GDP deflator between 2013 and 2014?
   c. What was real GDP in 2013 measured in 2007 prices?
   d. What was real GDP in 2014 measured in 2007 prices?
   e. What was the growth rate of real GDP between 2013 and 2014?
   f. Was the growth rate of nominal GDP higher or lower than the growth rate of real GDP? Explain.
8. If prices rise, people's income from selling goods increases. The growth of real GDP ignores this gain, however. Why, then, do economists prefer real GDP as a measure of economic well-being?
9. Revised estimates of Canadian GDP are usually released by Statistics Canada near the end of each month. Find a newspaper article that reports on the most recent release, or read the news release yourself at www.statcan.gc.ca, the website of Statistics Canada. Discuss the recent changes in real and nominal GDP and in the components of GDP.
10. Goods and services that are not sold in markets, such as food produced and consumed at home, are gene rally not included in GDP. Can you think of how this might cause the numbers in the second column of Table 5.4 to be misleading in a comparison of the economic well-being of Canada and India? Explain.
11. The participation of women in the Canadian labour force has risen dramatically since 1970.
   a. How do you think this rise affected GDP?
   b. Now imagine a measure of well-being that includes time spent working in the home and taking leisure time. How would the change in this measure of well-being compare to the change in GDP?
   c. Can you think of other aspects of well-being that are associated with the rise in women's labour-force participation? Would it be practical to construct a measure of well-being that includes these aspects?

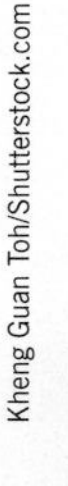
Kheng Guan Toh/Shutterstock.com

Measuring the Cost of Living

LEARNING **objectives**

In this chapter, you will ...

1. Learn how the consumer price index (CPI) is constructed
2. Consider why the CPI is an imperfect measure of the cost of living
3. Compare the CPI and the GDP deflator as measures of the overall price level
4. See how to use a price index to compare dollar figures from different times
5. Learn the distinction between real and nominal interest rates

In 1957 the price of gasoline was 43 cents per gallon, or 9.5 cents per litre. In 2014 the average price was around $1.30 per litre. Why did the price of gas increase so much relative to what it was 55 years previously? Do we blame the Organization of the Petroleum Exporting Countries (OPEC) for using its monopoly power to force up the price of crude oil? Did the big oil companies that buy the crude oil and sell gas at the pumps increase their markups? Or was this rise in the price of gas the inevitable result of rising demand from more people driving more cars, facing a diminishing supply of a nonrenewable natural resource?

At first sight, the increase in the price of gas might make you think that gas was a more scarce and valuable commodity in 2012 than it was in 1957. But, as everyone knows, the prices of nearly all goods and services have increased over time, and so have people's incomes. So it is not clear whether gas was more or less affordable in 2014 than it was in 1957. Did the value of gas increase or did the value of money decrease?

In the preceding chapter we looked at how economists use gross domestic product (GDP) to measure the quantity of goods and services that the economy is producing. This chapter examines how economists measure the overall cost of living. To compare 1957 prices and incomes with 2014 prices and incomes, we need to find some way of turning dollar figures into meaningful measures of purchasing power. That is exactly the job of a statistic called the *consumer price index*. After seeing how the consumer price index is constructed, we discuss how we can use such a price index to compare dollar figures from different points in time.

The consumer price index is used to monitor changes in the cost of living over time. When the consumer price index rises, the typical family has to spend more dollars to maintain the same standard of living. Economists use the term *inflation* to describe a situation in which the economy's overall price level is rising. The *inflation rate* is the percentage change in the price level from the previous period. As we will see in the coming chapters, inflation is a closely watched aspect of macroeconomic performance and is a key variable guiding macroeconomic policy. This chapter provides the background for that analysis by showing how economists measure the inflation rate using the consumer price index.

6-1 The Consumer Price Index

The **consumer price index (CPI)** is a measure of the overall cost of the goods and services bought by a typical consumer. Each month Statistics Canada computes and reports the consumer price index. In this section we discuss how the consumer price index is calculated and what problems arise in its measurement. We also consider how this index compares to the GDP deflator, another measure of the overall level of prices, which we examined in the preceding chapter.

consumer price index (CPI)
a measure of the overall cost of the goods and services bought by a typical consumer

6-1a How the Consumer Price Index Is Calculated

When Statistics Canada calculates the consumer price index and the inflation rate, it uses data on the prices of over 600 different goods and services. To see exactly how these statistics are constructed, let's consider a simple economy in which

TABLE 6.1

Calculating the Consumer Price Index and the Inflation Rate: An Example

This table shows how to calculate the consumer price index and the inflation rate for a hypothetical economy in which consumers buy only hot dogs and hamburgers.

Step 1: Survey Consumers to Determine a Fixed Basket of Goods

4 hot dogs, 2 hamburgers

Step 2: Find the Price of Each Good in Each Year

Year	Price of Hot Dog	Price of Hamburger
2013	$1	$2
2014	2	3
2015	3	4

Step 3: Compute the Cost of the Basket of Goods in Each Year

2013	($1 per hot dog × 4 hot dogs) + ($2 per hamburger × 2 hamburgers) = $8
2014	($2 per hot dog × 4 hot dogs) + ($3 per hamburger × 2 hamburgers) = $14
2015	($3 per hot dog × 4 hot dogs) + ($4 per hamburger × 2 hamburgers) = $20

Step 4: Choose One Year as a Base Year (2010) and Compute the Consumer Price Index in Each Year

2013	($8/$8) × 100 = 100
2014	($14/$8) × 100 = 175
2015	($20/$8) × 100 = 250

Step 5: Use the Consumer Price Index to Compute the Inflation Rate from Previous Year

2014	(175 − 100)/100 × 100 = 75%
2015	(250 − 175)/175 × 100 = 43%

consumers buy only two goods—hot dogs and hamburgers. Table 6.1 shows the five steps that Statistics Canada follows.

1. *Determine the basket*. The first step in computing the consumer price index is to determine which prices are most important to the typical consumer. If the typical consumer buys more hot dogs than hamburgers, then the price of hot dogs is more important than the price of hamburgers and, therefore, should be given greater weight in measuring the cost of living. Statistics Canada sets these weights by surveying consumers and finding the basket of goods and services that the typical consumer buys. In the example in the table, the typical consumer buys a basket of 4 hot dogs and 2 hamburgers.
2. *Find the prices*. The second step in computing the consumer price index is to find the price of each of the goods and services in the basket for each point in time. The table shows the prices of hot dogs and hamburgers for three different years.
3. *Compute the basket's cost*. The third step is to use the data on prices to calculate the cost of the basket of goods and services at different times. The table shows this calculation for each of the three years. Notice that only the prices in this calculation change. By keeping the basket of goods

the same (4 hot dogs and 2 hamburgers), we are isolating the effects of price changes from the effect of any quantity changes that might be occurring at the same time.

4. *Choose a base year and compute the index.* The fourth step is to designate one year as the base year, which is the benchmark against which other years are compared. (The choice of a base year is arbitrary, as the index is used to measure *changes* in the cost of living.) Once the base year is chosen, the index is calculated as follows:

$$\text{CPI} = \frac{\text{Price of basket of goods and services in current year}}{\text{Price of basket in base year}} \times 100$$

That is, the price of the basket of goods and services in each year is divided by the price of the basket in the base year, and this ratio is then multiplied by 100. The resulting number is the consumer price index.

In the example in the table, the year 2013 is the base year. In this year, the basket of hot dogs and hamburgers costs $8. Therefore, the price of the basket in all years is divided by $8 and multiplied by 100. The consumer price index is 100 in 2013. (The index is always 100 in the base year.) The consumer price index is 175 in 2014. This means that the price of the basket in 2014 is 175 percent of its price in the base year. Put differently, a basket of goods that costs $100 in the base year costs $175 in 2014. Similarly, the consumer price index is 250 in 2015, indicating that the price level in 2015 is 250 percent of the price level in the base year.

5. *Compute the inflation rate.* The fifth and final step is to use the consumer price index to calculate the **inflation rate**, which is the percentage change in the price index from the preceding period. That is, the inflation rate between two consecutive years is computed as follows:

inflation rate
the percentage change in the price index from the preceding period

$$\text{Inflation rate in year 2} = \frac{\text{CPI in year 2} - \text{CPI in year 1}}{\text{CPI in year 1}} \times 100$$

In our example, the inflation rate is 75 percent in 2014 and 43 percent in 2015.

Although this example simplifies the real world by including only two goods, it shows how Statistics Canada computes the consumer price index and the inflation rate. Statistics Canada collects and processes data on the prices of hundreds of goods and services every month and, by following the five foregoing steps, determines how quickly the cost of living for the typical consumer is rising. When Statistics Canada makes its monthly announcement of the consumer price index, you can usually hear the number on the evening radio or television news or see it in the next day's newspaper.

In addition to the consumer price index for the overall economy, Statistics Canada calculates several other price indexes. It reports the index for each province and territory and for 19 cities across Canada, as well as for some narrow categories of goods and services (such as food, clothing, and shelter). It also calculates the rate of "core" inflation, which excludes the most volatile components from the CPI basket of goods and services. The excluded components—fruit, vegetables, gasoline, fuel oil, natural gas, mortgage interest, intercity transportation, and tobacco products—account for 19 percent of the CPI basket. **Core inflation** is thought to be useful in predicting the underlying trend of inflation as measured by changes in the consumer price index. As we discuss later in Chapter 11, it is a measure of inflation that is the focus of policymakers.

core inflation
a measure of the underlying trend of inflation

FYI What Is in the CPI's Basket?

When constructing the consumer price index, Statistics Canada tries to include all the goods and services that the typical consumer buys. Thus, it tracks the prices of about 600 goods and services. Moreover, it tries to weight these goods and services according to how much consumers buy of each item.

Figure 6.1 shows the breakdown of consumer spending into the major categories of goods and services. The numbers show the percentage of expenditure on each category of goods and services for the average Canadian consumer in 2013. The largest category is shelter, which makes up 26.8 percent of the typical consumer's budget. This category includes the cost of renting an apartment or making mortgage payments on a house (which means that a rise in interest rates can directly affect the CPI).

The next largest category, at 19.1 percent, is transportation, which includes spending on cars, gasoline, airfares, buses, and so on. The next largest category, at 16.4 percent, is food; this includes both food eaten at home and restaurant meals. Next is the recreation, education, and reading category, which includes your university tuition fees and the price of this book. This category makes up 10.9 percent of the typical consumer's budget, but probably makes up a much larger percentage of your budget.

Unless you happen to buy exactly the same goods and services that the typical consumer is assumed to buy, changes in the CPI can never perfectly measure changes in your personal cost of living.

FIGURE 6.1

The Basket of Goods and Services

This figure shows how the typical Canadian consumer in 2013 divided his or her spending among various goods and services. These percentages are the weights that Statistics Canada uses to compute the CPI.

Source: *The Consumer Price Index*, Cat. 62-001, May 2015, Statistics Canada.

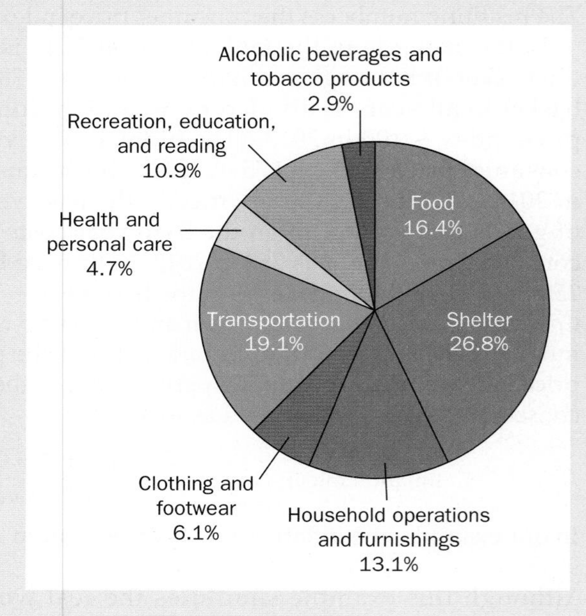

6-1b Problems in Measuring the Cost of Living

The goal of the consumer price index is to measure changes in the cost of living. In other words, the consumer price index tries to gauge how much incomes must rise in order to maintain a constant standard of living. The consumer price index, however, is not a perfect measure of the cost of living. Three problems with the index are widely acknowledged but difficult to solve.

The first problem is called *commodity substitution bias*. When prices change from one year to the next, they do not all change proportionately: Some prices rise more than others. Consumers respond to these differing price changes by buying less of the goods whose prices have risen by large amounts and by buying more of the goods whose prices have risen less or perhaps even have fallen. That is, consumers substitute toward goods that have become relatively less expensive. If a price index is computed assuming a fixed basket of goods, it ignores the possibility of consumer substitution and, therefore, overstates the increase in the cost of living from one year to the next.

Let's consider a simple example. Imagine that in the base year, apples are cheaper than pears, and so consumers buy more apples than pears. When Statistics Canada constructs the basket of goods, it will include more apples than pears. Suppose that next year pears are cheaper than apples. Consumers will naturally respond to the price changes by buying more pears and fewer apples. Yet, when computing the consumer price index, Statistics Canada uses a fixed basket, which in essence assumes that consumers continue buying the now expensive apples in the same quantities as before. For this reason, the index will measure a much larger increase in the cost of living than consumers actually experience. While Statistics Canada tries to minimize this problem by updating the CPI basket to reflect changes in spending patterns every four years, the bias remains within each four-year period.

The second problem with the consumer price index is the *introduction of new goods*. When a new good is introduced, consumers have more variety from which to choose. Greater variety, in turn, makes each dollar more valuable, so consumers need fewer dollars to maintain any given standard of living. To see why, consider a hypothetical situation: Suppose you could choose between a $100 gift certificate at a large store that offered a wide array of goods and a $100 gift certificate at a small store with the same prices but a more limited selection. Which would you prefer? Most people would pick the store with greater variety. In essence, the increased set of possible choices makes each dollar more valuable. The same is true with the evolution of an economy over time: As new goods are introduced, consumers have more choices and each dollar is worth more. Yet, because the consumer price index is based on a fixed basket of goods and services, it does not reflect the increase in the value of the dollar that arises from the introduction of new goods.

Again, let's consider an example. When the iPod was introduced in 2001, consumers found it more convenient to listen to their favourite music. Devices to play music were available previously, but they were not nearly as portable and versatile. The iPod was a new option that increased consumers' set of opportunities. For any given number of dollars, the introduction of the iPod made people better off; conversely, achieving the same level of economic well-being required a smaller number of dollars. A perfect cost-of-living index would have reflected the introduction of the iPod with a decrease in the cost of living. The consumer price index, however, did not decrease in response to the introduction of the iPod. Eventually, Statistics Canada revised the basket of goods to include the iPod, and subsequently, the index reflected changes in iPod prices. But the reduction in the cost of living associated with the initial introduction of the iPod never showed up in the index.

The third problem with the consumer price index is *unmeasured quality change*. If the quality of a good deteriorates from one year to the next, the value of a dollar falls, even if the price of the good stays the same. Similarly, if the quality rises from one year to the next, the value of a dollar rises. Statistics Canada does its best to account for quality change. When the quality of a good in the basket changes—for example, when a car model has more horsepower or uses less gas from one year to the next—Statistics Canada adjusts the price of the good to account for the quality change. It is, in essence, trying to compute the price of a basket of goods of constant quality. Despite these efforts, changes in quality remain a problem because quality is so hard to measure.

There is still debate among economists about how severe these measurement problems are and what should be done about them. Research done at the

Bank of Canada in 2012 suggests that the sources of bias identified above, taken together, cause the Canadian CPI to overstate increases in the cost of living by about 0.5 percentage points per year. The issue is important because private and public pension programs (Old Age Security and the Canada Pension Plan), personal income tax deductions, some government social payments, and many private-sector wage settlements are all adjusted upward using the CPI. The bias in the CPI suggests that adjustments to wages, pensions, and social payments that are based on the CPI may be larger than necessary to maintain the purchasing power of these wages and benefits.

6-1c The GDP Deflator versus the Consumer Price Index

In the preceding chapter, we examined another measure of the overall level of prices in the economy—the GDP deflator. The GDP deflator is the ratio of nominal GDP to real GDP. Because nominal GDP is current output valued at current prices and real GDP is current output valued at base-year prices, the GDP deflator reflects the current level of prices relative to the level of prices in the base year.

Economists and policymakers monitor both the GDP deflator and the consumer price index to gauge how quickly prices are rising. Usually, these two statistics tell a similar story. Yet there are two important differences that can cause them to diverge.

The first difference is that the GDP deflator reflects the prices of all goods and services *produced domestically*, whereas the consumer price index reflects the prices of all goods and services *bought by consumers*. For example, suppose that the price of an airplane produced by Bombardier and sold to the Canadian Forces rises. Even though the plane is part of GDP, it is not part of the basket of goods and services bought by a typical consumer. Thus, the price increase shows up in the GDP deflator but not in the consumer price index.

As another example, suppose that Volkswagen raises the price of its cars. Because Volkswagens are made in Germany, the car is not part of Canada's GDP. But Canadian consumers buy Volkswagens, so the car is part of the typical consumer's basket of goods. Hence, a price increase in an imported consumption good, such as a Volkswagen, shows up in the consumer price index but not in the GDP deflator.

The second and more subtle difference between the GDP deflator and the consumer price index concerns how various prices are weighted to yield a single number for the overall level of prices. The consumer price index compares the price of a *fixed* basket of goods and services to the price of the basket in the base year. Statistics Canada changes the basket of goods every two years. By contrast, the GDP deflator compares the price of *currently produced* goods and services to the price of the same goods and services in the base year. Thus, the group of goods and services used to compute the GDP deflator changes automatically over time. This difference is not important when all prices are changing proportionately. But if the prices of different goods and services are changing by varying amounts, the way we weight the various prices matters for the overall inflation rate.

Figure 6.2 shows the inflation rate as measured by both the GDP deflator and the consumer price index for each year since 1965. You can see that sometimes the two measures diverge. When they do diverge, it is possible to go behind these numbers and explain the divergence with the two differences we have discussed.

FIGURE 6.2

Two Measures of Inflation

This figure shows the inflation rate—the percentage change in the level of prices—as measured by the GDP deflator and the consumer price index using annual data since 1965. Notice that the two measures of inflation generally move together.

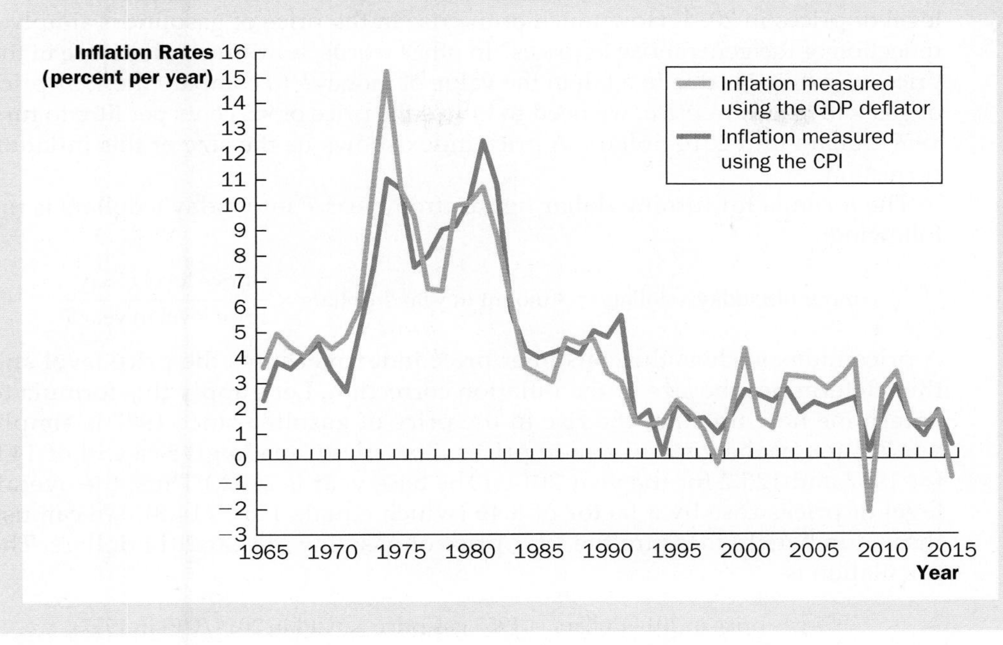

Source: Statistics Canada, CANSIM database.

For example, the sizable difference between the rate of inflation for 2009 measured by the CPI (+0.3 percent) and the rate measured using the GDP deflator (−2.1 percent) is likely due to the fall in the prices of certain key commodities—particularly oil and natural gas—affecting retail prices paid by consumers less than the prices paid by producers. The figure shows, however, that divergence between these two measures is the exception rather than the rule. In the late 1970s, both the GDP deflator and the consumer price index show high rates of inflation. Since the early 1990s, both measures show low rates of inflation.

QUICK **Quiz** *Explain briefly what the consumer price index is trying to measure and how it is constructed.*

6-2 Correcting Economic Variables for the Effects of Inflation

The purpose of measuring the overall level of prices in the economy is to permit comparison between dollar figures from different points in time. Now that we know how price indexes are calculated, let's see how we might use such an index to compare a dollar figure from the past to a dollar figure in the present.

6-2a Dollar Figures from Different Times

We return to the issue of the price of gasoline. Was the 1957 price of 9.5 cents per litre high or low compared with the 2014 price of gas ($1.30 per litre)?

To answer this question, we need to know the level of prices in 1957 and the level of prices in 2014. How much of the rise in the price of gasoline is simply a reflection of the general rise in prices? In other words, how much of the rise in the price of gasoline is due to a fall in the value of money? To compare the 1957 price of gas with the 2014 price, we need to inflate the price of 9.5 cents per litre to turn 1957 dollars into 2014 dollars. A price index shows us the size of this inflation correction.

The formula for turning dollar figures from year T into today's dollars is the following:

$$\text{Amount in today's dollars} = \text{Amount in year } T \text{ dollars} \times \frac{\text{Price level today}}{\text{Price level in year } T}.$$

A price index such as the consumer price index measures the price level and thus determines the size of the inflation correction. Let's apply this formula to determine how much of the rise in the price of gasoline since 1957 is simply a reflection of the general rise in prices. Statistics Canada gives a CPI of 14.8 for 1957 and 125.2 for the year 2014. (The base year is 2002.) Thus, the overall level of prices rose by a factor of 8.46 (which equals 125.2/14.8). We can use these numbers to measure the 1957 price of gasoline in year 2014 dollars. The calculation is

$$\begin{aligned}\text{1957 gas price in 2014 dollars} &= \text{1957 gas price} \times (\text{CPI in 2014/CPI in 1957}) \\ &= 9.5 \text{ cents} \times (125.2/14.8) \\ &= 80.4 \text{ cents}\end{aligned}$$

We find that the 1957 price of gasoline is equivalent to a price of 80.4 cents per litre in 2014. This is considerably less than the 2014 price of gas of $1.30 per litre. So, after adjusting for inflation, the price of gas in 2014 is considerably higher than it was 57 years earlier—by about 50 cents per litre. Over this 57-year period, then, the price of gasoline has on average increased somewhat faster than the price of all other goods and services.

FYI The Bank of Canada's Inflation Calculator

The Bank of Canada's website provides a great deal of information on interest rates, prices, inflation, money, and financial statistics. A useful tool for understanding the impact of inflation is the Bank's Inflation Calculator (www.bankofcanada.ca/en/rates/inflation-calculator). It uses the consumer price index to enable you to calculate what a basket of goods purchased in any year would have cost in any other year. For example, you can use the Inflation Calculator to show that a basket of goods purchased for $100 in 1914 would have cost $208.47 in 1950, $344.07 in 1970, and $2032.20 in 2014. It can also be used to measure rates of inflation over any period. For example, you can use the calculator to show that between 1970 and 1980 the rate of consumer price inflation in Canada averaged 7.89 percent per year, whereas between 2000 and 2014 it averaged only 2.03 percent per year.

Courtesy of Inflation Calculator.ca

case study

Mr. Index Goes to Hollywood

What was the most popular movie of all time? The answer might surprise you.

Movie popularity is usually gauged by box-office receipts. By that measure, as of June 2015, *Avatar* was the #1 movie of all time, followed by *Titanic* at #2. One of the very first movies ever made in colour, *Gone with the Wind* from 1939, barely registers in the list of top-grossing films at #206. But this ranking ignores an obvious but important fact: Prices, including those of movie tickets, have been rising over time. Inflation gives an advantage to newer films.

When we correct box-office receipts for the effects of inflation, the story is very different. *Titanic* now passes *Avatar* as the #1 movie of all time, and *Gone with the Wind* moves all the way up into the #2 spot. *Gone with the Wind* was released before everyone had television sets in their homes and at a time when far more people went to the cinema each week than even today. But the movies from that era rarely show up in popularity rankings because ticket prices were only a quarter. Scarlett and Rhett fare a lot better once we correct for the effects of inflation. ■

"Frankly, my dear, I don't care much for the effects of inflation."

6-2b Indexation

As we have just seen, price indexes are used to correct for the effects of inflation when comparing dollar figures from different times. This type of correction shows up in many places in the economy. When some dollar amount is automatically corrected for inflation by law or contract, the amount is said to be **indexed** for inflation.

indexation
the automatic correction of a dollar amount for the effects of inflation by law or contract

For example, many long-term contracts between firms and unions include partial or complete indexation of the wage to the consumer price index. Such a provision is called a *cost-of-living allowance*, or COLA. A COLA automatically raises the wage when the consumer price index rises.

Indexation is also a feature of many laws. Canada Pension Plan and Old Age Security benefits, for example, are adjusted every year to compensate the elderly for increases in prices. The brackets of the federal income tax—the income levels at which the tax rates change—are also indexed for inflation. There are, however, many ways in which the tax system is not indexed for inflation, even when perhaps it should be. We discuss these issues more fully when we discuss the costs of inflation later in this book.

6-2c Real and Nominal Interest Rates

Correcting economic variables for the effects of inflation is particularly important—and somewhat tricky—when we look at data on interest rates. When you deposit your savings into a bank account, you will earn interest on your deposit. Conversely, when you borrow from a bank to buy a car, you will pay interest on your car loan. Interest represents a payment in the future for a transfer of money in the past. As a result, interest rates always involve comparing amounts of money at different points in time. To fully understand interest rates, we need to know how to correct for the effects of inflation.

Let's consider an example. Suppose that Sally Saver deposits $1000 in a bank account that pays an annual interest rate of 10 percent. After a year passes, Sally has accumulated $100 in interest. Sally then withdraws her $1100. Is Sally $100 richer than she was when she made the deposit a year earlier?

The answer depends on what we mean by "richer." Sally does have $100 more than she had before. In other words, the number of dollars has risen by 10 percent. But Sally does not care about the amount of money itself: She cares about what she can buy with it. If prices have risen while her money was in the bank, each dollar now buys less than it did a year ago. In this case, her purchasing power—the amount of goods and services she can buy—has not risen by 10 percent.

To keep things simple, let's suppose that Sally is a music fan and buys only music CDs. When Sally made her deposit, a CD at her local music store cost $10. Her deposit of $1000 was equivalent to 100 CDs. A year later, after receiving her 10 percent interest, she has $1100. How many CDs can she buy now? It depends on what has happened to the price of a CD. Here are some examples:

- Zero inflation: If the price of a CD is still $10, the number of CDs she can buy has risen from 100 to 110. The 10 percent increase in the number of dollars means a 10 percent increase in her purchasing power.
- 6 percent inflation: If the price of a CD has increased from $10 to $10.60, then the number of CDs she can buy has risen from 100 to approximately 104. Her purchasing power has increased by about 4 percent.
- 10 percent inflation: If the price of a CD has increased from $10 to $11, then even though Sally's dollar wealth has risen from $1000 to $1100, she can still buy only 100 CDs. Her purchasing power is the same as it was a year earlier.
- 12 percent inflation: If the price of a CD has increased from $10 to $11.20, then even with her greater number of dollars, the number of CDs she can buy has fallen from 100 to approximately 98. Her purchasing power has decreased by about 2 percent.

And if Sally was living in an economy with deflation—falling prices—another possibility could arise:

- 2 percent deflation: If the price of a CD has fallen from $10 to $9.80, then the number of CDs she can buy rises from 100 to approximately 112. Her purchasing power increases by about 12 percent.

These examples show that the higher the rate of inflation, the smaller the increase in Sally's purchasing power. If the rate of inflation exceeds the rate of interest, her purchasing power actually falls. And if there is deflation (that is, a negative rate of inflation), her purchasing power rises by more than the rate of interest.

To understand how much a person earns in a savings account, we need to consider both the interest rate and the change in prices. The interest rate that measures the change in dollar amounts is called the **nominal interest rate**, and the interest rate corrected for inflation is called the **real interest rate**. The nominal interest rate, the real interest rate, and inflation are related approximately as follows:

nominal interest rate
the interest rate as usually reported without a correction for the effects of inflation

real interest rate
the interest rate corrected for the effects of inflation

$$\text{Real interest rate} = \text{Nominal interest rate} - \text{Inflation rate}$$

The real interest rate is the difference between the nominal interest rate and the rate of inflation. The nominal interest rate tells you how fast the number of dollars in your bank account rises over time. The rate of inflation tells you how fast the prices of things you want to buy with those dollars are rising. The real interest is the difference between these two measures; it tells you how fast the purchasing power of your bank account rises over time.

As this description suggests, it is the size of the real interest rate that is of crucial importance for economic decisions such as whether to buy a financial asset or to buy a home. A savings account promising to pay a 10 percent nominal interest rate seems like an attractive option when inflation is 2 percent but appears much less attractive if the rate of inflation is 9 percent. The reason is that, with inflation at 2 percent, the amount entering your savings account is growing much faster than the prices of things you want to buy. With inflation at 9 percent, the growth in your savings account is just barely keeping up with the prices of things you are hoping to buy. Clearly, the savings account promising a 10 percent rate of interest is far less attractive when inflation is high than when inflation is low. What matters is the difference—the real rate of interest. In the coming chapters, when we study the causes and effects of changes in interest rates, it will be important for us to keep in mind the distinction between real and nominal interest rates.

QUICK **Quiz** *Henry Ford paid his workers $5 a day in 1914. If the U.S. consumer price index was 10 in 1914 and 195 in 2005, how much is the Ford daily paycheque worth in 2005 dollars?*

Interest Rates in the Canadian Economy

Figure 6.3 shows real and nominal interest rates in the Canadian economy since 1965. The nominal interest rate in this figure is the interest rate on three-month corporate bonds (although data on other interest rates would be similar). The real interest rate is computed by subtracting the rate of inflation from this nominal interest rate. Here the inflation rate is measured as the percentage change in the consumer price index.

One feature of Figure 6.3 is that the nominal interest rate always exceeds the real interest rate. Recalling our discussion of the relationship between the real interest rate, the nominal interest rate, and the rate of inflation, we understand that this is the case because the Canadian economy has experienced positive rates of inflation in every year during the period. The higher the rate of inflation, the bigger the gap between the nominal and the real interest rate. So, as shown in the figure, in 1976 the real interest rate was well below the nominal interest rate because at that time the rate of inflation was quite high. By contrast, because the rate of inflation in 2003 was small, the gap between nominal and real interest rates was also small. As the rate of inflation has moderated, the gap between nominal and real interest rates has fallen since the 1980s.

It is noteworthy that in 1975 and again during the 2010 to 2012 period, the real interest rate turned negative. In 1975 this happened despite nominal interest rates being quite high (nearly 8 percent) and was the result of an even higher rate of inflation (nearly 11 percent). The result was a negative real interest rate (8 percent – 11 percent). During the 2010 to 2012 period, nominal interest rates were now low—averaging just over 1.0 percent—but the rate of inflation was now also low—averaging 2.5 percent—so that the real interest rate was again negative.

Many analysts believe the low value of the real interest rate contributed to a housing boom in Canada during the 2000s. Low real interest rates mean that people find the interest rates they must pay on their mortgage, when compared to the rate of inflation, to be particularly small and affordable. This makes buying a home relatively inexpensive and, not surprisingly, causes people to

FIGURE 6.3

Real and Nominal Interest Rates

Source: Statistics Canada, CANSIM database.

This figure shows nominal and real interest rates using annual data since 1965. The nominal interest rate is the rate on a three-month corporate bond. The real interest rate is the nominal interest rate minus the inflation rate as measured by the consumer price index. The rate of inflation is identified by the vertical distance between the two lines. Nominal and real interest rates often do not move together because of fluctuations in the rate of inflation.

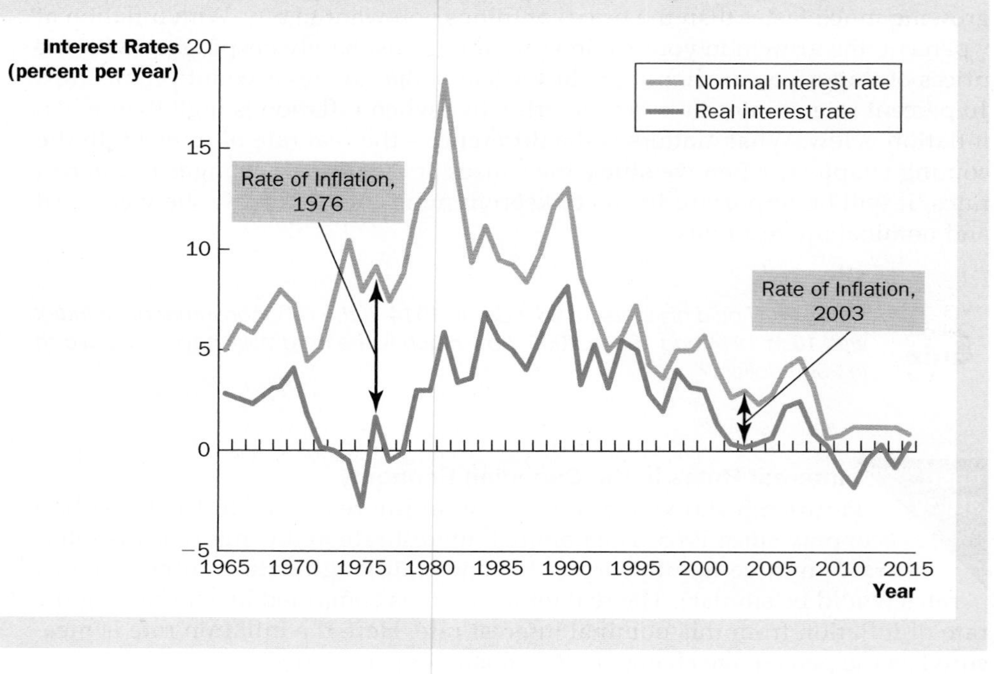

bid up the price of housing. In the coming chapters, we will examine the economic forces that determine both real and nominal interest rates as well as the rate of inflation and discuss the implications of these variables for economic outcomes. ■

6-3 Conclusion

"A nickel ain't worth a dime anymore," baseball player Yogi Berra once observed. Indeed, throughout recent history, the real values behind the nickel, the dime, and the dollar have not been stable. Persistent increases in the overall level of prices have been the norm. Such inflation reduces the purchasing power of each unit of money over time. When comparing dollar figures from different times, it is important to keep in mind that a dollar today is not the same as a dollar 20 years ago or, most likely, 20 years from now.

This chapter has discussed how economists measure the overall level of prices in the economy and how they use price indexes to correct economic variables for the effects of inflation. Price indexes allow us to compare dollar figures from different points in time, therefore giving us a better sense of how the economy is changing.

The discussion of price indexes in this chapter, together with the last chapter's discussion of GDP, is only a first step in the study of macroeconomics. We have not yet examined what determines a nation's GDP or the causes and effects of inflation. To do that, we need to go beyond issues of measurement. Indeed, that is our next task. Having explained how economists measure macroeconomic quantities and prices in the past two chapters, we are now ready to develop the models that explain movements in these variables.

Here is our strategy in the upcoming chapters. First, we look at the long-run determinants of real GDP and related variables, such as saving, investment, real interest rates, and unemployment. Second, we look at the long-run determinants of the price level and related variables, such as the money supply, inflation, and nominal interest rates. Finally, having seen how these variables are determined in the long run, we examine the more complex question of what causes short-run fluctuations in real GDP and the price level. In all of these chapters, the measurement issues we have just discussed will provide the foundation for the analysis.

summary

- The consumer price index shows the cost of a basket of goods and services relative to the cost of the same basket in the base year. The index is used to measure the overall level of prices in the economy. The percentage change in the consumer price index measures the inflation rate.
- The consumer price index is an imperfect measure of the cost of living for three reasons. First, it does not take into account consumers' ability to substitute toward goods that become relatively cheaper over time. Second, it does not take into account increases in the purchasing power of the dollar due to the introduction of new goods. Third, it is distorted by unmeasured changes in the quality of goods and services. While Statistics Canada tries to minimize the distortions to the CPI arising from these problems, they cannot be completely eliminated. For this reason, analysts believe that the CPI overstates the true rate of consumer price inflation by about 0.6 percentage points per year.
- Although the GDP deflator also measures the overall level of prices in the economy, it differs from the consumer price index because it includes goods and services produced rather than goods and services consumed. As a result, imported goods affect the consumer price index but not the GDP deflator. In addition, while the consumer price index uses a fixed basket of goods, the GDP deflator automatically changes the group of goods and services over time as the composition of GDP changes.
- Dollar figures from different points in time do not represent a valid comparison of purchasing power. To compare a dollar figure from the past to a dollar figure today, the older figure should be inflated using a price index.
- Various laws and private contracts use price indexes to correct for the effects of inflation. The tax laws, however, are only partially indexed for inflation.
- A correction for inflation is especially important when looking at data on interest rates. The nominal interest rate is the interest rate usually reported; it is the rate at which the number of dollars in a savings account increases over time. By contrast, the real interest rate takes into account changes in the value of the dollar over time. The real interest rate equals the nominal interest rate minus the rate of inflation.

KEY concepts

consumer price index (CPI), *p. 113*
inflation rate, *p. 115*
core inflation, *p. 115*
indexation, *p. 121*
nominal interest rate, *p. 122*
real interest rate, *p. 122*

QUESTIONS FOR **review**

1. Which do you think has a greater effect on the consumer price index: a 10 percent increase in the price of chicken or a 10 percent increase in the price of caviar? Why?
2. Describe the three problems that make the consumer price index an imperfect measure of the cost of living.
3. If the price of a military aircraft rises, is the consumer price index or the GDP deflator affected more? Why?
4. Over a long period of time, the price of a candy bar rose from $0.10 to $0.60. Over the same period, the consumer price index rose from 150 to 300. Adjusted for overall inflation, how much did the price of the candy bar change?
5. Explain the meaning of *nominal interest rate* and *real interest rate*. How are they related?

QUICK CHECK **multiple choice**

1. The consumer price index measures approximately the same economic phenomenon as which of the following?
   a. nominal GDP
   b. real GDP
   c. the GDP deflator
   d. the unemployment rate
2. What is the largest component in the basket of goods and services used to compute the CPI?
   a. food and beverages
   b. housing
   c. transportation
   d. apparel
3. If a Manitoba gun manufacturer raises the price of rifles it sells to the Canadian Army, which of the following will be increased by the price hikes?
   a. both the CPI and the GDP deflator
   b. neither the CPI nor the GDP deflator
   c. the CPI but not the GDP deflator
   d. the GDP deflator but not the CPI
4. Which of the following occurs because consumers can sometimes substitute cheaper goods for those that have risen in price?
   a. the CPI overstates inflation
   b. the CPI understates inflation
   c. the GDP deflator overstates inflation
   d. the GDP deflator understates inflation
5. If the consumer price index was 200 in 1980 and 300 today, then $600 in 1980 has the same purchasing power as what amount today?
   a. $400
   b. $500
   c. $700
   d. $900
6. You deposit $2000 in a savings account, and a year later you have $2100. Meanwhile, the consumer price index rises from 200 to 204. In this case, what are the nominal interest rate and the real interest rate, respectively?
   a. 1 percent; 5 percent
   b. 3 percent; 5 percent
   c. 5 percent; 1 percent
   d. 5 percent; 3 percent

PROBLEMS AND **applications**

1. Suppose that people consume only three goods, as shown in this table:

	Tennis Balls	Tennis Racquets	Gatorade
2014 price	$2	$40	$1
2014 quantity	100	10	200
2015 price	$2	$60	$2
2015 quantity	100	10	200

   a. What is the percentage change in the price of each of the three goods? What is the percentage change in the overall price level?
   b. Do tennis racquets become more or less expensive relative to Gatorade? Does the well-being of some people change relative to the well-being of others? Explain.
2. Suppose that the residents of Vegopia spend all of their income on cauliflower, broccoli, and carrots. In 2014 they buy 100 heads of cauliflower for $200, 50 bunches

of broccoli for $75, and 500 carrots for $50. In 2015 they buy 75 heads of cauliflower for $225, 80 bunches of broccoli for $120, and 500 carrots for $100. If the base year is 2014, what is the CPI in both years? What is the inflation rate in 2015?

3. Go to the website of Statistics Canada (www.statcan.gc.ca) and find data on the consumer price index. By how much has the index including all items risen over the past year? For which categories of spending have prices risen the most? The least? Have any categories experienced price declines? Can you explain any of these facts?

4. A small nation of ten people idolizes the TV show *Canadian Idol*. All that the ten people produce and consume are karaoke machines and CDs, in the following amounts:

	Karaoke Machines		CDs	
	Quantity	Price	Quantity	Price
2014	10	$40	30	$10
2015	12	60	50	12

a. Using a method similar to the consumer price index, compute the percentage change in the overall price level. Use 2014 as the base year, and fix the basket at 1 karaoke machine and 3 CDs.
b. Using a method similar to the GDP deflator, compute the percentage change of the overall price level. Also use 2014 as the base year.
c. Is the inflation rate in 2015 the same using the two methods? Explain why or why not.

5. Which of the problems in the construction of the CPI might be illustrated by each of the following situations? Explain.
a. The invention of the iPad
b. The introduction of air bags in cars
c. Increased personal computer purchases in response to a decline in the price
d. More scoops of raisins in each package of Raisin Bran
e. Greater use of fuel-efficient cars after gasoline prices increase

6. A single copy of the *Ottawa Citizen* cost $0.10 to purchase in 1970 and $0.50 in 1990. The average wage in manufacturing was $3.01 per hour in 1970 and $14.19 in 1990.
a. By what percentage did the price of a newspaper rise?
b. By what percentage did the wage rise?
c. In each year, how many minutes does a worker have to work to earn enough to buy a newspaper?
d. Did workers' purchasing power in terms of newspapers rise or fall?

7. The chapter explains that Canada Pension Plan benefits are increased each year in proportion to the increase in the CPI, even though most economists believe that the CPI overstates actual inflation.
a. If the elderly consume the same market basket as other people, does the Canada Pension Plan provide the elderly with an improvement in their standard of living each year? Explain.
b. In fact, the elderly consume more medicine than younger people, and medicine costs have risen faster than overall inflation. What would you do to determine whether the elderly are actually better off from year to year?

8. How do you think the basket of goods and services you buy differs from the basket bought by the typical Canadian household? Do you think you face a higher or lower inflation rate than is indicated by the CPI? Why?

9. Income tax brackets were not indexed until 2000. When inflation pushed up people's nominal incomes during the 1970s, what do you think happened to real tax revenue? (*Hint*: This phenomenon was known as "bracket creep.")

10. When deciding how much of their income to save for retirement, should workers consider the real or the nominal interest rate that their savings will earn? Explain.

11. Suppose that a borrower and a lender agree on the nominal interest rate to be paid on a loan. Then inflation turns out to be higher than they both expected.
a. Is the real interest rate on this loan higher or lower than expected?
b. Does the lender gain or lose from this unexpectedly high inflation? Does the borrower gain or lose?
c. Inflation during the 1970s was much higher than most people had expected when the decade began. How did this affect homeowners who obtained fixed-rate mortgages during the 1960s? How did it affect the banks that lent the money?

Production and Growth

LEARNING **objectives**

In this chapter, you will ...

1. See how economic growth differs around the world
2. Consider why productivity is the key determinant of a country's standard of living
3. Analyze the factors that determine a country's productivity
4. Examine how a country's policies influence its productivity growth

When you travel around the world, you see tremendous variation in the standard of living. The average person in a rich country, such as Canada, the United States, or Germany, has an income more than ten times as high as the average person in a poor country, such as India, Indonesia, or Nigeria. These large differences in income are reflected in large differences in the quality of life. Richer countries have more automobiles, more telephones, more televisions, better nutrition, safer housing, better health care, and longer life expectancy.

Even within a country, there are large changes in the standard of living over time. In Canada over the past century, average income as measured by real GDP per person has grown by about 2 percent per year. Although 2 percent might seem small, this rate of growth implies that average income doubles every 35 years. Because of this growth, average income today is about eight times as high as average income a century ago. As a result, the typical Canadian enjoys much greater economic prosperity than did his or her parents, grandparents, and great-grandparents.

Growth rates vary substantially from country to country. In some East Asian countries, such as Singapore, South Korea, and Taiwan, average income has risen about 7 percent per year in recent decades. At this rate, average income doubles every ten years. Over the past two decades, China has enjoyed an even higher rate of growth—about 12 percent per year, according to some estimates. A country experiencing such rapid growth can, in one generation, go from being among the poorest in the world to being among the richest. By contrast, in some nations in sub-Saharan Africa, average income has been stagnant for many years. Zimbabwe has had one of the worst growth experiences: From 1991 to 2011, income per person fell by a total of 38 percent.

What explains these diverse experiences? How can the rich countries ensure that they maintain their high standard of living? What policies should the poor countries pursue to promote more rapid growth in order to join the developed world? These are among the most important questions in macroeconomics. As Nobel Prize–winning economist Robert Lucas put it, "The consequences for human welfare in questions like these are simply staggering: Once one starts to think about them, it is hard to think about anything else."

In the previous two chapters we discussed how economists measure macroeconomic quantities and prices. In this chapter we start studying the forces that determine these variables. As we have seen, an economy's gross domestic product (GDP) measures both the total income earned in the economy and the total expenditure on the economy's output of goods and services. Although imperfect, the level of real GDP is a good gauge of economic prosperity, and the growth of real GDP is a good gauge of economic progress. Here we focus on the long-run determinants of the level and growth of real GDP. Later in this book we study the short-run fluctuations of real GDP around its long-run trend.

We proceed here in three steps. First, we examine international data on real GDP per person. These data will give you some sense of how much the level and growth of living standards vary around the world. Second, we examine the role of *productivity*—the amount of goods and services produced for each hour of a worker's time. In particular, we see that a nation's standard of living is determined by the productivity of its workers, and we consider the factors that determine a nation's productivity. Third, we consider the link between productivity and the economic policies that a nation pursues.

7-1 Economic Growth around the World

As a starting point for our study of long-run growth, let's look at the experiences of some of the world's economies. Table 7.1 shows data on real GDP per person for 13 countries. For each country, the data cover more than a century of history. The first and second columns of the table present the countries and time periods. (The time periods differ somewhat from country to country because of differences in data availability.) The third and fourth columns show estimates of real GDP per person for more than a century ago and for more recent years.

The data on real GDP per person show that living standards vary widely from country to country. Income per person in Canada, for instance, is about 5 times that in China and over 11 times that in India. The poorest countries have average levels of income that have not been seen in the developed world for many decades. The typical citizen of Indonesia in 2010 had real income less than that of the average citizen of the United Kingdom in 1870. The typical person in Pakistan in 2010 had a real income similar to that enjoyed by a typical Canadian 140 years previously.

The last column of the table shows each country's growth rate. The growth rate measures how rapidly real GDP per person grew in the typical year. In Canada, for example, real GDP per person was $2469 in 1870 and $39 528 in 2010. The growth rate was 2.0 percent per year. This means that if real GDP per person, beginning at $2469, were to increase by 2.0 percent for each of 140 years, it would end up at $39 528. Of course, real GDP per person did not actually rise exactly 2.0 percent every year: Some years it rose by more and other years by less. The growth rate of 2.0 percent per year ignores short-run fluctuations around the long-run trend and represents an average rate of growth for real GDP per person over many years.

TABLE 7.1

The Variety of Growth Experiences

Country	Period	Real GDP per Person at Beginning of Period*	Real GDP per Person at End of Period*	Growth Rate (per year)
Japan	1890–2010	$1 563	$35 861	2.65%
Brazil	1900–2010	809	11 311	2.43
Mexico	1900–2010	1 204	14 783	2.31
China	1900–2010	745	7 747	2.15
Germany	1870–2010	2 271	39 569	2.06
Canada	1870–2010	2 469	39 528	2.00
United States	1870–2010	4 166	48 635	1.77
Argentina	1900–2010	2 384	15 937	1.74
India	1900–2010	702	3 431	1.45
United Kingdom	1870–2010	4 999	36 695	1.43
Indonesia	1900–2010	926	4 306	1.41
Pakistan	1900–2010	766	2 843	1.20
Bangladesh	1900–2010	648	1 854	0.96

*Real GDP is measured in 2010 Canadian dollars.

Sources: Robert J. Barro and Xavier Sala-I-Martin, *Economic Growth* (New York: McGraw Hill, 1995), Tables 10.2 and 10.3; *World Development Indicators* online; and authors' calculations.

FYI Are You Richer Than the Richest American?

In October 1998 the magazine *American Heritage* published a list of the richest Americans of all time. The #1 spot went to John D. Rockefeller, the oil entrepreneur who lived from 1839 to 1937. According to the magazine's calculations, his wealth would today be the equivalent of $200 billion, significantly more than that of Bill Gates, the software entrepreneur who is today's richest American.

Keystone/Hulton Archive/Getty Images

John D. Rockefeller

Despite his great wealth, Rockefeller did not enjoy many of the conveniences that we now take for granted. He couldn't watch television, play video games, surf the Internet, or send an e-mail. During the heat of summer, he couldn't cool his home with air conditioning. For much of his life, he couldn't travel by car or plane, and he couldn't use a telephone to call friends or family. If he became ill, he couldn't take advantage of many medicines, such as antibiotics, that doctors today routinely use to prolong and enhance life.

Now consider: How much money would someone have to pay you to give up for the rest of your life all the modern conveniences that Rockefeller lived without? Would you do it for $200 billion? Perhaps not. And if you wouldn't, is it fair to say that you are better off than Rockefeller, allegedly the richest American ever?

The preceding chapter discussed how standard price indexes, which are used to compare sums of money from different points in time, fail to fully reflect the introduction of new goods in the economy. As a result, the rate of inflation is overestimated. The flip side of this observation is that the rate of real economic growth is underestimated. Pondering Rockefeller's life shows how significant this problem might be. Because of tremendous technological advances, the average American today is arguably "richer" than the richest American a century ago, even if that fact is lost in standard economic statistics.

The countries in Table 7.1 are ordered by their growth rate from the most to the least rapid. Japan tops the list, with a growth rate of 2.65 percent per year. In 1890, Japan was not a rich country. Japan's average income was only somewhat higher than Mexico's, and it was well behind Argentina's. To put the issue another way, Japan's income in 1890 was much less than India's income in 2010. But because of its spectacular growth, Japan is now an economic superpower, with average income only slightly behind that of Canada. At the bottom of the list of countries are Pakistan and Bangladesh, which experienced growth of only 1.20 and 0.96 percent, respectively, per year over more than a century. As a result, the typical resident of these countries continues to live in abject poverty.

Because of differences in growth rates, the ranking of countries by income changes substantially over time. As we have seen, Japan is a country that has risen relative to others. One country that has fallen behind is the United Kingdom. In 1870, the United Kingdom was the richest country in the world, with average income about 20 percent higher than that of the United States and more than twice that of Canada. Today, average income in the United Kingdom is well below the average income in the United States and noticeably less than that in Canada.

These data show that the world's richest countries have no guarantee they will stay the richest and that the world's poorest countries are not doomed forever to remain in poverty. But what explains these changes over time? Why do some countries zoom ahead while others lag behind? These are precisely the questions that we take up next.

QUICK **Quiz** *What is the approximate growth rate of real GDP per person in Canada? Name a country that has had faster growth and a country that has had slower growth.*

7-2 Productivity: Its Role and Determinants

Explaining the large variation in living standards around the world is, in one sense, very easy. As we will see, the explanation can be summarized in a single word—*productivity*. But, in another sense, the international variation is deeply puzzling. To explain why incomes are so much higher in some countries than in others, we must look at the many factors that determine a nation's productivity.

7-2a Why Productivity Is So Important

Let's begin our study of productivity and economic growth by developing a simple model based loosely on Daniel Defoe's famous novel *Robinson Crusoe*. Robinson Crusoe, as you may recall, is a sailor stranded on a desert island. Because Crusoe lives alone, he catches his own fish, grows his own vegetables, and makes his own clothes. We can think of Crusoe's activities—his production and consumption of fish, vegetables, and clothing—as being a simple economy. By examining Crusoe's economy, we can learn some lessons that also apply to more complex and realistic economies.

What determines Crusoe's standard of living? The answer is obvious. If Crusoe is good at catching fish, growing vegetables, and making clothes, he lives well. If he is bad at doing these things, he lives poorly. Because Crusoe gets to consume only what he produces, his living standard is tied to his productivity.

productivity
the quantity of goods and services produced from each hour of a worker's time

The term **productivity** refers to the quantity of goods and services that a worker can produce for each hour of work. In the case of Crusoe's economy, it is easy to see that productivity is the key determinant of living standards and that growth in productivity is the key determinant of growth in living standards. The more fish Crusoe can catch per hour, the more he eats at dinner. If Crusoe finds a better place to catch fish, his productivity rises. This increase in productivity makes Crusoe better off: He could eat the extra fish, or he could spend less time fishing and devote more time to making other goods he enjoys.

The key role of productivity in determining living standards is as true for nations as it is for stranded sailors. Recall that an economy's gross domestic product (GDP) measures two things at once: the total income earned by everyone in the economy and the total expenditure on the economy's output of goods and services. The reason why GDP can measure these two things simultaneously is that, for the economy as a whole, they must be equal. Put simply, an economy's income is the economy's output.

Like Crusoe, a nation can enjoy a high standard of living only if it can produce a large quantity of goods and services. Canadians live better than Nigerians because Canadian workers are more productive than Nigerian workers. The Japanese have enjoyed more rapid growth in living standards than Argentineans because Japanese workers have experienced more rapidly growing productivity. Indeed, one of the ten principles of economics in Chapter 1 is that a country's standard of living depends on its ability to produce goods and services.

Hence, to understand the large differences in living standards we observe across countries or over time, we must focus on the production of goods and services. But seeing the link between living standards and productivity is only the first step. It leads naturally to the next question: Why are some economies so much better at producing goods and services than others?

7-2b How Productivity Is Determined

Although productivity is uniquely important in determining Robinson Crusoe's standard of living, many factors determine Crusoe's productivity. Crusoe will be better at catching fish, for instance, if he has more fishing poles, if he has been trained in the best fishing techniques, if his island has a plentiful fish supply, and if he invents a better fishing lure. Each of these determinants of Crusoe's productivity—which we can call *physical capital, human capital, natural resources,* and *technological knowledge*—has a counterpart in more complex and realistic economies. Let's consider each of these factors in turn.

Physical Capital per Worker Workers are more productive if they have tools with which to work. The stock of equipment and structures that are used to produce goods and services is called **physical capital**, or just *capital.* For example, when woodworkers make furniture, they use saws, lathes, and drill presses. More tools allow work to be done more quickly and more accurately. That is, a worker with only basic hand tools can make less furniture each week than a worker with sophisticated and specialized woodworking equipment.

physical capital
the stock of equipment and structures that are used to produce goods and services

As you may recall from Chapter 2, the inputs used to produce goods and services—labour, capital, and so on—are called the *factors of production*. An important feature of capital is that it is a *produced* factor of production. That is, capital is an input into the production process that in the past was an output from the production process. The woodworker uses a lathe to make the leg of a table. Earlier the lathe itself was the output of a firm that manufactures lathes. The lathe manufacturer in turn used other equipment to make its product. Thus, capital is a factor of production used to produce all kinds of goods and services, including more capital.

Human Capital per Worker A second determinant of productivity is human capital. **Human capital** is the economist's term for the knowledge and skills that workers acquire through education, training, and experience. Human capital includes the skills accumulated in early childhood programs, grade school, high school, college or university, and on-the-job training for adults in the labour force.

human capital
the knowledge and skills that workers acquire through education, training, and experience

Although education, training, and experience are less tangible than lathes, bulldozers, and buildings, human capital is like physical capital in many ways. Like physical capital, human capital raises a nation's ability to produce goods and services. Also like physical capital, human capital is a produced factor of production. Producing human capital requires inputs in the form of teachers, libraries, and student time. Indeed, students can be viewed as "workers" who have the important job of producing the human capital that will be used in future production.

Natural Resources per Worker A third determinant of productivity is **natural resources**. Natural resources are inputs into production that are provided by nature, such as land, rivers, and mineral deposits. Natural resources take two forms: renewable and nonrenewable. A forest is an example of a renewable resource. When one tree is cut down, a seedling can be planted in its place to be harvested in the future. Oil is an example of a nonrenewable resource. Because oil is produced by nature over many thousands of years, there is only a limited supply. Once the supply of oil is depleted, it is impossible to create more.

natural resources
the inputs into the production of goods and services that are provided by nature, such as land, rivers, and mineral deposits

Differences in natural resources are responsible for some of the differences in standards of living around the world. The historical success of Canada was driven in part by the large supply of land well suited for agriculture and by an abundance of minerals, forests, and pools of oil and natural gas. Today, some countries in the Middle East, such as Kuwait and Saudi Arabia, are rich simply because they happen to be on top of some of the largest pools of oil in the world.

Although natural resources can be important, they are not necessary for an economy to be highly productive in producing goods and services. Japan, for instance, is one of the richest countries in the world, despite having few natural resources. International trade makes Japan's success possible. Japan imports many of the natural resources it needs, such as oil, and exports its manufactured goods to economies rich in natural resources.

technological knowledge
society's understanding of the best ways to produce goods and services

Technological Knowledge A fourth determinant of productivity is **technological knowledge**—the understanding of the best ways to produce goods and services. A hundred years ago, most Canadians worked on farms, because farm technology required a high input of labour in order to feed the entire population. Today, thanks to advances in the technology of farming, a small fraction of the population can produce enough food to feed the entire country. This technological change made labour available to produce other goods and services.

Technological knowledge takes many forms. Some technology is common knowledge—after it becomes used by one person, everyone becomes aware of it. For example, once Henry Ford successfully introduced production in assembly lines, other carmakers quickly followed suit. Other technology is proprietary—it is known only by the company that discovers it. Only the Coca-Cola Company, for instance, knows the secret recipe for making its famous soft drink. Still other

FYI The Production Function

Economists often use a *production function* to describe the relationship between the quantity of inputs used in production and the quantity of output from production. For example, suppose Y denotes the quantity of output, L the quantity of labour, K the quantity of physical capital, H the quantity of human capital, and N the quantity of natural resources. Then we might write

$$Y = A\,F(L, K, H, N)$$

where $F()$ is a function that shows how the inputs are combined to produce output. A is a variable that reflects the available production technology. As technology improves A rises, so the economy produces more output from any given combination of inputs.

Many production functions have a property called *constant returns to scale*. If a production function has constant returns to scale, then a doubling of all the inputs causes the amount of output to double as well. Mathematically, we write that a production function has constant returns to scale if, for any positive number x,

$$xY = A\,F(xL, xK, xH, xN)$$

A doubling of all inputs is represented in this equation by $x = 2$. The right-hand side shows the inputs doubling, and the left-hand side shows output doubling.

Production functions with constant returns to scale have an interesting implication. To see what it is, set $x = 1/L$. Then the equation above becomes

$$Y/L = A\,F(1, K/L, H/L, N/L)$$

Notice that Y/L is output per worker, which is a measure of productivity. This equation says that productivity depends on physical capital per worker (K/L), human capital per worker (H/L), and natural resources per worker (N/L). Productivity also depends on the state of technology, as reflected by the variable A. Thus, this equation provides a mathematical summary of the four determinants of productivity we have just discussed.

technology is proprietary for a short time. When a pharmaceutical company discovers a new drug, the patent system gives that company a temporary right to be its exclusive manufacturer. When the patent expires, however, other companies are allowed to make the drug. All these forms of technological knowledge are important for the economy's production of goods and services.

It is worthwhile to distinguish between technological knowledge and human capital. Although they are closely related, there is an important difference. Technological knowledge refers to society's understanding about how the world works. Human capital refers to the resources expended transmitting this understanding to the labour force. To use a relevant metaphor, knowledge is the quality of society's textbooks, whereas human capital is the amount of time that the population has devoted to reading them. Workers' productivity depends on both the quality of textbooks they have available and the amount of time they have spent studying them.

case study

Are Natural Resources a Limit to Growth?

Today, the world's population exceeds 7 billion, about four times what it was a century ago. At the same time, many people are enjoying a much higher standard of living than did their great-grandparents. A perennial debate concerns whether this growth in population and living standards can continue in the future.

esbobeldijk/Shutterstock.com

Technology can increase access to natural resources.

Many commentators have argued that natural resources provide a limit to how much the world's economies can grow. At first, this argument might seem hard to ignore. If the world has only a fixed supply of nonrenewable natural resources, how can population, production, and living standards continue to grow over time? Eventually, won't supplies of oil and minerals start to run out? When these shortages start to occur, won't they stop economic growth and, perhaps, even force living standards to fall?

Despite the apparent appeal of such arguments, most economists are less concerned about such limits to growth than one might guess. They argue that technological progress often yields ways to avoid these limits. If we compare the economy today to the economy of the past, we see various ways in which the use of natural resources has improved. Modern cars have better gas consumption. New houses have better insulation and require less energy to heat and cool them. Technological advances have also allowed us to access resources previously thought to be too difficult to extract. Such advances have, for example, made it possible to extract much more oil from the oil sands in Alberta than once was thought possible. Other technological advances have resulted in recycling, causing some nonrenewable resources to be reused. Finally, the development of alternative fuels, such as ethanol instead of gasoline, and solar power instead of electricity generated from burning natural gas, allows us to substitute renewable for nonrenewable resources.

Sixty years ago, some conservationists were concerned about the excessive use of tin and copper. At the time, these were crucial commodities: Tin was used to make many food containers and copper was used to make telephone wire. Some people advocated mandatory recycling and rationing of tin and copper so that supplies would be available for future generations. Today, however, plastic has replaced tin as a material for making many food containers, and phone calls often travel over fibre-optic cables, which are made from sand. Technological progress has made once-crucial natural resources less necessary.

But are all these efforts enough to permit continued economic growth? One way to answer this question is to look at the prices of natural resources. In a market economy, scarcity is reflected in market prices. If the world were running out of natural resources, then the prices of those resources would be rising over time. But, in fact, the opposite is more nearly true. The prices of most natural resources (adjusted for overall inflation) are stable or falling. It appears that our ability to conserve these resources is growing more rapidly than their supplies are dwindling. Market prices give no reason to believe that natural resources are a limit to economic growth. ■

List and describe four determinants of a country's productivity.

7-3 Economic Growth and Public Policy

So far, we have determined that a society's standard of living depends on its ability to produce goods and services and that its productivity depends on physical capital, human capital, natural resources, and technological knowledge. Let's now turn to the question faced by policymakers around the world: What can government policy do to raise productivity and living standards?

7-3a The Importance of Saving, Investment, and Stable Financial Markets

Because capital is a produced factor of production, a society can change the amount of capital it has. If today the economy produces a large quantity of new capital goods, then tomorrow it will have a larger stock of capital and be able to produce more of all types of goods and services. Thus, one way to raise future productivity is to invest more current resources in the production of capital.

One of the ten principles of economics presented in Chapter 1 is that people face tradeoffs. This principle is especially important when considering the accumulation of capital. Because resources are scarce, devoting more resources to producing capital requires devoting fewer resources to producing goods and services for current consumption. That is, for society to invest more in capital, it must consume less and save more of its current income. The growth that arises from capital accumulation is not a free lunch: It requires that society sacrifice consumption of goods and services in the present in order to enjoy higher consumption in the future.

A well-functioning and carefully regulated financial market, one that quickly and efficiently brings savings and investment together with minimal risk and in a transparent way, is a critical ingredient in the recipe for economic growth. This fact, which in modern market-based economies like Canada, the United States, and the countries of Europe has at times been forgotten and unappreciated, was made abundantly and dramatically clear in the financial crisis of 2007 to 2009. When, for reasons we will discuss in later chapters, people and firms lost faith in the transparency of financial markets, the world economy ground almost to a halt, and in the opinion of many economists only dramatic public policy responses ensured a recovery. Since that crisis, economists have paid closer attention to the importance of the design of financial institutions and the regulations that guide them—attention that many judge to be well overdue.

The next chapter examines in more detail how the economy's financial markets coordinate saving and investment. It also examines how government policies influence the amount of saving and investment that takes place. At this point it is important to note that encouraging saving and investment and maintaining well-functioning financial markets are important ways that a government can encourage growth and, in the long run, raise the economy's standard of living.

7-3b Diminishing Returns and the Catch-Up Effect

Suppose that a government pursues policies that raise the nation's saving rate—the percentage of GDP devoted to saving rather than consumption. What happens? With the nation saving more, fewer resources are needed to make consumption goods, and more resources are available to make capital goods. As a result, the capital stock increases, leading to rising productivity and more rapid growth in GDP. But how long does this higher rate of growth last? Assuming that the saving rate remains at its new higher level, does the growth rate of GDP stay high indefinitely or only for a period of time?

The traditional view of the production process is that capital is subject to **diminishing returns**: As the stock of capital rises, the extra output produced from an additional unit of capital falls. In other words, when workers already have a large quantity of capital to use in producing goods and services, giving them an additional unit of capital increases their productivity only slightly. This is illustrated in Figure 7.1, which shows how the amount of capital per worker

diminishing returns
the property whereby the benefit from an extra unit of an input declines as the quantity of the input increases

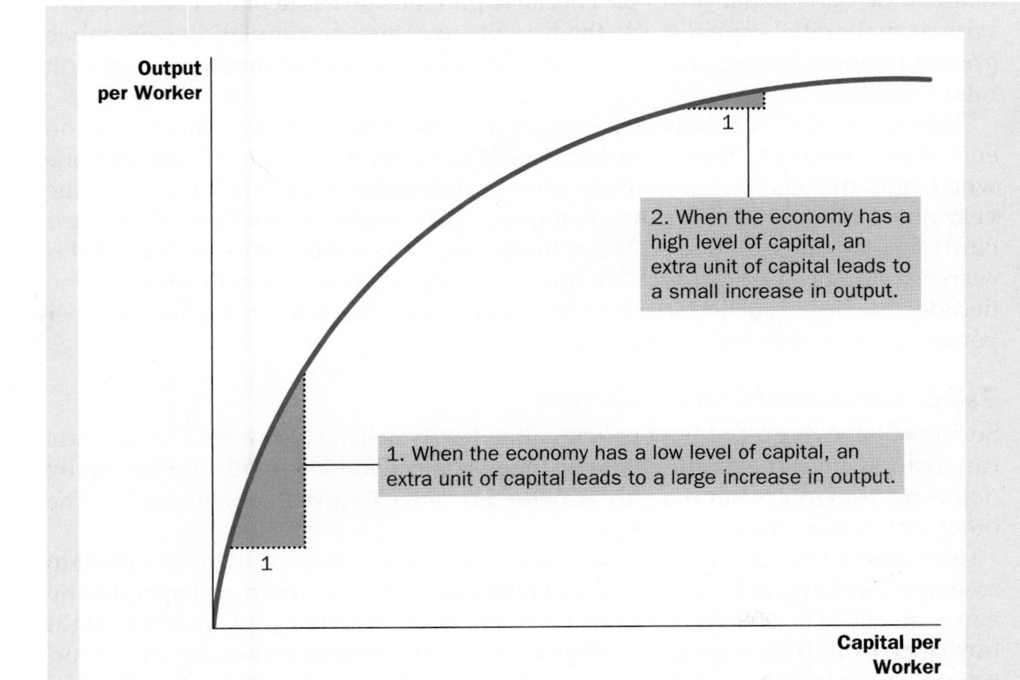

FIGURE 7.1

Illustrating the Production Function

This figure shows how the amount of capital per worker influences the amount of output per worker. Other determinants of output, including human capital, natural resources, and technology, are held constant. The curve becomes flatter as the amount of capital increases because of diminishing returns to capital.

determines the amount of output per worker, holding constant all the other determinants of output.

Because of diminishing returns, an increase in the saving rate leads to higher growth only for a while. As the higher saving rate allows more capital to be accumulated, the benefits from additional capital become smaller over time, and so growth slows down. *In the long run, the higher saving rate leads to a higher level of productivity and income, but not to higher growth in these variables*. Reaching this long run, however, can take quite a while. According to studies of international data on economic growth, increasing the saving rate can lead to substantially higher growth for a period of several decades.

The diminishing returns to capital has another important implication: Other things equal, it is easier for a country to grow fast if it starts out relatively poor. This effect of initial conditions on subsequent growth is sometimes called the **catch-up effect**. In poor countries, workers lack even the most rudimentary tools and, as a result, have low productivity. Small amounts of capital investment would substantially raise these workers' productivity. By contrast, workers in rich countries have large amounts of capital with which to work, and this partly explains their high productivity. Yet with the amount of capital per worker already so high, additional capital investment has a relatively small effect on productivity. Studies of international data on economic growth confirm this catch-up effect: Controlling for other variables, such as the percentage of GDP devoted to investment, poor countries do tend to grow at a faster rate than rich countries.

catch-up effect
the property whereby countries that start off poor tend to grow more rapidly than countries that start off rich

This catch-up effect can help explain some puzzling facts. From 1960 to 1990, Canada and South Korea devoted a similar share of GDP to investment. Yet Canada experienced only mediocre growth of about 2.5 percent, while South Korea experienced spectacular growth of more than 6 percent. The explanation is the catch-up effect. In 1960, South Korea had GDP per person less than one-tenth of the Canadian level, in part because previous investment had been so low. With a small initial capital stock, the benefits to capital accumulation were much greater in South Korea, and this gave South Korea a higher subsequent growth rate.

This catch-up effect shows up in other aspects of life. When a school gives an end-of-year award to the "Most Improved" student, that student is usually one who began the year with relatively poor performance. Students who began the year not studying find improvement easier than students who always worked hard. Note that it is good to be "Most Improved," given the starting point, but it is even better to be "Best Student." Similarly, economic growth over the past several decades has been much more rapid in South Korea than in Canada, but GDP per person is still higher in Canada.

7-3c Investment from Abroad

So far we have discussed how policies aimed at increasing a country's saving rate can increase investment and, thereby, long-term economic growth. Yet saving by domestic residents is not the only way for a country to invest in new capital. The other way is investment by foreigners.

Investment from abroad takes several forms. Bombardier might build a plant to assemble airplanes in Ireland. A capital investment that is owned and operated by a foreign entity is called *foreign direct investment*. Alternatively, a Canadian might buy stock in an Irish corporation (that is, buy a share in the ownership of the corporation); the Irish corporation can use the proceeds from the stock sale to build a new factory. An investment that is financed with foreign money but operated by domestic residents is called *foreign portfolio investment*. In both cases, Canadians provide the resources necessary to increase the stock of capital in Ireland. That is, Canadian saving is being used to finance Irish investment.

When foreigners invest in a country, they do so because they expect to earn a return on their investment. Bombardier's assembly plant increases Ireland's capital stock and, therefore, increases Ireland's productivity and Ireland's GDP. Yet Bombardier takes some of this additional income back to Canada in the form of profit. Similarly, when a Canadian investor buys Irish stock, the investor has a right to a portion of the profit that the Irish corporation earns.

Investment from abroad, therefore, does not have the same effect on all measures of economic prosperity. Recall that gross domestic product (GDP) is the income earned within a country by both residents and nonresidents. When Bombardier opens its assembly plant in Ireland, some of the income the plant generates accrues to people who do not live in Ireland. As a result, foreign investment in Ireland raises the income of Irish citizens by less than it raises the production in Ireland (measured by GDP).

Nonetheless, investment from abroad is one way for a country to grow. Even though some of the benefits from this investment flow back to the foreign owners, this investment does increase the economy's stock of capital, leading to higher productivity and higher wages. Moreover, investment from abroad is one way for poor countries to learn the state-of-the-art technologies developed and used in richer countries. For these reasons, many economists who advise governments in less-developed economies advocate policies that encourage investment from abroad. Often this means removing restrictions that governments have imposed on foreign ownership of domestic capital.

An organization that tries to encourage the flow of capital to poor countries is the World Bank. This international organization obtains funds from the world's advanced countries, such as Canada and the United States, and uses these resources to make loans to less-developed countries so that they can invest in roads, sewer systems, schools, and other types of capital. It also offers the countries advice about how the funds might best be used. The World Bank, together with its sister organization, the IMF, was set up after World War II. One lesson from the war was that economic distress often leads to political turmoil, international tensions, and military conflict. Thus, every country has an interest in promoting economic prosperity around the world. The World Bank and the IMF are aimed at achieving that common goal.

7-3d Education

Education—investment in human capital—is at least as important as investment in physical capital for a country's long-run economic success. In Canada, each year of schooling has historically raised a person's wage on average by about 10 percent. In less-developed countries, where human capital is especially scarce, the gap between the wages of educated and uneducated workers is even larger. Thus, one way in which government policy can enhance the standard of living is to provide good schools and to encourage the population to take advantage of them.

Investment in human capital, like investment in physical capital, has an opportunity cost. When students are in school, they forgo the wages they could have earned. In less-developed countries, children often drop out of school at an early age, even though the benefit of additional schooling is very high, simply because their labour is needed to help support the family.

Some economists have argued that human capital is particularly important for economic growth because human capital conveys positive externalities. An *externality* is the effect of one person's actions on the well-being of a bystander. An educated person, for instance, might generate new ideas about how best to produce goods and services. If these ideas enter society's pool of knowledge, so everyone can use them, then the ideas are an external benefit of education. In this case, the return to schooling for society is even greater than the return for the individual. This argument would justify the large subsidies to human-capital investment that we observe in the form of public education.

One problem facing some poor countries is the *brain drain*—the emigration of many of the most highly educated workers to rich countries, where these workers can enjoy a higher standard of living. If human capital does have positive externalities, then this brain drain makes those people left behind poorer than they otherwise would be. But it is not only poor countries that experience the economic effects of the brain drain. Canada is a rich country with a good system of higher education that attracts many of the best students from poor countries. In this way, Canada benefits from the brain drain suffered by poor countries. However, Canada also suffers a brain drain of its own as highly educated workers are attracted to high-paying jobs in the United States. Concern over the size of the brain drain to the United States has prompted some analysts to stress the need for Canada to cut taxes. They suggest this is necessary in order to make the after-tax incomes of skilled workers more comparable to those in the United States and in this way stem the flow of human capital out of Canada. Others suggest that instead of tax cuts, improvements to Canada's social programs as well as investments in better education and improved health care will also stem the flow of human capital to the United States. Finally, still other analysts are not convinced that the brain drain to the United States is so large as to justify any response at all.

7-3e Health and Nutrition

Although the term *human capital* usually refers to education, it can also be used to describe another type of investment in people: expenditures that lead to a healthier population. Other things equal, healthier workers are more productive. Making the right investments in the health of the population is one way for a nation to increase productivity and raise living standards.

Economic historian Robert Fogel has suggested that a significant factor in long-run economic growth is improved health from better nutrition. In his article "Health, Nutrition, and Economic Growth" (*Economic Development and Cultural Change*, University of Chicago Press, 2004), he estimated that in Great Britain in 1780, about one in five people were so malnourished that they were incapable of manual labour. Among those who could work, insufficient caloric intake substantially reduced the work effort they could put forth. As nutrition improved, so did workers' productivity.

Fogel studies these historical trends in part by looking at the height of the population. Short height can be an indicator of malnutrition, especially during pregnancy and the early years of life. Fogel finds that as nations develop economically, people eat more, and the population gets taller. From 1775 to 1975, the average caloric intake in Great Britain rose by 26 percent, and the height of the average man rose by 9.14 centimetres. Similarly, during the spectacular economic growth in South Korea from 1962 to 1995, caloric consumption rose

IN THE news Promoting Human Capital

Human capital is a key to economic growth. With this in mind, some developing countries now give parents an immediate financial incentive to keep their children in school.

Brazil Pays Parents to Help Poor Be Pupils, Not Wage Earners

By Celia W. Dugger

FORTALEZA, Brazil—Vandelson Andrade, 13, often used to skip school to work 12-hour days on the small, graceful fishing boats that sail from the picturesque harbor here. His meager earnings helped pay for rice and beans for his desperately poor family.

But this year he qualified for a small monthly cash payment from the government that his mother receives on the condition that he shows up in the classroom.

"I can't skip school anymore," said Vandelson, whose hand-me-down pants were so big that the crotch ended at his knees and the legs bunched up around his ankles. "If I miss one more day, my mother won't get the money."

This year, Vandelson will finally pass the fourth grade on his third try—a small victory in a new breed of social program that is spreading swiftly across Latin America. It is a developing-country version of American welfare reform: to break the cycle of poverty, the government gives the poor small cash payments in exchange for keeping their children in school and taking them for regular medical checkups.

"I think these programs are as close as you can come to a magic bullet in development," said Nancy Birdsall, president of the Center for Global Development, a nonprofit research group in Washington. "They're creating an incentive for families to invest in their own children's futures. Every decade or so, we see something that can really make a difference, and this is one of those things."...

Antônio Souza, 48, and Maria Torres, 37, are raising seven children in a mud hut a couple of hills away from Mr. Andrade. Every member of the family is sinewy and lean. The parents cannot remember the last time the family ate meat or vegetables. But their grant of $27 a month makes it possible to buy rice, sugar, pasta and oil.

Mr. Souza and Ms. Torres, illiterate believers in the power of education, have always sent their children to school. "If they don't study, they'll turn into dummies like me," said their father, whose weathered, deeply creased face broke into a wide smile as he surveyed his bright-eyed daughters, Ana Paula, 11, and Daniele, 8, among them. "All I can do is work in the fields."

His wife said proudly: "There are fathers who don't want their children to go to school. But this man here has done everything he could to send his children to school."

by 44 percent, and average male height rose by 5.08 centimetres. Of course, a person's height is determined by a combination of genetic predisposition and environment. But because the genetic makeup of a population is slow to change, such increases in average height are most likely due to changes in the environment—nutrition being the obvious explanation.

Moreover, studies have found that height is an indicator of productivity. Looking at data on a large number of workers at a point in time, researchers have found that taller workers tend to earn more. Because wages reflect a worker's productivity, this finding suggests that taller workers tend to be more productive. The effect of height on wages is especially pronounced in poorer countries, where malnutrition is a bigger risk.

Fogel won the Nobel Prize in Economic Sciences in 1993 for his work in economic history, which includes not only his studies of nutrition but also his studies of American slavery and the role of railroads in the development of the American economy. In the lecture he gave when he was awarded the prize, he reviewed the evidence on health and economic growth, concluding that "improved gross nutrition accounts for roughly 30 percent of the growth of per capita income in Britain between 1790 and 1980."

Today, malnutrition is fortunately rare in developed nations such as Great Britain, Canada, and the United States. (Obesity is a more widespread problem.) But for people in developing nations, poor health and inadequate nutrition remain obstacles to higher productivity and improved living standards. The United Nations recently estimated that almost a third of the population in sub-Saharan Africa is undernourished.

The causal link between health and wealth runs in both directions. Poor countries are poor in part because their populations are not healthy, and their populations are not healthy in part because they are poor and cannot afford adequate health care and nutrition. It is a vicious circle. But this fact opens the possibility of a virtuous circle: Policies that lead to more rapid economic growth would naturally improve health outcomes, which in turn would further promote economic growth.

7-3f Property Rights and Political Stability

Another way in which policymakers can foster economic growth is by protecting property rights and promoting political stability. This issue goes to the very heart of how market economies work.

Production in market economies arises from the interactions of millions of individuals and firms. When you buy a car, for instance, you are buying the output of a car dealer, a car manufacturer, a steel company, an iron ore mining company, and so on. This division of production among many firms allows the economy's factors of production to be used as effectively as possible. To achieve this outcome, the economy has to coordinate transactions among these firms, as well as between firms and consumers. Market economies achieve this coordination through market prices. That is, market prices are the instrument with which the invisible hand of the marketplace brings supply and demand into balance in each of the many thousands of markets that make up the economy.

An important prerequisite for the price system to work is an economy-wide respect for *property rights*: the ability of people to exercise authority over the resources they own. A mining company will not make the effort to mine iron ore if it expects the ore to be stolen. The company mines the ore only if it is confident that it will benefit from the ore's subsequent sale. For this reason, courts serve an important role in a market economy: They enforce property rights. Through the criminal justice system, the courts discourage direct theft. In addition, through the civil justice system, the courts ensure that buyers and sellers live up to their contracts.

Although those of us in developed countries tend to take property rights for granted, those living in less-developed countries understand that lack of property rights can be a major problem. In many countries, the system of justice does not work well. Contracts are hard to enforce, and fraud often goes unpunished. In more extreme cases, the government not only fails to enforce property rights but actually infringes on them. To do business in some countries, firms are expected to bribe powerful government officials. Such corruption impedes the coordinating power of markets. It also discourages domestic saving and investment from abroad.

One threat to property rights is political instability. When revolutions and coups are common, there is doubt about whether property rights will be respected in the future. If a revolutionary government might confiscate the capital of some businesses, as was often true after communist revolutions, domestic residents have less incentive to save, invest, and start new businesses. At the same time, foreigners have less incentive to invest in the country. Even the threat of revolution can act to depress a nation's standard of living.

Thus, economic prosperity depends in part on political prosperity. A country with an efficient court system, honest government officials, and a stable constitution will enjoy a higher economic standard of living than a country with a poor court system, corrupt officials, and frequent revolutions and coups.

7-3g Free Trade

Some of the world's poorest countries have tried to achieve more rapid economic growth by pursuing *inward-oriented policies*. These policies are aimed at raising productivity and living standards within the country by avoiding interaction with the rest of the world. This approach gets support from some domestic firms, which claim that they need protection from foreign competition in order to compete and grow. This infant-industry argument, together with a general distrust of foreigners, has at times led policymakers in less-developed countries to impose tariffs and other trade restrictions.

Most economists today believe that poor countries are better off pursuing *outward-oriented policies* that integrate these countries into the world economy. When we studied international trade earlier in the book, we showed how international trade can improve the economic well-being of a country's citizens. Trade is, in some ways, a type of technology. When a country exports wheat and imports steel, the country benefits in the same way as if it had invented a technology for turning wheat into steel. A country that eliminates trade restrictions will, therefore, experience the same kind of economic growth that would occur after a major technological advance.

The adverse impact of inward orientation becomes clear when one considers the small size of many less-developed economies. The total GDP of Argentina, for instance, is about that of Toronto. Imagine what would happen if the Toronto city council were to prohibit city residents from trading with people living outside the city limits. Without being able to take advantage of the gains from trade, Toronto would need to produce all the goods it consumes. It would also have to produce all its own capital goods, rather than importing state-of-the-art equipment from other cities. Living standards in Toronto would fall immediately, and the problem would likely only get worse over time. This is precisely what happened when Argentina pursued inward-oriented policies throughout much of the twentieth century. By contrast, countries pursuing outward-oriented policies, such as South Korea, Singapore, and Taiwan, have enjoyed high rates of economic growth.

The amount that a nation trades with others is determined not only by government policy but also by geography. Countries with good natural seaports find trade easier than countries without this resource. It is not a coincidence that many of the world's major cities, such as New York, London, and Hong Kong, are located next to oceans. Similarly, because landlocked countries find international trade more difficult, they tend to have lower levels of income than countries with easy access to the world's waterways. For example, countries with more than 80 percent of their population living within 100 kilometres of a coast have an average GDP per person about four times as large as countries with less than 20 percent of their population living near a coast. The critical importance of access to the sea helps explain why the African continent, which contains many landlocked countries, is so poor.

IN THE news

One Economist's Answer

MIT economist Daron Acemoğlu considers why some nations thrive while others do not.

What Makes a Nation Rich?

By Daron Acemoğlu

We are the rich, the haves, the developed. And most of the rest—in Africa, South Asia, and South America, the Somalias and Bolivias and Bangladeshes of the world—are the nots. It's always been this way, a globe divided by wealth and poverty, health and sickness, food and famine, though the extent of inequality across nations today is unprecedented: The average citizen of the United States is ten times as prosperous as the average Guatemalan, more than twenty times as prosperous as the average North Korean, and more than forty times as prosperous as those living in Mali, Ethiopia, Congo, or Sierra Leone.

The question social scientists have unsuccessfully wrestled with for centuries is, Why? But the question they should have been asking is How? Because inequality is not predetermined. Nations are not like children—they are not born rich or poor. Their governments make them that way.

You can chart the search for a theory of inequality to the French political philosopher Montesquieu, who in the mid-eighteenth century came up with a very simple explanation: People in hot places are inherently lazy. Other no less sweeping explanations soon followed: Could it be that Max Weber's Protestant work ethic is the true driver of economic success? Or perhaps the richest countries are those that were former British colonies? Or maybe it's as simple as tracing which nations have the largest populations of European descent? The problem with all of these theories is that while they superficially fit some specific cases, others radically disprove them.

It's the same with the theories put forth today. Economist Jeffrey Sachs, director of Columbia University's Earth Institute, attributes the relative success of nations to geography and weather: In the poorest parts of the world, he argues, nutrient-starved tropical soil makes agriculture a challenge, and tropical climates foment disease, particularly malaria. Perhaps if we were to fix these problems, teach the citizens of these nations better farming techniques, eliminate malaria, or at the very least equip them with artemisinin to fight this deadly disease, we could eliminate poverty. Or better yet, perhaps we just move these people and abandon their inhospitable land altogether.

Jared Diamond, the famous ecologist and best-selling author, has a different theory: The origin of world inequality stems from the historical endowment of plant and animal species and the advancement of technology. In Diamond's telling, the cultures that first learned to plant crops were the first to learn how to use a plow, and thus were first to adopt other technologies, the engine of every successful economy. Perhaps then the solution to world inequality rests in technology—wiring the developing world with Internet and cell phones.

And yet while Sachs and Diamond offer good insight into certain aspects of poverty, they share something in common with Montesquieu and others who followed: They ignore incentives. People need incentives to invest and prosper; they need to know that if they work hard, they can make money and actually keep that money. And the key to ensuring those incentives is sound institutions—the rule of law and security and a governing system that offers opportunities to achieve and innovate. That's what determines the haves from the have-nots—not geography or weather or technology or disease or ethnicity.

Put simply: Fix incentives and you will fix poverty. And if you wish to fix institutions, you have to fix governments.

7-3h Research and Development

The primary reason that living standards are higher today than they were a century ago is that technological knowledge has advanced. The telephone, the transistor, the computer, and the internal combustion engine are among the thousands of innovations that have improved the ability to produce goods and services.

Although most technological advance comes from private research by firms and individual inventors, there is also a public interest in promoting these efforts. To a large extent, knowledge is a *public good*: Once one person discovers an idea, the idea enters society's pool of knowledge, and other people can freely use it. Just as government has a role in providing a public good such as national defence, it also has a role in encouraging the research and development of new technologies.

The Canadian government has long played a role in creating and disseminating technological knowledge. Research at the Dominion Experimental Farms

How do we know that institutions are so central to the wealth and poverty of nations? Start in Nogales, a city cut in half by the Mexican-American border fence. There is no difference in geography between the two halves of Nogales. The weather is the same. The winds are the same, as are the soils. The types of diseases prevalent in the area given its geography and climate are the same, as is the ethnic, cultural, and linguistic background of the residents. By logic, both sides of the city should be identical economically.

And yet they are far from the same. On one side of the border fence, in Santa Cruz County, Arizona, the median household income is $30,000. A few feet away, it's $10,000. On one side, most of the teenagers are in public high school, and the majority of the adults are high school graduates. On the other side, few of the residents have gone to high school, let alone college. Those in Arizona enjoy relatively good health and Medicare for those over sixty-five, not to mention an efficient road network, electricity, telephone service, and a dependable sewage and public-health system. None of those things are a given across the border. There, the roads are bad, the infant-mortality rate high, electricity and phone service expensive and spotty.

The key difference is that those on the north side of the border enjoy law and order and dependable government services—they can go about their daily activities and jobs without fear for their life or safety or property rights. On the other side, the inhabitants have institutions that perpetuate crime, graft, and insecurity.

Nogales may be the most obvious example, but it's far from the only one. Take Singapore, a once-impoverished tropical island that became the richest nation in Asia after British colonialists enshrined property rights and encouraged trade. Or China, where decades of stagnation and famine were reversed only after Deng Xiaoping began introducing private-property rights in agriculture, and later in industry. Or Botswana, whose economy has flourished over the past forty years while the rest of Africa has withered, thanks to strong tribal institutions and farsighted nation building by its early elected leaders.

Now look at the economic and political failures. You can begin in Sierra Leone, where a lack of functioning institutions and an overabundance of diamonds have fueled decades of civil war and strife and corruption that continue unchecked today. Or take communist North Korea, a geographical, ethnic, and cultural mirror of its capitalist neighbor to the south, yet ten times poorer. Or Egypt, cradle of one of the world's great civilizations yet stagnant economically ever since its colonization by the Ottomans and then the Europeans, only made worse by its post-independence governments, which have restricted all economic activities and markets. In fact, the theory can be used to shed light on the patterns of inequality for much of the world.

If we know why nations are poor, the resulting question is what can we do to help them. Our ability to impose institutions from the outside is limited, as the recent U.S. experiences in Afghanistan and Iraq demonstrate. But we are not helpless, and in many instances, there is a lot to be done. Even the most repressed citizens of the world will stand up to tyrants when given the opportunity. We saw this recently in Iran and a few years ago in Ukraine during the Orange Revolution.

The U.S. must not take a passive role in encouraging these types of movements. Our foreign policy should encourage them by punishing repressive regimes through trade embargoes and diplomacy. . . . At the microlevel, we can help foreign citizens by educating them and arming them with the modern tools of activism, most notably the Internet, and perhaps even encryption technology and cell-phone platforms that can evade firewalls and censorship put in place by repressive governments, such as those in China or Iran, that fear the power of information.

There's no doubt that erasing global inequality, which has been with us for millennia and has expanded to unprecedented levels over the past century and a half, won't be easy. But by accepting the role of failed governments and institutions in causing poverty, we have a fighting chance of reversing it.

Source: "What Makes a Nation Rich," by Daron Acemoğlu. From *Esquire Magazine*, November 18, 2009. Reprinted by permission of the author.

led to the introduction of the Marquis strain of wheat to western Canada in 1911. Marquis matured earlier than other strains of wheat, making it feasible to cultivate much more of the Prairies than would otherwise have been possible. This research was therefore a significant contributor to Canada's early economic growth.

More recently, the Canadian government funded research that led to the development of the CANDU nuclear reactor. The government continues to encourage advances in knowledge with research grants from agencies such as the Natural Sciences and Engineering Research Council of Canada, the Canadian Institutes of Health Research, and the Social Sciences and Humanities Research Council of Canada. The federal, provincial, and territorial governments also encourage advances in knowledge by offering tax breaks to firms that engage in research and development.

Yet another way in which government policy encourages research is through the patent system. When a person or firm invents a new product, such as a new drug, the inventor can apply for a patent. If the product is deemed truly original, the government awards the patent, which gives the inventor the exclusive right to make the product for a specified number of years. In essence, the patent gives the inventor a property right over his invention, turning his new idea from a public good into a private good. By allowing inventors to profit from their inventions—even if only temporarily—the patent system enhances the incentive for individuals and firms to engage in research.

case study

Productivity Slowdowns and Speedups

The rate of productivity growth is not at all steady and reliable. As measured by real output per worker, productivity in Canada grew at a rate of 1.8 percent per year from 1966 to 1973. From 1974 to 1982, productivity slowed, growing by only 0.5 percent per year before speeding up to 1.7 percent per year over the 1983–88 period. Another productivity slowdown occurred during 1989–95 (0.9 percent per year) before another spurt of 2.1 percent annual growth was enjoyed from 1996 to 2000. Finally, from 2001 to 2014, Canada experienced yet another slowdown during which productivity growth averaged only 0.6 percent per year. Much of the slowdown during this period came in 2008 and 2009 in the midst of a financial crisis, during which a number of major lending institutions around the world either went bankrupt or required rescue by government.

The effects of these changes in productivity growth are easy to see. Productivity is reflected in real wages and family incomes. When productivity growth slowed, the typical worker received smaller inflation-adjusted raises, and many people experienced a general sense of economic anxiety. Accumulated over many years, even a small change in productivity growth has a large effect. For example, over the entire period of 1966 to 2014, output per worker grew at an average rate of 1.1 percent per year. If output per worker had continued to grow at the average rate enjoyed from 1966 to 1973 (1.8 percent per year), the income of the average Canadian would today be 41 percent higher than it is currently.

The causes of these changes in productivity growth are more elusive. One explanation that is sometimes offered is that productivity slowdowns are associated with technology shocks brought about by sharp increases in the price of energy. For example, the productivity slowdown over the period 1974–82 is often considered as being the result of the dramatic increase in oil prices precipitated by OPEC-driven supply shortages (we will discuss this in more detail in Chapter 14). By increasing the cost of a key input in the production process of most manufacturers, this price shock made previous oil-dependent technologies obsolete and so caused a fall in productivity during the transition to more energy-efficient technologies.

The significant fall in productivity suffered in 2008 and 2009 might similarly be explained as being the result of a shock to an input price—not oil this time, but rather the price of financial transactions. The collapse and near-collapse of a number of major lending institutions around the world forced financial institutions to change their lending practices and in so doing forced many firms to rely far less on financial capital to produce their products than they had previously. Finally, it has been suggested that the productivity speedup experienced over the period 1996–2000 was due to a significant fall in the price of computing that allowed firms to alter their production processes toward more capital-intensive processes. In this way, greater output was realized with relatively fewer additions of workers—a productivity improvement.

What does the future hold for technological progress and economic growth? History gives us little reason to be confident in any prediction. Neither the productivity slowdown nor the productivity speedup was foreseen by many forecasters before it arrived.

History can, however, give us a sense of what is a normal rate of technological progress in Canada. Between 1921 and 2014, the rate of growth in real GDP per worker averaged just less than 2 percent per year. That time span encompassed the dramatic slowdown in growth that occurred during the Great Depression of the 1930s, the equally dramatic increase in the rate of growth during and immediately following World War II, and the smaller slowdowns and speedups since 1960 described earlier. Over long periods, then, 2 percent annual growth in real output per worker might be considered the norm, but deviations from that long-term trend should not be considered surprising. ■

7-3i Population Growth

Economists and other social scientists have long debated how population affects a society. The most direct effect is on the size of the labour force: A large population means more workers to produce goods and services. The tremendous size of the Chinese population is one reason why China is such an important player in the world economy.

At the same time, however, a large population means more people to consume those goods and services. So while a large population means a larger total output of goods and services, it need not mean a higher standard of living for a typical citizen. Indeed, both large and small nations are found at all levels of economic development.

Beyond these obvious effects of population size, population growth interacts with the other factors of production in ways that are more subtle and open to debate.

Stretching Natural Resources Thomas Robert Malthus (1766–1834), an English minister and early economic thinker, is famous for his book called *An Essay on the Principle of Population as It Affects the Future Improvement of Society.* In it, Malthus offered what may be history's most chilling forecast. Malthus argued that an ever-increasing population would continually strain society's ability to provide for itself. As a result, mankind was doomed to forever live in poverty.

© Bettman/Corbis

Thomas Robert Malthus

Malthus's logic was simple. He began by noting that "food is necessary to the existence of man" and that "the passion between the sexes is necessary and will remain nearly in its present state." He concluded that "the power of population is infinitely greater than the power in the earth to produce subsistence for man." According to Malthus, the only check on population growth was "misery and vice." Attempts by charities or governments to alleviate poverty were counterproductive, he argued, because they merely allowed the poor to have more children, placing even greater strains on society's productive capabilities.

Malthus may have correctly described the world at the time when he lived but, fortunately, his dire forecast was far off the mark. Although the world population has increased about sixfold over the past two centuries, living standards around the world are on average much higher. As a result of economic growth, chronic hunger and malnutrition are less common now than they were in Malthus's day. Famines occur from time to time, but they are more often the result of an unequal income distribution or political instability than an inadequate production of food.

Where did Malthus go wrong? As we discussed in a case study earlier in this chapter, growth in mankind's ingenuity has offset the effects of a larger population. Pesticides, fertilizers, mechanized farm equipment, new crop varieties, and other technological advances that Malthus never imagined have allowed each farmer to feed ever-greater numbers of people. Even with more mouths to feed, fewer farmers are necessary because each farmer is so productive.

Diluting the Capital Stock Whereas Malthus worried about the effects of population on the use of natural resources, some modern theories of economic growth emphasize its effects on capital accumulation. According to these theories, high population growth reduces GDP per worker because rapid growth in the number of workers forces the capital stock to be spread more thinly. In other words, when population growth is rapid, each worker is equipped with less capital. A smaller quantity of capital per worker leads to lower productivity and lower GDP per worker.

This problem is most apparent in the case of human capital. Countries with high population growth have large numbers of school-age children. This places a larger burden on the educational system. It is not surprising, therefore, that educational attainment tends to be low in countries with high population growth.

The differences in population growth rates around the world are large. In many poor African countries, population grows at about 3 percent per year. At this rate, the population doubles every 23 years. This rapid population growth makes it harder to provide workers with the tools and skills they need to achieve high levels of productivity. By contrast, in developed countries, such as Canada, the United States, and Western Europe, the population growth rate has been only about 1 percent per year in recent decades. This rate of growth is below the rate necessary to maintain population at current levels. Policymakers in these countries are concerned that a shrinking population of working-age people will be unable to maintain economic growth rates. The result may be tax revenue that is insufficient to support a growing share of the population that is retired, hoping to collect public pensions, and expecting to be cared for in publicly funded hospitals.

Although rapid population growth is not the main reason that less-developed countries are poor, some analysts believe that reducing the rate of population growth would help these countries raise their standards of living. In some countries, this goal is accomplished directly with laws that regulate the number of children families may have. For instance, for many years in China, the government allowed only one child per family; couples who violated this rule were subject to substantial fines. In countries with greater freedom, the goal of reduced population growth is accomplished less directly by increasing awareness of birth control techniques.

Another way in which a country can influence population growth is to apply one of the ten principles of economics: People respond to incentives. Bearing a child, like any decision, has an opportunity cost. When the opportunity cost rises, people will choose to have smaller families. In particular, women with the opportunity to receive a good education and desirable employment tend to want fewer children than those with fewer opportunities outside the home. Hence, policies that foster equal treatment of women are one way for less-developed economies to reduce the rate of population growth and, perhaps, raise their standards of living.

Promoting Technological Progress Although rapid population growth may depress economic prosperity by reducing the amount of capital each worker has, it may also have some benefits. Some economists have suggested that world population growth has been an engine of technological progress and economic prosperity. The mechanism is simple: If there are more people, then there are more scientists, inventors, and engineers to contribute to technological advance, which benefits everyone.

Economist Michael Kremer has provided some support for this hypothesis in an article titled "Population Growth and Technological Change: One Million B.C. to 1990," which was published in the *Quarterly Journal of Economics* in 1993. Kremer begins by noting that over the broad span of human history, world growth rates have increased as world population has. For example, world growth was more rapid when the world population was 1 billion (which occurred around the year 1800) than it was when the population was only 100 million (around 500 B.C.). This fact is consistent with the hypothesis that having more people induces more technological progress.

Kremer's second piece of evidence comes from comparing regions of the world. The melting of the polar icecaps at the end of the ice age around 10 000 B.C. flooded the land bridges and separated the world into several distinct regions that could not communicate with one another for thousands of years. If technological progress is more rapid when there are more people to discover things, then larger regions should have experienced more rapid growth.

According to Kremer, that is exactly what happened. The most successful region of the world in 1500 (when Columbus reestablished contact) comprised the "Old World" civilizations of the large Eurasia–Africa region. Next in technological development were the Aztec and Mayan civilizations in the Americas, followed by the hunter-gatherers of Australia, and then the primitive people of Tasmania, who lacked even fire-making and most stone and bone tools.

The smallest isolated region was Flinders Island, a tiny island between Tasmania and Australia. With the smallest population, Flinders Island had the fewest opportunities for technological advance and, indeed, seemed to regress. Around 3000 B.C., human society on Flinders Island died out completely. A large population, Kremer concludes, is a prerequisite for technological advance.

Describe three ways in which a government policymaker can try to raise the growth in living standards in a society. Are there any drawbacks to these policies?

7-4 Conclusion: The Importance of Long-Run Growth

In this chapter we have discussed what determines the standard of living in a nation and how policymakers can endeavour to raise the standard of living through policies that promote economic growth. Most of this chapter is summarized in one of the ten principles of economics: A country's standard of living depends on its ability to produce goods and services. Policymakers who want to encourage growth in standards of living must aim to increase their nations' productive ability by encouraging rapid accumulation of the factors of production and ensuring that these factors are employed as effectively as possible.

Economists differ in their views of the role of government in promoting economic growth. At the very least, government can lend support to the invisible hand by maintaining property rights and political stability. More controversial is whether government should target and subsidize specific industries that might be especially important for technological progress. There is no doubt that these issues are among the most important in economics. The success of one generation's policymakers in learning and heeding the fundamental lessons about economic growth determines what kind of world the next generation will inherit.

summary

- Economic prosperity, as measured by GDP per person, varies substantially around the world. The average income in the world's richest countries is more than ten times that in the world's poorest countries. Because growth rates of real GDP also vary substantially, the relative positions of countries can change dramatically over time.
- The standard of living in an economy depends on the economy's ability to produce goods and services. Productivity, in turn, depends on the amounts of physical capital, human capital, natural resources, and technological knowledge available to workers.
- Government policies can try to influence the economy's growth rate in many ways: by encouraging saving and investment, encouraging investment from abroad, fostering education, maintaining property rights and political stability, allowing free trade, promoting the research and development of new technologies, and controlling population growth.
- The accumulation of capital is subject to diminishing returns: The more capital an economy has, the less additional output the economy gets from an extra unit of capital. Because of diminishing returns, higher saving leads to higher growth for a period of time, but growth eventually slows down as the economy approaches a higher level of capital, productivity, and income. Also because of diminishing returns, the return to capital is especially high in poor countries. Other things equal, these countries can grow faster because of the catch-up effect.
- Population growth has a variety of effects on economic growth. On one hand, more rapid population growth may lower productivity by stretching the supply of natural resources and by reducing the amount of capital available for each worker. On the other hand, a larger population may enhance the rate of technological progress because there are more scientists and engineers.

KEY **concepts**

productivity, *p. 132*
physical capital, *p. 133*
human capital, *p. 133*
natural resources, *p. 133*
technological knowledge, *p. 134*
diminishing returns, *p. 137*
catch-up effect, *p. 138*

QUESTIONS FOR **review**

1. What does the level of a nation's GDP measure? What does the growth rate of GDP measure? Would you rather live in a nation with a high level of GDP and a low growth rate, or in a nation with a low level of GDP and a high growth rate?
2. List and describe four determinants of productivity.
3. In what way is a university or college degree a form of capital?
4. Explain how higher saving leads to a higher standard of living. What might deter a policymaker from trying to raise the rate of saving?
5. Does a higher rate of saving lead to higher growth temporarily or indefinitely?

6. Why would removing a trade restriction, such as a tariff, lead to more rapid economic growth?
7. How does the rate of population growth influence the level of GDP per person?
8. Describe two ways in which the Canadian government tries to encourage advances in technological knowledge.

QUICK CHECK multiple choice

1. Over the past century real GDP per person in Canada has grown about ______ percent per year, which means it doubles about every ______ years.
   a. 2, 14
   b. 2, 35
   c. 5, 14
   d. 5, 35
2. The world's rich countries, such as Japan and Germany, have income per person that is about how many times the income per person in the world's poor countries, such as Pakistan and India?
   a. 3
   b. 6
   c. 12
   d. 36
3. Most economists are ___________ that natural resources will eventually limit economic growth. As evidence, they note that the prices of most natural resources, adjusted for overall inflation, have tended to ___________ over time.
   a. concerned, rise
   b. concerned, fall
   c. not concerned, rise
   d. not concerned, fall
4. Because capital is subject to diminishing returns, higher saving and investment does not lead to which of the following conditions?
   a. higher income in the long run
   b. higher income in the short run
   c. higher growth in the long run
   d. higher growth in the short run
5. When the Japanese car maker Toyota expands one of its car factories in Canada, what is the likely impact of this event on Canada's GDP?
   a. Canada's GDP rises.
   b. Canada's GDP falls because Toyota is a foreign-owned company.
   c. GDP falls in Canada and is unchanged in Japan.
   d. It is difficult to say what happens to Canada's GDP.
6. Thomas Robert Malthus believed that population growth would do which of the following?
   a. put stress on the economy's ability to produce food, dooming humans to remain in poverty
   b. spread the capital stock too thinly across the labour force, lowering each worker's productivity
   c. promote technological progress, because there would be more scientists and inventors
   d. eventually decline to sustainable levels, as birth control improved and people had smaller families

PROBLEMS AND applications

1. Most countries, including Canada, import substantial amounts of goods and services from other countries. Yet this chapter says that a nation can enjoy a high standard of living only if it can produce a large quantity of goods and services itself. Can you reconcile these two facts?
2. List the capital inputs necessary to produce each of the following.
   a. cars
   b. high-school education
   c. plane travel
   d. fruits and vegetables
3. Canadian income per person today is many times what it was a century ago. Many other countries have also experienced significant growth over that period. What are some specific ways in which your standard of living differs from that of your great-grandparents?
4. This chapter discusses how employment has declined relative to output in the farm sector. Can you think of another sector of the economy where the same phenomenon has occurred more recently? Would you consider the change in employment in this sector to represent a success or a failure from the standpoint of society as a whole?
5. Suppose that society decided to reduce consumption and increase investment.
   a. How would this change affect economic growth?
   b. What groups in society would benefit from this change? What groups might be hurt?

6. Societies choose what share of their resources to devote to consumption and what share to devote to investment. Some of these decisions involve private spending; others involve government spending.
   a. Describe some forms of private spending that represent consumption, and some forms that represent investment.
   b. Describe some forms of government spending that represent consumption, and some forms that represent investment.
7. What is the opportunity cost of investing in capital? Do you think a country can "overinvest" in capital? What is the opportunity cost of investing in human capital? Do you think a country can "overinvest" in human capital? Explain.
8. Suppose that an auto company owned entirely by German citizens opens a new factory in Quebec.
   a. What sort of foreign investment would this represent?
   b. What would be the effect of this investment on Canadian GDP? Would the effect on Canadian GNP be larger or smaller?
9. In the 1960s, American investors made significant direct and portfolio investments in Canada. At the time, many Canadians were unhappy that this investment was occurring.
   a. In what way was it better for Canada to receive this American investment than not to receive it?
   b. In what way would it have been better still for Canadians to have done this investing?
10. In the countries of South Asia in 1992, only 56 young women were enrolled in secondary school for every 100 young men. Describe several ways in which greater educational opportunities for young women could lead to faster economic growth in these countries.
11. How large will Canada's GDP be in 25 years? The answer depends on what the rate of growth in GDP will be over that 25-year period. A mathematical formula we can use for this calculation is the following:

$$GDP_{2041} = GDP_{2016}(1 + g)^{25}$$

where GDP_{2041} is the level of GDP in the year 2041, GDP_{2016} is the level of GDP in the year 2016, and g is the rate of growth in GDP. Assume that GDP in 2016 is $1000 million and assume that the value of g is 0.035 (3.5 percent per year). What will be the value of GDP in 2041? Now suppose that the value of g is 0.040 (4.0 percent per year). What will be the value of GDP in 2041 given this slightly larger rate of growth? What does this result say about the importance of policies that promote even slightly faster rates of growth in GDP?

rmnoa357/Shutterstock.com

CHAPTER

8

Saving, Investment, and the Financial System

LEARNING **objectives**

In this chapter, you will...

1. Learn about some of the important financial institutions in the Canadian economy
2. Consider how the financial system is related to key macroeconomic variables
3. Develop a model of the supply and demand for loanable funds in financial markets
4. Use a model to analyze various government policies
5. Consider how government budget deficits and surpluses affect the Canadian economy

Imagine that you have just graduated from university or college (with a degree in economics, of course) and you decide to start your own business—an economic forecasting firm. Before you make any money selling your forecasts, you have to incur substantial costs to set up your business. You have to buy computers with which to make your forecasts, as well as desks, chairs, and filing cabinets to furnish your new office. Each of these items is a type of capital that your firm will use to produce and sell its services.

How do you obtain the funds to invest in these capital goods? Perhaps you are able to pay for them out of your past savings. More likely, however, like most entrepreneurs, you do not have enough money of your own to finance the start of your business. As a result, you have to get the money you need from other sources.

There are various ways for you to finance these capital investments. You could borrow the money, perhaps from a bank or from a friend or relative. In this case, you would promise not only to return the money at a later date but also to pay interest for the use of the money. Alternatively, you could convince someone to provide the money you need for your business in exchange for a share of your future profits, whatever they might happen to be. In either case, your investment in computers and office equipment is being financed by someone else's saving.

financial system
the group of institutions in the economy that help to match one person's saving with another person's investment

The **financial system** consists of those institutions in the economy that help to match one person's saving with another person's investment. As we discussed in the previous chapter, saving and investment are key ingredients to long-run economic growth: When a country saves a large portion of its GDP, more resources are available for investment in capital, and higher capital raises a country's productivity and living standard. The previous chapter, however, did not explain how the economy coordinates saving and investment. At any time, some people want to save some of their income for the future, and others want to borrow in order to finance investments in new and growing businesses. What brings these two groups of people together? What ensures that the supply of funds from those who want to save balances the demand for funds from those who want to invest?

This chapter examines how the financial system works. First, we discuss the large variety of institutions that make up the financial system in our economy. Second, we discuss the relationship between the financial system and some key macroeconomic variables—notably saving and investment. Third, we develop a model of the supply and demand for funds in financial markets. In the model, the interest rate is the price that adjusts to balance supply and demand. The model shows how various government policies affect the interest rate and, thereby, society's allocation of scarce resources.

8-1 Financial Institutions in the Canadian Economy

At the broadest level, the financial system moves the economy's scarce resources from savers (people who spend less than they earn) to borrowers (people who spend more than they earn). Savers save for various reasons—to put a child through college or university in several years or to retire comfortably in several decades. Similarly, borrowers borrow for various reasons—to buy a house in which to live or to start a business with which to make a living. Savers supply their money to the financial system with the expectation that they will get it back with interest at a later date. Borrowers demand money from the financial system with the knowledge that they will be required to pay it back with interest at a later date.

The financial system is made up of various financial institutions that help coordinate savers and borrowers. A number of government regulators oversee these financial institutions. These regulators set the rules that guide the operation of a financial system that otherwise operates almost wholly within the private sector. The Office of the Superintendent of Financial Institutions (OSFI) is an independent agency of the federal government that reports to the Department of Finance Canada. The OSFI is the primary regulator of federally regulated banks, insurance companies, and pension plans in Canada. Credit unions and caisses populaires, securities dealers, and mutual funds are largely regulated by provincial governments. Finally, Canada's central bank, the Bank of Canada, also plays an important role in regulating the Canadian financial system. We will discuss more fully in Chapter 10 the crucial role that the Bank of Canada plays in the financial system. In the remainder of this chapter, and as a prelude to analyzing the economic forces that drive the financial system, we discuss the most important of the institutions operating in the private sector that make up the financial system.

Financial institutions can be grouped into two categories—financial markets and financial intermediaries. We consider each category in turn.

8-1a Financial Markets

Financial markets are the institutions through which a person who wants to save can directly supply funds to a person who wants to borrow. The two most important financial markets in our economy are the bond market and the stock market.

financial markets
financial institutions through which savers can directly provide funds to borrowers

The Bond Market When Intel, the giant maker of computer chips, wants to borrow to finance construction of a new factory, it can borrow directly from the public. It does this by selling bonds. A **bond** is a certificate of indebtedness that specifies the obligations of the borrower to the holder of the bond. Put simply, a bond is an IOU. It identifies the time at which the loan will be repaid, called the *date of maturity*, and the rate of interest that will be paid periodically until the loan matures. The buyer of a bond gives his or her money to Intel in exchange for this promise of interest and eventual repayment of the amount borrowed (called the *principal*). The buyer can hold the bond until maturity or can sell the bond at an earlier date to someone else.

bond
a certificate of indebtedness

There are literally millions of different bonds in the Canadian economy. When large corporations, the federal government, or any provincial or territorial governments need to borrow to finance the purchase of a new factory, a new jet fighter, or a new school, they usually do so by issuing bonds. If you look at the business section of your local newspaper, you will find a listing of the prices and interest rates of some of the most important bond issues. Although these bonds differ in many ways, two characteristics of bonds are most important.

The first characteristic is a bond's *term*—the length of time until the bond matures. Some bonds have short terms, such as a few months, while others have terms as long as 30 years. (The British government has even issued a bond that never matures, called a *perpetuity*. This bond pays interest forever, but the principal is never repaid.) The interest rate on a bond depends, in part, on its term. Long-term bonds are riskier than short-term bonds because holders of long-term bonds have to wait longer for repayment of principal. If a holder of a long-term bond needs his money earlier than the distant date of maturity, he has no choice but to sell the bond to someone else, perhaps at a reduced price. To compensate for this risk, long-term bonds usually pay higher interest rates than short-term bonds.

The second important characteristic of a bond is its *credit risk*—the probability that the borrower will fail to pay some of the interest or principal. Such a failure to pay is called a *default.* Borrowers can (and sometimes do) default on their loans by declaring bankruptcy. When bond buyers perceive that the probability of default is high, they demand a higher interest rate to compensate them for this credit risk.

Credit risk is affected by such things as the level of debt carried by the issuer of the bond, recent changes in the amount of debt carried, and the stability of the issuer's revenues. The Canadian government is considered a relatively safe credit risk because (as we'll see shortly) although it carries a lot of debt, the amount of debt it carries is small relative to its capacity to finance the debt.

Provincial and territorial governments also issue bonds, but provinces and territories are considered to be a somewhat greater credit risk than the federal government because provincial and territorial economies tend to be less diverse than the national economy and, as such, their revenues are more volatile. Since a sudden fall in revenue might cause a province or territory difficulty in paying its debts, the rate of interest paid on provincial or territorial bonds is somewhat higher than that paid on federal bonds with a similar term to maturity. The rate of interest paid on provincial and territorial bonds varies by province and territory, reflecting provincial and territorial differences in revenue volatility and provincial and territorial government debt.

Corporate bonds tend to pay higher rates of interest than provincial and territorial bonds because corporate revenues are likely to be more volatile than provincial and territorial revenues. Financially shaky corporations raise money by issuing *junk bonds*—which, as the name suggests, pay considerably higher interest rates than the bonds issued by more secure corporations and by governments.

Some idea of the role of credit risk in determining the interest rate paid on bonds is suggested by the fact that in June 2015, the interest rate paid on bonds maturing in 2037 was 2.32 percent on federal government bonds, 3.12 percent on Government of British Columbia bonds, and 4.37 percent on bonds issued by Suncor Energy Inc. Buyers of bonds can judge credit risk by checking with various private agencies, such as Standard & Poor's or Dominion Bond Rating Service, that rate the credit risk of different bonds.

stock
a claim to partial ownership in a firm

The Stock Market Another way for Intel to raise funds to build a new factory is to sell stock in the company. **Stock** represents ownership in a firm and is, therefore, a claim to the profits that the firm makes. For example, if Intel sells a total of 1 000 000 shares of stock, then each share represents ownership of 1/1 000 000 of the business.

The sale of stock to raise money is called *equity finance,* whereas the sale of bonds is called *debt finance.* Although corporations use both equity and debt finance to raise money for new investments, stocks and bonds are very different. The owner of shares of Intel stock is a part-owner of Intel; the owner of an Intel bond is a creditor of the corporation. If Intel is very profitable, the shareholders enjoy the benefits of these profits, whereas the bondholders get only the interest on their bonds. And if Intel runs into financial difficulty, the bondholders are paid what they are due before shareholders receive anything at all. Compared to bonds, stocks offer the holder both higher risk and potentially higher return.

After a corporation issues stock by selling shares to the public, these shares trade among shareholders on organized stock exchanges. In these transactions, the corporation itself receives no money when its stock changes hands. The most important stock exchanges in the U.S. economy are the New York Stock Exchange and NASDAQ (National Association of Securities Dealers Automatic Quotation system). In Canada, the Toronto Stock Exchange (TSX) is the most important. A more speculative stock exchange that raises money for junior companies is the TSX Venture Exchange, located in Calgary. Most of the world's countries have their own stock exchanges on which the shares of local companies trade.

The prices at which shares trade on stock exchanges are determined by the supply and demand for the stock in these companies. Because stock represents ownership in a corporation, the demand for a stock (and thus its price) reflects people's perception of the corporation's future profitability. When people become optimistic about a company's future, they raise their demand for its stock and thereby bid up the price of a share of stock. Conversely, when people come to expect a company to have little profit or even losses, the price of a share falls.

FYI How to Read Stock Tables

Some daily newspapers include stock tables, which contain information about recent trading in the stocks of several thousand companies. These numbers can also be easily obtained from online news services. Information pertaining to trading in four well-known Canadian stocks on June 18, 2012 is provided in the table below. The information provided about these stocks has the following meanings:

- *Price.* The single most important piece of information about a stock is the price of a share. The newspaper usually presents several prices. The "last" or "closing" price is the price of the last transaction that occurred before the stock exchange closed the previous day. Many newspapers also give the "high" and "low" prices over the past day of trading and, sometimes, over the past year as well.
- *Volume.* Most newspapers present the number of shares sold during the past day of trading. This figure is called the *daily volume.*
- *Dividend.* Corporations pay out some of their profits to their shareholders; this amount is called the *dividend.* (Profits not paid out are called *retained earnings* and are used by the corporation for additional investment.) Newspapers often report the dividend paid over the previous year for each share of stock. They sometimes report the *dividend yield,* which is the dividend expressed as a percentage of the stock's price.
- *Price/earnings ratio.* A corporation's earnings, or profit, is the amount of revenue it receives for the sale of its products minus its costs of production as measured by its accountants. *Earnings per share* is the company's total earnings divided by the number of shares of stock outstanding. Companies use some of their earnings to pay dividends to shareholders; the rest is kept in the firm to make new investments. The price/earnings ratio, often called the P/E, is the price of a corporation's stock divided by the amount the corporation earned per share over the past year. Historically, the typical price/earnings ratio is about 15. A higher P/E indicates that a corporation's stock is expensive relative to its recent earnings; this might indicate either that people expect earnings to rise in the future or that the stock is overvalued. Conversely, a lower P/E indicates that a corporation's stock is cheap relative to its recent earnings; this might indicate either that people expect earnings to fall or that the stock is undervalued.

Why does the newspaper report all these data every day? Many people who invest their savings in stock follow these numbers closely when deciding which stocks to buy and sell. By contrast, other shareholders follow a buy-and-hold strategy: They buy the stock of well-run companies, hold it for long periods of time, and do not respond to the daily fluctuations reported in the paper.

Highest and lowest price over the past year		Name of company	Symbol for company's stock	Dividend amount	Dividend yield	Price/earnings ratio	Trending volume over the previous day	Highest and lowest price over the previous day		Last price at which the stock traded	Change in closing price from the day before
365 Days											
High	Low	Stock	Sym	DIV	Yld %	P/E Ratio	Vol	High	Low	Close	Net Chg
247.56	192.79	Canadian Pacific Railway	CP	1.40	0.7	21.9	497 780	199.22	195.69	198.05	−0.9
260	141.41	Canadian Tire	CTC	2.10	0.9	31	161	232.5	232.5	232.5	6.39
58.2	49.67	TD Bank	TD	2.04	3.8	12.9	3 629 310	53.84	53.05	53.07	−1.27
34.95	25.85	WestJet Airlines	WJA	0.56	2.1	10	310 792	26.63	25.85	26.25	−0.11

Various stock indexes are available to monitor the overall level of stock prices. A *stock index* is computed as an average of a group of stock prices. The most famous stock index is the Dow Jones Industrial Average, which has been computed regularly since 1896. It is now based on the prices of the stocks of 30 major U.S. companies, such as Boeing, General Electric, Microsoft, Coca-Cola, AT&T, and IBM. The best-known and most closely watched stock index in Canada is the S&P/TSX Composite Index, which is currently based on the prices of over 200 major firms listed on the TSX. Because stock prices reflect expected profitability, these stock indexes are watched closely as possible indicators of future economic conditions.

8-1b Financial Intermediaries

financial intermediaries
financial institutions through which savers can indirectly provide funds to borrowers

Financial intermediaries are financial institutions through which savers can indirectly provide funds to borrowers. The term *intermediary* reflects the role of these institutions in standing between savers and borrowers. Here we consider two of the most important financial intermediaries—banks and mutual funds.

Banks If the owner of a small grocery store wants to finance an expansion of his business, he probably takes a strategy quite different from Intel. Unlike Intel, a small grocer would find it difficult to raise funds in the bond and stock markets. Most buyers of stocks and bonds prefer to buy those issued by larger, more familiar companies. The small grocer, therefore, most likely finances his business expansion with a loan from a local bank.

Banks are the financial intermediaries with which people are most familiar. A primary job of banks is to take in deposits from people who want to save and use these deposits to make loans to people who want to borrow. Banks pay depositors interest on their deposits and charge borrowers slightly higher interest on their loans. The difference between these rates of interest covers the banks' costs and returns some profit to the owners of the banks.

Besides being financial intermediaries, banks play a second important role in the economy: They facilitate purchases of goods and services by allowing people to write cheques against their deposits. In other words, banks help create a special asset that people can use as a medium of exchange. A *medium of exchange* is an item that people can easily use to engage in transactions. A bank's role in providing a medium of exchange distinguishes it from many other financial institutions. Stocks and bonds, like bank deposits, are a possible *store of value* for the wealth that people have accumulated in past saving, but access to this wealth is not as easy, cheap, and immediate as just writing a cheque. For now, we ignore this second role of banks, but we will return to it when we discuss the monetary system later in the book.

mutual fund
an institution that sells shares to the public and uses the proceeds to buy a portfolio of stocks and bonds

Mutual Funds A financial intermediary of increasing importance in the Canadian economy is the mutual fund. A **mutual fund** is an institution that sells shares to the public and uses the proceeds to buy a selection, or *portfolio,* of various types of stocks or bonds, or both stocks and bonds. The shareholder of the mutual fund accepts all the risk and return associated with the portfolio. If the value of the portfolio rises, the shareholder benefits; if the value of the portfolio falls, the shareholder suffers the loss.

The primary advantage of mutual funds is that they allow people with small amounts of money to diversify. Buyers of stocks and bonds are well advised to heed the adage: Don't put all your eggs in one basket. Because the value of any single stock or bond is tied to the fortunes of one company, holding a single kind of stock or bond is very risky. By contrast, people who hold a diverse portfolio of stocks and bonds face less risk because they have only a small stake in each company. Mutual funds make this diversification easy. With only a few hundred dollars, a person can buy shares in a mutual fund and, indirectly, become the part owner or creditor of hundreds of major companies. For this service, the company operating the mutual fund charges shareholders a fee, usually between 0.5 and 3.0 percent of assets each year.

A second advantage claimed by mutual fund companies is that mutual funds give ordinary people access to the skills of professional money managers. The managers of most mutual funds pay close attention to the developments and prospects of the companies in which they buy stock. These managers buy the stock of those companies that they view as having a profitable future and sell the stock of companies with less promising prospects. This professional management, it is argued, should increase the return that mutual fund depositors earn on their savings.

Financial economists, however, are often skeptical of this second argument. With thousands of money managers paying close attention to each company's prospects, the price of a company's stock is usually a good reflection of the company's true value. As a result, it is hard to "beat the market" by buying good stocks and selling bad ones. In fact, mutual funds called *index funds,* which buy all the stocks in a given stock index, perform somewhat better on average than mutual funds that take advantage of active management by professional money managers. The explanation for the superior performance of index funds is that they keep costs low by buying and selling very rarely and by not having to pay the salaries of the professional money managers.

8-1c Summing Up

The Canadian economy contains a large variety of financial institutions. In addition to the bond market, the stock market, banks, and mutual funds, there are also pension funds, credit unions and caisses populaires, insurance companies, and even the local loan shark. These institutions differ in many ways. When analyzing the macroeconomic role of the financial system, however, it is more important to keep in mind the similarity of these institutions than the differences. These financial institutions all serve the same goal—directing the resources of savers into the hands of borrowers.

QUICK **Quiz** *What is stock? What is a bond? How are they different? How are they similar?*

8-2 Saving and Investment in the National Income Accounts

Events that occur within the financial system are central to understanding developments in the overall economy. As we have just seen, the institutions that make up this system—the bond market, the stock market, banks, and mutual funds—have the role of coordinating the economy's saving and investment. And as we saw in the previous chapter, saving and investment are important determinants of long-run growth in GDP and living standards. As a result, macroeconomists need to understand how financial markets work and how various events and policies affect them.

FYI Financial Institutions in Crisis

Beginning in 2007, there were signs that the financial system in the United States was in trouble. Housing prices, which had peaked the previous summer, were now quickly falling. Holders of subprime mortgages, who had relied on rising house prices to refinance their homes, were now defaulting at record rates. On February 27, 2007, the Federal Home Loan Mortgage Corporation (popularly known as "Freddie Mac," this is a private company supported by the U.S. government and tasked with providing mortgages with advantageous interest rates and low down payments) announced that it would no longer buy such mortgages. In April, a leading lender of subprime mortgages in the United States fell into bankruptcy. By August, short-term interest rates had jumped dramatically upward, reflecting concerns over the ability of borrowers to repay loans. Between October 2007 and February 2009, the U.S. stock market (as measured by the Dow Jones Industrial Average index) had fallen by over 49 percent.

Canada was not immune to the crisis that had begun in the United States, as over the same period the S&P/TSX index fell by more than 44 percent. Financial markets around the world were seemingly under threat of collapse, and major firms were declaring bankruptcy. The largest carmaker in the world, General Motors, declared bankruptcy on June 1, 2009, as part of a restructuring that involved the governments of Canada, the United States, and Ontario taking significant ownership shares. World leaders and heads of the world's major central banks met to coordinate massive interventions designed to stabilize world financial markets. By the end of 2009, the worst of the financial crisis seemed to have passed but in its wake lay widespread bankruptcy, large government deficits, high unemployment rates, and the prospects of a long period of painful economic recovery.

What happened? The definitive history of these events has yet to be written, but many analysts emphasize that a major contributing factor was a failure of effective regulation in U.S. financial markets. At the heart of the problem was the development of complex financial instruments that enabled mortgage lenders to package high-risk (subprime) mortgages with other financial assets in a way that made it extremely difficult for anyone to understand who held the assets most likely to be defaulted on. When house prices in the United States began to fall, those holding subprime mortgages began to default on their loans. Soon, financial institutions became wary of lending to one another, as they were unsure who held those high-risk mortgages and so who was at risk of default. Firms that rely on the ability to borrow in order to finance their day-to-day operations quickly found it next to impossible to find a financial institution willing to lend to them. Borrowing and lending froze, followed by bankruptcies and fast-rising unemployment.

Norm Betts/Bloomberg/Getty Images

Those who have studied the financial crisis have suggested that Canadian financial institutions avoided the worst of the crisis because regulation of the mortgage market by the Bank of Canada and the Office of the Superintendent of Financial Institutions discouraged the proliferation of subprime mortgages and so the development of the complex financial instruments designed to make them more palatable to lenders. Consequently, as the world considers what can be done to avoid a repeat of the 2007–09 financial crisis, a good deal of attention is being paid to the regulations that guide the Canadian financial market.

Indeed, in November 2011 Mark Carney, at the time the governor of the Bank of Canada, was chosen by the leaders of the world's 20 largest economies as the chair of the Financial Stability Board (FSB). The FSB was established in 2009 to help develop and promote effective regulatory, supervisory, and other financial sector policies in the interest of financial stability. Its mandate is clearly reflective of the financial crisis of 2007–09 and Carney's appointment is an equally clear signal of the world community's recognition of the quality of financial regulations in Canada.

None of this should be taken to suggest, however, that the Canadian financial market is necessarily immune to financial crises. The Canadian financial system avoided the worst of the financial crisis because it had in place useful regulations governing the market for mortgages, which insulated it from the meltdown of the U.S. mortgage market. However, future financial crises may emanate from other sources—perhaps as a result of new exotic financial instruments to be invented in the future and perhaps from economic crises that emanate from foreign political choices. In June 2012, the world was holding its breath waiting for the outcome of a new financial crisis, this one having its origins in Europe and resulting from the challenges of governments having accumulated too much debt and now trying to rein in budget deficits while suffering the effects of recession. How this European crisis affects Canada will be determined in large part by the resilience of the Canadian financial system in the face of yet another shock. Clearly, the need for vigilance by Canadian financial market regulators remains.

An important lesson to be learned from the financial crisis of 2007–09 is that the financial system can act as an effective intermediary between savers and borrowers only if financial institutions are able to accurately judge the ability of one another to satisfy their obligations. As financial instruments become more complex, the importance of regulation by governments and central banks to ensure transparency in financial transactions grows. This is important not only for the financial intermediaries most directly involved in these transactions but also for the rest of the economy, which relies on a smoothly functioning financial system to create jobs, to save for the future, and to ensure future prosperity.

As a starting point for an analysis of financial markets, we discuss in this section the key macroeconomic variables that measure activity in these markets. Our emphasis here is not on behaviour but on accounting. *Accounting* refers to how various numbers are defined and added up. A personal accountant might help an individual add up her income and expenses. A national income accountant does the same thing for the economy as a whole. The national income accounts include, in particular, GDP and the many related statistics.

The rules of national income accounting include several important identities. Recall that an *identity* is an equation that must be true because of the way the variables in the equation are defined. Identities are useful to keep in mind because they clarify how different variables are related to one another. Here we consider some accounting identities that shed light on the macroeconomic role of financial markets.

8-2a Some Important Identities

Recall that gross domestic product (GDP) is both total income in an economy and the total expenditure on the economy's output of goods and services. GDP (denoted as Y) is divided into four components of expenditure: consumption (C), investment (I), government purchases (G), and net exports (NX). We write

$$Y = C + I + G + NX$$

This equation is an identity because every dollar of expenditure that shows up on the left-hand side also shows up in one of the four components on the right-hand side. Because of the way each of the variables is defined and measured, this equation must always hold.

In this chapter, we simplify our analysis by assuming that the economy we are examining is closed. A *closed economy* is one that does not interact with other economies. In particular, a closed economy does not engage in international trade in goods and services, nor does it engage in international borrowing and lending. Of course, actual economies are *open economies*—that is, they interact with other economies around the world. Nonetheless, assuming a closed economy is a useful simplification with which we can learn some lessons that apply to all economies. Moreover, this assumption applies perfectly to the world economy (because interplanetary trade is not yet common).

Because a closed economy does not engage in international trade, imports and exports are exactly zero. Therefore, net exports (NX) are also zero. In this case, we can write

$$Y = C + I + G$$

This equation states that GDP is the sum of consumption, investment, and government purchases. Each unit of output sold in a closed economy is consumed by a household, invested by a firm or a household, or bought by government.

To see what this identity can tell us about financial markets, subtract C and G from both sides of this equation. We obtain

$$Y - C - G = I$$

The left-hand side of this equation ($Y - C - G$) is the total income in the economy that remains after paying for consumption and government purchases: This

national saving (saving)
the total income in the economy that remains after paying for consumption and government purchases

amount is called **national saving**, or just **saving**, and is denoted S. Substituting S for $Y - C - G$, we can write the last equation as

$$S = I$$

This equation states that saving equals investment.

To understand the meaning of national saving, it is helpful to manipulate the definition a bit more. Let T denote the amount that the government collects from households in taxes minus the amount it pays back to households in the form of transfer payments (such as Employment Insurance and social assistance). We can then write national saving in either of two ways:

$$S = Y - C - G$$

or

$$S = (Y - T - C) + (T - G)$$

These equations are the same, because the two Ts in the second equation cancel each other, but each reveals a different way of thinking about national saving. In particular, the second equation separates national saving into two pieces: private saving $(Y - T - C)$ and public saving $(T - G)$.

private saving
the income that households have left after paying for taxes and consumption

public saving
the tax revenue that the government has left after paying for its spending

budget surplus
an excess of tax revenue over government spending

budget deficit
a shortfall of tax revenue from government spending

Consider each of these two pieces. **Private saving** is the amount of income that households have left after paying their taxes and paying for their consumption. In particular, because households receive income of Y, pay taxes of T, and spend C on consumption, private saving is $Y - T - C$. **Public saving** is the amount of tax revenue that the government has left after paying for its spending. The government receives T in tax revenue and spends G on goods and services. If T exceeds G, the government runs a **budget surplus** because it receives more money than it spends. This surplus of $T - G$ represents public saving. If the government spends more than it receives in tax revenue, then G is larger than T. In this case, the government runs a **budget deficit**, and public saving $T - G$ is a negative number.

Now consider how these accounting identities are related to financial markets. The equation $S = I$ reveals an important fact: *For the economy as a whole, saving must be equal to investment.* Yet this fact raises some important questions: What mechanisms lie behind this identity? What coordinates those people who are deciding how much to save and those people who are deciding how much to invest? The answer is the financial system. The bond market, the stock market, banks, mutual funds, and other financial markets and intermediaries stand between the two sides of the $S = I$ equation. They take in the nation's saving and direct it to the nation's investment.

8-2b The Meaning of Saving and Investment

The terms *saving* and *investment* can sometimes be confusing. Most people use these terms casually and sometimes interchangeably. By contrast, the macroeconomists who put together the national income accounts use these terms carefully and distinctly.

Consider an example. Suppose that Larry earns more than he spends and deposits his unspent income in a bank or uses it to buy a bond or some stock from a corporation. Because Larry's income exceeds his consumption, he adds to the nation's saving. Larry might think of himself as "investing" his money, but a macroeconomist would call Larry's act *saving* rather than *investment*.

In the language of macroeconomics, *investment* refers to the purchase of new capital, such as equipment or buildings. When Moe borrows from the bank to build himself a new house, he adds to the nation's investment. (Remember, the purchase of a new house is the one form of household spending that is investment rather than consumption.) Similarly, when the Curly Corporation sells some stock and uses the proceeds to build a new factory, it also adds to the nation's investment.

Although the accounting identity $S = I$ shows that saving and investment are equal for the economy as a whole, this does not have to be true for every individual household or firm. Larry's saving can be greater than his investment, and he can deposit the excess in a bank. Moe's saving can be less than his investment, and he can borrow the shortfall from a bank. Banks and other financial institutions make these individual differences between saving and investment possible by allowing one person's saving to finance another person's investment.

Define private saving, public saving, national saving, *and* investment. *How are they related?*

8-3 The Market for Loanable Funds

Having discussed some of the important financial institutions in our economy and the macroeconomic role of these institutions, we are ready to build a model of financial markets. Our purpose in building this model is to explain how financial markets coordinate the economy's saving and investment. The model also gives us a tool with which we can analyze various government policies that influence saving and investment.

To keep things simple, we assume that the economy has only one financial market, called the **market for loanable funds**. All savers go to this market to deposit their saving, and all borrowers go to this market to get their loans. Thus, the term *loanable funds* refers to all income that people have chosen to save and lend out, rather than use for their own consumption. In the market for loanable funds, there is one interest rate, which is both the return to saving and the cost of borrowing.

market for loanable funds
the market in which those who want to save supply funds and those who want to borrow to invest demand funds

The assumption of a single financial market, of course, is not literally true. As we have seen, the economy has many types of financial institutions. But, as we discussed in Chapter 2, the art in building an economic model is simplifying the world in order to explain it. For our purposes here, we can ignore the diversity of financial institutions and assume that the economy has a single financial market.

8-3a Supply and Demand for Loanable Funds

The economy's market for loanable funds, like other markets in the economy, is governed by supply and demand. To understand how the market for loanable funds operates, therefore, we first look at the sources of supply and demand in that market.

The supply of loanable funds comes from those people who have some extra income they want to save and lend out. This lending can occur directly, such as when a household buys a bond from a firm, or it can occur indirectly, such as when a household makes a deposit in a bank, which in turn uses the funds to make loans. In both cases, *saving is the source of the supply of loanable funds.*

The demand for loanable funds comes from households and firms who wish to borrow to make investments. This demand includes families taking out mortgages to buy homes. It also includes firms borrowing to buy new equipment or build factories. In both cases, *investment is the source of the demand for loanable funds.*

The interest rate is the price of a loan. It represents the amount that borrowers pay for loans and the amount that lenders receive on their saving. Because a high interest rate makes borrowing more expensive, the quantity of loanable funds demanded falls as the interest rate rises. Similarly, because a high interest rate makes saving more attractive, the quantity of loanable funds supplied rises as the interest rate rises. In other words, the demand curve for loanable funds slopes downward, and the supply curve for loanable funds slopes upward.

Figure 8.1 shows the interest rate that balances the supply and demand for loanable funds. In the equilibrium shown, the interest rate is 5 percent, and the quantity of loanable funds demanded and the quantity of loanable funds supplied both equal $120 billion.

The adjustment of the interest rate to the equilibrium level occurs for the usual reasons. If the interest rate were lower than the equilibrium level, the quantity of loanable funds supplied would be less than the quantity of loanable funds demanded. The resulting shortage of loanable funds would encourage lenders to raise the interest rate they charge. A higher interest rate would encourage saving (thereby increasing the quantity of loanable funds supplied) and discourage borrowing for investment (thereby decreasing the quantity of loanable funds demanded). Conversely, if the interest rate were higher than the equilibrium level, the quantity of loanable funds supplied would exceed the quantity of loanable funds demanded. As lenders competed for the scarce borrowers, interest rates would be driven down. In this way, the interest rate approaches the equilibrium level at which the supply and demand for loanable funds exactly balance.

Recall that economists distinguish between the real interest rate and the nominal interest rate. The nominal interest rate is the interest rate as usually reported—the

FIGURE 8.1

The Market for Loanable Funds

The interest rate in the economy adjusts to balance the supply and demand for loanable funds. The supply of loanable funds comes from national saving, including both private saving and public saving. The demand for loanable funds comes from firms and households that want to borrow for purposes of investment. Here the equilibrium interest rate is 5 percent, and $120 billion of loanable funds are supplied and demanded.

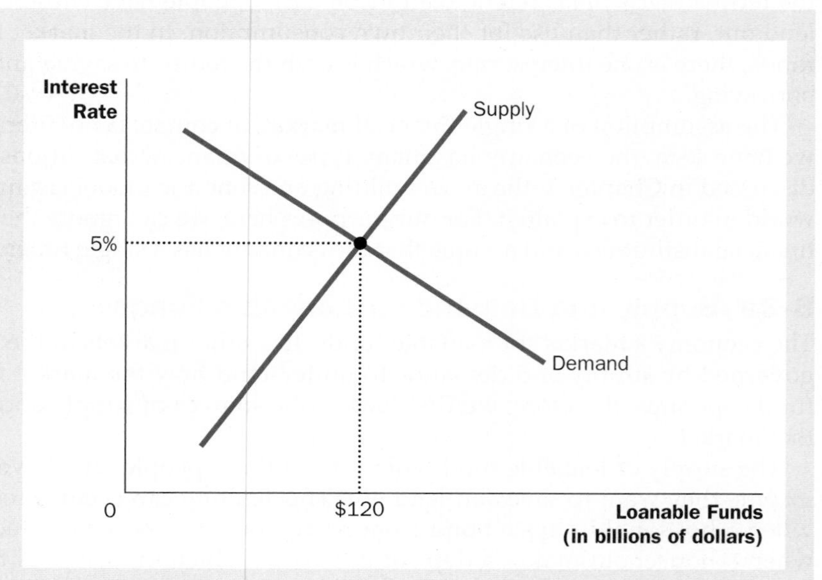

monetary return to saving and cost of borrowing. The real interest rate is the nominal interest rate corrected for inflation; it equals the nominal interest rate minus the inflation rate. Because inflation erodes the value of money over time, the real interest rate more accurately reflects the real return to saving and cost of borrowing. Therefore, the supply and demand for loanable funds depend on the real (rather than nominal) interest rate, and the equilibrium in Figure 8.1 should be interpreted as determining the real interest rate in the economy. For the rest of this chapter, when you see the term *interest rate,* you should remember that we are talking about the real interest rate.

This model of the supply and demand for loanable funds shows that financial markets work much like other markets in the economy. In the market for milk, for instance, the price of milk adjusts so that the quantity of milk supplied balances the quantity of milk demanded. In this way, the invisible hand coordinates the behaviour of dairy farmers and the behaviour of milk drinkers. Once we realize that saving represents the supply of loanable funds and investment represents the demand, we can see how the invisible hand coordinates saving and investment. When the interest rate adjusts to balance supply and demand in the market for loanable funds, it coordinates the behaviour of people who want to save (the suppliers of loanable funds) and the behaviour of people who want to invest (the demanders of loanable funds).

We can now use this analysis of the market for loanable funds to examine various government policies that affect the economy's saving and investment. Because this model is just supply and demand in a particular market, we analyze any policy using the three steps discussed in Chapter 4. First, we decide whether the policy shifts the supply curve or the demand curve. Second, we determine the direction of the shift. Third, we use the supply-and-demand diagram to see how the equilibrium changes.

8-3b Policy 1: Saving Incentives

Canadian families generally save a smaller fraction of their incomes than their counterparts in many other countries, such as Japan and Germany, but they usually save slightly more than families in the United States. Although the reasons for these international differences are unclear, many policymakers view the relatively low level of savings in Canada as a major problem. One of the ten principles of economics in Chapter 1 is that a country's standard of living depends on its ability to produce goods and services. And, as we discussed in the preceding chapter, saving is an important long-run determinant of a nation's productivity. If Canada could somehow raise its saving rate to the level that prevails in other countries, the growth rate of GDP would increase, and over time, Canadian citizens would enjoy a higher standard of living.

Another of the ten principles of economics is that people respond to incentives. Many economists have used this principle to suggest that the low saving rate in Canada is at least partly attributable to tax laws that discourage saving. The federal government, as well as all of the provincial and territorial governments, collects revenue by taxing income, including interest and dividend income. To see the effects of this policy, consider a 25-year-old who saves $1000 and buys a 30-year bond that pays an interest rate of 9 percent. In the absence of taxes, the $1000 grows to $13 268 when the individual reaches age 55. Yet if that interest is taxed at a rate of, say, 33 percent, then the after-tax interest rate is only 6 percent. In this case, the $1000 grows to only $5743 after 30 years. The tax on interest income substantially reduces the future payoff from current saving and, as a result, reduces the incentive for people to save.

In response to this problem, economists favour changes to the tax system that encourage greater saving. An important change to the Canadian tax system that most economists supported was the introduction of the federal Goods and Services Tax (GST) in 1991. The GST is a consumption tax. Under a consumption tax, income that is saved is not taxed, so the tax clearly encourages greater saving. The sales tax that provinces use to collect revenue is another example of a consumption tax. The only province not currently collecting a sales tax is Alberta, but the evidence in favour of collecting more revenue from a sales tax and less from the income taxes as a way of encouraging greater savings is so strong that tax economists have recently urged the province to introduce such a tax. Given economists' consistent and strong advocacy in favour of sales taxes, it is interesting that a newly elected federal government fulfilled a campaign promise to cut the GST from 7 percent to 6 percent, effective July 1, 2006. A further one percentage point cut in the GST, to 5 percent, was made effective January 1, 2008.

While economists generally disagree with the government cutting the GST from 7 percent to 5 percent, most support an increase in the amount that people can contribute to registered retirement savings plans (RRSPs). By buying an RRSP, people reduce the amount of their income that is subject to tax. In this way, saving is encouraged. For similar reasons, economists supported the introduction of Tax-Free Savings Accounts (TFSAs) in 2009. Income earned on savings that are held in a TFSA is not subject to tax, so people have yet another incentive to increase their savings. Let's consider the effect of introducing such saving incentives on the market for loanable funds, as illustrated in Figure 8.2.

First, which curve would these policies affect? Because the tax change would alter the incentive for households to save *at any given interest rate,* it would affect the quantity of loanable funds supplied at each interest rate. Thus, the supply of

FIGURE 8.2

An Increase in the Supply of Loanable Funds

A change in the tax laws to encourage Canadians to save more would shift the supply of loanable funds to the right from S_1 to S_2. As a result, the equilibrium interest rate would fall, and the lower interest rate would stimulate investment. Here the equilibrium interest rate falls from 5 percent to 4 percent, and the equilibrium quantity of loanable funds saved and invested rises from $120 billion to $160 billion.

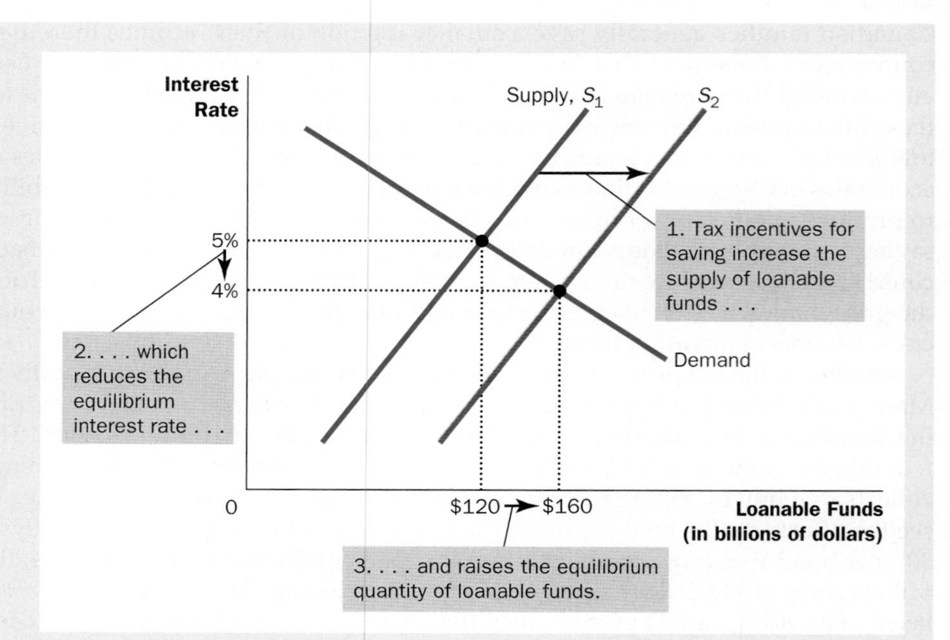

loanable funds would shift. The demand for loanable funds would remain the same, because the tax change would not directly affect the amount that borrowers want to borrow at any given interest rate.

Second, which way would the supply curve shift? Because saving would be taxed less heavily than under current law, households would increase their saving by consuming a smaller fraction of their income. Households would use this additional saving to increase their deposits in banks or to buy more bonds. The supply of loanable funds would increase, and the supply curve would shift to the right from S_1 to S_2, as shown in Figure 8.2.

Finally, we can compare the old and new equilibria. In the figure, the increased supply of loanable funds reduces the interest rate from 5 percent to 4 percent. The lower interest rate raises the quantity of loanable funds demanded from $120 billion to $160 billion. That is, the shift in the supply curve moves the market equilibrium along the demand curve. With a lower cost of borrowing, households and firms are motivated to borrow more to finance greater investment. Thus, *if a reform of the tax laws encouraged greater saving, the result would be lower interest rates and greater investment.*

Although this analysis of the effects of increased saving is widely accepted among economists, less consensus exists about what kinds of tax changes should be enacted. Many economists endorse tax reform aimed at increasing saving in order to stimulate investment and growth. Yet others are skeptical that these tax changes would have much effect on national saving. These skeptics also doubt the equity of the proposed reforms. They argue that, in many cases, the benefits of the tax changes would accrue primarily to the wealthy, who are least in need of tax relief. This argument would hold true, for example, with respect to increasing allowable RRSP contributions, because most RRSP contributions are made by those who are relatively wealthy. We examine this debate more fully in the final chapter of this book.

8-3c Policy 2: Investment Incentives

Suppose that Parliament passed a tax reform aimed at making investment more attractive. In essence, this is what Parliament does when it institutes an *investment tax credit,* which it does from time to time. An investment tax credit gives a tax advantage to any firm building a new factory or buying a new piece of equipment. Let's consider the effect of such a tax reform on the market for loanable funds, as illustrated in Figure 8.3.

First, would the law affect supply or demand? Because the tax credit would reward firms that borrow and invest in new capital, it would alter investment at any given interest rate and, thereby, change the demand for loanable funds. By contrast, because the tax credit would not affect the amount that households save at any given interest rate, it would not affect the supply of loanable funds.

Second, which way would the demand curve shift? Because firms would have an incentive to increase investment at any interest rate, the quantity of loanable funds demanded would be higher at any given interest rate. Thus, the demand curve for loanable funds would move to the right, as shown by the shift from D_1 to D_2 in the figure.

Third, consider how the equilibrium would change. In Figure 8.3, the increased demand for loanable funds raises the interest rate from 5 percent to 6 percent, and the higher interest rate in turn increases the quantity of loanable funds supplied from $120 billion to $140 billion, as households respond by increasing the amount

FIGURE 8.3

An Increase in the Demand for Loanable Funds

If the passage of an investment tax credit encouraged firms to invest more, the demand for loanable funds would increase. As a result, the equilibrium interest rate would rise, and the higher interest rate would stimulate saving. Here, when the demand curve shifts from D_1 to D_2, the equilibrium interest rate rises from 5 percent to 6 percent, and the equilibrium quantity of loanable funds saved and invested rises from \$120 billion to \$140 billion.

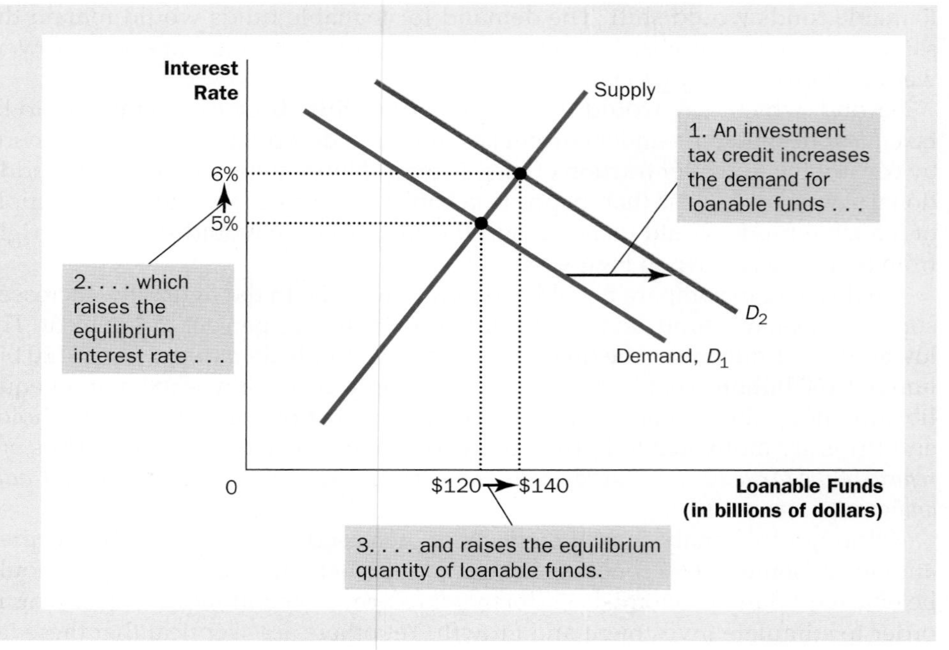

they save. This change in household behaviour is represented here as a movement along the supply curve. Thus, *if a reform of the tax laws encouraged greater investment, the result would be higher interest rates and greater saving.*

8-3d Policy 3: Government Budget Deficits and Surpluses

Many of the most pressing policy issues that have arisen over the past 30 years in Canada have either directly or indirectly resulted from large government budget deficits and the debt that accumulated as a result of these deficits. When a government spends more than it receives in tax revenue, the shortfall is called the government's *budget deficit*. When a government spends less than it receives in tax revenue, the excess is called the government's *budget surplus*. When a government spends exactly what it receives in tax revenue it is said to have a *balanced budget.* The sum of all past budget deficits minus the sum of all past budget surpluses is called the **government debt**.

government debt
the sum of all past budget deficits and surpluses

From 1975 to 1997 the federal government ran very large budget deficits, resulting in a rapidly growing federal government debt. During the same period, many provincial and territorial governments also ran large deficits, resulting in rapidly growing debts at the provincial/territorial level as well. During the early 2000s, Canadian governments realized sizable budget surpluses. This allowed them to retire some fraction of the debt they accumulated previously. Finally, since 2008, Canadian governments have again returned to deficits and debt accumulation. What has been the effect of all this on the Canadian market for loanable funds? We can use our model to find out.

Imagine that the government starts with a balanced budget and then, because of a tax cut or a spending increase, starts running a budget deficit. We can analyze the effects of the budget deficit by following our three steps in the market for loanable funds, as illustrated in Figure 8.4.

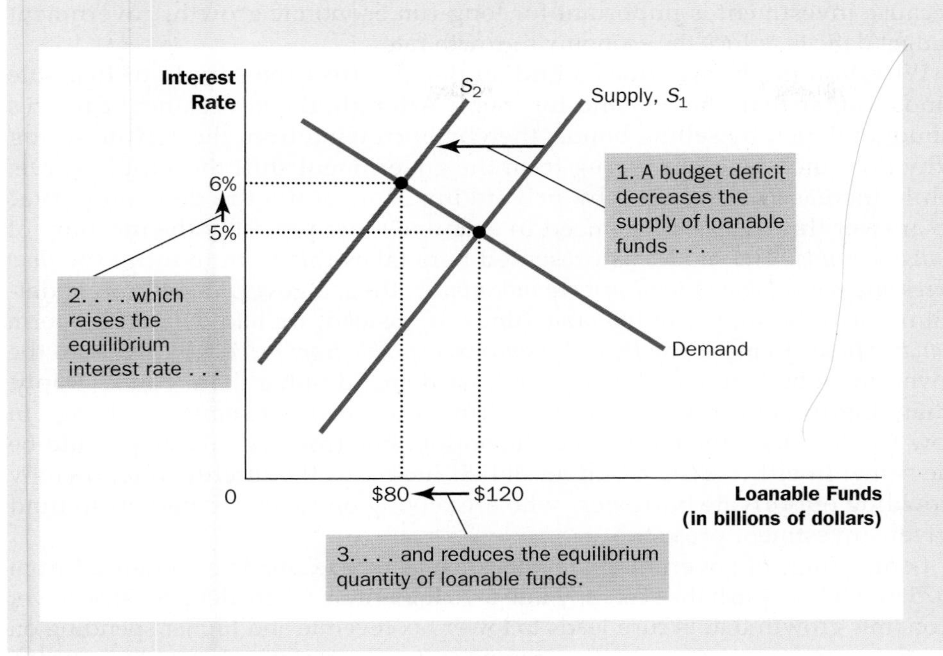

FIGURE 8.4

The Effect of a Government Budget Deficit

When the government spends more than it receives in tax revenue, the resulting budget deficit lowers national saving. The supply of loanable funds decreases, and the equilibrium interest rate rises. Thus, when the government borrows to finance its budget deficit, it crowds out households and firms that otherwise would borrow to finance investment. Here, when the supply shifts from S_1 to S_2, the equilibrium interest rate rises from 5 percent to 6 percent, and the equilibrium quantity of loanable funds saved and invested falls from $120 billion to $80 billion.

First, which curve shifts when the government starts running a budget deficit? Recall that national saving—the source of the supply of loanable funds—is composed of private saving and public saving. A change in the government budget balance represents a change in public saving and, thereby, in the supply of loanable funds. Because the budget deficit does not influence the amount that households and firms want to borrow to finance investment at any given interest rate, it does not alter the demand for loanable funds.

Second, which way does the supply curve shift? When the government runs a budget deficit, public saving is negative, and this reduces national saving. In other words, when the government borrows to finance its budget deficit, it reduces the supply of loanable funds available to finance investment by households and firms. Thus, a budget deficit shifts the supply curve for loanable funds to the left from S_1 to S_2, as shown in Figure 8.4.

Third, we can compare the old and new equilibria. In the figure, when the budget deficit reduces the supply of loanable funds, the interest rate rises from 5 percent to 6 percent. This higher interest rate then alters the behaviour of the households and firms that participate in the loan market. In particular, many demanders of loanable funds are discouraged by the higher interest rate. Fewer families buy new homes, and fewer firms choose to build new factories. The fall in investment because of government borrowing is called **crowding out** and is represented in the figure by the movement along the demand curve from a quantity of $120 billion in loanable funds to a quantity of $80 billion. That is, when the government borrows to finance its budget deficit, it crowds out private borrowers who are trying to finance investment.

crowding out
a decrease in investment that results from government borrowing

Thus, the most basic lesson about budget deficits follows directly from their effects on the supply and demand for loanable funds: *When the government reduces national saving by running a budget deficit, the interest rate rises, and investment falls.* Because investment is important for long-run economic growth, government budget deficits reduce the economy's growth rate.

Why, you might ask, does a budget deficit affect the supply of loanable funds, rather than the demand for them? After all, the government finances a budget deficit by selling bonds, thereby borrowing from the private sector. Why does increased borrowing from the government shift the supply curve, while increased borrowing by private investors shifts the demand curve? To answer this question, we need to examine more precisely the meaning of *loanable funds*. The model as presented here takes this term to mean the *flow of resources available to fund private investment*; thus, a government budget deficit reduces the supply of loanable funds. If, instead, we had defined the term *loanable funds* to mean the *flow of resources available from private saving*, then the government budget deficit would increase demand rather than reduce supply. Changing the interpretation of the term would cause a semantic change in how we described the model, but the bottom line from the analysis would be the same: In either case, a budget deficit increases the interest rate, thereby crowding out private borrowers who are relying on financial markets to fund private investment projects.

vicious circle
the cycle that results when deficits reduce the supply of loanable funds, increase interest rates, discourage investment, and result in slower economic growth; slower growth leads to lower tax revenue and higher spending on income-support programs, and the result can be even higher budget deficits

Long strings of government deficits such as those Canada experienced from 1975 to 1997 can push the economy into a **vicious circle** where deficits cause lower economic growth that in turn leads to lower tax revenue and higher spending on Employment Insurance and other income-support programs. Lower tax revenue and higher government spending lead to higher deficits and even slower economic growth. The only way to break out of this vicious circle is to raise tax rates and cut spending on government programs to eliminate the deficit and halt the circle of deficits, but this leads to slower economic growth and even higher deficits.

Most analysts believe that the long string of deficits incurred by Canadian governments from 1975 to 1997 caused Canada to become trapped in such a vicious circle. The rapid run-up in tax rates and the large cuts to government spending on health care, defence, social services, and education during the late 1980s and early 1990s were the inevitable responses of highly indebted governments.

Government budget surpluses work just the opposite as budget deficits. When government collects more in tax revenue than it spends, it saves the difference by retiring some of the outstanding government debt. This budget surplus, or public saving, contributes to national saving. Thus, *a budget surplus increases the supply of loanable funds, reduces the interest rate, and stimulates investment.* Higher investment, in turn, means greater capital accumulation and more rapid economic growth.

virtuous circle
the cycle that results when surpluses increase the supply of loanable funds, reduce interest rates, stimulate investment, and result in faster economic growth; faster growth leads to higher tax revenue and lower spending on income-support programs, and the result can be even higher budget surpluses

Just as long strings of government deficits can push the economy into a vicious circle of higher deficits leading to slower growth leading to even higher deficits, so can strings of government budget surpluses push the economy into a **virtuous circle**. In this case, by increasing the supply of loanable funds, reducing interest rates, and stimulating investment, surpluses encourage faster economic growth. Because this leads to higher tax revenues and lower spending on income-support programs, the government surplus grows over time. A virtuous circle produces very attractive choices: Should government cut tax rates, increase spending on social programs, or pay down accumulated debt?

By the end of the 1990s, the strong medicine required to break Canada out of the vicious circle had borne fruit in the form of large and growing government surpluses. Many analysts believe that the Canadian economy was enjoying a virtuous circle in the late 1990s and early 2000s. This enabled federal election campaigns during the early to mid-2000s to be fought over the choices that a virtuous circle provides: tax cuts versus spending increases versus debt reduction.

By 2008, the effects of a financial crisis that significantly slowed economic growth around the world began to be felt in Canadian government budgets. After 12 straight years of surpluses, the federal budget fell into deficit in 2009. At the time, most analysts believed the economy would require only a few years before it improved enough to return the budget to surplus. Early in 2016, however, a new government announced its intention to run large deficits in the hope of stimulating economic activity. The return to balanced federal budgets now seems unlikely for some years to come.

case study

The Accumulation of Government Debt in Canada

Budget deficits became a chronic problem in Canada only in the mid-1970s. From 1950 to 1974, the federal government ran budget surpluses as often as it ran budget deficits. These budget imbalances were generally small. In 1975, the federal government posted a large deficit and did so in every year until 1997. Between 1975 and 1997, the federal government accumulated about $550 billion in debt. In 1997, the string of deficits was broken and the federal government reported a budget surplus of $3.0 billion—the first time in 28 years that the federal government has actually paid down a portion of its debt. Between 1997 and 2008, the federal government ran a string of surpluses that enabled it to reduce its debt by over $90 billion. After 2008, however, the federal government returned to budget deficits. Between 2008 and 2014, the federal government added $166 billion to its net debt.

Figure 8.5 shows the net debt of the federal government and the combined net debts of the provinces and territories as a percentage of GDP. **Government net debt** is the difference between the value of the financial liabilities and the value of the financial assets it owns. Throughout the 1950s and until 1975, the federal government's debt-to-GDP ratio declined. Although the federal government ran budget deficits during many of these years, the deficits were small enough that the government's debt grew less rapidly than the overall economy. Because GDP is a rough measure of the government's ability to raise tax revenue, a declining debt-to-GDP ratio indicates that the economy is, in some sense, living within its means. By contrast, in the years following 1975 when the federal government's budget deficit ballooned, the debt started rising more rapidly than the overall economy. As a result, the debt-to-GDP ratio quickly increased. On three occasions—1982, 1989, and 1996—the federal government managed to halt the rise in its debt-to-GDP ratio. The first two efforts managed to halt the rise only temporarily. On both occasions, an economic slowdown caused government spending to increase and tax revenues to fall so that debt began to accumulate again. The effort initiated in 1996 proved more successful, and the federal government actually managed to reduce its debt-to-GDP ratio from its high of 73 percent in 1996 to 32 percent in 2009. Unfortunately, as a result of an economic slowdown that began in 2007, the federal budget returned to deficit in 2009. This pushed the federal debt-to-GDP ratio up to 37 percent by 2010 (from 32 percent in 2009). By 2014, the debt-to-GDP ratio had stabilized at 36 percent. In 2016, the federal government announced its intention to introduce significantly larger deficits than planned previously. Most analysts believe that despite this, so long as at least modest economic growth can be maintained, the debt-to-GDP ratio is not likely to rise significantly beyond what it was in 2014.

government net debt
the difference between the value of government financial liabilities and financial assets

FIGURE 8.5

Federal and Provincial/Territorial Net Debt in Canada

Sources: Authors' calculations, based on Statistics Canada Information. Net debt is measured as the difference between financial assets and direct liabilities. Since 1987 data on net debt are from Fiscal Reference Tables, October 2014, Department of Finance, www.fin.gc.ca. Data on GDP are from Statistics Canada, CANSIM database.

The net debt of the federal government and the combined net debts of the provincial and territorial governments are expressed here as a percentage of GDP. Data on provincial government debt are available only from 1970. The federal government debt fell dramatically following World War II, but then started to increase quickly in 1975 when the government began to run large and persistent deficits. Beginning in 1980, provincial and territorial governments also began to run sizable budget deficits and so saw their debts increase relative to GDP. Between 1997 and 2008, both levels of government—but, in particular, the federal government—managed to reduce the size of their debts relative to GDP. Beginning in 2009 a serious recession caused both levels of government to suffer sizable budget deficits, and as a result their debt-to-GDP ratios jumped up. Since then, the federal ratio has stabilized but at the provincial level it has continued to increase.

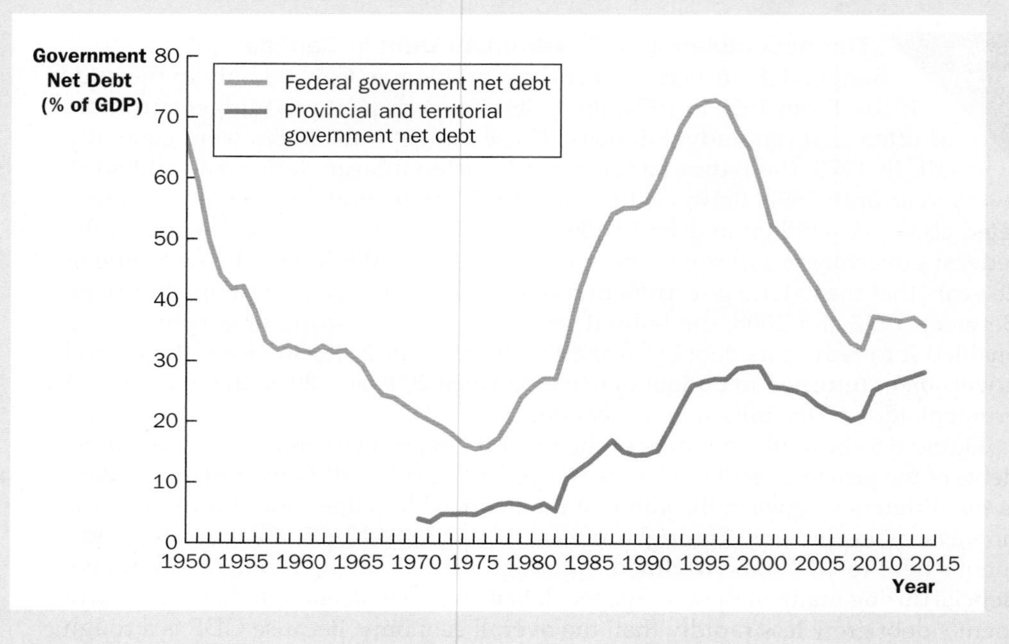

Until 1982, the provincial governments together maintained a fairly constant level of debt relative to the economy. Although the provinces ran budget deficits, these were not large enough to cause the combined debt of the provinces to grow faster than the overall economy. As a result, the provincial debt-to-GDP ratio stayed at roughly 6 percent of GDP from 1970 to 1982. In 1982, a major recession caused the provinces to run larger deficits and caused the provincial debt-to-GDP ratio to begin to climb. By 1999, the ratio reached its maximum of just under 30 percent. From 1999 to 2008, the debt-to-GDP ratio of the aggregate provincial government sector fell to under 21 percent. After 2009 the economic recession pushed the debt-to-GDP ratio of the provinces back up, and by 2014 it was over 28 percent and seemed poised to continue to increase. Unlike the case with the federal debt, the debt-to-GDP ratio of all provinces in aggregate seems unlikely to begin to fall without a concerted effort to reduce deficits or without a return of more vigorous economic growth. As signs mount in 2015 of a slowing economy the latter seems unlikely to occur, at least in the short term.

FYI How Large Is Government Debt?

This seems like an odd question to ask, given that the case study we just read presented a graph showing how government debt has changed over time. Surely we must have known the amount of government debt in order to draw that graph! It turns out, however, that there are different ways of thinking about and measuring government debt.

In the case study, we defined government net debt as the difference between the value of government financial assets—the "savings accounts" into which governments deposit tax revenues while they wait for the bills for spending programs to come due and for other purposes—and the value of government financial liabilities—the value of bonds that the government sometimes sells to finance new spending programs. In 2014, the federal government held $318 billion of financial assets and also owed $1001 billion in the form of bonds it would eventually need to repay. The difference in these amounts—$683 billion—was the size of the federal government's net debt as of March 31, 2014.

This seems like a sensible way of measuring net debt. Certainly it is the way most people would calculate their own net debt if they were asked for that number. They would likely take the value of their savings accounts and the value of their home and call that their financial assets. They might then calculate the amount still owing on their mortgage, their car loan, and maybe the amount owing on credit cards to determine their financial liabilities. The difference would be their net debt. This is the basic approach used to calculate the value of government net debt that was illustrated in Figure 8.5.

Economist William Robson of the C.D. Howe Institute suggests the measure of net debt presented in Figure 8.5 is just scraping the surface. Robson argues that measure is telling only part of the story because it focuses solely on *current* financial assets and liabilities. However, governments introduce spending programs that obligate taxpayers to pay the costs of those programs in the future. If the costs of spending programs are expected to grow faster than the tax revenues required to pay for them, taxpayers are said to face an *unfunded financial liability*.

For example, the publicly funded health care system governed by the Canada Health Act guarantees that government will pay for the cost of health care for all Canadians. When the act was introduced in 1984, the median age in Canada was 30.6 years. That is, half of Canadians were younger than that and half were older. Those aged 65 years and older made up just 10 percent of the population. As of 2013, the median age of Canada's population was estimated to be 40.2 years, with seniors making up 15.3 percent of the population. By 2036, it is estimated that the median age will be between 42 and 45 years and seniors will make up between 23 and 25 percent of the population. The fact that the population is growing older is important because about 44 percent of publicly funded health care spending is devoted to the care of those aged 65 years and above, so as the population ages, health care costs will likely rise as well.

Robson uses facts like these to point out that the public health care system as currently designed obligates Canadian taxpayers to fund a great deal of health care spending in the future. Of course, an aging population also means governments will need to spend less on things like primary education. However, Robson's calculations show that on balance government spending in the future will need to be considerably higher than it is now. Since the tax system as currently designed will not raise sufficient revenue to pay these projected costs, taxpayers are said to face an unfunded liability (and future tax increases). Robson, writing in 2004, estimated that unfunded liabilities increased the standard measure of government net debt by about a third.

As well as increasing our estimate of government debt, these calculations of unfunded liabilities have another serious implication. The fact that taxes must rise in the future to pay for this unfunded liability means that future taxpayers—today's young people—face the prospect of carrying a significantly heavier tax burden than current taxpayers. Much of this extra tax burden is due to the unfunded liability attached to publicly funded health care. In debates over health care provision and financing, the young and healthy therefore have a lot at stake: It is they who will have to pay the cost, and they will likely have to pay that cost well before they reach the age when the benefits of a well-operated health care system are most appreciated.

As of March 31, 2011, adding together the debts of the federal government and the debts of all provincial, territorial, and local governments, Canadian governments carried just over $1100 billion in net debt. That amounted to 65 percent of Canada's GDP. One way of gauging the size of that debt is to compare it to past values. In 1996, the aggregate amount of government debt was equal to 102 percent of GDP. Much progress has therefore been made since 1996, but if we look back farther, we find the debt-to-GDP ratio was only 22 percent in 1975. Going back still farther, however, it was certainly over 100 percent immediately following World War II.

"Our debt-reduction plan is simple, but it will require a great deal of money."

Another way of gauging the size of Canadian government debt is to compare it to the level of debt carried by governments in other countries. It is difficult to compare levels of debt across countries because definitions differ, but it is safe to say that in 2015 the debt-to-GDP ratio in Canada was below that in the United States, and well below that in countries like Greece and Spain.

Still one more measure of the size of government debt is to compare default risk across countries. As of 2012, Canada was one of only nine countries (along with Australia, Germany, Luxembourg, Singapore, Switzerland, Norway, Denmark, and Sweden) that seemed secure in being able to retain its triple-A credit rating with the three main rating agencies: Moody's, Standard & Poor's, and Fitch.

By all of these measures, the level of government debt in Canada is not extraordinarily large, either historically or in comparison to other countries.

As we saw in the previous chapter, national saving is a key ingredient in long-run economic growth. By using some of the private sector's saving to finance budget deficits, governments pull resources away from investment in new capital and, by doing so, depress the living standard of future generations. In recent years, all political parties in Canada have come to recognize this basic argument and now view persistent budget deficits as an important policy problem. As a result, Canadians have over the past decade seen governments of all political stripes endeavour to avoid budget deficits. Indeed, no major political party in Canada advocates a return to large and persistent government deficits. ■

If more Canadians adopted a "live for today" approach to life, how would this affect saving, investment, and the interest rate?

8-4 Conclusion

"Neither a borrower nor a lender be," Polonius advises his son in Shakespeare's *Hamlet*. If everyone followed this advice, this chapter would have been unnecessary.

Few economists would agree with Polonius. In our economy, people borrow and lend often, and usually for good reason. You may borrow one day to start your own business or to buy a home. And people may lend to you in the hope that the interest you pay will allow them to enjoy a more prosperous retirement. The financial system has the job of coordinating all this borrowing and lending activity.

In many ways, financial markets are like other markets in the economy. The price of loanable funds—the interest rate—is governed by the forces of supply and demand, just as other prices in the economy are. And we can analyze shifts in supply or demand in financial markets as we do in other markets. One of the ten principles of economics introduced in Chapter 1 is that markets are usually a good way to organize economic activity. This principle applies to financial markets as well. When financial markets bring the supply and demand for loanable funds into balance, they help allocate the economy's scarce resources to their most efficient use.

In one way, however, financial markets are special. Financial markets, unlike most other markets, serve the important role of linking the present and the future. Those who supply loanable funds—savers—do so because they want to convert some of their current income into future purchasing power. Those who demand loanable funds—borrowers—do so because they want to invest today in order to have additional capital in the future to produce goods and services. Thus, well-functioning financial markets are important not only for current generations but also for future generations who will inherit many of the resulting benefits.

summary

- The Canadian financial system is made up of many types of financial institutions, such as the bond market, the stock market, banks, and mutual funds. All these institutions act to direct the resources of households who want to save some of their income into the hands of households and firms who want to borrow.
- National income accounting identities reveal some important relationships among macroeconomic variables. In particular, for a closed economy, national saving must equal investment. Financial institutions are the mechanism through which the economy matches one person's saving with another person's investment.
- The interest rate is determined by the supply and demand for loanable funds. The supply of loanable funds comes from households that want to save some of their income and lend it out. The demand for loanable funds comes from households and firms that want to borrow for investment. To analyze how any policy or event affects the interest rate, one must consider how it affects the supply and demand for loanable funds.
- National saving equals private saving plus public saving. A government budget deficit represents negative public saving and, therefore, reduces national saving and the supply of loanable funds available to finance investment. When a government budget deficit crowds out investment, it reduces the growth of productivity and GDP.

KEY concepts

financial system, *p. 154*
financial markets, *p. 155*
bond, *p. 155*
stock, *p. 156*
financial intermediaries, *p. 158*
mutual fund, *p. 158*
national saving (saving), *p. 162*
private saving, *p. 162*
public saving, *p. 162*
budget surplus, *p. 162*
budget deficit, *p. 162*
market for loanable funds, *p. 163*
government debt, *p. 168*
crowding out, *p. 169*
vicious circle, *p. 170*
virtuous circle, *p. 170*
government net debt, *p. 171*

QUESTIONS FOR review

1. What is the role of the financial system? Name and describe two markets that are part of the financial system in our economy. Name and describe two financial intermediaries.
2. Why is it important for people who own stocks and bonds to diversify their holdings? What type of financial institution makes diversification easier?
3. What is national saving? What is private saving? What is public saving? How are these three variables related?
4. What is investment? How is it related to national saving?
5. Describe a change in the tax laws that might increase private saving. If this policy were implemented, how would it affect the market for loanable funds?
6. What is a government budget deficit? How does it affect interest rates, investment, and economic growth?
7. How does government accumulate debt? If the government maintains a budget surplus, what happens to its debt? What if it maintains a budget deficit?

QUICK CHECK multiple choice

1. Nina wants to buy and operate an ice-cream truck but doesn't have the financial resources to start the business. She borrows $5000 from her friend Max, to whom she promises an interest rate of 7 percent, and gets another $10 000 from her friend David, to whom she promises a third of her profits. Which of the following best describes this situation?
   a. Max is a shareholder, and Nina is a bondholder.
   b. Max is a shareholder, and David is a bondholder.
   c. David is a shareholder, and Nina is a bondholder.
   d. David is a shareholder, and Max is a bondholder.
2. Which of the following occurs when the government collects more in tax revenue than it spends, and households consume more than they get in after-tax income?
   a. private and public saving are both positive
   b. private and public saving are both negative
   c. private saving is positive, but public saving is negative
   d. private saving is negative, but public saving is positive
3. A closed economy has income of $1000, government spending of $200, taxes of $150, and investment of $250. What is private saving?
   a. $100
   b. $200
   c. $300
   d. $400
4. If a popular TV show on personal finance convinces more Canadians about the importance of saving for retirement, the _____ curve for loanable funds would shift, driving the equilibrium interest rate _____.
   a. supply, up
   b. supply, down
   c. demand, up
   d. demand, down
5. If the business community becomes more optimistic about the profitability of capital, the _____ curve for loanable funds would shift, driving the equilibrium interest rate _____.
   a. supply, up
   b. supply, down
   c. demand, up
   d. demand, down
6. Which of the following describes the ratio of federal government debt to GDP in Canada from 1996 to 2009?
   a. it increased markedly
   b. it decreased markedly
   c. it was stable at a historically high level
   d. it was stable at a historically low level

PROBLEMS AND applications

1. For each of the following pairs, which bond would you expect to pay a higher interest rate? Explain.
   a. a bond of the Canadian government or a bond of an East European government
   b. a bond that repays the principal in year 2015 or a bond that repays the principal in year 2025
   c. a bond from Coca-Cola or a bond from a software company you run in your garage
   d. a bond issued by the federal government or a bond issued by Prince Edward Island
2. Check a newspaper or the Internet for the stock listings of two companies you know something about (perhaps as a customer). What is the price/earnings ratio for each company? Why do you think they differ? If you were to buy one of these stocks, which would you choose? Why?
3. Theodore Roosevelt once said, "There is no moral difference between gambling at cards or in lotteries or on the race track and gambling in the stock market." What social purpose do you think is served by the existence of the stock market?
4. Declines in stock prices are sometimes viewed as harbingers of future declines in real GDP. Why do you suppose that might be true?
5. When the Russian government defaulted on its debt to foreigners in 1998, interest rates rose on bonds issued by many other developing countries. Why do you suppose this happened?
6. Many workers hold large amounts of stock issued by the firms for which they work. Why do you suppose companies encourage this behaviour? Why might a person *not* want to hold stock in the company where he works?
7. Explain the difference between saving and investment as defined by a macroeconomist. Which of the following situations represent investment? Saving? Explain.
   a. Your family takes out a mortgage and buys a new house.
   b. You use your $200 paycheque to buy stock in Bombardier.

c. Your roommate earns $100 and deposits it into her account at a bank.
d. You borrow $1000 from a bank to buy a car to use in your pizza delivery business.

8. Suppose GDP is $800 billion, taxes are $150 billion, private saving is $50 billion, and public saving is $20 billion. Assuming this economy is closed, calculate consumption, government purchases, national saving, and investment.

9. Suppose that Intel is considering building a new chip-making factory.
   a. Assuming that Intel needs to borrow money in the bond market, why would an increase in interest rates affect Intel's decision about whether to build the factory?
   b. If Intel has enough of its own funds to finance the new factory without borrowing, would an increase in interest rates still affect Intel's decision about whether to build the factory? Explain.

10. Suppose the government borrows $20 billion more next year than this year.
    a. Use a supply-and-demand diagram to analyze this policy. Does the interest rate rise or fall?
    b. What happens to investment? To private saving? To public saving? To national saving? Compare the size of the changes to the $20 billion of extra government borrowing.
    c. How does the elasticity of supply of loanable funds affect the size of these changes?
    d. How does the elasticity of demand for loanable funds affect the size of these changes?
    e. Suppose households believe that greater government borrowing today implies higher taxes to pay off the government debt in the future. What does this belief do to private saving and the supply of loanable funds today? Does it increase or decrease the effects you discussed in parts (a) and (b)?

11. Over the past ten years, new computer technology has enabled firms to reduce substantially the amount of inventories they hold for each dollar of sales. Illustrate the effect of this change on the market for loanable funds. (*Hint:* Expenditure on inventories is a type of investment.) What do you think has been the effect on investment in factories and equipment?

12. "Some economists worry that the aging populations of industrial countries are going to start running down their savings just when the investment appetite of emerging economies is growing" (*The Economist*, May 6, 1995). Illustrate the effect of this phenomenon on the world market for loanable funds.

13. This chapter explains that investment can be increased both by reducing taxes on private saving and by reducing the government budget deficit.
    a. Why is it difficult to implement both of these policies at the same time?
    b. What would you need to know about private saving in order to judge which of these two policies would be a more effective way to raise investment?

Monkey Business Images/Shutterstock.com

Unemployment and Its Natural Rate

LEARNING **objectives**

In this chapter, you will ...

1. Learn about the data used to measure the amount of unemployment
2. Consider how unemployment arises from the process of job search
3. Consider how unemployment can result from minimum-wage laws
4. See how unemployment can arise from bargaining between firms and unions
5. Examine how unemployment results when firms choose to pay efficiency wages

Losing a job can be the most distressing economic event in a person's life. Most people rely on their labour earnings to maintain their standard of living, and many people get from their work not only income but also a sense of personal accomplishment. A job loss means a lower living standard in the present, anxiety about the future, and reduced self-esteem. It is not surprising, therefore, that politicians campaigning for office often speak about how their proposed policies will help create jobs.

In previous chapters we have seen some of the forces that determine the level and growth of a country's standard of living. A country that saves and invests a high fraction of its income, for instance, enjoys more rapid growth in its capital stock and its GDP than a similar country that saves and invests less. An even more obvious determinant of a country's standard of living is the amount of unemployment it typically experiences. People who would like to work but cannot find jobs are not contributing to the economy's production of goods and services. Although some degree of unemployment is inevitable in a complex economy with thousands of firms and millions of workers, the amount of unemployment varies substantially over time and across countries. When a country keeps its workers as fully employed as possible, it achieves a higher level of GDP than it would if it left many of its workers idle.

This chapter begins our study of unemployment. The problem of unemployment is usefully divided into two categories—the long-run problem and the short-run problem. The economy's *natural rate of unemployment* refers to the amount of unemployment that the economy normally experiences. *Cyclical unemployment* refers to the year-to-year fluctuations in unemployment around its natural rate, and it is closely associated with the short-run ups and downs of economic activity. Cyclical unemployment has its own explanation, which we will defer until we study short-run economic fluctuations later in this book. In this chapter we discuss the determinants of an economy's natural rate of unemployment. As we will see, the designation *natural* does not imply that this rate of unemployment is desirable. Nor does it imply that it is constant over time or impervious to economic policy. It merely means that this unemployment does not go away on its own even in the long run.

We begin the chapter by looking at some of the relevant facts that describe unemployment. In particular, we examine three questions: How does the government measure the economy's rate of unemployment? What problems arise in interpreting the unemployment data? How long are the unemployed typically without work?

We then turn to the reasons why economies always experience some unemployment and the ways in which policymakers can help the unemployed. We discuss four explanations for the economy's natural rate of unemployment: job search, minimum-wage laws, unions, and efficiency wages. As we will see, long-run unemployment does not arise from a single problem that has a single solution. Instead, it reflects a variety of related problems. As a result, there is no easy way for policymakers to reduce the economy's natural rate of unemployment and, at the same time, to alleviate the hardships experienced by the unemployed.

9-1 Identifying Unemployment

We begin this chapter by examining more precisely what the term *unemployment* means. We consider how the government measures unemployment, what problems arise in interpreting the unemployment data, how long the typical spell of unemployment lasts, and why there will always be some people unemployed.

9-1a How Is Unemployment Measured?

Measuring unemployment is the job of Statistics Canada. Every month Statistics Canada produces data on unemployment and on other aspects of the labour market, such as types of employment, length of the average workweek, and the duration of unemployment. These data come from a regular survey of about 54 000 households, called the *Labour Force Survey.*

Based on the answers to survey questions, Statistics Canada places each adult (aged 15 and older) in each surveyed household into one of three categories:

- employed
- unemployed
- not in the labour force

A person is considered employed if he or she spent some of the previous week working at a paid job. A person is unemployed if he or she is on temporary layoff or is looking for a job. A person who fits neither of the first two categories, such as a full-time student, homemaker, or retiree, is not in the labour force. Figure 9.1 shows this breakdown for 2014.

Once Statistics Canada has placed all the individuals covered by the survey in a category, it computes various statistics to summarize the state of the labour market. Statistics Canada defines the **labour force** as the sum of the employed and the unemployed:

labour force
the total number of workers, including both the employed and the unemployed

Labour force = Number of employed + Number of unemployed

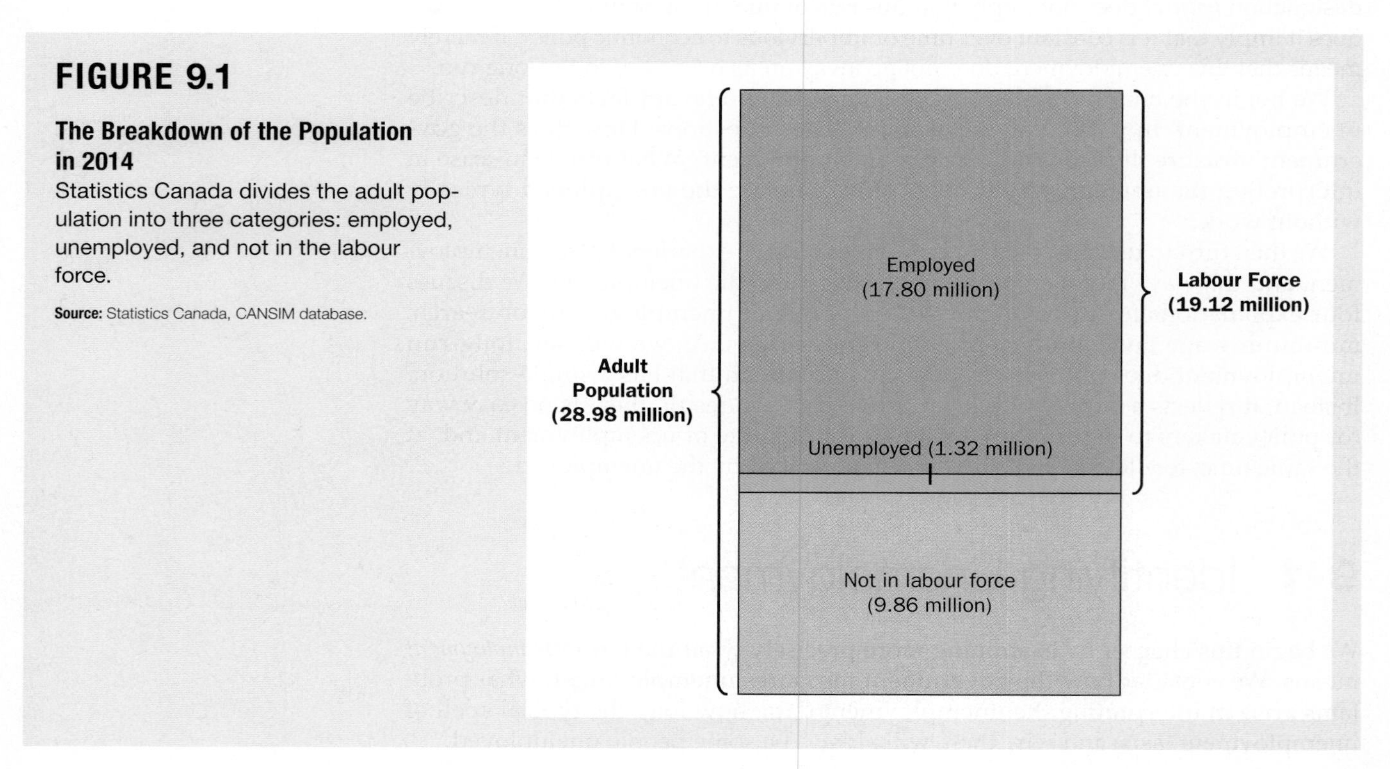

FIGURE 9.1

The Breakdown of the Population in 2014

Statistics Canada divides the adult population into three categories: employed, unemployed, and not in the labour force.

Source: Statistics Canada, CANSIM database.

Statistics Canada defines the **unemployment rate** as the percentage of the labour force that is unemployed:

unemployment rate
the percentage of the labour force that is unemployed

$$\text{Unemployment rate} = \frac{\text{Number of unemployed}}{\text{Labour force}} \times 100$$

Statistics Canada computes unemployment rates for the entire adult population and for more narrowly defined groups—young, old, men, women, and so on.

Statistics Canada uses the same survey to produce data on labour-force participation. The **labour-force participation rate** measures the percentage of the total adult population of Canada that is in the labour force:

labour-force participation rate
the percentage of the adult population that is in the labour force

$$\text{Labour-fource participation rate} = \frac{\text{Labour force}}{\text{Adult population}} \times 100$$

This statistic tells us the fraction of the population that has chosen to participate in the labour market. The labour-force participation rate, like the unemployment rate, is computed both for the entire adult population and for more specific groups.

To see how these data are computed, consider the figures for 2014. In that year, 17.80 million people were employed, and 1.32 million people were unemployed. The labour force was

$$\text{Labour force} = 17.80 + 1.32 = 19.12 \text{ million.}$$

The unemployment rate was

$$\text{Unemployment rate} = (1.32/19.12) \times 100 = 6.90 \text{ percent.}$$

Because the adult population was 28.98 million, the labour-force participation rate was

$$\text{Labour-force participation rate} = (19.12/28.98) \times 100 = 65.98 \text{ percent.}$$

Hence, in 2014, two-thirds of Canada's adult population were participating in the labour market, and 6.9 percent of those labour-market participants were without work.

Table 9.1 compares statistics on unemployment and labour-force participation for two groups within the Canadian population: between men and women and

TABLE 9.1

The Labour-Market Experiences of Various Demographic Groups
This table shows the unemployment rate and the labour-force participation rate of various groups in the population for 2014.

Demographic Group	Unemployment Rate	Labour-Force Participation Rate
Both sexes, 15 years and over	6.9%	66.0%
Males, 15–24 years	15.0	63.8
Males, 25–44 years	6.4	91.2
Males, 45–64 years	5.9	80.1
Females, 15–24 years	11.9	64.6
Females, 25–44 years	5.6	82.0
Females, 45–64 years	5.3	71.0

Source: Statistics Canada, CANSIM database.

between young and old. Three interesting facts are revealed by these statistics. First, the labour-force participation rate of young women (aged 15–24) is very similar to that of young men, but for other age groups women have noticeably lower rates of labour-force participation than men. This has been a fairly constant trend over time but, as we will see in a case study a little later, the gap is closing. Second, young people aged 15 to 24 have much higher rates of unemployment than older people. Third, similarly aged men and women tend to have similar rates of unemployment. Although this third fact has proven to be generally true over time, it is interesting to note that since about 2009 the unemployment rate of males has proven to be noticeably higher than the unemployment rate of similarly aged females. This result has prompted some labour economists to label the 2008–09 recession a *mancession* because it affected the unemployment rates of males more than the unemployment rates of females. Since the end of that recession the difference in unemployment rates for similarly aged men and women has remained, suggesting that perhaps the unemployment rate for females will remain persistently below that of males.

Labour-force data also allow economists and policymakers to monitor changes in the economy over time. Figure 9.2 shows the unemployment rate for Canada and for groupings of provinces: Atlantic Canada (Newfoundland and Labrador, Prince Edward Island, Nova Scotia, and New Brunswick), Central Canada (Ontario and Quebec), and Western Canada (Manitoba, Saskatchewan, Alberta, and British Columbia). The figure shows that the economy always has some unemployment and that the amount changes from year to year.

Figure 9.2 also shows that both the unemployment rate and the amount by which it changes from year to year vary widely for different regions of the country. The unemployment rate in Atlantic Canada is consistently higher than in the rest of the country. Furthermore, the difference between the unemployment rate in Atlantic Canada and that in the rest of the country, while quite

FIGURE 9.2

Canadian and Regional Unemployment Rates, 1966–2014

Sources: Statistics Canada, CANSIM database and authors' calculations.

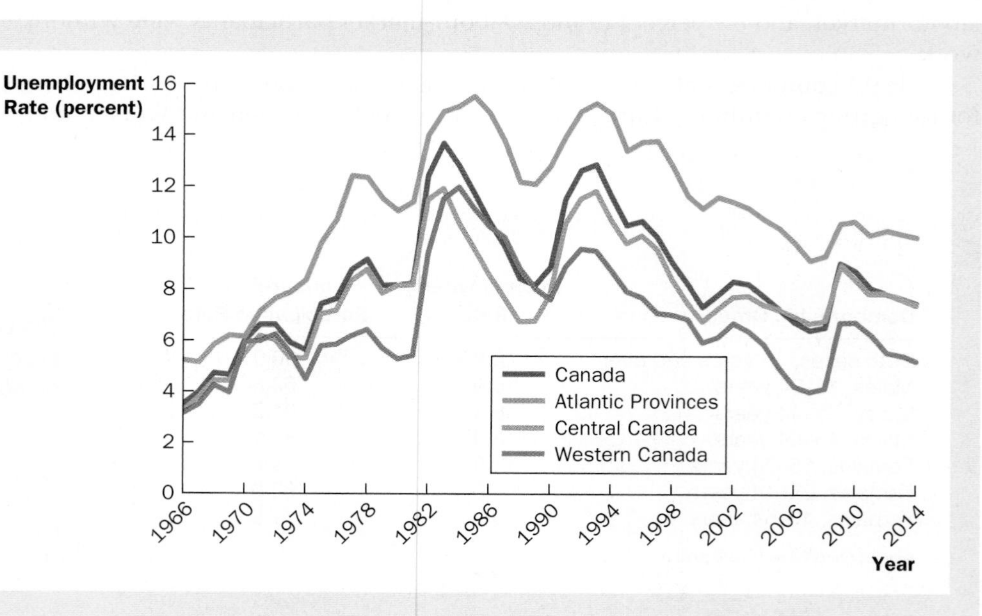

small in 1970, has grown since then. The unemployment rate in Western Canada has generally been lower than in the rest of the country. During the mid- to late 1980s, however, Western Canada's unemployment rate increased to become roughly equal to the Canadian average. This was mainly due to a fall in oil and natural gas prices—an event that harmed the economies in Western Canada but benefited those in the rest of the country. Finally, the unemployment rate in Central Canada closely follows the national unemployment rate. This is to be expected, since Central Canada comprises more than 60 percent of the Canadian labour force.

A final point worth making about measuring unemployment is that it is sometimes misleading to make international comparisons. In the United States, for example, the unemployment rate is defined slightly differently than it is in Canada. One example of the difference is that in the United States, the labour force is defined as the number of people aged 16 years and above actively seeking employment, whereas in Canada the age cut-off is 15 years and above. Differences in definitions like these have a significant effect. In 2014, for example, while the official Canadian unemployment rate was 6.9 percent, if it was measured according to definitions used in the United States it would have been only 5.9 percent.

case study: Labour-Force Participation of Men and Women in the Canadian Economy

Women's role in Canadian society has changed dramatically over the past century. Social commentators have pointed to many causes for this change. In part, it is attributable to new technologies, such as the washing machine, clothes dryer, refrigerator, freezer, and dishwasher, which have reduced the amount of time required to complete routine household tasks. In part, it is attributable to improved birth control, which has reduced the number of children born to the typical family. And, of course, this change in women's role is also partly attributable to changing political and social attitudes. Together these developments have had a profound impact on society in general and on the economy in particular.

Nowhere is that impact more obvious than in data on labour-force participation. Figure 9.3 shows the labour-force participation rates of men and women in Canada since 1951. Just after World War II, men and women had very different roles in society. Only 24 percent of women were working or looking for work, in contrast to 84 percent of men. Over the past several decades, the difference between the participation rates of men and women has gradually diminished, as growing numbers of women have entered the labour force and some men have left it. Data for 2014 show that 62 percent of women were in the labour force, in contrast to 71 percent of men. As measured by labour-force participation, men and women are now playing a more equal role in the economy.

The increase in women's labour-force participation is easy to understand, but the fall in men's may seem puzzling. There are several reasons for this decline. First, young men now stay in school longer than their fathers and grandfathers did. Second, older men now retire earlier and live longer. Third, with more women employed, more fathers now stay at home to raise their children. Full-time students, retirees, and stay-at-home fathers are all counted as out of the labour force. ■

FIGURE 9.3

Labour-Force Participation Rates for Men and Women since 1951

Sources: Data for 1966–2014 are from Statistics Canada, CANSIM database. Observations for 1951 and 1961 are from F.H. Leacy, ed., *Historical Statistics of Canada*, 2nd ed. (Ottawa: Statistics Canada, 1983). Values for 1952:60 and 1962:65 are linear interpolations from the 1951, 1961, and 1966 observations.

This figure shows the percentage of adult men and women who are members of the labour force. It shows that over the past several decades, women have entered the labour force, and men have left it.

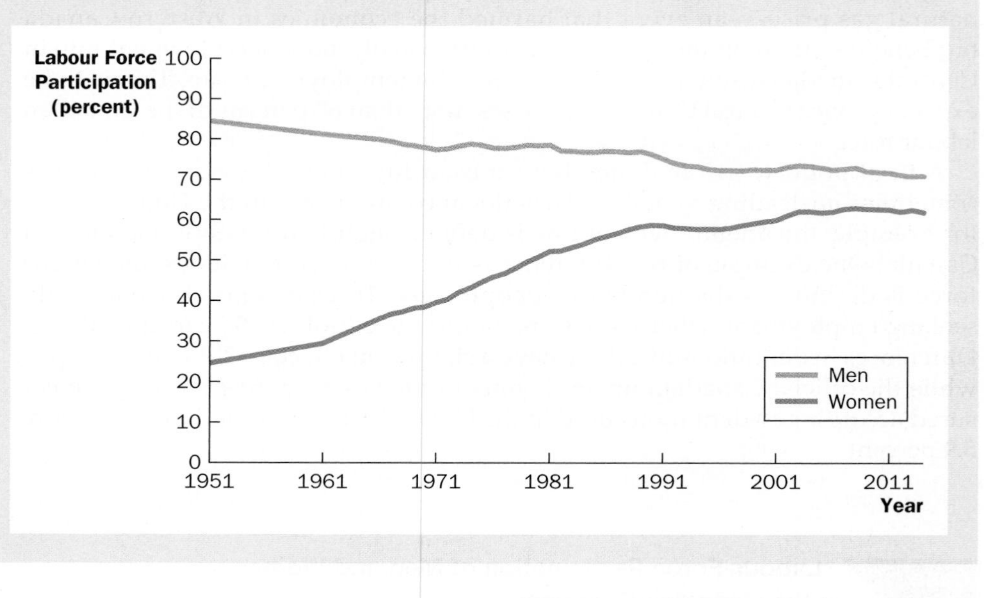

9-1b Does the Unemployment Rate Measure What We Want It To?

Measuring the amount of unemployment in the economy might seem straightforward. In fact, it is not. While it is easy to distinguish between a person with a full-time job and a person who is not working at all, it is much harder to distinguish between a person who is unemployed and a person who is not in the labour force.

Movements into and out of the labour force are, in fact, common. More than one-third of the unemployed are recent entrants into the labour force. These entrants include young workers looking for their first jobs, such as recent university and college graduates. They also include, in greater numbers, older workers who had previously left the labour force but have now returned to look for work. Moreover, not all unemployment ends with the job seeker finding a job. Almost half of all spells of unemployment end when the unemployed person leaves the labour force.

Because people move into and out of the labour force so often and for such a variety of reasons, statistics on unemployment can be difficult to interpret. On the one hand, some of those who report being unemployed may not, in fact, be trying hard to find a job; for example, they might be on temporary layoff and are waiting to be recalled to work. Or perhaps they are calling themselves unemployed because they want to qualify for Employment Insurance or because they are actually working and being paid "under the table." It may be more realistic to view these individuals as out of the labour force or, in some cases, employed.

TABLE 9.2

Alternative Measures of Labour Underutilization

This table shows various measures of joblessness for the Canadian economy. The data are averages for 2014. Figures may fail to sum exactly due to rounding.

Measure and Description	Percentage of the Labour Force
Unemployed 1 to 4 weeks	2.3%
Unemployed 5 to 13 weeks	2.3
Unemployed 14 to 25 weeks	1.9
Unemployed 26 to 52 weeks	1.0
Unemployed more than 52 weeks	0.8
Official Unemployment Rate	6.9
Discouraged searchers	0.1
Those awaiting recall	0.5
Involuntary part-time workers	1.8
Official rate + discouraged searchers + those awaiting recall + involuntary part-time workers	9.3

Sources: Statistics Canada, CANSIM database and authors' calculations.

On the other hand, some of those who report being out of the labour force may, in fact, want to work. These individuals may have tried to find a job but have given up after an unsuccessful search. Such individuals, labelled **discouraged searchers** by Statistics Canada, do not show up in unemployment statistics, even though they are truly workers without jobs. Similarly, some workers may be working part-time when, in fact, they want to work full-time. Although such workers are working less than they want to and so are underemployed, they do not show up in unemployment statistics.

discouraged searchers
individuals who would like to work but have given up looking for a job

The bottom part of Table 9.2, which provides 2014 data, shows the official unemployment rate for Canada as well as several alternative measures of labour underutilization calculated by Statistics Canada. The table shows that these alternative measures can paint quite a different picture of the unemployment situation. In the end, it is best to view the official unemployment rate as a useful but imperfect measure of joblessness.

9-1c How Long Are the Unemployed without Work?

In 2014, the average spell of unemployment in Canada lasted 20.8 weeks. Unfortunately, averages can hide a lot of interesting variation. For example, the Canadian average hides the fact that the average spell of unemployment varied widely across the country. In 2014, the average spell of unemployment ranged from a low of 13.5 weeks in Saskatchewan to a high of 22.9 weeks in Quebec. Average values also hide the fact that there may be a wide dispersion of unemployment experiences across individuals. Consider a simple example: Suppose that Bart experiences an unemployment spell lasting 51 weeks while Lisa, Otto, Edna, and Willie all experience spells of unemployment lasting just one week. While it is true that in this example the average unemployed person suffered 11 weeks of unemployment, this summary statistic seems inadequate for describing the true picture. In particular, by looking only at the average we would fail to learn that unemployment is a short-term and a relatively minor problem for Lisa, Otto, Edna, and Willie, while unemployment is a long-term and much more serious problem for Bart.

FYI The Employment Rate

How does one evaluate the health of an economy? There are many answers to this question, but a simple and reasonably comprehensive measure of success is the employment ratio. The employment ratio measures the fraction of those of working age (aged 15–64 years) who have found employment and so are able to support themselves or their families. It also provides insight into whether the community is able to fund social programs, a quality health care system, effective policing and courts, and more without unduly high tax rates. In short, a high employment ratio is a good indicator of a successful economy along many dimensions.

Alberta has typically had the highest employment rate amongst Canadian provinces. The employment rate in Alberta peaked at 80 percent in 2008. In that year, then, 80 percent of those aged 15–64 years in Alberta were employed.

Figure 9.4 shows the employment rate for Saskatchewan, Ontario, and Newfoundland and Labrador from 1976 to 2014. At the beginning of this period, Saskatchewan and Ontario had virtually the same employment rates but over time the rates have diverged. Whereas in Saskatchewan the employment rate has increased more or less steadily from 66 percent to 77 percent, in Ontario the employment rate has grown much less quickly and in 2014 was noticeably below that in Saskatchewan. But the biggest story is Newfoundland and Labrador. Starting from a woefully low level in 1976, when fewer than half of the working-age population were employed, the economy of Newfoundland and Labrador has undergone a remarkable transformation. In 2014, 65 percent of working-aged people had found employment, a level not far below the Canadian average of 72 percent. This transformation of the Newfoundland and Labrador economy has taken place just in the period since 1996; a period that corresponds to the development of off-shore oil fields and which has occurred despite the collapse of the cod fishery in 1992.

FIGURE 9.4

The Employment Rate in Three Provinces since 1976

This figure shows the percentage of the working-age population that is employed in Saskatchewan, Ontario, and Newfoundland and Labrador. It shows that since 1976 the employment rate has grown steadily in Saskatchewan, less quickly in Ontario, and, since 1996, remarkably quickly in Newfoundland and Labrador.

Sources: Statistics Canada, CANSIM database and authors' calculations.

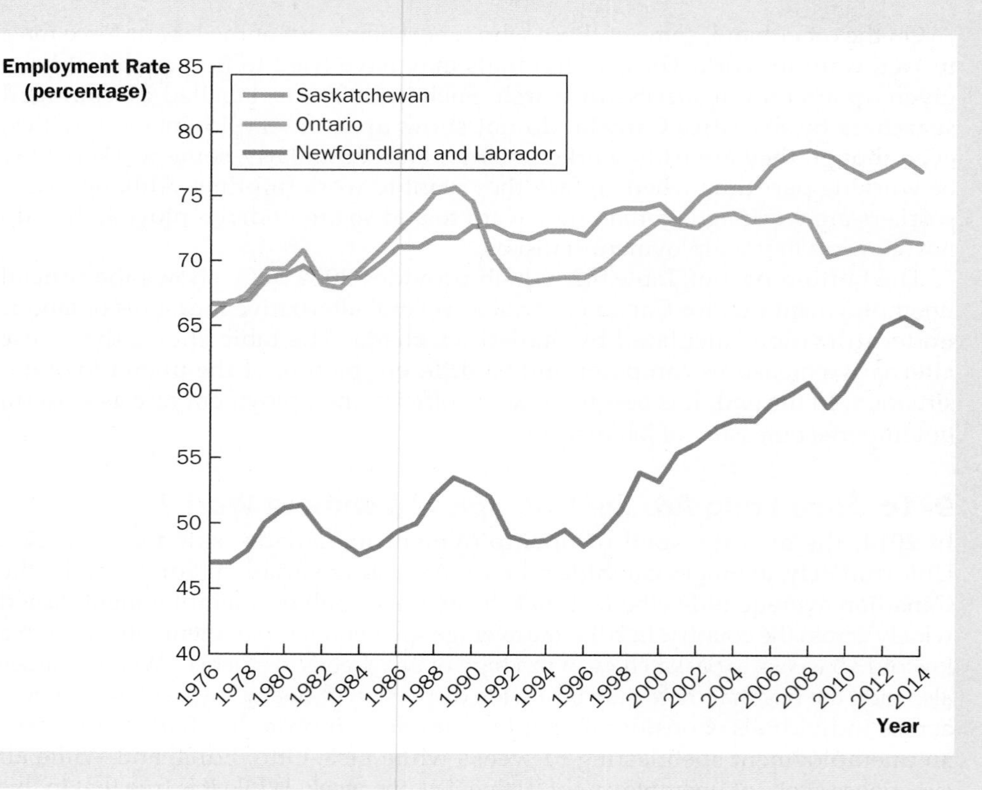

In our simple example, most spells of unemployment were quite short; for four of the five people in the example, unemployment lasted just one week. The figures in the top part of Table 9.2 indicate this is also true in Canada: One-third of those suffering through a spell of unemployment are unemployed for a month or less and three-fifths are unemployed for less than three months. While being unemployed for up to three months is by no means a minor problem, it is a far less serious problem than that faced by those suffering unemployment spells lasting longer than three months and certainly a less serious problem than that faced by those suffering unemployment spells lasting more than a year.

The figures in Table 9.2 suggest that economists and policymakers must be careful when interpreting data on unemployment and when designing policies to help the unemployed. Most people who become unemployed will soon find jobs. Policy solutions directed toward fixing the unemployment problem should be directed toward those suffering prolonged spells of unemployment.

9-1d Why Are There Always Some People Unemployed?

We have discussed how the government measures the amount of unemployment, the problems that arise in interpreting unemployment statistics, and the findings of labour economists on the duration of unemployment. You should now have a good idea about what unemployment is.

This discussion, however, has not explained why economies experience unemployment. In most markets in the economy, prices adjust to bring quantity supplied and quantity demanded into balance. In an ideal labour market, wages would adjust to balance the quantity of labour supplied and the quantity of labour demanded. This adjustment of wages would ensure that all workers are always fully employed.

Of course, reality does not resemble this ideal. There are always some workers without jobs, even when the overall economy is doing well. Figure 9.5 shows Canada's observed unemployment rate and an estimate of Canada's natural unemployment rate. The **natural rate of unemployment** is what economists judge to be the rate of unemployment to which the economy tends to return in the long run. The exact value of the natural unemployment rate is unknown, but most economists estimate the rate in Canada to be currently 6 to 7 percent. Economists form estimates of the natural unemployment rate based on those variables they believe are the underlying determinants of the natural rate of unemployment. We will discuss these underlying determinants in the remainder of this chapter.

natural rate of unemployment
the rate of unemployment to which the economy tends to return in the long run

The values of the natural unemployment rate shown in Figure 9.5 represent the authors' opinions. Because the natural unemployment rate is only an estimate, there may be some dispute about the level of the rate at any particular time. However, the movements shown in the figure represent a fairly widespread view among economists about what has happened to Canada's natural unemployment rate since 1966. During the 1970s and 1980s, the natural unemployment rate roughly doubled from about 4 percent to over 8 percent, and began falling in the mid-1990s. Most economists would agree that by 2014, the natural rate had fallen to between 6 percent and 7 percent.

Figure 9.5 also shows that the observed unemployment rate fluctuates around the natural rate. The observed unemployment rate differs from the natural rate due to the existence of **cyclical unemployment**. Cyclical unemployment arises due to short-run economic fluctuations. Later in this book we discuss short-run economic fluctuations, including the year-to-year fluctuations in unemployment around its natural rate. In the rest of this chapter, however, we ignore the short-run fluctuations and examine why unemployment is a chronic problem for market economies. That is, we will examine the determinants of the natural unemployment rate.

cyclical unemployment
the deviation of unemployment from its natural rate

FIGURE 9.5

Observed and Natural Unemployment Rates, 1966–2014

Sources: Statistics Canada, CANSIM database and authors' assumptions.

Most economists agree that the natural unemployment rate increased during the 1970s, stabilized at about 8 percent in the 1980s, and has followed a slow downward path since the mid-1990s. The difference between the observed unemployment rate and the natural unemployment rate is the cyclical unemployment rate. The recessions in the early 1980s, the early 1990s, and most recently in 2008–09 are identified in this figure by the jump in the observed unemployment rate well above the natural unemployment rate.

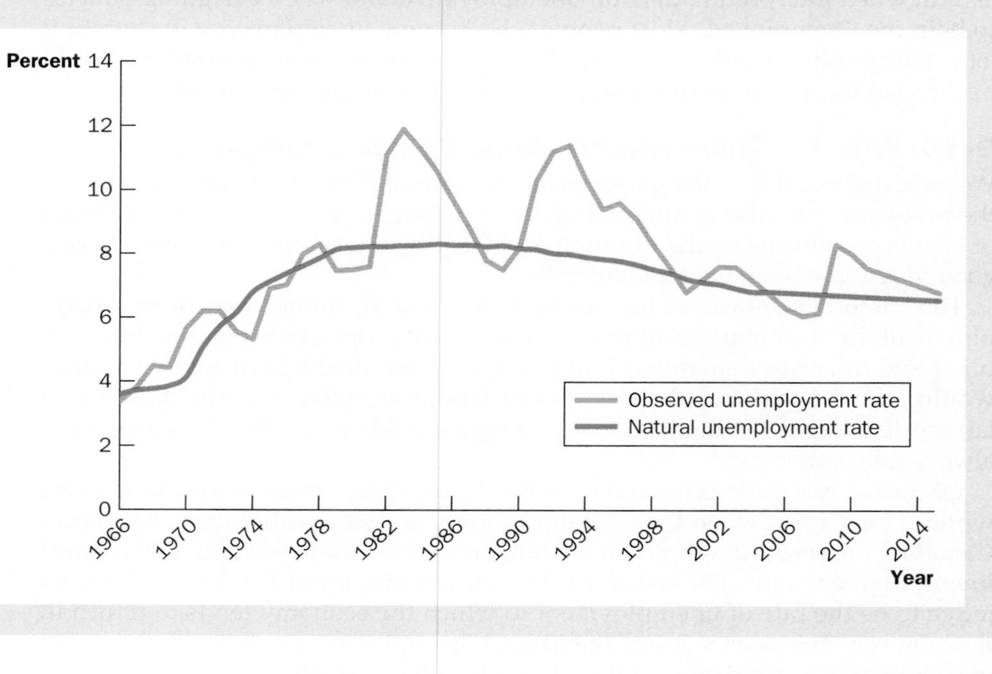

To preview our conclusions, we will find that there are four ways to explain unemployment in the long run. The first explanation is that it takes time for workers to search for the jobs that are best suited for them. The unemployment that results from the process of matching workers and jobs is sometimes called **frictional unemployment**, and it is often thought to explain relatively short spells of unemployment.

frictional unemployment
unemployment that results because it takes time for workers to search for the jobs that best suit their tastes and skills

The next three explanations for unemployment suggest that the number of jobs available in some labour markets may be insufficient to give a job to everyone who wants one. This occurs when the quantity of labour supplied exceeds the quantity demanded. Unemployment of this sort is sometimes called **structural unemployment**, and it is often thought to explain longer spells of unemployment. As we will see, this kind of unemployment results when wages are, for some reason, set above the level that brings supply and demand into equilibrium. Later in this section, we will examine three possible reasons for an above-equilibrium wage: minimum-wage laws, unions, and efficiency wages.

structural unemployment
unemployment that results because the number of jobs available in some labour markets is insufficient to provide a job for everyone who wants one

How is the unemployment rate measured? • How might the unemployment rate overstate the amount of joblessness? How might it understate it?

FYI A Tale of Two Recessions

The Canadian labour market is made up of many local labour markets. Statistics Canada defines 70 local labour market regions and reports employment, labour force, and unemployment statistics in each. In each of these 70 labour markets, the local demand for labour meets the local supply of labour. The implication is that the unemployment rate for Canada is, actually, an average of the unemployment rates in each of these 70 local labour markets.

The differences across local labour markets can be sizable. For example, over the five-month period from January to May 2012, among the 11 labour market regions that Statistics Canada defines in Ontario, the rate of employment growth ranged from a low of −3.9 percent in the labour region called Northwest Ontario to a high of +2.6 percent in the labour region of Ottawa.

Differences like these suggest that when we hear reports like "Canada has entered into recession," we should be aware that this may not be true for all parts of Canada. Some regions of the country may experience a recession that is considerably deeper or much milder than the Canadian average. Some regions might not suffer a recession at all.

An important reason for this is that regions of the country differ by their industrial composition. A fall in oil prices is more likely to cause a recession in oil-producing provinces like Alberta, Saskatchewan, and Newfoundland and Labrador than it is in Ontario, which relies heavily on automobile manufacturing and so benefits from lower oil and gasoline prices. On the other hand, a recession sparked by a fall in demand for automobiles is likely to mainly impact Ontario, while having little influence on unemployment rates in Manitoba.

To illustrate how areas of the country may experience different labour market effects of a recession, Table 9.3 presents data on how much unemployment rates in each province increased during the first year of two recessionary periods: the recession of 1990–91 and the recession of 2008–09.

During the first year of these two recessions, the unemployment rate in Canada increased by almost the same amounts—just over two percentage points on it. But while the 1990–91 downturn had a relatively mild impact on Alberta, British Columbia, and Newfoundland and Labrador, those provinces fared considerably worse during the 2008–09 downturn. The labour markets in New Brunswick and Saskatchewan came through both periods relatively unscathed, while in both recessions, Ontario suffered more than suggested by the Canadian average.

An implication of these results is that the federal government, which generally introduces tax policy changes and changes in spending programs that affect all Canadians, will find it difficult to target recession-fighting policies toward those areas of the country that need it most.

TABLE 9.3

A Tale of Two Recessions

	% Change in Unemployment Rate	
	1990–91	**2008–09**
Newfoundland and Labrador	1.0%	2.3%
Prince Edward Island	2.3	1.2
Nova Scotia	1.4	1.5
New Brunswick	0.6	0.3
Quebec	1.7	1.2
Ontario	3.4	2.5
Manitoba	1.2	1.0
Saskatchewan	0.3	0.7
Alberta	1.3	2.9
British Columbia	1.5	3.1
CANADA	2.2	2.1

Source: Statistics Canada, CANSIM database and authors' calculations.

9-2 Job Search

One reason why economies always experience some unemployment is job search. **Job search** is the process of matching workers with appropriate jobs. If all workers and all jobs were the same, so that all workers were equally well suited for all jobs, job search would not be a problem. Laid-off workers would quickly find new jobs that were well suited for them. But, in fact, workers differ in their tastes and skills, jobs differ in their attributes, and information about job candidates and job vacancies is disseminated slowly among the many firms and households in the economy.

job search
the process by which workers find appropriate jobs given their tastes and skills

9-2a Why Some Frictional Unemployment Is Inevitable

Frictional unemployment is often the result of changes in the demand for labour among different firms. When consumers decide that they prefer Hewlett-Packard over Dell computers, Hewlett-Packard increases employment, and Dell lays off workers. The former Dell workers must now search for new jobs, and Hewlett-Packard must decide which new workers to hire for the various jobs that have opened up. The result of this transition is a period of unemployment.

Similarly, because different regions of the country produce different goods, employment can rise in one region while it falls in another. Consider, for instance, what happens when the world price of oil falls. Oil-producing firms in Alberta respond to the lower price by cutting back on production and employment. At the same time, cheaper gasoline stimulates car sales, so auto-producing firms in Ontario raise production and employment. Changes in the composition of demand among industries or regions are called *sectoral shifts*. Because it takes time for workers to search for jobs in the new sectors, sectoral shifts temporarily cause unemployment.

Frictional unemployment is inevitable simply because the economy is always changing. Only 90 years ago, car manufacturing, petroleum, and aircraft manufacturing industries were very minor sources of employment in Canada. Today, these are three of the largest employers in the Canadian economy. At the same time, agriculture has fallen from being the largest single source of employment in Canada in 1911 to being only a minor source of employment today. As this transition took place, jobs were created in some industries and destroyed in others. The end result of this process has been higher productivity and higher living standards. But, along the way, workers in declining industries found themselves out of work and searching for new jobs.

Some idea of the size of the flow of employees from shrinking to expanding firms can be understood from Table 9.4. Gross job creation is the sum of the increase in the number of jobs across all new and established firms in a given year. Gross job destruction is the sum of the job losses across all firms that either reduce their employment or go out of business altogether in that year. Net employment growth is the difference between job creation and job destruction in that year. The numbers in the table measure the size of employment changes as a percentage of the average level of employment in the current and the previous year.

The table shows that in 2009, for example, employment increased by 9.4 percent because new jobs were created by new firms and by existing firms which expanded employment. In the same year, 12.6 percent of existing jobs were lost because existing firms reduced employment or went out of business altogether. In 2009, the net effect of job creation and destruction was a loss of 3.2 percent of existing jobs.

TABLE 9.4

Job Creation and Destruction

	2009	2010	2011	2012	2013
Gross job creation	9.4	9.8	10.6	9.8	9.4
Gross job destruction	12.6	9.2	8.5	7.9	8.1
Net employment growth	−3.2	0.6	2.2	1.9	1.4

Source: Statistics Canada, CANSIM database.

In 2009, Canada was in a serious recession and so it is not surprising that net employment growth was negative. What is perhaps surprising is that even in the midst of a serious recession, the economy continued to create new employment. After 2009, the economy was in recovery and so net employment growth was positive. Perhaps surprising here is that even in the midst of a strong recovery, in 2011 a large percentage of jobs were nonetheless lost.

In recent years total employment in Canada has been about 17.8 million. The figures in the table suggest that even in a year when net employment growth might be zero, there are nonetheless very large movements of people from failing and shrinking firms to new and growing firms. If we assume each of these flows is about 10 percent of employment, then even in a year when net employment growth is zero approximately 1.75 million employees are moving from failing to growing firms.

Not surprisingly, when Statistics Canada does its monthly survey of households, it will find that some people will report being unemployed because they are searching for re-employment with a growing firm after having been let go by a failing firm. This is the source of what economists refer to as frictional unemployment.

Because frictional unemployment is the result of a well-functioning economy that rewards innovation and new ideas, we should always expect frictional unemployment to be greater than zero.

9-2b Public Policy and Job Search

Even if some frictional unemployment is inevitable, the precise amount is not. The faster information spreads about job openings and worker availability, the more rapidly the economy can match workers and firms. The Internet, for instance, may help facilitate job search and reduce frictional unemployment. In addition, public policy may play a role. If policy can reduce the time it takes unemployed workers to find new jobs, it can reduce the economy's natural rate of unemployment.

Government programs try to facilitate job search in various ways. One way is through government-run employment agencies, which give out information about job vacancies. Another way is through public training programs, which aim to ease the transition of workers from declining to growing industries and to help disadvantaged groups escape poverty. Government training programs in Canada are, for the most part, conducted through the federal government's Employment Insurance program. Recent reforms to this program have reallocated funds away from the payment of benefits to unemployed people and toward the funding of training programs.

Advocates of government programs designed to facilitate job search believe that the programs make the economy operate more efficiently by keeping the labour force more fully employed, and reduce the inequities inherent in a constantly changing market economy. These supporters also stress that in certain circumstances the private sector is incapable of helping those who lose their jobs. This is the case when job loss is the result of disasters, such as the collapse of the cod fishery in Newfoundland. It is argued that the virtual disappearance of an industry that is central to the economy of an entire region demands government involvement. In such cases, the solution is not simply for workers to find a similar job in the next company down the street, but rather to retrain for a new job in a new industry in a new area of the country. Government retraining and relocation programs may play a useful role in these cases, one that the private sector may be incapable of playing.

Critics of these programs question whether the government should get involved with the process of job search. They argue that it is better to let the private market match workers and jobs. In fact, most job search in our economy takes place without intervention by the government. Newspaper ads, Internet job sites, university and college placement offices, headhunters, and word of mouth all help spread information about job openings and job candidates. Similarly, much worker education is done privately, either through schools or through on-the-job training. These critics contend that the government is no better—and most likely worse—at disseminating the right information to the right workers and deciding what kinds of worker training would be most valuable. They claim that these decisions are best made privately by workers and employers.

9-2c Employment Insurance

Employment Insurance (EI)
a government program that partially protects workers' incomes when they become unemployed

In Canada, the federal government maintains an **Employment Insurance (EI)** program. This program is intended to ease the burden of those who find themselves unemployed, by temporarily providing them with income. Canada's EI program is expensive (in 2014, the government budgeted over $17 billion for the EI program) and controversial. Many economists believe that, while EI eases the burden of being unemployed, it may also cause the unemployment rate to be higher than it would be otherwise. Thus, the program may increase the amount of frictional unemployment without intending to do so.

Since 1971, two considerations have determined when and for how long someone can collect EI benefits: the number of hours worked in the past year and the unemployment rate in the area of residence. More hours of work make a claimant eligible to collect EI benefits for a longer period of time. The higher the local unemployment rate, the longer a claimant can collect and the fewer hours the claimant must work in order to become eligible. The details of the program have changed a great deal since 1971, and revisions to the program occur frequently.

Current EI regulations require that workers who live in a region where the unemployment rate exceeds 16 percent have to work only 420 hours (for example, 12 weeks of full-time, 35-hours-per-week employment) to become eligible for 37 weeks of benefits. Workers who live in a region where the unemployment rate is 6 percent or less have to work a minimum of 700 hours (for example, 20 weeks of full-time employment) to become eligible for benefits, and this minimum amount of work makes claimants eligible for just 19 weeks of insurance. In regions of the country with high unemployment rates, therefore, relatively few hours of work are needed to be eligible for EI, and EI benefits can be collected for a long time. In regions of the country with low unemployment rates, many more hours of work are needed to be eligible for EI, and EI benefits can be collected for a much shorter time. Legislation that was introduced in 2012 and took effect in 2013 modified some features of the EI program. In particular, it changed the definition of what is deemed to be "suitable work" and "reasonable job search" in ways intended to make the collection of EI benefits more challenging.

These features of the program suggest that while EI reduces the hardship of unemployment, it can also increase the amount of unemployment. The explanation is based on one of the ten principles of economics in Chapter 1: People respond to incentives. Because EI benefits stop when a worker takes a new job, we might expect that the unemployed would devote less effort to job search and be more likely to turn down unattractive job offers. In addition, the design of the program provides an incentive for people to enter the labour force when they might not otherwise have done so. The reason is that the EI program increases the total income people receive by working: They not only earn a wage while working, but also become eligible to collect EI benefits should they leave the job.

Many studies by labour economists have examined the incentive effects of programs like EI. The results of these studies confirm economists' expectations of how such programs influence labour market behaviours, finding, for example, that job duration is affected by the length of time required to become eligible to collect benefits. In particular, those who collect benefits tend to quit their jobs sooner than they would otherwise have done. Studies have also found that employers initiate layoffs only after workers become eligible for EI benefits. This is presumably done as a benefit to workers who in return accept lower wages.

Other studies have found that success at finding employment while collecting EI benefits is affected by the number of weeks of benefits remaining on the individual's claim: The likelihood of finding new employment increases as EI recipients near the end of their benefits. Finally, many studies have confirmed that joining the labour force is significantly influenced by the availability and generosity of EI benefits. These results all suggest that the design of the EI program influences behaviour in ways that increase the unemployment rate.

Even though EI increases the unemployment rate, we should not necessarily conclude that the program is a bad one. EI does achieve its primary goal of reducing the income uncertainty faced by unemployed people. What's more, studies have found that EI allows unemployed people to conduct a more thorough job search, resulting in a higher wage in their new job than would otherwise have been the case. On the basis of such results, some economists have argued that EI improves the ability of the economy to match each worker with the most appropriate job.

As mentioned above, the design of Canada's EI program has changed considerably over time. Changes introduced in 1971 made it substantially easier to become eligible to collect EI benefits and to collect it for a long time. Most economists believe these changes were responsible for a large increase in Canada's natural unemployment rate. Since 1990, many changes introduced to the program have had the opposite effect. The conditions under which one is eligible to collect EI benefits, and the length of time one is able to collect them, are now more stringent than they were in 1971. Economists believe these changes have contributed to a fall in Canada's natural unemployment rate from a peak reached in the late 1980s.

The study of EI shows that the unemployment rate is an imperfect measure of a nation's overall level of economic well-being. Most economists agree that eliminating EI would reduce the amount of unemployment in the economy. Yet economists disagree on whether economic well-being would be enhanced or diminished by this change in policy.

How would an increase in the world price of oil affect the amount of frictional unemployment? Is this unemployment undesirable? What public policies might affect the amount of unemployment caused by this price change?

9-3 Minimum-Wage Laws

Having seen how frictional unemployment results from the process of matching workers and jobs, let's now examine how structural unemployment results when the number of jobs is insufficient for the number of workers.

To understand structural unemployment, we begin by reviewing how unemployment arises from minimum-wage laws. Although minimum wages are not the predominant reason for unemployment in our economy, they have an important effect on certain groups with particularly high unemployment rates. Moreover, the analysis of minimum wages is a natural place to start because, as we will see, it can be used to understand some of the other reasons for structural unemployment.

Figure 9.6 reviews the basic economics of a minimum wage. When a minimum-wage law forces the wage to remain above the level that balances supply and demand, it raises the quantity of labour supplied and reduces the quantity of labour demanded compared to the equilibrium level. There is a surplus of labour. Because there are more workers willing to work than there are jobs, some workers are unemployed.

It is important to note that minimum-wage laws are not a predominant reason for unemployment in the economy because most workers in the economy earn wages well above the legal minimum. Minimum-wage laws are binding most often for the least skilled and least experienced members of the labour force, such as teenagers. It is only among these workers that minimum-wage laws explain the existence of unemployment.

Although Figure 9.6 is drawn to show the effects of a minimum-wage law, it also illustrates a more general lesson: *If the wage is kept above the equilibrium level for any reason, the result is unemployment.* Minimum-wage laws are just one reason

FIGURE 9.6

Unemployment from a Wage above the Equilibrium Level
In this labour market, the wage at which supply and demand balance is W_E. At this equilibrium wage, the quantity of labour supplied and the quantity of labour demanded both equal L_E. By contrast, if the wage is forced to remain above the equilibrium level, perhaps because of a minimum-wage law, the quantity of labour supplied rises to L_S, and the quantity of labour demanded falls to L_D. The resulting surplus of labour, $L_S - L_D$, represents unemployment.

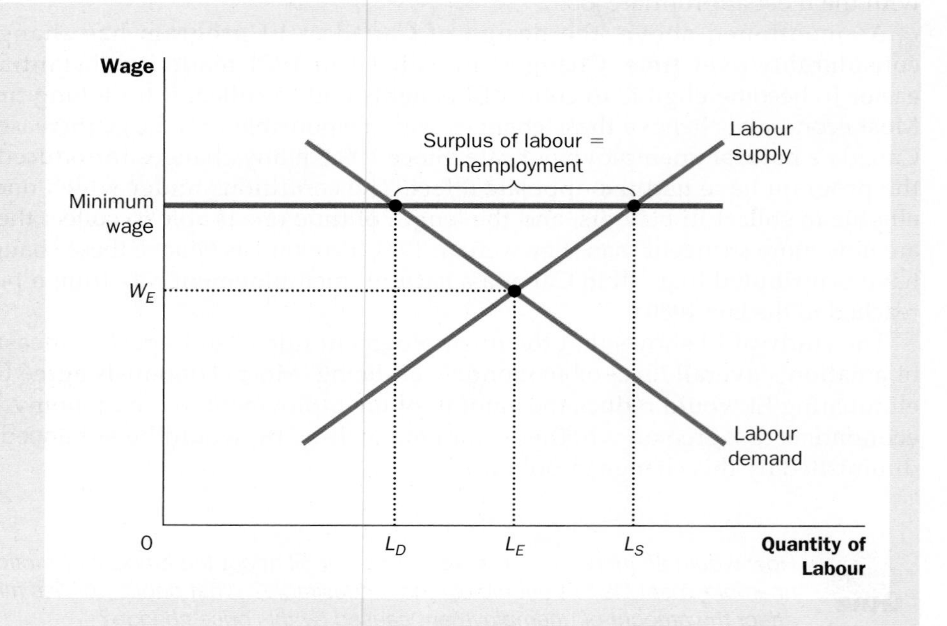

why wages may be "too high." In the remaining two sections of this chapter, we consider two other reasons why wages may be kept above the equilibrium level—unions and efficiency wages. The basic economics of unemployment in these cases is the same as that shown in Figure 9.6, but these explanations of unemployment can apply to many more of the economy's workers.

At this point, however, we should stop and notice that the structural unemployment that arises from an above-equilibrium wage is, in an important sense, different from the frictional unemployment that arises from the process of job search. The need for job search is not due to the failure of wages to balance labour supply and labour demand. When job search is the explanation for unemployment, workers are *searching* for the jobs that best suit their tastes and skills. By contrast, when the wage is above the equilibrium level, the quantity of labour supplied exceeds the quantity of labour demanded, and workers are unemployed because they are *waiting* for jobs to open up.

Draw the supply curve and the demand curve for a labour market in which the wage is fixed above the equilibrium level. Show the quantity of labour supplied, the quantity demanded, and the amount of unemployment.

9-4 Unions and Collective Bargaining

A **union** is a worker association that bargains with employers over wages and working conditions. As of 2013, 30 percent of all employed workers in Canada belonged to unions. In the 1940s and 1950s, union membership as a fraction of the labour force was considerably smaller, at just 10 percent in 1941 and 20 percent in 1951. While union membership in Canada is larger now than it was 70 years ago, the opposite is true in the United States. Union membership in the United States peaked in the 1950s at about one-third of the labour force and has fallen ever since. Today, only about 12 percent of U.S. workers are union members. In contrast to North American rates, European union membership rates are quite high. For example, in Sweden and Denmark, more than 75 percent of all workers belong to unions.

union
a worker association that bargains with employers over wages and working conditions

Union membership as a fraction of the labour force varies by province and by occupation. Using data from 2012, union membership is highest in Quebec, where 40 percent of the labour force is unionized, and lowest in Alberta, where only 23 percent of the labour force is unionized. In the public sector, 71 percent of workers are unionized, while only 16 percent in the private sector are unionized. Unionization is highest in industries in the public sector (education, public administration, and health care) and lowest in the food and accommodation industry.

9-4a The Economics of Unions

A union is a type of cartel. Like any cartel, a union is a group of sellers acting together in the hope of exerting their joint market power. Most workers in the Canadian economy discuss their wages, benefits, and working conditions with their employers as individuals. By contrast, workers in a union do so as a group. The process by which unions and firms agree on the terms of employment is called **collective bargaining**.

collective bargaining
the process by which unions and firms agree on the terms of employment

When a union bargains with a firm, it asks for higher wages, better benefits, and better working conditions than the firm would offer in the absence of a

strike
the organized withdrawal of labour from a firm by a union

union. If the union and the firm do not reach agreement, the union can organize a withdrawal of labour from the firm, called a **strike**. Because a strike reduces production, sales, and profit, a firm facing a strike threat is likely to agree to pay higher wages than it otherwise would. Economists who study the effects of unions typically find that union workers earn about 10 to 20 percent more than similar workers who do not belong to unions.

When a union raises the wage above the equilibrium level, it raises the quantity of labour supplied and reduces the quantity of labour demanded, resulting in unemployment. Those workers who remain employed are better off, but those who were previously employed and are now unemployed at the higher wage are worse off. Indeed, unions are often thought to cause conflict between different groups of workers—between the *insiders* who benefit from high union wages and the *outsiders* who do not get the union jobs.

The outsiders can respond to their status in one of two ways. Some of them remain unemployed and wait for the chance to become insiders and earn the high union wage. Others take jobs in firms that are not unionized. Thus, when unions raise wages in one part of the economy, the supply of labour increases in other parts of the economy. This increase in labour supply, in turn, reduces wages in industries that are not unionized. In other words, workers in unions reap the benefit of collective bargaining, while workers not in unions bear some of the cost.

The role of unions in the economy depends in part on the laws that govern union organization and collective bargaining. Normally, explicit agreements among members of a cartel are illegal. If firms that sell a common product were to agree to set a high price for that product, the agreement would be a "conspiracy to unduly limit competition." The government would prosecute these firms in civil and criminal court for violating Canada's competition laws. By contrast, unions are exempt from these laws. The policymakers who wrote Canada's competition laws believed that workers needed greater market power as they bargained with employers. Indeed, various laws are designed to encourage the formation of unions. In particular, the National War Labour Order of 1944 provided private-sector employees with the right to union representation and collective bargaining. The Public Service Staff Relations Act of 1967 extended these rights to federal public-sector employees. Similar acts of provincial legislatures have extended these rights to provincial public-sector employees. Given these pieces of legislation, it is not surprising that 70 percent of public-sector employees are unionized.

In the private sector, unions must approach workers in nonunionized companies and try to convince a majority of those workers of the benefits of union membership. While these membership drives are often unsuccessful, the very threat of such attempts at unionization likely have the effect of causing firms to increase wages and improve working conditions as a way of discouraging workers from joining a union.

9-4b Are Unions Good or Bad for the Economy?

Economists disagree about whether unions are good or bad for the economy as a whole. Let's consider both sides of the debate.

Critics of unions argue that unions are merely a type of cartel. When unions raise wages above the level that would prevail in competitive markets, they reduce the quantity of labour demanded, cause some workers to be unemployed, and reduce the wages in the rest of the economy. The resulting allocation of labour is, critics argue, both inefficient and inequitable. It is inefficient because high union wages

FYI Who Earns the Minimum Wage?

In Canada, provincial and territorial governments establish the minimum before-tax hourly wage that can be paid by employers in that jurisdiction. The federal and provincial tax systems then determine how much tax is paid and so determine the after-tax wage actually received. The table reports the before-tax and after-tax minimum wage, and the amount of taxes paid per hour, in each province as of July 2015. The calculations assume a single wage earner working 2000 hours per year (40 hours per week for 50 weeks).

	Before-Tax Wage	Before-Tax Rank	Taxes Paid per Hour	After-Tax Wage	After-Tax Rank
Ontario	$11.25	1	$1.79	$9.46	1
Manitoba	10.70	2	$1.89	8.81	5
Nova Scotia	10.60	3	$2.21	8.39	9
Quebec	10.55	4	$1.71	8.84	4
Newfoundland and Labrador	10.50	5	$1.94	8.56	7
Prince Edward Island	10.50	5	$2.28	8.22	10
British Columbia	10.45	7	$1.46	8.99	3
New Brunswick	10.30	8	$1.81	8.49	8
Saskatchewan	10.20	9	$1.47	8.73	6
Alberta	10.20	9	$1.20	9.00	2

Source: Alberta Jobs, Skills, Training and Labour (2015), *Alberta Minimum Wage Profile April 2014–March 2015, Appendix C: Interprovincial Minimum Wage Comparisons 2015*, p. 7. https://work.alberta.ca/documents/alberta-minimim-wage-profile.pdf

In the table, before-tax minimum wages are listed from highest (Ontario) to lowest (Saskatchewan and Alberta). The ranking of provinces changes once taxes are taken into consideration. Ontario remains number one with the highest after-tax minimum wage but Alberta, at the bottom of the before-tax rankings, moves up to number two. Going the other way is Nova Scotia, which falls to number nine in the after-tax ranking from number three in the before-tax ranking. The change in rank that results when we take taxes into consideration is almost wholly due to differences in provincial tax systems. Alberta moves up the ranking, and Nova Scotia moves down, when we look at the after-tax minimum wage because the taxes paid by a minimum-wage earner in Alberta are much lower than those paid by a minimum-wage earner in Nova Scotia. These movements suggest that governments anxious to help the working poor can accomplish a great deal by changing the tax they impose on those earning low incomes.

The government of Alberta increased its before-tax minimum wage to $11.20 on October 1, 2015. That change moved Alberta into the number two position for before-tax minimum wages and into top place with respect to the after-tax wage.

The reason most people give for suggesting that governments establish or increase a minimum wage is that this is a useful tool for fighting poverty. If only working people earned a higher wage, goes the argument, they would be able to lift themselves out of poverty. To evaluate the potential impact on poverty of changes to minimum-wage legislation, it is important to understand who works for minimum wage and what types of jobs they hold. In 2010, Statistics Canada released a study from its series called *Perspectives on Labour and Income* that examined just that. Here is a summary of its findings.

- In 2009, the percentage of all employees working at or below the minimum wage varied widely by province, from just 1.3 percent in Alberta to 9.3 percent in Newfoundland and Labrador. For Canada as a whole, 5.8 percent of all employees in Canada worked at or below the minimum-wage rate set by their province.
- Those working at minimum wage tend to be young. In 2009, about 41 percent of all those working at minimum wage were aged 15 to 19 years, and 18 percent were aged 20 to 24 years. Nearly 60 percent of all those working for minimum wage were therefore aged 15 to 24 years.
- The majority of young people earning the minimum wage (80 percent of those aged 15–19 years and 60 percent of those aged 20–24 years) were attending school.
- Minimum-wage workers were more likely to be working part-time (60 percent) than full-time. Of those working for minimum wage, 47 percent had been in their current job for one year or less.
- Finally, most (56 percent) minimum-wage workers were living at home with their parents.

These facts provided by the Statistics Canada study raise questions about the effectiveness of minimum-wage laws for reducing poverty. A significant percentage of minimum-wage earners are young people living at home and attending school. The face of poverty looks very different from this. Poverty is greatest amongst those dealing with disabilities and those unable to find employment. Neither of these groups benefits from minimum-wage policies.

reduce employment in unionized firms below the efficient, competitive level. It is inequitable because some workers benefit at the expense of other workers.

Advocates of unions contend that unions are a necessary antidote to the market power of the firms that hire workers. The extreme case of this market power is the "company town," where a single firm does most of the hiring in a geographic region. In a company town, if workers do not accept the wages and working conditions that the firm offers, they have little choice but to move or stop working. In the absence of a union, therefore, the firm could use its market power to pay lower wages and offer worse working conditions than would prevail if it had to compete with other firms for the same workers. In this case, a union may balance the firm's market power and protect the workers from being at the mercy of the firm owners.

Advocates of unions also claim that unions are important for helping firms respond efficiently to workers' concerns. Whenever a worker takes a job, the worker and the firm must agree on many attributes of the job in addition to the wage: hours of work, overtime, vacations, sick leave, health benefits, promotion schedules, job security, and so on. By representing workers' views on these issues, unions allow firms to provide the right mix of job attributes. Even if unions have the adverse effect of pushing wages above the equilibrium level and causing unemployment, they have the benefit of helping firms keep a happy and productive workforce.

In the end, there is no consensus among economists about whether unions are good or bad for the economy. Like many institutions, their influence is probably beneficial in some circumstances and adverse in others.

How does a union in the auto industry affect wages and employment at General Motors and Ford? How does it affect wages and employment in other industries?

9-5 The Theory of Efficiency Wages

efficiency wages
above-equilibrium wages paid by firms in order to increase worker productivity

A fourth reason why economies always experience some unemployment—in addition to job search, minimum-wage laws, and unions—is suggested by the theory of **efficiency wages**. According to this theory, firms operate more efficiently if wages are above the equilibrium level. Therefore, it may be profitable for firms to keep wages high even in the presence of a surplus of labour.

In some ways, the unemployment that arises from efficiency wages is similar to the unemployment that arises from minimum-wage laws and unions. In all three cases, unemployment is the result of wages above the level that balances the quantity of labour supplied and the quantity of labour demanded. Yet there is also an important difference. Minimum-wage laws and unions prevent firms from lowering wages in the presence of a surplus of workers. Efficiency-wage theory states that such a constraint on firms is unnecessary in many cases because firms may be better off keeping wages above the equilibrium level.

Why should firms want to keep wages high? This decision may seem odd at first, because wages are a large part of firms' costs. Normally, we expect profit-maximizing firms to want to keep costs—and therefore wages—as low as possible. The novel insight of efficiency-wage theory is that paying high wages might be profitable because they might raise the efficiency of a firm's workers.

There are several types of efficiency-wage theory. Each type suggests a different explanation for why firms may want to pay high wages. Let's now consider four of these types.

9-5a Worker Health

The first and simplest type of efficiency-wage theory emphasizes the link between wages and worker health. Better paid workers eat a more nutritious diet, and workers who eat a better diet are healthier and more productive. A firm may find it more profitable to pay high wages and have healthy, productive workers than to pay lower wages and have less healthy, less productive workers.

This type of efficiency-wage theory can be relevant for explaining unemployment in less developed countries where inadequate nutrition can be a problem. In these countries, firms may fear that cutting wages would, in fact, adversely influence their workers' health and productivity. In other words, nutrition concerns may explain why firms maintain above-equilibrium wages despite a surplus of labour. Worker health concerns are far less relevant for firms in rich countries such as Canada, where the equilibrium wages for most workers are well above the level needed for an adequate diet.

9-5b Worker Turnover

A second type of efficiency-wage theory emphasizes the link between wages and worker turnover. Workers quit jobs for many reasons—to take jobs in other firms, to move to other parts of the country, to leave the labour force, and so on. The frequency with which they quit depends on the entire set of incentives they face, including the benefits of leaving and the benefits of staying. The more a firm pays its workers, the less often its workers will choose to leave. Thus, a firm can reduce turnover among its workers by paying them a high wage.

Why do firms care about turnover? The reason is that it is costly for firms to hire and train new workers. Moreover, even after they are trained, newly hired workers are not as productive as experienced workers. Firms with higher turnover, therefore, will tend to have higher production costs. Firms may find it profitable to pay wages above the equilibrium level in order to reduce worker turnover.

9-5c Worker Effort

A third type of efficiency-wage theory emphasizes the link between wages and worker effort. In many jobs, workers have some discretion over how hard to work. As a result, firms monitor the efforts of their workers, and workers caught shirking their responsibilities are fired. But not all shirkers are caught immediately because monitoring workers is costly and imperfect. A firm in such a circumstance always looks for ways to deter shirking.

One solution is to pay wages above the equilibrium level. High wages make workers more eager to keep their jobs, giving workers an incentive to put forward their best efforts. If the wage was at the level that balanced supply and demand, workers would have less reason to work hard because if they were fired, they could quickly find new jobs at the same wage. Therefore, firms raise wages above the equilibrium level, providing an incentive for workers not to shirk their responsibilities.

9-5d Worker Quality

A fourth and final type of efficiency-wage theory emphasizes the link between wages and worker quality. All firms want workers who are talented, and they try to pick the best applicants to fill job openings. But because firms cannot perfectly gauge the quality of applicants, hiring has a degree of randomness to it. When a firm pays a high wage, it attracts a better pool of workers to apply for its jobs and thereby increases the quality of its workforce. If the firm responded to a surplus of labour by reducing the wage, the most competent applicants—who are more likely to have better alternative opportunities than less competent applicants—may choose not to apply. If this influence of the wage on worker quality is strong enough, it may be profitable for the firm to pay a wage above the level that balances supply and demand.

case study

Henry Ford and the Very Generous $5-a-Day Wage

Henry Ford was an industrial visionary. As founder of the Ford Motor Company, he was responsible for introducing modern techniques of production. Rather than building cars with small teams of skilled craftsmen, Ford built cars on assembly lines in which unskilled workers were taught to perform the same simple tasks over and over again. The output of this assembly process was the Model T Ford, one of the most famous early automobiles.

In 1914, Ford introduced another innovation: the $5 workday. This might not seem like much today, but back then $5 was about twice the going wage. It was also far above the wage that balanced supply and demand. When the new $5-a-day wage was announced, long lines of job seekers formed outside the Ford factories. The number of workers willing to work at this wage far exceeded the number of workers Ford needed.

AFP/Getty Images

Ford's high-wage policy had many of the effects predicted by efficiency-wage theory. Turnover fell, absenteeism fell, and productivity rose. Workers were so much more efficient that Ford's production costs were lower even though wages were higher. Thus, paying a wage above the equilibrium level was profitable for the firm. Henry Ford himself called the $5-a-day wage "one of the finest cost-cutting moves we ever made."

Historical accounts of this episode are also consistent with efficiency-wage theory. A historian of the early Ford Motor Company wrote, "Ford and his associates freely declared on many occasions that the high-wage policy turned out to be good business. By this they meant that it had improved the discipline of the workers, given them a more loyal interest in the institution, and raised their personal efficiency."

Why did it take Henry Ford to introduce this efficiency wage? Why were other firms not already taking advantage of this seemingly profitable business strategy? According to some analysts, Ford's decision was closely linked to his use of the

FYI Minimum, Efficiency, and Living Wages

In this chapter, we have discussed minimum wages and efficiency wages. Many antipoverty advocates argue for consideration of yet another type of wage: the *living wage*. How are these three concepts related?

Those who advocate for the living wage typically define it as the wage level that allows the earner to afford shelter, food, and the other necessities of life. Often it is defined as a wage sufficient to ensure that no more than 30 percent of it needs to be spent on shelter. Most advocates recognize this would require defining a living wage in excess of the minimum-wage rates listed in the FYI feature "Who Earns the Minimum Wage?" earlier in this chapter. Interestingly, some who argue in favour of increases to the minimum wage also suggest it is necessary to ensure a decent standard of living. The arguments for a minimum wage and those for a living wage therefore sound like very much alike. How, then, does the *living* wage differ from the *minimum* wage?

The difference is that while the minimum wage applies to all employees in a jurisdiction (in Canada, these are provinces and territories), a living wage is defined by a municipal ordinance that applies only to firms hoping to win contracts with, or receive subsidies from, the municipal government in a particular municipality. The idea is that taxpayers, as represented by their municipal government, should not be dealing with firms that pay a wage too low for their employees to afford a decent standard of living in that municipality.

Supporters of living-wage ordinances often suggest that by forcing firms to pay a higher wage, the municipal government will help not only employees of those firms but also the firms themselves. The argument is that if the firm pays a higher wage it will experience lower rates of employment turnover and that saves the firm training and recruitment costs. What's more, paying a living wage may increase worker morale, leading to higher productivity. All of this is good for the firm and provides an important offsetting benefit to the cost to the firm of paying the higher living wage.

If those arguments in favour of living-wage policies sound familiar, it is because these are the same sorts of ideas that have been used to support suggestions that private firms may choose to pay *efficiency* wages—wages in excess of the equilibrium level. Since many economists recognize the possibility that firms will choose to pay efficiency wages, does this suggest that economic theory supports the use of living-wage ordinances?

Not really. The concept of an efficiency wage is based on the notion that a firm may find it in its own best interest to pay a wage in excess of what it otherwise needs to pay (the equilibrium wage). Doing so may enable the firm to enjoy lower worker turnover and higher productivity. A living-wage ordinance, on the other hand, coerces firms to pay a wage higher than they have found to be in their own best interests. It seems difficult to argue that firms need to be coerced to pay a higher wage if they would in fact benefit by doing so. If coercion is necessary, it seems likely that a living-wage ordinance will result in the sorts of changes we described earlier with respect to the minimum wage—lower employment, particularly for young and inexperienced workers.

Advocates of higher minimum wages and living wages often admit these policies may result in lower employment, but they believe these effects to be small and that, all things considered, a higher wage makes the poor better off. Opponents of minimum-wage and living-wage ordinances contend that even if employment effects are in fact small, these approaches are not effective ways of combatting poverty. They suggest that if the goal is poverty reduction, then efforts would be better spent advocating for well-targeted income-support programs that benefit not only those earning low wages but also those who, perhaps due to physical or neurodevelopmental disorders, are unable to find employment at all.

assembly line. Workers organized in an assembly line are highly interdependent. If one worker is absent or works slowly, other workers are less able to complete their own tasks. Thus, while assembly lines made production more efficient, they also raised the importance of low worker turnover, high worker quality, and high worker effort. As a result, paying efficiency wages may have been a better strategy for the Ford Motor Company than for other businesses at the time. ■

Give four explanations for why firms might find it profitable to pay wages above the level that balances quantity of labour supplied and quantity of labour demanded.

9-6 Conclusion

In this chapter we discussed the measurement of unemployment and the reasons why economies always experience some degree of unemployment. We have seen how job search, minimum-wage laws, unions, and efficiency wages can all help explain why some workers do not have jobs. Which of these four explanations for the natural rate of unemployment are the most important for the Canadian economy and other economies around the world? Unfortunately, there is no easy way to tell. Economists differ in which of these explanations of unemployment they consider most important.

The analysis of this chapter yields an important lesson: Although the economy will always have some unemployment, its natural rate does change over time. Many events and policies can change the amount of unemployment the economy typically experiences. As the information revolution changes the process of job search, as governments adjust the minimum wage and alter the eligibility requirements for Employment Insurance, as workers form or quit unions, and as firms alter their reliance on efficiency wages, the natural rate of unemployment evolves. Unemployment is not a simple problem with a simple solution. But how we choose to organize our society can profoundly influence how prevalent a problem it is.

summary

- The unemployment rate is the percentage of those who would like to work but do not have jobs. Statistics Canada calculates this statistic monthly based on a survey of thousands of households.
- The unemployment rate is an imperfect measure of joblessness. Some people who call themselves unemployed may actually not want to work, and some people who would like to work have left the labour force after an unsuccessful search.
- In the Canadian economy, most people who become unemployed find work within a fairly short period of time. The fraction of those who find themselves unemployed for periods longer than six months is relatively small. Public policy solutions to the unemployment problem should be directed toward providing help to those experiencing long bouts of unemployment.
- One reason for unemployment is the time it takes for workers to search for jobs that best suit their tastes and skills. Employment Insurance is a government policy that, while protecting workers' incomes, increases the amount of frictional unemployment.
- The second reason why our economy always has some unemployment is minimum-wage laws. By raising

the wage of unskilled and inexperienced workers above the equilibrium level, minimum-wage laws raise the quantity of labour supplied and reduce the quantity demanded. The resulting surplus of labour represents unemployment.

- The third reason for unemployment is the market power of unions. When unions push the wages in unionized industries above the equilibrium level, they create a surplus of labour.
- The fourth reason for unemployment is suggested by the theory of efficiency wages. According to this theory, firms find it profitable to pay wages above the equilibrium level. High wages can improve worker health, lower worker turnover, increase worker effort, and raise worker quality.

KEY **concepts**

labour force, *p. 180*
unemployment rate, *p. 181*
labour-force participation rate, *p. 181*
discouraged searchers, *p. 185*
natural rate of unemployment, *p. 187*
cyclical unemployment, *p. 187*
frictional unemployment, *p. 188*
structural unemployment, *p. 188*
job search, *p. 189*
Employment Insurance (EI), *p. 192*
union, *p. 195*
collective bargaining, *p. 195*
strike, *p. 196*
efficiency wages, *p. 198*

QUESTIONS FOR **review**

1. What are the three categories into which Statistics Canada divides everyone? How does Statistics Canada compute the labour force, the unemployment rate, and the labour-force participation rate?
2. Employment Insurance provides an economic incentive that encourages people to enter the labour force. Explain.
3. Why is frictional unemployment inevitable? How might the government reduce the amount of frictional unemployment?
4. Are minimum-wage laws a better explanation for structural unemployment among teenagers or among postsecondary graduates? Why?
5. How do unions affect the natural rate of unemployment?
6. What claims do advocates of unions make to argue that unions are good for the economy?
7. Explain four ways in which a firm might increase its profits by raising the wages it pays.

QUICK CHECK **multiple choice**

1. The population of Ectenia is 100 people: 40 work full-time, 20 work half-time but would prefer to work full-time, 10 are looking for a job, 10 would like to work but are so discouraged they have given up looking, 10 are not interested in working because they are full-time students, and 10 are retired. What is the number of unemployed in Ectenia?
   a. 10
   b. 20
   c. 30
   d. 40
2. Using the numbers in the preceding question, what is the size of Ectenia's labour force?
   a. 50
   b. 60
   c. 70
   d. 80
3. The main policy goal of the employment insurance system is to reduce which of the following?
   a. the search effort of the unemployed
   b. the income uncertainty that workers face
   c. the role of unions in wage setting
   d. the amount of frictional unemployment
4. According to the most recent data, among workers who are paid at an hourly rate, about what percent have jobs that pay at or below the minimum wage?
   a. 2 percent
   b. 6 percent
   c. 15 percent
   d. 40 percent

5. Unionized workers are paid more than similar non-union workers by about what percent?
   a. 2 to 5 percent
   b. 5 to 10 percent
   c. 10 to 20 percent
   d. 40 percent

6. Which of the following is true according to the theory of efficiency wages?
   a. firms may find it profitable to pay above-equilibrium wages
   b. an excess supply of labour puts downward pressure on wages
   c. sectoral shifts are the main source of frictional unemployment
   d. right-to-work laws reduce the bargaining power of unions

PROBLEMS AND **applications**

1. Statistics Canada announced that in May 2015, of all Canadians aged 15 years and older, 17 953 800 were employed, 1 307 600 were unemployed, and 9 970 800 were not in the labour force. How big was the labour force? What was the labour-force participation rate? What was the unemployment rate?

2. As shown in Figure 9.3, the overall labour-force participation rate of men declined between 1976 and 1997. This overall decline reflects different patterns for different age groups, however, as shown in the following table.

	All Men	Men 15–24	Men 25–54	Men 55 and Over
1976	78%	68%	95%	48%
1997	72	63	91	33

   Which group experienced the largest decline? Given this information, what factor may have played an important role in the decline in overall male labour-force participation over this period?

3. The labour-force participation rate of women increased sharply between 1976 and 1997, as shown in Figure 9.3. As with men, however, there were different patterns for different age groups, as shown in this table:

	All Women	Women 15–24	Women 25–54	Women 55 and Over
1976	46%	58%	52%	18%
1997	57	59	76	17

   Why do you think that younger women experienced a bigger increase in labour-force participation than older women?

4. Between 2008 and 2009, total employment in Canada decreased by 277 000 workers, but the number of unemployed workers increased by 400 000. How are these numbers consistent with each other?

5. Go to the Government of Canada's website at http://srv129.services.gc.ca/rbin/eng/postalcode_search.aspx and enter your postal code. You will be told the unemployment rate in your region, the number of hours of employment you will need to qualify for EI benefits, and the number of weeks you will be eligible to collect EI, depending on your recent employment history. Now enter a postal code for someone living in an area of the country with a much different unemployment rate from that in your area. How might these differences influence labour market behaviour in one region versus the other?

6. Are the following workers more likely to experience short-term or long-term unemployment? Explain.
   a. a construction worker laid off because of bad weather
   b. a manufacturing worker who loses her job at a plant in an isolated area
   c. a stagecoach-industry worker laid off because of competition from railroads
   d. a short-order cook who loses his job when a new restaurant opens across the street
   e. an expert welder with little formal education who loses her job when the company installs automatic welding machinery

7. Using a diagram of the labour market, show the effect of an increase in the minimum wage on the wage paid to workers, the number of workers supplied, the number of workers demanded, and the amount of unemployment.

8. Do you think that firms in small towns or in cities have more market power in hiring? Do you think that firms generally have more market power in hiring today than 50 years ago, or less? How do you think this change over time has affected the role of unions in the economy? Explain.

9. Consider an economy with two labour markets, neither of which is unionized. Now suppose a union is established in one market.
   a. Show the effect of the union on the market in which it is formed. In what sense is the quantity of labour employed in this market an inefficient quantity?
   b. Show the effect of the union on the nonunionized market. What happens to the equilibrium wage in this market?
10. It can be shown that an industry's demand for labour will become more elastic when the demand for the industry's product becomes more elastic. Let's consider the implications of this fact for the Canadian automobile industry and Unifor, the union that represents Canadian autoworkers.
    a. What happened to the elasticity of demand for Canadian cars when the Japanese developed a strong auto industry? What happened to the elasticity of demand for Canadian autoworkers? Explain.
    b. As the chapter explains, a union generally faces a tradeoff in deciding how much to raise wages because a larger increase is better for workers who remain employed but also results in a greater reduction in employment. How did the rise in auto imports from Japan affect the wage–employment tradeoff faced by Unifor?
    c. Do you think the growth of the Japanese auto industry increased or decreased the gap between the competitive wage and the wage negotiated by Unifor? Explain.
11. Some workers in the economy are paid a flat salary and some are paid by commission. Which compensation scheme would require more monitoring by supervisors? In which case do firms have an incentive to pay more than the equilibrium level (as in the worker-effort variant of efficiency-wage theory)? What factors do you think determine the type of compensation firms choose?
12. Structural unemployment is sometimes said to result from a mismatch between the job skills that employers want and the job skills that workers have. To explore this idea, consider an economy with two industries: auto manufacturing and aircraft manufacturing.
    a. If workers in these two industries require similar amounts of training, and if workers at the beginning of their careers could choose which industry to train for, what would you expect to happen to the wages in these two industries? How long would this process take? Explain.
    b. Suppose that one day the economy opens itself to international trade and, as a result, starts importing autos and exporting aircraft. What would happen to demand for labour in these two industries?
    c. Suppose that workers in one industry cannot be quickly retrained for the other. How would these shifts in demand affect equilibrium wages both in the short run and in the long run?
    d. If for some reason wages fail to adjust to the new equilibrium levels, what would occur?
13. (This problem is challenging.) Suppose that Parliament passes a law requiring employers to provide employees some benefit (such as dental care) that raises the cost of an employee by $4 per hour.
    a. What effect does this employer mandate have on the demand for labour? (In answering this and the following questions, be quantitative when you can.)
    b. If employees place a value on this benefit exactly equal to its cost, what effect does this employer mandate have on the supply of labour?
    c. If the wage is free to balance supply and demand, how does this law affect the wage and the level of employment? Are employers better or worse off? Are employees better or worse off?
    d. If a minimum-wage law prevents the wage from balancing supply and demand, how does the employer mandate affect the wage, the level of employment, and the level of unemployment? Are employers better or worse off? Are employees better or worse off?
    e. Now suppose that workers do not value the mandated benefit at all. How does this alternative assumption change your answers to parts (b), (c), and (d) above?

CHAPTER 10

The Monetary System

LEARNING **objectives**

In this chapter, you will ...

1. Consider the nature of money and its functions in the economy
2. Learn about the Bank of Canada
3. Study how the banking system helps determine the supply of money
4. Examine the tools used by the Bank of Canada to alter the supply of money

When you walk into a restaurant to buy a meal, you get something of value—a full stomach. To pay for this service, you might hand the restaurateur several worn-out pieces of coloured paper decorated with strange symbols, birds, government buildings, and the portrait of the Queen or a dead prime minister. Or you might hand him a piece of paper with the name of a bank and your signature, or a plastic card. Whether you pay by cash, cheque, or debit card, the restaurateur is happy to work hard to satisfy your gastronomical desires in exchange for these pieces of paper and plastic that, in and of themselves, are worthless.

To anyone who has lived in a modern economy, this social custom is not at all odd. Even though paper money has no intrinsic value, the restaurateur is confident that, in the future, some third person will accept it in exchange for something that the restaurateur does value. And that third person is confident that some fourth person will accept the money, with the knowledge that yet a fifth person will accept the money ... and so on. To the restaurateur and to other people in our society, your cash, cheque, or debit card represents a claim to goods and services in the future.

The social custom of using money for transactions is extraordinarily useful in a large, complex society. Imagine, for a moment, that there was no item in the economy widely accepted in exchange for goods and services. People would have to rely on *barter*—the exchange of one good or service for another—to obtain the things they need. To get your restaurant meal, for instance, you would have to offer the restaurateur something of immediate value. You could offer to wash some dishes, clean his car, or give him your family's secret recipe for meat loaf. An economy that relies on barter will have trouble allocating its scarce resources efficiently. In such an economy, trade is said to require the *double coincidence of wants*—the unlikely occurrence that two people each have a good or service that the other wants.

The existence of money makes trade easier. The restaurateur does not care whether you can produce a valuable good or service for him. He is happy to accept your money, knowing that other people will do the same for him. Such a convention allows trade to be roundabout. The restaurateur accepts your money and uses it to pay his chef; the chef uses her paycheque to send her child to daycare; the daycare centre uses this tuition to pay a teacher; and the teacher hires you to mow his lawn. As money flows from person to person in the economy, it facilitates production and trade, thereby allowing each person to specialize in what he or she does best and raising everyone's standard of living.

In this chapter we begin to examine the role of money in the economy. We discuss what money is, the various forms that money takes, how the banking system helps create money, and how the government controls the quantity of money in circulation. Because money is so important in the economy, we devote much effort in the rest of this book to learning how changes in the quantity of money affect various economic variables, including inflation, interest rates, production, and employment. Consistent with our long-run focus in the previous chapters, in the next chapter we will examine the long-run effects of changes in the quantity of money. The short-run effects of monetary changes are a more complex topic, which we will take up later in the book. This chapter provides the background for all of this further analysis.

10-1 The Meaning of Money

What is money? This might seem like an odd question. When you read that billionaire Bill Gates has a lot of money, you know what that means: He is so rich that he can buy almost anything he wants. In this sense, the term *money* is used to mean *wealth.*

money
the set of assets in an economy that people regularly use to buy goods and services from other people

Economists, however, use the word in a more specific sense: **Money** is the set of assets in the economy that people regularly use to buy goods and services from other people. The cash in your wallet is money because you can use it to buy a meal at a restaurant or a shirt at a clothing store. By contrast, if you happened to own most of Microsoft Corporation, as Bill Gates does, you would be wealthy, but this asset is not considered a form of money. You could not buy a meal or a shirt with this wealth without first obtaining some cash. According to the economist's definition, money includes only those few types of wealth that are regularly accepted by sellers in exchange for goods and services.

10-1a The Functions of Money

Money has three functions in the economy: It is a *medium of exchange,* a *unit of account,* and a *store of value*. These three functions together distinguish money from other assets in the economy, such as stocks, bonds, real estate, art, and even hockey cards. Let's examine each of these functions of money in turn.

medium of exchange
an item that buyers give to sellers when they want to purchase goods or services

A **medium of exchange** is an item that buyers give to sellers when they purchase goods and services. When you buy a shirt at a clothing store, the store gives you the shirt, and you give the store your money. This transfer of money from buyer to seller allows the transaction to take place. When you walk into a store, you are confident that the store will accept your money for the items it is selling because money is the commonly accepted medium of exchange.

unit of account
the yardstick people use to post prices and record debts

A **unit of account** is the yardstick people use to post prices and record debts. When you go shopping, you might observe that a shirt costs $20 and a hamburger costs $2. Even though it would be accurate to say that the price of a shirt is 10 hamburgers and the price of a hamburger is 1/10 of a shirt, prices are never quoted in this way. Similarly, if you take out a loan from a bank, the size of your future loan repayments will be measured in dollars, not in a quantity of goods and services. When we want to measure and record economic value, we use money as the unit of account.

store of value
an item that people can use to transfer purchasing power from the present to the future

A **store of value** is an item that people can use to transfer purchasing power from the present to the future. When a seller accepts money today in exchange for a good or service, that seller can hold the money and become a buyer of another good or service at another time. Of course, money is not the only store of value in the economy, because a person can also transfer purchasing power from the present to the future by holding other assets. The term *wealth* is used to refer to the total of all stores of value, including both money and nonmonetary assets.

liquidity
the ease with which an asset can be converted into the economy's medium of exchange

Economists use the term **liquidity** to describe the ease with which an asset can be converted into the economy's medium of exchange. Because money is the economy's medium of exchange, it is the most liquid asset available. Other assets vary widely in their liquidity. Most stocks and bonds can be sold easily with small cost, so they are relatively liquid assets. By contrast, selling a house, a Rembrandt painting, or a 1966 Bobby Orr hockey card requires more time and effort, so these assets are less liquid.

When people decide in what form to hold their wealth, they have to balance the liquidity of each possible asset against the asset's usefulness as a store of value. Money is the most liquid asset, but it is far from perfect as a store of value. When prices rise, the value of money falls. In other words, when goods and services become more expensive, each dollar in your wallet can buy less. This link between the price level and the value of money will turn out to be important for understanding how money affects the economy.

10-1b The Kinds of Money

When money takes the form of a commodity with intrinsic value, it is called **commodity money**. The term *intrinsic value* means that the item would have value even if it were not used as money. One example of commodity money is gold. Gold has intrinsic value because it is used in industry and in the making of jewellery. Although today we no longer use gold as money, historically gold has been a common form of money because it is relatively easy to carry, measure, and verify for impurities. When an economy uses gold as money (or uses paper money that is convertible into gold on demand), it is said to be operating under a *gold standard.*

commodity money
money that takes the form of a commodity with intrinsic value

Another example of commodity money is cigarettes. In prisoner-of-war camps during World War II, prisoners traded goods and services with one another using cigarettes as the store of value, unit of account, and medium of exchange. Similarly, as the Soviet Union was breaking up in the late 1980s, cigarettes started replacing the ruble as the preferred currency in Moscow. In both cases, even nonsmokers were happy to accept cigarettes in an exchange, knowing that they could use the cigarettes to buy other goods and services.

Money without intrinsic value is called **fiat money**. A *fiat* is simply an order or decree, and fiat money is established as money by government decree. For example, compare the paper dollars in your wallet (printed by the Canadian government) and the paper dollars from a game of Monopoly (printed by the Parker Brothers game company). Why can you use the first to pay your bill at a restaurant but not the second? The answer is that the Canadian government has decreed its dollars to be valid money. Each paper dollar in your wallet reads: "This note is legal tender."

fiat money
money without intrinsic value that is used as money because of government decree

Although the government is central to establishing and regulating a system of fiat money (by prosecuting counterfeiters, for example), other factors are also required for the success of such a monetary system. To a large extent, the acceptance of fiat money depends as much on expectations and social convention as on government decree. The Soviet government in the 1980s never abandoned the ruble as the official currency. Yet the people of Moscow preferred to accept cigarettes (or even American dollars) in exchange for goods and services, because they were more confident that these alternative monies would be accepted by others in the future.

10-1c Money in the Canadian Economy

As we will see, the quantity of money circulating in the economy, called the *money stock,* has a powerful influence on many economic variables. But before we consider why that is true, we need to ask a preliminary question: What is the quantity of money? In particular, suppose you were given the task of measuring how much money there is in the Canadian economy. What would you include in your measure?

The most obvious asset to include is **currency**—the paper bills and coins in the hands of the public. Currency is clearly the most widely accepted medium of exchange in our economy. There is no doubt that it is part of the money stock.

currency
the paper bills and coins in the hands of the public

IN THE **news**

Why Gold?

For many centuries, when societies have used a form of commodity money, the most common choice has been the gold standard. This outcome may have a sound scientific basis.

A Chemist Explains Why Gold Beat Out Lithium, Osmium, Einsteinium ...

By Jacob Goldstein and David Kestenbaum

The periodic table lists 118 different chemical elements. And yet, for thousands of years, humans have really, really liked one of them in particular: gold. Gold has been used as money for millennia, and its price has been going through the roof.

Why gold? Why not osmium, lithium, or ruthenium?

We went to an expert to find out: Sanat Kumar, a chemical engineer at Columbia University. We asked him to take the periodic table, and start eliminating anything that wouldn't work as money.

The periodic table looks kind of like a bingo card. Each square has a different element in it—one for carbon, another for gold, and so on.

Sanat starts with the far-right column of the table. The elements there have a really appealing characteristic: They're not going to change. They're chemically stable.

But there's also a big drawback: They're gases. You could put all your gaseous money in a jar, but if you opened the jar, you'd be broke. So Sanat crosses out the right-hand column.

Then he swings over to the far left-hand column, and points to one of the elements there: Lithium.

"If you expose lithium to air, it will cause a huge fire that can burn through concrete walls," he says.

Money that spontaneously bursts into flames is clearly a bad idea. In fact, you don't want your money undergoing any kind of spontaneous chemical reactions. And it turns out that a lot of the elements in the periodic table are pretty reactive.

Not all of them burst into flames. But sometimes they corrode, start to fall apart.

So Sanat crosses out another 38 elements, because they're too reactive.

Then we ask him about those two weird rows at the bottom of the table. They're always broken out separately from the main table, and they have some great names—promethium, einsteinium. But it turns out they're radioactive—put some einsteinium in your pocket, and a year later, you'll be dead.

So we're down from 118 elements to 30, and we've come up with a list of three key requirements:

1. Not a gas.
2. Doesn't corrode or burst into flames.
3. Doesn't kill you.

Now Sanat adds a new requirement: You want the thing you pick to be rare. This lets him cross off a lot of the boxes near the top of the table, because the elements clustered there tend to be more abundant.

TAGSTOCK1/Shutterstock.com. Coin images © 2016 Royal Canadian Mint. All rights reserved.

At the same time, you don't want to pick an element that's too rare. So osmium—which apparently comes to earth via meteorites—gets the axe.

That leaves us with just five elements: rhodium, palladium, silver, platinum and gold. And all of them, as it happens, are considered precious metals.

But even here we can cross things out. Silver has been widely used as money, of course. But it's reactive—it tarnishes. So Sanat says it's not the best choice.

Early civilizations couldn't have used rhodium or palladium, because they weren't discovered until the early 1800s.

That leaves platinum and gold, both of which can be found in rivers and streams.

But if you were in the ancient world and wanted to make platinum coins, you would have needed some sort of magic furnace from the future. The melting point for platinum is over 3,000 degrees Fahrenheit.

Gold happens to melt at a much lower temperature, which made it much easier for pre-industrial people to work with.

So we ask Sanat: If we could run the clock back and start history again, could things go a different way, or would gold emerge again as the element of choice?

"For the earth, with every parameter we have, gold is the sweet spot," he says. "It would come out no other way."

Yet currency is not the only asset that you can use to buy goods and services. Many stores also accept personal cheques and debit cards. Wealth held in your chequing account is almost as convenient for buying things as wealth held in your wallet. To measure the money stock, therefore, you might want to include **demand deposits**—balances in bank accounts that depositors can access on demand simply by writing a cheque or using a debit card.

demand deposits
balances in bank accounts that depositors can access on demand by writing a cheque or using a debit card

Once you start to consider balances in chequing accounts as part of the money stock, you are led to consider the large variety of other accounts that people hold at banks and other financial institutions. Bank depositors can often write cheques against the balances in their savings accounts, and they can easily transfer funds from savings into chequing accounts. In addition, depositors in money market mutual funds can sometimes write cheques against their balances. Thus, these other accounts should plausibly be part of the Canadian money stock.

In a complex economy such as ours, it is not easy to draw a line between assets that can be called "money" and assets that cannot. The coins in your pocket are clearly part of the money stock, and the CN Tower clearly is not, but there are many assets in between these extremes for which the choice is less clear. Therefore, various measures of the money stock are available for the Canadian economy. Figure 10.1 shows two important measures, designated M1+ and M2. Each of these measures uses a slightly different criterion for distinguishing monetary and nonmonetary assets.

For our purposes in this book, we need not dwell on the differences between the various measures of money. The important point is that the money stock for the Canadian economy includes not just currency but also deposits in banks and other financial institutions that can be readily accessed and used to buy goods and services.

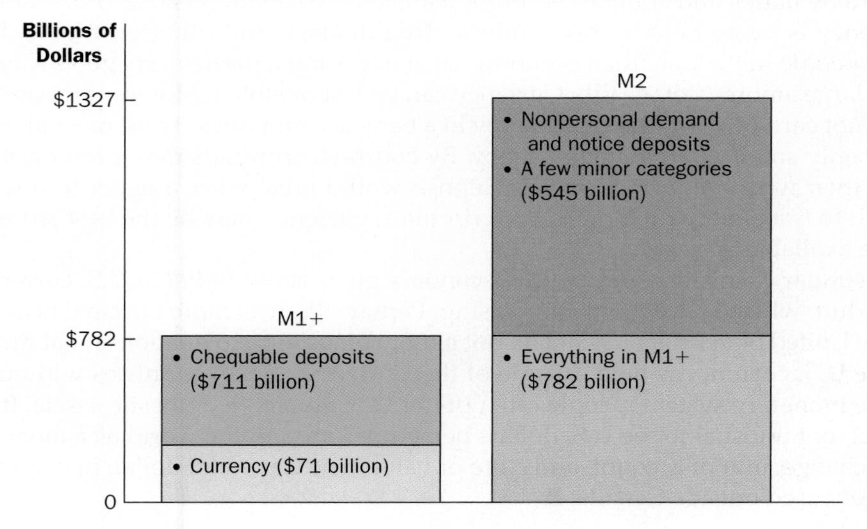

FIGURE 10.1

Two Measures of the Money Stock for the Canadian Economy

Two important measures of the money stock are what the Bank of Canada defines as M1+ and M2. This figure shows the size of each measure in June 2015.

Source: Bank of Canada.

FYI Credit Cards, Debit Cards, and Money

It might seem natural to include credit cards as part of the economy's stock of money. After all, people use credit cards to make many of their purchases. Aren't credit cards, therefore, a medium of exchange?

Although at first this argument may seem persuasive, credit cards are excluded from all measures of the quantity of money. The reason is that credit cards are not really a method of payment but a method of *deferring* payment. When you buy a meal with a credit card, the bank that issued the card pays the restaurant what it is due. At a later date, you will have to repay the bank (perhaps with interest). When the time comes to pay your credit card bill, you will probably do so by writing a cheque against your chequing account. The balance in this chequing account is part of the economy's stock of money.

Notice that credit cards are very different from debit cards, which automatically withdraw funds from a bank account to pay for items bought. Rather than allowing the user to postpone payment for a purchase, a debit card allows the user immediate access to deposits in a bank account. In this sense, a debit card is more similar to a cheque than to a credit card. The account balances that lie behind debit cards are included in measures of the quantity of money.

Even though credit cards are not considered a form of money, they are nonetheless important for analyzing the monetary system. People who have credit cards can pay many of their bills all at once at the end of the month, rather than sporadically as they make purchases. As a result, people who have credit cards probably hold less money on average than people who do not have credit cards. Thus, the introduction and increased popularity of credit cards may reduce the amount of money that people choose to hold.

case study — Where Is All the Currency?

One puzzle about the money stock of the Canadian economy concerns the amount of currency. In 2015, there was about $71 billion of currency outstanding. To put this number in perspective, we can divide it by 28.9 million, the number of adults (aged 18 and over) in Canada in 2015. This calculation implies that the average adult holds about $2457 of currency. Most people are surprised to learn that our economy has so much currency because they carry far less than this in their wallets.

Who is holding all this currency? No one knows for sure. Some of the currency is held by banks and companies, but a plausible explanation is that much of the currency is being held by tax evaders, drug dealers, and other criminals. For most people in the Canadian economy, currency is not a particularly good way to hold large amounts of wealth. Currency can be lost or stolen. Moreover, currency does not earn interest, whereas money in a bank account does. Thus, most people hold only small amounts of currency. By contrast, criminals may prefer not to hold their wealth in banks. A bank deposit would give police a paper trail with which to trace illegal activities. For criminals, currency may be the best store of value available.

A similar calculation for the U.S. economy gives about $4490 in U.S. currency per adult, which is even more surprising. Perhaps there is more criminal activity in the United States than in Canada but a more plausible explanation is that much of the U.S. currency is held outside of the United States. In countries without a stable monetary system, people often prefer U.S. dollars to domestic assets. It is, in fact, not unusual to see U.S. dollars being used around the world as a medium of exchange, unit of account, and store of value. The Canadian dollar, in contrast, is rarely used outside Canada. ■

Martin Novak/Shutterstock.com

List and describe the three functions of money.

10-2 The Bank of Canada

Whenever an economy relies on a system of fiat money, as the Canadian economy does, some organization must be responsible for controlling the stock of money. In Canada, that organization is the **Bank of Canada**. If you look at a Canadian bank note, you will see on it the words "Bank of Canada" and the signatures of the governor and the deputy governor of the Bank of Canada. The Bank of Canada is an example of a **central bank**—an institution designed to control the quantity of money in the economy. Other major central banks around the world include the Bank of England, the Bank of Japan, the European Central Bank, and the Federal Reserve of the United States.

Bank of Canada
the central bank of Canada

central bank
an institution designed to regulate the quantity of money in the economy

10-2a The Bank of Canada Act

Until the Great Depression of the 1930s, Canada had no central bank. Bank notes were issued by the Department of Finance and by the large commercial banks, like the Bank of Montreal. The monetary system was regulated by the Department of Finance, acting in concert with those large commercial banks. The gold standard ensured that bank notes could normally be exchanged for a fixed quantity of gold. The economic problems of the Great Depression, and the need to control the quantity of fiat money when the gold standard collapsed, led the government to set up a royal commission to study the issues. The commission recommended that a central bank be established. As a result, in 1934 Parliament enacted the Bank of Canada Act, which laid down the responsibilities of the Bank of Canada. The Bank was established in 1935 and nationalized in 1938, so it is now owned by the Canadian government.

The Bank of Canada is managed by a board of directors composed of the governor, the senior deputy governor, and 12 directors, including the deputy minister of Finance. All members of the board of directors are appointed by the minister of Finance, with seven-year terms for the governor and senior deputy governor and three-year terms for the other directors.

The significance of this management structure is that ultimately the Bank of Canada is controlled by the Canadian government; the government not only appoints the board of directors but can, as a last resort, issue a written directive to the governor with which he or she must comply. In practice, however, the Bank of Canada is largely independent of the Canadian government. Just as Supreme Court judges are appointed for life to insulate them from politics, the seven-year term of the governor of the Bank of Canada provides insulation from short-term political pressures when the governor formulates monetary policy. And it is generally accepted that the governor would immediately resign if issued with a written directive from the minister of Finance. The threat of the turmoil in financial markets that would follow the governor's resignation means that the Finance minister would use this weapon only as a last resort.

Commercial banks, like the "Big 5"—Bank of Montreal, Royal Bank, TD Bank, CIBC, and Scotiabank—are owned by their individual shareholders. The primary responsibility of these commercial banks is to maximize the profits they earn on behalf of these shareholders. Central banks like the Bank of Canada are owned by the government and hand over to the government any profits they earn. Their primary responsibility, however, is not to maximize profits but to act in the national interest. The preamble to the Bank of Canada Act reads:

> "Whereas it is desirable to establish a central bank in Canada to regulate credit and currency in the best interests of the economic life of the nation, to control and protect the external value of the national monetary unit and to mitigate by its influence fluctuations in the general level of production, trade, prices and employment, so far as may be possible within the scope of monetary action, and generally to promote the economic and financial welfare of Canada...."
>
> **Source:** Bank of Canada Act [R.S.C. 1985, c. B-2].

The Bank of Canada has four related jobs. The first is to issue currency. The Bank of Canada Act gives the Bank a monopoly over the right to issue notes for circulation in Canada. The second job is to act as banker to the commercial banks. Just as you may have a demand deposit at the Bank of Montreal, so the Bank of Montreal (and the other large commercial banks) has a demand deposit at the Bank of Canada. These deposits at the Bank of Canada enable the commercial banks to make payments to each other. The Bank of Canada makes daily loans to banks when banks themselves need to borrow money to make payments to other banks. Also, when financially troubled banks find themselves short of cash, the Bank of Canada may occasionally act as a lender of last resort—a lender to those who cannot borrow anywhere else—in order to maintain stability in the overall banking system. The third job is to act as banker to the Canadian government. The Government of Canada has a demand deposit at the Bank of Canada as well as demand deposits at the large commercial banks. The Bank of Canada manages the government's bank accounts, and also manages Canada's foreign exchange reserves and national debt on behalf of the government.

The Bank of Canada's fourth and most important job is to control the quantity of money that is made available to the economy, called the **money supply**. Decisions by policymakers concerning the money supply constitute **monetary policy**.

money supply
the quantity of money available in the economy

monetary policy
the setting of the money supply by policymakers in the central bank

10-2b Monetary Policy

The Bank of Canada has the power to increase or decrease the number of dollars in the economy. In simple metaphorical terms, you can imagine the Bank of Canada printing up $20 bills and dropping them around the country by helicopter. Similarly, you can imagine the Bank of Canada using a giant vacuum cleaner to suck $20 bills out of people's wallets. Although in practice the Bank of Canada's methods of controlling the money supply are more complex and subtle than this, the helicopter–vacuum metaphor is a good first approximation of the meaning of *monetary policy*. We discuss later how the Bank of Canada actually changes the money supply.

The Bank of Canada is an important institution because changes in the money supply can profoundly affect the economy. One of the ten principles of economics identified in Chapter 1 is that prices rise when the government prints too much money. Another of these ten principles is that society faces a short-run tradeoff between inflation and unemployment. The power of the Bank of Canada rests on these principles.

For reasons we discuss more fully in coming chapters, the Bank of Canada's policy decisions have an important influence on the economy's rate of inflation in the long run and the economy's employment and production in the short run. Indeed, the governor of the Bank of Canada might be called the second most powerful person in Canada. To learn more about the Bank of Canada, check out its website at www.bankofcanada.ca.

What is the difference between a central bank like the Bank of Canada and a commercial bank like the Bank of Montreal?

10-3 Commercial Banks and the Money Supply

So far we have introduced the concept of "money" and discussed the role of the Bank of Canada. Although the Bank of Canada alone is responsible for Canadian monetary policy, the central bank can control the supply of money only through its influence on the entire banking system. We now look at the role played by commercial banks (which include credit unions, caisses populaires, and trust companies) in the monetary system.

Recall that the amount of money you hold includes both currency (the bills in your wallet and coins in your pocket) and demand deposits (the balance in your chequing account). Because demand deposits are held in banks, the behaviour of banks can influence the quantity of demand deposits in the economy and, therefore, the money supply. This section examines how banks affect the money supply and, in doing so, how they complicate the Bank of Canada's job of controlling the money supply.

10-3a The Simple Case of 100 Percent-Reserve Banking

To see how banks influence the money supply, it is useful to imagine first a world without any banks at all. In this simple world, currency is the only form of money. To be concrete, let's suppose that the total quantity of currency is $100. The supply of money is, therefore, $100.

Now suppose that someone opens a bank, appropriately called First National Bank. First National Bank is only a depository institution—that is, it accepts deposits but does not make loans. The purpose of the bank is to give depositors a safe place to keep their money. Whenever a person deposits some money, the bank keeps the money in its vault until the depositor comes to withdraw it or writes a cheque against his or her balance. Deposits that banks have received but have not loaned out are called **reserves**. In this imaginary economy, all deposits are held as reserves, so this system is called *100 percent-reserve banking.*

reserves
deposits that banks have received but have not loaned out

We can express the financial position of First National Bank with a *T-account*, which is a simplified accounting statement that shows changes in a bank's assets and liabilities. Here is the T-account for First National Bank if the economy's entire $100 of money is deposited in the bank:

FIRST NATIONAL BANK

Assets		Liabilities	
Reserves	$100.00	Deposits	$100.00

On the left-hand side of the T-account are the bank's assets of $100 (the reserves it holds in its vaults). On the right-hand side of the T-account are the bank's liabilities of $100 (the amount it owes to its depositors). Notice that the assets and liabilities of First National Bank exactly balance.

Now consider the money supply in this imaginary economy. Before First National Bank opens, the money supply is the $100 of currency that people are holding. After the bank opens and people deposit their currency, the money supply is the $100 of demand deposits. (There is no longer any currency outstanding, because it is all in the bank vault.) Each deposit in the bank reduces currency and raises demand deposits by exactly the same amount, leaving the money supply unchanged. Thus, *if banks hold all deposits in reserve, banks do not influence the supply of money.*

10-3b Money Creation with Fractional-Reserve Banking

Eventually, the bankers at First National Bank may start to reconsider their policy of 100 percent-reserve banking. Leaving all that money sitting idle in their vaults seems unnecessary. Why not use some of it to make loans? Families buying houses and firms building new factories would be happy to pay interest to borrow some of that money for a while. Of course, First National Bank has to keep some reserves so that currency is available if depositors want to make withdrawals. But if the flow of new deposits is roughly the same as the flow of withdrawals, First National needs to keep only a fraction of its deposits in reserve. Thus, First National adopts a system called **fractional-reserve banking**.

fractional-reserve banking
a banking system in which banks hold only a fraction of deposits as reserves

reserve ratio
the fraction of deposits that banks hold as reserves

The fraction of total deposits that a bank holds as reserves is called the **reserve ratio**. This ratio is determined by a combination of government regulation and bank policy. As we discuss more fully later in the chapter, some central banks place a minimum on the amount of reserves that banks hold, called a *reserve requirement*. In addition, banks may hold reserves above the legal minimum, called *excess reserves*, so they can be more confident that they will not run short of cash. For our purpose here, we just take the reserve ratio as given and examine what fractional-reserve banking means for the money supply.

Let's suppose that First National has a reserve ratio of 10 percent. This means that it keeps 10 percent of its deposits in reserve and loans out the rest. Now let's look again at the bank's T-account:

FIRST NATIONAL BANK

Assets		Liabilities	
Reserves	$10.00	Deposits	$100.00
Loans	90.00		

First National still has $100 in liabilities because making the loans did not alter the bank's obligation to its depositors. But now the bank has two kinds of assets: It has $10 of reserves in its vault, and it has loans of $90. (These loans are liabilities of the people taking out the loans but they are assets of the bank making the loans, because the borrowers will later repay the bank.) In total, First National's assets still equal its liabilities.

Once again consider the supply of money in the economy. Before First National makes any loans, the money supply is the $100 of deposits in the bank. Yet when First National makes these loans, the money supply increases. The depositors still have demand deposits totalling $100, but now the borrowers hold $90 in currency. The money supply (which equals currency plus demand deposits) equals $190. Thus, *when banks hold only a fraction of deposits in reserve, banks create money.*

At first, this creation of money by fractional-reserve banking may seem too good to be true because it appears that the bank has created money out of thin air. To make this creation of money seem less miraculous, note that when First National Bank loans out some of its reserves and creates money, it does not create any wealth. Loans from First National give the borrowers some currency and thus the ability to buy goods and services. Yet the borrowers are also taking on debts, so the loans do not make them any richer. In other words, as a bank creates the asset of money, it also creates a corresponding liability for its borrowers. At the end of this process of money creation, the economy is more liquid in the sense that there is more of the medium of exchange, but the economy is no wealthier than before.

10-3c The Money Multiplier

The creation of money does not stop with First National Bank. Suppose the borrower from First National uses the $90 to buy something from someone who then deposits the currency in Second National Bank. Here is the T-account for Second National Bank:

SECOND NATIONAL BANK

Assets		Liabilities	
Reserves	$9.00	Deposits	$90.00
Loans	81.00		

After the deposits, this bank has liabilities of $90. If Second National also has a reserve ratio of 10 percent, it keeps assets of $9 in reserve and makes $81 in loans. In this way, Second National Bank creates an additional $81 of money. If this $81 is eventually deposited in Third National Bank, which also has a reserve ratio of 10 percent, this bank keeps $8.10 in reserve and makes $72.90 in loans. Here is the T-account for Third National Bank:

THIRD NATIONAL BANK

Assets		Liabilities	
Reserves	$8.10	Deposits	$81.00
Loans	72.90		

The process goes on and on. Each time that money is deposited and a bank loan is made, more money is created.

How much money is eventually created in this economy? Let's add it up:

Original deposit	= $100.00
First National lending	= $90.00 [= 0.9 × $100.00]
Second National lending	= $81.00 [= 0.9 × $90.00]
Third National lending	= $72.90 [= 0.9 × $81.00]
⋮	⋮
Total money supply	= $1000.00

It turns out that even though this process of money creation can continue forever, it does not create an infinite amount of money. If you laboriously add the infinite sequence of numbers in the foregoing example, you find the $100 of reserves generates $1000 of money. The amount of money the banking system generates with each dollar of reserves is called the **money multiplier**. In this imaginary economy, where the $100 of reserves generates $1000 of money, the money multiplier is 10.

money multiplier
the amount of money the banking system generates with each dollar of reserves

What determines the size of the money multiplier? It turns out that the answer is simple: *The money multiplier is the reciprocal of the reserve ratio.* If R is the reserve ratio for all banks in the economy, then each dollar of reserves generates $1/R$ dollars of money. In our example, $R = 1/10$, so the money multiplier is 10.

This reciprocal formula for the money multiplier makes sense. If a bank holds $1000 in deposits, then a reserve ratio of 1/10 (10 percent) means that the bank must hold $100 in reserves. The money multiplier just turns this idea around: If the banking system as a whole holds a total of $100 in reserves, it can have only $1000 in deposits. In other words, if R is the ratio of reserves to deposits at each bank (that is, the reserve ratio), then the ratio of deposits to reserves in the banking system (that is, the money multiplier) must be $1/R$.

This formula shows how the amount of money that banks create depends on the reserve ratio. If the reserve ratio was only 1/20 (5 percent), then the banking system would have 20 times as much in deposits as in reserves, implying a money multiplier of 20. Each dollar of reserves would generate $20 of money. Similarly, if the reserve ratio was 1/5 (20 percent), deposits would be 5 times reserves, the money multiplier would be 5, and each dollar of reserves would generate $5 of money. *Thus, the higher the reserve ratio, the less of each deposit banks loan out, and the smaller the money multiplier.* In the special case of 100 percent-reserve banking, the reserve ratio is 1, the money multiplier is 1, and banks do not make loans or create money.

10-3d Bank Capital, Leverage, and the Financial Crisis of 2007–09

In the previous sections, we have seen a very simplified explanation of how banks work. The reality of modern banking, however, is a bit more complicated, and this complex reality played a leading role in the financial crisis of 2007–09. Before looking at that crisis, we need to learn a bit more about how banks actually function.

In the bank balance sheets you have seen so far, a bank accepts deposits and uses those deposits either to make loans or to hold reserves. More realistically, a bank gets financial resources not only from accepting deposits but also, like other companies, from issuing equity and debt. The resources that a bank obtains from issuing equity to its owners are called **bank capital**. A bank uses these financial resources in various ways to generate profit for its owners. It not only makes loans and holds reserves but also buys financial securities, such as stocks and bonds.

bank capital
the resources a bank's owners have put into the institution

Here is a more realistic example of a bank's balance sheet:

MORE REALISTIC NATIONAL BANK

Assets		Liabilities and Owners' Equity	
Reserves	$200	Deposits	$800
Loans	700	Debt	150
Securities	100	Capital (owners' equity)	50

On the right side of this balance sheet are the bank's liabilities and capital (also known as *owners' equity*). This bank obtained $50 of resources from its owners. It also took in $800 of deposits and issued $150 of debt. The total of $1000 was put to use in three ways; these are listed on the left side of the balance sheet, which shows the bank's assets. This bank held $200 in reserves, made $700 in bank loans, and used $100 to buy financial securities, such as government or corporate bonds. The bank decides how to allocate its resources among asset classes based on their risk and return, as well as on any regulations that restrict the bank's choices.

By the rules of accounting, the reserves, loans, and securities on the left side of the balance sheet must always equal, in total, the deposits, debt, and capital on the right side of the balance sheet. There is no magic in this equality. It occurs because the value of the owners' equity is, by definition, the value of the bank's assets (reserves, loans, and securities) minus the value of its liabilities (deposits and debt). Therefore, the left and right sides of the balance sheet always sum to the same total.

Many businesses in the economy rely on **leverage**, the use of borrowed money to supplement existing funds for investment purposes. Indeed, whenever anyone uses debt to finance an investment project, he is applying leverage. Leverage is particularly important for banks, however, because borrowing and lending are at the heart of what they do. To fully understand banking, therefore, it is crucial to understand how leverage works.

leverage
the use of borrowed money to supplement existing funds for purposes of investment

The **leverage ratio** is the ratio of the bank's total assets to bank capital. In this example, the leverage ratio is $1000/$50, or 20. A leverage ratio of 20 means that for every dollar of capital that the bank owners have contributed, the bank has $20 of assets. Of the $20 of assets, $19 are financed with borrowed money—either by taking in deposits or issuing debt.

leverage ratio
the ratio of assets to bank capital

You may have learned in a science class that a lever can amplify a force: A boulder that you cannot move with your arms alone will move more easily if you use a lever. A similar result occurs with bank leverage. To see how this works, let's continue with this numerical example. Suppose that the bank's assets were to rise in value by 5 percent because, say, some of the securities the bank was holding rose in price. Then the $1000 of assets would now be worth $1050. Because the depositors and debt holders are still owed $950, the bank capital rises from $50 to $100. So when the leverage rate is 20, a 5 percent increase in the value of assets increases the owners' equity by 100 percent.

The same principle works on the downside, but with troubling consequences. Suppose that some people who borrowed from the bank default on their loans, reducing the value of the bank's assets by 5 percent, to $950. Because the depositors and debt holders have the legal right to be paid before the bank owners are paid, the value of the owners' equity falls to zero. So when the leverage ratio is 20, a 5 percent fall in the value of the bank assets leads to a 100 percent fall in bank capital. If the value of assets were to fall by more than 5 percent, the bank's assets would fall below its liabilities. In this case, the bank would be *insolvent*, and it would be unable to pay off its debt holders and depositors in full.

Bank regulators require banks to hold a certain amount of capital. The goal of such a **capital requirement** is to ensure that banks will be able to pay off their depositors (without having to resort to government-provided deposit insurance funds). The amount of capital required depends on the kind of assets a bank holds. If the bank holds safe assets such as government bonds, regulators require

capital requirement
a government regulation specifying a minimum amount of bank capital

less capital than if the bank holds risky assets such as loans to borrowers whose credit is of dubious quality.

In 2008 and 2009, many banks in the United States found themselves with too little capital after they had incurred losses on some of their assets—specifically, mortgage loans and securities backed by mortgage loans. The shortage of capital induced those banks to reduce their lending, a phenomenon sometimes called a *credit crunch,* which in turn contributed to a severe downturn in economic activity. To address this problem, the U.S. Treasury, working with the Federal Reserve, put many billions of dollars of public funds into the banking system to increase the amount of bank capital. As a result, it temporarily made the U.S. taxpayer a part owner of many banks. The goal of this unusual policy was to recapitalize the banking system so that bank lending could return to a more normal level, which, in fact, occurred by late 2009. Canadian banks weathered the financial crisis far better than U.S. banks, in part because the Office of the Superintendent of Financial Institutions (OSFI) had required they maintain higher capital requirements. The Canadian banks therefore proved to be more resilient to the financial crisis because they were able to maintain sufficient capital even as they suffered losses on some of their assets.

Late in 2010, an international agreement (known as *Basel III* after the town in Switzerland where an international committee on bank supervision meets) required that central banks impose higher minimum capital requirements on their national banks. The impact on Canadian banks of imposing these new minimum requirements is expected to be small because the new requirements are largely in line with OSFI requirements already in place.

10-3e The Bank of Canada's Tools of Monetary Control

As we have already discussed, the Bank of Canada is responsible for controlling the supply of money in the economy. Now that we understand how fractional-reserve banking works, we are in a better position to understand how the Bank of Canada can carry out this job. Because banks create money in a system of fractional-reserve banking, the Bank of Canada's control of the money supply is indirect. When the Bank of Canada decides to change the money supply, it must consider how its actions will work through the banking system.

Over its history, the Bank of Canada has used different methods of controlling the money supply. Different central banks around the world likewise use different tools of monetary control. Central banks have three main tools in their toolbox: open-market operations, changes in reserve requirements, and changes in the overnight rate. The Bank of Canada currently uses changes in the overnight rate to control the money supply, so let's start there.

Changing the Overnight Rate Central banks like the Bank of Canada act as bankers to the commercial banks. These banks hold demand deposits at the Bank of Canada, which are part of their reserves.

If Muriel, who has a chequing account at the Bank of Montreal, buys a car for $5000 from Julia, who has a chequing account at the TD Bank, the Bank of Montreal will deduct $5000 from Muriel's chequing account and pay $5000 to the TD Bank so that the TD Bank in turn can credit Julia's chequing account. Transfers between banks are done by the Bank of Canada. The Bank of Canada will deduct $5000 from the Bank of Montreal's demand deposit and add $5000 to the TD Bank's demand deposit. What happens if the Bank of Montreal doesn't have $5000 in its demand deposit at the Bank of Canada? The Bank of Montreal may then borrow from the Bank of Canada—in effect, it must get an overdraft. The rate of interest that central banks charge commercial banks for these loans is called the *discount rate* in some countries. In Canada it is called the **bank rate**.

bank rate
the interest rate charged by the Bank of Canada on loans to the commercial banks

Since 1998 the Bank of Canada has allowed commercial banks to borrow freely at the bank rate, and has paid commercial banks the bank rate, minus half a percent, on their deposits at the Bank of Canada. For example, if the bank rate is 5 percent, this means the Bank of Montreal must pay 5 percent interest if it needs to borrow from the Bank of Canada. And the Bank of Canada would pay 4.5 percent interest if the Bank of Montreal had a positive balance in its demand deposit at the Bank of Canada. What is called the *operating band* is then from 4.5 to 5 percent, which sets the pattern for all short-term interest rates in Canada.

Commercial banks never need to pay more than the bank rate for short-term loans, because they can always borrow from the Bank of Canada instead. Conversely, commercial banks never need to accept less than the bank rate, minus half a percent, when they make short-term loans, because they can always lend to the Bank of Canada instead. In practice, the **overnight rate**, which is the rate of interest on very short-term loans between commercial banks, stays very close to the middle of the operating band, so the overnight rate will always be about one-quarter of a percent below the bank rate.

overnight rate
the interest rate on very short-term loans between commercial banks

The Bank of Canada can alter the money supply by changing the bank rate, which in turn causes an equal change in the overnight rate. A higher overnight rate discourages banks from borrowing reserves from the Bank of Canada. Thus, an increase in the overnight rate reduces the quantity of reserves in the banking system, which in turn reduces the money supply. Conversely, a lower overnight rate encourages banks to borrow from the Bank of Canada, increases the quantity of reserves, and increases the money supply.

The Bank of Canada lowers the overnight rate whenever it wants the money supply to expand, and raises the overnight rate whenever it wants the money supply to contract. Because the overnight rate not only affects the money supply but also sets the pattern for all Canadian interest rates, changes in the overnight rate are a closely watched indicator of the Bank of Canada's views about the sort of monetary policy the Canadian economy needs. Since December 2000, the Bank of Canada has fixed eight dates each year, roughly six weeks apart, on which it announces whether it will raise the overnight rate, lower the overnight rate, or leave the overnight rate unchanged. It can also change the overnight rate at any time, if extraordinary action is needed.

Figure 10.2 shows values of the Bank of Canada's overnight rate from January 2008 to August 2015. The Bank responded strongly to the onset of recession in 2008 by quickly reducing the overnight rate and, consequently, causing the money supply to grow. By the middle of 2010 the Bank judged the economy to have recovered sufficiently that it could start to increase the overnight rate to more normal levels. From September 2010 to January 2015 the Bank held the overnight rate at 1.00 percent, but in January 2015, worried by signs of weak economic performance, it again reduced the overnight rate. A second reduction in the overnight rate was announced in July 2015 as the Bank continued its efforts to increase the money supply.

FIGURE 10.2

The Bank of Canada's Overnight Rate since 2008

At the beginning of 2008, the Bank of Canada quickly reduced the overnight rate in response to a recession. Renewed concern over the possibility of recession prompted the Bank to reduce the overnight rate in January and July of 2015. Reductions in the overnight rate increase the money supply.

Source: Bank of Canada, Canadian Interest Rates and Monetary Policy Variables: 10-Year Lookup, http://www.bankofcanada.ca/rates/interest-rates/canadian-interest-rates/

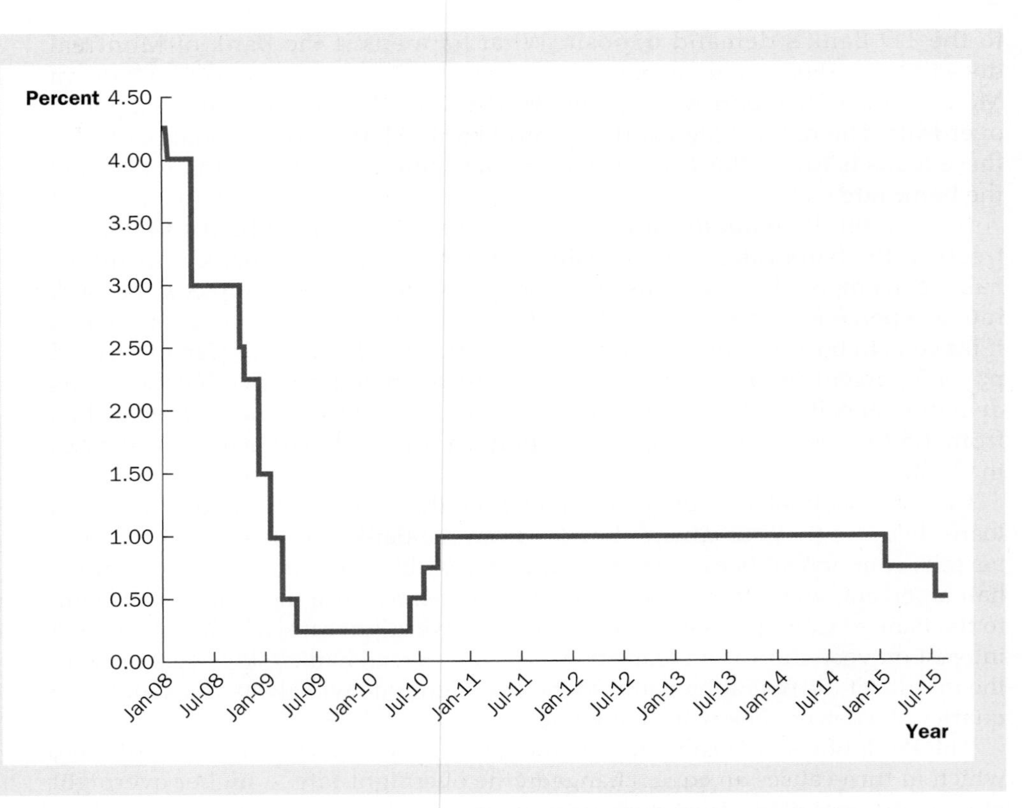

Open-Market Operations Central banks can increase the supply of money in circulation by buying something. They can decrease the supply of money by selling something. It really doesn't matter what the Bank of Canada buys or sells. For example, if the Bank of Canada buys a new computer for its researchers with $1000 of newly printed currency, the firm that sold the computer to the Bank of Canada now holds an extra $1000 cash, so the money supply increases by $1000 immediately. If the Bank of Canada sells a used computer for $200 cash, the quantity of currency in circulation will immediately decrease by $200.

Since the Bank of Canada does not buy or sell a large quantity of computers, any changes in the money supply from buying or selling computers are small enough to be ignored. But the Bank of Canada does buy from and sell to the public a large quantity of Canadian government bonds; these transactions are called **open-market operations**. To increase the money supply, the Bank of Canada periodically buys Treasury bills (a Treasury bill is just a short-term government bond). The dollars the Bank of Canada pays for the bonds increase the number of dollars in circulation. Some of these new dollars are held as currency; some are deposited in banks. Each new dollar held as currency increases the money supply by exactly $1. Each new dollar deposited in a bank increases the money supply by a greater extent because it increases reserves and, thereby, the amount of money that a fractional-reserve banking system can create.

open-market operations
the purchase or sale of government of Canada bonds by the Bank of Canada

To reduce the money supply, the Bank of Canada can do just the opposite: It can sell government bonds to the public. The public pays for these bonds with its holdings of currency and bank deposits, directly reducing the amount of money in circulation. In addition, as people make withdrawals from banks, banks find themselves with a smaller quantity of reserves. In response, banks reduce the amount of lending, and the process of money creation reverses itself.

While open-market operations are normally conducted using short-term government securities (Treasury bills), there is no reason why the Bank of Canada could not buy and sell government securities with longer maturities or even buy and sell nongovernment securities. Open-market operations that involve nongovernment securities or government securities with long terms to maturity have become known as **quantitative easing**. During the 2007–09 financial crisis, the U.S. Federal Reserve made use of quantitative easing as a way of increasing bank capital. By temporarily purchasing private bank assets, the Federal Reserve enabled private banks to meet their capital requirements and so continue to make savings available to borrowers.

quantitative easing
the purchase and sale by the central bank of nongovernment securities or government securities with long maturity terms

The Bank of Canada did not need to rely on quantitative easing during the financial crisis, as Canadian banks proved better able to maintain bank capital and so weather the crisis without intervention by the central bank. Quantitative easing is a tool of monetary control normally used only in extraordinary circumstances. It nonetheless is a tool of monetary policy that the Bank of Canada can employ if needed.

Another important market in which the Bank of Canada buys and sells things is the foreign exchange market, where its purchases and sales of foreign moneys are called **foreign exchange market operations**. If the Bank of Canada buys $100 million U.S. dollars in the foreign exchange market for $110 million Canadian, the Canadian money supply increases immediately by $110 million. If the Bank of Canada sells foreign currency from its foreign exchange reserves, it gets Canadian dollars in exchange. Those Canadian dollars are withdrawn from circulation, so the Canadian money supply is reduced.

foreign exchange market operations
the purchase or sale of foreign money by the Bank of Canada

Sometimes the Bank of Canada wants to sell foreign currency in the foreign exchange market to support the Canadian dollar's exchange rate, but does not want the money supply to fall. To do this, it uses the Canadian dollars it acquires in the foreign exchange market to buy Canadian government bonds, thus putting the Canadian dollars back into circulation. This process of offsetting a foreign exchange market operation with an open-market operation is called **sterilization**. Currently, the Bank of Canada routinely sterilizes foreign exchange market operations.

sterilization
the process of offsetting foreign exchange market operations with open-market operations, so that the effect on the money supply is cancelled out

Changing Reserve Requirements Some central banks around the world also influence the money supply with **reserve requirements**, which are regulations on the minimum amount of reserves that banks must hold against deposits. Reserve requirements influence how much money the banking system can create with each dollar of reserves. An increase in reserve requirements means that banks must hold more reserves and, therefore, can loan out less of each dollar that is deposited; as a result, it raises the reserve ratio, lowers the money multiplier, and decreases the money supply. Conversely, a decrease in reserve requirements lowers the reserve ratio, raises the money multiplier, and increases the money supply.

reserve requirements
regulations on the minimum amount of reserves that banks must hold against deposits

The Bank of Canada has rarely used changes in reserve requirements to control the money supply, because frequent changes would disrupt the business of banking. Indeed, since 1994 the Bank of Canada has phased out reserve requirements altogether to give banks a level playing field with other financial institutions, which are not required to hold reserves. This means that the Bank of Canada does not currently use changes in reserve requirements to change the money supply.

10-3f Problems in Controlling the Money Supply

The Bank of Canada has at its disposal a powerful set of tools that enables it to influence the size of the money supply. Yet the Bank of Canada's control of the money supply is not precise. The Bank of Canada must wrestle with two problems, each of which arises because much of the money supply is created by our system of fractional-reserve banking.

The first problem is that the Bank of Canada does not control the amount of money that households choose to hold as deposits in banks. The more money that households deposit, the more reserves banks have, and the more money

FYI

The Bank of Canada's Response to the 2007–09 Financial Crisis

While in normal times the Bank of Canada's tools for controlling the money supply are very effective at influencing the state of the economy and keeping it running smoothly, on rare occasions extraordinary additional steps are required. Such a rare occasion arose as a result of a financial crisis that began in 2007 and had its origins in the U.S. financial system.

In Chapter 8 (FYI: Financial Institutions in Crisis), we described how a crisis in the U.S. financial system triggered a series of events that would lead to widespread bankruptcies both within and outside the financial sector, a dramatic fall in stock prices, rapidly increasing unemployment rates, and concerns that the world's financial system was about to collapse. We described how most analysts believe the Canadian financial system avoided the worst of the financial crisis thanks in part to the tighter regulations imposed on Canadian financial institutions by the Bank of Canada and the Office of the Superintendent of Financial Institutions (OSFI).

But as well as relying on tighter regulations already in place, the Bank of Canada took a number of extraordinary steps designed to calm financial markets and better enable the Canadian financial system to weather the financial crisis. These extraordinary steps, which we describe here, are generally understood to have significantly lessened the impacts of the financial crisis.

An important role of the Bank of Canada is to ensure that financial institutions are able to interact with one another smoothly and efficiently. As described earlier, the Bank provides short-term loans (typically of one day or less) to private banks when a customer of one bank cashes a cheque drawn on an account held at a second bank. Should the second bank not have sufficient reserves with the Bank of Canada, where such exchanges are cleared, the Bank offers a loan and charges an interest rate known as the *overnight rate*. Essentially, the Bank makes it easier for financial institutions to convert any asset into money—the financial asset that all are readily willing to accept. In other words, the Bank adds *liquidity* to the financial system and so keeps it running smoothly.

Figure 10.2 shows that in 2008 and 2009, the Bank was responding to the financial crisis with a series of large reductions in its overnight rate. In normal times, such a large reduction in the overnight rate would have been sufficient to introduce the needed liquidity into the economy. Unfortunately, the financial crisis that began in 2007 ushered in a period that was far from normal. Financial institutions, unsure of their exposure to subprime mortgages and other so-called "toxic" assets, stopped trading with one another. Companies found it extremely difficult to secure loans to fund their day-to-day operations and so started to fail. The degree of liquidity in the system—the ease with which assets could be converted to money—quickly fell despite the fall in the overnight rate.

In the midst of this crisis, the Bank introduced extraordinary measures to add liquidity to the financial system. First, the Bank extended beyond one business day the length of time it would offer short-term loans to financial institutions. Second, the Bank expanded the set of assets it would accept as collateral for these short-term loans and in this way made the loans easier to obtain. Third, the Bank expanded the list of financial market participants to whom it would extend short-term loans. Finally, the Bank significantly increased the amount of liquidity it offered to financial institutions. By December 2008, the Bank was providing $41 billion of liquidity support to a far wider range of participants in the financial system than it had ever done previously.

Financial conditions improved throughout 2009, and as a consequence the Bank of Canada was able to begin to unwind its extraordinary measures. By early 2010, the financial crisis had subsided and financial conditions improved significantly in Canada and around the world. By the fall of 2010, the Bank of Canada was able to have completely unwound its extraordinary measures to maintain liquidity in the private banking sector.

Although the financial crisis has left behind higher unemployment rates, government deficits, and bankruptcies, the general consensus is that were it not for the innovative policies of the Bank of Canada and other major central banks around the world, the impacts would have been significantly worse. Indeed, given concerns that the financial crisis would precipitate an economic downturn similar to that experienced in the Great Depression of the 1930s, the actions of central banks would seem to have been highly successful.

the banking system can create. And the less money that households deposit, the less reserves banks have, and the less money the banking system can create. To see why this is a problem, suppose that one day people begin to lose confidence in the banking system and, therefore, decide to withdraw deposits and hold more currency. When this happens, the banking system loses reserves and creates less money. The money supply falls, even without any Bank of Canada action.

The second problem with monetary control is that the Bank of Canada does not control the amount that commercial bankers choose to lend. Once money is deposited in a bank, it creates more money only when the bank loans it out. Because banks can choose to hold excess reserves, the Bank of Canada cannot be sure how much money the banking system will create. For instance, suppose that one day bankers become more cautious about economic conditions and decide to make fewer loans and hold greater reserves. When this happens, the banking system creates less money than it otherwise would. Because of the bankers' decision, the money supply falls.

Hence, in a system of fractional-reserve banking, the amount of money in the economy depends in part on the behaviour of depositors and bankers. Because the Bank of Canada cannot control or perfectly predict this behaviour, it cannot perfectly control the money supply. But these problems need not be large. The Bank of Canada collects data on deposits every week, so it is quickly aware of any changes in the money supply caused by changes in depositor or banker behaviour. If the Bank of Canada discovers that the money supply is growing too fast, it can raise the overnight rate to slow it down. If the Bank of Canada discovers that the money supply is growing too slowly, or falling, it can lower the overnight rate to increase the money supply. The Bank of Canada is like the driver of a car using the gas pedal to control her speed. Many things may cause the car to speed up or slow down, but by watching the speedometer and adjusting the gas pedal accordingly, the driver can keep her speed close to the level she chooses.

case study

Bank Runs and the Money Supply

Although you have probably never witnessed a bank run in real life, you may have seen one depicted in movies such as *Mary Poppins* or *It's a Wonderful Life.* A bank run occurs when depositors suspect that a bank may go bankrupt and, therefore, "run" to the bank to withdraw their deposits. Canada has not seen a major bank run in recent history, but in the United Kingdom, a bank called Northern Rock experienced a run in 2007 and, as a result, was eventually taken over by the government. In 2012, fears about the viability of banks in Greece and Spain were causing significant numbers of depositors to withdraw their savings, raising the spectre of bank runs in those countries. Similar fears, particularly with respect to banks in Greece, caused another run on banks in that country in 2015 and prompted the government to limit the size of withdrawals.

Bank runs are a problem for banks under fractional-reserve banking. Because a bank holds only a fraction of its deposits in reserve, it cannot satisfy withdrawal requests from all depositors. Even if the bank is in fact solvent (meaning that its assets exceed its liabilities), it will not have enough cash on hand to allow all depositors immediate access to all of their money. When a run occurs, the bank is forced to close its doors until some bank loans are repaid or until some lender of last resort (such as the Bank of Canada) provides it with the currency it needs to satisfy depositors.

Bank runs complicate the control of the money supply. An important example of this problem occurred in the United States during the Great Depression in the early 1930s. After a wave of bank runs and bank closings, households and bankers became more cautious. Households withdrew their deposits from banks, preferring to hold their money in the form of currency. This decision reversed the process of money creation, as bankers responded to falling reserves by reducing bank loans. At the same time, bankers increased their reserve ratios so that they would have enough cash on hand to meet their depositors' demands in any future bank runs. The higher reserve ratio reduced the money multiplier, which also reduced the money supply. From 1929 to 1933, the U.S. money supply fell by 28 percent, even without the Federal Reserve (the U.S. central bank) taking any deliberate contractionary action. Many economists point to this massive fall in the U.S. money supply to explain the high unemployment and falling prices that prevailed during this period. (In future chapters we examine the mechanisms by which changes in the money supply affect unemployment and prices.)

Canadian banks in the 1930s were larger, more diversified, and safer than American banks. Canada did not experience the wave of bank runs and bank failures that happened in the United States. In Canada, banks' reserve ratios increased only slightly, and the decline in the Canadian money supply was much smaller. But the Great Depression was as bad in Canada as it was in the United States, perhaps because the Canadian economy was more dependent on international trade and exports of primary products, whose value dropped considerably during the Great Depression.

Today, bank runs are not a major problem for the banking system or the Bank of Canada. A few small banks did fail in the 1980s, but there were no major bank runs. The Office of the Superintendent of Financial Institutions monitors financial institutions in Canada to try to prevent bankruptcies. Also, the federal government now guarantees the safety of deposits up to $100 000 at Canadian banks through the Canada Deposit Insurance Corporation (CDIC). Small depositors do not run on their banks because they are confident that even if their banks go bankrupt the CDIC will make good on the deposits. As a result, most people see bank runs only in the movies. ■

Describe how banks create money. If the Bank of Canada wanted to use all three of its policy tools to decrease the money supply, what would it do?

10-4 Conclusion

Whenever we buy or sell anything, we are relying on the extraordinarily useful social convention called *money*. Now that we know what money is and what determines its supply, we can discuss how changes in the quantity of money affect the economy. We begin to address that topic in the next chapter.

summary

- The term *money* refers to assets that people regularly use to buy goods and services.
- Money serves three functions. As a medium of exchange, it provides the item used to make transactions. As a unit of account, it provides the way in which prices and other economic values are recorded. As a store of value, it provides a way of transferring purchasing power from the present to the future.
- Commodity money, such as gold, is money that has intrinsic value: It would be valued even if it was not used as money. Fiat money, such as paper dollars, is money without intrinsic value: It would be worthless if it was not used as money.
- In the Canadian economy, money takes the form of currency and various types of bank deposits, such as chequing accounts.
- The Bank of Canada, Canada's central bank, is responsible for controlling the supply of money in Canada. The governor and senior deputy governor of the Bank of Canada are appointed for seven-year terms, and the other directors are appointed for three-year terms. All these appointments are made by the Canadian government, which owns the Bank of Canada.
- Bank depositors provide resources to banks by depositing their funds into bank accounts. These deposits are part of a bank's liabilities. Bank owners also provide resources (called bank capital) for the bank. Because of leverage (the use of borrowed funds for investment), a small change in the value of a bank's assets can lead to a large change in the value of the bank's capital. To protect depositors, bank regulators require banks to hold a certain minimum amount of capital.
- The Bank of Canada controls the supply of money primarily through changes in the overnight rate. Lowering the overnight rate increases the money supply, and raising the overnight rate reduces the money supply. The Bank of Canada may also control the money supply through open-market operations. The purchase of government of Canada bonds increases the money supply, and the sale of these bonds reduces the money supply.
- When banks loan out some of their deposits, they increase the quantity of money in the economy. Because of this role of banks in determining the money supply, the Bank of Canada's control of the money supply is imperfect.

KEY concepts

QUESTIONS FOR review

1. What distinguishes money from other assets in the economy?
2. What is commodity money? What is fiat money? Which kind do we use?
3. What are demand deposits, and why should they be included in the stock of money?
4. Who is responsible for setting monetary policy in Canada?
5. If the Bank of Canada wants to increase the money supply with open-market operations, what does it do?
6. Why don't banks hold 100 percent reserves? How is the amount of reserves banks hold related to the amount of money the banking system creates?
7. Bank A has a leverage ratio of 10, while Bank B has a leverage ratio of 20. Similar losses on bank loans at the two banks cause the value of their assets to fall by

7 percent. Which bank shows a larger change in bank capital? Does either bank remain solvent? Explain.

8. What is the overnight rate? What happens to the money supply when the Bank of Canada raises the overnight rate?

9. What are reserve requirements? What happens to the money supply when a central bank raises reserve requirements?

10. Why can't the Bank of Canada control the money supply perfectly?

QUICK CHECK **multiple choice**

1. The money supply includes all EXCEPT which of the following?
   a. metal coins
   b. paper currency
   c. lines of credit accessible with credit cards
   d. bank balances accessible with debit cards

2. Chloe takes $100 of currency from her wallet and deposits it into her chequing account. If the bank adds the entire $100 to reserves, the money supply _____, but if the bank lends out some of the $100, the money supply _____.
   a. increases, increases even more
   b. increases, increases by less
   c. is unchanged, increases
   d. decreases, decreases by less

3. If the reserve ratio is 1/4 and the central bank increases the quantity of reserves in the banking system by $120, the money supply increases by what amount?
   a. $90 c. $160
   b. $150 d. $480

4. A bank has capital of $200 and a leverage ratio of 5. If the value of the bank's assets declines by 10 percent, then its capital will be reduced to what amount?
   a. $100 c. $180
   b. $150 d. $185

5. Which of the following actions by the Bank of Canada would reduce the money supply?
   a. an open-market purchase of government bonds
   b. a reduction in banks' reserve requirements
   c. an increase in the interest rate paid on reserves
   d. a decrease in the discount rate on Bank of Canada lending

6. In a system of fractional-reserve banking, even without any action by the central bank, the money supply declines if households choose to hold _____ currency or if banks choose to hold _____ excess reserves.
   a. more, more c. less, more
   b. more, less d. less, less

PROBLEMS AND **applications**

1. Which of the following are money in the Canadian economy? Which are not? Explain your answers by discussing each of the three functions of money.
   a. a Canadian dollar coin
   b. a Mexican peso
   c. a Picasso painting
   d. a plastic credit card

2. Every month *Yankee* magazine includes a "Swopper's [*sic*] Column" of offers to barter goods and services. Here is an example: "Will swop custom-designed wedding gown and up to 6 bridesmaids' gowns for 2 round-trip plane tickets and 3 nights' lodging in the countryside of England." Why would it be difficult to run our economy using a "Swopper's Column" instead of money? In light of your answer, why might the *Yankee* "Swopper's Column" exist?

3. What characteristics of an asset make it useful as a medium of exchange? As a store of value?

4. Consider how the following situations would affect the economy's monetary system.
   a. Suppose that the people on Yap discovered an easy way to make limestone wheels. How would this development affect the usefulness of stone wheels as money? Explain.
   b. Suppose that someone in Canada discovered an easy way to counterfeit $100 bills. How would this development affect the Canadian monetary system? Explain.

5. Go to the website of the Bank of Canada at www.bankofcanada.ca and find the following information:
   a. data on the recent history of the overnight rate
   b. the next fixed announcement date

c. the Bank's latest press release about overnight rates, and why the Bank decided to change, or not change, its target for the overnight rate

6. Your uncle repays a $100 loan from Tenth National Bank by writing a $100 cheque on his TNB chequing account. Use T-accounts to show the effect of this transaction on your uncle and on TNB. Has your uncle's wealth changed? Explain.

7. Beleaguered Provincial Bank (BPB) holds $250 million in deposits and maintains a reserve ratio of 10 percent.
   a. Show a T-account for BPB.
   b. Now suppose that BPB's largest depositor withdraws $10 million in cash from her account. If BPB decides to restore its reserve ratio by reducing the amount of loans outstanding, show its new T-account.
   c. Explain what effect BPB's action will have on other banks.
   d. Why might it be difficult for BPB to take the action described in part (b)? Discuss another way for BPB to return to its original reserve ratio.

8. You take $100 you had kept under your mattress and deposit it in your bank account. If this $100 stays in the banking system as reserves and if banks hold reserves equal to 10 percent of deposits, by how much does the total amount of deposits in the banking system increase? By how much does the money supply increase?

9. The Bank of Canada conducts a $10 million open-market purchase of government bonds. If the required reserve ratio is 10 percent, what is the largest possible increase in the money supply that could result? Explain. What is the smallest possible increase? Explain.

10. Suppose that the T-account for First National Bank is as follows:

Assets		Liabilities	
Reserves	$100 000	Deposits	$500 000
Loans	400 000		

   a. If the Bank of Canada requires banks to hold 5 percent of deposits as reserves, how much in excess reserves does First National now hold?
   b. Assume that all other banks hold only the required amount of reserves. If First National decides to reduce its reserves to only the required amount, by how much would the economy's money supply increase?

11. Suppose there is a reserve requirement for private banks set at 10 percent of deposits. Also assume that banks do not hold any excess reserves.
   a. If the Bank of Canada sells $1 million of government bonds, what is the effect on the economy's reserves and money supply?
   b. Now suppose the Bank of Canada lowers the reserve requirement to 5 percent, but banks choose to hold another 5 percent of deposits as excess reserves. Why might banks do so? What is the overall change in the money multiplier and the money supply as a result of these actions?

12. Assume there is a reserve requirement of 20 percent. Also assume that banks do not hold excess reserves and there is no cash held by the public. The Bank of Canada decides that it wants to expand the money supply by $40 million.
   a. If the Bank of Canada is using open-market operations, will it buy or sell bonds?
   b. What quantity of bonds does the Bank of Canada need to buy or sell to accomplish the goal? Explain your reasoning.

13. Suppose that the Bank of Canada sells 100 million pounds sterling from its foreign exchange reserves, and that the exchange rate is $1.60 Canadian per pound sterling.
   a. Explain what happens to the Canadian money supply.
   b. Now suppose that the Bank of Canada does not want the money supply to change. What would it need to do to sterilize its foreign exchange market operation?

14. (This problem is challenging.) The economy of Elmendyn contains 2000 $1 bills.
   a. If people hold all money as currency, what is the quantity of money?
   b. If people hold all money as demand deposits and banks maintain 100 percent reserves, what is the quantity of money?
   c. If people hold equal amounts of currency and demand deposits and banks maintain 100 percent reserves, what is the quantity of money?
   d. If people hold all money as demand deposits and banks maintain a reserve ratio of 10 percent, what is the quantity of money?
   e. If people hold equal amounts of currency and demand deposits and banks maintain a reserve ratio of 10 percent, what is the quantity of money?

Maciej Korzekwa/Getty Images

CHAPTER 11

Money Growth and Inflation

LEARNING **objectives**

In this chapter, you will ...

1. See why inflation results from rapid growth in the money supply
2. Learn the meaning of the classical dichotomy and monetary neutrality
3. See why some countries print so much money that they experience hyperinflation
4. Examine how the nominal interest rate responds to the inflation rate
5. Consider the various costs that inflation imposes on society

Although today you need a dollar or two to buy yourself an ice-cream cone, life was very different 70 years ago. In one Trenton, New Jersey, candy store (run, incidentally, by one author's grandmother in the 1930s), ice-cream cones came in two sizes. A cone with a small scoop of ice cream cost three cents. Hungry customers could buy a large scoop for a nickel.

You are probably not surprised at the increase in the price of ice cream. In our economy, most prices tend to rise over time. This increase in the overall level of prices is called *inflation.* Earlier in the book we examined how economists measure the inflation rate as the percentage change in the consumer price index, the GDP deflator, or some other index of the overall price level. These price indexes show that, over the past 70 years, prices have risen on average about 4 percent per year. Accumulated over so many years, a 4 percent annual inflation rate leads to a 16-fold increase in the price level.

Inflation may seem natural and inevitable to a person who grew up in Canada during the second half of the twentieth century, but in fact it is not inevitable at all. There were long periods in the nineteenth century during which most prices fell—a phenomenon called *deflation.* The average level of prices in the Canadian economy was 37 percent lower in 1933 than in 1920, and this deflation was a major problem. Farmers, who had accumulated large debts, were suffering when the fall in crop prices reduced their incomes and thus their ability to pay off their debts. They advocated government policies to reverse the deflation. Japan has also experienced some deflation in recent years.

Although inflation has been the norm in more recent history, there has been substantial variation in the rate at which prices rise. During the 1990s, prices rose at an average rate of about 2 percent per year. By contrast, in the 1970s, prices rose by 7 percent per year, which meant a doubling of the price level over the decade. The public often views such high rates of inflation as a major economic problem.

International data show an even broader range of inflation experiences. In 2012, while the inflation rate in Canada was about 1.2 percent, inflation was –0.1 percent in Japan, 5.1 percent in Russia, 9.3 percent in India, and 21.1 percent in Venezuela. And even the high inflation rates in India and Venezuela are moderate by some standards. In February 2008, the central bank of Zimbabwe announced the inflation rate in its economy had reached 24 000 percent, while some independent estimates put the figure even higher. An extraordinarily high rate of inflation such as this is called *hyperinflation*.

What determines whether an economy experiences inflation and, if so, how much? This chapter answers this question by developing the *quantity theory of money.* Chapter 1 summarized this theory as one of the ten principles of economics: Prices rise when the government prints too much money. This insight has a long and venerable tradition among economists. The quantity theory was discussed by the famous eighteenth-century philosopher David Hume and has been advocated more recently by the prominent economist Milton Friedman. This theory of inflation can explain both moderate inflations, such as those we have experienced in Canada, and hyperinflations.

After developing a theory of inflation, we turn to a related question: Why is inflation a problem? At first glance, the answer to this question may seem obvious: Inflation is a problem because people don't like it. In the 1970s, when Canada experienced a relatively high rate of inflation, opinion polls placed inflation as the most important issue facing the nation. Perhaps in response to these polls, from 1975 to 1978 the federal government imposed rules and regulations that limited the size of wage and price increases in an effort to reduce the rate of inflation.

But what, exactly, are the costs that inflation imposes on a society? The answer may surprise you. Identifying the various costs of inflation is not as straightforward as it first appears. As a result, although all economists decry hyperinflation, some economists argue that the costs of moderate inflation are not nearly as large as the general public believes.

11-1 The Classical Theory of Inflation

We begin our study of inflation by developing the quantity theory of money. This theory is often called "classical" because it was developed by some of the earliest thinkers about economic issues. Most economists today rely on this theory to explain the long-run determinants of the price level and the inflation rate.

11-1a The Level of Prices and the Value of Money

Suppose we observe over some period of time the price of an ice-cream cone rising from a nickel to a dollar. What conclusion should we draw from the fact that people are willing to give up so much more money in exchange for a cone? It is possible that people have come to enjoy ice cream more (perhaps because some chemist has developed a miraculous new flavour). Yet that is probably not the case. It is more likely that people's enjoyment of ice cream has stayed roughly the same and that, over time, the money used to buy ice cream has become less valuable. Indeed, the first insight about inflation is that it is more about the value of money than about the value of goods.

This insight helps point the way toward a theory of inflation. When the consumer price index and other measures of the price level rise, commentators are often tempted to look at the many individual prices that make up these price indexes: "The CPI rose by 3 percent last month, led by a 20 percent rise in the price of coffee and a 30 percent rise in the price of heating oil." Although this approach does contain some interesting information about what's happening in the economy, it also misses a key point: Inflation is an economy-wide phenomenon that concerns, first and foremost, the value of the economy's medium of exchange.

The economy's overall price level can be viewed in two ways. So far, we have viewed the price level as the price of a basket of goods and services. When the price level rises, people have to pay more for the goods and services they buy. Alternatively, we can view the price level as a measure of the value of money. A rise in the price level means a lower value of money because each dollar in your wallet now buys a smaller quantity of goods and services.

It may help to express these ideas mathematically. Suppose P is the price level as measured, for instance, by the consumer price index or the GDP deflator. Then P measures the number of dollars needed to buy a basket of goods and services. Now turn this idea around: The quantity of goods and services that can be bought with \$1 equals $1/P$. In other words, if P is the price of goods and services measured in terms of money, $1/P$ is the value of money measured in terms of goods and services.

This math is simplest to understand in an economy that produces only a single good, say, ice-cream cones. In that case, P would be the price of a cone. When the price of a cone (P) is \$2, then the value of a dollar ($1/P$) is half a cone. When the price (P) rises to \$3, the value of a dollar ($1/P$) falls to a third of a cone. The actual economy produces thousands of goods and services, so we use a price index rather than the price of a single good. But the logic remains the same: When the overall price level rises, the value of money falls.

11-1b Money Supply, Money Demand, and Monetary Equilibrium

What determines the value of money? The answer to this question, like many in economics, is supply and demand. Just as the supply and demand for bananas determines the price of bananas, the supply and demand for money determines the value of money. Thus, our next step in developing the quantity theory of money is to consider the determinants of money supply and money demand.

First, consider money supply. In the preceding chapter we discussed how the Bank of Canada, together with the banking system, determines the supply of money. When it increases the overnight rate, the Bank of Canada discourages banks from borrowing reserves from it. Thus, an increase in the overnight rate reduces the quantity of reserves in the banking system, which in turn reduces the money supply. Conversely, a lower overnight rate encourages banks to borrow from the Bank of Canada, increases the quantity of reserves, and increases the money supply. In the same way, if the Bank of Canada sells bonds in an open-market operation, it receives dollars in exchange and contracts the money supply. If instead it buys bonds in an open-market operation, the Bank of Canada pays out dollars and expands the money supply. For our purposes in this chapter, we ignore the complications introduced by the banking system and simply take the quantity of money supplied as a policy variable that the Bank of Canada controls.

Now consider money demand. Most fundamentally, the demand for money reflects how much wealth people want to hold in liquid form. For that reason, discussions of the demand for money are sometimes referred to as discussions of "liquidity preference." Many factors influence the quantity of money demanded or, if you like, the preference for holding wealth in liquid form. The amount of currency that people hold in their wallets, for instance, depends on how much they rely on credit cards and on whether an automated teller machine is easy to find. And, as we will emphasize in Chapter 15, the quantity of money demanded depends on the interest rate that a person could earn by using the money to buy an interest-bearing bond rather than leaving it in a wallet or low-interest chequing account.

Although many variables affect the demand for money, one variable stands out in importance: the average level of prices in the economy. People hold money because it is the medium of exchange. Unlike other assets, such as bonds or stocks, people can use money to buy the goods and services on their shopping lists. How much money they choose to hold for this purpose depends on the prices of those goods and services. The higher prices are, the more money the typical transaction requires, and the more money people will choose to hold in their wallets and chequing accounts. That is, a higher price level (a lower value of money) increases the quantity of money demanded.

What ensures that the quantity of money the Bank of Canada supplies balances the quantity of money people demand? The answer, it turns out, depends on the time horizon being considered. Later in this book we will examine the short-run answer, and we will see that interest rates play a key role. In the long run, however, the answer is different and much simpler. *In the long run, the overall level of prices adjusts to the level at which the demand for money equals the supply.* If the price level is above the equilibrium level, people will want to hold more money than the Bank of Canada has created, so the price level must fall to balance supply and demand. If the price level is below the equilibrium level, people will want to hold less money than the Bank of Canada has created, and the price level must rise to balance supply and demand. At the equilibrium price level, the quantity of money that people want to hold exactly balances the quantity of money supplied by the Bank of Canada.

Figure 11.1 illustrates these ideas. The horizontal axis of this graph shows the quantity of money. The left-hand vertical axis shows the value of money $1/P$, and the right-hand vertical axis shows the price level P. Notice that the price-level axis on the right is inverted: A low price level is shown near the top of this axis, and a high price level is shown near the bottom. This inverted axis illustrates that when the value of money is high (as shown near the top of the left axis), the price level is low (as shown near the top of the right axis).

The two curves in this figure are the supply and demand curves for money. The supply curve is vertical because the Bank of Canada has fixed the quantity of money available. The demand curve for money is downward sloping, indicating that when the value of money is low (and the price level is high), people demand a larger quantity of it to buy goods and services. At the equilibrium, shown in the figure as point A, the quantity of money demanded balances the quantity of money supplied. This equilibrium of money supply and money demand determines the value of money and the price level.

FIGURE 11.1

How the Supply and Demand for Money Determine the Equilibrium Price Level

The horizontal axis shows the quantity of money. The left vertical axis shows the value of money, and the right vertical axis shows the price level. The supply curve for money is vertical because the quantity of money supplied is fixed by the Bank of Canada. The demand curve for money is downward sloping because people want to hold a larger quantity of money when each dollar buys less. At the equilibrium, point A, the value of money (on the left axis) and the price level (on the right axis) have adjusted to bring the quantity of money supplied and the quantity of money demanded into balance.

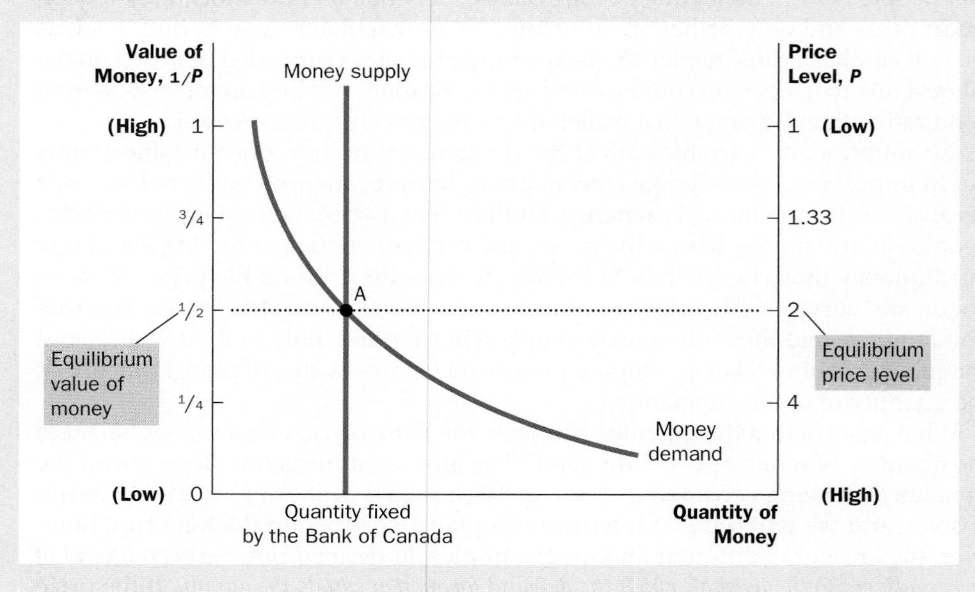

11-1c The Effects of a Monetary Injection

Let's now consider the effects of a change in monetary policy. To do so, imagine that the economy is in equilibrium and then, suddenly, the Bank of Canada doubles the supply of money by printing some dollar bills and dropping them around the country from helicopters. (Or, less dramatically and more realistically, the Bank of Canada could lower the overnight rate and, in so doing, cause the money supply to increase.) What happens after such a monetary injection? How does the new equilibrium compare to the old one?

Figure 11.2 shows what happens. The monetary injection shifts the supply curve to the right from MS_1 to MS_2, and the equilibrium moves from point A to point B. As a result, the value of money (shown on the left axis) decreases from 1/2 to 1/4, and the equilibrium price level (shown on the right axis) increases from 2 to 4. In other words, when an increase in the money supply makes dollars more plentiful, the result is an increase in the price level that makes each dollar less valuable.

This explanation of how the price level is determined and why it might change over time is called the **quantity theory of money**. According to the quantity theory, the quantity of money available in the economy determines the value of money, and growth in the quantity of money is the primary cause of inflation. As economist Milton Friedman once put it, "Inflation is always and everywhere a monetary phenomenon."

quantity theory of money
a theory asserting that the quantity of money available determines the price level and that the growth rate in the quantity of money available determines the inflation rate

11-1d A Brief Look at the Adjustment Process

So far we have compared the old equilibrium and the new equilibrium after an injection of money. How does the economy get from the old to the new

FIGURE 11.2

An Increase in the Money Supply

When the Bank of Canada increases the supply of money, the money supply curve shifts from MS_1 to MS_2. The value of money (on the left axis) and the price level (on the right axis) adjust to bring supply and demand back into balance. The equilibrium moves from point A to point B. Thus, when an increase in the money supply makes dollars more plentiful, the price level increases, making each dollar less valuable.

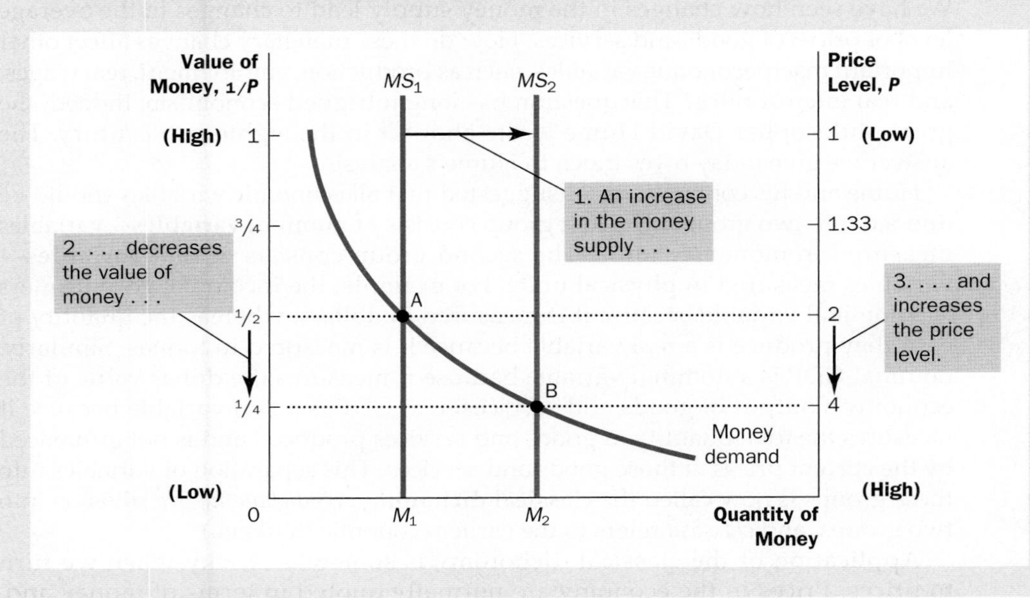

equilibrium? A complete answer to this question requires an understanding of short-run fluctuations in the economy, which we examine later in this book. Yet, even now, it is instructive to consider briefly the adjustment process that occurs after a change in money supply.

The immediate effect of a monetary injection is to create an excess supply of money. Before the injection, the economy was in equilibrium (point A in Figure 11.2). At the prevailing price level, people had exactly as much money as they wanted. But after the helicopters drop the new money and people pick it up off the streets, people have more dollars in their wallets than they want. At the prevailing price level, the quantity of money supplied now exceeds the quantity demanded.

People try to get rid of this excess supply of money in various ways. They might buy goods and services with their excess holdings of money. Or they might use this excess money to make loans to others by buying bonds or by depositing the money into a bank savings account. These loans allow other people to buy goods and services. In either case, the injection of money increases the demand for goods and services.

The economy's ability to supply goods and services, however, has not changed. As we saw in the chapter on production and growth, the economy's output of goods and services is determined by the available labour, physical capital, human capital, natural resources, and technological knowledge. None of these is altered by the injection of money.

Thus, the greater demand for goods and services causes the prices of goods and services to increase. The increase in the price level, in turn, increases the quantity of money demanded because people are using more dollars for every transaction. Eventually, the economy reaches a new equilibrium (point B in Figure 11.2) at which the quantity of money demanded again equals the quantity of money supplied. In this way, the overall price level for goods and services adjusts to bring money supply and money demand into balance.

11-1e The Classical Dichotomy and Monetary Neutrality

We have seen how changes in the money supply lead to changes in the average level of prices of goods and services. How do these monetary changes affect other important macroeconomic variables, such as production, employment, real wages, and real interest rates? This question has long intrigued economists. Indeed, the great philosopher David Hume wrote about it in the eighteenth century. The answer we give today owes much to Hume's analysis.

nominal variables
variables measured in monetary units

real variables
variables measured in physical units

classical dichotomy
the theoretical separation of nominal and real variables

Hume and his contemporaries suggested that all economic variables should be divided into two groups. The first group consists of **nominal variables**—variables measured in monetary units. The second group consists of **real variables**—variables measured in physical units. For example, the income of corn farmers is a nominal variable because it is measured in dollars, whereas the quantity of corn they produce is a real variable because it is measured in tonnes. Similarly, nominal GDP is a nominal variable because it measures the dollar value of the economy's output of goods and services; real GDP is a real variable because it measures the total quantity of goods and services produced and is not influenced by the current prices of those goods and services. This separation of variables into these groups is now called the **classical dichotomy**. (A *dichotomy* is a division into two groups, and *classical* refers to the earlier economic thinkers.)

Application of the classical dichotomy is somewhat tricky when we turn to prices. Prices in the economy are normally quoted in terms of money and, therefore, are nominal variables. For instance, when we say that the price of corn is $200 per tonne or that the price of wheat is $100 per tonne, both prices are nominal variables. But what about a *relative* price—the price of one thing compared to another? In our example, we could say that the price of a tonne of corn is two tonnes of wheat. Notice that this relative price is no longer measured in terms of money. When comparing the prices of any two goods, the dollar signs cancel, and the resulting number is measured in physical units. The lesson is that dollar prices are nominal variables, whereas relative prices are real variables.

This lesson has several important applications. For instance, the real wage (the dollar wage adjusted for inflation) is a real variable because it measures the rate at which the economy exchanges goods and services for each unit of labour. Similarly, the real interest rate (the nominal interest rate adjusted for inflation) is a real variable because it measures the rate at which the economy exchanges goods and services produced today for goods and services produced in the future.

Why bother separating variables into these two groups? The classical dichotomy is useful in analyzing the economy because different forces influence real and nominal variables. In particular, nominal variables are heavily influenced by developments in the economy's monetary system, whereas in the long run, the quantity of money is largely irrelevant for understanding the determinants of important real variables.

This idea was implicit in our earlier discussions of the real economy in the long run. In previous chapters, we examined how real GDP, saving, investment, real interest rates, and unemployment are determined without any mention of the existence of money. As explained in that analysis, the economy's production of goods and services depends on productivity and factor supplies, the real interest rate adjusts to balance the supply and demand for loanable funds, the real wage adjusts to balance the supply and demand for labour, and unemployment results when the real wage is for some reason kept above its equilibrium level. These important conclusions have nothing to do with the quantity of money supplied.

Changes in the supply of money, according to classical analysis, affect nominal variables but not real variables. When the central bank doubles the money supply, the price level doubles, the dollar wage doubles, and all other dollar values double. Real variables, such as production, employment, real wages, and real interest rates, are unchanged. This irrelevance of monetary changes for real variables in the long run is called **monetary neutrality**.

monetary neutrality
the proposition that changes in the money supply do not affect real variables

An analogy sheds light on the meaning of monetary neutrality. Recall that, as the unit of account, money is the ruler we use to measure economic transactions. When a central bank doubles the money supply, all prices double and the value of the unit of account falls by half. A similar change would occur if the government were to reduce the length of the metre from 100 to 50 cm: As a result of the new unit of measurement, all *measured* distances (nominal variables) would double, but the *actual* distances (real variables) would remain the same. The dollar, like the metre, is merely a unit of measurement, so a change in its value should not have important real effects.

Is this conclusion of monetary neutrality a realistic description of the world in which we live? The answer is: not completely. A change in the length of the metre from 100 to 50 cm would not matter much in the long run, but in the short run it would certainly lead to confusion and various mistakes. Similarly, most economists today believe that over short periods of time—within the span of a year or two—there is reason to think that monetary changes do have important effects on real variables. Hume himself also doubted that monetary neutrality would apply in the short run. (We will turn to the study of short-run nonneutrality later in the book, and this topic will shed light on the reasons why the Bank of Canada changes the supply of money over time.)

Yet classical analysis is right about the economy in the long run. Over the course of a decade, for instance, monetary changes have important effects on nominal variables (such as the price level) but only negligible effects on real variables (such as real GDP). When studying long-run changes in the economy, the neutrality of money offers a good description of how the world works.

11-1f Velocity and the Quantity Equation

We can obtain another perspective on the quantity theory of money by considering the following question: How many times per year is the typical dollar used to pay for a newly produced good or service? The answer to this question is given by a variable called the **velocity of money**. In physics, the term *velocity* refers to the speed at which an object travels. In economics, the velocity of money refers to the speed at which the typical dollar travels around the economy from wallet to wallet.

velocity of money
the rate at which money changes hands

To calculate the velocity of money, we divide the nominal value of output (nominal GDP) by the quantity of money. If P is the price level (the GDP deflator), Y the quantity of output (real GDP), and M the quantity of money, then velocity is

$$V = (P \times Y)/M$$

To see why this makes sense, imagine a simple economy that produces only pizza. Suppose that the economy produces 100 pizzas in a year, that a pizza sells for $10, and that the quantity of money in the economy is $50. Then the velocity of money is

$$V = (\$10 \times 100)/\$50 = 20$$

In this economy, people spend a total of $1000 per year on pizza. For this $1000 of spending to take place with only $50 of money, each dollar must change hands on average 20 times per year.

With slight algebraic rearrangement, this equation can be rewritten as

$$M \times V = P \times Y$$

This equation states that the quantity of money (M) times the velocity of money (V) equals the price of output (P) times the amount of output (Y). It is called the **quantity equation** because it relates the quantity of money (M) to the nominal value of output ($P \times Y$). The quantity equation shows that an increase in the quantity of money in an economy must be reflected in one of the other three variables: The price level must rise, the quantity of output must rise, or the velocity of money must fall.

quantity equation
the equation $M \times V = P \times Y$, which relates the quantity of money, the velocity of money, and the dollar value of the economy's output of goods and services

In many cases, it turns out that the velocity of money is relatively stable. For example, Figure 11.3 shows nominal GDP, the quantity of money (as measured by M2), and the velocity of money for the Canadian economy since 1968. Although the velocity of money is not exactly constant, it has not changed dramatically. By contrast, the money supply and nominal GDP during this period have increased more than tenfold. Thus, for some purposes, the assumption of constant velocity may be a good approximation.

This figure shows the nominal value of output as measured by nominal GDP, the quantity of money as measured by M2, and the velocity of money as measured by their ratio. For comparability, all three series have been scaled to equal 100 in 1968. Notice that nominal GDP and the quantity of money have grown dramatically over this period, while velocity has been relatively stable. The recession of 2009 is apparent in the fall in the value of GDP in that year.

FIGURE 11.3

Nominal GDP, the Quantity of Money, and the Velocity of Money

Sources: Statistics Canada, CANSIM database and authors' calculations.

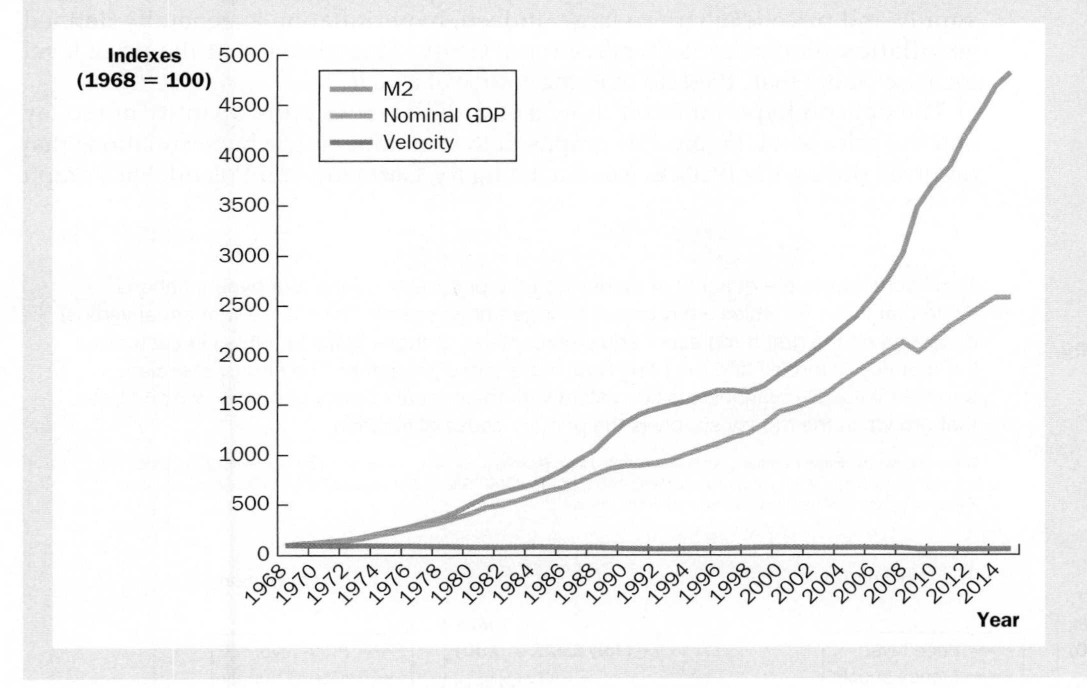

We now have all the elements necessary to explain the equilibrium price level and inflation rate. Here they are:

1. The velocity of money is relatively stable over time.
2. Because velocity is stable, when the central bank changes the quantity of money (M), it causes proportionate changes in the nominal value of output ($P \times Y$).
3. The economy's output of goods and services (Y) is primarily determined by factor supplies (labour, physical capital, human capital, and natural resources) and the available production technology. In particular, because money is neutral, money does not affect output.
4. With output (Y) determined by factor supplies and technology, when the central bank alters the money supply (M) and induces proportional changes in the nominal value of output ($P \times Y$), these changes are reflected in changes in the price level (P).
5. Therefore, when the central bank increases the money supply rapidly, the result is a high rate of inflation.

These five steps are the essence of the quantity theory of money.

case study

Money and Prices during Hyperinflations

Although earthquakes can wreak havoc on a society, they have the beneficial by-product of providing much useful data for seismologists. These data can shed light on alternative theories and, thereby, help society predict and deal with future threats. Similarly, hyperinflations offer monetary economists a natural experiment they can use to study the effects of money on the economy.

Hyperinflations are interesting in part because the changes in the money supply and price level are so large. Indeed, hyperinflation is generally defined as inflation that exceeds 50 percent *per month.* This means that the price level increases more than 100-fold over the course of a year.

The data on hyperinflation show a clear link between the quantity of money and the price level. Figure 11.4 graphs data from four classic hyperinflations that occurred during the 1920s in Austria, Hungary, Germany, and Poland. Each graph

FIGURE 11.4

Money and Prices during Four Hyperinflations

This figure shows the quantity of money and the price level during four hyperinflations. (Note that these variables are graphed on logarithmic scales. This means that equal vertical distances on the graph represent equal percentage changes in the variable.) In each case, the quantity of money and the price level move closely together. The strong association between these two variables is consistent with the quantity theory of money, which states that growth in the money supply is the primary cause of inflation.

Sources for Austria, Hungary, Germany, and Poland: Adapted from Thomas J. Sargent, "The End of Four Big Inflations," in Robert Hall, ed., *Inflation* (Chicago: University of Chicago Press, 1983), pp. 41–93.

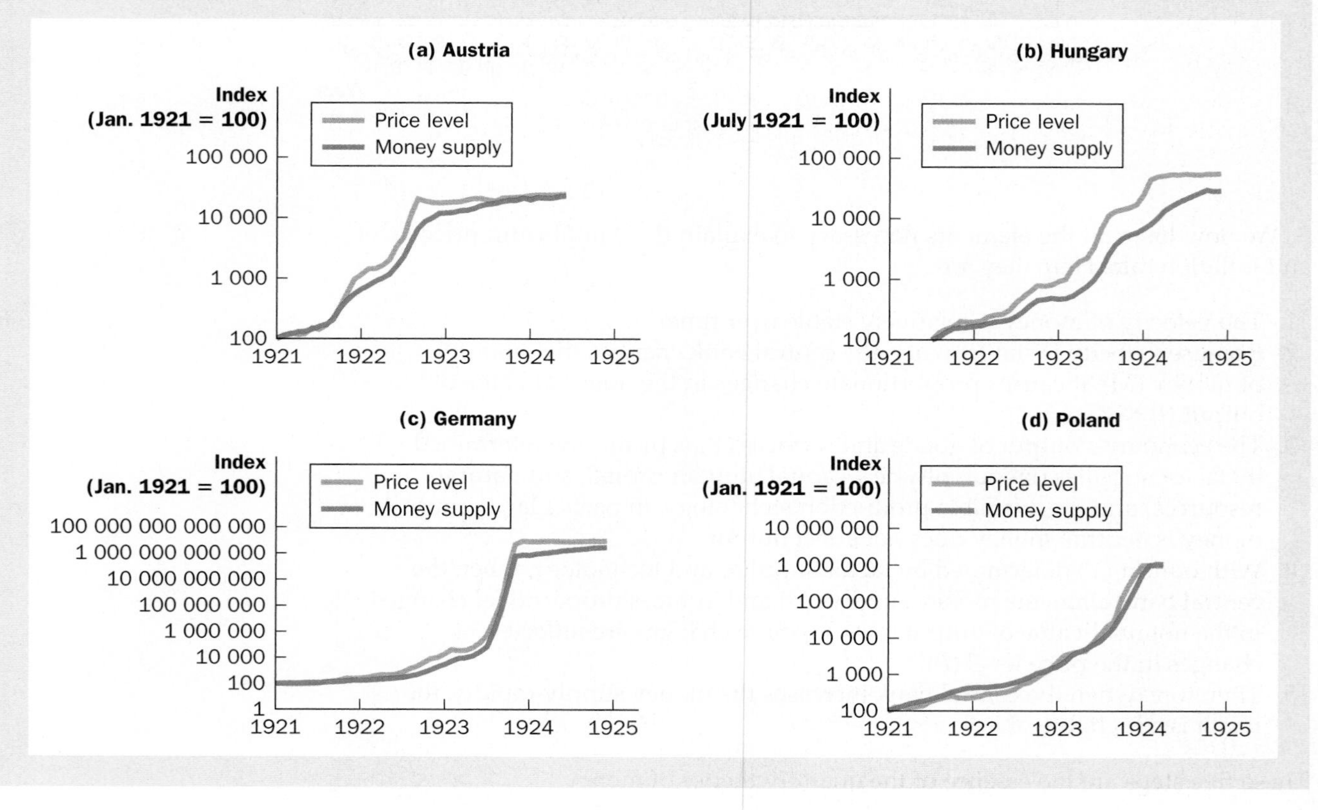

shows the quantity of money in the economy and an index of the price level. The slope of the money line represents the rate at which the quantity of money was growing, and the slope of the price line represents the inflation rate. The steeper the lines, the higher the rates of money growth or inflation.

Notice that in each graph the quantity of money and the price level are almost parallel. In each instance, growth in the quantity of money is moderate at first, and so is inflation. But over time, the quantity of money in the economy starts growing faster and faster. At about the same time, inflation also takes off. Then when the quantity of money stabilizes, the price level stabilizes as well. These episodes illustrate well one of the ten principles of economics: Prices rise when the government prints too much money.

In case you think that hyperinflations are ancient history, more recent examples have been observed. For example, during the period 1971–73, inflation reached levels of 500 percent per year in Chile. Just over a decade later, in 1985, the rate of inflation exceeded 11 000 percent per year in Bolivia. Since 2000, the government of Zimbabwe has printed trillions of Zimbabwe dollars, resulting in rates of inflation hitting 98 percent *per day*—the equivalent of over 35 000 percent per year.

It is also important to emphasize the long-term impact of hyperinflations. The memory of hyperinflation in Europe during the 1920s guides the current policy choices of the European Central Bank, policy choices that emphasize the need to limit growth in the money supply and to keep inflation low. The hyperinflation in Chile led to a military coup that ushered in a period of corruption and human rights violations, and the hyperinflation in Zimbabwe impoverished the people of that country. From this perspective, more than just inflation is on the line when governments choose to print too much money. ■

11-1g The Inflation Tax

If inflation is so easy to explain, why do countries experience hyperinflation? That is, why do the central banks of these countries choose to print so much money that its value is certain to fall rapidly over time?

The answer is that the governments of these countries are using money creation as a way to pay for their spending. When the government wants to build roads, pay salaries to police officers, or give transfer payments to the poor or elderly, it first has to raise the necessary funds. Normally, the government does this by levying taxes, such as income and sales taxes, and by borrowing from the public by selling government bonds. Yet the government can also pay for spending by simply printing the money it needs.

When the government raises revenue by printing money, it is said to levy an **inflation tax**. The inflation tax is not exactly like other taxes, however, because no one receives a bill from the government for this tax. Instead, the inflation tax is more subtle. When the government prints money, the price level rises, and the dollars in your pocket are less valuable. Thus, *the inflation tax is like a tax on everyone who holds money.*

inflation tax
the revenue the government raises by creating money

The importance of the inflation tax varies from country to country and over time. In Canada, the inflation tax is now a trivial source of revenue: It currently accounts for less than 1 percent of government revenue. During the 1770s, however, the Continental Congress of the fledgling United States relied heavily on the inflation tax to pay for military spending. Because the new government had a limited ability to raise funds through regular taxes or borrowing, printing dollars was the easiest way to pay the American soldiers. As the quantity theory predicts, the result was a high rate of inflation: Prices measured in terms of the continental dollar rose more than 100-fold over a few years.

Almost all hyperinflations follow the same pattern as the hyperinflation during the American Revolution. The government has high spending, inadequate tax revenue, and limited ability to borrow. As a result, it turns to the printing press to pay for its spending. The massive increases in the quantity of money lead to massive inflation. The inflation ends when the government institutes fiscal reforms—such as cuts in government spending—that eliminate the need for the inflation tax.

11-1h The Fisher Effect

According to the principle of monetary neutrality, an increase in the rate of money growth raises the rate of inflation but does not affect any real variable. An important application of this principle concerns the effect of money on interest rates. Interest rates are important variables for macroeconomists to understand because they link the economy of the present and the economy of the future through their effects on saving and investment.

To understand the relationship between money, inflation, and interest rates, recall the distinction between the nominal interest rate and the real interest rate. The *nominal interest rate* is the interest rate you hear about at your bank. If you have a savings account, for instance, the nominal interest rate tells you how fast the number of dollars in your account will rise over time. The *real interest rate* corrects the nominal interest rate for the effect of inflation in order to tell you how fast the purchasing power of your savings account will rise over time. The real interest rate is the nominal interest rate minus the inflation rate:

$$\text{Real interest rate} = \text{Nominal interest rate} - \text{Inflation rate}$$

For example, if the bank posts a nominal interest rate of 7 percent per year and the inflation rate is 3 percent per year, then the real value of the deposits grows by 4 percent per year.

We can rewrite this equation to show that the nominal interest rate is the sum of the real interest rate and the inflation rate:

$$\text{Nominal interest rate} = \text{Real interest rate} + \text{Inflation rate}$$

This way of looking at the nominal interest rate is useful because different economic forces determine each of the two terms on the right-hand side of this equation. As we discussed earlier in the book, the supply and demand for loanable funds determine the real interest rate. And, according to the quantity theory of money, growth in the money supply determines the inflation rate.

Let's now consider how the growth in the money supply affects interest rates. In the long run over which money is neutral, a change in money growth should not affect the real interest rate. The real interest rate is, after all, a real variable. For the real interest rate not to be affected, the nominal interest rate must adjust one-for-one to changes in the inflation rate. Thus, *when the Bank of Canada increases the rate of money growth, the result is both a higher inflation rate and a higher nominal interest rate.* This adjustment of the nominal interest rate to the inflation rate is called the **Fisher effect**, after economist Irving Fisher (1867–1947), who first studied it.

Fisher effect
the one-for-one adjustment of the nominal interest rate to the inflation rate

Keep in mind that our analysis of the Fisher effect has maintained a long-run perspective. The Fisher effect does not hold in the short run to the extent that inflation is unanticipated. A nominal interest rate is a payment on a loan, and it

IN THE news

A Recipe for Economic Disaster

Step 1: Print a lot of money. Step 2: Try to stop inflation by controlling prices. Step 3: Watch the laws of economics unfold.

Freeze on Wages Is Latest Step to Stanch Inflation in Zimbabwe

By Michael Wines

Zimbabwe's government slapped a six-month freeze on wages, rents, and service fees on Friday, the latest step in what some analysts call an increasingly desperate campaign to sustain an economy gutted by hyperinflation.

Even as President Robert G. Mugabe declared the freeze, however, Zimbabwean newspapers suggested that the government's two-month-old drive against inflation had backfired by drying up tax revenues needed to run the government.

The new freeze, announced in Friday's editions of government-controlled newspapers, is intended to combat an annual inflation rate that the government says exceeds 7,600 percent, and private economists say is twice that. It bars businesses from indexing wages or fees to inflation, a method employed in many wage agreements.

All increases must now be approved by a government commission, the state-run *Herald* newspaper reported.

The freeze follows a decree issued in late June that forced merchants and wholesalers to reduce all prices by at least 50 percent. Shoppers stripped store shelves of clothes, meat, and other basic goods after that decree, and producers have largely failed to ship new stock because goods now sell for less than it costs to make them.

© AP Photo/Tsvangirayi Mukwazhi

Most commodities are now available only on the black market, where prices have continued to skyrocket. Moreover, as the last remaining stocks of goods trickle out of factory warehouses and onto the market, Zimbabwe could soon see the start of an inflationary spiral that would make today's prices seem cheap, John Robertson, a Harare economist, said in an interview.

"It could go much higher—10 times as much for some things in the next couple of weeks, as goods cease to exist," he said.

Mr. Robertson said idle producers had been forced to lay off workers to cut costs, cutting the government's payroll tax receipts, and that sales-tax revenues were plummeting because stores had little to buy.

Harare's *Financial Gazette* newspaper, which is controlled by the president of the government's reserve bank, Gideon Gono, reported in this week's edition that value-added tax receipts had dropped by up to 90 percent since the price-cutting campaign began.

The Zimbabwe *Independent*, one of the few newspapers not under government ownership, reported that the price cuts had cost the government 13 trillion Zimbabwe dollars in lost tax revenue. At current black market rates, that totals about $55 million—a vast sum for a government that is already technically bankrupt.

The government continues to function by printing money to pay its bills, but as the currency has dwindled in value, state workers have increasingly demanded regular raises. Zimbabwe's 100,000 teachers, all government employees, have been threatening to strike if their pay is not increased.

The military, which is among Mr. Mugabe's most reliable supporters, is also asking for wage increases for soldiers. A report issued this week by the Parliament's Defense and Home Affairs Committee warned that the military was running out of money to pay foreign suppliers and maintain its infrastructure.

Source: From *The New York Times*, September 1, 2007

is typically set when the loan is first made. If inflation catches the borrower and lender by surprise, the nominal interest rate they set will fail to reflect the higher inflation. But if inflation remains high, people will eventually come to expect it, and loan agreements will reflect this expectation. To be precise, therefore, the Fisher effect states that the nominal interest rate adjusts to expected inflation.

FIGURE 11.5

The Nominal Interest Rate and the Inflation Rate

This figure uses annual data since 1968 to show the nominal interest rate on three-month corporate bonds and the inflation rate as measured by the consumer price index. The close association between these two variables over the long run is evidence for the Fisher effect: When the inflation rate rises, so does the nominal interest rate.

Sources: Statistics Canada, CANSIM database.

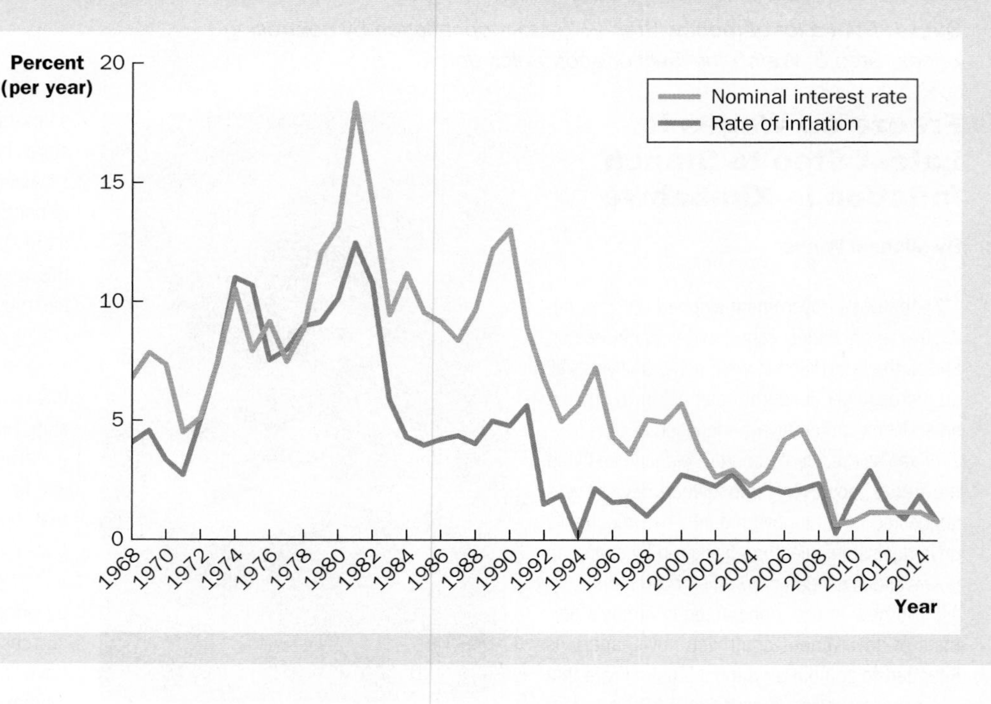

Expected inflation moves with actual inflation in the long run, but that is not necessarily true in the short run.

The Fisher effect is crucial for understanding changes over time in the nominal interest rate. Figure 11.5 shows the nominal interest rate and the inflation rate in the Canadian economy since 1968. The close association between these two variables is clear. The nominal interest rate rose throughout the 1970s because inflation was also rising during this time. Similarly, the nominal interest rate fell from the early 1980s through to 2012 because the Bank of Canada got inflation under control. In recent years, both the nominal interest rate and the inflation rate have been low by historical standards.

The government of a country increases the growth rate of the money supply from 5 percent per year to 50 percent per year. What happens to prices? What happens to nominal interest rates? Why might the government be doing this?

11-2 The Costs of Inflation

In the late 1970s, when the Canadian inflation rate reached levels in excess of 10 percent per year, inflation dominated debates over economic policy. And even though inflation has remained low since the early 1990s, it remains a closely watched macroeconomic variable. Inflation is closely watched and widely discussed because it is thought to be a serious economic problem. But is that true? And if so, why?

11-2a A Fall in Purchasing Power? The Inflation Fallacy

If you ask the typical person why inflation is bad, he will tell you that the answer is obvious: Inflation robs him of the purchasing power of his hard-earned dollars. When prices rise, each dollar of income buys fewer goods and services. Thus, it might seem that inflation directly lowers living standards.

Yet further thought reveals a fallacy in this answer. When prices rise, buyers of goods and services pay more for what they buy. At the same time, however, sellers of goods and services get more for what they sell. Because most people earn their incomes by selling their services, such as their labour, inflation in incomes goes hand in hand with inflation in prices. Thus, *inflation does not in itself reduce people's real purchasing power.*

People believe the inflation fallacy because they do not appreciate the principle of monetary neutrality. A worker who receives an annual raise of 10 percent tends to view that raise as a reward for her own talent and effort. When an inflation rate of 6 percent reduces the real value of that raise to only 4 percent, the worker might feel that she has been cheated of what is rightfully her due. In fact, as we discussed in the chapter on production and growth, real incomes are determined by real variables, such as physical capital, human capital, natural resources, and the available production technology. Nominal incomes are determined by those factors and the overall price level. If the Bank of Canada were to lower the inflation rate from 6 percent to zero, our worker's annual raise would fall from 10 percent to 4 percent. She might feel less robbed by inflation, but her real income would not rise more quickly.

If nominal incomes tend to keep pace with rising prices, why then is inflation a problem? It turns out that there is no single answer to this question. Instead, economists have identified several costs of inflation. Each of these costs shows some way in which persistent growth in the money supply does, in fact, have some effect on real variables.

11-2b Shoeleather Costs

As we have discussed, inflation is like a tax on the holders of money. The tax itself is not a cost to society: It is only a transfer of resources from households to the government. Yet most taxes give people an incentive to alter their behaviour to avoid paying the tax, and this distortion of incentives causes deadweight losses for society as a whole. Like other taxes, the inflation tax also causes deadweight losses because people waste scarce resources trying to avoid it.

How can a person avoid paying the inflation tax? Because inflation erodes the real value of the money in your wallet, you can avoid the inflation tax by holding less money. One way to do this is to go to the bank more often. For example, rather than withdrawing $200 every four weeks, you might withdraw $50 once a week. By making more frequent trips to the bank, you can keep more of your wealth in your interest-bearing savings account and less in your wallet, where inflation erodes its value.

The cost of reducing your money holdings is called the **shoeleather cost** of inflation because making more frequent trips to the bank causes your shoes to wear out more quickly. Of course, this term is not to be taken literally: The actual cost of reducing your money holdings is not the wear and tear on your shoes but the time and convenience you must sacrifice to keep less money on hand than you would if there were no inflation.

shoeleather costs
the resources wasted when inflation encourages people to reduce their money holdings

The shoeleather costs of inflation may seem trivial. And, in fact, they are in the Canadian economy, which has had only moderate inflation in recent years. But this cost is magnified in countries experiencing hyperinflation. Here is a description of one person's experience in Bolivia during its hyperinflation (as reported in the August 13, 1985, issue of *The Wall Street Journal,* p. 1):

> When Edgar Miranda gets his monthly teacher's pay of 25 million pesos, he hasn't a moment to lose. Every hour, pesos drop in value. So, while his wife rushes to market to lay in a month's supply of rice and noodles, he is off with the rest of the pesos to change them into black-market dollars.
>
> Mr. Miranda is practicing the First Rule of Survival amid the most out-of-control inflation in the world today. Bolivia is a case study of how runaway inflation undermines a society. Price increases are so huge that the figures build up almost beyond comprehension. In one six-month period, for example, prices soared at an annual rate of 38,000 percent. By official count, however, last year's inflation reached 2,000 percent, and this year's is expected to hit 8,000 percent—though other estimates range many times higher. In any event, Bolivia's rate dwarfs Israel's 370 percent and Argentina's 1,100 percent—two other cases of severe inflation.
>
> It is easier to comprehend what happens to the thirty-eight-year-old Mr. Miranda's pay if he doesn't quickly change it into dollars. The day he was paid 25 million pesos, a dollar cost 500,000 pesos. So he received $50. Just days later, with the rate at 900,000 pesos, he would have received $27.*

As this story shows, the shoeleather costs of inflation can be substantial. With the high inflation rate, Mr. Miranda does not have the luxury of holding the local money as a store of value. Instead, he is forced to convert his pesos quickly into goods or into U.S. dollars, which offer a more stable store of value. The time and effort that Mr. Miranda expends to reduce his money holdings are a waste of resources. If the monetary authority pursued a low-inflation policy, Mr. Miranda would be happy to hold pesos, and he could put his time and effort to more productive use. In fact, shortly after this article was written, the Bolivian inflation rate was reduced substantially with more restrictive monetary policy.

11-2c Menu Costs

Most firms do not change the prices of their products every day. Instead, firms often announce prices and leave them unchanged for weeks, months, or even years. The typical Canadian firm changes its prices about once a year.

menu costs
the costs of changing prices

Firms change prices infrequently because there are costs of changing prices. Costs of price adjustment are called **menu costs**, a term derived from a restaurant's cost of printing a new menu. Menu costs include the cost of deciding on new prices, the cost of printing new price lists and catalogues, the cost of sending these new price lists and catalogues to dealers and customers, the cost of advertising the new prices, and even the cost of dealing with customer annoyance over price changes.

Inflation increases the menu costs that firms must bear. In the current Canadian economy, with its low inflation rate, annual price adjustment is an appropriate business strategy for many firms. But when high inflation makes firms' costs

---

rise rapidly, annual price adjustment is impractical. During hyperinflations, for example, firms must change their prices daily or even more often just to keep up with all the other prices in the economy.

11-2d Relative-Price Variability and the Misallocation of Resources

Suppose that the Eatabit Eatery prints a new menu with new prices every January and then leaves its prices unchanged for the rest of the year. If there is no inflation, Eatabit's relative prices—the prices of its meals compared to other prices in the economy—would be constant over the course of the year. By contrast, if the inflation rate is 12 percent per year, Eatabit's relative prices will automatically fall by 1 percent each month. The restaurant's relative prices (that is, its prices compared with others in the economy) will be high in the early months of the year, just after it has printed a new menu, and low in the later months. And the higher the inflation rate, the greater is this automatic variability. Thus, because prices change only once in a while, inflation causes relative prices to vary more than they otherwise would.

Why does this matter? The reason is that market economies rely on relative prices to allocate scarce resources. Consumers decide what to buy by comparing the quality and prices of various goods and services. Through these decisions, they determine how the scarce factors of production are allocated among industries and firms. When inflation distorts relative prices, consumer decisions are distorted, and markets are less able to allocate resources to their best use.

11-2e Inflation-Induced Tax Distortions

Almost all taxes distort incentives, cause people to alter their behaviour, and lead to a less efficient allocation of the economy's resources. Many taxes, however, become even more problematic in the presence of inflation. The reason is that lawmakers often fail to take inflation into account when writing the tax laws; economists who have studied the issue conclude that inflation tends to raise the tax burden on income earned from savings.

One example of how inflation discourages saving is the tax treatment of *capital gains*—the profits made by selling an asset for more than its purchase price. Suppose that in 1980 you used some of your savings to buy shares in Microsoft Corporation for $10 and that in 2010 you sold the shares for $50. According to the tax law, you have earned a capital gain of $40, which you must include in your income when computing how much income tax you owe. But suppose the overall price level doubled from 1980 to 2010. In this case, the $10 you invested in 1980 is equivalent (in terms of purchasing power) to $20 in 2010. When you sell your shares for $50, you have a real gain (an increase in purchasing power) of only $30. The tax laws, however, do not take account of inflation and assesses you a tax on a gain of $40. Thus, inflation exaggerates the size of capital gains and inadvertently increases the tax burden on this type of income.

Another example is the tax treatment of interest income. The income tax treats the *nominal* interest earned on savings as income, even though part of the nominal interest rate merely compensates for inflation. To see the effects of this policy, consider the numerical example in Table 11.1. The table compares two economies, both of which tax interest income at a rate of 25 percent. In Economy A, inflation is zero, and the nominal and real interest rates are both 4 percent. In this case, the 25 percent tax on interest income reduces the real interest rate from 4 percent to 3 percent. In Economy B, the real interest rate is again 4 percent, but the inflation rate is 8 percent. As a result of the Fisher effect, the nominal interest rate is

TABLE 11.1

How Inflation Raises the Tax Burden on Saving

In the presence of zero inflation, a 25 percent tax on interest income reduces the real interest rate from 4 percent to 3 percent. In the presence of 8 percent inflation, the same tax reduces the real interest rate from 4 percent to 1 percent.

	Economy A (price stability)	Economy B (inflation)
Real interest rate	4%	4%
Inflation rate	0	8
Nominal interest rate (real interest rate + inflation rate)	4	12
Reduced interest due to 25 percent tax (0.25 × nominal interest rate)	1	3
After-tax nominal interest rate (0.75 × nominal interest rate)	3	9
After-tax real interest rate (after-tax nominal interest rate − inflation rate)	3	1

12 percent. Because the income tax treats this entire 12 percent interest as income, the government takes 25 percent of it, leaving an after-tax nominal interest rate of only 9 percent and an after-tax real interest rate of only 1 percent. In this case, the 25 percent tax on interest income reduces the real interest rate from 4 percent to 1 percent. Because the after-tax real interest rate provides the incentive to save, saving is much less attractive in the economy with inflation (Economy B) than in the economy with stable prices (Economy A).

The taxes on nominal capital gains and on nominal interest income are two examples of how tax law interacts with inflation. There are many others. Because of these inflation-induced tax changes, higher inflation tends to discourage people from saving. Recall that the economy's saving provides the resources for investment, which in turn is a key ingredient to long-run economic growth. Thus, when inflation raises the tax burden on saving, it tends to depress the economy's long-run growth rate. There is, however, no consensus among economists about the size of this effect.

One solution to this problem, other than eliminating inflation, is to index the tax system. That is, the tax laws could be rewritten to take account of the effects of inflation. In the case of capital gains, for example, the tax laws could adjust the purchase price using a price index and assess the tax only on the real gain. In the case of interest income, the government could tax only real interest income by excluding that portion of the interest income that merely compensates for inflation. To some extent, the tax laws have moved in the direction of indexation. For example, the income levels at which income tax rates change are adjusted automatically each year based on changes in the consumer price index. Yet many other aspects of the tax laws—such as the tax treatment of capital gains and interest income—are not indexed.

In an ideal world, the tax laws would be written so that inflation would not alter anyone's real tax liability. In the world in which we live, however, tax laws are far from perfect. More complete indexation would probably be desirable, but it would further complicate tax laws that many people already consider too complex.

11-2f Confusion and Inconvenience

Imagine that we took a poll and asked people the following question: "This year the metre is 100 cm. How long do you think it should be next year?" Assuming we could get people to take us seriously, they would tell us that the metre should stay the same length—100 cm. Anything else would just complicate life needlessly.

What does this finding have to do with inflation? Recall that money, as the economy's unit of account, is what we use to quote prices and record debts. In other words, money is the ruler with which we measure economic transactions. The job of the Bank of Canada is a bit like the job of Measurement Canada—to ensure the reliability of a commonly used unit of measurement. When the Bank of Canada increases the money supply and creates inflation, it erodes the real value of the unit of account.

It is difficult to judge the costs of the confusion and inconvenience that arise from inflation. Earlier we discussed how tax law incorrectly measures real incomes in the presence of inflation. Similarly, accountants incorrectly measure firms' earnings when prices are rising over time. Because inflation causes dollars at different times to have different real values, computing a firm's profit—the difference between its revenue and costs—is more complicated in an economy with inflation. Therefore, to some extent, inflation makes investors less able to sort out successful from unsuccessful firms, which in turn impedes financial markets in their role of allocating the economy's saving to alternative types of investment.

11-2g A Special Cost of Unexpected Inflation: Arbitrary Redistributions of Wealth

So far, the costs of inflation we have discussed occur even if inflation is steady and predictable. Inflation has an additional cost, however, when it comes as a surprise. Unexpected inflation redistributes wealth among the population in a way that has nothing to do with either merit or need. These redistributions occur because many loans in the economy are specified in terms of the unit of account—money.

Consider an example. Suppose that Sam takes out a $20 000 loan at a 7 percent interest rate from Bigbank to expand his business. In ten years, the loan will come due. After his debt has compounded interest for ten years at 7 percent, Sam will owe Bigbank about $40 000. The real value of this debt will depend on inflation over the decade. If Sam is lucky, the economy will have a hyperinflation. In this case, wages and prices will rise so high that Sam will be able to pay the $40 000 debt out of pocket change. By contrast, if the economy goes through a major deflation, then wages and prices will fall, and Sam will find the $40 000 debt a greater burden than he anticipated.

This example shows that unexpected changes in prices redistribute wealth among debtors and creditors. A hyperinflation enriches Sam at the expense of Bigbank because it diminishes the real value of the debt; Sam can repay the loan in less valuable dollars than he anticipated. Deflation enriches Bigbank at Sam's expense because it increases the real value of the debt; in this case, Sam has to repay the loan in more valuable dollars than he anticipated. If inflation were predictable, then Bigbank and Sam could take inflation into account when setting the nominal interest rate. (Recall the Fisher effect.) But if inflation is hard to predict, it imposes risk on Sam and Bigbank that both would prefer to avoid.

This cost of unexpected inflation is important to consider together with another fact: Inflation is especially volatile and uncertain when the average rate of inflation is high. This is seen most simply by examining the experience of different countries. Countries with low average inflation, such as Germany in the late twentieth century, tend to have stable inflation. Countries with high average inflation, such as many countries in Latin America, tend also to have unstable inflation. There are no known examples of economies with high, stable inflation.

This relationship between the level and volatility of inflation points to another cost of inflation: If a country pursues a high-inflation monetary policy, it will have to bear not only the costs of high expected inflation but also the arbitrary redistributions of wealth associated with unexpected inflation.

11-2h Inflation Is Bad, but Deflation May Be Worse

In recent Canadian history, inflation has been the norm but the level of prices has fallen at times, such as during the late nineteenth century and early 1930s. Moreover, Japan has experienced declines in its overall price level in recent years. So, as we conclude our discussion of the costs of inflation, we should briefly consider the costs of deflation as well.

Some economists have suggested that a small and predictable amount of deflation may be desirable. Milton Friedman pointed out that deflation would lower the nominal interest rate (recall the Fisher effect) and that a lower nominal interest rate would reduce the cost of holding money. The shoeleather costs of holding money would, he argued, be minimized by a nominal interest rate close to zero, which in turn would require deflation equal to the real interest rate. This prescription for moderate deflation is called the *Friedman rule*.

Yet there are also costs of deflation. Some of these mirror the costs of inflation. For example, just as a rising price level induces menu costs and relative-price variability, so does a falling price level. Moreover, in practice, deflation is rarely as steady and predictable as Friedman recommended. More often, it comes as a surprise, resulting in the redistribution of wealth toward creditors and away from debtors. Because debtors are often poorer, these redistributions in wealth are particularly harmful.

Perhaps most important, deflation often arises because of broader macroeconomic difficulties. As we will see in future chapters, falling prices result when some event, such as a monetary contraction, reduces the overall demand for goods and services in the economy. This fall in aggregate demand can lead to falling incomes and rising unemployment. In other words, deflation is often a symptom of deeper economic problems.

case study

Money Growth, Inflation, and the Bank of Canada

In the early 1970s, Canada had a quickly growing money supply, and the inflation rate rose to over 10 percent. At the same time, an economic viewpoint known as "monetarism" was becoming increasingly influential. One of the main recommendations of monetarists was that central banks should keep the supply of money growing at a slow, constant rate.

In response to the problem of inflation and influenced by the monetarist perspective, the Bank of Canada adopted a policy of "monetary gradualism." The central bank announced a target path for the future supply of money, along which the growth rate of M1 would gradually be reduced. It hoped that the inflation rate would also gradually fall. The results were not as expected. At first inflation stayed high, despite the slowdown in money growth. Then in the early 1980s, inflation fell much more quickly than money growth. The link between money growth and inflation was seen as not precise enough to rely on, so the central bank abandoned its policy of monetary gradualism. In the words of the then governor of the Bank of Canada, Gerald Bouey: "We did not abandon M1. M1 abandoned us."

Africa Studio/Shutterstock.com

When we look at different countries over long periods of time, we see great variation in the growth rates of money supply. Variations in velocity are small in comparison, so the link between money growth and inflation can be seen clearly.

This is especially true during periods of hyperinflation. But in any one country, over a few years, if the money supply does not vary much, variations in velocity become relatively more important. Fluctuations in velocity mean that the Canadian inflation rate could fluctuate in the short run even if the Bank of Canada kept the money growth rate constant.

Since 1992, the Bank of Canada has explicitly rejected targeting the supply of money and has instead announced a target rate of inflation, currently 2 percent. Under this policy of inflation targeting, which is now the policy of many of the world's central banks, the Bank of Canada adjusts monetary policy, by changing the overnight rate of interest, to try to ensure that inflation will stay at or near the 2 percent target.

The money supply is just one of many sources of information the Bank of Canada considers when setting the overnight rate. After looking at all of its information, if the central bank thinks that there is a danger of inflation rising above the 2 percent target, it raises the overnight rate, which reduces the growth rate of the money supply and also reduces future inflation. If the central bank thinks there is a danger of inflation falling below the 2 percent target, it lowers the overnight rate, which increases the growth rate of the money supply and also increases future inflation.

Since 1992, the Bank of Canada has successfully used monetary policy to keep inflation close to its 2 percent target. (Refer to Figure 11.6 below.) But the central bank looks at a very wide range of information when deciding whether to raise

FIGURE 11.6

Total and Core CPI Inflation

Source: Statistics Canada, CANSIM database and authors' calculations.

The Bank of Canada maintains a target for total CPI inflation of 2 percent. It is also guided in its monetary policy by the rate of change in core CPI inflation; a measure that excludes eight of the most volatile prices in the CPI basket and the effects of certain tax changes. This figure shows the average annual rate of change in inflation as measured by total and core measures of CPI since 1993.

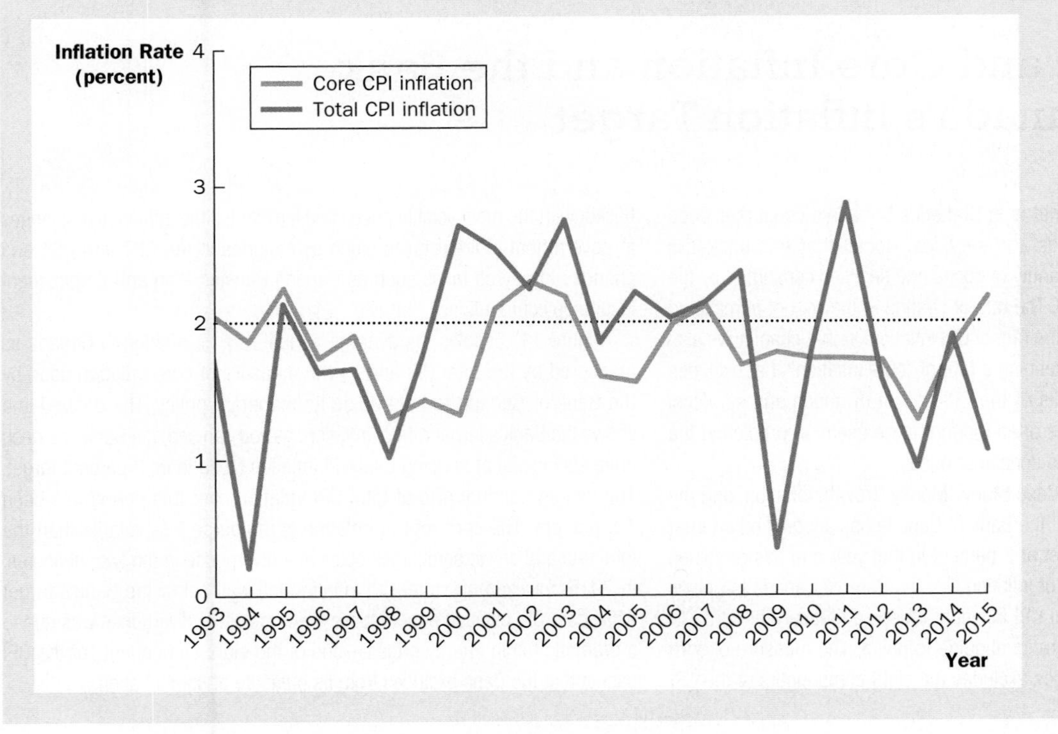

or lower the overnight rate, and there has sometimes been little or no relationship between money growth and inflation during that time. Does this mean that money growth is not very important as a cause of inflation? And if money growth is not very important as a cause of inflation, how has the Bank of Canada, using only monetary policy, been able to keep inflation so close to target?

Milton Friedman, one of the founders of monetarism, offered an analogy to help us better understand the relationship between money growth and inflation. In a house with a good thermostat, set at a constant 20°C, we will see fluctuations in the outside temperature and compensating fluctuations in the amount of natural gas burned in the furnace, but very small fluctuations in the temperature inside the house and little or no relationship between the amount of natural gas burned in the furnace and the inside temperature. Similarly, in a country with a good inflation-targeting central bank, we will see fluctuations in velocity and compensating fluctuations in money growth, but very small fluctuations in inflation and little or no relationship between money growth and inflation.

Other things equal, an increase in the amount of natural gas burned in the furnace will cause an increase in the inside temperature. Similarly, other things equal, an increase in money growth will cause an increase in inflation. But a good thermostat will never increase the quantity of natural gas burned in the furnace except when other things (like the outside temperature) are *not* equal. Similarly, a good inflation-targeting central bank will never increase money growth except when the other things (like velocity) are *not* equal. You could observe the true relationship between natural gas consumption and inside temperature only by random experiments with the thermostat. Similarly, you could observe the true relationship between money growth and inflation only by random experiments with monetary policy. Although economists might love to learn the results by conducting random experiments with monetary policy, the Bank of Canada is understandably reluctant! ■

FYI Total and Core Inflation and the Bank of Canada's Inflation Target

In Chapter 6 we defined what is in Statistics Canada's consumer price index (CPI) basket of goods and services. Recall that this basket is intended to represent the quantity of goods and services consumed by the average Canadian household. The rate of change in the cost of purchasing this basket of goods defines the rate of CPI inflation. In that chapter we also discussed the possibility of defining a rate of "core inflation" that excludes the most volatile components of the CPI basket of goods and services. A measure of core inflation is often thought to be useful in predicting the underlying trend of changes in consumer prices.

As just discussed in the Case Study "Money Growth, Inflation, and the Bank of Canada," since 1992 the Bank of Canada has announced a target of inflation. The target was set at 2 percent in that year and has remained so ever since. While the rate of inflation that the Bank of Canada targets is measured by the rate of total CPI inflation, it uses a measure of core CPI inflation as a short-term operational guide to policy. The measure of core CPI inflation that the Bank uses excludes the eight components of the CPI basket with the most volatile prices and it excludes the influence of changes in government indirect taxes (such as changes in the GST and HST and changes in payroll taxes such as Canada Pension Plan and Employment Insurance contributions).

Figure 11.6 shows the average annual rate of inflation in Canada as measured by the total CPI and by the measure of core inflation used by the Bank of Canada to help guide its monetary policy. The dashed line shows the Bank's target rate of inflation. As you can see, the Bank has been quite successful at keeping total CPI inflation close to its 2 percent target. The average annual rate of total CPI inflation over this period has been 1.8 percent. The core rate of inflation is of course less volatile than the total rate and so we sometimes observe a divergence in the two measures. In 2015, for example, total CPI inflation fell well below the Bank's target while core CPI inflation edged above the target. This divergence was due to a dramatic fall in energy prices—one of the eight components of the CPI basket that the Bank excludes from its measure of core inflation.

QUICK **Quiz** *List and describe six costs of inflation.*

11-3 Conclusion

This chapter discussed the causes and costs of inflation. Over the long term, the primary cause of inflation is simply growth in the quantity of money. When the central bank creates money in large quantities, the value of money falls quickly. To maintain stable prices, the central bank must maintain strict control over the money supply.

The costs of inflation are more subtle. They include shoeleather costs, menu costs, increased variability of relative prices, unintended changes in tax liabilities, confusion and inconvenience, and arbitrary redistributions of wealth. Are these costs, in total, large or small? All economists agree that they become huge during hyperinflation. But their size for moderate inflation—when prices rise by less than 10 percent per year—is more open to debate.

Although this chapter presented many of the most important lessons about inflation, the discussion is incomplete. When the central bank reduces the rate of money growth, prices rise less rapidly, as the quantity theory suggests. Yet as the economy makes the transition to this lower inflation rate, the change in monetary policy will have disruptive effects on production and employment. That is, even though monetary policy is neutral in the long run, it has profound effects on real variables in the short run. Later in this book we will examine the reasons for short-run monetary nonneutrality in order to enhance our understanding of the causes and costs of inflation.

summary

- The overall level of prices in an economy adjusts to bring money supply and money demand into balance. When the central bank increases the supply of money, it causes the price level to rise. Persistent growth in the quantity of money supplied leads to continuing inflation.
- The principle of monetary neutrality asserts that changes in the quantity of money influence nominal variables but not real variables. Most economists believe that monetary neutrality approximately describes the behaviour of the economy in the long run.
- A government can pay for some of its spending simply by printing money. When countries rely heavily on this "inflation tax," the result is hyperinflation.
- One application of the principle of monetary neutrality is the Fisher effect. According to the Fisher effect, when the inflation rate rises, the nominal interest rate rises by the same amount, so that the real interest rate remains the same.
- Many people think that inflation makes them poorer because it raises the cost of what they buy. This view is a fallacy, however, because inflation also raises nominal incomes.
- Economists have identified six costs of inflation: shoeleather costs associated with reduced money holdings, menu costs associated with more frequent adjustment of prices, increased variability of relative prices, unintended changes in tax liabilities due to nonindexation of the tax laws, confusion and inconvenience resulting from a changing unit of account, and arbitrary redistributions of wealth between debtors and creditors. Many of these costs are large during hyperinflation, but the size of these costs for moderate inflation is less clear.

KEY concepts

quantity theory of money, *p. 235*
nominal variables, *p. 236*
real variables, *p. 236*
classical dichotomy, *p. 236*
monetary neutrality, *p. 237*
velocity of money, *p. 238*
quantity equation, *p. 238*
inflation tax, *p. 241*
Fisher effect, *p. 242*
shoeleather costs, *p. 245*
menu costs, *p. 246*

QUESTIONS FOR review

1. Explain how an increase in the price level affects the real value of money.
2. According to the quantity theory of money, what is the effect of an increase in the quantity of money?
3. Explain the difference between nominal and real variables, and give two examples of each. According to the principle of monetary neutrality, which variables are affected by changes in the quantity of money?
4. In what sense is inflation like a tax? How does thinking about inflation as a tax help explain hyperinflation?
5. According to the Fisher effect, how does an increase in the inflation rate affect the real interest rate and the nominal interest rate?
6. What are the costs of inflation? Which of these costs do you think are most important for the Canadian economy?
7. If inflation is less than expected, who benefits—debtors or creditors? Explain.

QUICK CHECK multiple choice

1. The classical principle of monetary neutrality states that changes in the money supply do not influence ___ variables and is thought most applicable in the ___ run.
   a. nominal, short
   b. nominal, long
   c. real, short
   d. real, long
2. According to the quantity theory of money, if nominal GDP is $400, real GDP is $200, and the money supply is $100, then which of the following is correct?
   a. the price level is 1/2, and velocity is 2
   b. the price level is 1/2, and velocity is 4
   c. the price level is 2, and velocity is 2
   d. the price level is 2, and velocity is 4
3. According to the quantity theory of money, which variable in the quantity equation is most stable over long periods of time?
   a. money
   b. velocity
   c. price level
   d. output
4. Hyperinflations occur when the government runs a large budget ___, which the central bank finances with a substantial monetary ___.
   a. deficit, contraction
   b. deficit, expansion
   c. surplus, contraction
   d. surplus, expansion
5. According to the quantity theory of money and the Fisher effect, what happens if the central bank increases the rate of money growth?
   a. inflation and the nominal interest rate both increase
   b. inflation and the real interest rate both increase
   c. the nominal interest rate and the real interest rate both increase
   d. inflation, the real interest rate, and the nominal interest rate all increase
6. If an economy always has inflation of 10 percent per year, which of the following costs of inflation will it NOT suffer?
   a. shoeleather costs from reduced holdings of money
   b. menu costs from more frequent price adjustment
   c. distortions from the taxation of nominal capital gains
   d. arbitrary redistributions between debtors and creditors

PROBLEMS AND **applications**

1. Using the quantity theory of money, suppose that this year's money supply is $50 billion, nominal GDP is $1 trillion, and real GDP is $500 billion.
   a. What is the price level? What is the velocity of money?
   b. Suppose that velocity is constant and the economy's output of goods and services rises by 5 percent each year. What will happen to nominal GDP and the price level next year if the Bank of Canada keeps the money supply constant?
   c. What money supply should the Bank of Canada set next year if it wants to keep the price level stable?
   d. What money supply should the Bank of Canada set next year if it wants inflation of 10 percent?
2. Suppose that changes in bank regulations expand the availability of credit cards, so that people need to hold less cash.
   a. How does this event affect the demand for money?
   b. If the Bank of Canada does not respond to this event, what will happen to the price level?
   c. If the Bank of Canada wants to keep the price level stable, what should it do?
3. It is often suggested that the Bank of Canada try to achieve zero inflation. If we assume that velocity is constant, does this zero-inflation goal require that the rate of money growth equal zero? If yes, explain why. If no, explain what the rate of money growth should equal.
4. The economist John Maynard Keynes wrote in *The Economic Consequences of the Peace* (1919): "Lenin is said to have declared that the best way to destroy the capitalist system was to debauch the currency. By a continuing process of inflation, governments can confiscate, secretly and unobserved, an important part of the wealth of their citizens." Justify Lenin's assertion.
5. Suppose that a country's inflation rate increases sharply. What happens to the inflation tax on the holders of money? Why is wealth that is held in savings accounts *not* subject to a change in the inflation tax? Can you think of any way in which holders of savings accounts are hurt by the increase in the inflation rate?
6. Hyperinflations are extremely rare in countries whose central banks are independent of the rest of the government. Why might this be so?
7. Let's consider the effects of inflation in an economy comprising only two people: Bob, a bean farmer, and Rita, a rice farmer. Bob and Rita both always consume equal amounts of rice and beans. In year 2015, the price of beans was $1, and the price of rice was $3.
   a. Suppose that in 2016 the price of beans was $2 and the price of rice was $6. What was inflation? Was Bob better off, worse off, or unaffected by the changes in prices? What about Rita?
   b. Now suppose that in 2016 the price of beans was $2 and the price of rice was $4. What was inflation? Was Bob better off, worse off, or unaffected by the changes in prices? What about Rita?
   c. Finally, suppose that in 2016 the price of beans was $2 and the price of rice was $1.50. What was inflation? Was Bob better off, worse off, or unaffected by the changes in prices? What about Rita?
   d. What matters more to Bob and Rita—the overall inflation rate or the relative price of rice and beans?
8. If the tax rate is 40 percent, compute the before-tax real interest rate and the after-tax real interest rate in each of the following cases.
   a. The nominal interest rate is 10 percent and the inflation rate is 5 percent.
   b. The nominal interest rate is 6 percent and the inflation rate is 2 percent.
   c. The nominal interest rate is 4 percent and the inflation rate is 1 percent.
9. What are your shoeleather costs of going to the bank? How might you measure these costs in dollars? How do you think the shoeleather costs of the president of your school differ from your own?
10. Recall that money serves three functions in the economy. What are those functions? How does inflation affect the ability of money to serve each of these functions?
11. Suppose that people expect inflation to equal 3 percent, but in fact prices rise by 5 percent. Describe how this unexpectedly high inflation rate would help or hurt the following:
    a. the government
    b. a homeowner with a fixed-rate mortgage
    c. a union worker in the second year of a labour contract
    d. a college or university that has invested some of its endowment in government bonds
12. Explain one harm associated with unexpected inflation that is *not* associated with expected inflation. Then explain one harm associated with both expected and unexpected inflation.
13. Explain whether the following statements are true, false, or uncertain.
    a. "Inflation hurts borrowers and helps lenders, because borrowers must pay a higher rate of interest."
    b. "If prices change in a way that leaves the overall price level unchanged, then no one is made better or worse off."
    c. "Inflation does not reduce the purchasing power of most workers."

Thinkstock

CHAPTER 12

Open-Economy Macroeconomics: Basic Concepts

LEARNING **objectives**

In this chapter, you will ...

1. Learn how net exports measure the international flow of goods and services
2. Learn how net capital outflow measures the international flow of capital
3. Consider why net exports must always equal net capital outflow
4. See how saving, domestic investment, and net foreign investment are related
5. Learn the meaning of the nominal exchange rate and the real exchange rate
6. Examine purchasing-power parity as a theory of how exchange rates are determined
7. Learn that Canada is a small open economy and the implications of perfect capital mobility

When you decide to buy a car, you may compare the latest models offered by Ford and Toyota. When you take your next vacation, you may consider spending it on a ski hill in British Columbia or on a beach in Mexico. When you start saving for your retirement, you may choose between a mutual fund that buys stock in Canadian companies and one that buys stock in foreign companies. In all of these cases, you are participating not just in the Canadian economy but in economies around the world.

Clear benefits exist to being open to international trade: Trade allows people to produce what they produce best and to consume the great variety of goods and services produced around the world. Indeed, one of the ten principles of economics highlighted in Chapter 1 is that trade can make everyone better off. As we saw in Chapter 3, international trade can raise living standards in all countries by allowing each country to specialize in producing those goods and services in which it has a comparative advantage.

So far our development of macroeconomics has largely ignored the economy's interaction with other economies around the world. For most questions in macroeconomics, international issues are peripheral. For instance, when we discussed the natural rate of unemployment in Chapter 9 and the causes of inflation in Chapter 11, the effects of international trade could safely be ignored. Indeed, to keep their analysis simple, macroeconomists often assume a **closed economy**—an economy that does not interact with other economies.

closed economy
an economy that does not interact with other economies in the world

Yet when macroeconomists study an **open economy**—an economy that interacts freely with other economies around the world—they encounter a whole set of new issues. This chapter and the next one provide an introduction to open-economy macroeconomics. We begin in this chapter by discussing the key macroeconomic variables that describe an open economy's interactions in world markets. You may have noticed mention of these variables—exports, imports, the trade balance, and exchange rates—when reading the newspaper or watching the nightly news. Our first job is to understand what these data mean. In the next chapter we develop a model to explain how these variables are determined and how they are affected by various government policies.

open economy
an economy that interacts freely with other economies around the world

12-1 The International Flows of Goods and Capital

An open economy interacts with other economies in two ways: It buys and sells goods and services in world product markets, and it buys and sells capital assets such as stocks and bonds in world financial markets. Here we discuss these two activities and the close relationship between them.

12-1a The Flow of Goods: Exports, Imports, and Net Exports

As we first noted in Chapter 3, **exports** are domestically produced goods and services that are sold abroad, and **imports** are foreign-produced goods and services that are sold domestically. When Bombardier, the Canadian aircraft manufacturer, builds a plane and sells it to Air France, the sale is an export for Canada and an import for France. When Volvo, the Swedish car manufacturer, makes a car and sells it to a Canadian resident, the sale is an import for Canada and an export for Sweden.

exports
goods and services produced domestically and sold abroad

imports
goods and services produced abroad and sold domestically

net exports
the value of a nation's exports minus the value of its imports; also called the *trade balance*

trade balance
the value of a nation's exports minus the value of its imports; also called *net exports*

trade surplus
an excess of exports over imports

trade deficit
an excess of imports over exports

balanced trade
a situation in which exports equal imports

The **net exports** of any country are the value of its exports minus the value of its imports:

Net exports = Value of country's exports − Value of country's imports

The Bombardier sale raises Canada's net exports, and the Volvo sale reduces Canada's net exports. Because net exports tell us whether a country is, in total, a seller or a buyer in world markets for goods and services, net exports are also called the **trade balance**. If net exports are positive, exports are greater than imports, indicating that the country sells more goods and services abroad than it buys from other countries. In this case, the country is said to run a **trade surplus**. If net exports are negative, exports are less than imports, indicating that the country sells fewer goods and services abroad than it buys from other countries. In this case, the country is said to run a **trade deficit**. If net exports are zero, its exports and imports are exactly equal, and the country is said to have **balanced trade**.

In the next chapter we develop a theory that explains an economy's trade balance, but even at this early stage it is easy to think of many factors that might influence a country's exports, imports, and net exports. Those factors include the following:

- tastes of consumers for domestic and foreign goods
- prices of goods at home and abroad
- exchange rates at which people can use domestic currency to buy foreign currencies
- incomes of consumers at home and abroad
- cost of transporting goods from country to country
- government policies toward international trade

As these variables change over time, so does the amount of international trade.

case study

The Increasing Openness of the Canadian Economy

An important change in the Canadian economy since 1960 has been the increasing importance of international trade and finance. This change is illustrated in Figure 12.1, which shows the total value of goods and services exported to other countries and imported from other countries expressed as a percentage of gross domestic product. In the 1960s, exports of goods and services averaged less than 20 percent of GDP. By 2000, they were nearly 50 percent of GDP. Imports of goods and services changed by similar amounts. While the share of international trade in GDP has fallen since it peaked in 2000, exports and imports remain much higher today than they were in the 1960s.

Figure 12.1 also shows the value of Canadian exports to and imports from the United States as a percentage of gross domestic product. Clearly, Canada's trade with the United States is the largest part of Canada's total trade. What's more, fluctuations in Canada's total exports and imports over time are mainly due to fluctuations in Canadian exports to and imports from the United States.

This increase in international trade is partly due to improvements in transportation. In 1950 the average merchant ship carried less than 10 000 tonnes of cargo; today, many ships carry more than 100 000 tonnes. The long-distance jet was introduced in 1958 and the wide-body jet in 1967, making air transport far cheaper. Because of these developments, goods that once had to be produced locally can now be traded around the world. Cut flowers, for instance, are now

FIGURE 12.1

The Internationalization of the Canadian Economy

This figure shows the value of Canada's exports and imports as a percentage of GDP since 1960. It shows the value of exports and imports to the whole world and the value of exports and imports to the United States. The substantial increase over time shows the increasing importance of international trade, particularly with the United States. The dramatic increase in trade following the signing of the Canada–U.S. Free Trade Agreement in 1989 is especially noteworthy.

Source: Statistics Canada, CANSIM database and authors' calculations.

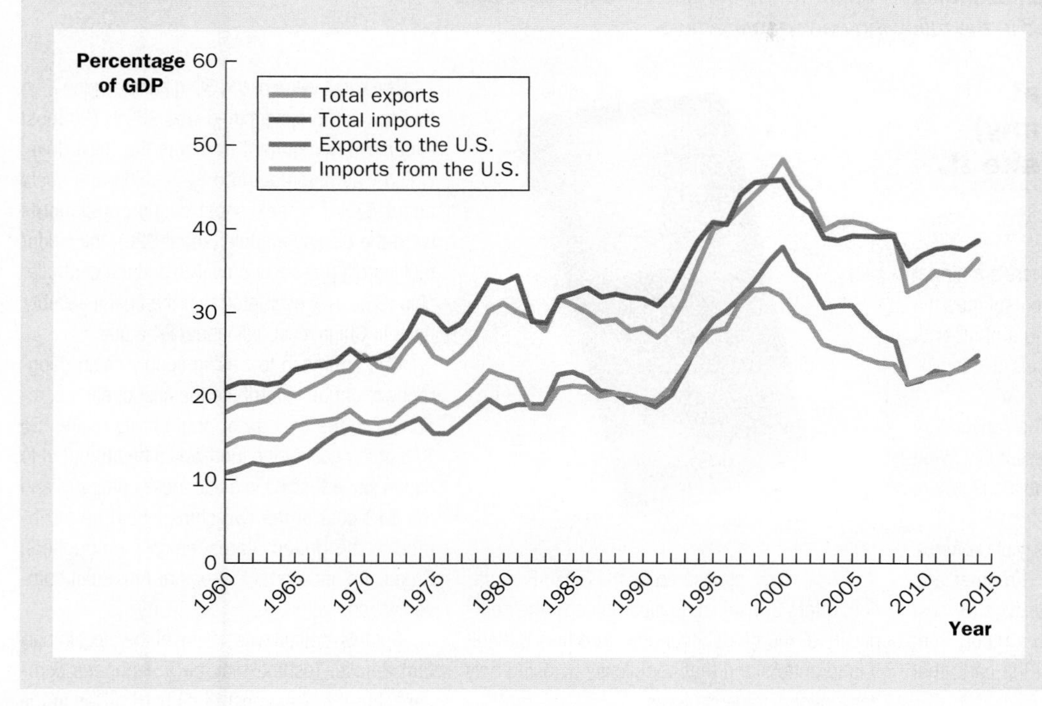

grown in Israel and flown to Canada to be sold. Fresh fruits and vegetables that can grow only in summer can now be consumed in winter as well, because they can be shipped to Canada from countries in the southern hemisphere.

The increase in international trade has also been influenced by advances in telecommunications, which have allowed businesses to reach overseas customers more easily. For example, the first transatlantic telephone cable was not laid until 1956. As recently as 1966, the technology allowed only 138 simultaneous conversations between North America and Europe. Today, communications satellites permit more than 1 million conversations to occur at the same time.

Technological progress has also fostered international trade by changing the kinds of goods that economies produce. When bulky raw materials (such as steel) and perishable goods (such as foodstuffs) were a large part of the world's output, transporting goods was often costly and sometimes impossible. By contrast, goods produced with modern technology are often light and easy to transport. Consumer electronics, for instance, have low weight for every dollar of value, which makes them easy to produce in one country and sell in another. An even more extreme example is the film industry. Once a studio in Hollywood makes a movie, it can send copies of the film around the world at almost zero cost. And, indeed, movies are a major export of the United States.

Government trade policies have also been a factor in increasing international trade. For example, the Canada–U.S. Auto Pact, signed in 1965, made it possible

IN THE **news**

Breaking Up the Chain of Production

Some goods are manufactured not in one country, but in many. The free flow of goods and services between countries—free trade—is conducive to the specialization in production described in the following newspaper article.

An iPod Has Global Value. Ask the (Many) Countries That Make It.

By Hal R. Varian

Who makes the Apple iPod? Here's a hint: It is not Apple. The company outsources the entire manufacture of the device to a number of Asian enterprises, among them Asus-tek, Inventec Appliances and Foxconn.

But this list of companies isn't a satisfactory answer either: They only do final assembly. What about the 451 parts that go into the iPod? Where are they made and by whom?

Three researchers at the University of California, Irvine—Greg Linden, Kenneth L. Kraemer and Jason Dedrick—applied some investigative cost accounting to this question, using a report from Portelligent Inc. that examined all the parts that went into the iPod.

Fairfax Media/Getty Images

Their study, sponsored by the Sloan Foundation, offers a fascinating illustration of the complexity of the global economy, and how difficult it is to understand that complexity by using only conventional trade statistics.

The retail value of the 30-gigabyte video iPod that the authors examined was $299. The most expensive component in it was the hard drive, which was manufactured by Toshiba and costs about $73. The next most costly components were the display module (about $20), the video/multimedia processor chip ($8) and the controller chip ($5). They estimated that the final assembly, done in China, cost only about $4 a unit.

One approach to tracing supply chain geography might be to attribute the cost of each component to the country of origin of its maker. So $73 of the cost of the iPod would be attributed to Japan since Toshiba is a Japanese company, and the $13 cost of the two chips would be attributed to the United States, since the suppliers, Broadcom and Portal Player, are American companies, and so on.

But this method hides some of the most important details. Toshiba may be a Japanese company, but it makes most of its hard drives in the

for automobile manufacturers to move auto parts and finished automobiles across the Canada–U.S. border without having to pay import duties. The Auto Pact is largely responsible for the establishment in Canada of a large automobile manufacturing industry. In 1989, Canada signed the Canada–U.S. Free Trade Agreement, which called for the gradual elimination of tariffs on a much larger scale. This agreement was followed in 1994 by the North American Free Trade Agreement (NAFTA) among Canada, the United States, and Mexico. The effect of these free trade agreements on Canadian exports and imports is clear from Figure 12.1. Beginning in 1989, Canada's exports and imports dramatically increased, with most of the increase coming as a result of growing trade with the United States. This growth in trade peaked in 2000, however, and has fallen since, suggesting that considerations other than the signing of free trade agreements play a role in explaining changes in the importance of international trade. For example, the effect of the recession that struck the United States, Canada, and most of the world's major economies in 2009 is reflected in the sharp fall in Canadian exports and imports in that year. During that recession people stopped buying goods and services wherever in the world they were produced.

Philippines and China. So perhaps we should also allocate part of the cost of that hard drive to one of those countries. The same problem arises regarding the Broadcom chips, with most of them manufactured in Taiwan. So how can one distribute the costs of the iPod components across the countries where they are manufactured in a meaningful way?

To answer this question, let us look at the production process as a sequence of steps, each possibly performed by a different company operating in a different country. At each step, inputs like computer chips and a bare circuit board are converted into outputs like an assembled circuit board. The difference between the cost of the inputs and the value of the outputs is the "value added" at that step, which can then be attributed to the country where that value was added.

The profit margin on generic parts like nuts and bolts is very low, since these items are produced in intensely competitive industries and can be manufactured anywhere. Hence, they add little to the final value of the iPod. More specialized parts, like the hard drives and controller chips, have much higher value added.

According to the authors' estimates, the $73 Toshiba hard drive in the iPod contains about $54 in parts and labor. So the value that Toshiba added to the hard drive was $19 plus its own direct labor costs. This $19 is attributed to Japan since Toshiba is a Japanese company.

Continuing in this way, the researchers examined the major components of the iPod and tried to calculate the value added at different stages of the production process and then assigned that value added to the country where the value was created. This isn't an easy task, but even based on their initial examination, it is quite clear that the largest share of the value added in the iPod goes to enterprises in the United States, particularly for units sold here.

The researchers estimated that $163 of the iPod's $299 retail value in the United States was captured by American companies and workers, breaking it down to $75 for distribution and retail costs, $80 to Apple, and $8 to various domestic component makers. Japan contributed about $26 to the value added (mostly via the Toshiba disk drive), while Korea contributed less than $1.

The unaccounted-for parts and labor costs involved in making the iPod came to about $110. The authors hope to assign those labor costs to the appropriate countries, but as the hard drive example illustrates, that's not so easy to do.

This value added calculation illustrates the futility of summarizing such a complex manufacturing process by using conventional trade statistics. Even though Chinese workers contribute only about 1 percent of the value of the iPod, the export of a finished iPod to the United States directly contributes about $150 to our bilateral trade deficit with the Chinese.

Ultimately, there is no simple answer to who makes the iPod or where it is made. The iPod, like many other products, is made in several countries by dozens of companies, with each stage of production contributing a different amount to the final value.

The real value of the iPod doesn't lie in its parts or even in putting those parts together. The bulk of the iPod's value is in the conception and design of the iPod. That is why Apple gets $80 for each of these video iPods it sells, which is by far the largest piece of value added in the entire supply chain.

Those clever folks at Apple figured out how to combine 451 mostly generic parts into a valuable product. They may not make the iPod, but they created it. In the end, that's what really matters.

Source: From *The New York Times,* June 28, 2007

Since 2009 the volume of trade measured as a percentage of GDP has recovered somewhat.

As we discussed earlier in this book, economists have long believed that free trade between countries is mutually beneficial. Over time, policymakers around the world have come to accept these conclusions. International agreements, such as NAFTA and those negotiated with the World Trade Organization, have gradually lowered tariffs, import quotas, and other trade barriers. The pattern of generally increasing trade illustrated in Figure 12.1 is a phenomenon that most economists and policymakers endorse and encourage. ■

12-1b The Flow of Financial Resources: Net Capital Outflow

So far we have been discussing how residents of an open economy participate in world markets for goods and services. In addition, residents of an open economy participate in world financial markets. A Canadian resident with $20 000 could use that money to buy a car from Toyota, but he could instead use that money to buy stock in the Toyota corporation. The first transaction would represent a flow of goods, whereas the second would represent a flow of capital.

net capital outflow
the purchase of foreign assets by domestic residents minus the purchase of domestic assets by foreigners

The term **net capital outflow** refers to the purchase of foreign assets by domestic residents minus the purchase of domestic assets by foreigners:

$$\text{Net capital outflow} = \begin{array}{l}\text{Purchase of foreign assets by domestic residents} \\ -\ \text{Purchase of domestic assets by foreigners}\end{array}$$

When a Canadian buys stock in Telmex, the Mexican phone company, the purchase raises Canadian net capital outflow. When a Japanese resident buys a bond issued by the Canadian government, the purchase reduces Canadian net capital outflow.

Recall that the flow of capital abroad takes two forms. If Tim Hortons opens a fast-food outlet in Russia, that is an example of *foreign direct investment.* Alternatively, if a Canadian buys stock in a Russian corporation, that is an example of *foreign portfolio investment.* In the first case, the Canadian owner is actively managing the investment, whereas in the second case the Canadian owner has a more passive role. In both cases, Canadian residents are buying assets located in another country, so both purchases increase Canadian net capital outflow.

The net capital outflow (sometimes called *net foreign investment*) can be either positive or negative. When it is positive, domestic residents are buying more foreign assets than foreigners are buying domestic assets. Capital is said to be flowing out of the country. When the net capital outflow is negative, domestic residents are buying less foreign assets than foreigners are buying domestic assets. Capital is said to be flowing into the country. That is, when net capital outflow is negative, a country is experiencing a capital inflow.

We develop a theory to explain net capital outflow in the next chapter. Here, let's consider briefly some of the more important variables that influence net capital outflow:

- real interest rates being paid on foreign assets
- real interest rates being paid on domestic assets
- perceived economic and political risks of holding assets abroad
- government policies that affect foreign ownership of domestic assets

For example, consider Canadian investors deciding whether to buy Mexican government bonds or Canadian government bonds. (Recall that a bond is, in effect, an IOU of the issuer.) To make this decision, Canadian investors compare the real interest rates offered on the two bonds. The higher a bond's real interest rate, the more attractive it is. While making this comparison, however, Canadian investors must also take into account the risk that one of these governments might *default* on its debt (that is, not pay interest or principal when it is due), as well as any restrictions that the Mexican government has imposed, or might impose in the future, on foreign investors in Mexico.

12-1c The Equality of Net Exports and Net Capital Outflow

We have seen that an open economy interacts with the rest of the world in two ways—in world markets for goods and services and in world financial markets. Net exports and net capital outflow each measure a type of imbalance in these markets. Net exports measure an imbalance between a country's exports and its imports. Net capital outflow measures an imbalance between the amount of foreign assets bought by domestic residents and the amount of domestic assets bought by foreigners.

An important but subtle fact of accounting states that, for an economy as a whole, these two imbalances must offset each other. That is, net capital outflow (NCO) always equals net exports (NX):

$$NCO = NX$$

This equation holds because every transaction that affects one side of this equation must also affect the other side by exactly the same amount. This equation is an *identity*—an equation that must hold because of the way the variables in the equation are defined and measured.

To see why this accounting identity is true, consider an example. Suppose that Bombardier, the Canadian aircraft maker, sells some planes to a Japanese airline. In this sale, a Canadian company gives planes to a Japanese company, and a Japanese company gives yen to a Canadian company. Notice that two things have occurred simultaneously. Canada has sold to a foreigner some of its output (the planes), and this sale increases Canadian net exports. In addition, Canada has acquired some foreign assets (the yen), and this acquisition increases Canada's net capital outflow.

Although Bombardier most likely will not hold on to the yen it has acquired in this sale, any subsequent transaction will preserve the equality of net exports and net capital outflow. For example, Bombardier may exchange its yen for dollars with a Canadian mutual fund that wants the yen to buy stock in Sony Corporation, the Japanese maker of consumer electronics. In this case, Bombardier's net export of planes equals the mutual fund's net capital outflow in Sony stock. Hence, NX and NCO rise by an equal amount.

Alternatively, Bombardier may exchange its yen for dollars with another Canadian company that wants to buy computers from Toshiba, the Japanese computer maker. In this case, Canada's imports (of computers) exactly offset Canada's exports (of planes). The sales by Bombardier and Toshiba together affect neither Canada's net exports nor Canada's net capital outflow. That is, NX and NCO are the same as they were before these transactions took place.

The equality of net exports and net capital outflow follows from the fact that every international transaction is an exchange. When a seller country transfers a good or service to a buyer country, the buyer country gives up some asset to pay for this good or service. The value of that asset equals the value of the good or service sold. When we add everything up, the net value of goods and services sold by a country (NX) must equal the net value of assets acquired (NCO). We can generalize from these examples to the economy as a whole.

- When a nation is running a trade surplus ($NX > 0$), it is selling more goods and services to foreigners than it is buying from them. What is it doing with the foreign currency it receives from the net sale of goods and services abroad? It must be using it to buy foreign assets. Capital is flowing out of the country ($NCO > 0$).
- When a nation is running a trade deficit ($NX < 0$), it is buying more goods and services from foreigners than it is selling to them. How is it financing the net purchase of these goods and services in world markets? It must be selling assets abroad. Capital is flowing into the country ($NCO < 0$).

The international flow of goods and services and the international flow of capital are two sides of the same coin.

FYI The Current Account Balance

Net capital outflow (*NCO*) defines the difference between the dollar value of foreign assets purchased by domestic residents and the dollar value of domestic assets purchased by foreigners. Thus, when a Mexican spends $100 to purchase 10 shares of Tim Hortons (at $10 per share), there is a $100 inflow of financial capital into Canada. When a Canadian spends $160 to purchase 40 shares of Mexican phone company Telmex (at $4 per share), there is a $160 outflow of financial capital from Canada. The net effect of these two trades is a net capital outflow of $60.

Another pair of financial flows will eventually be associated with these two stock trades. At some time in the future, Tim Hortons might pay a dividend to the Mexican who purchased 10 shares of Tim Hortons stock. Let's suppose that this dividend is equal to 3 percent of the share price. The payment of this dividend will result in a future outflow of financial capital equal to $0.30 per share, or $3 in total. Similarly, at some time in the future Telmex might pay a dividend to the Canadian who purchased stock in Telmex. Assuming Telmex pays a 5 percent dividend, the Canadian will at some point in the future receive $0.20 per share, or $8 in total. These two payments will together result in a future net inflow of $5 worth of dividend payments. Other transactions may involve the purchase and sale of bonds. These transactions will in the future result in interest payments being paid.

We account for the share purchases—which in our example resulted in a net capital outflow of $60—in our measure of *NCO*. Where do we account for the future flow of financial capital that will result from the payment of dividends? Similarly, while the initial purchase and sale of bonds are measured in *NCO*, where do we account for the net flow of interest payments that will eventually result?

The answer is that they are accounted for in what is called the *current account balance*. The current account balance is defined as

$$\text{Current account balance} = \begin{matrix}\text{Net exports} + \text{Net inflow of dividends and} \\ \text{interest payments}\end{matrix}$$

Thus, the current account balance measures payments received from abroad in exchange for goods and services—including interest and dividend payments—minus analogous payments made to foreigners. We discussed the most important part of the current account balance when we discussed exports, imports, and their difference, net exports. We did not explicitly discuss the net flow of dividends and interest payments for two reasons. First, as our example shows, they are small relative to the net capital outflow (*NCO*) that gives rise to them: In our example, the *NCO* of $60 will in the future give rise to a net inflow of dividend payments of just $5. Second, the fact that the flow of dividends and interest payments occurs only in the future, and the fact those payments are ongoing for many periods in the future (for as long as the Mexican owns Tim Hortons stock and for as long as the Canadian owns Telmex stock) complicates any effort to determine the full impact of any event that might give rise to an *NCO*. For these reasons, this part of the current account balance is often ignored in basic analyses of open economies. It is worth noting, however, that in producing Figure 12.1, we were careful to include receipts on interest and dividend payments in our measure of exports and to include payments of interest and dividend payments in our measure of imports.

12-1d Saving, Investment, and Their Relationship to the International Flows

A nation's saving and investment are, as we have seen in earlier chapters, crucial to its long-run economic growth. Let's therefore consider how these variables are related to the international flows of goods and capital as measured by net exports and net capital outflow. We can do this most easily with the help of some simple mathematics.

As you may recall, the term *net exports* first appeared earlier in the book when we discussed the components of gross domestic product. The economy's gross domestic product (Y) is divided among four components: consumption (C), investment (I), government purchases (G), and net exports (NX). We write this as

$$Y = C + I + G + NX$$

Total expenditure on the economy's output of goods and services is the sum of expenditure on consumption, investment, government purchases, and net exports. Because each dollar of expenditure is placed into one of these four components, this equation is an accounting identity: It must be true because of the way the variables are defined and measured.

Recall that national saving is the income of the nation that is left after paying for current consumption and government purchases. National saving (S) equals $Y - C - G$. If we rearrange the above equation to reflect this fact, we obtain

$$Y - C - G = I + NX$$
$$S = I + NX$$

Because net exports (NX) also equal NCO, we can write this equation as

$$S = I + NCO$$

Saving = Domestic investment + Net capital investment outflow

This equation shows that a nation's saving must equal its domestic investment plus its net capital outflow. In other words, when Canadian citizens save a dollar of their income for the future, that dollar can be used to finance accumulation of domestic capital or it can be used to finance the purchase of capital abroad.

This equation should look somewhat familiar. Earlier in the book, when we analyzed the role of the financial system, we considered this identity for the special case of a closed economy. In a closed economy, net capital outflow is zero ($NCO = 0$), so saving equals investment ($S = I$). By contrast, an open economy has two uses for its saving: domestic investment and net capital outflow.

As before, we can view the financial system as standing between the two sides of this identity. For example, suppose the Smith family decides to save some of its income for retirement. This decision contributes to national saving, the left-hand side of our equation. If the Smiths deposit their saving in a mutual fund, the mutual fund may use some of the deposit to buy stock issued by Cameco, which uses the proceeds to develop a new uranium mine in Saskatchewan. In addition, the mutual fund may use some of the Smiths' deposit to buy stock issued by Toyota, which uses the proceeds to build a steel plant in Osaka. These transactions show up on the right-hand side of the equation. From the standpoint of Canadian accounting, the expenditure by Cameco on a new uranium mine is domestic investment, and the purchase of Toyota stock by a Canadian resident is net capital outflow. Thus, all saving in the Canadian economy shows up as investment in the Canadian economy or as Canadian net capital outflow.

The bottom line is that saving, investment, and international capital flows are inextricably linked. When a nation's saving exceeds its domestic investment its net capital outflow is positive, indicating that the nation is using some of its saving to buy assets abroad. When a nation's domestic investment exceeds its saving its net capital outflow is negative, indicating that foreigners are financing some of this investment by purchasing domestic assets.

12-1e Summing Up

Table 12.1 summarizes many of the ideas presented so far in this chapter. It describes the three possibilities for an open economy: a country with a trade deficit, a country with balanced trade, and a country with a trade surplus.

Consider first a country with a trade surplus. By definition, a trade surplus means that the value of exports exceeds the value of imports. Because net exports are exports minus imports, net exports (NX) are greater than zero. As a result, income ($Y = C + I + G + NX$) must be greater than domestic spending ($C + I + G$). But if Y is more than $C + I + G$, then $Y - C - G$ must be more than I. That is, saving ($S = Y - C - G$) must exceed investment. Because the country is saving

TABLE 12.1

International Flows of Goods and Capital: Summary
This table shows the three possible outcomes for an open economy.

Trade Deficit	Balanced Trade	Trade Surplus
Exports < Imports	Exports = Imports	Exports > Imports
Net exports < 0	Net exports = 0	Net exports > 0
$Y < C + I + G$	$Y = C + I + G$	$Y > C + I + G$
Saving < Investment	Saving = Investment	Saving > Investment
Net capital outflow < 0	Net capital outflow = 0	Net capital outflow > 0

more than it is investing, it must be sending some of its saving abroad. That is, the net capital outflow must be greater than zero.

The converse logic applies to a country with a trade deficit. By definition, a trade deficit means that the value of exports is less than the value of imports. Because net exports are exports minus imports, net exports (*NX*) are negative. Thus, income ($Y = C + I + G + NX$) must be less than domestic spending ($C + I + G$). But if Y is less than $C + I + G$, then $Y - C - G$ must be less than I. That is, saving must be less than investment. The net capital outflow must be negative.

A country with balanced trade is between these cases. Exports equal imports, so net exports are zero. Income equals domestic spending, and saving equals investment. The net capital outflow equals zero.

case study

Saving, Investment, and Net Capital Outflow of Canada

Canada is a net debtor in world financial markets. This means that foreigners own more Canadian assets than Canadians own foreign assets. In the 1960s and 1970s, much concern was expressed about the extent of foreign investment in Canada. At the time, many people advocated restrictions on foreign ownership of Canadian assets. Was this a sensible policy to recommend? Is the fact that Canada is a net debtor a legitimate source of concern?

To answer these questions, let's see what these macroeconomic accounting identities tell us about the Canadian economy. Panel (a) of Figure 12.2 shows national saving and domestic investment as a percentage of GDP since 1961. Panel (b) shows net capital outlflow as a percentage of GDP. Notice that, as the identities require, net capital outflow always equals national saving minus domestic investment.

Panel (b) shows that over the period 1961 to 1998, Canada typically experienced negative net capital outflow (*NCO*). That is, it was typically true that, each year, foreigners purchased more Canadian assets than Canadians purchased foreign assets. This net purchase of Canadian assets by foreigners allowed domestic investment in Canada to exceed Canada's national saving by an average of 2.3 percent of GDP over the period 1961 to 1998. Because net exports must equal net foreign investment, net exports in Canada were also typically negative over this period, as we saw in Figure 12.1.

Starting in 1999, a significant change occurred in Canada's net capital outflow: It turned positive. Whereas for almost all of the previous 40 years capital was flowing into Canada (that is, *NCO* was negative), beginning in 1999 capital began to flow out of Canada (*NCO* turned positive). Although positive values of net capital outflow had occurred previously in 1970, 1982, and 1996, the change in 1999 proved to be longer lasting and the size of the net capital outflow was much larger than in those earlier periods. What happened to cause that change and what happened in 2009 to cause it to reverse direction once again?

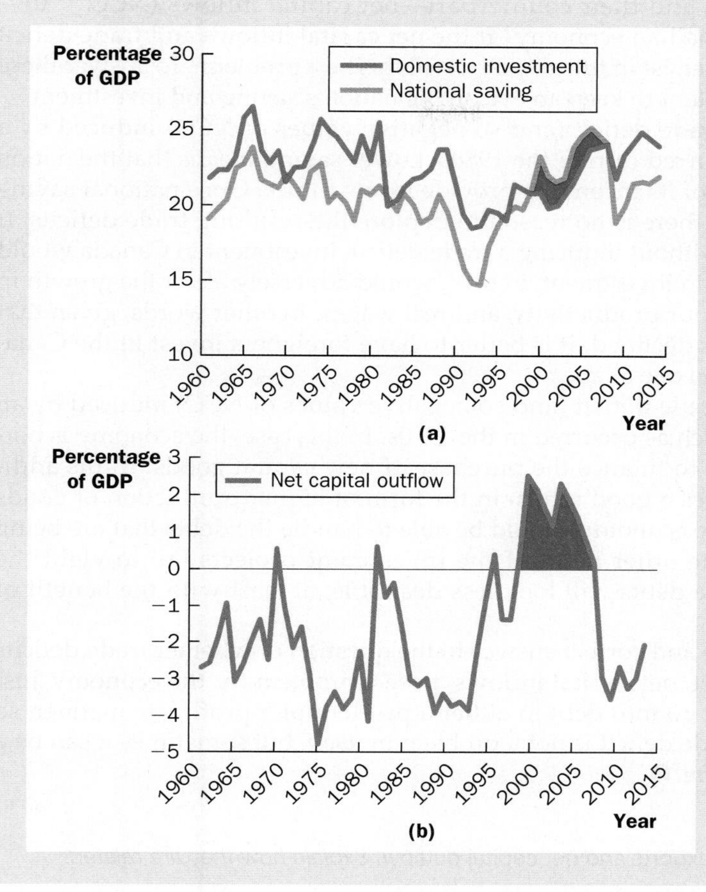

FIGURE 12.2

National Saving, Domestic Investment, and Net Capital Outflow

Panel (a) shows national saving and domestic investment as a percentage of GDP. Panel (b) shows net capital outflow as a percentage of GDP. In all but three years from 1961 to 1998, net capital outflow was negative and large in absolute value. From 1999 to 2008, net capital outflow turned positive thanks to increases in national saving that made it possible for Canadians to not only satisfy the demand for domestic investment but also to purchase foreign assets. A recession in 2009 caused national saving to fall and so caused net capital outflow to become negative again.

Source: Statistics Canada, CANSIM database and authors' calculations.

As seen in panel (a) of Figure 12.2, national saving increased from 15 percent of GDP in 1993 to over 24 percent in 2005, where it remained until 2009. In large part, this was due to steady economic growth that assisted the efforts of the federal government and most provincial and territorial governments to eliminate their budget deficits over that period. The resulting increase in national saving was sufficiently large that, despite a significant increase in domestic investment, Canadians' savings were more than sufficient to meet the demands of domestic firms for investment funds. As a result, Canadians' savings were available for lending to foreigners and a large and persistent net capital outflow followed.

Net capital inflows (that is, negative values for *NCO*) returned in 2009. This was the result of a fall in domestic investment but an even larger fall in national saving. Both of these declines were the result of the economic recession that Canada suffered in that year. The recession caused tax revenues to fall and demands for government spending to increase, both of which caused government budgets to move into deficit and so reduce national saving. At the same time, the financial crisis that caused the recession induced firms to reduce investment spending. Since the fall in national saving exceeded the fall in domestic investment, net capital outflow turned negative. Because net exports must equal net capital outflow, net exports also turned negative in 2009, as we saw in Figure 12.1.

Are trade deficits and their counterpart—net capital inflows ($NCO < 0$)—problems for the Canadian economy? If the net capital inflows and trade deficit observed after 2009 persist in future years, will this be a problem? To answer these questions, it is important to keep an eye on the nation's saving and investment.

Consider first a trade deficit (and so negative values of *NCO*) induced by a fall in saving, as occurred during the 1980s. Lower saving means that the nation is putting away less of its income to provide for its future. Once national saving has fallen, however, there is no reason to deplore the resulting trade deficits. If national saving fell without inducing a trade deficit, investment in Canada would have to fall. This fall in investment, in turn, would adversely affect the growth in the capital stock, labour productivity, and real wages. In other words, given that Canadian saving has declined, it is better to have foreigners invest in the Canadian economy than no one at all.

Now consider a trade deficit (and so negative values of *NCO*) induced by an investment boom, such as occurred in the 1970s. In this case, the economy is borrowing from abroad to finance the purchase of new capital goods. If this additional capital provides a good return in the form of higher production of goods and services, then the economy should be able to handle the debts that are being accumulated. On the other hand, if the investment projects fail to yield the expected returns, the debts will look less desirable, at least with the benefit of hindsight.

There is no simple and correct answer to the question of whether trade deficits and their counterpart, net capital inflows, pose a problem for the economy. Just as an individual can go into debt in either a prudent or a profligate manner, so can a nation. The trade deficit is not a problem in itself, but sometimes it can be a symptom of a problem. ■

Define net exports *and* net capital outflow. *Explain how they are related.*

12-2 The Prices for International Transactions: Real and Nominal Exchange Rates

So far we have discussed measures of the flow of goods and services and the flow of capital across a nation's border. In addition to these quantity variables, macroeconomists also study variables that measure the prices at which these international transactions take place. Just as the price in any market serves the important role of coordinating buyers and sellers in that market, international prices help coordinate the decisions of consumers and producers as they interact in world markets. Here we discuss the two most important international prices—the nominal and real exchange rates.

nominal exchange rate
the rate at which a person can trade the currency of one country for the currency of another

12-2a Nominal Exchange Rates

The **nominal exchange rate** is the rate at which a person can trade the currency of one country for the currency of another. For example, if you go to a bank, you might see a posted exchange rate of 80 yen per dollar. If you give the bank one Canadian dollar, it will give you 80 Japanese yen; and if you give the bank

80 Japanese yen, it will give you one Canadian dollar. (In actuality, the bank will post slightly different prices for buying and selling yen. The difference gives the bank some profit for offering this service. For our purposes here, we can ignore these differences.)

An exchange rate can always be expressed in two ways. If the exchange rate is 80 yen per dollar, it is also 1/80 (= 0.0125) dollar per yen. Throughout this book, we always express the nominal exchange rate as units of foreign currency per Canadian dollar, such as 80 yen per dollar.

If the exchange rate changes so that a dollar buys more foreign currency, that change is called an **appreciation** of the dollar. If the exchange rate changes so that a dollar buys less foreign currency, that change is called a **depreciation** of the dollar. For example, when the exchange rate rises from 80 to 90 yen per dollar, the dollar is said to appreciate. At the same time, because a Japanese yen now buys less of the Canadian currency, the yen is said to depreciate. When the exchange rate falls from 80 to 70 yen per dollar, the dollar is said to depreciate, and the yen is said to appreciate.

appreciation
an increase in the value of a currency as measured by the amount of foreign currency it can buy

depreciation
a decrease in the value of a currency as measured by the amount of foreign currency it can buy

At times you may have heard the media report that the dollar is either "strong" or "weak." These descriptions usually refer to recent changes in the nominal exchange rate. When a currency appreciates, it is said to *strengthen* because it can then buy more foreign currency. Similarly, when a currency depreciates, it is said to *weaken* because it can then buy fewer units of foreign currency. The use of the terms "weak" and "strong" is unfortunate, as they confer meanings that are unintended. There is nothing inherently good about a currency becoming "stronger" or inherently bad about a currency becoming "weaker." An exchange rate is a price, and like any price, an increase in its value is good for someone but bad for someone else. Thus, while farmers appreciate a "stronger" price for wheat, consumers of bread prefer a "weaker" price. In a similar way, a stronger Canadian dollar is good for those buying foreign currencies but bad for those trying to sell foreign currencies. Whether a "stronger" or a "weaker" price is desirable depends on which side of the transaction you stand.

For any country, there are many nominal exchange rates. The Canadian dollar can be used to buy Japanese yen, British pounds, Mexican pesos, U.S. dollars, and so on. When economists study changes in the exchange rate, they often use indexes that average these many exchange rates. Just as the consumer price index turns the many prices in the economy into a single measure of the price level, an exchange rate index turns these many exchange rates into a single measure of the international value of the currency. So when economists talk about the dollar appreciating or depreciating, they often are referring to an exchange rate index that takes into account many individual exchange rates.

The Bank of Canada provides a measure of just such an index. The Canadian-dollar effective exchange-rate index (CERI) is a weighted average of the exchange rates between the Canadian dollar and the currencies of Canada's major trading partners. The index is currently based on six foreign currencies: the U.S. dollar, the European Union euro, the Japanese yen, the U.K. pound, the Chinese yuan, and the Mexican peso. The importance of each of these currencies in the CERI depends on the amount of trade that Canada does with those countries. Since about 80 percent of Canada's trade is with the United States, it is not surprising that movements in the CERI closely mimic changes in the value of the Canada–U.S. exchange rate.

12-2b Real Exchange Rates

real exchange rate
the rate at which a person can trade the goods and services of one country for the goods and services of another

The **real exchange rate** is the rate at which a person can trade the goods and services of one country for the goods and services of another. For example, suppose you go shopping and find that a case of German beer is twice as expensive as a case of Canadian beer. We would then say that the real exchange rate is half of a case of German beer per case of Canadian beer. Notice that, like the nominal exchange rate, we express the real exchange rate as units of the foreign item per unit of the domestic item. But in this instance the item is a good rather than a currency.

Real and nominal exchange rates are closely related. To see how, consider an example. Suppose that a bushel of Canadian wheat sells for $200, and a bushel of Russian wheat sells for 1600 rubles. What is the real exchange rate between Canadian and Russian wheat? To answer this question, we must first use the nominal exchange rate to convert the prices into a common currency. If the nominal exchange rate is 4 rubles per dollar, then a price for Canadian wheat of $200 per bushel is equivalent to 800 rubles per bushel. Canadian wheat is half as expensive as Russian wheat. The real exchange rate is one-half bushel of Russian wheat per bushel of Canadian wheat.

We can summarize this calculation for the real exchange rate with the following formula:

$$\text{Real exchange rate} = \frac{\text{Nominal exchange rate} \times \text{Domestic price}}{\text{Foreign price}}$$

Using the numbers in our example, the formula applies as follows:

$$\begin{aligned}\text{Real exchange rate} &= \frac{(\text{4 rubles per dollar}) \times (\text{\$200 per bushel of Canadian wheat})}{\text{1600 rubles per bushel of Russian wheat}}\\ &= \frac{\text{800 rubles per bushel of Canadian wheat}}{\text{1600 rubles per bushel of Russian wheat}}\\ &= \tfrac{1}{2}\ \text{bushel of Russian wheat per bushel of Canadian wheat}\end{aligned}$$

Thus, the real exchange rate depends on the nominal exchange rate and on the prices of goods in the two countries measured in the local currencies.

Why does the real exchange rate matter? As you might guess, the real exchange rate is a key determinant of how much a country exports and imports. When Catelli is deciding whether to buy Canadian wheat or Russian wheat to make pasta, for example, it will ask which wheat is cheaper. The real exchange rate gives the answer. As another example, imagine that you are deciding whether to take a seaside vacation in Tofino, British Columbia, or in Cancun, Mexico. You might ask your travel agent the price of a hotel room in Tofino (measured in dollars), the price of a hotel room in Cancun (measured in pesos), and the exchange rate between pesos and dollars. If you decide where to vacation by comparing costs, you are basing your decision on the real exchange rate.

When studying an economy as a whole, macroeconomists focus on overall prices rather than the prices of individual items. That is, to measure the real exchange rate, they use price indexes, such as the consumer price index, that measure the price of a basket of goods and services. By using a price index for a Canadian basket (P), a price index for a foreign basket (P^*), and the nominal exchange rate between the Canadian dollar and foreign currencies (e), we can compute the overall real exchange rate between Canada and other countries as follows:

$$\text{Real exchange rate} = (e \times P)/P^*$$

FYI The Value of the Canadian Dollar

When Canadians think about the value of the Canadian dollar, they typically compare it with the U.S. dollar. This is not surprising, given that when they leave Canada on holiday or on business, the vast majority of Canadians go to the United States. The value of the Canadian dollar relative to the U.S. dollar is therefore foremost in the minds of Canadians.

It is important to remember, however, that there is a nominal exchange rate between the Canadian dollar and the currency of every other country. What's more, Canada trades with many countries other than the United States. There are, then, many ways of defining the value of the Canadian dollar. We can compare it with the U.S. dollar, the British pound, or any other currency in the world.

The four graphs in Figure 12.3 show how the exchange rate has changed recently between the Canadian dollar and four currencies: the U.S. dollar, the British pound, the Japanese yen, and the Australian dollar. The graph in panel (a) shows that from January 2000 to August 2015, the Canadian dollar first slowly fell in value relative to the U.S. dollar, then soared in relative value beginning in 2003, plummeted between late 2008 and early 2009, and then increased in relative value during 2009, 2010, and the early part of 2011. From mid 2011 to late 2015 the Canadian dollar has fallen in value relative to the U.S. dollar. A similar pattern evolved with respect to the Japanese yen [panel (c)], at least up to 2009. The Canadian dollar increased in value relative to the yen until mid 2007 but this was followed by a precipitous fall in value relative to the yen until 2009. Since that time, the Canadian dollar has gained in value relative to the Japanese currency. With respect to the Australian dollar [panel (d)], the value of the Canadian dollar has followed a saw-toothed pattern of rises and falls. More recently, the Canadian dollar has more or less steadily increase in value relative to the Australian dollar since 2014. With respect to the British pound [panel (b)], the Canadian dollar increased in value until 2014 but has steadily lost relative value since 2013.

Information on exchange rates is useful to Canadians wondering where to go on their next holiday. These graphs suggest, for example, that a trip to Great Britain was considerably cheaper from 2010 to 2013 than at any time before or since.

FIGURE 12.3
The Value of the Canadian Dollar

These graphs show how the value of the Canadian dollar has changed relative to the values of other currencies from January 2000 to August 2015.

Source: Statistics Canada.

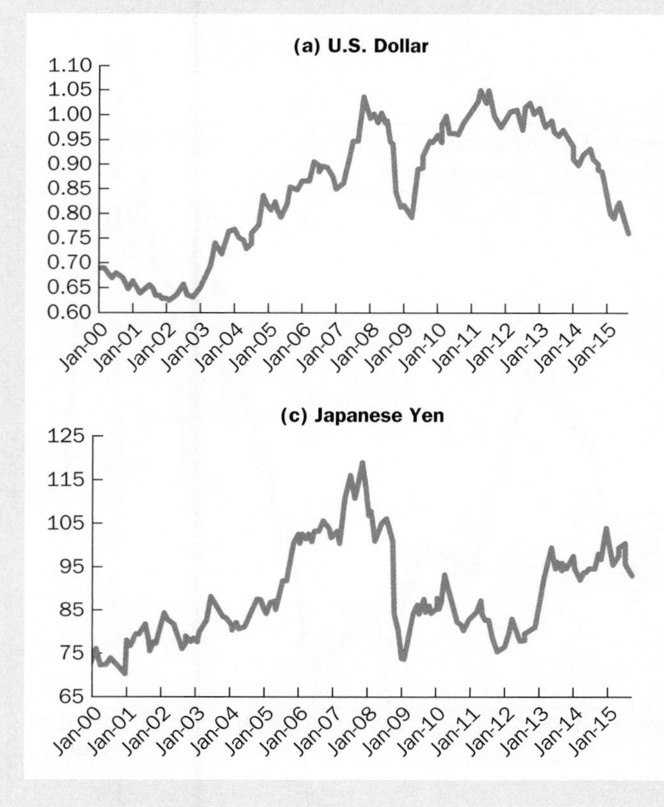

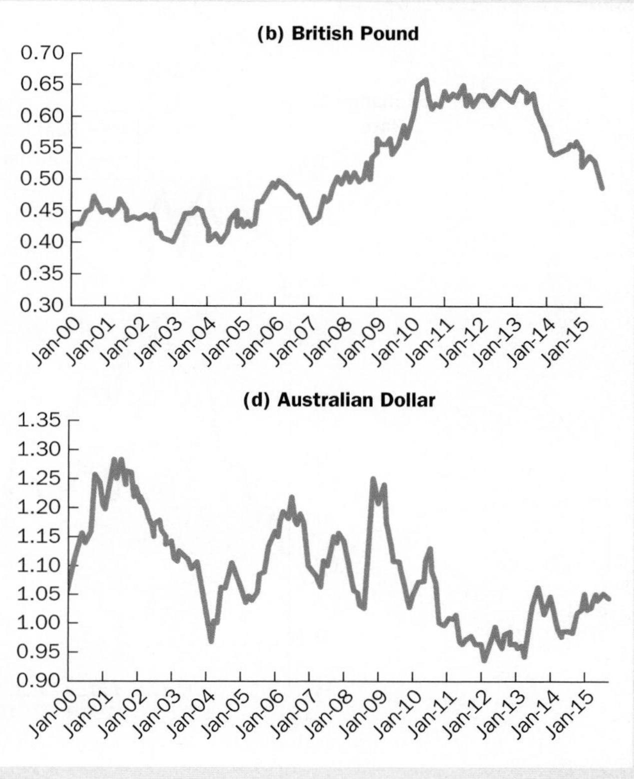

This real exchange rate measures the price of a basket of goods and services available domestically relative to a basket of goods and services available abroad.

Figure 12.4 presents data on the real and the nominal exchange rate between the Canadian and the U.S. dollar. The exchange rates move closely with one another because the price level in Canada (P) and the price level in the United States (P^*) tend to move together, so most of the variation is due to changes in the nominal exchange rate (e). Since, as noted earlier, most of Canada's trade is with the United States, movements in the real exchange rate between Canadian and U.S. currencies is a good indication of changes in the price of Canadian goods relative to those abroad.

As we examine more fully in the next chapter, a country's real exchange rate is a key determinant of its net exports of goods and services. A depreciation (fall) in Canada's real exchange rate means that Canadian goods have become cheaper relative to foreign goods. This change encourages consumers both at home and abroad to buy more Canadian goods and fewer goods from other countries. As a result, Canada's exports rise and Canada's imports fall, and both of these changes

FIGURE 12.4

Real and Nominal Exchange Rates

Source: U.S. Bureau of Labor Statistics and Statistics Canada.

This figure shows values of the nominal (e) and the real [$(e \times P)/P^*$] exchange rate between the Canadian and the U.S. dollar from 1970 to 2015. The two exchange rates usually move together because prices in Canada and the United States are usually closely related.

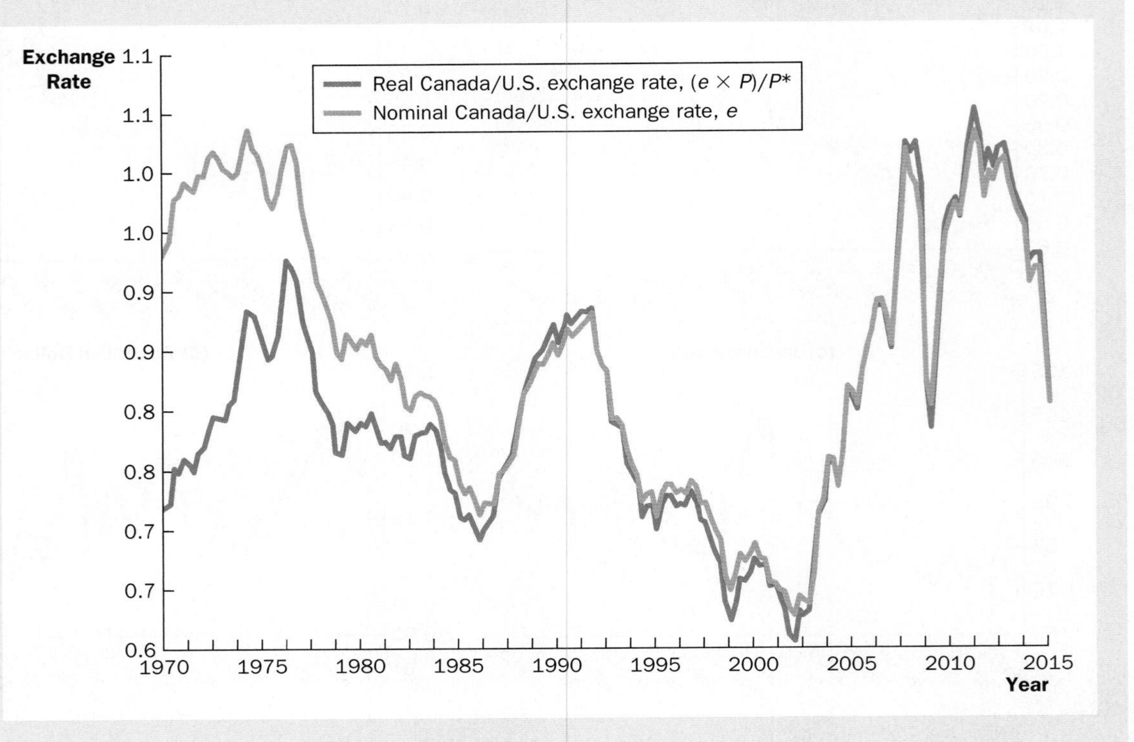

FYI The Euro

You may have once heard of, or perhaps even seen, currencies such as the French franc, the German mark, or the Italian lira. These types of money no longer exist. During the 1990s, many European nations decided to give up their national currencies and use a common currency called the *euro.* The euro started circulating on January 1, 2002. Monetary policy for the euro area is now set by the European Central Bank (ECB), with representatives from all of the participating countries. The ECB issues the euro and controls the supply of this money, much as the Bank of Canada controls the supply of dollars in the Canadian economy.

Why did these countries adopt a common currency? One benefit of a common currency is that it makes trade easier. Imagine that each of the ten Canadian provinces and three territories had a different currency. Every time you crossed a provincial or territorial border you would need to change your money and perform the kind of exchange-rate calculations discussed in the text. This would be inconvenient, and it might deter you from buying goods and services outside your own province or territory. The countries of Europe decided that as their economies became more integrated, it would be better to avoid this inconvenience.

To some extent, the adoption of a common currency in Europe was a political decision based on concerns beyond the scope of standard economics. Some advocates of the euro wanted to reduce nationalistic feelings and to make Europeans appreciate more fully their shared history and destiny. A single money for most of the continent, they argued, would help achieve this goal.

There are, however, costs of choosing a common currency. If the nations of Europe have only one money, they can have only one monetary policy. If they disagree about which monetary policy is best, they will have to reach some kind of agreement, rather than each nation going its own way. Because adopting a single money has both benefits and costs, there is debate among economists about whether Europe's adoption of the euro was a good decision.

Beginning in 2010, the euro question heated up as several European nations dealt with a variety of economic difficulties. Greece, in particular, had run up a large government debt and found itself facing possible default. As a result, it had to raise taxes and cut back government spending substantially. Some observers suggested that dealing with these problems would have been easier if the government had an additional tool—a national monetary policy. The possibility of Greece leaving the euro area and reintroducing its own currency was debated in 2012 and again in 2015 and was part of the debate in the Greek elections held in those years. As this book was going to press, the question of whether Greece will remain in the euro area was by no means assured.

Hub.-Wilh. Domrose/
Shutterstock.com

raise Canada's net exports. Conversely, an appreciation (rise) in Canada's real exchange rate means that Canadian goods have become more expensive compared to foreign goods, so Canada's net exports fall.

QUICK **Quiz**

Define nominal exchange rate *and* real exchange rate, *and explain how they are related. • If the nominal exchange rate goes from 100 to 120 yen per dollar, has the dollar appreciated or depreciated?*

12-3 A First Theory of Exchange-Rate Determination: Purchasing-Power Parity

Exchange rates vary substantially over time. In 1970, a Canadian dollar could be used to buy 3.49 German marks or 600 Italian lira. In 2001, as both Germany and Italy were getting ready to adopt the euro as their common currency, a Canadian dollar bought 1.41 German marks or 1397 Italian lira. In other words, over this period the value of the dollar fell by more than half compared to the mark, while it more than doubled compared to the lira.

What explains these large and opposite changes? Economists have developed many models to explain how exchange rates are determined, each emphasizing just some of the many forces at work. Here we develop the simplest theory of exchange rates, called **purchasing-power parity**. This theory states that a unit of any given currency should be able to buy the same quantity of goods in all countries. Many economists believe that purchasing-power parity describes the forces that determine exchange rates in the long run. We now consider the logic on which this long-run theory of exchange rates is based, as well as the theory's implications and limitations.

purchasing-power parity
a theory of exchange rates whereby a unit of any given currency should be able to buy the same quantity of goods in all countries

12-3a The Basic Logic of Purchasing-Power Parity

The theory of purchasing-power parity is based on a principle called the *law of one price.* This law asserts that a good must sell for the same price in all locations. Otherwise, opportunities for profit would be left unexploited. For example, suppose that coffee beans sold for less in Vancouver than in Halifax. A person could buy coffee in Vancouver for, say, $4 a kilo and then sell it in Halifax for $5 per kilo, making a profit of $1 per kilo from the difference in price. The process of taking advantage of differences in prices in different markets is called *arbitrage.* In our example, as people took advantage of this arbitrage opportunity, they would increase the demand for coffee in Vancouver and increase the supply in Halifax. The price of coffee would rise in Vancouver (in response to greater demand) and fall in Halifax (in response to greater supply). This process would continue until, eventually, the prices were the same in the two markets.

Now consider how the law of one price applies to the international marketplace. If a dollar (or any other currency) could buy more coffee in Canada than in Japan, international traders could profit by buying coffee in Canada and selling it in Japan. This export of coffee from Canada to Japan would drive up the Canadian price of coffee and drive down the Japanese price. Conversely, if a dollar could buy more coffee in Japan than in Canada, traders could buy coffee in Japan and sell it in Canada. This import of coffee into Canada from Japan would drive down the Canadian price of coffee and drive up the Japanese price. In the end, the law of one price tells us that a dollar must buy the same amount of coffee in all countries.

This logic leads us to the theory of purchasing-power parity. According to this theory, a currency must have the same purchasing power in all countries. That is, a Canadian dollar must buy the same quantity of goods in Canada and Japan, and a Japanese yen must buy the same quantity of goods in Japan and Canada. Indeed, the name of this theory describes it well. *Parity* means equality, and *purchasing power* refers to the value of money. *Purchasing-power parity* states that a unit of all currencies must have the same real value in every country.

12-3b Implications of Purchasing-Power Parity

What does the theory of purchasing-power parity say about exchange rates? It tells us that the nominal exchange rate between the currencies of two countries depends on the price levels in those countries. If a dollar buys the same quantity of goods in Canada (where prices are measured in dollars) as in Japan (where prices are measured in yen), then the number of yen per dollar must reflect the prices of goods in Canada and Japan. For example, if a kilo of coffee costs 500 yen in Japan and $5 in Canada, then the nominal exchange rate must be 100 yen per dollar (500 yen/$5 = 100 yen per dollar). Otherwise, the purchasing power of the dollar would not be the same in the two countries.

To see more fully how this works, it is helpful to use just a bit of mathematics. Suppose that P is the price of a basket of goods in Canada (measured in dollars), P^* is the price of a basket of goods in Japan (measured in yen), and e is the nominal exchange rate (the number of yen a dollar can buy). Now consider the quantity of goods a dollar can buy at home and abroad. At home, the price level is P, so the purchasing power of $1 at home is $1/P$. Abroad, a dollar can be exchanged into e units of foreign currency, which in turn have purchasing power e/P^*. For the purchasing power of a dollar to be the same in the two countries, it must be the case that

$$1/P = e/P^*$$

With rearrangement, this equation becomes

$$1 = eP/P^*$$

Notice that the left-hand side of this equation is a constant, and the right-hand side is the real exchange rate. Thus, if the purchasing power of the dollar is always the same at home and abroad, then the real exchange rate—the relative price of domestic and foreign goods—cannot change.

To see the implication of this analysis for the nominal exchange rate, we can rearrange the last equation to solve for the nominal exchange rate:

$$e = P^*/P$$

That is, the nominal exchange rate equals the ratio of the foreign price level (measured in units of the foreign currency) to the domestic price level (measured in units of the domestic currency). *According to the theory of purchasing-power parity, the nominal exchange rate between the currencies of two countries must reflect the different price levels in those countries.*

A key implication of this theory is that nominal exchange rates change when price levels change. As we saw in the preceding chapter, the price level in any country adjusts to bring the quantity of money supplied and the quantity of money demanded into balance. Because the nominal exchange rate depends on the price levels, it also depends on the money supply and money demand in each country. When a central bank in any country increases the money supply and causes the price level to rise, it also causes that country's currency to depreciate relative to other currencies in the world. In other words, *when the central bank prints large quantities of money, that money loses value both in terms of the goods and services it can buy and in terms of the amount of other currencies it can buy.*

We can now answer the question that began this section: Why did the Canadian dollar lose value compared to the German mark and gain value compared to the Italian lira? The answer is that Germany pursued a less inflationary monetary policy than Canada, and Italy pursued a more inflationary monetary policy. From 1970 to 2001, inflation in Canada was 5.2 percent per year. By contrast, inflation was 3.3 percent in Germany, and 9.5 percent in Italy. As Canadian prices rose relative to German prices, the value of the dollar fell relative to the mark. Similarly, as Canadian prices fell relative to Italian prices, the value of the dollar rose relative to the lira.

Germany and Italy now have a common currency—the euro. This means that the two countries share a single monetary policy and that the inflation rates in the two countries will be closely linked. But the historical lessons of the lira and the mark will apply to the euro as well. Whether the Canadian dollar buys more or fewer euros 20 years from now than it does today depends on whether the European Central Bank produces more or less inflation in Europe than the Bank of Canada does in Canada.

Albert Harlingue/Roger Viollet/Getty Images

case study — The Nominal Exchange Rate during a Hyperinflation

Macroeconomists can only rarely conduct controlled experiments. Most often, they must glean what they can from the natural experiments that history gives them. One natural experiment is hyperinflation—the high inflation that arises when a government turns to the printing press to pay for large amounts of government spending. Because hyperinflations are so extreme, they illustrate some basic economic principles with clarity.

Consider the German hyperinflation of the early 1920s. Figure 12.5 shows the German money supply, the German price level, and the nominal exchange rate (measured as U.S. cents per German mark) for that period. Notice that these series move closely together. When the supply of money starts growing quickly, the price level also takes off, and the German mark depreciates. When the money supply stabilizes, so does the price level and the exchange rate.

The pattern shown in this figure appears during every hyperinflation. It leaves no doubt that there is a fundamental link among money, prices, and the nominal exchange rate. The quantity theory of money discussed in the previous chapter explains how the money supply affects the price level. The theory of purchasing-power parity discussed here explains how the price level affects the nominal exchange rate. ■

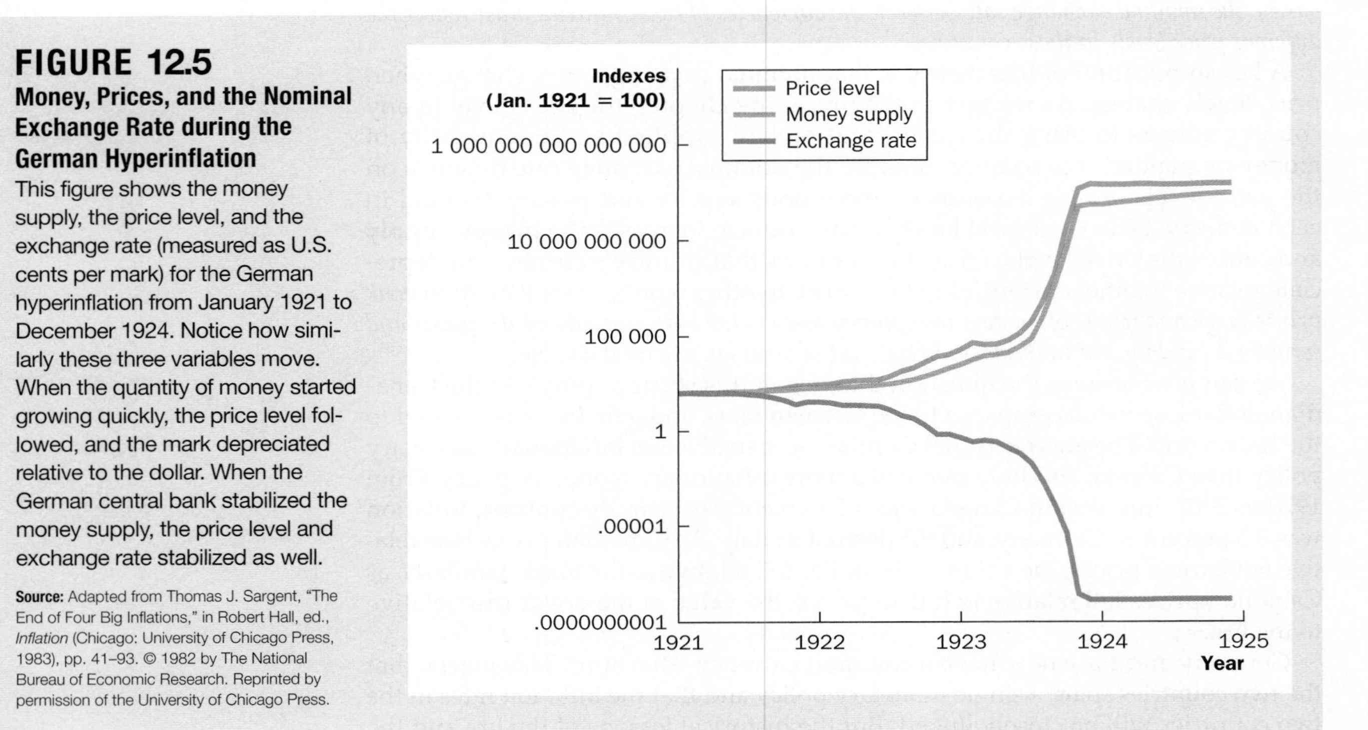

FIGURE 12.5

Money, Prices, and the Nominal Exchange Rate during the German Hyperinflation

This figure shows the money supply, the price level, and the exchange rate (measured as U.S. cents per mark) for the German hyperinflation from January 1921 to December 1924. Notice how similarly these three variables move. When the quantity of money started growing quickly, the price level followed, and the mark depreciated relative to the dollar. When the German central bank stabilized the money supply, the price level and exchange rate stabilized as well.

Source: Adapted from Thomas J. Sargent, "The End of Four Big Inflations," in Robert Hall, ed., *Inflation* (Chicago: University of Chicago Press, 1983), pp. 41–93. © 1982 by The National Bureau of Economic Research. Reprinted by permission of the University of Chicago Press.

12-3c Limitations of Purchasing-Power Parity

Purchasing-power parity provides a simple model of how exchange rates are determined. For understanding many economic phenomena, the theory works well. In particular, it can explain many long-term trends, such as the depreciation of the Canadian dollar against the German mark and the appreciation of the Canadian dollar against the Italian lira discussed earlier. It can also explain the major changes in exchange rates that occur during hyperinflations.

Yet the theory of purchasing-power parity is not completely accurate. That is, exchange rates do not always move to ensure that a dollar has the same real value in all countries all the time. There are two reasons why the theory of purchasing-power parity does not always hold in practice.

The first reason is that many goods are not easily traded. Imagine, for instance, that haircuts are more expensive in Paris than in Montreal. International travellers might avoid getting their haircuts in Paris, and some haircutters might move from Montreal to Paris. Yet such arbitrage would probably be too limited to eliminate the differences in prices. Thus, the deviation from purchasing-power parity might persist, and a dollar (or euro) would continue to buy less of a haircut in Paris than in Montreal.

The second reason why purchasing-power parity does not always hold is that even tradable goods are not always perfect substitutes when they are produced in different countries. For example, some consumers prefer German beer, and others prefer Canadian beer. Moreover, consumer tastes can change over time. If German beer suddenly becomes more popular, the increase in demand will drive up the price of German beer compared to Canadian beer. But despite this difference in prices in the two markets, there might be no opportunity for profitable arbitrage because consumers do not view the two beers as equivalent.

Thus, both because some goods are not tradable and because some tradable goods are not perfect substitutes with their foreign counterparts, purchasing-power parity is not a perfect theory of exchange-rate determination. For these reasons, real exchange rates fluctuate over time. Nonetheless, the theory of purchasing-power parity does provide a useful first step in understanding exchange rates. The basic logic is persuasive: As the real exchange rate drifts from the level predicted by purchasing-power parity, people have greater incentive to move goods across national borders. Even if the forces of purchasing-power parity do not completely fix the real exchange rate, they provide a reason to expect that changes in the real exchange rate are most often small or temporary. As a result, large and persistent movements in nominal exchange rates typically reflect changes in price levels at home and abroad.

© Jeff Greenberg/PhotoEdit

In Canada the 2015 price of a Big Mac was $5.85; in Japan it was 370 yen.

case study

The Hamburger Standard

When economists apply the theory of purchasing-power parity to explain exchange rates, they need data on the prices of a basket of goods available in different countries. One analysis of this sort is conducted by *The Economist*, an international newsmagazine. The magazine occasionally collects data on a basket of goods consisting of "two all-beef patties, special sauce, lettuce, cheese, pickles, onions, on a sesame seed bun." It's called the "Big Mac" and is sold by McDonald's around the world.

Once we have the prices of Big Macs in two countries denominated in the local currencies, we can compute the exchange rate predicted by the theory of purchasing-power parity. The predicted exchange rate is the one that makes the cost of the Big Mac the same in the two countries. For instance, if the price of a

Big Mac is $2 in the United States and 200 yen in Japan, purchasing-power parity would predict an exchange rate of 100 yen per U.S. dollar.

How well does purchasing-power parity work when applied using Big Mac prices? Here are some examples from an *Economist* article published on July 16, 2015, when the price of a Big Mac was $4.79 in the United States:

Country	Price of a Big Mac	Predicted Exchange Rate	Actual Exchange Rate
Canada	5.85 $CDN	1.22 $CDN/$US	1.29 $CDN/$US
South Korea	4300 won	898 won/$US	1143 won/$US
Japan	370 yen	77.2 yen/$US	123.9 yen/$US
Sweden	43.7 kronor	9.1 kronor/$US	8.5 kronor/$US
Mexico	48 pesos	10.2 pesos/$US	15.7 pesos/$US
Euro area	3.7 euros	0.77 euro/$US	0.91 euro/$US
Britain	2.89 pounds	0.60 pounds/$US	0.64 pounds/$US

Source: © The Economist Newspaper Limited, London. "The Big Mac Index," July 16, 2015. http://www.economist.com/content/big-mac-index

You can see that the predicted and actual exchange rates are not always exactly the same. After all, international arbitrage in Big Macs is not easy. Yet the predicted and the actual exchange rates are usually in the same ballpark. Purchasing-power parity is not a precise theory of exchange rates, but it often provides a reasonable first approximation. ■

Over the past 20 years, Brazil has experienced relatively high inflation while Japan has experienced relatively low inflation. What do you think has happened to the number of Brazilian reais a person can buy with a Japanese yen?

12-4 Interest Rate Determination in a Small Open Economy with Perfect Capital Mobility

When they want to predict whether Canadian interest rates will rise or fall, Canadian economists tend to pay a lot of attention to anticipated changes in U.S. interest rates. They do so because interest rates in Canada tend to increase when interest rates in the United States increase and fall when interest rates in the United States fall.

Why do interest rates in Canada and the United States tend to move up and down together? Recall our earlier discussion of the market for loanable funds, which we used to explain the determination of the real interest rate. That discussion assumed a closed economy—one that does not trade goods and services with other economies. This assumption is not appropriate for describing the Canadian economy. As we saw earlier in this chapter, Canada is an open economy in which trade with other countries makes up a very large part of GDP. For this reason, economists prefer to use a model of the Canadian economy that takes into consideration these trade flows. The model most economists prefer to use is one that describes Canada as a *small open economy with perfect capital mobility.*

In this section, we take a first step toward modifying our description of the market for loanable funds in a small open economy with perfect capital mobility. We will see that determining the real interest rate in such an economy is pretty straightforward. In the next chapter we will make use of this discussion to modify our discussion of the market for loanable funds in a way that is appropriate for a small open economy.

12-4a A Small Open Economy

What do we mean when we say Canada is a **small open economy** with perfect capital mobility? By "small" we mean an economy that is a small part of the world economy. In particular, we are describing an economy that, by itself, has only a negligible effect on the prices of goods and services and on interest rates in the rest of the world. Thus, for example, an increase in demand for computer chips by Canadians is unlikely to have an effect on the world price for computer chips. Canada's share of the total world demand for computer chips is too small for such a change to have anything but a negligible effect on the world price. Canadian financial markets are also "small" in this sense. An increase in the supply of Canadian bonds has a negligible effect on the total world supply of bonds. Changes in Canadian financial markets therefore have negligible effects on world interest rates.

small open economy
an economy that trades goods and services with other economies and, by itself, has a negligible effect on world prices and interest rates

12-4b Perfect Capital Mobility

By **perfect capital mobility** we mean that Canadians have full access to world financial markets and that people in the rest of the world have full access to the Canadian financial market.

perfect capital mobility
full access to world financial markets

The implication of perfect capital mobility for a small open economy like Canada's is that the real interest rate in Canada should equal the real interest rate prevailing in world financial markets. In simple mathematical terms, if r is the Canadian real interest rate and r^w is the world real interest rate, then

$$r = r^w$$

Why should this be so? Some examples will illustrate. If $r^w = 8$ percent and $r = 5$ percent, this situation cannot persist. The reason is simple: With full access to world financial markets, Canadian savers would prefer to buy foreign assets that pay an interest rate of 8 percent than Canadian assets that pay an interest rate of just 5 percent. We would expect to see savers sell their Canadian assets and buy foreign assets instead. The sale of Canadian assets then forces Canadian borrowers to offer a more attractive interest rate. Indeed, we would expect them to offer an interest rate of 8 percent, the world interest rate.

Similarly, if $r^w = 5$ percent and $r = 8$ percent, this situation cannot persist either. With full access to world financial markets, Canadian borrowers would prefer to borrow from foreigners at an interest rate of 5 percent than from Canadians at an interest rate of 8 percent. In order to find someone to whom to lend money, Canadian savers would have to offer to lend their savings at 5 percent, the world interest rate. As long as the Canadian and the foreign assets are close substitutes, the difference in interest rates provides an arbitrage opportunity for either borrowers or savers.

The logic by which the real interest rates in Canada should adjust to equal the real interest rate in the rest of the world should remind you of our discussion of the law of one price and purchasing-power parity. This is because the concepts are closely related. Just as we discussed earlier in the context of the prices of goods, people taking advantage of arbitrage opportunities will ensure that price differentials disappear. The only difference is that here the price we are talking about is the price of borrowing: the real interest rate. The theory that the real interest rate in Canada should equal that in the rest of the world is known as **interest rate parity**.

interest rate parity
a theory of interest rate determination whereby the real interest rate on comparable financial assets should be the same in all economies with full access to world financial markets

12-4c Limitations to Interest Rate Parity

Just as there are limitations to purchasing-power parity explaining how exchange rates are determined, there are also limitations to interest rate parity explaining how real interest rates are determined. The real interest rate in Canada is not always equal to the real interest rate in the rest of the world, for two key reasons.

The first reason is that financial assets carry with them the possibility of default. That is, while the seller of a financial asset promises to repay the buyer at some future date, the possibility always exists that the seller may not do so. If the seller does, in fact, renege on this agreement, the seller is said to be in default of the loan. Buyers of financial assets are therefore said to incur a *default risk*. Buyers of financial assets try to learn about relative levels of default risk in order to better evaluate the relative attractiveness of different financial assets. The higher the default risk, the higher the interest rate that asset buyers (savers) demand from asset sellers (borrowers). If the seller of one financial asset is perceived to be more likely to default than the seller of another otherwise similar asset, the difference in the rate of interest paid on these assets may not necessarily represent an arbitrage opportunity. For this reason, interest rate differences may persist.

The second reason why interest rate parity does not always hold in practice is because financial assets offered for sale in different countries are not necessarily perfect substitutes for one another. For example, the manner in which governments tax the returns earned on financial assets differs across countries. While similar assets in two countries may pay the same rate of pre-tax return, different tax regimes in these two countries may result in different after-tax returns. Those seeking arbitrage opportunities look only at after-tax returns. Thus, while after-tax returns will be equalized internationally, differences in pre-tax rates of return will persist.

Because of the differences in default risk and in tax treatments, interest rate parity is not a perfect theory of real interest rate determination in a small open economy. For this reason, we do not expect real interest rates in Canada to exactly equal those in the rest of the world. Nonetheless, interest rate parity does offer a persuasive argument for believing that the difference in real interest rates in Canada versus the rest of the world will be relatively small, and that Canadian interest rates will fluctuate with those in the rest of the world.

The data bear this out. Over the 32-year period of 1984–2015, the real interest rates paid on long-term government debt in Canada and the United States have tended to move up and down together. The average real interest rate over this period was 3.7 percent in Canada and 3.0 percent in the United States. The 0.7 percentage-point difference is a measure of how much more, on average, Canadian lenders had to offer to compensate borrowers for higher default risk and higher tax rates in Canada. This difference grew wider during the 1980s and early 1990s as Canadian tax rates increased relative to those in the United States and as frequent constitutional crises and growing levels of government debt raised concerns in the minds of lenders about the possibility of the Canadian government defaulting on its debt.

Since 1996 the difference in interest rates has grown much smaller. Over the period 1996–2015, the difference in real interest rates has fallen in half and averaged just 0.4 percentage points. This change reflects less frequent constitutional crises over this period and the fact that Canadian governments reined in their deficits and began to reduce their debt loads relative to levels of U.S. government debt. If we interpret the U.S. interest rate as the "world" interest rate, r^w, then these data provide support for our imposing the interest rate parity condition on our model. That will be our strategy when we turn to the macroeconomic theory of the open economy.

12-5 Conclusion

The purpose of this chapter has been to develop some basic concepts that macroeconomists use to study open economies. You should now understand why a nation's net exports must equal its net capital outflow, and why national saving must equal domestic investment plus net capital outflow. You should understand that when a nation is running a trade surplus, it must be sending capital abroad, and that when it is running a trade deficit, it must be experiencing a net capital inflow. You should also understand the meaning of the nominal and real exchange rates, as well as the implications and limitations of purchasing-power parity as a theory of how exchange rates are determined. Finally, you should understand why real interest rates in Canada tend to rise and fall with interest rates in the rest of the world.

The macroeconomic variables defined here offer a starting point for analyzing an open economy's interactions with the rest of the world. In the next chapter we develop a model that can explain what determines these variables. We can then discuss how various events and policies affect a country's trade balance and the rate at which nations make exchanges in world markets.

summary

- Net exports are the value of domestic goods and services sold abroad minus the value of foreign goods and services sold domestically. Net capital outflow is the acquisition of foreign assets by domestic residents minus the acquisition of domestic assets by foreigners. Because every international transaction involves an exchange of an asset for a good or service, an economy's net capital outflow always equals its net exports.
- An economy's saving can be used either to finance investment at home or to buy assets abroad. Thus, national saving equals domestic investment plus net capital outflow.
- The nominal exchange rate is the relative price of the currency of two countries, and the real exchange rate is the relative price of the goods and services of two countries. When the nominal exchange rate changes so that each dollar buys more foreign currency, the dollar is said to *appreciate* or *strengthen.* When the nominal exchange rate changes so that each dollar buys less foreign currency, the dollar is said to *depreciate* or *weaken.*
- According to the theory of purchasing-power parity, a dollar (or a unit of any other currency) should be able to buy the same quantity of goods in all countries. This theory implies that the nominal exchange rate between the currencies of two countries should reflect the price levels in those countries. As a result, countries with relatively high inflation should have depreciating currencies, and countries with relatively low inflation should have appreciating currencies.
- Most economists prefer to use a model that describes Canada as a small open economy with perfect capital mobility. In such economies, interest rate parity is expected to hold. Interest rate parity is a theory that predicts interest rates in Canada will equal those in the rest of the world. Due to differences in tax rates and concerns about default risk, interest rates in Canada are not expected to exactly equal those in the rest of the world, but we do expect Canadian interest rates to rise and fall with increases and decreases in world interest rates.

KEY concepts

closed economy, *p. 257*
open economy, *p. 257*
exports, *p. 257*
imports, *p. 257*
net exports, *p. 258*
trade balance, *p. 258*

trade surplus, *p. 258*
trade deficit, *p. 258*
balanced trade, *p. 258*
net capital outflow, *p. 262*
nominal exchange rate, *p. 268*
appreciation, *p. 269*
depreciation, *p. 269*
real exchange rate, *p. 270*
purchasing-power parity, *p. 274*
small open economy, *p. 279*
perfect capital mobility, *p. 279*
interest rate parity, *p. 279*

QUESTIONS FOR **review**

1. Define net exports and net capital outflow. Explain how and why they are related.
2. Explain the relationship among saving, investment, and net capital outflow.
3. If a car in Japan costs 500 000 yen, a similar car in Canada costs $10 000, and a dollar can buy 100 yen, what are the nominal and real exchange rates?
4. Describe the economic logic behind the theory of purchasing-power parity.
5. If the Bank of Canada started printing large quantities of Canadian dollars, what would happen to the number of Japanese yen a dollar could buy?
6. Describe the economic logic behind the theory of interest rate parity.

QUICK CHECK **multiple choice**

1. Comparing the Canadian economy today to that of 1950, what does one find to be true about exports and imports today as a percentage of GDP?
   a. exports and imports are both higher
   b. exports and imports are both lower
   c. exports are higher, and imports are lower
   d. exports are lower, and imports are higher
2. In an open economy, national saving equals domestic investment
   a. plus the net outflow of capital abroad.
   b. minus the net exports of goods and services.
   c. plus the government's budget deficit.
   d. minus foreign portfolio investment.
3. If the value of a nation's imports exceeds the value of its exports, which of the following is NOT true?
   a. Net exports are negative.
   b. GDP is less than the sum of consumption, investment, and government purchases.
   c. Domestic investment is greater than national saving.
   d. The nation is experiencing a net outflow of capital.
4. If a nation's currency doubles in value on foreign exchange markets, the currency is said to___, reflecting a change in the ___ exchange rate.
   a. appreciate, nominal
   b. appreciate, real
   c. depreciate, nominal
   d. depreciate, real
5. If a cup of coffee costs 2 euros in Paris and $6 in Toronto and purchasing-power parity holds, what is the exchange rate?
   a. 1/4 euro per dollar
   b. 1/3 euro per dollar
   c. 3 euros per dollar
   d. 4 euros per dollar
6. The theory of purchasing-power parity says that higher inflation in a nation causes the nation's currency to___, leaving the ___ exchange rate unchanged.
   a. appreciate, nominal
   b. appreciate, real
   c. depreciate, nominal
   d. depreciate, real

PROBLEMS AND **applications**

1. How would the following transactions affect Canada's exports, imports, and net exports?
   a. A Canadian art professor spends the summer touring museums in Europe.
   b. Students in Paris flock to the latest Diana Krall concert.
   c. Your uncle buys a new Volvo.
   d. The student bookstore at Oxford University sells a pair of Bauer hockey skates.
   e. A Canadian citizen shops at a store in northern Vermont to avoid Canadian sales taxes.
2. International trade in each of the following products has increased over time. Suggest some reasons why this might be so.
   a. wheat
   b. banking services
   c. computer software
   d. automobiles

3. Describe the difference between foreign direct investment and foreign portfolio investment. Who is more likely to engage in foreign direct investment—a corporation or an individual investor? Who is more likely to engage in foreign portfolio investment?
4. How would the following transactions affect Canada's net capital outflow? Also, state whether each involves direct investment or portfolio investment.
   a. A Canadian cellular phone company establishes an office in the Czech Republic.
   b. Harrod's of London sells shares to the Ontario Teachers' Pension Plan.
   c. Honda expands its factory in Alliston, Ontario.
   d. A Bank of Montreal mutual fund sells its Volkswagen shares to a French investor.
5. Holding national saving constant, does an increase in net capital outflow increase, decrease, or have no effect on a country's accumulation of domestic capital?
6. The business section of most major newspapers contains a table showing Canadian exchange rates. Find such a table and use it to answer the following questions.
   a. Does this table show nominal or real exchange rates? Explain.
   b. What are the exchange rates between the United States and Canada and between Canada and Japan? Calculate the exchange rate between the United States and Japan.
   c. If Canadian inflation exceeds Japanese inflation over the next year, would you expect the Canadian dollar to appreciate or depreciate relative to the Japanese yen?
7. Would each of the following groups be happy or unhappy if the Canadian dollar appreciated? Explain.
   a. Dutch pension funds holding Canadian government bonds
   b. Canadian manufacturing industries
   c. Australian tourists planning a trip to Canada
   d. A Canadian firm trying to purchase property overseas
8. What is happening to Canada's real exchange rate in each of the following situations? Explain.
   a. Canada's nominal exchange rate is unchanged, but prices rise faster in Canada than abroad.
   b. Canada's nominal exchange rate is unchanged, but prices rise faster abroad than in Canada.
   c. Canada's nominal exchange rate declines, and prices are unchanged in Canada and abroad.
   d. Canada's nominal exchange rate declines, and prices rise faster abroad than in Canada.
9. List three goods for which the law of one price is likely to hold, and three goods for which it is not. Justify your choices.
10. A can of pop costs $0.75 in Canada and 12 pesos in Mexico. What would the peso–dollar exchange rate be if purchasing-power parity holds? If a monetary expansion caused all prices in Mexico to double, so that the price of pop rose to 24 pesos, what would happen to the peso–dollar exchange rate?
11. Assume that Canadian wheat sells for $100 per bushel, Russian wheat sells for 1600 rubles per bushel, and the nominal exchange rate is 4 rubles per dollar.
    a. Explain how you could make a profit from this situation. What would be your profit per bushel of wheat? If other people exploit the same opportunity, what would happen to the price of wheat in Russia and the price of wheat in Canada?
    b. Suppose that wheat is the only commodity in the world. What would happen to the real exchange rate between Canada and Russia?
12. A case study in the chapter analyzed purchasing-power parity for several countries using the price of Big Macs. Here are data for a few more countries:

Country	Price of a Big Mac		Predicted Exchange Rate	Actual Exchange Rate
Indonesia	30 500 rupiah	___	rupiah/$US	13 344 rupiah/$US
Hungary	900 forint	___	forint/$US	283 forint/$US
Czech Republic	70.0 koruna	___	koruna/$US	24.7 koruna/$US
Thailand	108 baht	___	baht/$US	34.1 baht/$US
China	17.0 yuan	___	yuan/$US	6.21 yuan/$US

Source: Based on data from "The Big Mac Index," The Economist Newspaper Limited, London. July 16, 2015. http://www.economist.com/content/big-mac-index

   a. For each country, compute the predicted exchange rate of the local currency per U.S. dollar. (Recall that the U.S. price of a Big Mac was $4.79.) How well does the theory of purchasing-power parity explain exchange rates?
   b. According to purchasing-power parity, what is the predicted exchange rate between the Hungarian forint and the Chinese yuan? What is the actual exchange rate?

Taina Sohlman/Shutterstock.com

A Macroeconomic Theory of the Small Open Economy

LEARNING **objectives**

In this chapter, you will ...

1. Build a model to explain an open economy's trade balance and exchange rate
2. Use the model to analyze the effects of government budget deficits
3. Use the model to analyze the macroeconomic effects of trade policies
4. Use the model to analyze political instability and capital flight

Issues related to international trade are of constant concern to Canadians. In part this is because many Canadians are employed in industries that depend on international trade, and because all Canadians consume goods and services that are available only because of trade. Trade issues are also of concern to Canadians because these issues are often the sources of conflict with our trading partners. For example, softwood lumber producers in the United States have often claimed that Canadian softwood lumber producers receive an unfair competitive advantage due to the nature of certain government policies. Canadians, in turn, complain about the frequent imposition of "Buy American" laws that prohibit Canadian firms from selling in the United States. More recently, attention has focused on the Trans-Pacific Partnership (TPP), an agreement involving Canada and 11 other countries intended to lower barriers to trade. Like all trade agreements, the TPP raises concerns about what it means for employment, prices, and the viability of certain industries in the Canadian economy.

In addition to concerns about international trade in goods and services, Canadians have also often expressed concern about the purchase of Canadian assets by foreigners. As we have seen, Canada's net capital outflow (*NCO*) has been negative for much of the past 40 years. Over that period, foreigners purchased more Canadian assets than Canadians purchased foreign assets. As a result, many firms located in Canada are owned by foreigners. In the past, this situation has prompted the government to introduce legislation designed to limit the extent of foreign ownership. As we showed in the previous chapter, in 1999, Canada's *NCO* turned large and positive and remained so until 2008. During that ten-year period, Canadians were buying more foreign assets than foreigners were buying Canadian assets. To some, this situation is also indicative of economic problems: Canadians' savings are going abroad to purchase foreign assets.

Imagine that you are the prime minister and some people are demanding that you do something about the fact that Canada's net capital outflow is positive, while others are ready to criticize if net capital outflow returns to negative values. What should you do? Should you try to place limits on international trade? Should you discourage or encourage foreigners to buy Canadian steel or oil and gas firms?

To understand what factors determine a country's trade balance and how government policies can affect it, we need a macroeconomic theory of the open economy. The preceding chapter introduced some of the key macroeconomic variables that describe an economy's relationship with other economies—including net exports, net capital outflow, and the real and nominal exchange rates. The preceding chapter also described Canada as a "small" open economy—an open economy for which the world interest rate and the world price of goods and services are unaffected by what happens in Canada. This chapter develops a model that identifies the forces that determine these variables and shows how these variables are related to one another, all in the context of a small open economy like Canada.

To develop this macroeconomic model of a small open economy, we build on our previous analysis in three important ways. First, the model takes the economy's GDP as given. We assume that the economy's output of goods and services, as measured by real GDP, is determined by the supplies of the factors of production and by the available production technology that turns these inputs into output. Second, the model takes the economy's price level as given. We assume that the price level adjusts to bring the supply and demand for money into balance. Third, the model takes the real interest rate as given. The real interest rate is assumed to equal the world interest rate because of perfect capital mobility. In other words, this chapter takes as a starting point the lessons learned in previous chapters about the determination of the economy's output, interest rate, and price level.

The goal of the model in this chapter is to highlight the forces that determine the economy's trade balance and exchange rate. In one sense, the model is simple: It applies the tools of supply and demand to an open economy. Yet the model is also more complicated than others we have seen because it involves looking simultaneously at two related markets—the market for loanable funds and the market for foreign-currency exchange. After we develop this model of the small open economy, we use it to examine how various events and policies affect the economy's trade balance and exchange rate.

13-1 Supply and Demand for Loanable Funds and for Foreign-Currency Exchange

To understand the forces at work in an open economy, we focus on supply and demand in two markets. The first is the market for loanable funds, which coordinates the economy's saving, investment, and the flow of loanable funds abroad (called the *net capital outflow*). The second is the market for foreign-currency exchange, which coordinates people who want to exchange the domestic currency for the currency of other countries. In this section we discuss supply and demand in each of these markets. In the next section we put these markets together to explain the overall equilibrium for an open economy.

13-1a The Market for Loanable Funds

When we first analyzed the role of the financial system in Chapter 8, we made the simplifying assumption that the financial system consists of only one market, called the *market for loanable funds*. All savers go to this market to deposit their saving, and all borrowers go to this market to get their loans. In this market, there is one interest rate, which is both the return to saving and the cost of borrowing.

To understand the market for loanable funds in an open economy, the place to start is the identity discussed in the preceding chapter:

$$S = I + NCO$$

$$\text{Saving} = \text{Domestic investment} + \text{Net capital outflow}$$

This identity emphasizes that in an open economy the amount that a nation saves does not have to equal the amount it spends to purchase domestic capital. If the amount of national saving exceeds the amount needed to finance the purchase of domestic capital, the amount left over can be used to finance the purchase of an asset abroad. In this case, net capital outflow (NCO) is a positive number. If national saving is insufficient to finance the purchase of domestic capital, the shortfall can be met by the savings of foreigners. In this case, NCO is a negative number. The equation identifies the three components of the market for loanable funds in an open economy and shows how they are related. The demand for loanable funds comes from domestic investment (I).

In Canada, the supply of loanable funds from national saving (S) has at times not been sufficient to satisfy the demand for loanable funds for domestic investment (I), so we have had $S < I$. In those cases, the shortfall has been met by the savings of foreigners and *net capital outflow* has been negative. For much of the past 40 years, that situation described the Canadian experience. At other times in Canada, the supply of loanable funds from national saving (S) has been more than sufficient to satisfy the demand for loanable funds for domestic investment (I), so $S > I$. In those cases, Canadian savings have been used to purchase foreign assets and *NCO* has been positive. That situation described the Canadian experience over the 1999–2008 period. In both of these cases, the identity relating values of national saving (S), domestic investment (I), and net capital outflow (*NCO*) was satisfied.

The next step in understanding the market for loanable funds in a small open economy is to recall our discussion from the preceding chapter on interest rate determination. We found that in a small open economy with perfect capital mobility, like Canada, if we ignore differences in tax treatments and default risk, the domestic interest rate will equal the world interest rate. The reason for this is simple. Suppose that the Canadian interest rate is 5 percent and the world interest rate is 8 percent. This situation cannot persist because with full access to world financial markets, Canadian savers would prefer to buy foreign assets that pay the higher interest rate. We would expect to see savers sell their holdings of Canadian assets and buy foreign assets instead. To halt the sale of Canadian assets, Canadian borrowers would have to offer to pay the more attractive world interest rate of 8 percent. Similarly, if the world interest rate is 5 percent and the Canadian interest rate is 8 percent, Canadian borrowers would prefer to borrow from foreigners. In order to find someone to whom to lend money, Canadian savers would have to offer to lend their savings at 5 percent, the world interest rate.

Now we are ready to put these ideas to work in a simple diagram. The market for loanable funds is represented in the familiar supply-and-demand diagram in Figure 13.1. As in our earlier analysis of the financial system, the demand curve slopes downward because a higher real interest rate makes borrowing to finance capital projects more costly; thus, it discourages investment and reduces the quantity of loanable funds demanded. The supply curve slopes upward because a higher real interest rate encourages people to save and, therefore, raises the quantity of loanable funds made available by national saving. Unlike the situation in our previous discussion, however, in a small open economy with perfect capital mobility, the supply curve represents only part of the supply of loanable funds available. The supply curve shows the amount of national saving—the savings of Canadians—available at every real interest rate. It shows, then, that a higher interest rate increases the quantity of loanable funds made available by Canadians. If we were discussing a closed economy, we would need to consider only the supply of loanable funds made available by the savings of Canadians. In that case we would conclude that the real rate of interest would be determined by the intersection of the demand and supply curves for loanable funds. In a small open economy with perfect capital mobility, however, the interest rate is equal to the world interest rate, and we need to also consider the role played by the savings of foreigners.

In panel (a) of Figure 13.1, the world interest rate is greater than the Canadian interest rate would be if this were a closed economy. Because there is perfect capital mobility, the Canadian interest rate is given by the world interest rate. At this interest rate, the demand for loanable funds in Canada (I) is \$100 billion, and the supply of loanable funds that Canadians make available (S) is \$150 billion. At this world interest rate, the supply of Canadians' savings is more than enough to satisfy the demand for loanable funds in Canada. The excess supply of loanable funds, \$50 billion, is therefore available to purchase foreign assets. In this

FIGURE 13.1

The Market for Loanable Funds

In a small open economy with perfect capital mobility, like Canada, the domestic real interest rate is equal to the world real interest rate. Domestic investment determines the demand for loanable funds. National saving determines the supply of loanable funds provided by Canadians. In panel (a), at the world interest rate, domestic investment is $100 billion and Canadians save $150 billion. The difference between domestic investment and national saving, $50 billion, is net capital outflow. It measures the value of foreign assets purchased by Canadians. In panel (b), at the world interest rate, domestic investment is $130 billion and Canadians save only $90 billion. The shortfall of national saving relative to domestic investment, $40 billion, is made up by the savings of foreigners. In this case, net capital outflow is negative, indicating that foreigners are purchasing more Canadian assets than Canadians are purchasing foreign assets.

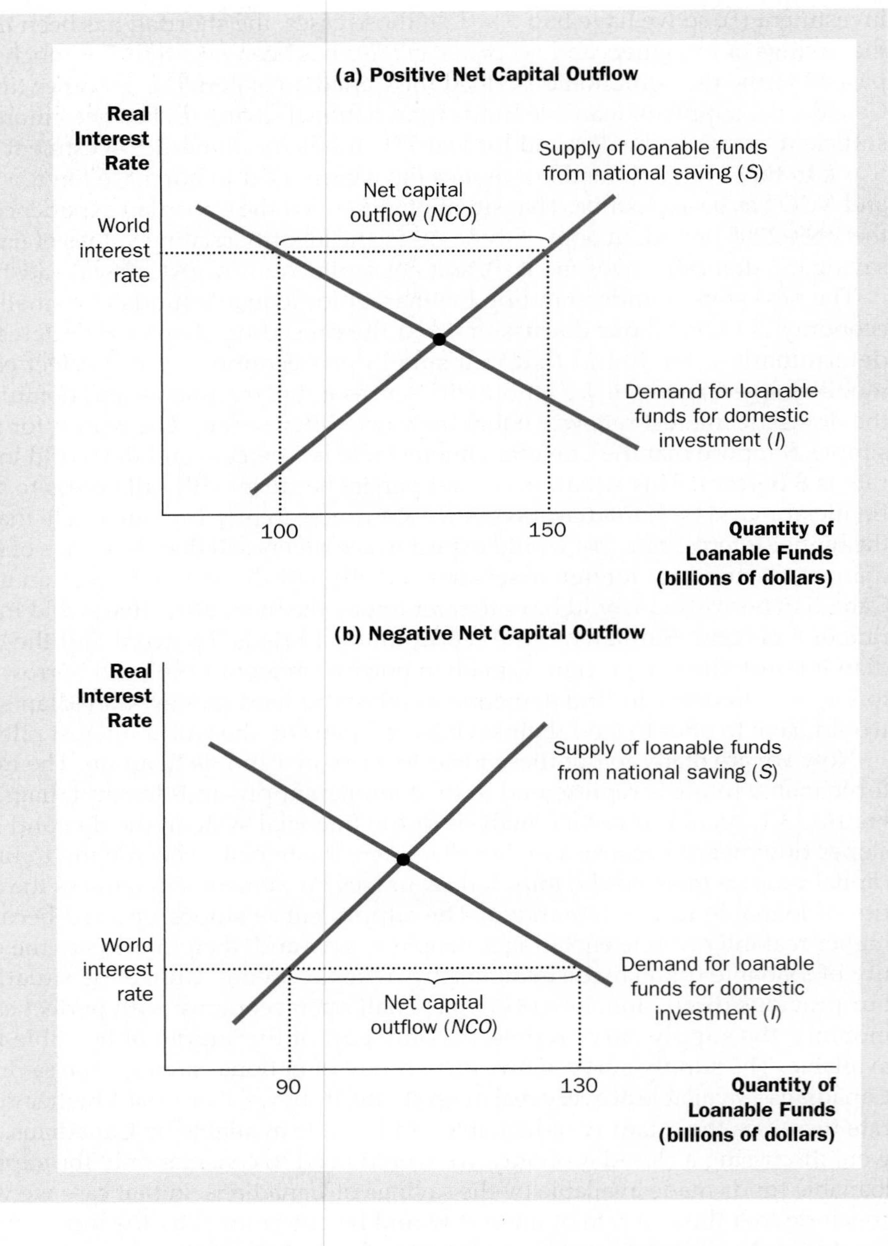

situation, net capital outflow (*NCO*) is $50 billion. Note that $S = I + NCO$, as required by our accounting identity.

In panel (b) of Figure 13.1, the world interest rate is shown as being less than the interest rate would be if this were a closed economy. At this world interest rate, the demand for loanable funds in Canada (*I*) is now $130 billion, and the supply of loanable funds that Canadians make available (*S*) is $90 billion. At this world interest rate, the supply of Canadians' savings is not enough to satisfy the demand for loanable funds in Canada. The excess demand for loanable funds, $40 billion, must therefore be satisfied by the savings of foreigners. In this situation, *NCO* takes on a negative value: −$40 billion. (Don't be confused by the negative number. We have defined net capital outflow as the amount of foreign assets that Canadians purchase minus the amount of Canadian assets that foreigners buy. A negative value simply indicates a net purchase of Canadian assets by foreigners.) Note that, once again, $S = I + NCO$ as required by our accounting identity.

These two diagrams show that the market for loanable funds in a small open economy with perfect capital mobility is different from that in a closed economy. In particular, the interest rate is no longer determined by the demand and supply of loanable funds. Instead, the interest rate is equal to the world interest rate. As a result, the quantity of loanable funds made available by the savings of Canadians does not have to equal the quantity of loanable funds demanded for domestic investment. The difference between these two amounts is net capital outflow. Net capital outflow is determined by the difference between the supply of loanable funds due to national saving (S) and the demand for loanable funds (I) at the world interest rate. If we recall another identity from the preceding chapter,

$$NCO = NX$$

Net capital outflow = Net exports

we can also state this result as follows: Net exports are determined by the difference between the supply of loanable funds due to national saving (S) and the demand for loanable funds (I) at the world interest rate. These two statements are equivalent because net exports must equal net capital outflow.

13-1b The Market for Foreign-Currency Exchange

The second market in our model of the open economy is the market for foreign-currency exchange. The market for foreign exchange exists because people want to trade goods, services, and financial assets with people in other countries, but they want to be paid for these things in their own currency. This means that, for a Canadian to purchase a good, service, or financial asset from someone in another country, the Canadian must purchase the other country's currency as well. Similarly, for a foreigner to purchase a good, service, or financial asset from someone in Canada, the foreigner must purchase Canadian dollars. The need to make these currency exchanges means that a market must exist where the exchanges can take place. This is the foreign-currency exchange market. In this section we will describe the market in which Canadian dollars are traded for foreign currencies.

To understand the market for foreign-currency exchange, we begin with the accounting identity we just discussed:

$$NCO = NX$$

Net capital outflow = Net exports

If we combine this identity with the identity we discussed earlier,

$$S = I + NCO$$

Saving = Domestic investment + Net capital outflow

we see that

$$S - I = NX$$

Saving − Domestic investment = Net exports

Each of these statements is an identity and, as such, each describes a relationship that must be true. The last identity is useful for describing the market for foreign-currency exchange. This identity states that the imbalance between the domestic supply of loanable funds that is due to national saving (S) and the demand for loanable funds for domestic investment (I) must equal the imbalance between exports and imports (NX). This must be true because, as we have just seen, the imbalance between the domestic supply and demand for loanable funds must equal net capital outflow (NCO), which in turn must equal net exports.

We can view the two sides of this identity as representing the two sides of the market for foreign-currency exchange. The difference between national saving and domestic investment represents net capital outflow. This difference, then, represents the quantity of dollars supplied in the market for foreign-currency exchange for the purpose of buying foreign assets. For example, when a Canadian mutual fund wants to buy a Japanese government bond, it needs to exchange dollars for yen, so it *supplies* dollars in a market for foreign-currency exchange. Net exports represent the quantity of dollars demanded in that market for the purpose of buying Canadian net exports of goods and services. For example, when a Japanese airline wants to buy a plane made by Bombardier, it needs to exchange its yen for dollars, so it *demands* dollars in the market for foreign-currency exchange.

What price balances the supply and demand in the market for foreign-currency exchange? The answer is the real exchange rate. As we saw in the preceding chapter, the real exchange rate is the relative price of domestic and foreign goods and, therefore, is a key determinant of net exports. When Canada's real exchange rate appreciates, Canadian goods become more expensive relative to foreign goods, making Canadian goods less attractive to consumers both at home and abroad. As a result, exports from Canada fall, and imports into Canada rise. For both reasons, net exports fall. Hence, an appreciation of the real exchange rate reduces the quantity of dollars demanded in the market for foreign-currency exchange.

Figure 13.2 shows supply and demand in the market for foreign-currency exchange. The demand curve slopes downward for the reason we just discussed: A higher real exchange rate makes Canadian goods more expensive and reduces the quantity of dollars demanded to buy those goods. The supply curve is vertical because the quantity of dollars supplied for net capital outflow does not depend on the real exchange rate. (As discussed earlier, net capital outflow depends on the real interest rate. When discussing the market for foreign-currency exchange, we take the real interest rate and net capital outflow as given.)

It might seem strange at first that net capital outflow does not depend on the exchange rate. After all, a higher exchange value of the Canadian dollar not only makes foreign goods less expensive for Canadian buyers but also makes foreign assets less expensive. One might guess that this would make foreign assets more attractive. But remember that a Canadian investor will eventually want to turn the foreign asset, as well as any profits earned on it, back into dollars. For example, a high value of the dollar makes it less expensive for a Canadian to buy stock in a Japanese company, but when that stock pays dividends, those will be in yen. As these yen are exchanged for dollars, the high value of the dollar means that the dividend will buy fewer dollars. Thus, changes in the exchange rate influence both the cost of buying foreign assets and the benefit of owning them, and these two effects offset each other. For these reasons, our model of the open economy posits that net capital outflow does not depend on the real exchange rate, as represented by the vertical supply curve in Figure 13.2.

The real exchange rate adjusts to balance the supply and demand for dollars just as the price of any good adjusts to balance supply and demand for that good. If the real exchange rate was below the equilibrium level, the quantity of dollars

FIGURE 13.2

The Market for Foreign-Currency Exchange

The real exchange rate is determined by the supply and demand for foreign-currency exchange. The supply of dollars to be exchanged into foreign currency comes from net capital outflow. Net capital outflow, in turn, equals the difference between the demand for loanable funds (domestic investment) and the supply of loanable funds made available by the savings of Canadians. Because neither domestic savings nor domestic investment depends on the real exchange rate, the supply curve is vertical. The demand for dollars to be exchanged into foreign currency comes from net exports. Because a lower real exchange rate stimulates net exports (and thus increases the quantity of dollars demanded to pay for these net exports), the demand curve is downward sloping. At the equilibrium real exchange rate, the number of dollars people supply to buy foreign assets exactly balances the number of dollars people demand to buy net exports.

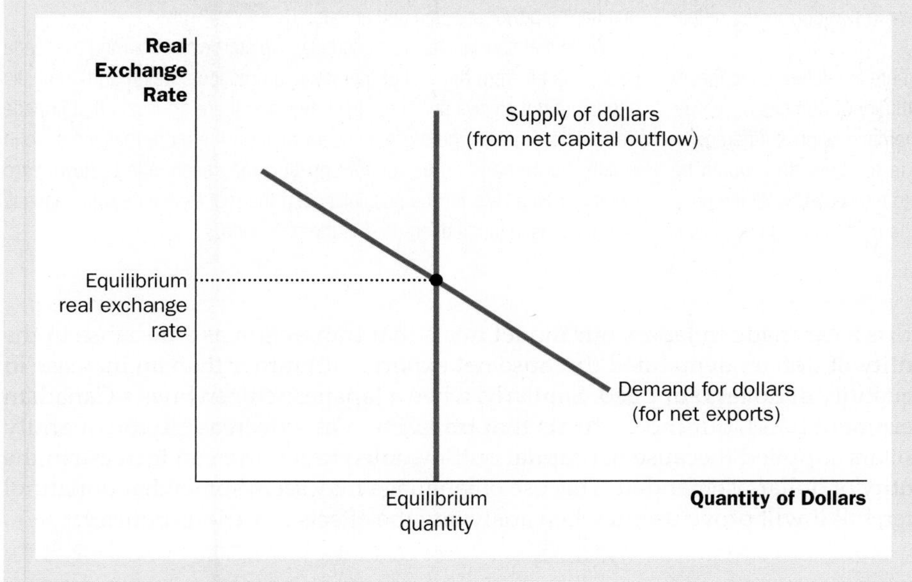

supplied would be less than the quantity demanded. The resulting shortage of dollars would push the value of the dollar upward. Conversely, if the real exchange rate was above the equilibrium level, the quantity of dollars supplied would exceed the quantity demanded. The surplus of dollars would drive the value of the dollar downward. *At the equilibrium real exchange rate, the demand for dollars to buy net exports exactly balances the supply of dollars to be exchanged into foreign currency to buy assets abroad.*

13-1c Disentangling Supply and Demand in the Market for Foreign-Currency Exchange

Suppose the owner of an apple orchard decides to consume some of his own apples. Does this decision represent an increase in the demand for apples or a decrease in the supply? Either answer is defensible, and as long as we are careful in our subsequent analysis, nothing important will hinge on which answer we choose. Sometimes how we divide things between supply and demand is a bit arbitrary.

This is the case in the market for foreign-currency exchange described in Figure 13.2. In our model, net exports are the source of the demand for dollars, and net capital outflow is the source of the supply. Thus, when a Canadian resident

FYI Purchasing-Power Parity as a Special Case

An alert reader of this book might ask: Why are we developing a theory of the exchange rate here? Didn't we already do that in the preceding chapter?

As you may recall, the preceding chapter developed a theory of the exchange rate called *purchasing-power parity*. This theory asserts that a dollar (or any other currency) must buy the same quantity of goods and services in every country. As a result, the real exchange rate is fixed, and all changes in the nominal exchange rate between two currencies reflect changes in the price levels in the two countries.

The model of the exchange rate developed here is related to the theory of purchasing-power parity. According to the theory of purchasing-power parity, international trade responds quickly to international price differences. If goods were cheaper in one country than in another, they would be exported from the first country and imported into the second until the price difference disappeared. In other words, the theory of purchasing-power parity assumes that net exports are highly responsive to small changes in the real exchange rate. If net exports were in fact so responsive, the demand curve in Figure 13.2 would be horizontal.

Thus, the theory of purchasing-power parity can be viewed as a special case of the model considered here. In that special case, the demand curve for foreign-currency exchange, rather than being downward sloping, is horizontal at the level of the real exchange rate that ensures parity of purchasing power at home and abroad.

While that special case is a good place to start when studying exchange rates, it is far from the end of the story. In practice, foreign and domestic goods are not always perfect substitutes, and there are costs that impede trade. This chapter, therefore, concentrates on the more realistic case in which the demand curve for foreign-currency exchange is downward sloping. This allows for the possibility that the real exchange rate changes over time, as in fact it often does in the real world.

imports a car made in Japan, our model treats that transaction as a decrease in the quantity of dollars demanded (because net exports fall) rather than an increase in the quantity of dollars supplied. Similarly, when a Japanese citizen buys a Canadian government bond, our model treats that transaction as a decrease in the quantity of dollars supplied (because net capital outflow falls) rather than an increase in the quantity of dollars demanded. This use of language may seem somewhat unnatural at first, but it will prove useful when analyzing the effects of various policies.

Describe the sources of supply and demand in the market for loanable funds and the market for foreign-currency exchange.

13-2 Equilibrium in the Small Open Economy

So far we have discussed supply and demand in two markets—the market for loanable funds and the market for foreign-currency exchange. Let's now consider how these markets are related to each other.

13-2a Net Capital Outflow: The Link between the Two Markets

We begin by recapping what we've learned so far in this chapter. We have been discussing how the economy coordinates four important macroeconomic variables: national saving (S), domestic investment (I), net capital outflow (NCO), and net exports (NX). Keep in mind the following identities:

$$S = I + NCO$$

and

$$NCO = NX$$

In the market for loanable funds, national saving provides the domestic supply, demand comes from domestic investment, and net capital outflow is the difference between the two at the world interest rate. In the market for foreign-currency exchange, supply comes from net capital outflow, demand comes from net exports, and the real exchange rate balances supply and demand.

Net capital outflow is the variable that links these two markets. In the market for loanable funds, net capital outflow is the difference between domestic investment and national saving at the world interest rate. A change in domestic investment, national saving, or the world interest rate will cause net capital outflow to change. A change in net capital outflow means a Canadian is buying or selling foreign assets. Because a person who wants to buy an asset in another country must supply dollars in order to exchange them for the currency of that country, a change in net capital outflow affects the market for foreign-currency exchange.

The key determinant of net capital outflow, as we have discussed, is the world interest rate. When the world interest rate is higher than the interest rate that equates the demand for loanable funds in Canada to the supply of loanable funds coming from the savings of Canadians, as in panel (a) of Figure 13.1, net capital outflow is positive and is equal to the difference between national saving and the domestic demand for loanable funds. When the world interest rate is lower than the interest rate that equates the demand for loanable funds in Canada to the supply of loanable funds coming from the savings of Canadians, as in panel (b) of Figure 13.1, net capital outflow is negative and is equal to the difference between national saving and the domestic demand for loanable funds.

13-2b Simultaneous Equilibrium in Two Markets

We can now put all the pieces of our model together in Figure 13.3. This figure shows how the market for loanable funds and the market for foreign-currency exchange jointly determine the important macroeconomic variables of an open economy.

Panel (a) of Figure 13.3 shows the market for loanable funds (taken from Figure 13.1). As before, national saving measures the supply of loanable funds made available by the savings of Canadians. Domestic investment is the source of the demand for loanable funds. The world interest rate determines the quantity of loanable funds demanded ($100 billion) and the quantity of loanable funds supplied by the savings of Canadians ($150 billion). The difference between these amounts, $50 billion, measures the amount of national saving available to purchase foreign assets. Because national saving is more than sufficient to provide loanable funds for domestic investment, the excess is used to buy foreign assets. This is net capital outflow.

Panel (b) of the figure shows the market for foreign-currency exchange (taken from Figure 13.2). Because national saving is more than enough to provide for domestic investment, Canadians are purchasing foreign assets. Since to do so they must purchase foreign currency, they must sell Canadian dollars in the market for foreign exchange. For this reason, the quantity of net capital outflow from panel (a) determines the supply of dollars to be exchanged into foreign currencies. The real exchange rate does not affect net capital outflow, so the supply curve is vertical. The demand for dollars comes from net exports. Because a depreciation of the real exchange rate increases net exports, the demand curve for foreign-currency exchange slopes downward. The equilibrium real exchange rate (E_1) brings into balance the quantity of dollars supplied and the quantity of dollars demanded in the market for foreign-currency exchange.

FIGURE 13.3

The Real Equilibrium in a Small Open Economy

In panel (a), the real interest rate is determined by the world real interest rate. At the world interest rate, national saving (*S*) exceeds the demand for loanable funds for domestic investment (*I*). The difference ($S - I$) measures net capital outflow. In panel (b), net capital outflow determines the supply of Canadian dollars offered for sale in the market for foreign-currency exchange. The demand for foreign-currency exchange is determined by Canada's net exports. The equilibrium real exchange rate (E_1) brings into balance the quantity of dollars supplied and the quantity of dollars demanded in the market for foreign-currency exchange.

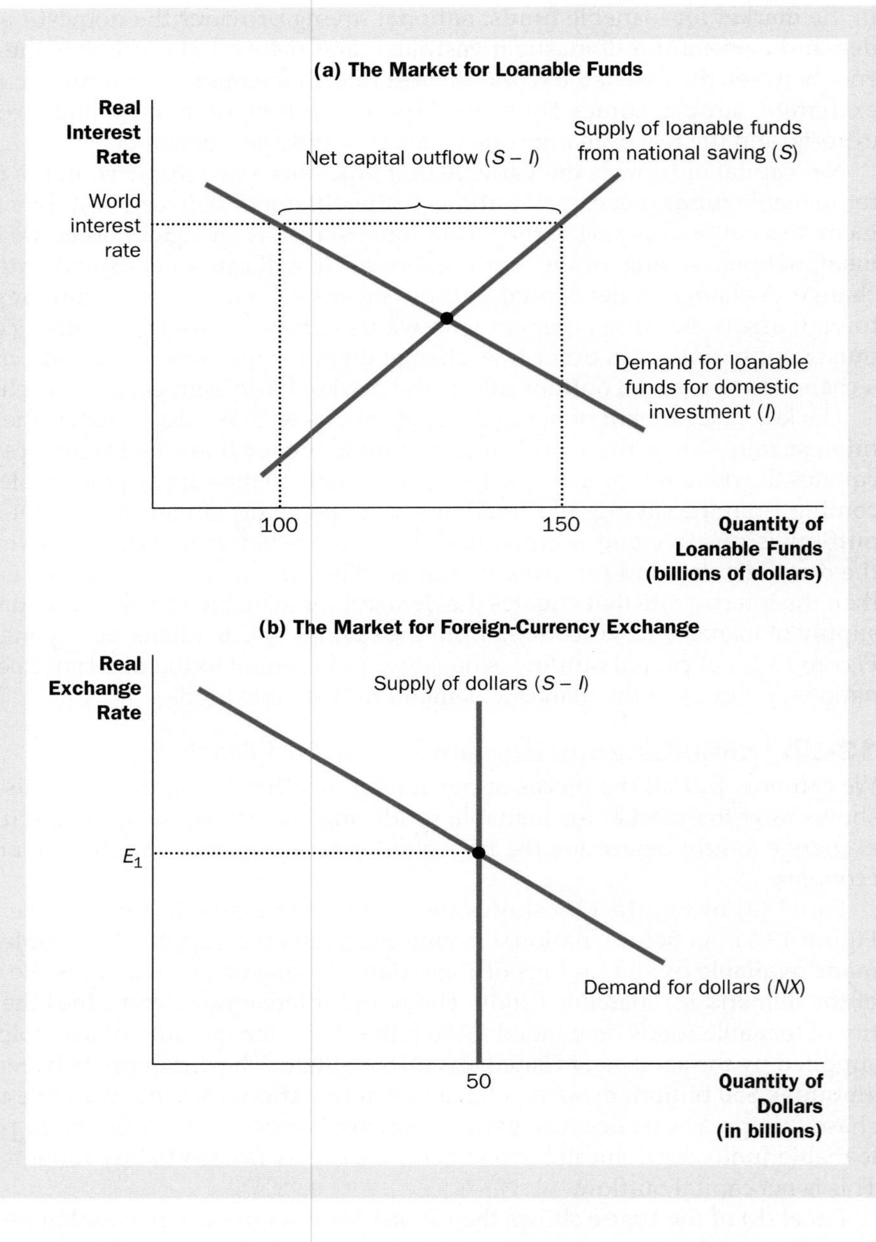

The two markets shown in Figure 13.3 determine the real exchange rate, national saving, domestic investment, and the size of net capital outflow. National saving, domestic investment, and net capital outflow are determined in panel (a). National saving and domestic investment are determined by the world interest rate. Net capital outflow is the difference between these amounts. The real exchange rate determined in panel (b) is the price of domestic goods and services relative to foreign goods and services. We will use this model soon to see how all of these variables change when some policy or event causes one of these curves to shift.

In the model of the open economy just developed, two markets determine one price and the value of three variables. What are the markets? What three variables are determined? What price is determined?

13-3 How Policies and Events Affect a Small Open Economy

Having developed a model to explain how key macroeconomic variables are determined in an open economy, we can now use the model to analyze how changes in policy and other events alter the economy's equilibrium. As we proceed, keep in mind that our model is just supply and demand in two markets—the market for loanable funds and the market for foreign-currency exchange. When using the model to analyze any event, we can apply the three steps outlined in Chapter 4. First, we determine which of the supply and demand curves the event affects. Second, we determine which way the curves shift. Third, we use the supply-and-demand diagrams to examine how these shifts alter the economy's equilibrium.

13-3a Increase in World Interest Rates

We have seen that in a small open economy with perfect capital mobility, the real interest rate is equal to the world real interest rate. One implication of this fact is that events outside Canada that cause the world interest rate to change can

FYI Negative Values of Net Capital Outflow

In this section we use our model to analyze how policy changes and economic events alter the economy's equilibrium. Throughout this section we will be considering a small open economy such as the one described in Figure 13.3, an economy in which net capital outflow is a positive amount. Earlier, we saw evidence that in the past Canada's *NCO* has often been negative. How would our analyses in this section change for this case?

The answer is: Very little. The difference is that now national saving is insufficient to provide for domestic investment, and Canada must rely on the savings of foreigners to make up the difference. This is net capital outflow again, but this time it is a negative number. Since *NCO* must equal net exports, net exports must be negative too. This means that foreigners are seeking to buy Canadian assets and therefore want to purchase Canadian dollars in the foreign-currency exchange market. On the goods side, Canadians are buying more foreign goods than foreigners are buying Canadian goods. Thus, Canadians want to purchase foreign currencies and to do so they must sell Canadian dollars in the foreign-currency exchange market. Now the demand for dollars is coming from net capital outflow, while the supply is coming from net exports.

photographereddie/Thinkstock

It is worth repeating what we noted earlier—the division of transactions between "supply" and "demand" in the market for foreign-currency exchange is somewhat artificial. Whether net capital outflow is a source of supply to this market or a source of demand depends on whether it takes on a positive or a negative value. Similarly, whether the value of net exports is a source of supply or demand in this market depends on whether net exports are positive or negative. It is essential to understand that the real exchange rate is determined by the supply and demand for foreign-currency exchange and that the supply and demand of foreign-currency exchange come from net capital outflow and net exports.

Fortunately for our purposes in this section, whether net capital outflow and net exports are positive or negative is not relevant. All that matters is the *direction of change* in these values. For this reason, we rely on presentations that involve positive values of net capital outflow and net exports because this makes for an easier discussion. However, the results we derive in this section would be exactly the same whether we assumed positive or negative values of net capital outflow and net exports.

have important effects on the Canadian economy. This explains why Canadian newspapers so often report changes to interest rates in the United States. Because the United States is the largest economy in the world, movements in U.S. interest rates are responsible in large part for movements in the world interest rate. Indeed, it is not unreasonable to treat the U.S. interest rate as the world interest rate. Changes in U.S. interest rates therefore have important implications for Canada.

Figure 13.4 shows the effect of an increase in the world interest rate on a small open economy with perfect capital mobility. In panel (a), which shows the market for loanable funds, no curves shift. Instead, the increase in the world interest rate

FIGURE 13.4

The Effects of an Increase in the World Interest Rate
When the world interest rate increases, it increases the supply of loanable funds made available by Canadians and reduces the quantity of loanable funds demanded for domestic investment. For both of these reasons, net capital outflow increases. An increase in the supply of dollars in the market for foreign-currency exchange causes the Canadian dollar to depreciate. The depreciation of the dollar causes net exports to rise.

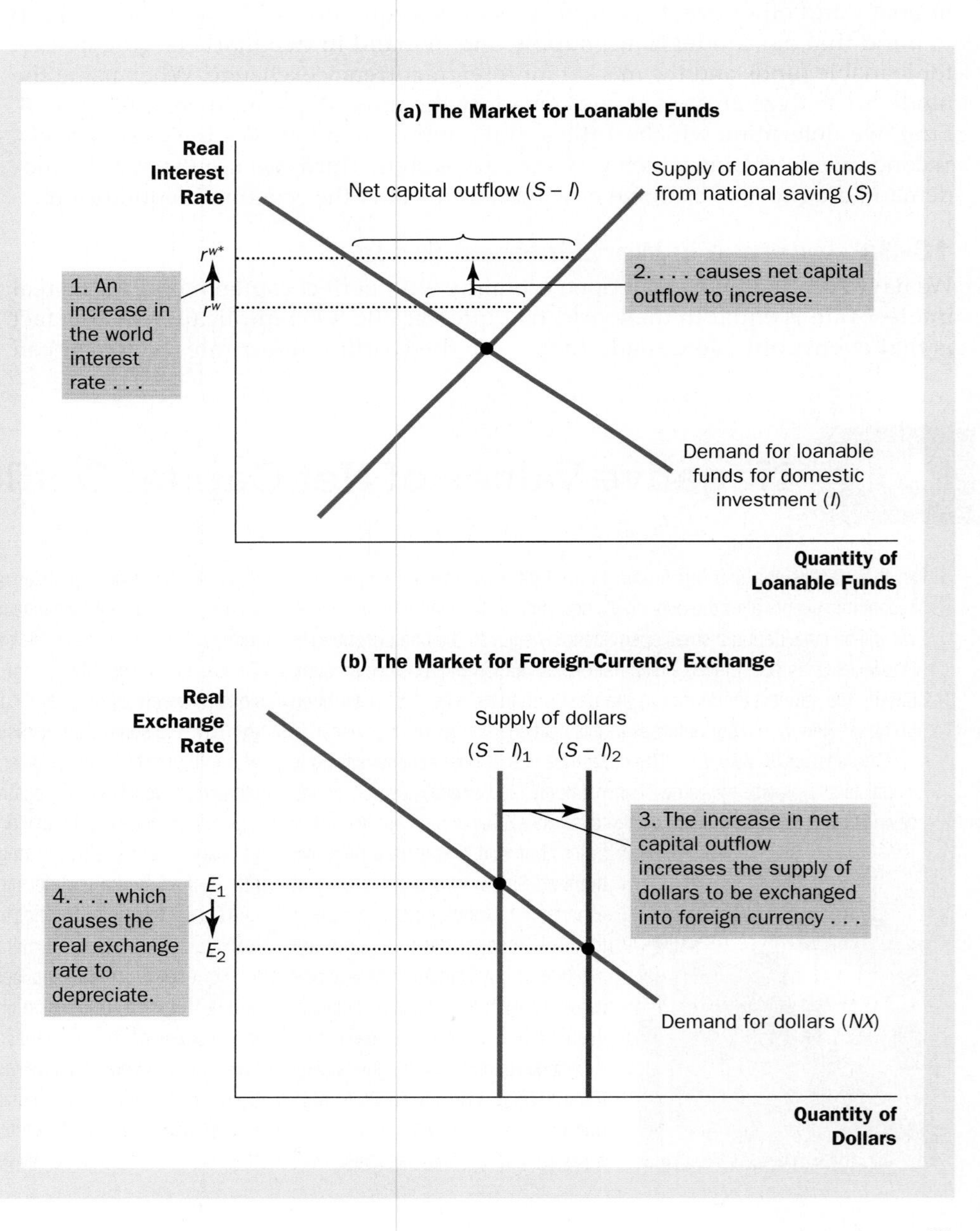

causes a slide up the supply and demand curves for loanable funds. The quantity of loanable funds made available by the savings of Canadians rises. The quantity of loanable funds demanded for domestic investment falls. Both of these changes cause an increase in the amount by which the savings of Canadians exceed the demand for loanable funds in Canada. This excess is net capital outflow, and it measures the amount of Canadian saving that is available to purchase foreign assets.

In panel (b), the increase in net capital outflow shifts the curve that measures the supply of dollars to be exchanged in the market for foreign-currency exchange to the right, from $(S - I)_1$ to $(S - I)_2$. The increased supply of dollars causes the real exchange rate to depreciate from E_1 to E_2. That is, the dollar becomes less valuable relative to other currencies. This depreciation, in turn, makes Canadian goods less expensive compared with foreign goods. Because people both at home and abroad switch their purchases toward the less expensive Canadian goods, exports from Canada rise and imports into Canada fall. For both reasons, Canada's net exports rise. Hence, *in a small open economy with perfect capital mobility, an increase in the world interest rate crowds out domestic investment, causes the dollar to depreciate, and causes net exports to rise.*

This analysis indicates why it is not surprising to find Canadians closely watching movements in world interest rates. Such movements are of interest to exporters, importers, Canadian consumers, and Canadian firms. An increase in world interest rates, by causing the Canadian dollar to depreciate, benefits exporters by making goods priced in Canadian dollars cheaper to foreigners. At the same time, the depreciation of the dollar hurts Canadian importers by making goods priced in foreign currencies more expensive to Canadians. Given the large quantity of foreign goods they purchase, Canadian consumers are also hurt by increase in world interest rates. Finally, of course, those Canadian firms planning new investment projects must now pay a higher rate of interest on funds they borrow for that purpose.

13-3b Government Budget Deficits and Surpluses

When we first discussed the supply and demand for loanable funds earlier in the book, we examined the effects of government budget deficits, which occur when government spending exceeds government revenue. Because a government budget deficit represents *negative* public saving, it reduces national saving (the sum of public and private saving). Thus, a government budget deficit reduces the supply of loanable funds, drives up the interest rate, and crowds out investment.

Now let's consider the effects of a budget deficit in an open economy. First, which curve in our model shifts? As in a closed economy, the initial impact of the budget deficit is on national saving and, therefore, on the supply curve for loanable funds. Second, which way does this supply curve shift? Again as in a closed economy, a budget deficit represents *negative* public saving, so it reduces national saving and shifts the supply curve for loanable funds to the left. This is shown as the shift to the left of the curve that measures the supply of loanable funds available from national saving in panel (a) of Figure 13.5.

Our third and final step is to compare the old and new equilibria. Panel (a) of Figure 13.5 shows the impact of an increase in a Canadian government budget deficit on the Canadian market for loanable funds. At the world interest rate, national saving is less now than it was before. This decrease in national saving is shown by the movement from point A to point B. As a result of this shift, the excess of national saving over domestic investment, which was initially given by

FIGURE 13.5

The Effects of an Increase in the Government Budget Deficit

An increase in the size of the government budget deficit reduces the supply of loanable funds available from national saving. As a result, the supply curve shifts to the left, as shown in panel (a). Net capital outflow therefore also decreases from the amount given by the distance between points A and C to the amount given by the distance between points B and C. In panel (b), the decrease in net capital outflow reduces the supply of dollars in the market for foreign exchange. This decrease in the supply of dollars causes the supply curve to shift to the left, from $(S - I)_1$ to $(S - I)_2$, and causes the real exchange rate to appreciate from E_1 to E_2. The appreciation of the exchange rate causes net exports to fall.

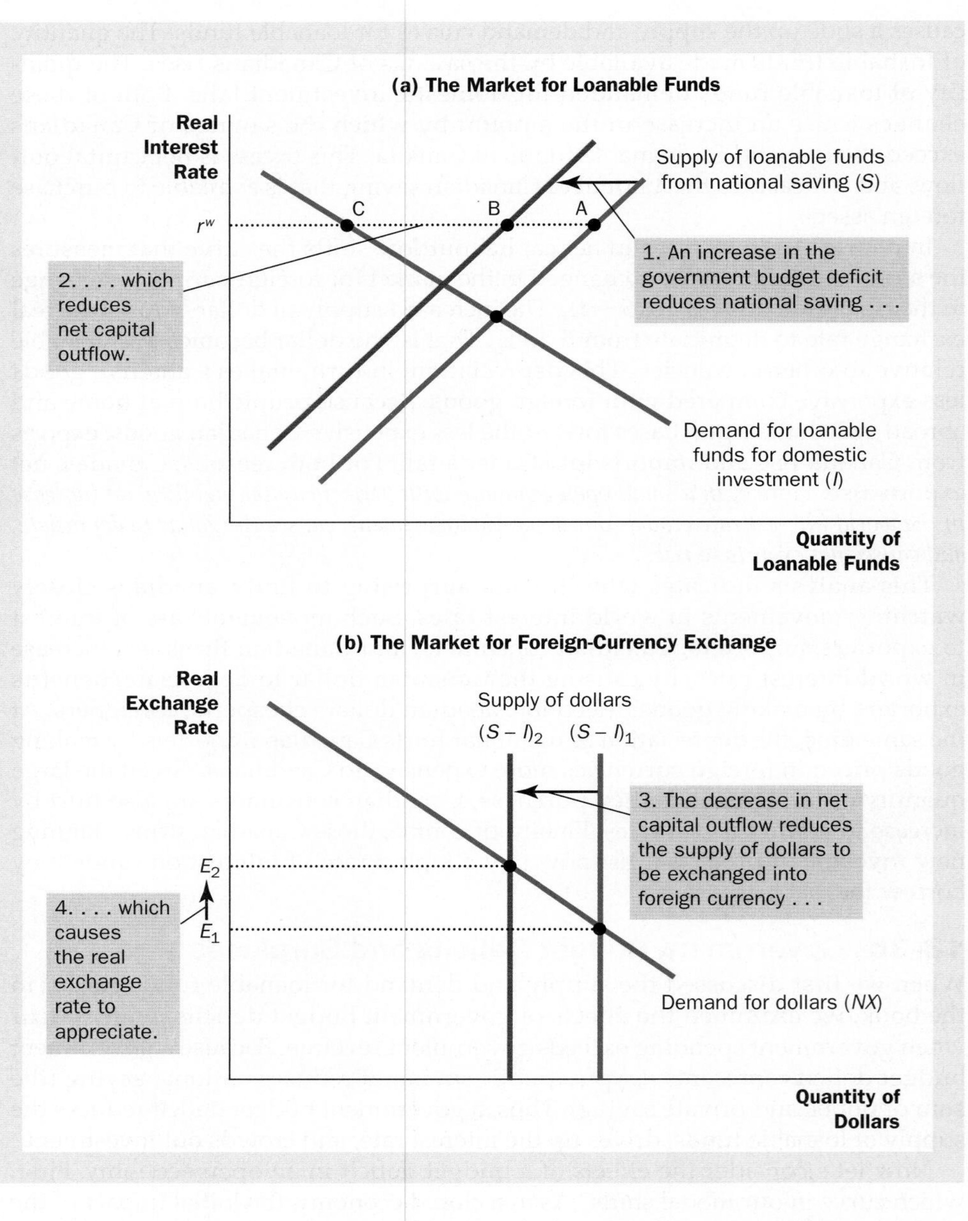

the distance between points A and C, is now given by the distance between points B and C. The increase in the government deficit reduces the excess of national saving over domestic investment and therefore causes net capital outflow to fall.

Panel (b) shows how the increase in the budget deficit affects the market for foreign-currency exchange. Because net capital outflow is reduced, the supply of Canadian dollars offered for sale in the market for foreign-currency exchange is reduced. This decrease in the supply of dollars is shown by the movement of the supply curve from $(S - I)_1$ to $(S - I)_2$. The reduced supply of dollars causes the real exchange rate to appreciate from E_1 to E_2. That is, the dollar becomes more valuable relative to foreign currencies. This appreciation, in turn, makes Canadian goods more expensive compared with foreign goods. Because people both at home and abroad switch their purchases away from more expensive Canadian goods, exports from Canada fall and imports to Canada rise. For both reasons, Canada's net exports fall. Hence, *in a small open economy with perfect capital mobility, an increase in government budget deficits causes the dollar to appreciate and causes net exports to fall.*

This analysis shows how decisions made in the past that caused government deficits to increase have affected Canada's real exchange rate and net exports. Since the mid-1990s, and until a serious recession that began in 2009, Canadian federal, provincial, and territorial governments eliminated deficits and introduced budget surpluses. We can understand the implications of the introduction of budget surpluses by reversing the movements described in Figure 13.5 and discussed above. A decrease in government budget deficits increases national saving. At the world interest rate, the excess of national saving over domestic investment increases, which is equivalent to saying that net capital outflow increases. The increase in net capital outflow increases the supply of dollars in the market for foreign-currency exchange, which causes the real exchange rate to depreciate. This depreciation, in turn, makes Canadian goods less expensive compared with foreign goods. Because people both at home and abroad switch their purchases toward less expensive Canadian goods, exports from Canada rise and imports to Canada fall. For both reasons, Canada's net exports rise. Hence, *in a small open economy with perfect capital mobility, a decrease in government budget deficits causes the dollar to depreciate and causes net exports to rise.*

This analysis shows why it is important for Canadians to closely watch movements in government budget balances. Swings in budget balances between deficit and surplus have effects on the value of the Canadian dollar and so affect the price of imported goods purchased by Canadians and the price of exported goods that Canadian firms hope to sell abroad.

13-3c Trade Policy

A **trade policy** is a government policy that directly influences the quantity of goods and services that a country imports or exports. Trade policy takes various forms. One common trade policy is a **tariff**, a tax on imported goods. Another is an **import quota**, a limit on the quantity of a good that can be produced abroad and sold domestically. Trade policies are common throughout the world, although sometimes they are disguised. For example, the Canadian and U.S. governments have in the past pressured Japanese automakers to reduce the number of cars they sell in North America. These so-called "voluntary export restrictions" are not really voluntary and, in essence, are a form of import quota.

trade policy
a government policy that directly influences the quantity of goods and services that a country imports or exports

tariff
a tax on goods produced abroad and sold domestically

import quota
a limit on the quantity of a good that is produced abroad and sold domestically

Let's consider the macroeconomic impact of trade policy. Suppose that the North American auto industry, concerned about competition from Japanese automakers, convinces the Canadian government to impose a quota on the number of cars that can be imported from Japan. In making their case, lobbyists for the auto industry assert that the trade restriction would shrink the size of the Canadian trade deficit. Are they right? Our model, as illustrated in Figure 13.6, offers an answer.

The first step in analyzing the trade policy is to determine which curve shifts. The initial impact of the import restriction is, not surprisingly, on imports. Because net exports equal exports minus imports, the policy also affects net exports. And because net exports are the source of demand for dollars in the market for foreign-currency exchange, the policy affects the demand curve in this market.

The second step is to determine which way this demand curve shifts. Because the quota restricts the number of Japanese cars sold in Canada, it reduces imports at any given real exchange rate. Net exports, which equal exports minus imports,

FIGURE 13.6

The Effects of an Import Quota

When the Canadian government imposes a quota on the import of Japanese cars, nothing happens in the market for loanable funds in panel (a) or to the supply of dollars in the market for foreign-currency exchange in panel (b). The only effect is a rise in net exports (exports minus imports) for any given exchange rate. As a result, the demand for dollars in the market for foreign-currency exchange rises, as shown by the shift of the demand curve in panel (b). This increase in the demand for dollars causes the value of the dollar to appreciate from E_1 to E_2. This appreciation in the value of the dollar tends to reduce net exports, offsetting the direct effect of the import quota on the trade balance.

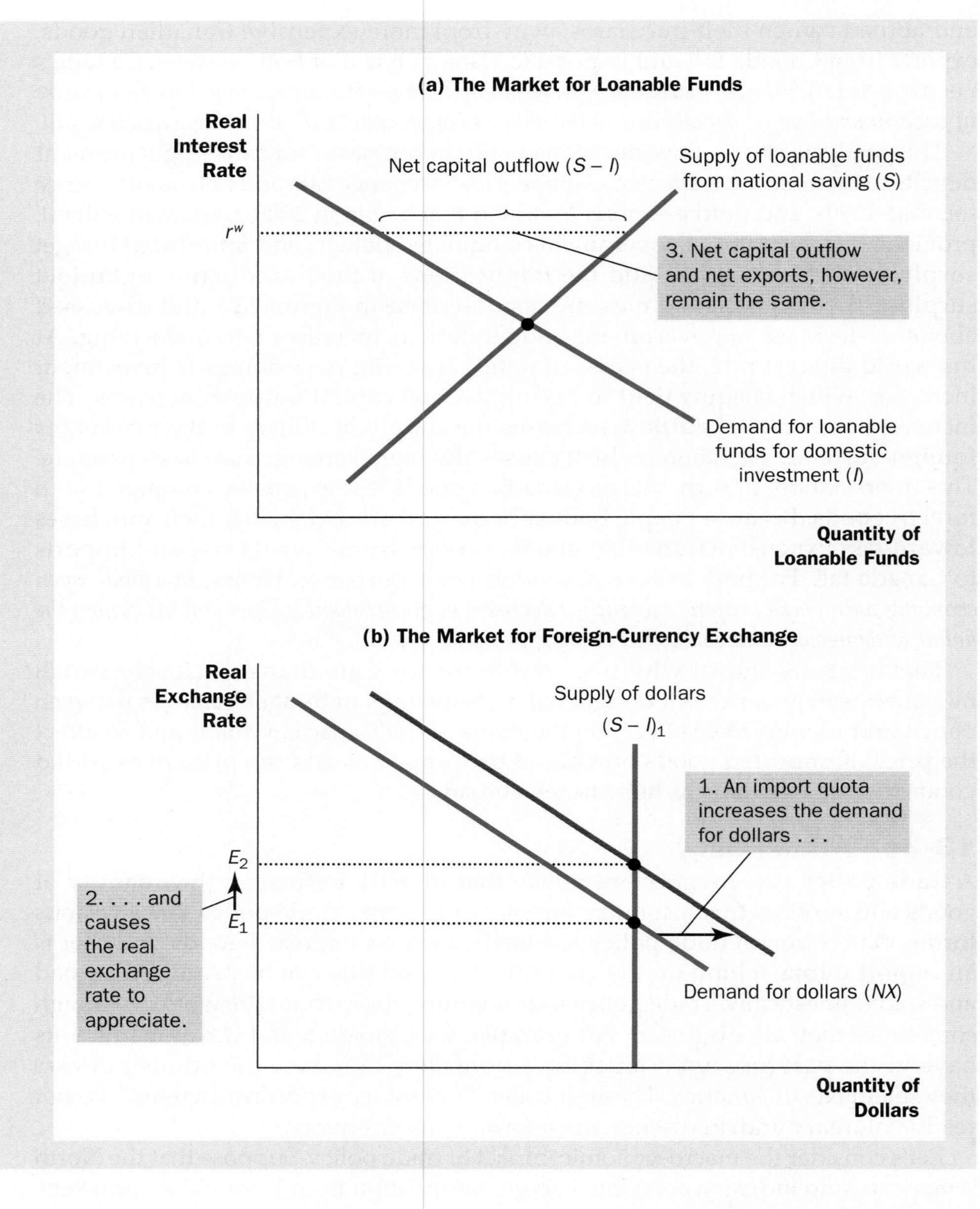

will therefore *rise* for any given real exchange rate. Because foreigners need dollars to buy Canada's net exports, there is an increased demand for dollars in the market for foreign-currency exchange. This increase in the demand for dollars is shown in panel (b) of Figure 13.6 as the shift to the right of the demand curve.

The third step is to compare the old and new equilibria. As we can see in panel (b), the increase in the demand for dollars causes the real exchange rate to appreciate from E_1 to E_2. Because nothing has happened in the market for loanable funds in panel (a), there is no change in net capital outflow. And because there is no change in net capital outflow, there can be no change in net exports, even though the import quota has reduced imports.

The reason why net exports can stay the same while imports fall is explained by the change in the real exchange rate: When the dollar appreciates in value in the market for foreign-currency exchange, domestic goods become more expensive relative to foreign goods. This appreciation encourages imports and discourages exports—and both of these changes work to offset the direct increase in net exports due to the import quota. In the end, an import quota reduces both imports and exports, but net exports (exports minus imports) are unchanged.

We have thus come to a surprising implication: *Trade policies do not affect the trade balance.* That is, policies that directly influence exports or imports do not alter net exports. This conclusion seems less surprising if one recalls the accounting identity:

$$NX = NCO = S - I$$

Net exports equal net capital outflow, which equals national saving minus domestic investment. Trade policies do not alter the trade balance because they do not alter national saving or domestic investment. For given levels of national saving and domestic investment, the real exchange rate adjusts to keep the trade balance the same, regardless of the trade policies the government puts in place.

Although trade policies do not affect a country's overall trade balance, these policies do affect specific firms, industries, and countries. When the Canadian government imposes an import quota on Japanese cars, General Motors has less competition from abroad and will sell more cars. At the same time, because the dollar has appreciated in value, Bombardier, the Canadian aircraft maker, will find it harder to compete with Embraer, the Brazilian aircraft maker. Canadian exports of aircraft will fall, and Canadian imports of aircraft will rise. In this case, the import quota on Japanese cars will increase net exports of cars and decrease net exports of planes. In addition, it will increase net exports from Canada to Japan and decrease net exports from Canada to Brazil. The overall trade balance of the Canadian economy, however, stays the same.

The effects of trade policies are, therefore, more microeconomic than macroeconomic. Although advocates of trade policies sometimes claim (incorrectly) that these policies can alter a country's trade balance, they are usually more motivated by concerns about particular firms or industries. One should not be surprised, for instance, to hear an executive from General Motors advocating import quotas for Japanese cars. Economists almost always oppose such trade policies. Free trade allows economies to specialize in doing what they do best—making residents of all countries better off. Trade restrictions interfere with these gains from trade and, thus, reduce overall economic well-being.

13-3d Political Instability and Capital Flight

In 1994, political instability in Mexico, including the assassination of a prominent political leader, made world financial markets nervous. People began to view Mexico as a much less stable country than they had previously thought. They decided to pull some of their assets out of Mexico in order to move these funds to the United States and other "safe havens." Such a large and sudden movement of funds out of a country is called **capital flight**. To see the implications of capital flight for the Mexican economy, we again follow our three steps for analyzing a change in equilibrium, but this time we apply our model of the open economy from the perspective of Mexico rather than Canada.

capital flight
a large and sudden reduction in the demand for assets located in a country

Panel (a) of Figure 13.7 shows the market for loanable funds in Mexico before the flight of capital. At the world interest rate, r^w, the supply of loanable funds

FIGURE 13.7

The Effects of Capital Flight

If Mexico is judged to be a risky place to keep savings, savers in Mexico and elsewhere will demand that they receive a risk premium if they are to continue to hold Mexican assets. The response of Mexican savers is shown in panel (a) by the upward shift in the curve that represents the supply of loanable funds available from the savings of Mexicans. Because borrowers in Mexico must now pay a higher interest rate, $r^w + \gamma$, than they paid before the crisis of confidence, the quantity of loanable funds demanded for domestic investment falls. The increase in the interest rate paid by Mexican borrowers and the shift of the supply curve causes an increase in the net capital outflow of Mexico. Net capital outflow increases from an amount measured by the distance between points A and B to an amount measured by the distance between points X and Y. The increase in net capital outflow means that the supply of pesos in the market for foreign-currency exchange increases. This is shown in panel (b) by the shift to the right of the supply curve from $(S - I)_1$ to $(S - I)_2$. This increase in the supply of pesos causes the peso to depreciate from E_1 to E_2, so the peso becomes less valuable compared with other currencies.

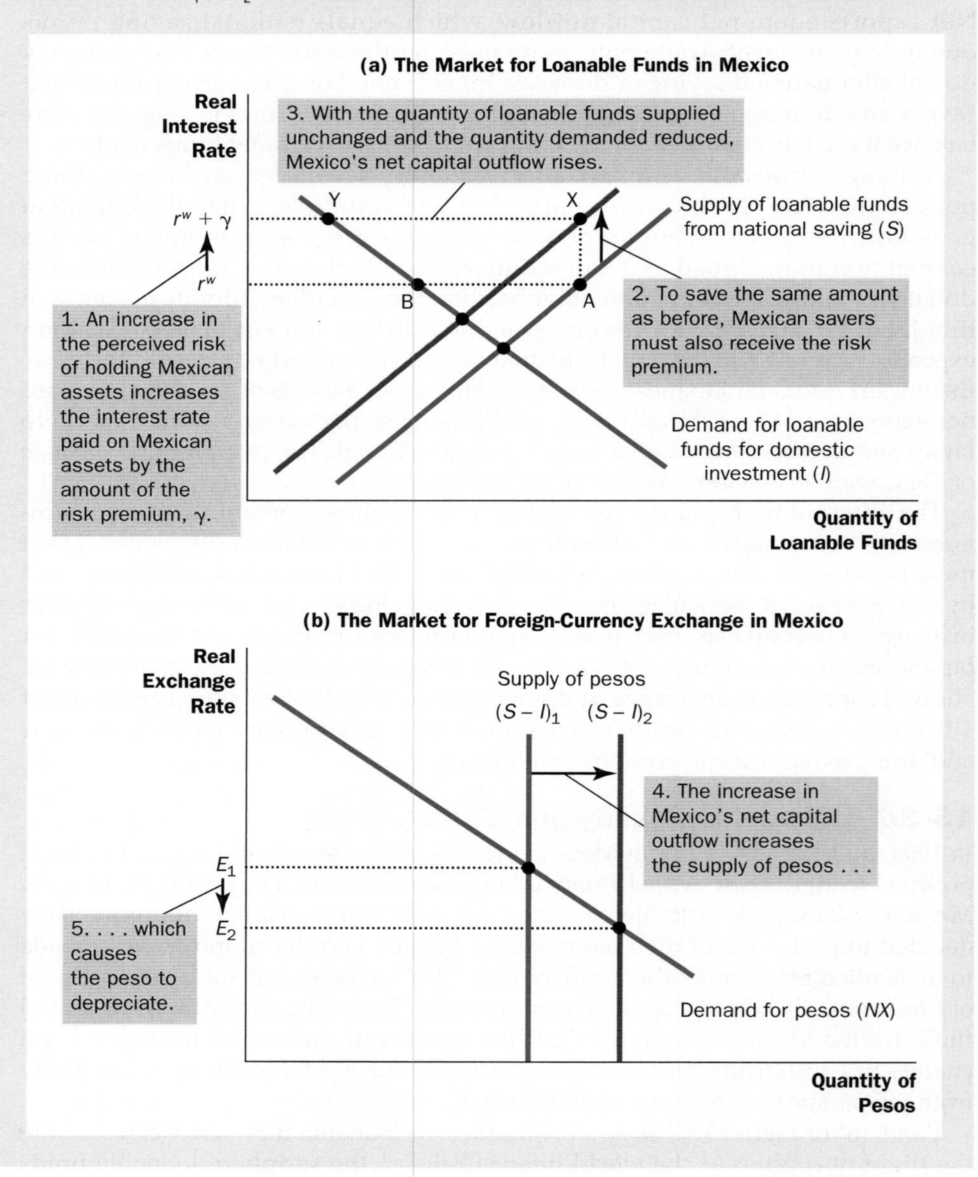

made available by the savings of Mexicans is greater than the demand for loanable funds for investment in Mexico. The difference is the amount of Mexican saving that is available to purchase foreign assets—in other words, Mexico's net capital outflow. Mexico's net capital outflow is shown in panel (a) by the distance between points A and B. The level of net capital outflow determines the supply of pesos in the market for foreign-currency exchange. This is shown in panel (b) by the curve $(S - I)_1$. The point at which the demand and supply of pesos are in equilibrium determines the real exchange rate, E_1.

Now consider which curves are affected, and which way the affected curves shift, if the world financial community suddenly loses confidence in the Mexican economy. As we have seen previously, if lenders lose confidence in the ability of a borrower to repay debts, they will demand that that borrower pay them a higher interest rate. Lenders, then, by receiving a higher interest rate, are compensated for the greater default risk that they incur. If the world financial community begins to question the ability of Mexico to repay its debts, lenders will hold Mexican debt only if they receive a higher interest rate than they can receive in other countries. In a small open economy like Mexico, this requires that Mexican borrowers offer to pay an interest rate greater than the world interest rate.

Let's define γ as the extra amount lenders need to receive from Mexican borrowers if they are to hold Mexican debt. This amount is commonly referred to as the *risk premium* that risky borrowers must pay. To prevent the sale of all Mexican assets, borrowers in Mexico must now pay the world interest rate, r^w, plus the risk premium, γ. To save the same quantity of loanable funds as before the confidence crisis, Mexican savers also demand that they receive $r^w + \gamma$. This response of Mexican savers is shown in panel (a) by a shift upward of the curve that represents the supply of loanable funds made available by Mexicans. The curve shifts up by the amount of the risk premium to indicate that Mexicans will choose to contribute the same quantity of their savings to the Mexican market for loanable funds only if they are compensated for the greater risk they incur by doing so. After all, Mexican savers could otherwise put their savings into Canada's, Japan's, or some other country's market for loanable funds. Paying the risk premium enables Mexican borrowers to halt the sale of Mexican assets, and receiving the risk premium causes Mexicans to save the same quantity of loanable funds as they did before the capital flight. Thus, the capital flight stops.

However, as we can see from panel (a), the addition of the risk premium also reduces domestic investment. The net effect of these changes is that net capital outflow has increased by the time the sale of Mexican assets has been halted. In panel (a), Mexico's net capital outflow is now represented by the distance between points X and Y. In panel (b), the increase in net capital outflow increases the supply of pesos in the market for foreign-currency exchange from $(S - I)_1$ to $(S - I)_2$. That is, the rush to sell Mexican assets causes a large increase in the supply of pesos to be converted into dollars. This increase in supply causes the peso to depreciate from E_1 to E_2. Thus, *capital flight from Mexico increases Mexican interest rates and decreases the value of the Mexican peso in the market for foreign-currency exchange.* This is exactly what was observed in 1994. From November 1994 to March 1995, the interest rate on short-term Mexican government bonds rose from 14 percent to 70 percent, and the peso depreciated in value from 40 to 21 Canadian cents per peso.

These price changes that result from capital flight influence some key macroeconomic quantities. The depreciation of the currency makes exports cheaper and imports more expensive, thus causing net exports to increase. Most important, and most damaging, is the effect of the increase in the interest rate. By reducing domestic investment, the increase in the interest rate caused by capital flight slows capital accumulation and economic growth.

The events that we have been describing in Mexico could happen to any economy in the world, and in fact they do from time to time. In 1997, the world learned that the banking systems of several Asian economies, including Thailand, South Korea, and Indonesia, were at or near the point of bankruptcy, and this news induced capital to flee from these nations. In 1998, the Russian government defaulted on its debt, inducing international investors to take whatever money they could and run. A similar (but more complicated) set of events unfolded in Argentina in 2002. In each of these cases of capital flight, the results were much as our model predicts: rising interest rates and a falling currency. More recently, in 2012 and again in 2015, citizens of Greece were reported to be withdrawing their savings from Greek banks because they feared that Greece would leave the European Union. Interest rates in Greece increased as a result. At the time of this writing, events in Greece continue to unfold and it was unclear what impact this capital flight would ultimately have.

IN THE **news**

The Open-Economy Trilemma

The following newspaper article discusses how different nations adopt different policies toward the value of their currencies in foreign-exchange markets. The article explains why. The description of the choice made by the United States accurately describes the choice made by Canada.

The Coins That Have Three Sides

By N. Gregory Mankiw

As the world economy struggles to recover from its various ailments, the international financial order is coming under increased scrutiny. Currencies and exchange rates, in particular, are getting a hard look.

Various pundits and politicians, including President Obama himself, have complained that the Chinese renminbi is undervalued and impeding a global recovery. The problems in Greece have caused many people to wonder whether the euro is a failed experiment and whether Europe's nations would have been better off maintaining their own currencies.

In thinking about these issues, the place to start is what economists call the *fundamental trilemma of international finance*. Yes, *trilemma* really is a word. It has been a term of art for logicians since the 17th century, according to the *Oxford English Dictionary*, and it describes a situation in which someone faces a choice among three options, each of which comes with some inevitable problems.

What is the trilemma in international finance? It stems from the fact that, in most nations, economic policy makers would like to achieve these three goals:

- *Make the country's economy open to international flows of capital.* Capital mobility lets a nation's citizens diversify their holdings by investing abroad. It also encourages foreign investors to bring their resources and expertise into the country.
- *Use monetary policy as a tool to help stabilize the economy.* The central bank can then increase the money supply and reduce interest rates when the economy is depressed, and reduce money growth and raise interest rates when it is overheated.
- *Maintain stability in the currency exchange rate.* A volatile exchange rate, at times driven by speculation, can be a source of broader economic volatility. Moreover, a stable rate makes it easier for households and businesses to engage in the world economy and plan for the future.

But here's the rub: You can't get all three. If you pick two of these goals, the inexorable logic of economics forces you to forgo the third.

In the United States, we have picked the first two. Any American can easily invest abroad, simply by sending cash to an international mutual fund, and foreigners are free to buy stocks and bonds on domestic exchanges. Moreover, the Federal Reserve sets monetary policy to try to maintain full employment and price stability. But a result of this decision is volatility in the value of the dollar in foreign exchange markets.

Could the events that occurred in Mexico, Southeast Asia, and Russia ever happen in Canada? Although the Canadian economy has long been viewed as a safe place in which to invest, political developments in Canada have at times induced small amounts of capital flight. For example, past referendums held on the question of Quebec separation, and the possibility of future referendums, are generally acknowledged to have caused interest rates to be higher in Canada than they would otherwise have been. Because the issue of Quebec separation has led some international investors to wonder whether Canada will continue to exist as a country, Canadian borrowers have had to pay a risk premium to Canadian and international lenders. In addition to causing Canadian interest rates to be higher, the uncertainty about Canada's political future has caused domestic investment and the value of the Canadian dollar to be lower, as our model has predicted.

Economic developments in Canada have also been the source of capital flight. High levels of government debt have at times caused international investors to express concern about the wisdom of placing their savings in Canada. Their

By contrast, China has chosen a different response to the trilemma. Its central bank conducts monetary policy and maintains tight control over the exchange value of its currency. But to accomplish these two goals, it has to restrict the international flow of capital, including the ability of Chinese citizens to move their wealth abroad. Without such restrictions, money would flow into and out of the country, forcing the domestic interest rate to match those set by foreign central banks.

Most of Europe's nations have chosen the third way. By using the euro to replace the French franc, the German mark, the Italian lira, the Greek drachma and other currencies, these countries have eliminated all exchange-rate movements within their zone. In addition, capital is free to move among nations. Yet the cost of making these choices has been to give up the possibility of national monetary policy.

The European Central Bank sets interest rates for Europe as a whole. But if the situation in one country—Greece, for example—differs from that in the rest of Europe, that country no longer has its own monetary policy to address national problems.

Is there a best way to deal with this trilemma? Perhaps not surprisingly, many American economists argue for the American system of floating exchange rates determined by market forces. This preference underlies much of the criticism of China's financial policy. It also led to skepticism when Europe started down the path toward a common currency in the early 1990s. Today, those euro skeptics feel vindicated by the problems in Greece.

But economists should be cautious when recommending exchange-rate policy, because it is far from obvious what is best. In fact, Americans' embrace of floating exchange rates is relatively recent. From World War II to the early 1970s, the United States participated in the Bretton Woods system, which fixed exchange rates among the major currencies. Moreover, in 1998, as much of Asia was engulfed in a financial crisis, Robert E. Rubin, then the Treasury secretary, praised China's exchange-rate policy as an "island of stability" in a turbulent world.

Even the euro experiment is based in part on an American model. Anyone taking a trip across the United States doesn't need to change money with every crossing of a state border. A common currency among the 50 states has served Americans well. Europeans were aspiring for similar benefits.

To be sure, Europe is different from the United States, which has a large central government that can redistribute resources

among regions as needed. More important, our common language and heritage allow labor to move freely among regions in a way that will always be harder in Europe. The United States of Europe may have been too much to hope for.

Without doubt, the world financial system presents policy makers with difficult tradeoffs. Americans shouldn't be too harsh when other nations facing the trilemma reach conclusions different from ours. In this area of economic policy, as well as many others, there is room for reasonable nations to disagree.

Source: From *The New York Times,* July 10, 2010

concern has forced Canadian borrowers to offer a risk premium to international investors and this has resulted in all of the effects described above: an increase in net capital outflow, a lower value for the Canadian dollar, higher interest rates, and slower economic growth.

Even a large economy like the United States can suffer the consequences of capital flight. Periodic budget battles between the president and Congress have at times been associated with jumps in the interest rate on U.S. government bonds because investors feared a possible default on government debt. Many analysts believe something similar may happen again as a consequence of the 2009 recession. As discussed in Chapter 8, the spark that ignited this widespread recession originated in the U.S. financial system. The Government of the United States responded with an unprecedented increase in its budget deficit, a deficit that analysts believe will be deeper and more persistent than in other countries around the world. This perception gained credence when credit rating agencies downgraded U.S. federal government debt in August 2011. The implication is that the U.S. economy may be about to enter a period during which U.S. borrowers will be required to offer a risk premium to international investors nervous about the U.S. government's ability to pay its debts. If this is so, then our model predicts that the U.S. economy may be about to enter a period of increased net capital outflow, a lower value to the U.S. dollar, higher interest rates, and slower economic growth.

Suppose that Canadians decided to spend a smaller fraction of their incomes. What would be the effect on saving, domestic investment, net capital outflow, the real exchange rate, and the trade balance?

13-4 Conclusion

International economics is a topic of increasing importance. More and more, Canadian citizens are buying goods produced abroad and producing goods to be sold overseas. Through mutual funds and other financial institutions, they borrow and lend in world financial markets. As a result, a full analysis of the Canadian economy requires an understanding of how the Canadian economy interacts with other economies in the world. This chapter has provided a basic model for thinking about the macroeconomics of open economies.

It is worth noting, however, that the model that has been presented in this chapter is just that—a model. As such, it relies on a number of assumptions and simplifications. These assumptions and simplifications produce answers that need to be modified when these assumptions and simplifications are relaxed. There is nothing unusual about this. (Recall our discussion in Chapter 2 when we talked about the scientific method and the role of models.) The model presented in this chapter dispenses with various details that, for some purposes, are significant. More complex models of the type you will see in future courses in macroeconomics will include, for example, the role of people's expectations in relation to the future and the longer-run implications of capital flows. More complex models may also allow for a relaxation of our assumption of perfectly mobile capital. Having said that, it is nonetheless true that the basic model presented in this chapter provides a very useful way of thinking about the macroeconomics of a small open economy.

Although the study of international economics is valuable, we should be careful not to exaggerate its importance. Policymakers and commentators are often quick to blame foreigners for problems facing the Canadian economy. By contrast, economists more often view these problems as homegrown. For example, politicians often discuss foreign competition as a threat to Canadian living standards. Economists are more likely to lament the low level of national saving. Low saving impedes growth in capital, productivity, and living standards, regardless of whether the economy is open or closed. Foreigners are a convenient target for politicians because blaming foreigners provides a way to avoid responsibility without insulting any domestic constituency. Whenever you hear popular discussions of international trade and finance, therefore, it is especially important to try to separate myth from reality. The tools you have learned in the past two chapters should help in that endeavour.

summary

- Most economists prefer to use a model that describes Canada as a small open economy with perfect capital mobility. This means that borrowers must pay, and lenders demand that they receive, the world interest rate. In the analysis of the macroeconomics of such an economy, two markets are central—the market for loanable funds and the market for foreign-currency exchange. In the market for loanable funds, the world interest rate determines the quantity of loanable funds demanded for domestic investment and the quantity of loanable funds made available from national saving. The difference between the quantity of loanable funds demanded and the quantity of loanable funds supplied at the world interest rate is net capital outflow. In the market for foreign-currency exchange, the real exchange rate adjusts to balance the supply of dollars (from net capital outflow) and the demand for dollars (from net exports). Because net capital outflow is determined in the market for loanable funds and provides the supply of dollars for foreign-currency exchange, it is the variable that connects these two markets.
- An increase in a government budget deficit reduces the supply of loanable funds available from national saving. This reduces net capital outflow and in turn reduces the supply of dollars in the market for foreign-currency exchange. The fall in the supply of dollars causes the real exchange rate to appreciate and therefore causes net exports to fall. A decrease in a government deficit, or an increase in a government surplus, increases the supply of loanable funds and increases net capital outflow. The increase in the supply of dollars in the market for foreign-currency exchange causes the real exchange rate to depreciate and net exports to rise.
- Although restrictive trade policies, such as tariffs or quotas on imports, are sometimes advocated as a way to alter the trade balance, they do not necessarily have that effect. A trade restriction increases net exports for a given exchange rate and, therefore, increases the demand for dollars in the market for foreign-currency exchange. As a result, the dollar appreciates in value, making domestic goods more expensive relative to foreign goods. This appreciation offsets the initial impact of the trade restriction on net exports.
- When investors change their attitudes about holding assets of a country, the ramifications for the country's economy can be profound. In particular, political instability can lead to capital flight, which tends to increase interest rates and cause the currency to depreciate.

KEY concepts

trade policy, *p. 299*

tariff, *p. 299*

import quota, *p. 299*

capital flight, *p. 301*

QUESTIONS FOR **review**

1. Describe supply and demand in the market for loanable funds and the market for foreign-currency exchange. How are these markets linked?
2. How would a fall in U.S. interest rates affect Canadian investment, saving, and net capital outflow, and the Canadian real exchange rate?
3. Suppose that a textile workers' union encourages people to buy only Canadian-made clothes. What would this policy do to the trade balance and the real exchange rate? What is the impact on the textile industry? What is the impact on the auto industry?
4. What is capital flight? When a country experiences capital flight, what is the effect on its interest rate and the value of the currency?

QUICK CHECK **multiple choice**

1. Holding other things constant, an increase in the world interest rate increases which of the following?
   a. national saving and domestic investment
   b. national saving and the net capital outflow
   c. domestic investment and the net capital outflow
   d. national saving only
2. An appreciation of a nation's currency can be the result of which of the following?
   a. an increase in net exports
   b. a decrease in net exports
   c. a fall in national saving
   d. a decrease in domestic demand for investment
3. The government in an open economy increases spending. As a result, the supply of loanable funds from national saving ___, leading to a(n) ___ net capital outflow ___ and a real exchange rate ___.
   a. falls, reduced, appreciation
   b. falls, increased, depreciation
   c. increases, increased, appreciation
   d. increases, decreases, depreciation
4. The nation of Ectenia has long banned the export of its highly prized puka shells. A newly elected president, however, removes the export ban. This change in policy will cause the nation's currency to ___, making the goods Ectenia imports ___ expensive.
   a. appreciate, less
   b. appreciate, more
   c. depreciate, less
   d. depreciate, more
5. A civil war abroad causes foreign investors to seek a safe haven for their funds in Canada, leading to ___ Canadian interest rates and a ___ Canadian dollar.
   a. higher, weaker
   b. higher, stronger
   c. lower, weaker
   d. lower, stronger
6. If business leaders in Great Britain become more confident in their economy, their optimism will induce them to increase investment, causing the British pound to ___ and pushing the British trade balance toward ___.
   a. appreciate, deficit
   b. appreciate, surplus
   c. depreciate, deficit
   d. depreciate, surplus

PROBLEMS AND **applications**

1. Japan generally runs a significant trade surplus. Do you think this is most related to high foreign demand for Japanese goods, low Japanese demand for foreign goods, a high Japanese saving rate relative to Japanese investment, or structural barriers against imports into Japan? Explain your answer.
2. How would an increase in foreigners' incomes affect Canada's net exports curve? How would this affect the value of the dollar in the market for foreign-currency exchange?
3. Suppose that Parliament passes an investment tax credit, which subsidizes domestic investment. How does this policy affect national saving, domestic investment, net capital outflow, the interest rate, the exchange rate, and the trade balance?
4. Economists generally favour reductions in trade restrictions. Many policymakers, however, insist that any lowering of Canadian import restrictions must be accompanied by reductions in other countries' import quotas on Canadian exports. Only in this way,

these policymakers believe, can Canadian exporters benefit from a lowering of Canadian import quotas. Explain how a reduction in import restrictions will benefit exporters even if other countries do not follow Canada's example and reduce their import quotas on Canadian exports.

5. In fiscal year 2009–10, the Government of Canada incurred a budget deficit of $56 billion, an increase of about $50 billion from the year before.
   a. What effect should we expect this increase in the government's deficit to have had on Canada's net exports?
   b. If large deficits were to persist for many years, what would we expect would happen to levels of foreign investment in Canada?
6. Economists often lament the low level of national saving. Low saving impedes capital growth, productivity, and living standards. For this reason, economists tend to favour policies designed to increase saving. Suppose that all Canadians choose to increase their saving. What would be the effect of increased saving on the value of the dollar and on net exports?
7. Changes in government deficits are closely related to changes in net exports. In particular, increases in government deficits lead to reductions in net exports, while reductions in government deficits lead to increases in net exports. Use a two-panel diagram to explain this important relationship.
8. Suppose the French suddenly develop a strong taste for British Columbia wines. Answer the following questions in words and using a diagram:
   a. What happens to the demand for dollars in the market for foreign-currency exchange?
   b. What happens to the value of dollars in the market for foreign-currency exchange?
   c. What happens to the quantity of net exports?
9. A Member of Parliament (MP) renounces her past support for protectionism: "Canada's trade deficit must be reduced, but import quotas only annoy our trading partners. If we subsidize Canadian exports instead, we can reduce the trade deficit by increasing our competitiveness." Using a two-panel diagram, show the effect of an export subsidy on net exports and the real exchange rate. Do you agree with the MP?
10. Suppose that the federal government increases the tax on corporate profits. Such a tax has the effect of reducing domestic investment. What effect would this tax increase have on Canada's real exchange rate and net exports?
11. Suppose that the world interest rate rises.
    a. If the elasticity of national saving in relation to the world interest rate is very high, will this rise in the world interest rate have a large or small effect on Canada's net capital outflow?
    b. If the elasticity of Canada's exports in relation to the real exchange rate is very low, will this rise in the world interest rate have a large or small effect on Canada's real exchange rate?
12. Suppose that Europeans suddenly become very interested in investing in Canada.
    a. What happens to Canadian net capital outflow?
    b. What effect does this have on Canadian private saving and Canadian domestic investment?
    c. What is the long-run effect on the Canadian capital stock?
13. During the 1960s, a commonly held concern among Canadians was that Americans were "buying Canada." This concern stemmed from the fact that Canada's net capital outflow during the 1960s was consistently negative. As a result, foreigners, particularly Americans, were buying more Canadian assets than Canadians were buying foreign assets. Because many of these assets were firms operating in Canada, Canadians were concerned that eventually all of Canada would be owned by Americans. In response to this concern, the federal government of the time passed legislation limiting the amount that foreigners could invest in certain sectors of the economy. How do you think this legislation affected investment in Canada? What do you think happened to Canada's real exchange rate and net exports as a result?
14. Figure 13.4 shows the effect of an increase in the world interest rate on a small open economy with perfect capital mobility. In the figure, we assumed that net capital outflow (*NCO*) was positive. For most of the past 40 years, however, Canada's *NCO* has been negative. Redraw the two panels of Figure 13.4, but this time assume that *NCO* is negative at the world interest rate. Now suppose that the world interest rate increases. What happens to national saving (S)? What happens to domestic investment (I)? What happens to *NCO* and the real exchange rate? Does the conclusion we reached in our discussion of Figure 13.4—that an increase in world interest rates causes the Canadian dollar to depreciate and net exports to increase—still hold?

iStockphoto.com/Devonyu

Aggregate Demand and Aggregate Supply

LEARNING **objectives**

In this chapter, you will ...

1. Learn three key facts about short-run economic fluctuations
2. Consider how the economy in the short run differs from the economy in the long run
3. Use the model of aggregate demand and aggregate supply to explain economic fluctuations
4. See how shifts in aggregate demand or aggregate supply can cause booms and recessions

Economic activity fluctuates from year to year. In most years, the production of goods and services rises. Because of increases in the labour force, increases in the capital stock, and advances in technological knowledge, the economy can produce more and more over time. This growth allows everyone to enjoy a higher standard of living. We saw in Chapter 7 that since 1870, the level of production in the Canadian economy, as measured by real GDP per person, has grown by about 2 percent per year.

In some years, however, this normal growth does not occur. Firms find themselves unable to sell all of the goods and services they have to offer, so they cut back on production. Workers are laid off, unemployment rises, and factories are left idle. With the economy producing fewer goods and services, real GDP and other measures of income fall. Such a period of falling incomes and rising unemployment is called a **recession** if it is relatively mild and a **depression** if it is more severe.

recession
a period of declining real incomes and rising unemployment

depression
a severe recession

An example of such a downturn occurred in 2008 and 2009. From the fourth quarter of 2008 to the second quarter of 2009, real GDP for the Canadian economy fell by 3 percent. The national rate of unemployment rose from 6.1 percent in October 2008 to 8.7 percent in August 2009. In some areas of the country, the recession was felt even more severely: the unemployment rate in Ontario, for example, increased from 5.9 percent to 10.0 percent over this same period. Not surprisingly, students graduating during this time found that desirable jobs were hard to find.

What causes short-run fluctuations in economic activity? What, if anything, can public policy do to prevent periods of falling incomes and rising unemployment? When recessions and depressions occur, how can policymakers reduce their length and severity? These are the questions that we take up now.

The variables that we study are largely those we have already seen in previous chapters. They include GDP, unemployment, interest rates, exchange rates, and the price level. Also familiar are the policy instruments of government spending, taxes, and the money supply. What differs from our earlier analysis is the time horizon. So far, our focus has been on the behaviour of the economy in the long run. Our focus now is on the economy's short-run fluctuations around its long-run trend.

Although there remains some debate among economists about how to analyze short-run fluctuations, most economists use the *model of aggregate demand and aggregate supply.* Learning how to use this model for analyzing the short-run effects of various events and policies is the primary task ahead. This chapter introduces the model's two key pieces—the aggregate-demand curve and the aggregate-supply curve. But before turning to the model, let's look at some of the key facts that describe the ups and downs of the economy.

14-1 Three Key Facts about Economic Fluctuations

Short-run fluctuations in economic activity occur in all countries and in all times throughout history. As a starting point for understanding these year-to-year fluctuations, let's discuss some of their most important properties.

14-1a Fact 1: Economic Fluctuations Are Irregular and Unpredictable

Fluctuations in the economy are often called the *business cycle.* As this term suggests, economic fluctuations correspond to changes in business conditions. When real GDP grows rapidly, business is good. During such periods of economic expansion, firms find that customers are plentiful and that profits are growing.

On the other hand, when real GDP falls during recessions, businesses have trouble. During such periods of economic contraction, most firms experience declining sales and dwindling profits.

The term *business cycle* is somewhat misleading, however, because it seems to suggest that economic fluctuations follow a regular, predictable pattern. In fact, economic fluctuations are not at all regular, and they are almost impossible to predict with much accuracy. Panel (a) of Figure 14.1 shows the real GDP of the Canadian economy since 1966. The shaded areas represent times of recession. As the figure shows, recessions do not come at regular intervals. Sometimes recessions are close together, such as the recessions of 1980 and 1982. Sometimes the economy goes many years without a recession. From 1991 to the fall of 2008, Canada enjoyed a recession-free period of economic growth.

14-1b Fact 2: Most Macroeconomic Quantities Fluctuate Together

Real GDP is the variable that is most commonly used to monitor short-run changes in the economy because it is the most comprehensive measure of economic activity. Real GDP measures the value of all final goods and services produced within a given period of time. It also measures the total income (adjusted for inflation) of everyone in the economy.

FIGURE 14.1

A Look at Short-Run Economic Fluctuations

Source: Statistics Canada, CANSIM database.

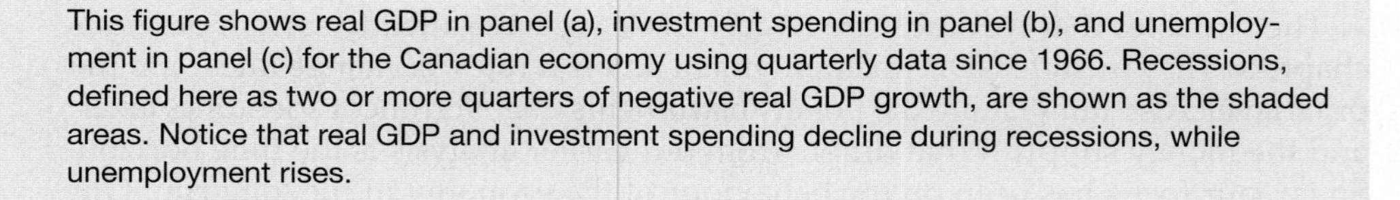

This figure shows real GDP in panel (a), investment spending in panel (b), and unemployment in panel (c) for the Canadian economy using quarterly data since 1966. Recessions, defined here as two or more quarters of negative real GDP growth, are shown as the shaded areas. Notice that real GDP and investment spending decline during recessions, while unemployment rises.

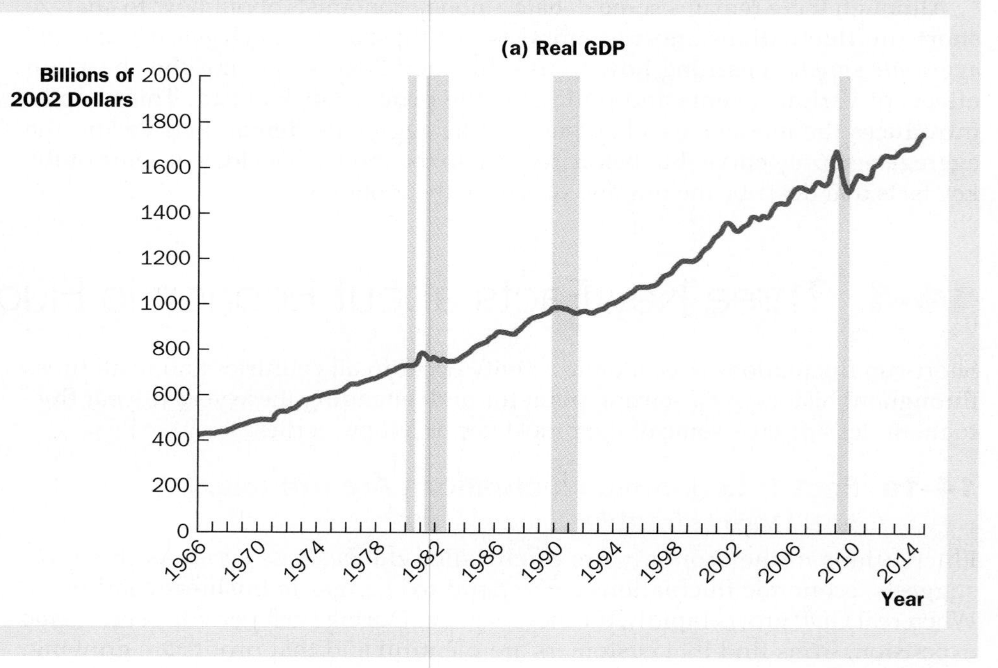

FIGURE 14.1 (Continued)

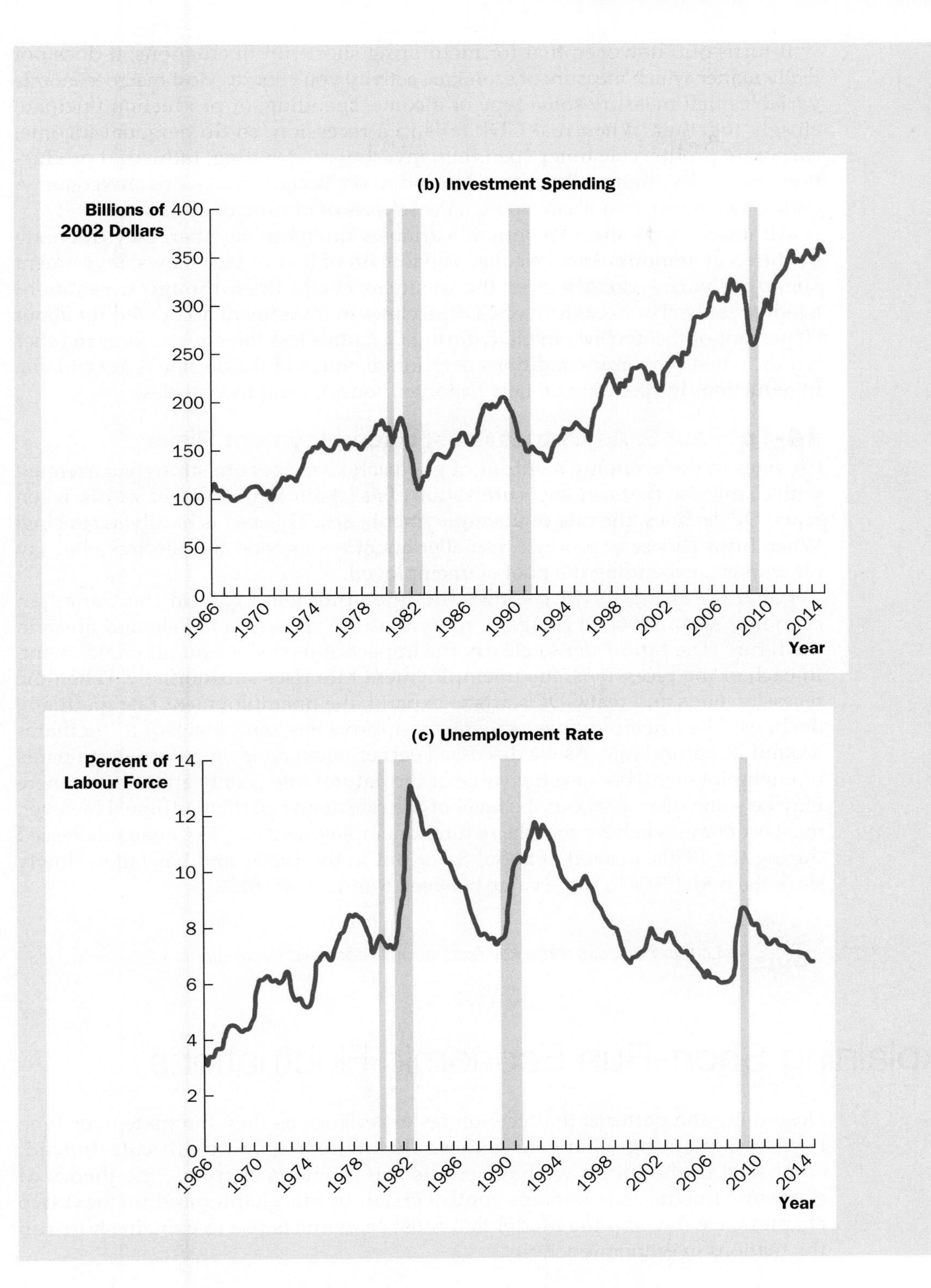

It turns out, however, that for monitoring short-run fluctuations, it does not really matter which measure of economic activity you choose. Most macroeconomic variables that measure some type of income, spending, or production fluctuate closely together. When real GDP falls in a recession, so do personal income, corporate profits, consumer spending, investment spending, industrial production, retail sales, home sales, auto sales, and so on. Because recessions are economy-wide phenomena, they show up in many sources of macroeconomic data.

Although many macroeconomic variables fluctuate together, they fluctuate by different amounts. In particular, as panel (b) of Figure 14.1 shows, investment spending varies greatly over the business cycle. Even though investment averages only about one-fifth of GDP, declines in investment accounted for about 80 percent of the declines in GDP during Canada's last three recessions. In other words, when economic conditions deteriorate, much of the decline is attributable to reductions in spending on new factories, housing, and inventories.

14-1c Fact 3: As Output Falls, Unemployment Rises

Changes in the economy's output of goods and services are strongly correlated with changes in the economy's utilization of its labour force. In other words, when real GDP declines, the rate of unemployment rises. This fact is hardly surprising: When firms choose to produce a smaller quantity of goods and services, they lay off workers, expanding the pool of unemployed.

Panel (c) of Figure 14.1 shows the unemployment rate in the Canadian economy since 1966. Once again, recessions are shown as the shaded areas in the figure. The figure shows clearly the impact of recessions on unemployment. In each of the recessions, the unemployment rate rises substantially. When the recession ends and real GDP starts to expand, the unemployment rate gradually declines. The unemployment rate never approaches zero; instead, it fluctuates around its natural rate. As we discussed earlier when reviewing the determinants of unemployment, because the value of the natural rate is only an estimate, there may be some dispute about the level of the rate at any particular time. However, most economists believe that the natural unemployment rate in Canada increased during the 1970s, peaked at about 8 percent in the 1980s, and has fallen slowly since the mid-1990s to some value between 6 and 7 percent.

List and discuss three key facts about economic fluctuations.

14-2 Explaining Short-Run Economic Fluctuations

Describing the patterns that economies experience as they fluctuate over time is easy. Explaining what causes these fluctuations is more difficult. Indeed, compared to the topics we have studied in previous chapters, the theory of economic fluctuations remains controversial. In this chapter and the next two chapters, we develop the model that most economists use to explain short-run fluctuations in economic activity.

14-2a The Assumptions of Classical Economics

In previous chapters we developed theories to explain what determines most important macroeconomic variables in the long run. Chapter 7 explained the level and growth of productivity and real GDP. Chapter 8 explained how the financial system works and how the real interest rate adjusts to balance saving and investment in a closed economy. Chapter 9 explained why there is always some unemployment in the economy. Chapters 10 and 11 explained the monetary system and how changes in the money supply affect the price level, the inflation rate, and the nominal interest rate. Chapters 12 and 13 extended this analysis to open economies in order to explain the trade balance and the exchange rate. There we learned that, as a result of perfect capital mobility, the real interest rate in Canada must increase and decrease with increases and decreases in the value of the world real interest rate.

All of this previous analysis was based on two related ideas—the classical dichotomy and monetary neutrality. Recall that the classical dichotomy is the separation of variables into real variables (those that measure quantities or relative prices) and nominal variables (those measured in terms of money). According to classical macroeconomic theory, changes in the money supply affect nominal variables but not real variables. As a result of this monetary neutrality, Chapters 7 through 9 were able to examine the determinants of real variables (real GDP, the real interest rate, and unemployment) without introducing nominal variables (the money supply and the price level).

In a sense, money does not matter in a classical economic world. If the quantity of money in the economy were to double, everything would cost twice as much, and everyone's income would be twice as high. But so what? The change would be *nominal* (in the sense of being nearly insignificant). The things that people *really* care about—whether they have a job, how many goods and services they can afford, and so on—would be exactly the same.

This classical view is sometimes described by the saying, "Money is a veil." That is, nominal variables may be the first things we see when we observe an economy because economic variables are often expressed in units of money. But what's important are the real variables and the economic forces that determine them. According to classical theory, to understand these real variables, we need to look beneath the veil.

14-2b The Reality of Short-Run Fluctuations

Do these assumptions of classical macroeconomic theory apply to the world in which we live? The answer to this question is of central importance to understanding how the economy works. *Most economists believe that classical theory describes the world in the long run, but not in the short run.*

Consider again the impact of money on the economy. Most economists believe that, beyond a period of several years, changes in the money supply affect prices and other nominal variables, but do not affect real GDP, unemployment, or other real variables—just as classical theory says. When studying year-to-year changes in the economy, however, the assumption of monetary neutrality is no longer appropriate. In the short run, real and nominal variables are highly intertwined, and changes in the money supply can temporarily push real GDP away from its long-run trend.

Even the classical economists themselves, such as David Hume, realized that classical economic theory did not hold in the short run. From his vantage point in eighteenth-century England, Hume observed that when the money supply expanded after gold discoveries, it took some time for prices to rise, and in the meantime, the economy enjoyed higher employment and production.

IN THE news

The Social Influences of Economic Downturns

Recessions have broad impacts beyond those that can be described by unemployment rates and falling GDP. They also affect society more broadly.

Everybody Hurts in a Social Recession

By Michael Kirby

U.S. public officials have been comparing the mental-health impact of the recession and unemployment crisis to a natural disaster, like Hurricane Katrina. The parallels are obvious: In both natural disasters and man-made economic ones, people lose businesses, jobs, homes, hopes, lives. Each type wreaks a devastating toll on the mental health of its victims—lost jobs and livelihoods cause great psychological distress and increased rates of anxiety, depression, child neglect, family violence, substance abuse, crime and suicide.

Even before the recession, our world was a complex and confusing place for many people. Now, the economic crisis is adding a whole new layer of pressures. The United Nations International Labour Organization estimates that 40 million people worldwide could lose their jobs this year, and each victim has colleagues, families and friends whose lives are also affected.

There is very solid data correlating unemployment and personal financial stress with increased mental-health problems, including higher rates of depression and suicide. In Windsor, Ont., where the auto industry was hit early and hard by the recession, demand for mental-health services has jumped 50 per cent in the past year. The Canadian Medical Association reported recently that 40 per cent of Canadians are feeling stressed or overwhelmed by financial concerns. And in a recent survey, 88 per cent of family physicians in Canada said that since the recession began, they have been seeing patients with stress problems that can be attributed to the economy.

luxorphoto/Shutterstock.com

So, in addition to the global economic recession, it appears we are now experiencing what the World Health Organization has called a "social recession," in which the daily lives of individuals, their families and whole communities are torn asunder by financial loss, unemployment, fear and declining physical and mental health.

At a unique international roundtable this past week in Ottawa organized by the Mental Health Commission of Canada, mental-health and public-policy experts from Canada, the United States, Europe, New Zealand, and Australia discussed the toll the recession is taking on working men and women and their families and what action society should be taking to address the crisis.

We learned that even though we are starting to see hope for economic recovery, no government should be lulled into thinking that the social recession will end any time soon. After the last economic recession in Australia, it took more than 14 years for employment levels to recover. We learned that social agencies around the world are seeing a new group of people seeking help: members of the middle class who have never needed assistance before.

Where do we go from here? The answer is a challenge to both the public and private sector.

We should put an end to the sort of short-term thinking that caused the crisis, and focus on strengthening the resources that are of greatest strategic importance. A good place to start is with our human capital, because knowledge societies and knowledge economies need strong mental health capital.

As a priority, we need to improve the delivery of mental-health services to the groups in society that are most vulnerable. One of these is the 18- to 25-year-olds who are being hit hardest by unemployment. No society can afford to have an entire generation of disillusioned young people.

We should also urge employers to put workplace mental health at the top of the agenda. And when workers are laid off, we need to ensure that, in addition to employment insurance, they also gain access to psychological support.

And instead of cutting social-service budgets in times of crisis, we should nurture a culture of community support for the unemployed. This will help them cope with the initial impact of unemployment and assist the transition back to work.

By taking these and other actions, Canada will be in a much stronger position to address mental-health issues at every point in the economic cycle so we can avoid a social recession even if we can't avoid an economic hurricane.

Michael Kirby is chair of the Mental Health Commission of Canada.

Source: "Everybody Hurts in a Social Recession," by Michael Kirby, ***The Globe and Mail,*** August 26, 2009. Reprinted by permission of the author.

To understand how the economy works in the short run, we need a new model. This new model can be built using many of the tools we developed in previous chapters, but it must abandon the classical dichotomy and the neutrality of money. We can no longer separate our analysis of real variables such as output and employment from our analysis of nominal variables such as money and the price level. Our new model focuses on how real and nominal variables interact.

14-2c The Model of Aggregate Demand and Aggregate Supply

Our model of short-run economic fluctuations focuses on the behaviour of two variables. The first variable is the economy's output of goods and services, as measured by real GDP. The second variable is the overall price level, as measured by the CPI or the GDP deflator. Notice that output is a real variable, whereas the price level is a nominal variable. By focusing on the relationship between these two variables, we are departing from the classical assumption that real and nominal variables can be studied separately.

We analyze fluctuations in the economy as a whole with the **model of aggregate demand and aggregate supply,** which is illustrated in Figure 14.2. On the vertical axis is the overall price level in the economy. On the horizontal axis is the overall quantity of goods and services. The **aggregate-demand curve** shows the quantity of goods and services that households, firms, and the government want to buy at each price level. The **aggregate-supply curve** shows the quantity of goods and services that firms produce and sell at each price level. According to this model, the price level and the quantity of output adjust to bring aggregate demand and aggregate supply into balance.

It may be tempting to view the model of aggregate demand and aggregate supply as nothing more than a large version of the model of market demand and market supply, which we introduced in Chapter 4. Yet, in fact, this model is quite

model of aggregate demand and aggregate supply
the model that most economists use to explain short-run fluctuations in economic activity around its long-run trend

aggregate-demand curve
a curve that shows the quantity of goods and services that households, firms, and the government want to buy at each price level

aggregate-supply curve
a curve that shows the quantity of goods and services that firms choose to produce and sell at each price level

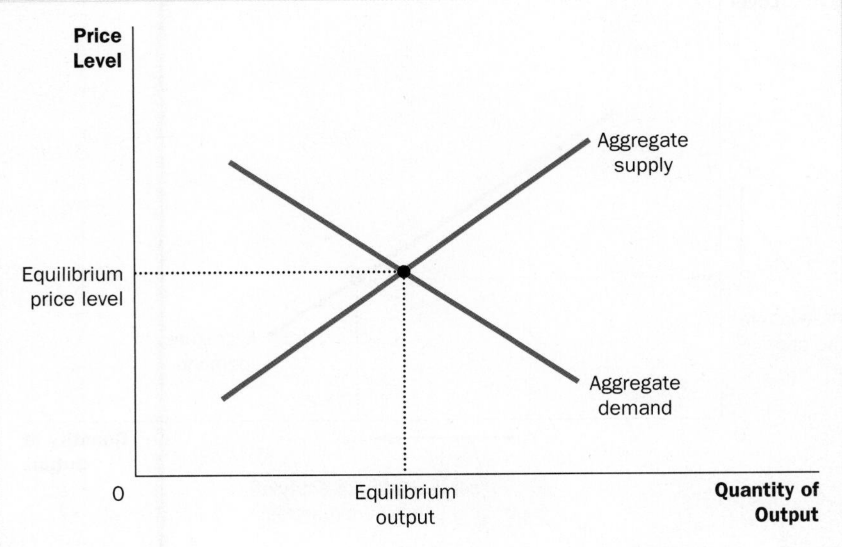

FIGURE 14.2

Aggregate Demand and Aggregate Supply
Economists use the model of aggregate demand and aggregate supply to analyze economic fluctuations. On the vertical axis is the overall level of prices. On the horizontal axis is the economy's total output of goods and services. Output and the price level adjust to the point at which the aggregate-supply and aggregate-demand curves intersect.

different. When we consider demand and supply in a particular market—ice cream, for instance—the behaviour of buyers and sellers depends on the ability of resources to move from one market to another. When the price of ice cream rises, the quantity demanded falls because buyers will use their incomes to buy products other than ice cream. Similarly, a higher price of ice cream raises the quantity supplied because firms that produce ice cream can increase production by hiring workers away from other parts of the economy. This *microeconomic* substitution from one market to another is impossible when we are analyzing the economy as a whole. After all, the quantity that our model is trying to explain—real GDP—measures the total quantity produced in all of the economy's markets. To understand why the aggregate-demand curve is downward sloping and why the aggregate-supply curve is upward sloping, we need a *macroeconomic* theory. Developing such a theory is our next task.

How does the economy's behaviour in the short run differ from its behaviour in the long run? • Draw the model of aggregate demand and aggregate supply. What variables are on the two axes?

14-3 The Aggregate-Demand Curve

The aggregate-demand curve tells us the quantity of all goods and services demanded in the economy at any given price level. As Figure 14.3 illustrates, the aggregate-demand curve is downward sloping. This means that, other things equal, a fall in the economy's overall level of prices (from, say, P_1 to P_2) tends to raise the quantity of goods and services demanded (from Y_1 to Y_2). Conversely, an increase in the price level reduces the quantity of goods and services demanded.

FIGURE 14.3

The Aggregate-Demand Curve

A fall in the price level from P_1 to P_2 increases the quantity of goods and services demanded from Y_1 to Y_2. There are three reasons for this negative relationship. As the price level falls, real wealth rises, interest rates fall, and the exchange rate depreciates. These effects stimulate spending on consumption, investment, and net exports. Increased spending on these components of output means a larger quantity of goods and services demanded.

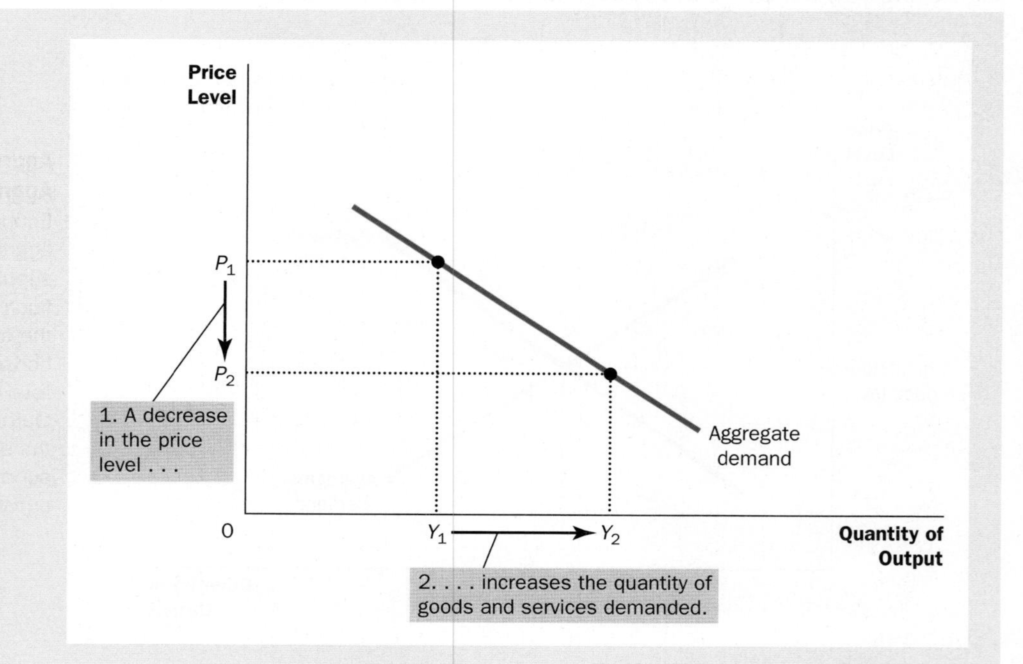

14-3a Why the Aggregate-Demand Curve Slopes Downward

Why does a fall in the price level raise the quantity of goods and services demanded? To answer this question, it is useful to recall that GDP (which we denote as Y) is the sum of consumption (C), investment (I), government purchases (G), and net exports (NX):

$$Y = C + I + G + NX$$

Each of these four components contributes to the aggregate demand for goods and services. For now, we assume that government spending is fixed by policy. The other three components of spending—consumption, investment, and net exports—depend on economic conditions and, in particular, on the price level. To understand the downward slope of the aggregate-demand curve, therefore, we must examine how the price level affects the quantity of goods and services demanded for consumption, investment, and net exports.

The Price Level and Consumption: The Wealth Effect Consider the money that you hold in your wallet and your bank account. The nominal value of this money is fixed: One dollar is always worth one dollar. Yet the *real* value of a dollar is not fixed. If a candy bar costs one dollar, then a dollar is worth one candy bar. If the price of a candy bar falls to 50 cents, then one dollar is worth two candy bars. Thus, when the price level falls, the dollars you are holding rise in value, which increases your real wealth and your ability to buy goods and services.

This logic gives us the first reason the aggregate-demand curve is downward sloping. *A decrease in the price level makes consumers wealthier, which in turn encourages them to spend more. The increase in consumer spending means a larger quantity of goods and services demanded. Conversely, an increase in the price level reduces the real value of money, in turn reducing wealth, consumer spending, and the quantity of goods and services demanded.*

The Price Level and Investment: The Interest Rate Effect As we discussed in Chapter 11, the price level is one determinant of the quantity of money demanded. The lower the price level, the less money households need to hold to buy the goods and services they want. When the price level falls, therefore, households try to reduce their holdings of money by lending some of it out. For instance, a household might use its excess money to buy interest-bearing bonds. Or it might deposit its excess money in an interest-bearing savings account, and the bank would use these funds to make more loans. In either case, as households try to convert some of their money into interest-bearing assets, they drive down interest rates. (The next chapter analyzes this process in more detail.)

Interest rates, in turn, affect spending on goods and services. Because a lower interest rate makes borrowing less expensive, it encourages firms to borrow more to invest in new plants and equipment, and it encourages households to borrow more to invest in new housing. (A lower interest rate might also stimulate consumer spending, especially spending on large durable purchases such as cars, which are often bought on credit.) Thus, a lower interest rate increases the quantity of goods and services demanded.

This logic gives us a second reason the aggregate-demand curve is downward sloping: *A lower price level reduces the interest rate, encourages greater spending on investment goods, and thereby increases the quantity of goods and services demanded. Conversely, a higher price level raises the interest rate, discourages investment spending, and decreases the quantity of goods and services demanded.*

The Price Level and Net Exports: The Real Exchange-Rate Effect In Chapter 12, we saw that by using a price index for a Canadian basket of goods and services (P), a price index for a foreign basket (P^*), and the nominal exchange rate between the Canadian dollar and foreign currencies (e), we can compute the real exchange rate between Canada and other countries as follows:

$$\text{Real exchange rate} = (e \times P)/P^*$$

The real exchange rate measures the rate at which a person can trade Canadian-produced goods and services for the goods and services of other countries. For a given nominal exchange rate, a lower price level reduces the real exchange rate. This depreciation makes Canadian-produced goods and services cheaper relative to foreign-produced goods and services. As a result, Canadians and foreigners substitute away from foreign-produced goods and services in favour of Canadian-produced goods and services.

This logic yields a third reason the aggregate-demand curve is downward sloping: *A fall in the Canadian price level causes the real exchange rate to depreciate, and this depreciation stimulates Canadian net exports and thereby increases the quantity of goods and services demanded. Conversely, an increase in the Canadian price level causes the real exchange rate to appreciate, and this appreciation reduces Canadian net exports and thereby decreases the quantity of goods and services demanded.*

Summary There are, therefore, three distinct but related reasons why a fall in the price level increases the quantity of goods and services demanded:

1. Consumers are wealthier, which stimulates the demand for consumption goods.
2. Interest rates fall, which stimulates the demand for investment goods.
3. The exchange rate depreciates, which stimulates the demand for net exports.

For all three reasons, the aggregate-demand curve slopes downward. The same three effects work in reverse: When the price level rises, decreased wealth depresses consumer spending, higher interest rates depress investment spending, and a currency appreciation depresses net exports.

Here is a thought experiment to hone your intuition about these effects. Imagine that one day you wake up and notice that, for some mysterious reason, the prices of all goods and services have doubled, so the dollars you are holding are worth half as much. In real terms, you now have half as much money as you had when you went to bed the night before. What might you do? You could reduce the amount you spend at your favourite restaurant, decreasing consumer spending. You could reduce your savings (by reducing your deposits at your bank), increasing interest rates and so reducing investment spending. Or you could respond to the resulting higher real exchange rate by increasing your purchases of foreign-produced goods and thereby contribute to a reduction in Canada's net exports. Whichever of these three responses you choose, the increase in the price level leads to a decrease in the quantity of Canadian-produced goods and services demanded. This is what the downward slope of the aggregate-demand curve represents.

It is important to keep in mind that the aggregate-demand curve (like all demand curves) is drawn holding "other things equal." In particular, our three explanations of the downward-sloping aggregate-demand curve assume that the money supply is fixed. That is, we have been considering how a change in the price level affects the demand for goods and services, holding the amount of money in the economy constant. As we will see, a change in the quantity of money shifts the aggregate-demand curve. At this point, just keep in mind that the aggregate-demand curve is drawn for a given quantity of money.

14-3b Why the Aggregate-Demand Curve Might Shift

The downward slope of the aggregate-demand curve shows that a fall in the price level raises the overall quantity of goods and services demanded. Many other factors, however, affect the quantity of goods and services demanded at a given price level. When one of these other factors changes, the aggregate-demand curve shifts.

Let's consider some examples of events that shift aggregate demand. We can categorize them according to which component of spending is most directly affected.

Shifts Arising from Changes in Consumption Suppose Canadians suddenly become more concerned about saving for retirement and, as a result, reduce their current consumption. This concern about retirement savings might arise because of a fall in stock prices that makes people feel less wealthy. Because the quantity of goods and services demanded at any price level is lower, the aggregate-demand curve shifts to the left. Conversely, imagine that a stock market boom makes people wealthier and less concerned about saving. The resulting increase in consumer spending means a greater quantity of goods and services demanded at any given price level, so the aggregate-demand curve shifts to the right.

Thus, any event that changes how much people want to consume at a given price level shifts the aggregate-demand curve. One policy variable that has this effect is the level of taxation. When the government cuts taxes, it encourages people to spend more, so the aggregate-demand curve shifts to the right. When the government raises taxes, people cut back on their spending, and the aggregate-demand curve shifts to the left.

case study

Housing Wealth

Consumption expenditures are in part influenced by how wealthy people feel they are. Falls in the stock market, general concerns about the adequacy of retirement savings, even the arrival of a new child and all the future expenditures that entails are reasons why people might feel less wealthy than otherwise. Increases in the stock market, an inheritance, and the graduation of a son or daughter from university are reasons why people might suddenly feel wealthier.

An important consideration that influences how wealthy people feel they are is the value of what is typically their largest asset: their house. Figure 14.4 shows the year-over-year percentage change in the prices of new and resale homes in Canada since 1993. The period from 1997 to 2008 was one of generally rapidly rising house prices. In 2006, for example, the price of both new and resale house prices increased by over 11 percent. In 2009, however, house prices stopped increasing and instead fell. This period of falling house prices was short-lived. By 2010, the prices of new houses were again increasing by roughly 2 percent per year. Resale housing, however, returned to annual increases of about 6 percent

FIGURE 14.4

Canadian House Prices, 1993–2015

Sources: Bank of Canada, Indicators of Capacity and Inflation Pressures for Canada: http:www.bankofcanada.ca/en/rates/indinf/real_data_en.html

This figure shows the annual percentage change in the prices of new and resale houses in Canada from 1993 to 2015. The large annual increases in house prices during the early 2000s may, by causing people to feel wealthier, have caused household spending to also increase during that period. The sudden fall in house prices in 2009 likely contributed to a fall in household spending and so contributed to the severity of the 2008–09 recession.

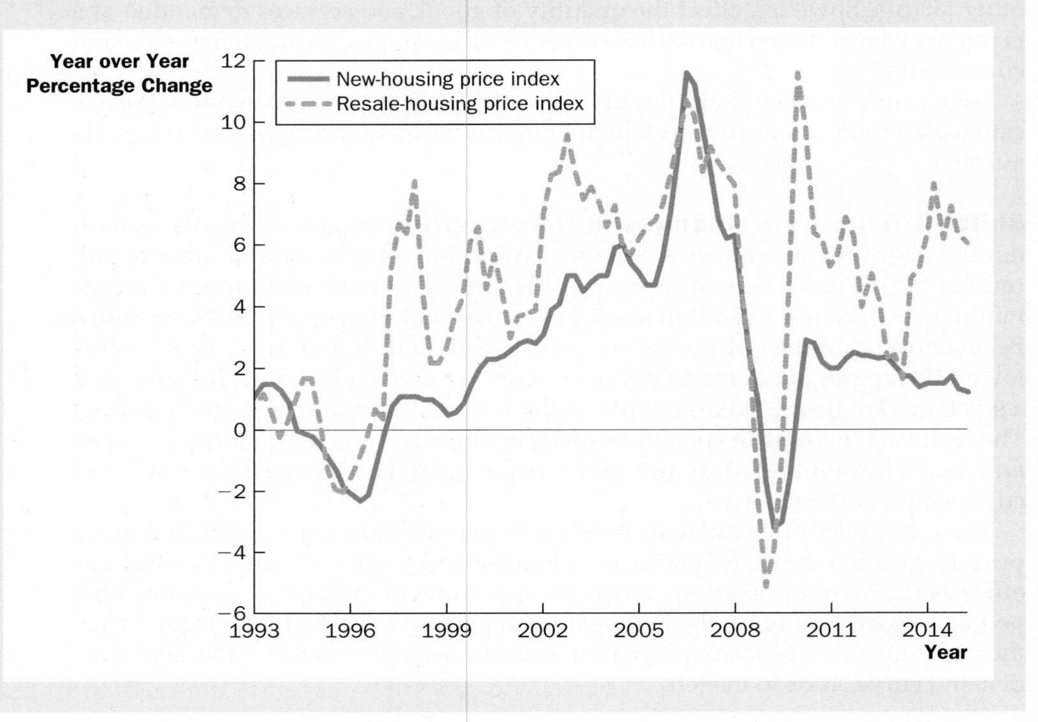

per year. The data presented in Figure 14.4 are, of course, averages of how much house prices increased across Canada. In certain housing markets the rate of change in prices was much greater than in other local housing markets.

Large increases and decreases in housing prices are a concern of policymakers not only because of the potential effect on consumption spending, but also due to worries about the resilience of mortgage holders to absorb the financial consequences if interest rates rise or housing prices take a sudden drop. For all of these reasons, the Bank of Canada and the government keep a close watch on the housing market.

As large as these changes in Canadian house prices were during this period, in the United States they were much larger. The impact of the fall in house prices on U.S. household consumption during the 2008–09 recession is believed to have imposed a significant drag on the economic recovery in the United States. ■

Shifts Arising from Changes in Investment Any event that changes how much firms want to invest at a given price level also shifts the aggregate-demand curve. For instance, imagine that the computer industry introduces a faster line of computers and many firms decide to invest in new computer systems. Because the quantity of goods and services demanded at any price level is higher, the aggregate-demand curve shifts to the right. Conversely, if firms become pessimistic about future business conditions, they may cut back on investment spending, shifting the aggregate-demand curve to the left.

Tax policy can also influence aggregate demand through investment. As we saw in Chapter 8, an investment tax credit (a tax rebate tied to a firm's investment spending) increases the quantity of investment goods that firms demand at any given interest rate. It therefore shifts the aggregate-demand curve to the right. The repeal of an investment tax credit reduces investment and shifts the aggregate-demand curve to the left.

Another policy variable that can influence investment and aggregate demand is the money supply. As we discuss in more detail in the next chapter, an increase in the money supply lowers the interest rate in the short run. This makes borrowing less costly, which stimulates investment spending and thereby shifts the aggregate-demand curve to the right. Conversely, a decrease in the money supply raises the interest rate, discourages investment spending, and thereby shifts the aggregate-demand curve to the left. Many economists believe that throughout Canada's history, changes in monetary policy have been an important source of shifts in aggregate demand.

Shifts Arising from Changes in Government Purchases The most direct way that policymakers shift the aggregate-demand curve is through government purchases. For example, suppose Parliament decides to increase purchases of new equipment for Canada's armed forces. Because the quantity of goods and services demanded at any price level is higher, the aggregate-demand curve shifts to the right. Conversely, if provincial governments choose to spend less on highway construction, the result is a smaller quantity of goods and services demanded at any price level, so the aggregate-demand curve shifts to the left.

Shifts Arising from Changes in Net Exports Any event that changes net exports for a given price level also shifts aggregate demand. For instance, when the United States experiences a recession, it buys fewer goods from Canada. This reduces Canada's net exports and shifts the aggregate-demand curve for the Canadian economy to the left. When the United States recovers from its recession, it starts buying Canadian goods again, shifting the aggregate-demand curve to the right.

Net exports sometimes change because of movements in the exchange rate. Suppose, for instance, that international speculators bid up the value of the Canadian dollar in the market for foreign-currency exchange. This appreciation of the dollar would make Canadian goods more expensive compared to foreign goods, which would depress net exports and shift the aggregate-demand curve to the left. Conversely, a depreciation of the dollar stimulates net exports and shifts the aggregate-demand curve to the right.

Summary In the next chapter we analyze the aggregate-demand curve in more detail. There we examine more precisely how the tools of monetary and fiscal policy can shift aggregate demand and whether policymakers should use these tools for that purpose. At this point, however, you should have some idea about why the aggregate-demand curve slopes downward and what kinds of events and policies can shift this curve. Table 14.1 summarizes what we have learned so far.

TABLE 14.1

The Aggregate-Demand Curve: Summary

Why Does the Aggregate-Demand Curve Slope Downward?

1. *The Wealth Effect:* A lower price level increases real wealth, which encourages spending on consumption.
2. *The Interest Rate Effect:* A lower price level reduces the interest rate, which encourages spending on investment.
3. *The Real Exchange-Rate Effect:* A lower price level causes the real exchange rate to depreciate, which encourages spending on net exports.

Why Might the Aggregate-Demand Curve Shift?

1. *Shifts Arising from Changes in Consumption:* An event that makes consumers spend more at a given price level (a tax cut, a stock market boom) shifts the aggregate-demand curve to the right. An event that makes consumers spend less at a given price level (a tax hike, a stock market decline) shifts the aggregate-demand curve to the left.
2. *Shifts Arising from Changes in Investment:* An event that makes firms invest more at a given price level (optimism about the future, a fall in interest rates due to an increase in the money supply) shifts the aggregate-demand curve to the right. An event that makes firms invest less at a given price level (pessimism about the future, a rise in interest rates due to a decrease in the money supply) shifts the aggregate-demand curve to the left.
3. *Shifts Arising from Changes in Government Purchases:* An increase in government purchases of goods and services (greater spending on defence or highway construction) shifts the aggregate-demand curve to the right. A decrease in government purchases of goods and services (a cutback in defence or highway spending) shifts the aggregate-demand curve to the left.
4. *Shifts Arising from Changes in Net Exports:* An event that raises spending on net exports at a given price level (a boom experienced by a major trading partner, an exchange-rate depreciation) shifts the aggregate-demand curve to the right. An event that reduces spending on net exports at a given price level (a recession experienced by a major trading partner, an exchange-rate appreciation) shifts the aggregate-demand curve to the left.

Explain the three reasons why the aggregate-demand curve slopes downward. • Give an example of an event that would shift the aggregate-demand curve. Which way would this event shift the curve?

14-4 The Aggregate-Supply Curve

The aggregate-supply curve tells us the total quantity of goods and services that firms produce and sell at any given price level. Unlike the aggregate-demand curve, which is always downward sloping, the aggregate-supply curve shows a relationship that depends crucially on the time horizon being examined. *In the long run, the aggregate-supply curve is vertical, whereas in the short run, the aggregate-supply curve is upward sloping.* To understand short-run economic fluctuations, and how the short-run behaviour of the economy deviates from its long-run behaviour, we need to examine both the long-run aggregate-supply curve and the short-run aggregate-supply curve.

14-4a Why the Aggregate-Supply Curve Is Vertical in the Long Run

What determines the quantity of goods and services supplied in the long run? We implicitly answered this question earlier in the book when we analyzed the process of economic growth. *In the long run, an economy's production of goods and services (its real GDP) depends on its supplies of labour, capital, and natural resources and on the available technology used to turn these factors of production into goods and services.*

When we analyzed these forces that govern long-run growth, we did not need to make any reference to the overall level of prices. We examined the price level in a separate chapter, where we saw that it was determined by the quantity of money. We learned that if two economies were identical except that one had twice as much money in circulation as the other, the price level would be twice as high in the economy with more money, but the output of goods and services would be the same.

Because the price level does not affect these long-run determinants of real GDP, the long-run aggregate-supply curve is vertical, as in Figure 14.5. In other words, in the long run, the economy's labour, capital, natural resources, and technology determine the total quantity of goods and services supplied, and this quantity supplied is the same regardless of what the price level happens to be.

The vertical long-run aggregate-supply curve is a graphical representation of the classical dichotomy and monetary neutrality. As we have already discussed, classical macroeconomic theory is based on the assumption that real variables do not depend on nominal variables. The long-run aggregate-supply curve is consistent with this idea because it implies that the quantity of output (a real variable) does not depend on the level of prices (a nominal variable). As noted earlier, most economists believe that this principle works well when studying the economy over a period of many years, but not when studying year-to-year changes. Thus, the aggregate-supply curve is vertical only in the long run.

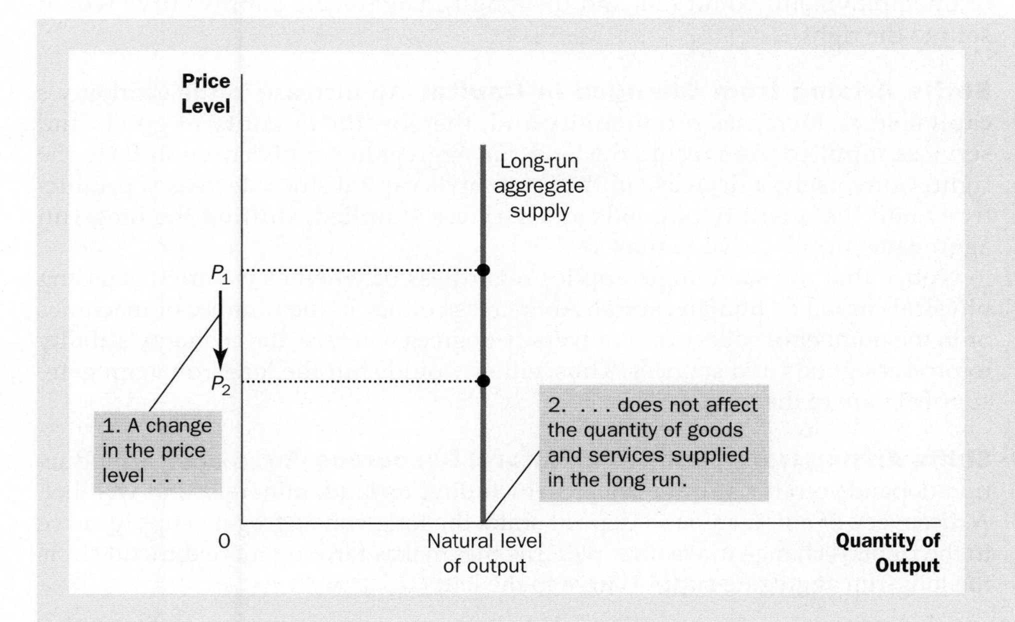

FIGURE 14.5

The Long-Run Aggregate-Supply Curve

In the long run, the quantity of output supplied depends on the economy's quantities of labour, capital, and natural resources and on the technology for turning these inputs into output. The quantity supplied does not depend on the overall price level. As a result, the long-run aggregate-supply curve is vertical at the natural level of output.

14-4b Why the Long-Run Aggregate-Supply Curve Might Shift

Classical macroeconomic theory predicts the quantity of goods and services produced by an economy in the long run, so it also explains the position of the long-run aggregate-supply curve. The long-run level of production is sometimes called *potential output* or *full-employment output*. To be more accurate, we call it the **natural level of output** because it shows what the economy produces when unemployment is at its natural, or normal, rate. The natural level of output is the level of production toward which the economy gravitates in the long run.

natural level of output
the production of goods and services that an economy achieves in the long run when unemployment is at its normal rate

Any change in the economy that alters the natural level of output shifts the long-run aggregate-supply curve. Because output in the classical model depends on labour, capital, natural resources, and technological knowledge, we can categorize shifts in the long-run aggregate-supply curve as arising from these four sources.

Shifts Arising from Changes in Labour Imagine that an economy experiences an increase in immigration from abroad. Because there would be a greater number of workers, the quantity of goods and services supplied would increase. As a result, the long-run aggregate-supply curve would shift to the right. Conversely, if many workers left the economy to go abroad, the long-run aggregate-supply curve would shift to the left.

The position of the long-run aggregate-supply curve also depends on the natural rate of unemployment, so any change in the natural rate of unemployment shifts the long-run aggregate-supply curve. For example, if provincial and territorial governments were to raise the minimum wage substantially, the natural rate of unemployment would rise, and the economy would produce a smaller quantity of goods and services. As a result, the long-run aggregate-supply curve would shift to the left. Conversely, if a reform of the Employment Insurance system were to encourage unemployed workers to search harder for new jobs, the natural rate of unemployment would fall, and the long-run aggregate-supply curve would shift to the right.

Shifts Arising from Changes in Capital An increase in the economy's capital stock increases productivity and, thereby, the quantity of goods and services supplied. As a result, the long-run aggregate-supply curve shifts to the right. Conversely, a decrease in the economy's capital stock decreases productivity and the quantity of goods and services supplied, shifting the long-run aggregate-supply curve to the left.

Notice that the same logic applies regardless of whether we are discussing physical capital or human capital. An increase either in the number of machines or in the number of college and university degrees will raise the economy's ability to produce goods and services. Thus, either would shift the long-run aggregate-supply curve to the right.

Shifts Arising from Changes in Natural Resources An economy's production depends on its natural resources, including its land, minerals, and weather. A discovery of a new mineral deposit shifts the long-run aggregate-supply curve to the right. A change in weather patterns that makes farming more difficult shifts the long-run aggregate-supply curve to the left.

In many countries, important natural resources are imported from abroad. A change in the availability of these resources can also shift the aggregate-supply curve. As we discuss later in this chapter, events occurring in the world oil market have historically been an important source of shifts in aggregate supply.

Shifts Arising from Changes in Technological Knowledge Perhaps the most important reason that the economy today produces more than it did a generation ago is that our technological knowledge has advanced. The invention of the computer, for instance, has allowed us to produce more goods and services from any given amounts of labour, capital, and natural resources. As a result, it has shifted the long-run aggregate-supply curve to the right.

Although not literally technological, there are many other events that act like changes in technology. For example, opening up international trade has effects similar to inventing new production processes because it allows a country to specialize in higher-productivity industries, so it also shifts the long-run aggregate-supply curve to the right. Conversely, if the government passed new regulations preventing firms from using some production methods, perhaps because they produced too much pollution, the result would be a leftward shift in the long-run aggregate-supply curve.

Summary The long-run aggregate-supply curve reflects the classical model of the economy we developed in previous chapters. Any policy or event that raised real GDP in previous chapters can now be viewed as increasing the quantity of goods and services supplied and shifting the long-run aggregate-supply curve to the right. Any policy or event that lowered real GDP in previous chapters can now be viewed as decreasing the quantity of goods and services supplied and shifting the long-run aggregate-supply curve to the left.

14-4c Using Aggregate Demand and Aggregate Supply to Depict Long-Run Growth and Inflation

Having introduced the economy's aggregate-demand curve and the long-run aggregate-supply curve, we now have a new way to describe the economy's long-run trends. Figure 14.6 illustrates the changes that occur in the economy from decade to decade. Notice that both curves are shifting. Although there are many forces that govern the economy in the long run and can in principle cause such shifts, the two most important in practice are technology and monetary policy. Technological progress enhances the economy's ability to produce goods and services, and this continually shifts the long-run aggregate-supply curve to the right. At the same time, because the Bank of Canada increases the money supply over time, the aggregate-demand curve also shifts to the right.

Figure 14.6 illustrates the aggregate-demand curve shifting farther to the right than the aggregate-supply curve. The result is trend growth in output (as shown by increasing Y) and inflation (as shown by increasing P). If the Bank of Canada introduced smaller increases in the money supply, the shifts to the right in the aggregate-demand curve would also be smaller. The result would be lower inflation (as shown by smaller increases in P) but no change in the trend growth in output. This is just another way of representing the classical analysis of growth and inflation we conducted in Chapters 7 and 11. It also effectively summarizes what we learned previously about inflation and one of

FIGURE 14.6

Long-Run Growth and Inflation in the Model of Aggregate Demand and Aggregate Supply

As the economy becomes better able to produce goods and services over time, primarily because of technological progress, the long-run aggregate-supply curve shifts to the right. At the same time, as the Bank of Canada increases the money supply, the aggregate-demand curve also shifts to the right. In this figure, output grows from Y_{1980} to Y_{1990} and then to Y_{2000}, and the price level rises from P_{1980} to P_{1990} and then to P_{2000}. Thus, the model of aggregate demand and aggregate supply offers a new way to describe the classical analysis of growth and inflation.

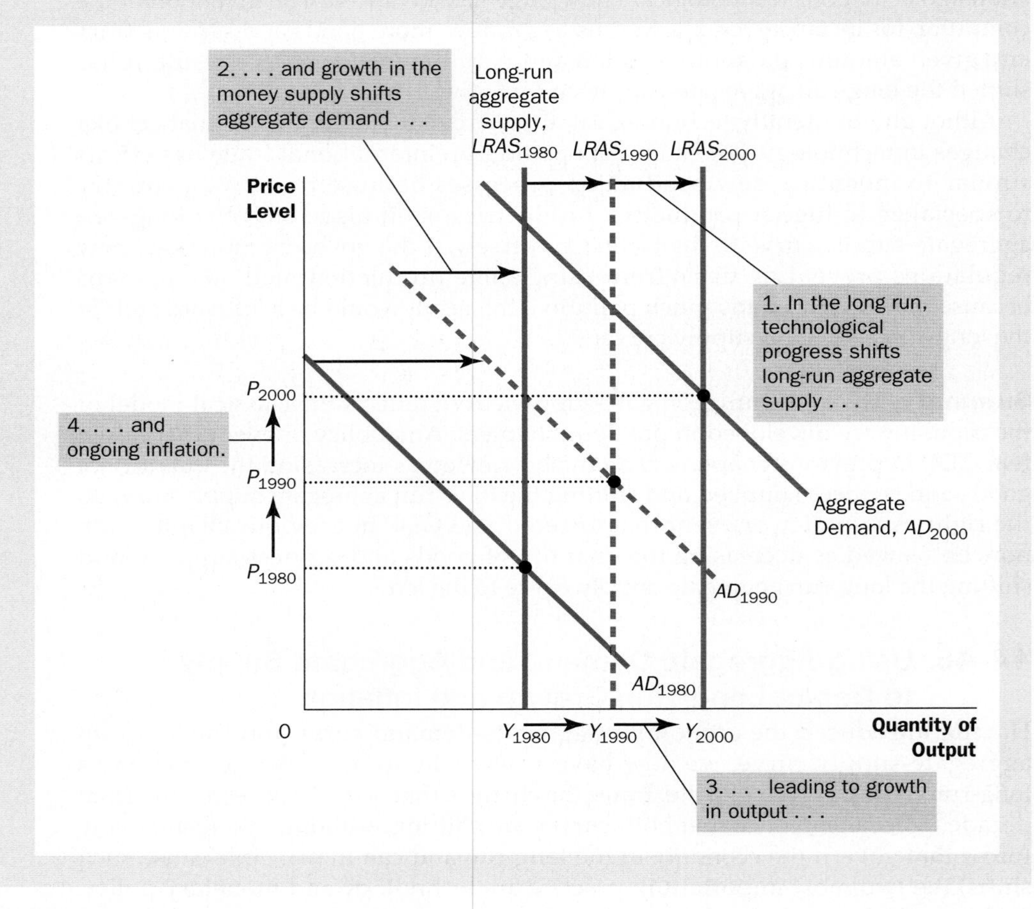

our ten principles of economics: Prices rise when the government prints too much money. In particular, as we illustrate in Figure 14.6, the primary cause of inflation is simply growth in the quantity of money that is faster than growth in output.

The purpose of developing the model of aggregate demand and aggregate supply, however, is not to dress our long-run conclusions in new clothing. Instead, it is to provide a framework for short-run analysis, as we will see soon. As we develop the short-run model, we keep the analysis simple by not showing the continuing growth and inflation depicted in Figure 14.6. But always remember that long-run trends provide the background for short-run fluctuations. *Short-run fluctuations in output and the price level should be viewed as deviations from the continuing long-run trends.*

14-4d Why the Aggregate-Supply Curve Slopes Upward in the Short Run

We now come to the key difference between the economy in the short run and in the long run: the behaviour of aggregate supply. As we have already discussed, the long-run aggregate-supply curve is vertical because, in the long run, the overall level of prices does not affect the economy's ability to produce goods and services. By contrast, in the short run, the price level *does* affect the economy's output. That is, over a period of a year or two, an increase in the overall level of prices in the economy tends to raise the quantity of goods and services supplied, and a decrease in the level of prices tends to reduce the quantity of goods and services supplied. As a result, the short-run aggregate-supply curve is upward sloping, as shown in Figure 14.7.

Why do changes in the price level affect output in the short run? Macroeconomists have proposed three theories for the upward slope of the short-run aggregate-supply curve. In each theory, a specific market imperfection causes the supply side of the economy to behave differently in the short run than it does in the long run. Although each of the following theories will differ in detail, they share a common theme: *The quantity of output supplied deviates from its long-run, or "natural," level when the actual price level deviates from the price level that people expected to prevail.* When the price level rises above the expected level, output rises above its natural level, and when the price level falls below the expected level, output falls below its natural level.

The Sticky-Wage Theory The first and simplest explanation of the upward slope of the short-run aggregate-supply curve is the sticky-wage theory. Because this theory is the simplest of the three approaches to aggregate supply, it is the one we emphasize in this book.

According to this theory, the short-run aggregate-supply curve slopes upward because nominal wages are slow to adjust to changing economic conditions. In other words, wages are "sticky" in the short run. To some extent, the slow

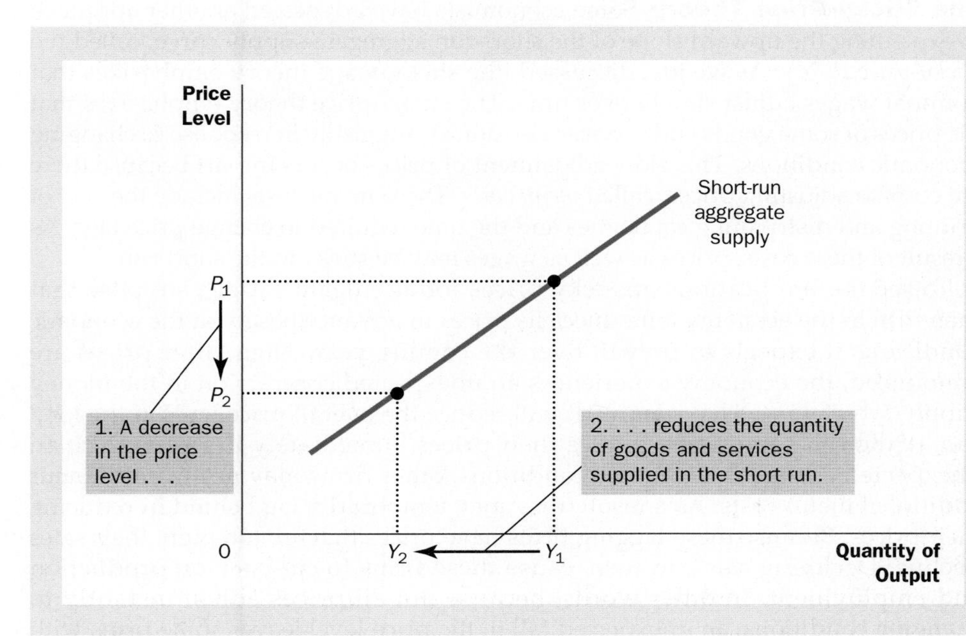

FIGURE 14.7

The Short-Run Aggregate-Supply Curve

In the short run, a fall in the price level from P_1 to P_2 reduces the quantity of output supplied from Y_1 to Y_2. This positive relationship could be due to sticky wages, sticky prices, or misperceptions. Over time, wages, prices, and perceptions adjust, so this positive relationship is only temporary.

adjustment of nominal wages is attributable to long-term contracts between workers and firms that fix nominal wages, sometimes for three years or longer. In addition, this slow adjustment may be attributable to social norms and notions of fairness that influence wage setting and that change only slowly over time.

An example helps explain how sticky nominal wages can result in a short-run aggregate-supply curve that slopes upward. Imagine that a year ago, a firm expected the price level to be 100 and, based on this expectation, it signed a contract with its workers agreeing to pay them, say, $20 per hour. In fact, the price level, P, turns out to be only 95. Because prices have fallen below expectations, the firm gets 5 percent less than expected for each unit of its product that it sells. The cost of labour used to make the output, however, is stuck at $20 per hour. Production is now less profitable, so the firm hires fewer workers and reduces the quantity of output supplied. Over time, the labour contract will expire, and the firm can renegotiate with its workers for a lower wage (which they may accept because prices are lower), but in the meantime, employment and production will remain below their long-run levels.

The same logic works in reverse. Suppose the price level turns out to be 105, and the wage remains stuck at $20. The firm sees that the amount it is paid for each unit sold is up by 5 percent, while its labour costs are not. In response, it hires more workers and increases the quantity supplied. Eventually, the workers will demand higher nominal wages to compensate for the higher price level, but for a while, the firm can take advantage of the profit opportunity by increasing employment and the quantity of output supplied above its long-run levels.

In short, according to the sticky-wage theory, the short-run aggregate-supply curve is upward sloping because nominal wages are based on expected prices and do not respond immediately when the actual price level turns out to be different from what was expected. This stickiness of wages gives firms an incentive to produce less than the natural level of output when the price level turns out to be lower than expected and to produce more when the price level turns out to be higher than expected.

The Sticky-Price Theory Some economists have advocated another approach to explaining the upward slope of the short-run aggregate-supply curve, called the *sticky-price theory.* As we just discussed, the sticky-wage theory emphasizes that nominal wages adjust slowly over time. The sticky-price theory emphasizes that the prices of some goods and services also adjust sluggishly in response to changing economic conditions. This slow adjustment of prices occurs in part because there are costs to adjusting prices, called *menu costs.* These menu costs include the cost of printing and distributing catalogues and the time required to change price tags. As a result of these costs, prices as well as wages may be sticky in the short run.

To see the implications of sticky prices for aggregate supply, suppose that each firm in the economy announces its prices in advance based on the economic conditions it expects to prevail over the coming year. Then, after prices are announced, the economy experiences an unexpected contraction in the money supply, which (as we have learned) will reduce the overall price level in the long run. Although some firms reduce their prices immediately in response to an unexpected change in economic conditions, other firms may not want to incur additional menu costs. As a result, they may temporarily lag behind in reducing their prices. Because these lagging firms have prices that are too high, their sales decline. Declining sales, in turn, cause these firms to cut back on production and employment. In other words, because not all prices adjust instantly to changing conditions, an unexpected fall in the price level leaves some firms with higher-than-desired prices, and these higher-than-desired prices depress sales and induce firms to reduce the quantity of goods and services they produce.

The same reasoning applies when the money supply and price level turn out to be above what firms expected when they originally set their prices. While some firms raise their prices immediately in response to the new economic environment, other firms lag behind, keeping their prices at the lower-than-desired levels. These low prices attract customers, which induces these firms to increase employment and production. Thus, during the time that these lagging firms are operating with outdated prices, there is a positive association between the overall price level and the quantity of output. This positive association is represented by the upward slope of the short-run aggregate-supply curve.

The Misperceptions Theory A third approach to explaining the upward slope of the short-run aggregate-supply curve is the misperceptions theory. According to this theory, changes in the overall price level can temporarily mislead suppliers about what is happening in the individual markets in which they sell their output. As a result of these short-run misperceptions, suppliers respond to changes in the level of prices, and this response leads to an upward-sloping aggregate-supply curve.

To see how this might work, suppose the overall price level falls below the level that people expected. When suppliers see the prices of their products fall, they may mistakenly believe that their *relative* prices have fallen. For example, wheat farmers may notice a fall in the price of wheat before they notice a fall in the prices of the many items they buy as consumers. They may infer from this observation that the reward from producing wheat is temporarily low, and they may respond by reducing the quantity of wheat they supply. Similarly, workers may notice a fall in their nominal wages before they notice a fall in the prices of the goods they buy. They may infer that the reward from working is temporarily low and respond by reducing the quantity of labour they supply. In both cases, a lower price level causes misperceptions about relative prices, and these misperceptions induce suppliers to respond to the lower price level by decreasing the quantity of goods and services supplied.

Similar misperceptions arise when the price level is above what was expected. Suppliers of goods and services may notice the price of their output rising and infer, mistakenly, that their relative prices are rising. They would conclude that it is a good time to produce. Until their misperceptions are corrected, they respond to the higher price level by increasing the quantity of goods and services supplied. This behaviour results in a short-run aggregate-supply curve that slopes upward.

Summary There are three alternative explanations for the upward slope of the short-run aggregate-supply curve: (1) sticky wages, (2) sticky prices, and (3) misperceptions. Economists debate which of these theories is correct, and it is very possible that each contains an element of truth. For our purposes in this book, the similarities of the theories are more important than the differences. All three theories suggest that output deviates from its natural level when the price level deviates from the price level that people expected. We can express this mathematically as follows:

$$\begin{array}{c}\text{Quantity}\\ \text{of output}\\ \text{supplied}\end{array} = \begin{array}{c}\text{Natural}\\ \text{level of}\\ \text{output}\end{array} + a\left(\begin{array}{c}\text{Actual}\\ \text{price}\\ \text{level}\end{array} - \begin{array}{c}\text{Expected}\\ \text{price}\\ \text{level}\end{array}\right)$$

where a is a number that determines how much output responds to unexpected changes in the price level.

Notice that each of the three theories of short-run aggregate supply emphasizes a problem that is likely to be only temporary. Whether the upward slope of the aggregate-supply curve is attributable to sticky wages, sticky prices, or misperceptions, these conditions will not persist forever. Eventually, as people adjust their expectations, nominal wages adjust, prices become unstuck, and misperceptions about relative prices will be corrected. In other words, it is reasonable to assume that in the long run, wages and prices are flexible rather than sticky and that people are not confused about relative prices. This means that the expected and actual price levels are equal in the long run. In the long run, then, our mathematical statement becomes

Quantity of output supplied = Natural level of output

which indicates that the aggregate-supply curve is vertical rather than upward sloping. This is the mathematical description of the long-run aggregate-supply curve drawn in Figure 14.5.

14-4e Why the Short-Run Aggregate-Supply Curve Might Shift

The short-run aggregate-supply curve tells us the quantity of goods and services supplied in the short run for any given level of prices. We can think of this curve as similar to the long-run aggregate-supply curve but made upward sloping by the presence of sticky wages, sticky prices, and misperceptions. Thus, when thinking about what shifts the short-run aggregate-supply curve, we have to consider all those variables that shift the long-run aggregate-supply curve plus a new variable—the expected price level—that influences the wages that are stuck, the prices that are stuck, and the perceptions about relative prices.

Let's start with what we know about the long-run aggregate-supply curve. As we discussed earlier, shifts in the long-run aggregate-supply curve normally arise from changes in labour, capital, natural resources, or technological knowledge. These same variables shift the short-run aggregate-supply curve. For example, when an increase in the economy's capital stock increases productivity, both the long-run and short-run aggregate-supply curves shift to the right. When a substantial increase in the minimum wage raises the natural rate of unemployment, both the long-run and short-run aggregate-supply curves shift to the left.

The important new variable that affects the position of the short-run aggregate-supply curve is the price level that people expected to prevail. As we have discussed, the quantity of goods and services supplied depends, in the short run, on sticky wages, sticky prices, and misperceptions. Yet wages, prices, and perceptions are set on the basis of expectations of the price level. So when people change their expectations of the price level, the short-run aggregate-supply curve shifts.

To make this idea more concrete, let's consider a specific theory of aggregate supply—the sticky-wage theory. According to this theory, when workers and firms expect the price level to be high, they are more likely to negotiate high nominal wages. High wages raise firms' costs and, for any given actual price level, reduce the quantity of goods and services that firms supply. Thus, when the expected price level rises, wages are higher, costs increase, and firms supply a smaller quantity of goods and services at any given actual price level. Thus, the short-run aggregate-supply curve shifts to the left. Conversely, when the expected price level falls, wages are lower, costs decline, firms increase production at any given price level, and the short-run aggregate-supply curve shifts to the right.

A similar logic applies in each theory of aggregate supply. The general lesson is the following: *An increase in the expected price level reduces the quantity of goods and services supplied and shifts the short-run aggregate-supply curve to the left. A decrease in the expected price level raises the quantity of goods and services supplied and shifts the short-run aggregate-supply curve to the right.* As we will see in the next section, this influence of expectations on the position of the short-run aggregate-supply curve plays a key role in explaining how the economy makes the transition from the short run to the long run. In the short run, expectations are fixed, and the economy finds itself at the intersection of the aggregate-demand curve and the short-run aggregate-supply curve. In the long run, if people observe that the price level is different from what they expected, their expectations adjust, and the short-run aggregate-supply curve shifts. This shift ensures that the economy eventually finds itself at the intersection of the aggregate-demand curve and the long-run aggregate-supply curve.

You should now have some understanding about why the short-run aggregate-supply curve slopes upward and what events and policies can cause this curve to shift. Table 14.2 summarizes our discussion.

TABLE 14.2

The Short-Run Aggregate-Supply Curve: Summary

Why Does the Short-Run Aggregate-Supply Curve Slope Upward?

1. *The Sticky-Wage Theory:* An unexpectedly low price level raises the real wage, which causes firms to hire fewer workers and produce a smaller quantity of goods and services.
2. *The Sticky-Price Theory:* An unexpectedly low price level leaves some firms with higher-than-desired prices, which depresses their sales and leads them to cut back production.
3. *The Misperceptions Theory:* An unexpectedly low price level leads some suppliers to think their relative prices have fallen, which induces a fall in production.

Why Might the Short-Run Aggregate-Supply Curve Shift?

1. *Shifts Arising from Changes in Labour:* An increase in the quantity of labour available (perhaps due to a fall in the natural rate of unemployment) shifts the aggregate-supply curve to the right. A decrease in the quantity of labour available (perhaps due to a rise in the natural rate of unemployment) shifts the aggregate-supply curve to the left.
2. *Shifts Arising from Changes in Capital:* An increase in physical or human capital shifts the aggregate-supply curve to the right. A decrease in physical or human capital shifts the aggregate-supply curve to the left.
3. *Shifts Arising from Changes in Natural Resources:* An increase in the availability of natural resources shifts the aggregate-supply curve to the right. A decrease in the availability of natural resources shifts the aggregate-supply curve to the left.
4. *Shifts Arising from Changes in Technology:* An advance in technological knowledge shifts the aggregate-supply curve to the right. A decrease in the available technology (perhaps due to government regulation) shifts the aggregate-supply curve to the left.
5. *Shifts Arising from Changes in the Expected Price Level:* A decrease in the expected price level shifts the short-run aggregate-supply curve to the right. An increase in the expected price level shifts the short-run aggregate-supply curve to the left.

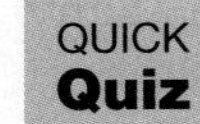

QUICK Quiz *Explain why the long-run aggregate-supply curve is vertical. • Explain three theories for why the short-run aggregate-supply curve is upward sloping.*

14-5 Two Causes of Economic Fluctuations

Now that we have introduced the model of aggregate demand and aggregate supply, we have the basic tools we need to analyze fluctuations in economic activity. In particular, we can use what we have learned about aggregate demand and aggregate supply to examine the two basic causes of short-run fluctuations: shifts in aggregate demand and shifts in aggregate supply.

To keep things simple, we assume the economy begins in long-run equilibrium, as shown in Figure 14.8. Equilibrium output and the price level are determined by the intersection of the aggregate-demand curve and the long-run aggregate-supply curve, shown as point A in the figure. At this point, output is at its natural level. The short-run aggregate-supply curve passes through this point as well, indicating that wages, prices, and perceptions have fully adjusted to this long-run equilibrium. That is, when an economy is in its long-run equilibrium, wages, prices, and perceptions must have adjusted so that the intersection of aggregate demand with short-run aggregate supply is the same as the intersection of aggregate demand with long-run aggregate supply.

14-5a The Effects of a Shift in Aggregate Demand

Suppose that a wave of pessimism suddenly overtakes the economy. The cause might be a crash in the stock market or the outbreak of war overseas. Because of this event, many people lose confidence in the future and alter their plans. Households cut back on their spending and delay major purchases, and firms put off buying new equipment.

FIGURE 14.8

The Long-Run Equilibrium
The long-run equilibrium of the economy is found where the aggregate-demand curve crosses the long-run aggregate-supply curve (point A). When the economy reaches this long-run equilibrium, wages, prices, and perceptions will have adjusted so that the short-run aggregate-supply curve crosses this point as well.

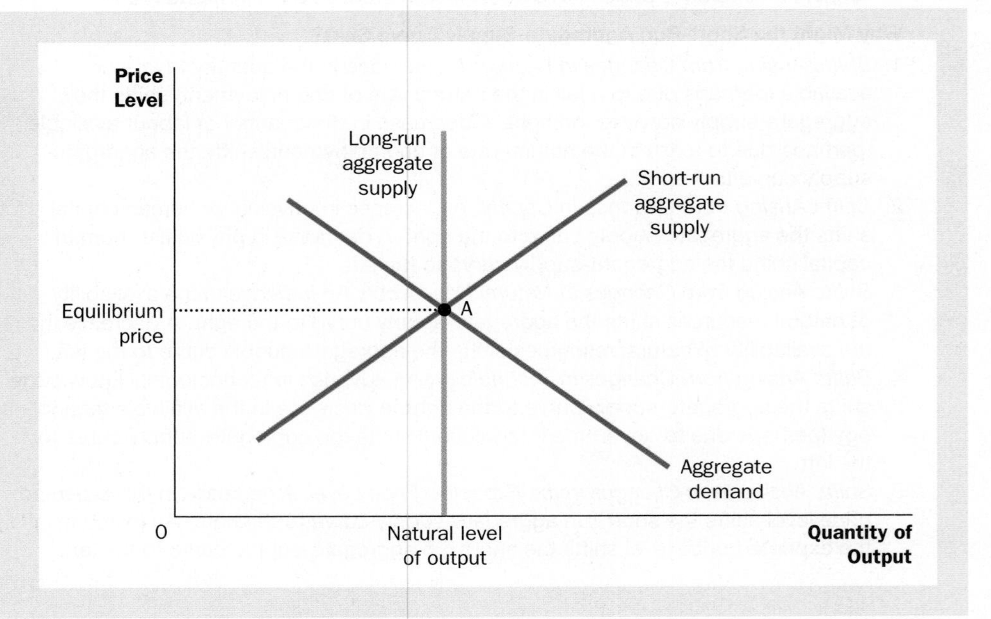

TABLE 14.3

Four Steps for Analyzing Macroeconomic Fluctuations

1. Decide whether the event shifts the aggregate-demand curve or the aggregate-supply curve (or perhaps both).
2. Decide in which direction the curve shifts.
3. Use the diagram of aggregate demand and aggregate supply to see how the shift changes output and the price level in the short run.
4. Use the diagram of aggregate demand and aggregate supply to analyze how the economy moves from its new short-run equilibrium to its long-run equilibrium.

What is the macroeconomic impact of such a wave of pessimism? In answering this question, we can follow the three steps we used in Chapter 4 when analyzing supply and demand in specific markets. First, we determine whether the event affects aggregate demand or aggregate supply. Second, we decide in which direction the curve shifts. Third, we use the diagram of aggregate demand and aggregate supply to compare the initial and the new equilibrium. The new wrinkle is that we need to add a fourth step: We have to keep track of a new short-run equilibrium, a new long-run equilibrium, and the transition between them. Table 14.3 summarizes the four steps to analyze economic fluctuations.

The first two steps in Table 14.3 are easy. First, because the wave of pessimism affects spending plans, it affects the aggregate-demand curve. Second, because households and firms now want to buy a smaller quantity of goods and services for any given price level, the event reduces aggregate demand. As Figure 14.9 shows, the aggregate-demand curve shifts to the left from AD_1 to AD_2.

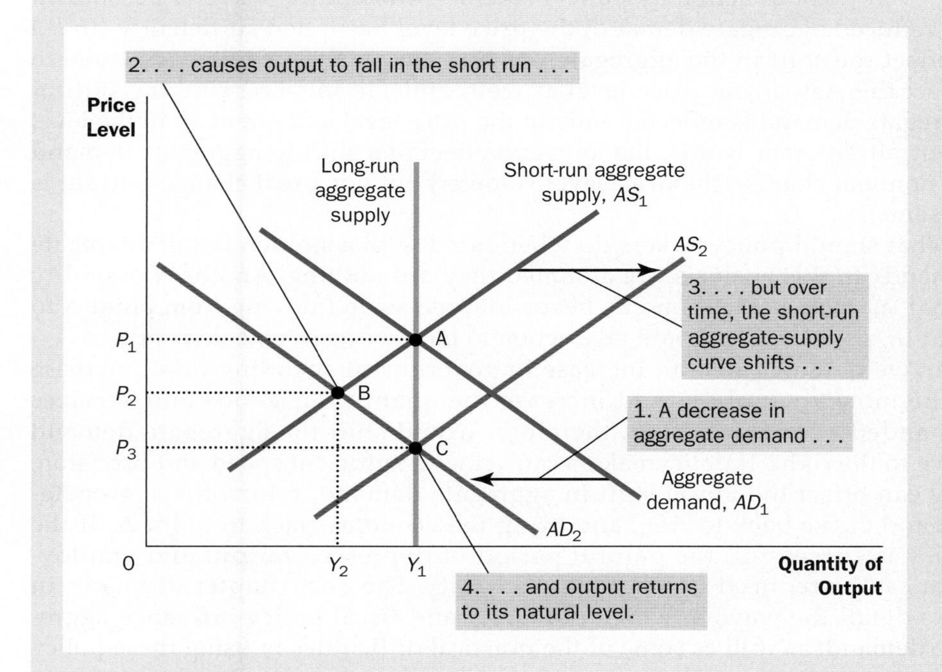

FIGURE 14.9

A Contraction in Aggregate Demand

A fall in aggregate demand, which might be due to a wave of pessimism in the economy, is represented with a leftward shift in the aggregate-demand curve from AD_1 to AD_2. The economy moves from point A to point B. Output falls from Y_1 to Y_2, and the price level falls from P_1 to P_2. Over time, as wages, prices, and perceptions adjust, the short-run aggregate-supply curve shifts to the right from AS_1 to AS_2, and the economy reaches point C, where the new aggregate-demand curve crosses the long-run aggregate-supply curve. The price level falls to P_3, and output returns to its natural level, Y_1.

With this figure, we can perform step three: By comparing the initial and new equilibrium, we can see the effects of the fall in aggregate demand. In the short run, the economy moves along the initial short-run aggregate-supply curve, AS_1, going from point A to point B. As the economy moves between these two points, output falls from Y_1 to Y_2, and the price level falls from P_1 to P_2. The falling level of output indicates that the economy is in a recession. Although not shown in the figure, firms respond to lower sales and production by reducing employment. Thus, the pessimism that caused the shift in aggregate demand is, to some extent, self-fulfilling: Pessimism about the future leads to falling incomes and rising unemployment.

Now comes step four—the transition from the short-run equilibrium to the long-run equilibrium. Because of the reduction in aggregate demand, the price level initially falls from P_1 to P_2. The price level is thus below the level that people had come to expect (P_1) before the sudden fall in aggregate demand. Although people are surprised in the short run, they will not remain surprised. Over time, expectations catch up with this new reality, and the expected price level falls as well. The fall in the expected price level alters wages, prices, and perceptions, which in turn influence the position of the short-run aggregate-supply curve. For example, according to the sticky-wage theory, once workers and firms come to expect a lower level of prices, the firms begin to bargain for lower nominal wages; a reduction in labour costs encourages firms to hire more workers and expands production at any given level of prices. Thus, the fall in the expected price level shifts the short-run aggregate-supply curve to the right from AS_1 to AS_2 in Figure 14.9. This shift allows the economy to approach point C, where the new aggregate-demand curve (AD_2) crosses the long-run aggregate-supply curve.

In the new long-run equilibrium, point C, output is back to its natural level. The economy has corrected itself: The decline in output is reversed in the long run, even without action by policymakers. Although the wave of pessimism has reduced aggregate demand, the price level has fallen sufficiently (to P_3) to offset the shift in the aggregate-demand curve, and people have come to expect this new lower price level as well. Thus, in the long run, the shift in aggregate demand is reflected fully in the price level and not at all in the level of output. In other words, the long-run effect of a shift in aggregate demand is a nominal change (the price level is lower) but not a real change (output is the same).

What should policymakers do when faced with a sudden fall in aggregate demand? In this analysis, we assumed they did nothing. Another possibility is that, as soon as the economy heads into recession (moving from point A to point B), policymakers could take action to increase aggregate demand.

As we noted earlier, an increase in government spending or an increase in the money supply would increase the quantity of goods and services demanded at any price and, therefore, would shift the aggregate-demand curve to the right. If policymakers can act with sufficient speed and precision, they can offset the initial shift in aggregate demand, return the aggregate-demand curve back to AD_1, and bring the economy back to point A. If the policy is successful, the painful period of depressed output and employment can be reduced in length and severity. The next chapter discusses in more detail the ways in which monetary and fiscal policy influence aggregate demand, as well as some of the practical difficulties in using these policy instruments.

FYI Monetary Neutrality Revisited

According to classical economic theory, money is neutral. That is, changes in the quantity of money affect nominal variables such as the price level but not real variables such as output. Earlier in this chapter, we noted that most economists accept this conclusion as a description of how the economy works in the long run but not in the short run. With the model of aggregate demand and aggregate supply, we can illustrate this conclusion and explain it more fully.

Suppose that the Bank of Canada reduces the quantity of money in the economy. What effect does this change have? As we discussed, the money supply is one determinant of aggregate demand. The reduction in the money supply shifts the aggregate-demand curve to the left.

The analysis looks just like Figure 14.9. Even though the cause of the shift in aggregate demand is different, we would observe the same effects on output and the price level. In the short run, both output and the price level fall. The economy experiences a recession. But, over time, the expected price level falls as well. Firms and workers respond to their new expectations by, for instance, agreeing to lower nominal wages. As they do so, the short-run aggregate-supply curve shifts to the right. Eventually, the economy finds itself back on the long-run aggregate-supply curve.

Figure 14.9 shows when money matters for real variables and when it does not. In the long run, money is neutral, as represented by the movement of the economy from point A to point C. But, in the short run, a change in the money supply has real effects, as represented by the movement of the economy from point A to point B. An old saying summarizes the analysis: "Money is a veil, but when the veil flutters, real output sputters."

To sum up, this story about shifts in aggregate demand has three important lessons:

1. In the short run, shifts in aggregate demand cause fluctuations in the economy's output of goods and services.
2. In the long run, shifts in aggregate demand affect the overall price level but do not affect output.
3. Policymakers who influence aggregate demand can potentially mitigate the severity of economic fluctuations.

case study Big Shifts in Aggregate Demand: Two Depressions and World War II

At the beginning of this chapter, we established three key facts about economic fluctuations by looking at data since 1966. Let's now take a much longer look at Canadian economic history. Figure 14.10 shows data since 1880 on the percentage change in real GDP per person over three years prior to each reported year. In an average three-year period, real GDP per capita grew just under 6 percent—or about 2 percent per year. The business cycle, however, caused fluctuations around this average. Three episodes stand out as being particularly significant—the large drop in real GDP following World War I, another large drop in the early 1930s, and the rapid increase in real GDP in the 1940s. All three of these events are attributable to shifts in aggregate demand.

In what was until then the most severe recession in Canada's history, real GDP per person fell by 27 percent between 1917 and 1921. The view of economic historians is that the 1917–21 depression was the result of two key events. One was the end of an investment and export boom. From 1900 to 1914, huge investments were made in settling western Canada, mainly in the form of railway construction. This investment and the settlement that accompanied

FIGURE 14.10

Canadian Real GDP per Person since 1870

Sources: Data for 1870-1925 from M.C. Urquhart, "New Estimates of Gross National Product, Canada, 1870–1926: Some Implications for Canadian Development" in S. Engerman and R. Gallman, eds., *Long-Term Factors in American Economic Growth* (Chicago: University of Chicago Press, 1986): data for 1926–1960 from F.H. Leacy, ed., *Historical Statistics of Canada*, 2nd ed. (Ottawa: Statistics Canada, 1983); data for 1961–2014 from Statistics Canada CANSIM database.

Over the course of Canadian economic history, three fluctuations stand out as being especially large. Following World War I and during the Great Depression of the 1930s, the economy suffered through the two worst depressions in Canadian history. During World War II, the economy experienced rapid economic growth. These major fluctuations are usually explained as resulting from large shifts in aggregate demand. These three major fluctuations are identified in the figure by the vertical coloured bars. Canada's most recent recessions, in 1981, 1991, and 2009, are also identified in this manner.

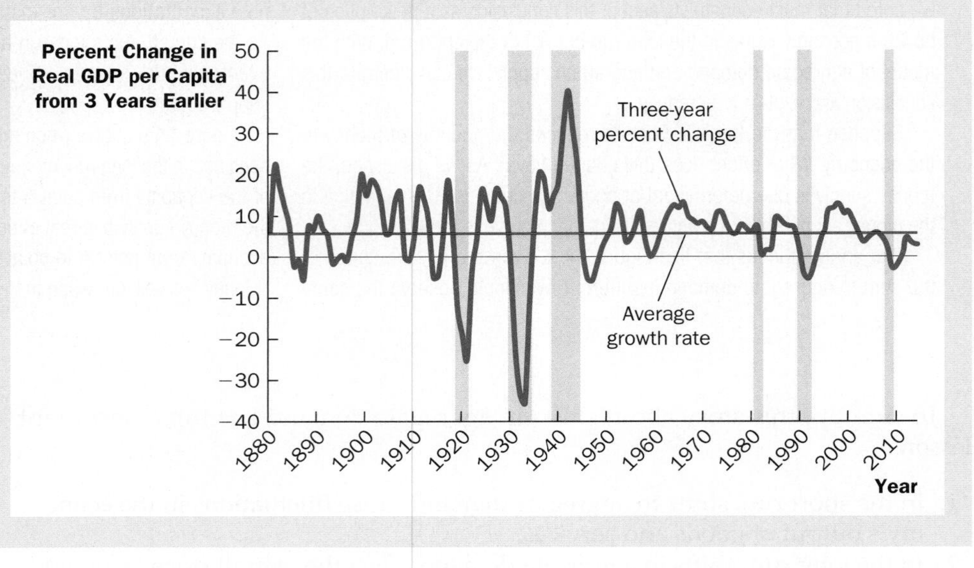

it, both of which were driven by a rapid increase in wheat prices, sparked a tremendous increase in Canadian exports. By 1914 this boom was ending, but by then a second source of increase in aggregate demand arose: World War I. The war brought with it a tremendous expansion of industry, which enabled growth in per capita GDP to continue. The end of the war, however, meant an end to war production. Now the industrial expansion of the war years was mirrored by industrial contraction following them. The end of the war and the end of the earlier investment and export boom resulted in a major contraction of aggregate demand and fall in GDP.

The economic calamity of the early 1930s is called the Great Depression, and as Figure 14.10 indicates, it was the largest economic downturn in Canadian history. Real GDP per person fell by 30 percent from 1929 to 1933, and the unemployment rate rose from 4 percent to 25 percent. At the same time, the price level fell by 19 percent over these four years. Many other countries experienced similar declines in output and prices during this period.

Peake & Whittingham/Library and Archives Canada/PA-068220

Wars: One way to stimulate aggregate demand.

Economic historians continue to debate the causes of the Great Depression in Canada, but most explanations centre on a large decline in aggregate demand. What caused this decline is still the subject of disagreement.

Many economists emphasize the decline in the money supply, which from 1929 to 1933 fell by 16 percent. As households' savings fell and bankers became more cautious and started holding greater reserves, the process of money creation under fractional-reserve banking went into reverse. Many economists suggest that the Great Depression was so severe because Canada did not have a central bank (the Bank of Canada was not created until 1935) that could have offset this fall in the money supply with expansionary open-market operations. Indeed, it was the economic problems of the Great Depression that led the government to establish the Bank of Canada.

Other economists emphasize that Canada's exposure to the U.S. economy because of the large amount of trade Canada has with the United States was an important cause of the Great Depression. Thus, a fall in aggregate demand arising from a fall in net exports is also a likely contributor.

Finally, still other economists suggest the collapse of the stock market in 1929 as an explanation for the Great Depression. Stock prices fell by 90 percent during this period, depressing household wealth and thereby consumer spending. The collapse in stock prices may also have made it difficult for firms to finance new investment projects, leading to a fall in investment spending. Of course, all of these forces may have acted together to contract aggregate demand during the Great Depression.

The third significant episode indicated in Figure 14.10—the economic boom of the 1940s—is easier to explain. The obvious cause of this boom was World War II. As Canada entered the war in 1939, the federal government had to devote more resources to the military. Government spending dramatically increased from 1939 to 1944. The huge expansion of aggregate demand increased real GDP per person by 60 percent over this period, and the unemployment rate fell from 15 percent to under 2 percent, the lowest in Canada's history.

Canada's latest recessions, in 1981, 1991, and 2009, are also identified in Figure 14.10. Note how much smaller the fall in the growth rate of GDP was during these recessions. By comparison to the deep recessions of the 1920s and 1930s, recent recessions have exhibited relatively mild slowdowns in economic growth. That fact, plus the smaller fluctuations in the growth rate of GDP around the long-run average, indicates that the amplitude of economic cycles in Canada has grown smaller over time. ■

case study

The Recession of 2008–09

Following a very long economic expansion, the Canadian economy fell into recession in the fall of 2008. In earlier chapters, we described the recession as being the product of a crisis in the U.S. financial system, a crisis most economists believe developed because of a failure of effective financial market regulation, which allowed high-risk (subprime) mortgages and other exotic types of financial instruments to proliferate. A downturn in the U.S. housing market caused many to default on their mortgages and so exposed the risk involved in holding these financial assets. Almost immediately a number of large companies in the financial sector began to fail. These failures effectively "froze" the financial system, as lenders and borrowers became wary of one another; no one was sure who owned these "toxic" financial assets and who did not. As a result, lending virtually stopped and firms that rely on the ability to borrow in order to finance their day-to-day operations started to fail, resulting in fast-rising unemployment.

Although originating in the U.S. financial system, the effects of the financial crisis quickly spread around the world, including to Canada. While Canada's better-regulated financial system weathered the crisis better than financial systems in other parts of the world, the negative impact was considerable nonetheless. Two key impacts were felt. First, the amount of liquidity in the economy fell, so that firms found it extremely difficult to borrow to invest in new capital or even to simply maintain current levels of output. Second, the downturn in the U.S. economy meant that Canadian exports, most of which go to the United States, fell. Both of these effects can be represented in our model as a shift to the left of the aggregate-demand curve.

This description means that we can use Figure 14.9, which shows the effect of a contraction in aggregate demand, to understand the 2008–09 recession. Referring to that diagram, the financial crisis resulted in a shift of aggregate-demand curve from AD_1 to AD_2 and an adjustment from point A to point B. In our earlier discussion of what would happen next in Figure 14.9, we made the assumption that policymakers did nothing in response to the fall in aggregate demand. We noted, however, that another possibility is that policymakers could take action as soon as the economy heads into recession (moving from point A to point B). This, in fact, is what policymakers did in 2008 and 2009.

As noted earlier, the Bank of Canada reacted to the financial crisis by increasing the amount of liquidity in the financial sector. This made it significantly easier for firms to borrow and so enabled them to finance new investment spending as well as their day-to-day operations. At the same time, the Canadian government, in a coordinated effort with other governments around the world, increased spending and offered a number of tax incentives to encourage citizens to increase their own spending on goods and services. These joint efforts of monetary and fiscal policy are represented in our model by a shift to the right of the aggregate-demand curve. In terms of Figure 14.9, these policies shifted the aggregate-demand curve from AD_2 back toward its initial position, AD_1, and caused an adjustment from point B back toward point A.

At the time this case study was being written (November 2015), the Canadian economy continued a halting recovery from the financial crisis. As we saw in Figure 14.1, real GDP and investment spending stopped falling by the end of 2009 and have since been growing steadily though with some slowing in 2015. The unemployment rate stopped rising, and since 2009 has fallen slowly but more or less steadily. These outcomes suggest that the policy actions may indeed have been successful in minimizing the length of the painful period of depressed output and rising unemployment that might otherwise have been experienced.

More reason for believing these policy responses have had beneficial effects is just how similar our description of the causes of the 2008–09 recession is to the causes of the Great Depression of the 1930s described in the previous case study. The same factors—a failure in the financial sector, a fall in wealth due to a precipitous fall in the stock market, and a fall in exports to the United States—resulted in the worst recession in Canada's history during the 1930s but a much shallower and shorter recession in 2008–09. The fact that monetary and fiscal policymakers, both in Canada and abroad, acted much more strongly and quickly in 2008–09 than they did in the 1930s suggests these actions had beneficial effects.

The recession of 2008–09, resulting as it did from a fall in U.S. housing prices and the unexpected contagion effect that this would have on financial systems around the world, is a reminder of the many kinds of events that can influence aggregate demand and, thus, the direction of the Canadian economy.

Central banks around the world continue to dissect the causes and implications of the 2008–09 financial crisis. In October 2015, Stephen Poloz, the Governor of the Bank of Canada, presented a speech in which he emphasized a major lesson to be drawn from the crisis is the need to integrate financial stability into monetary policy and a need to recognize that uncertainty and risk must always be recognized and confronted when designing policy responses:

> Through painful experience, we have been reminded that a well-functioning financial system is critical for economic activity and the transmission of monetary policy. We saw the emergence of excessive risk taking, aided by financial engineering and shortcomings of oversight, during an extended period of low and stable inflation and low volatility. The crisis showed us how financial imbalances in one sector of one economy could be amplified and propagated across the entire financial system, leading to the worst global downturn since the Great Depression. So what I will discuss today is how central banks integrate financial stability concerns into the pursuit of our goals of price stability and macroeconomic stabilization. This exercise is fraught with risks and uncertainties and it is complicated by the fact that macroeconomic and financial stability objectives are not always consistent with each other. Coping with this becomes a problem not of policy optimization, but of risk management. In other words, we put aside the idea of engineering the perfect policy and focus instead on the more realistic goal of finding an appropriate policy setting, given the risks and uncertainties.* ■

14-5b The Effects of a Shift in Aggregate Supply

Imagine once again an economy in its long-run equilibrium. Now suppose that suddenly some firms experience an increase in their costs of production. For example, bad weather might destroy some crops, driving up the cost of producing food products. Or a war in the Middle East might interrupt the shipping of crude oil, driving up the cost of producing oil products.

To analyze the macroeconomic impact of such an increase in production costs, we follow the same four steps as we always do. First, which curve is affected? Because production costs affect the firms that supply goods and services, changes in production costs alter the position of the aggregate-supply curve. Second, which direction does the curve shift? Because higher production costs make selling goods and services less profitable, firms now supply a smaller quantity of output for any given price level.

Thus, as Figure 14.11 shows, the short-run aggregate-supply curve shifts to the left from AS_1 to AS_2. (Depending on the event, the long-run aggregate-supply curve might also shift. To keep things simple, however, we will assume that it does not.)

Figure 14.11 allows us to perform step three of comparing the initial and new equilibrium. In the short run, the economy moves along the existing aggregate-demand curve, going from point A to point B. The output of the economy falls from Y_1 to Y_2, and the price level rises from P_1 to P_2. Because the economy is experiencing both *stagnation* (falling output) and *inflation* (rising prices), such an event is sometimes called **stagflation.**

stagflation
a period of falling output and rising prices

Now consider step four—the transition from the short-run equilibrium to the long-run equilibrium. According to the sticky-wage theory, the key issue is how stagflation affects nominal wages. Firms and workers may at first respond

* Stephen S. Poloz, Governor of the Bank of Canada, remarks at the Institute of International Finance, Lima, Peru, 10 October 2015, "Integrating Financial Stability into Monetary Policy." © Bank of Canada. Reproduced by permission.

FIGURE 14.11

An Adverse Shift in Aggregate Supply
When some event increases firms' costs, the short-run aggregate-supply curve shifts to the left from AS_1 to AS_2. The economy moves from point A to point B. The result is stagflation: Output falls from Y_1 to Y_2, and the price level rises from P_1 to P_2.

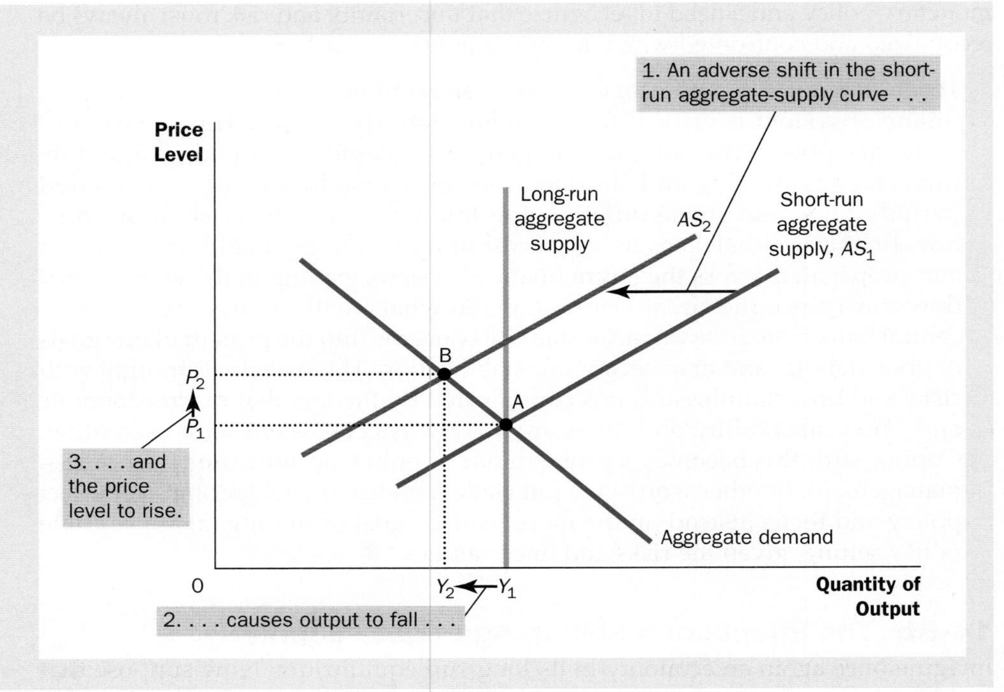

to the higher level of prices by raising their expectations of the price level and setting higher nominal wages. In this case, firms' costs will rise yet again, and the short-run aggregate-supply curve will shift farther to the left, making the problem of stagflation even worse. This phenomenon of higher prices leading to higher wages, in turn leading to even higher prices, is sometimes called a *wage–price spiral*.

At some point, this spiral of ever-rising wages and prices will slow. The low level of output and employment will put downward pressure on workers' wages because workers have less bargaining power when unemployment is high. As nominal wages fall, producing goods and services becomes more profitable, and the short-run aggregate-supply curve shifts to the right. As it shifts back toward AS_1, the price level falls, and the quantity of output approaches its natural level. In the long run, the economy returns to point A, where the aggregate-demand curve crosses the long-run aggregate-supply curve.

This transition back to the initial equilibrium assumes, however, that aggregate demand is held constant throughout the process. In the real world, that may not be the case. Policymakers who control monetary and fiscal policy might attempt to offset some of the effects of the shift in the short-run aggregate-supply curve by shifting the aggregate-demand curve. This possibility is shown in Figure 14.12. In this case, changes in policy shift the aggregate-demand curve to the right from AD_1 to AD_2—exactly enough to prevent the shift in aggregate supply from affecting output. The economy moves directly from point A to point C. Output remains at its natural level, and the price level rises from P_1 to P_3. In this case, policymakers are said to *accommodate* the shift in aggregate supply. An accommodative policy accepts a permanently higher level of prices to maintain a higher level of output and employment.

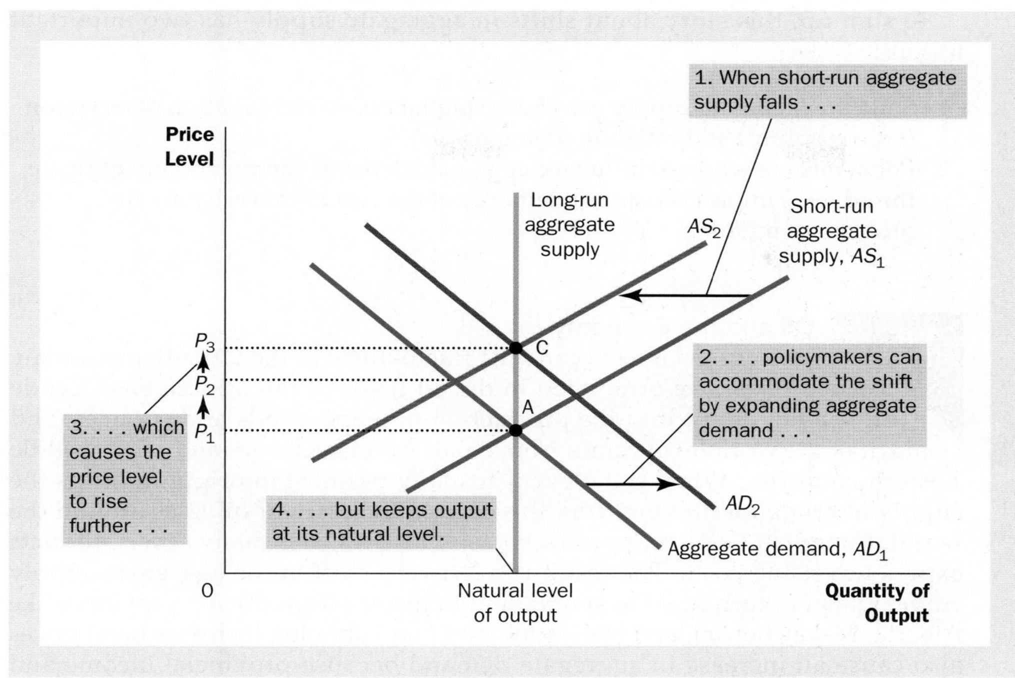

FIGURE 14.12

Accommodating an Adverse Shift in Aggregate Supply

Faced with an adverse shift in aggregate supply from AS_1 to AS_2, policymakers who can influence aggregate demand might try to shift the aggregate-demand curve to the right from AD_1 to AD_2. The economy would move from point A to point C. This policy would prevent the supply shift from reducing output in the short run, but the price level would permanently rise from P_1 to P_3.

FYI The Origins of Aggregate Demand and Aggregate Supply

Now that we have a preliminary understanding of the model of aggregate demand and aggregate supply, it is worthwhile to step back from it and consider its history. How did this model of short-run fluctuations develop? The answer is that this model, to a large extent, is a by-product of the Great Depression of the 1930s. Economists and policymakers at the time were puzzled about what had caused this calamity and were uncertain about how to deal with it.

John Maynard Keynes

In 1936, economist John Maynard Keynes published a book entitled *The General Theory of Employment, Interest and Money*, which attempted to explain short-run economic fluctuations in general and the Great Depression in particular. Keynes's primary message was that recessions and depressions can occur because of inadequate aggregate demand for goods and services.

Keynes had long been a critic of classical economic theory—the theory we examined earlier in the book—because it could explain only the long-run effects of policies. A few years before offering *The General Theory*, Keynes had written the following about classical economics:

> *The long run is a misleading guide to current affairs. In the long run we are all dead. Economists set themselves too easy, too useless a task if in tempestuous seasons they can only tell us when the storm is long past, the ocean will be flat.*

Keynes's message was aimed at policymakers as well as economists. As the world's economies suffered with high unemployment, Keynes advocated policies to increase aggregate demand, including government spending on public works.

In the next chapter we examine in detail how policymakers can try to use the tools of monetary and fiscal policy to influence aggregate demand. The analysis in the next chapter, as well as in this one, owes much to the legacy of John Maynard Keynes.

To sum up, this story about shifts in aggregate supply has two important lessons:

1. Shifts in aggregate supply can cause stagflation—a combination of recession (falling output) and inflation (rising prices).
2. Policymakers who can influence aggregate demand can potentially mitigate the adverse impact on output, but only at the cost of exacerbating the problem of inflation.

case study

Oil and the Economy

Some of the largest economic fluctuations in the Canadian economy since 1970 have originated in the oil fields of the Middle East. Crude oil is a key input into the production of many goods and services, and much of the world's oil comes from Saudi Arabia, Kuwait, and other Middle Eastern countries. When some event (usually political in origin) reduces the supply of crude oil flowing from this region, the price of oil rises around the world. Canadian firms that produce gasoline, tires, and many other products experience rising costs. The result is a leftward shift in the aggregate-supply curve, which in turn leads to stagflation. In major oil-producing provinces like Alberta, Saskatchewan, and Newfoundland and Labrador, increases in oil prices also cause an increase in aggregate demand because provincial income and provincial net exports rise. In those provinces, the net effect of the leftward shift in aggregate supply and the rightward shift in aggregate demand is to increase real output and put upward pressure on prices.

The first episode of this sort occurred in the mid-1970s. The countries with large oil reserves got together as members of the Organization of the Petroleum Exporting Countries (OPEC). OPEC was a *cartel*—a group of sellers that attempts to thwart competition and reduce production in order to raise prices. And, indeed, oil prices rose substantially. From 1973 to 1975, the world price of oil almost tripled. Oil-importing countries around the world experienced simultaneous inflation and recession. In Canada, the inflation rate as measured by the GDP price deflator exceeded 14 percent in 1974. The unemployment rate rose from 5.5 percent in 1973 to 7.0 percent in 1975. Not surprisingly, the effects of the increase in oil prices differed considerably across oil-exporting and oil-importing provinces. For example, from 1973 to 1975, the unemployment rate in Alberta fell from 5.3 percent to 4.1 percent, while the unemployment rate in Ontario increased from 4.3 percent to 6.3 percent.

Almost the same thing happened again a few years later. In the late 1970s, the OPEC countries again restricted the supply of oil to raise the price. From 1978 to 1981, the price of oil more than doubled. Once again, costs increased for firms that used oil as an input in the production process. This second shock to oil prices prompted the federal government to introduce the National Energy Program (NEP) in 1980. The NEP was intended to slow the growth in oil prices in Canada to below the rate of growth in world markets, and thereby minimize the stagflation effects of the most recent jump in oil prices. The NEP helped industries that used oil as an input, but it also harmed industries that produced oil. As a result, although this policy response to the OPEC price shock reduced the stagflation effects for Canada on average, it did so by favouring some industries over others and, in oil-producing provinces, caused a great deal of bitterness toward the federal government.

Laurent VAN DER STOCKT/Gamma-Rapho/Getty Images

Changes in Middle East oil production are one source of Canadian economic fluctuations.

The world market for oil can also be a source of favourable shifts in aggregate supply. In 1986 squabbling broke out among members of OPEC. Member countries reneged on their agreements to restrict oil production. In the world market for crude oil, prices fell by about half. This fall in oil prices reduced costs to firms that used oil as an input in the production process. As a result, Canada's aggregate-supply curve shifted to the right and the Canadian economy experienced the opposite of stagflation: Output grew rapidly, and the Canadian unemployment rate fell from 10.5 percent in 1985 to 7.5 percent in 1989. Once again, however, the effects of the decrease in oil prices differed considerably across oil-exporting and oil-importing provinces. For example, from 1985 to 1987, the unemployment rate in Alberta remained constant at about 10.0 percent, while the unemployment rate in Ontario fell from 8.0 percent to 6.1 percent.

Clearly, the world market for crude oil is often very volatile. This volatility is in part a reflection of the inherent instability of cartels. Members of cartels have an incentive to undercut the agreed-upon price and, in doing so, increase their share of the market. Because all members of the cartel face this incentive, the price agreed on by the cartel occasionally collapses. The volatility of crude oil prices also reflects the political turmoil associated with the Middle East in recent years. Both of these influences were behind the collapse of world oil prices in early 1998. Between October 1997 and December 1998, the price of crude oil fell by 41 percent. Soon after this collapse in prices, however, OPEC met and decided to restrict output. The result was that from December 1998 to November 2000 the price of crude oil *increased* by 200 percent.

After a period of relative stability, the price of West Texas Intermediate (WTI)—a price that is widely used to measure the world price of oil—has recently become quite volatile again. After falling as low as $49 per barrel in February 2009, the WTI price more than doubled to exceed $100 per barrel early in 2011. From 2011 to the middle of 2014, the price fluctuated between $85 and $95 per barrel but then quickly fell as an increase in supply from the Middle East and from new oil shale developments in the United States struck the market. By January 2016, the price of WTI oil had fallen to $30 per barrel, well below the price observed in 2009.

There are many explanations for the instability of oil prices. Technological advances that have made it profitable to develop oil sands and shale oil are certainly behind a recent oil glut that has resulted in recent price reductions. Price volatility is also related to fluctuations in the rate of growth in major economies like the United States, the European Union, and China with the recent slowdown in China's economy contributing to low prices. The price at which Canadian producers can sell oil is also related to their ability to ship oil to the U.S. market and to overseas markets. Efforts to expand Canada's access to foreign markets to sell oil are behind recent efforts to build the Keystone XL pipeline into the United States, the Energy East pipeline project from western Canada to the east coast, and the Northern Gateway pipeline from Alberta to the west coast. Trying to expand the market for Canadian oil by building new pipelines has met with considerable opposition from environmental groups and it is by no means certain these projects will go ahead. Indeed, in November 2015 the U.S. government denied the permits required for the construction of the Keystone XL pipeline. Whether these projects do or do not eventually go ahead will play an important role in determining at what price Canadian producers can sell their oil.

What does this mean for the Canadian economy? Oil prices, whether high or low, are never good (or bad) for everyone. When prices are high, certain sources of oil—such as the oil sands in Alberta and the oil fields offshore Newfoundland

and Labrador—become profitable to develop and this creates thousands of jobs. On the other hand, high prices drive up the costs of those firms that use oil as an input and for consumers of oil in the form of heating fuel and gasoline. When prices are low, the billions of dollars invested in developing the oil sands and offshore oil projects become unprofitable and must be shut down while firms that use oil as an input enjoy lower production costs and so expand.

Fortunately, conservation efforts and changes in technology have reduced the economy's dependence on oil as an input into production. For each dollar of real GDP produced, Canada uses less than half the amount of oil that it did before the first OPEC price shock in 1973. As a result, changes in the price of oil now have a smaller impact on those firms that use oil as an input into the production process. What's more, increases in the price of oil discourage consumption of oil-based products and so results in a reduction in carbon emissions. For both these reasons, increases in the price of oil are increasingly of net benefit to the Canadian economy. ■

Suppose that the election of a popular prime minister suddenly increases people's confidence in the future. Use the model of aggregate demand and aggregate supply to analyze the effect on the economy.

14-6 Conclusion

This chapter has achieved two goals. First, we have discussed some of the important facts about short-run fluctuations in economic activity. Second, we have introduced a basic model to explain those fluctuations, called the *model of aggregate demand and aggregate supply.* We continue our study of this model in the next chapter in order to understand more fully what causes fluctuations in the economy and how policymakers might respond to these fluctuations.

summary

- All societies experience short-run economic fluctuations around long-run trends. These fluctuations are irregular and largely unpredictable. When recessions do occur, real GDP and other measures of income, spending, and production fall, and unemployment rises.
- Classical economic theory is based on the assumption that nominal variables such as the money supply and the price level do not influence real variables such as output and employment. Most economists believe that this assumption is accurate in the long run but not in the short run. Economists analyze short-run economic fluctuations using the model of aggregate demand and aggregate supply. According to this model, the output of goods and services and the overall level of prices adjust to balance aggregate demand and aggregate supply.
- The aggregate-demand curve slopes downward for three reasons. First, a lower price level raises the real value of households' money holdings, which stimulates consumer spending. Second, a lower price level reduces the quantity of money households demand; as households try to convert money into interest-bearing assets interest rates fall, which stimulates investment spending. Third, a lower price level reduces the real exchange rate. This depreciation makes Canadian-produced goods and services cheaper relative to foreign-produced goods and services, and in this way stimulates net exports.
- Any event or policy that raises consumption, investment, government purchases, or net exports at a given price level increases aggregate demand. Any event or policy that reduces consumption, investment, government purchases, or net exports at a given price level decreases aggregate demand.
- The long-run aggregate-supply curve is vertical. In the long run, the quantity of goods and services

supplied depends on the economy's labour, capital, natural resources, and technology, but not on the overall level of prices.

- Three theories have been proposed to explain the upward slope of the short-run aggregate-supply curve. According to the sticky-wage theory, an unexpected fall in the price level temporarily raises real wages, which induces firms to reduce employment and production. According to the sticky-price theory, an unexpected fall in the price level leaves some firms with prices that are temporarily too high, which reduces their sales and causes them to cut back production. According to the misperceptions theory, an unexpected fall in the price level leads suppliers to mistakenly believe that their relative prices have fallen, which induces them to reduce production. All three theories imply that output deviates from its natural level when the price level deviates from the price level that people expected.
- Events that alter the economy's ability to produce output, such as changes in labour, capital, natural resources, or technology, shift the short-run aggregate-supply curve (and may shift the long-run aggregate-supply curve as well). In addition, the position of the short-run aggregate-supply curve depends on the expected price level.
- One possible cause of economic fluctuations is a shift in aggregate demand. When the aggregate-demand curve shifts to the left, for instance, output and prices fall in the short run. Over time, as a change in the expected price level causes wages, prices, and perceptions to adjust, the short-run aggregate-supply curve shifts to the right, and the economy returns to its natural level of output at a new, lower price level.
- A second possible cause of economic fluctuations is a shift in aggregate supply. When the aggregate-supply curve shifts to the left, the short-run effect is falling output and rising prices—a combination called *stagflation*. Over time, as wages, prices, and perceptions adjust, the price level falls back to its original level, and output recovers.

KEY **concepts**

recession, *p. 311*
depression, *p. 311*
model of aggregate demand and aggregate supply, *p. 317*
aggregate-demand curve, *p. 317*
aggregate-supply curve, *p. 317*
natural level of output, *p. 326*
stagflation, *p. 341*

QUESTIONS FOR **review**

1. Name two macroeconomic variables that decline when the economy goes into a recession. Name one macroeconomic variable that rises during a recession.
2. Draw a diagram with aggregate demand, short-run aggregate supply, and long-run aggregate supply. Be careful to label the axes correctly.
3. List and explain the three reasons why the aggregate-demand curve is downward sloping.
4. Explain why the long-run aggregate-supply curve is vertical.
5. List and explain the three theories for why the short-run aggregate-supply curve is upward sloping.
6. What might shift the aggregate-demand curve to the left? Use the model of aggregate demand and aggregate supply to trace through the effects of such a shift.
7. What might shift the aggregate-supply curve to the left? Use the model of aggregate demand and aggregate supply to trace through the effects of such a shift.

QUICK CHECK **multiple choice**

1. When the economy goes into a recession, real GDP ________ and unemployment ________.
   a. rises, rises
   b. rises, falls
   c. falls, rises
   d. falls, falls
2. Which of the following is shifted by a sudden crash in the stock market?
   a. the aggregate-demand curve
   b. the short-run aggregate-supply curve, but not the long-run aggregate-supply curve
   c. the long-run aggregate-supply curve, but not the short-run aggregate-supply curve
   d. both the short-run and the long-run aggregate-supply curves

3. Which of the following is shifted by a change in the expected price level?
   a. the aggregate-demand curve
   b. the short-run aggregate-supply curve, but not the long-run aggregate-supply curve
   c. the long-run aggregate-supply curve, but not the short-run aggregate-supply curve
   d. both the short-run and the long-run aggregate-supply curves
4. An increase in the aggregate demand for goods and services has a larger impact on output ________ and a larger impact on the price level ________.
   a. in the short run, in the long run
   b. in the long run, in the short run
   c. in the short run, also in the short run
   d. in the long run, also in the long run
5. Which of the following causes stagflation?
   a. a leftward shift in the aggregate-demand curve
   b. a rightward shift in the aggregate-demand curve
   c. a leftward shift in the aggregate-supply curve
   d. a rightward shift in the aggregate-supply curve
6. The idea that economic downturns result from an inadequate aggregate demand for goods and services is derived from the work of which economist?
   a. Adam Smith
   b. David Hume
   c. David Ricardo
   d. John Maynard Keynes

PROBLEMS AND **applications**

1. Why do you think that investment is more variable over the business cycle than consumer spending? Which category of consumer spending do you think would be most volatile: durable goods (such as furniture and car purchases), nondurable goods (such as food and clothing), or services (such as haircuts and dental care)? Why?
2. Suppose that the economy is in a long-run equilibrium.
   a. Use a diagram to illustrate the state of the economy. Be sure to show aggregate demand, short-run aggregate supply, and long-run aggregate supply.
   b. Now suppose that a stock market crash causes aggregate demand to fall. Use your diagram to show what happens to output and the price level in the short run. What happens to the unemployment rate?
   c. Use the sticky-wage theory of aggregate supply to explain what will happen to output and the price level in the long run (assuming there is no change in policy). What role does the expected price level play in this adjustment? Be sure to illustrate your analysis in a graph.
3. Explain whether each of the following events will increase, decrease, or have no effect on long-run aggregate supply.
   a. Canada experiences a wave of immigration.
   b. Provincial and territorial governments raise the minimum wage to $15 per hour.
   c. Intel invents a new and more powerful computer chip.
   d. A severe hurricane damages factories along the east coast.
4. Suppose an economy is in long-run equilibrium.
   a. Use the model of aggregate demand and aggregate supply to illustrate the initial equilibrium (call it point A). Be sure to include both short-run and long-run aggregate supply.
   b. The central bank raises the money supply by 5 percent. Use your diagram to show what happens to output and the price level as the economy moves from the initial to the new short-run equilibrium (call it point B).
   c. Now show the new long-run equilibrium (call it point C). What causes the economy to move from point B to point C?
   d. According to the sticky-wage theory of aggregate supply, how do nominal wages at point A compare to nominal wages at point B? How do nominal wages at point A compare to nominal wages at point C?
   e. According to the sticky-wage theory of aggregate supply, how do real wages at point A compare to real wages at point B? How do real wages at point A compare to real wages at point C?
   f. Judging by the impact of the money supply on nominal and real wages, is this analysis consistent with the proposition that money has real effects in the short run but is neutral in the long run?
5. Explain why the following statements are false.
   a. "The aggregate-demand curve slopes downward because it is the horizontal sum of the demand curves for individual goods."
   b. "The long-run aggregate-supply curve is vertical because economic forces do not affect long-run aggregate supply."

   c. "If firms adjusted their prices every day, then the short-run aggregate-supply curve would be horizontal."
   d. "Whenever the economy enters a recession, its long-run aggregate-supply curve shifts to the left."

6. For each of the three theories for the upward slope of the short-run aggregate-supply curve, carefully explain the following.
   a. how the economy recovers from a recession and returns to its long-run equilibrium without any policy intervention
   b. what determines the speed of that recovery

7. Suppose the Bank of Canada expands the money supply, but because the public expects this action, it simultaneously raises the public's expectation of the price level. What will happen to output and the price level in the short run? Compare this result to the outcome if the Bank of Canada expanded the money supply but the public didn't change its expectation of the price level.

8. Suppose that the economy is currently in a recession. If policymakers take no action, how will the economy evolve over time? Explain in words and using an aggregate-demand/aggregate-supply diagram.

9. Suppose workers and firms suddenly believe that inflation will be quite high over the coming year. Suppose also that the economy begins in long-run equilibrium, and the aggregate-demand curve does not shift.
   a. What happens to nominal wages? What happens to real wages?
   b. Using an aggregate-demand/aggregate-supply diagram, show the effect of the change in expectations on both the short-run and long-run levels of prices and output.
   c. Were the expectations of high inflation accurate? Explain.

10. For each of the following events explain the effect, if any, on the position of the short- and long-run aggregate-supply curves and the aggregate-demand curve.
   a. In the summer of 2003, a single cow in Alberta was found to suffer from BSE, or mad cow disease. As a consequence, many countries stopped importing Canadian beef and Canadian ranchers found that, at any price, they could sell much less beef than they could previously.
   b. Over the past decade, prospectors have discovered diamonds in Canada. The development of these diamond mines has progressed to the point that today Canada produces roughly 10 percent of the world's diamonds.
   c. Ongoing crises in the Middle East and the high price of oil have encouraged firms to significantly expand plants for the extraction of oil from the oil sands region of Alberta.
   d. In 2003, an outbreak of severe acute respiratory syndrome (SARS) in the Toronto region resulted in a significant reduction in the number of tourists visiting Canada.

11. Explain whether each of the following events shifts the short-run aggregate-supply curve, the aggregate-demand curve, both, or neither. For each event that does shift a curve, use a diagram to illustrate the effect on the economy.
   a. Households decide to save a larger share of their income.
   b. Okanagan peach orchards suffer a prolonged period of below-freezing temperatures.
   c. Increased job opportunities overseas cause many people to leave Canada.

12. For each of the following events, explain the short-run and long-run effects on output and the price level, assuming policymakers take no action.
   a. The stock market declines sharply, reducing consumers' wealth.
   b. The federal government increases spending on national defence.
   c. A technological improvement raises productivity.
   d. A recession overseas causes foreigners to buy fewer Canadian goods.

13. Suppose that firms become very optimistic about future business conditions and invest heavily in new capital equipment.
   a. Use an aggregate-demand/aggregate-supply diagram to show the short-run effect of this optimism on the economy. Label the new levels of prices and real output. Explain in words why the aggregate quantity of output *supplied* changes.
   b. Now use the diagram from part (a) to show the new long-run equilibrium of the economy. (For now, assume there is no change in the long-run aggregate-supply curve.) Explain in words why the aggregate quantity of output *demanded* changes between the short run and the long run.
   c. How might the investment boom affect the long-run aggregate-supply curve? Explain.

14. In Economy A, all workers agree in advance on the nominal wages that their employers will pay them. In Economy B, half of all workers have these nominal wage contracts, while the other half have indexed employment contracts, so their wages rise and fall automatically with the price level. According to the sticky-wage theory of aggregate supply, which economy has a more steeply sloped short-run aggregate-supply curve? In which economy would a 5 percent increase in the money supply have a larger impact on output? In which economy would it have a larger impact on the price level? Explain.

Derek R. Audette/Shutterstock.com

The Influence of Monetary and Fiscal Policy on Aggregate Demand

LEARNING **objectives**

In this chapter, you will ...

1. Learn the theory of liquidity preference as a short-run theory of the interest rate
2. Analyze how monetary policy affects interest rates and aggregate demand in open and closed economies
3. Analyze how fiscal policy affects interest rates and aggregate demand in open and closed economies
4. Discuss the debate over whether policymakers should try to stabilize the economy

Imagine that you are the governor of the Bank of Canada and therefore are in charge of setting monetary policy. You observe that the economy is slowing down and unemployment is rising. What should the Bank of Canada do? Imagine now that you are the federal government's Minister of Finance in charge of setting fiscal policy. What should you do, given the evidence of an economic slowdown? Does the choice of the governor of the Bank of Canada depend on the choice made by the Minister of Finance?

To answer these questions, you need to consider the impact of monetary and fiscal policy on the economy. In the preceding chapter we saw how to explain short-run economic fluctuations using the model of aggregate demand and aggregate supply. When the aggregate-demand curve or the aggregate-supply curve shifts, the result is fluctuations in the economy's overall output of goods and services and in its overall level of prices. As we noted in the previous chapter, monetary and fiscal policy can each influence aggregate demand. Thus, a change in one of these policies can lead to short-run fluctuations in output and prices. Policymakers will want to anticipate this effect and, perhaps, adjust the other policy in response.

In this chapter we examine in more detail how the government's tools of monetary and fiscal policy influence the position of the aggregate-demand curve. We have previously discussed the long-run effects of these policies. In Chapters 7 and 8 we saw how fiscal policy affects saving, investment, and long-run economic growth. In Chapters 10 and 11 we saw how the Bank of Canada controls the money supply and how the money supply affects the price level in the long run. In Chapters 12 and 13 we looked at macroeconomic relationships in open economies and saw how the real exchange rate, net exports, and net foreign investment are determined.

In this chapter we will also see how the tools of monetary and fiscal policy can shift the aggregate-demand curve and, in doing so, affect short-run economic fluctuations. We will also see that the effect of policy tools on the position of the aggregate-demand curve depends on the degree to which the economy is closed or open to trade in goods, services, and financial capital. We begin our discussion of the influence of monetary and fiscal policy on aggregate demand by assuming a closed economy. This approach simplifies the analysis and puts us on the road to understanding what will happen in a small open economy. We will then show the implications for fiscal and monetary policy of Canada's being a small open economy.

As we have already learned, many factors influence aggregate demand besides monetary and fiscal policy. In particular, desired spending by households and firms determines the overall demand for goods and services. When desired spending changes, aggregate demand shifts. If policymakers do not respond, such shifts in aggregate demand cause short-run fluctuations in output and employment. As a result, monetary and fiscal policymakers sometimes use the policy levers at their disposal to try to offset these shifts in aggregate demand and thereby stabilize the economy. Here we discuss the theory behind these policy actions and some of the difficulties that arise in using this theory in practice.

It may seem like a lot to present, all in one chapter, how both fiscal and monetary policy, in both open and closed economies, influence aggregate demand. But as you will see, the model that economists use for examining influences on aggregate demand allows for a step-by-step approach which emphasizes that what happens in an open economy builds on our understanding of what happens in a closed economy. What's more, we benefit from presenting how fiscal policy influences aggregate demand at the same time we present how monetary policy influences aggregate demand because by doing so we more clearly see the ways in which these policy tools are similar and how they are different. In this way we gain an understanding of why policymakers may in certain circumstances prefer to adjust one policy lever over the other.

15-1 How Monetary Policy Influences Aggregate Demand

The aggregate-demand curve shows the total quantity of goods and services demanded in the economy for any price level. As you may recall from the preceding chapter, the aggregate-demand curve slopes downward for three reasons:

1. *The wealth effect:* A lower price level raises the real value of households' money holdings, and higher real wealth stimulates consumer spending.
2. *The interest-rate effect:* A lower price level lowers the interest rate as people try to lend out their excess money holdings, and the lower interest rate stimulates investment spending.
3. *The real exchange-rate effect:* A lower price level reduces the real exchange rate. This depreciation makes Canadian-produced goods and services cheaper relative to foreign-produced goods and services. As a result, Canadian net exports rise.

These three effects should not be viewed as alternative theories. Instead, they occur simultaneously to increase the quantity of goods and services demanded when the price level falls and to decrease it when the price level rises.

Although all three effects work together in explaining the downward slope of the aggregate-demand curve, they are not of equal importance. Because money holdings are a small part of household wealth, the wealth effect is the least important of the three. In a closed economy, the real exchange-rate effect is nonexistent, leaving the interest rate effect as the most important reason for the downward slope of the aggregate-demand curve. Since it is our goal to begin our discussion of the influence of monetary and fiscal policy on aggregate demand by first assuming a closed economy, we examine the interest rate effect in more detail. When thinking about Canada, however, we need to keep in mind that exports and imports make up a large proportion of the Canadian economy. As a result, the real exchange-rate effect is an important explanation for why Canada's aggregate-demand curve slopes downward.

To begin developing an understanding of how policy influences aggregate demand, we examine the interest rate effect in more detail. This will involve discussing the **theory of liquidity preference**. This theory of interest rate determination will help explain the downward slope of the aggregate-demand curve, as well as how monetary and fiscal policy can shift this curve. By shedding new light on aggregate demand, the theory of liquidity preference expands our understanding of what causes short-run economic fluctuations and what policymakers can potentially do about them.

theory of liquidity preference
Keynes's theory that the interest rate adjusts to bring money supply and money demand into balance

15-1a The Theory of Liquidity Preference

In his classic book *The General Theory of Employment, Interest and Money,* John Maynard Keynes proposed the theory of liquidity preference to explain what factors determine the economy's interest rate. The theory is, in essence, just an application of supply and demand. According to Keynes, the interest rate adjusts to balance the supply and demand for money.

You may recall that economists distinguish between two interest rates: The *nominal interest rate* is the interest rate as usually reported, and the *real interest rate* is the interest rate corrected for the effects of inflation. When there is no inflation, the two rates are the same. But when borrowers and lenders expect prices to rise over the course of a loan, they agree to a nominal interest rate that exceeds the real interest rate by the expected rate of inflation. The higher nominal interest rate compensates for the fact that they expect the loan to be repaid in less valuable dollars.

Which interest rate are we now trying to explain with the theory of liquidity preference? The answer is both. In the analysis that follows, we hold constant the expected rate of inflation. This assumption is reasonable for studying the economy in the short run because expected inflation is typically stable over short periods of time. In this case, nominal and real interest rates differ by a constant. When the nominal interest rate rises or falls, the real interest rate that people expect to earn rises or falls as well. For the rest of this chapter, when we refer to changes in the interest rate, you should envision the real and nominal interest rates moving in the same direction.

Let's now develop the theory of liquidity preference by considering the supply and demand for money and how each depends on the interest rate.

Money Supply The first piece of the theory of liquidity preference is the supply of money. As we first discussed in Chapter 10, the money supply in the Canadian economy is controlled by the Bank of Canada. The Bank of Canada alters the money supply using two methods. The predominant method the Bank of Canada uses to alter the money supply is by changing the bank rate. The bank rate is the interest rate on the loans that the Bank of Canada makes to commercial banks. Commercial banks may borrow from the Bank of Canada if they find that their reserves are inadequate. By increasing the bank rate, the Bank of Canada makes such loans more expensive and thus discourages commercial banks from borrowing reserves. Therefore, an increase in the bank rate effectively reduces the quantity of reserves in the banking system, which in turn reduces the money supply. Similarly, a decrease in the bank rate makes it less expensive for banks to borrow from the Bank of Canada and thus effectively increases the quantity of reserves in the banking system, which in turn increases the money supply.

The second method the Bank of Canada can use to alter the money supply is to change the quantity of reserves in the banking system through what is known as an *open-market operation*. One form that open-market operations take involves the Bank of Canada buying and selling federal government bonds in the bond market. When the Bank of Canada buys government bonds, the dollars it pays for the bonds are typically deposited in banks, and these dollars are added to bank reserves. When the Bank of Canada sells government bonds, the dollars it receives for the bonds are withdrawn from the banking system, and bank reserves fall. These changes in bank reserves, in turn, lead to changes in banks' ability to make loans and create money.

A different form of open-market operation involves the Bank of Canada buying and selling foreign currencies in the market for foreign-currency exchange. These sales and purchases are referred to as *foreign exchange market operations*.

As we discussed in Chapter 10, if the Bank of Canada buys US$100 million in the market for foreign-currency exchange for CDN$150 million, the Canadian money supply increases immediately by $150 million. If the Bank of Canada sells foreign currency from its foreign exchange reserves, it receives Canadian dollars in exchange. Those Canadian dollars are withdrawn from circulation, so the Canadian money supply is reduced.

Open-market operations and changing the bank rate are the most important methods available to the Bank of Canada for changing the money supply. As we will see, the Bank of Canada's decision on whether or not to buy and sell dollars in the market for foreign-currency exchange has important implications for the effect of monetary and fiscal policy on aggregate demand.

These details of monetary control are important for the implementation of Bank of Canada policy, but they are not crucial for the analysis in this chapter. Our goal here is to examine how changes in the money supply affect the aggregate demand for goods and services. For this purpose, we can ignore the details of how Bank of Canada policy is implemented and assume that the Bank controls the money supply directly. In other words, the quantity of money supplied in the economy is fixed at whatever level the Bank of Canada decides to set it.

The relationship between money demand and money supply is shown in Figure 15.1, with the quantity of money on the horizontal axis and the interest rate on the vertical axis. We assume that the Bank of Canada controls the money supply directly. In particular, we assume that the supply of money is not affected at all by changes in the interest rate. Once the Bank has made its policy decision, the quantity of money supplied is the same, regardless of the prevailing interest rate. For this reason, the money-supply curve is drawn as a vertical line.

Money Demand The second piece of the theory of liquidity preference is the demand for money. As a starting point for understanding money demand, recall

FIGURE 15.1

The Supply of Money
The supply of money in an economy is fixed by the central bank, which in Canada is the Bank of Canada. Because the quantity of money supplied does not depend on the interest rate, the supply curve is vertical.

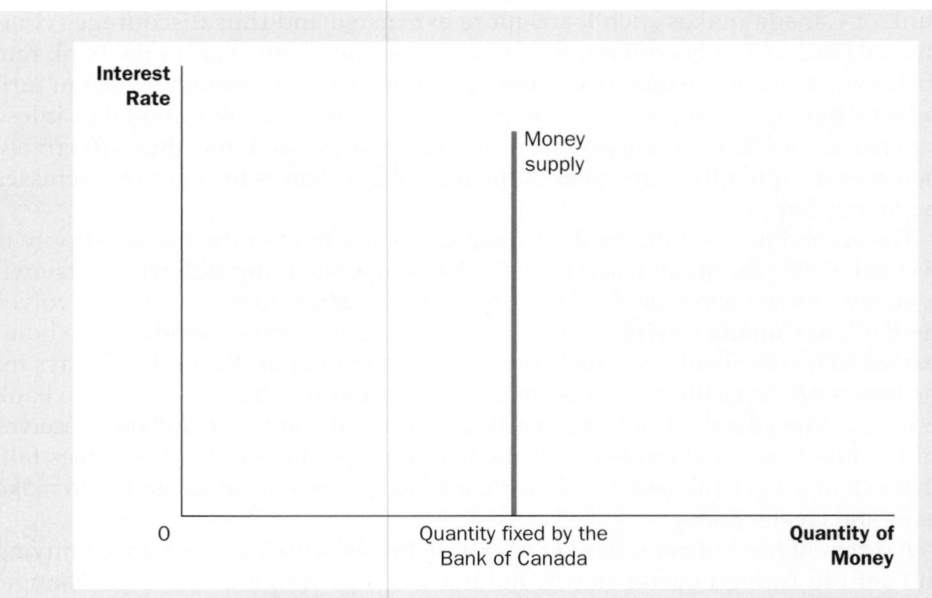

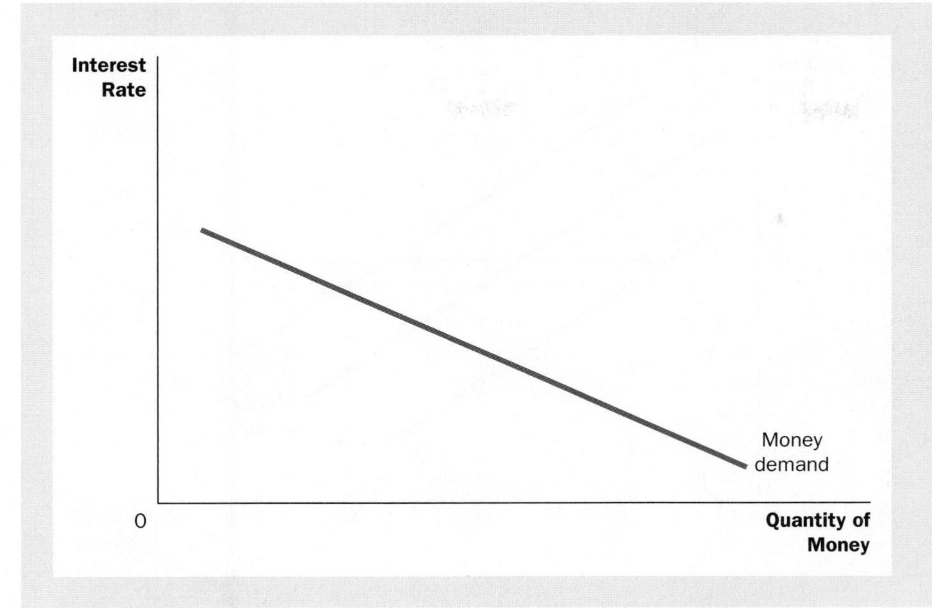

FIGURE 15.2

The Demand for Money
Because the interest rate measures the opportunity cost of holding noninterest-bearing money instead of interest-bearing bonds, an increase in the interest rate reduces the quantity of money demanded. A downward-sloping demand curve represents this negative relationship.

that any asset's *liquidity* refers to the ease with which that asset is converted into the economy's medium of exchange. Money is the economy's medium of exchange, so it is by definition the most liquid asset available. The liquidity of money explains the demand for it: People choose to hold money instead of other assets that offer higher rates of return because money can be used to buy goods and services.

Although many factors determine the quantity of money demanded, the one emphasized by the theory of liquidity preference is the interest rate. The reason is that the interest rate is the opportunity cost of holding money. That is, when you hold wealth as cash in your wallet, instead of as an interest-bearing bond, you lose the interest you could have earned. An increase in the interest rate raises the cost of holding money and, as a result, reduces the quantity of money demanded. A decrease in the interest rate reduces the cost of holding money and raises the quantity demanded. Thus, as shown in Figure 15.2, the money-demand curve slopes downward.

The other key determinant of the quantity of money demanded is the fact that money is used to buy goods and services. As a result, when either the quantity or the price of goods and services increases, people need to hold more of their assets in the form of money. The quantity of goods and services that people buy is simply equal to real GDP. The price of goods and services in the economy is represented by a price index such as the consumer price index or the GDP deflator. The product of these two measures is the dollar value of all transactions in the economy. Figure 15.3 shows the influence on money demand of an increase in either the price level or the level of real GDP. For a given interest rate, an increase in the dollar value of transactions causes the demand for money to increase. As a result, the money-demand curve shifts to the right. For a given interest rate, a decrease in the dollar value of transactions causes the demand for money to decrease. As a result, the money-demand curve shifts to the left.

FIGURE 15.3

Shifts in the Demand for Money
People hold money in order to buy goods and services. If the dollar value of transactions increases because of an increase in either prices or real GDP, then for any interest rate (r_1), people will hold more of their assets as money (increasing from M_1^d to M_3^d). As a result, the money-demand curve shifts to the right. If the dollar value of transactions decreases because of a decrease in either price or real GDP, then for any interest rate (r_1) people will hold less of their assets as money (decreasing from M_1^d to M_2^d). As a result, the money-demand curve shifts to the left.

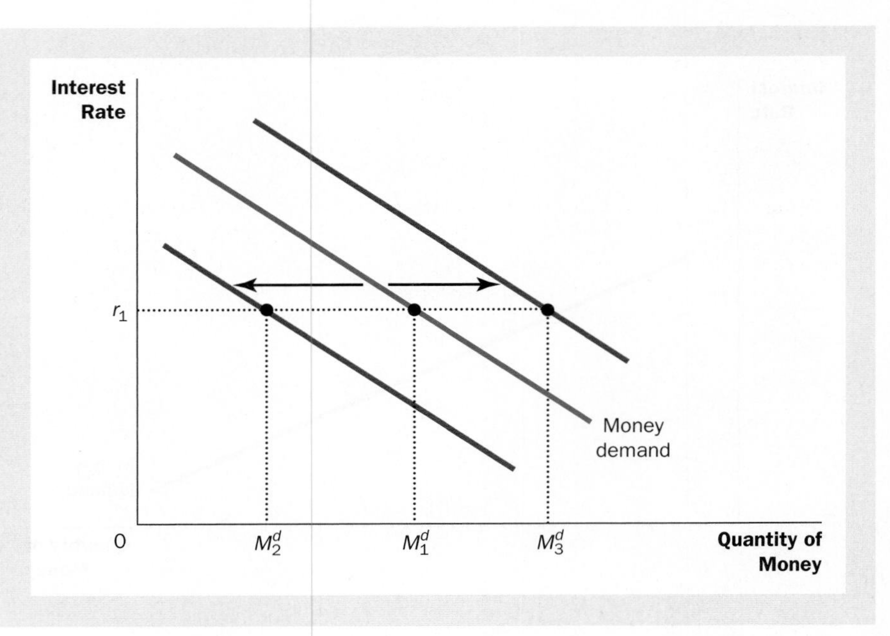

Equilibrium in the Money Market According to the theory of liquidity preference, the interest rate adjusts to balance the supply and demand for money. There is one interest rate, called the *equilibrium interest rate,* at which the quantity of money demanded exactly balances the quantity of money supplied. If the interest rate is at any other level, people will try to adjust their portfolios of assets and, as a result, drive the interest rate toward the equilibrium.

For example, suppose that the interest rate is above the equilibrium level, such as r_1 in Figure 15.4. In this case, the quantity of money that people want to hold, M_1^d, is less than the quantity of money that the Bank of Canada has supplied. Those people who are holding the surplus of money will try to get rid of it by buying interest-bearing bonds or by depositing it in an interest-bearing bank account. Because bond issuers and banks prefer to pay lower interest rates, they respond to this surplus of money by lowering the interest rates they offer. As the interest rate falls, people become more willing to hold money until, at the equilibrium interest rate, people are happy to hold exactly the amount of money the Bank of Canada has supplied.

Conversely, at interest rates below the equilibrium level, such as r_2 in Figure 15.4, the quantity of money that people want to hold, M_2^d, is greater than the quantity of money that the Bank of Canada has supplied. As a result, people try to increase their holdings of money by reducing their holdings of bonds and other interest-bearing assets. As people cut back on their holdings of bonds, bond issuers find that they have to offer higher interest rates to attract buyers. Thus, the interest rate rises and approaches the equilibrium level.

15-1b The Downward Slope of the Aggregate-Demand Curve

Having seen how the theory of liquidity preference explains the economy's equilibrium interest rate, we now consider its implications for the aggregate demand

FIGURE 15.4

Equilibrium in the Money Market

According to the theory of liquidity preference, the interest rate adjusts to bring the quantity of money supplied and the quantity of money demanded into balance. If the interest rate is above the equilibrium level (such as at r_1), the quantity of money people want to hold (M_1^d) is less than the quantity the Bank of Canada has created, and this surplus of money puts downward pressure on the interest rate. Conversely, if the interest rate is below the equilibrium level (such as at r_2), the quantity of money people want to hold (M_2^d) is greater than the quantity the Bank of Canada has created, and this shortage of money puts upward pressure on the interest rate. Thus, the forces of supply and demand in the market for money push the interest rate toward the equilibrium interest rate, at which people are content holding the quantity of money the Bank of Canada has created.

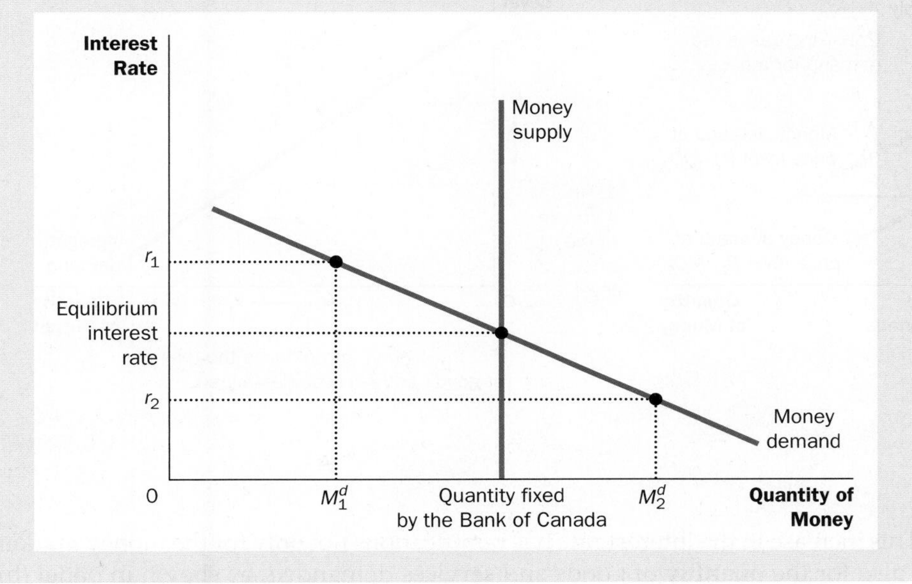

for goods and services. As a warm-up exercise, let's begin by using the theory to reexamine a topic we already understand—the interest rate effect and the downward slope of the aggregate-demand curve. In particular, suppose that the overall level of prices in the economy rises. What happens to the interest rate that balances the supply and demand for money, and how does that change affect the quantity of goods and services demanded?

As we have just discussed, the price level is one determinant of the quantity of money demanded. At higher prices, more money is exchanged every time a good or service is sold. As a result, people will choose to hold a larger quantity of money. That is, a higher price level increases the quantity of money demanded for any given interest rate. Thus, an increase in the price level from P_1 to P_2 shifts the money-demand curve to the right from MD_1 to MD_2, as shown in panel (a) of Figure 15.5.

Notice how this shift in money demand affects the equilibrium in the money market. For a fixed money supply, the interest rate must rise to balance money supply and money demand. The higher price level has increased the amount of money people want to hold and has shifted the money demand curve to the right. Yet the quantity of money supplied is unchanged, so the interest rate must rise from r_1 to r_2 to discourage the additional demand.

FIGURE 15.5

The Money Market and the Slope of the Aggregate-Demand Curve

An increase in the price level from P_1 to P_2 shifts the money-demand curve to the right, as in panel (a). This increase in money demand causes the interest rate to rise from r_1 to r_2. Because the interest rate is the cost of borrowing, the increase in the interest rate reduces the quantity of goods and services demanded from Y_1 to Y_2. This negative relationship between the price level and quantity demanded is represented with a downward-sloping aggregate-demand curve, as in panel (b).

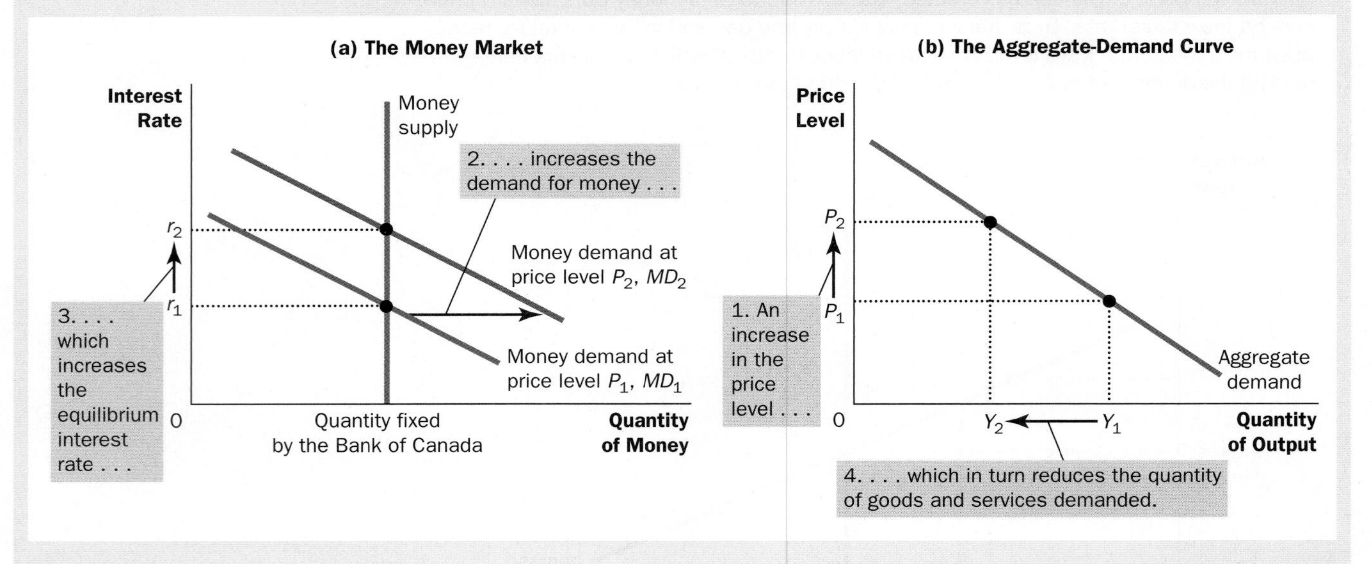

This increase in the interest rate has ramifications not only for the money market but also for the quantity of goods and services demanded, as shown in panel (b) of Figure 15.5. At a higher interest rate, the cost of borrowing and the return to saving are greater. Fewer households choose to borrow to buy a new house, and those who do buy smaller houses, so the demand for residential investment falls. Fewer firms choose to borrow to build new factories and buy new equipment, so business investment falls. Thus, when the price level rises from P_1 to P_2, increasing money demand from M_1^d to M_2^d and raising the interest rate from r_1 to r_2, the quantity of goods and services demanded falls from Y_1 to Y_2.

Hence, this analysis of the interest rate effect can be summarized in three steps: (1) A higher price level raises money demand. (2) Higher money demand leads to a higher interest rate. (3) A higher interest rate reduces the quantity of goods and services demanded. Of course, the same logic works in reverse as well: A lower price level reduces money demand, which leads to a lower interest rate, and this in turn increases the quantity of goods and services demanded. The end result of this analysis is a negative relationship between the price level and the quantity of goods and services demanded, which is illustrated with a downward-sloping aggregate-demand curve.

In an open economy, the other important influence is the real exchange-rate effect. An increase in the price level causes the real exchange rate to increase. Because this makes Canadian-produced goods more expensive relative to foreign-produced goods, both foreigners and Canadians substitute away from Canadian-produced goods. As a result, Canada's net exports fall. For this additional reason, then, in a small open economy an increase in the price level causes the quantity of

Canadian-produced goods and services demanded to fall. Whether it is due primarily to the interest rate effect or to the real exchange-rate effect, the end result of this analysis is a negative relationship between the price level and the quantity of goods and services demanded. This relationship is illustrated with a downward-sloping aggregate-demand curve.

15-1c Changes in the Money Supply

So far we have used the theory of liquidity preference to explain in more detail how the total quantity demanded of goods and services in the economy changes as the price level changes. That is, we have examined movements along the downward-sloping aggregate-demand curve. The theory also sheds light, however, on some of the other events that alter the quantity of goods and services demanded. Whenever the quantity of goods and services demanded changes *for a given price level,* the aggregate demand curve shifts. As we will see, how the economy responds to changes in the quantity of goods and services demanded depends on whether the economy is closed or open. It is worth repeating that our strategy will be to first show what happens in a closed economy. We will then turn to open-economy considerations. This is a useful way of proceeding because what happens in an open economy is essentially the same as what happens in a closed economy but with one or two additional considerations. Thus, the closed-economy discussion is a helpful stepping stone to understanding what happens in an open economy like Canada.

One important variable that shifts the aggregate-demand curve is monetary policy. To see how monetary policy affects the economy in the short run, suppose that the Bank of Canada causes the money supply to increase. (Why the Bank of Canada might do this will become clear later after we understand the effects of such a move.) Let's consider how this monetary injection influences the equilibrium interest rate for a given price level. This will tell us what the injection does to the position of the aggregate-demand curve.

As panel (a) of Figure 15.6 shows, an increase in the money supply shifts the money-supply curve to the right from MS_1 to MS_2. Because the money-demand curve has not changed, the interest rate falls from r_1 to r_2 to balance money supply and money demand. That is, the interest rate must fall to induce people to hold the additional money the Bank of Canada has created.

Once again, the interest rate influences the quantity of goods and services demanded, as shown in panel (b) of Figure 15.6. The lower interest rate reduces the cost of borrowing and the return to saving. Households buy more and larger houses, stimulating the demand for residential investment. Firms spend more on new factories and new equipment, stimulating business investment. For all of these reasons, the quantity of goods and services demanded at the given price level, $\overline{P}$, rises. The increase in demand for goods and services increases the demand for money from MD_1 to MD_2, causing the interest rate to rise slightly from r_2 to r_3. This partial reversal in the fall in the interest rate reduces somewhat the stimulative effect on residential and firm investment. As a result, the shift in aggregate demand is smaller than it would otherwise have been. The net effect is an increase in the quantity of goods and services demanded at the given price level, $\overline{P}$, from Y_1 to Y_2, and thus a shift to the right of the aggregate-demand curve from AD_1 to AD_2. Of course, there is nothing special about $\overline{P}$: The monetary injection raises the quantity of goods and services demanded at every price level. Thus, the entire aggregate-demand curve shifts to the right.

FIGURE 15.6

A Monetary Injection in a Closed Economy

In panel (a), an increase in the money supply from MS_1 to MS_2 reduces the equilibrium interest rate from r_1 to r_2. Because the interest rate is the cost of borrowing, the fall in the interest rate raises the quantity of goods and services demanded at a given price level. At the same time, the increase in output requires that people hold more money. This causes the demand for money to increase from MD_1 to MD_2 and causes a partial reversal in the interest rate, from r_2 to r_3. As a result, the increase in the quantity demanded of goods and services is smaller than it would otherwise have been. In the end, the aggregate-demand curve shifts to the right from AD_1 to AD_2, and we move from point A to point B in panels (a) and (b).

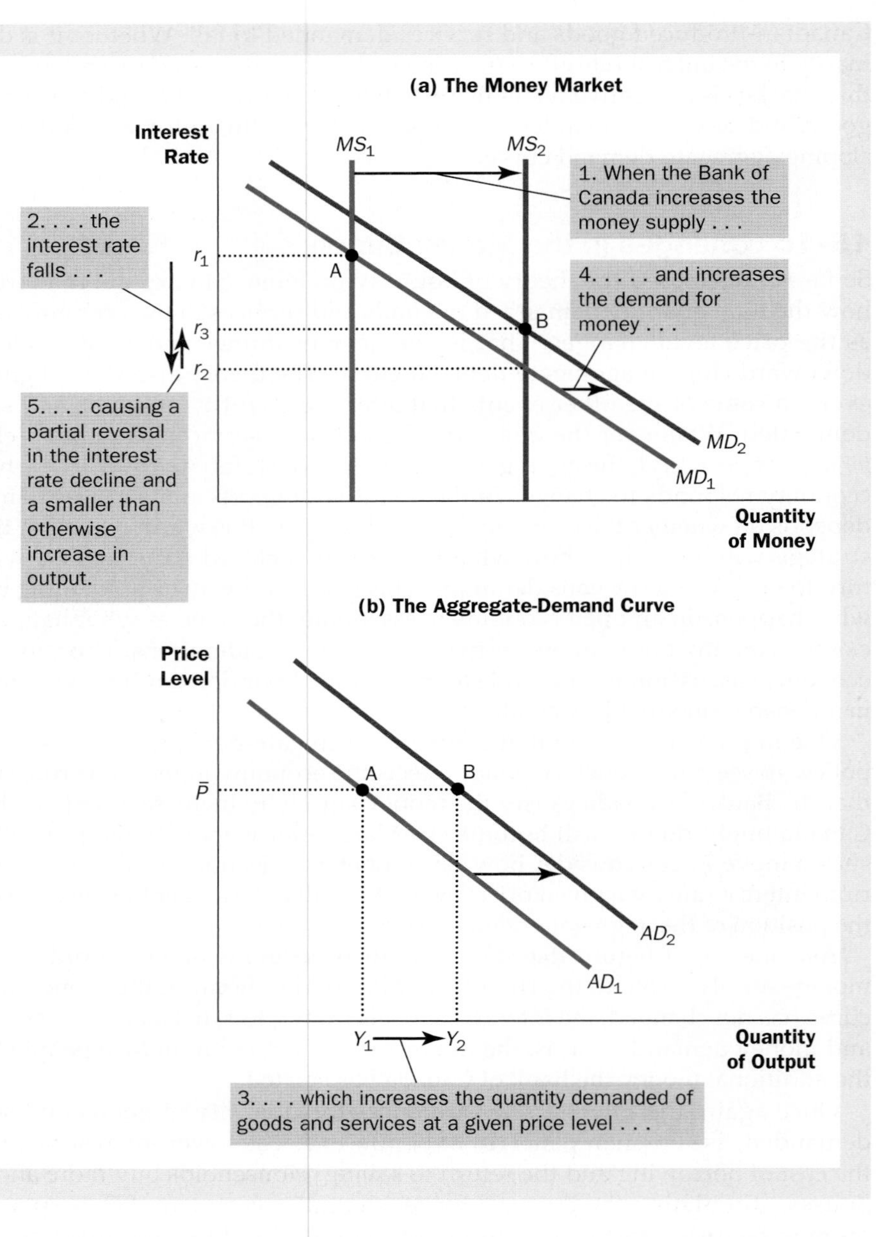

To sum up: *When the Bank of Canada increases the money supply, it lowers the interest rate and increases the quantity of goods and services demanded for any given price level, shifting the aggregate-demand curve to the right. Conversely, when the Bank of Canada contracts the money supply, it raises the interest rate and reduces the quantity of goods and services demanded for any given price level, shifting the aggregate-demand curve to the left.*

15-1d Open-Economy Considerations

Our discussion of how monetary policy affects aggregate demand so far has ignored open-economy considerations. Earlier we discussed how Canada is described by macroeconomists as a small open economy with perfect capital mobility. We saw that one implication of this is that Canada's interest rate must move up and down with changes in the world interest rate. Canada's interest rate differs from the world interest rate only by an amount reflecting differences in the tax treatment of financial capital and differences in default risk in Canada versus the rest of the world. For simplicity, we will ignore these differences and thus assume that Canada's interest rate adjusts to equal the world interest rate. We turn now to the question of how a monetary injection affects the aggregate-demand curve in a small open economy. We will see that the story we have told so far, while correct for a closed economy, is incomplete for a small open economy like Canada.

Panel (a) of Figure 15.7 shows money-demand and money-supply curves intersecting at the world interest rate, r^w. Because eventually Canada's interest rate

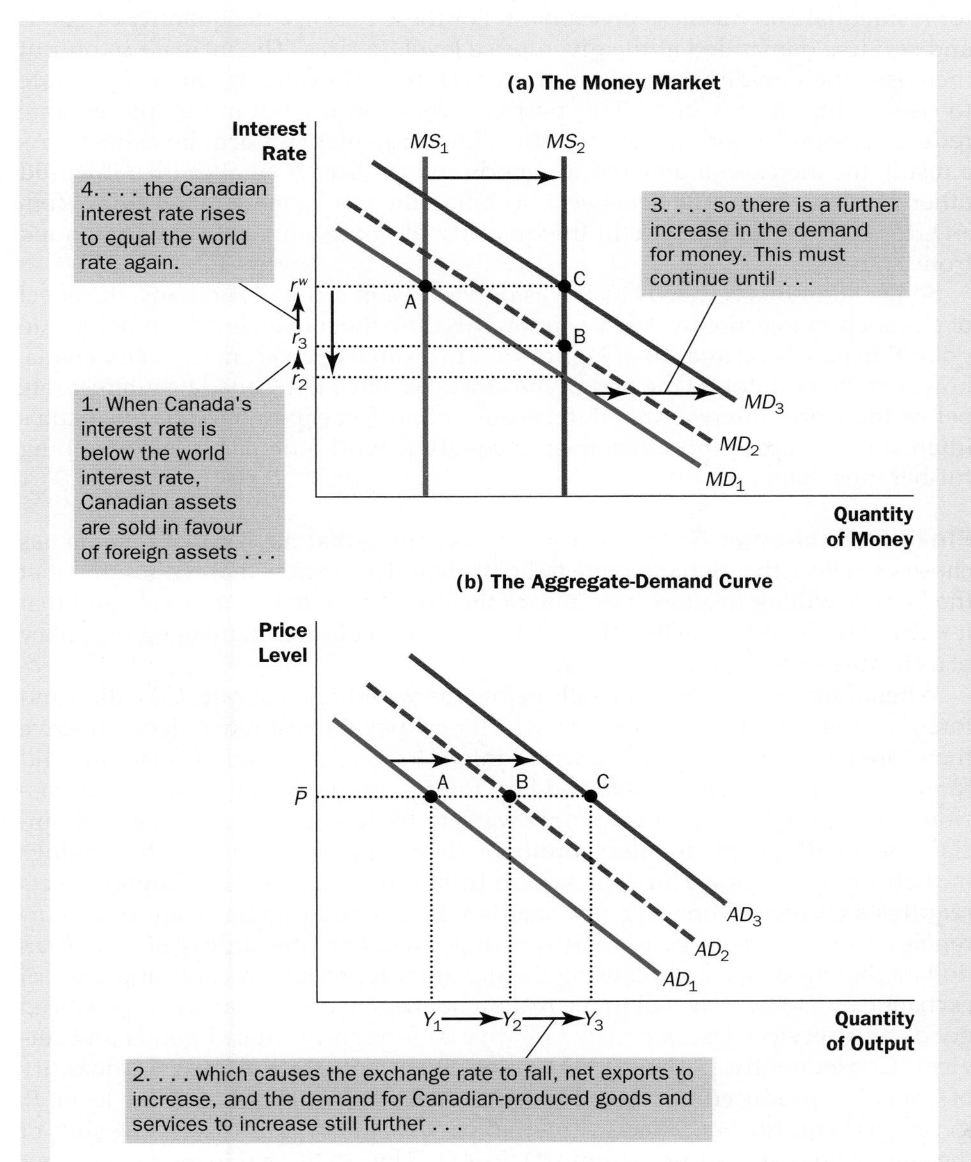

FIGURE 15.7

A Monetary Injection in an Open Economy

In a closed economy, a monetary injection causes the interest rate to fall and output to increase. This is shown by the movements from point A to point B in panels (a) and (b). In a small open economy, the fact that the domestic interest rate, r_3, is less than the world interest rate, r^w, means that the rate must be further adjusted. Canadian and foreign savers find the Canadian interest rate less attractive than the world rate. As a result, they sell Canadian assets to buy foreign assets. This increases the supply of Canadian dollars in the market for foreign-currency exchange and causes the exchange rate to fall. Because the fall in the exchange rate increases net exports, the demand for Canadian-produced goods and services rises from AD_2 to AD_3 in panel (b). The expansion of output from Y_2 to Y_3 requires that people hold more money to make transactions. This is shown by the increase in the demand for money from MD_2 to MD_3 and the increase in the Canadian interest rate from r_3 to r^w in panel (a). In the end, the economy adjusts to point C in both panels. The interest rate returns to the world interest rate, and output increases by more than it would in a closed economy.

must equal the world interest rate, we begin our discussion of how monetary policy affects aggregate demand from this point. To obtain a true measure of the impact of monetary policy, we must show all of the adjustments in the economy that return Canada's interest rate to the world interest rate.

An increase in the money supply shifts the money-supply curve to the right, from MS_1 to MS_2. Because the money-demand curve has not changed, the interest rate falls below the world interest rate to r_2 in order to balance money supply and money demand. That is, the Canadian interest rate must fall to induce people to hold the additional money the Bank of Canada has created.

Once again, the interest rate influences the quantity of goods and services demanded, as shown in panel (b) of Figure 15.7. By lowering the cost of borrowing and the return to saving, the lower interest rate stimulates the demand for residential and business investment. For these reasons, the quantity of goods and services demanded at the given price level, $\overline{P}$, rises. The increase in output increases the demand for money from MD_1 to MD_2, causing the interest rate to rise slightly from r_2 to r_3. This partial reversal in the fall in the interest rate reduces somewhat the stimulative effect on residential and firm investment. As a result, the increase in demand for goods and services is smaller than it would otherwise have been. The net effect is a shift in the aggregate-demand curve from AD_1 to AD_2 and an increase in the quantity of goods and services demanded from Y_1 to Y_2.

So far, all of this is exactly as it was previously. In a closed economy, the effect of a monetary injection would be summarized by the movement from point A to point B in panels (a) and (b) of Figure 15.7. In a small open economy like Canada, however, this cannot be the end of the story. We have left Canada's interest rate below the world interest rate. But, because of perfect capital mobility, Canada's interest rate must eventually adjust to equal the world interest rate. Something further must happen.

Flexible Exchange Rate We begin by assuming that the Bank of Canada has chosen to allow the exchange rate to be flexible. This means that we assume that the Bank is willing to allow the value of the exchange rate to vary freely and that it will not try to influence its value. The Bank of Canada has maintained the policy of a **flexible exchange rate** since 1970.

flexible exchange rate
a policy by which the value of the exchange rate is allowed to vary without interference by the central bank

When Canada's interest rate falls below the world interest rate, Canadian and foreign savers find Canadian assets, which now pay interest rate r_3, less attractive than foreign assets that pay the world interest rate. As a result, Canadians and foreigners sell Canadian assets and buy foreign assets. Recall from our discussion in Chapter 13 that while people want to trade goods, services, and financial assets with people in other countries, they want to be paid for these things in their own currency. Thus, the switch from Canadian assets to foreign assets requires a corresponding sale of Canadian dollars and purchase of foreign currencies. In the market for foreign-currency exchange, the supply of Canadian dollars therefore increases, causing the dollar to depreciate in value and the real exchange rate to fall. The fall in the real exchange rate makes Canadian-produced goods and services less expensive relative to foreign-produced goods and services. Consequently, Canada's net exports increase, which causes the quantity of Canadian-produced goods and services demanded at the given price level, $\overline{P}$, to increase still further. This is shown in panel (b) of Figure 15.7 by the shift of the aggregate-demand curve from AD_2 to AD_3. This additional increase in output increases the demand for money, which causes the interest rate to rise still further.

This is shown in panel (a) of Figure 15.7 by the shift of the money-demand curve from MD_2 to MD_3. This shift must be such that Canada's interest rate is once again equal to the world interest rate. The end result of all of these adjustments is an increase in the demand for money to MD_3, a return of Canada's interest rate to the world interest rate, an increase in the quantity of goods and services demanded to Y_3, and a shift in the aggregate-demand curve to AD_3.

To sum up: *In a small open economy with a flexible exchange rate, a monetary injection by the Bank of Canada causes the dollar to depreciate in value. Because this depreciation of the dollar causes net exports to rise, there is an additional increase in demand for Canadian-produced goods and services that is not realized in a closed economy. In the end, a monetary injection in an open economy shifts the aggregate-demand curve farther to the right than it does in a closed economy.*

Fixed Exchange Rate Now we consider the effect of monetary policy on aggregate demand in an open economy when the Bank of Canada has chosen to fix the value of the exchange rate. The Bank of Canada maintained a policy of a **fixed exchange rate** from 1962 to 1970.

fixed exchange rate
a policy by which the value of the exchange rate is held fixed by the central bank

As we explained in Chapter 10, the Bank of Canada can, if it wishes, buy and sell foreign currencies in what are known as *foreign exchange market operations.* Foreign exchange market operations are very similar to open-market operations in that they both involve the central bank buying or selling something. When the central bank buys something, whether it is a government bond or foreign currency, it causes the money supply to increase. When the Bank sells something, whether it is a government bond or foreign currency, it causes the money supply to decrease. Now consider what would happen if the Bank of Canada wanted to expand the money supply while maintaining a constant value of the Canadian dollar.

By lowering the Canadian interest rate, a monetary injection causes Canadians and foreigners to sell Canadian assets in preference for foreign assets. This switch out of Canadian assets and into foreign assets increases the supply of Canadian dollars in the market for foreign-currency exchange, which causes the exchange rate to fall. If the Bank of Canada wanted to prevent this fall in the exchange rate, it would enter the market for foreign-currency exchange to sell foreign currency it holds and purchase Canadian dollars. This purchase of dollars would increase the demand for dollars in the market for foreign-currency exchange and offset the increased supply of dollars caused by Canadians and foreigners selling Canadian assets. In this way, the value of the Canadian dollar remains unchanged. But the sale of foreign currency by the Bank of Canada would also decrease the money supply. To prevent a fall in the value of the Canadian dollar, then, the Bank of Canada would need to contract the Canadian money supply. Because the purpose of the monetary injection was to expand the money supply, it would be counterproductive indeed for the Bank of Canada to try to prevent the value of the dollar from changing. Table 15.1 summarizes what we have learned so far.

This explanation of why the Bank of Canada must allow the exchange rate to vary freely if it wants to change the money supply teaches an important lesson: *The Bank of Canada cannot simultaneously choose the size of the money supply and the value of the Canadian dollar.* By choosing to change the money supply, the Bank of Canada must allow the exchange rate to vary.

QUICK **Quiz** *Explain how a decrease in the money supply affects the money market and the position of the aggregate-demand curve. What is the effect for a closed economy and for a small open economy?*

TABLE 15.1

The Effects of a Monetary Injection: Summary

How Does a Monetary Injection Shift the Aggregate-Demand Curve in a Closed Economy?

1. An increase in money supply causes the interest rate to fall.
2. The fall in the interest rate stimulates investment and consumption of durable goods. The increase in spending increases the demand for money, causing a partial reversal of the fall in the interest rate.
3. The increase in spending shifts the aggregate-demand curve to the right.

How Does a Monetary Injection Shift the Aggregate-Demand Curve in an Open Economy?

1. Due to perfect capital mobility, and ignoring differences in default risk and taxes, Canada's interest rate must equal the world interest rate. We begin with $r = r^w$.
2. An increase in the money supply causes Canada's interest rate to fall below r^w.
3. The fall in the interest rate stimulates investment and consumption of durable goods. The increase in spending increases the demand for money, causing a partial reversal of the fall in the interest rate. Canada's interest rate remains below r^w.
4. With $r < r^w$, Canadian assets are sold in favour of buying foreign assets. The switch from Canadian to foreign assets requires that dollars be sold in the market for foreign-currency exchange. The real exchange rate falls.
5. The fall in the real exchange rate increases net exports, causing the aggregate-demand curve to shift even farther to the right.
6. This additional stimulus to spending increases the demand for money until $r = r^w$.
7. It makes sense for the Bank of Canada to cause a monetary injection only if it allows the exchange rate to be flexible.

FYI The Zero Lower Bound

As we have just seen, monetary policy works through interest rates. This conclusion raises a question: What if the Bank of Canada's target interest rate has fallen as far as it can? What, if anything, can monetary policy do then to stimulate the economy?

Some economists describe this situation as a *liquidity trap.* According to the theory of liquidity preference, expansionary monetary policy works by reducing interest rates and stimulating investment spending. But if interest rates have already fallen almost to zero, then perhaps monetary policy is no longer effective. Nominal interest rates cannot fall below zero: Rather than making a loan at a negative nominal interest rate, a person would just hold cash. In this environment, expansionary monetary policy raises the supply of money, making the public's asset portfolio more liquid, but because interest rates can't fall any further, the extra liquidity might not have any effect. Aggregate demand, production, and employment may be "trapped" at low levels.

Other economists are skeptical about the relevance of liquidity traps and believe that a central bank continues to have tools to expand the economy, even after its interest rate target hits its lower bound of zero. One possibility is that the central bank could raise inflation expectations by committing itself to future monetary expansion. Even if nominal interest rates cannot fall any further, higher expected inflation can lower real interest rates by making them negative, which would stimulate investment spending.

A second possibility is that the central bank could conduct expansionary open-market operations with a larger variety of financial instruments than it normally uses. For example, it could buy mortgages and corporate debt and thereby lower the interest rates on these kinds of loans. We described this approach earlier, in Chapter 10, as an open-market operation known as *quantitative easing.* The U.S. Federal Reserve actively pursued the quantitative easing option during the downturn of 2008 and 2009. During this same period, the Bank of Canada indicated that it was willing to use this approach if necessary.

Some economists have suggested that the possibility of hitting the zero lower bound for interest rates justifies setting the target rate of inflation well above zero. Under zero inflation, the real interest rate, like the nominal interest rate, can never fall below zero. But if the normal rate of inflation is, say, 4 percent, then the central bank can easily push the real interest rate to negative 4 percent by lowering the nominal interest rate toward zero. Thus, moderate inflation gives monetary policymakers more room to stimulate the economy when needed, reducing the risk of hitting the zero lower bound and having the economy fall into a liquidity trap.

case study

Why Central Banks Watch the Stock Market (and Vice Versa)

"Irrational exuberance." That was how U.S. Federal Reserve Chairman Alan Greenspan once described the booming stock market of the late 1990s. He was right about the market being exuberant: Average stock prices in the United States increased about fourfold during the 1990s. While somewhat less exuberant, the average stock price in Canada nonetheless increased 2.5 times over this period. And perhaps stock markets were even irrational: In 2001 and 2002, stock markets took back some of these large gains, as stock prices experienced a pronounced decline. More recently, in response to the financial crisis originating in U.S. financial markets in 2007, stock markets again suffered a large loss, only to reverse that selloff almost immediately. As a result, between October 2007 and February 2009, the S&P/TSX index fell by more than 44 percent, but then the index recovered and increased by 45 percent between February and December 2009.

Regardless of how they view booming (or crashing) stock markets, how should central banks respond to stock market fluctuations? Central banks have no reason to care about stock prices in themselves, but they do have the job of monitoring and responding to developments in the overall economy, and the stock market is a piece of the puzzle. When the stock market booms, households become wealthier, and this increased wealth stimulates consumer spending. In addition, a rise in stock prices makes it more attractive for firms to sell new shares of stock, and this stimulates investment spending. For both reasons, a booming stock market expands the aggregate demand for goods and services.

As we discuss more fully later in the chapter, one of a central bank's goals is to stabilize aggregate demand because greater stability in aggregate demand means greater stability in output and the price level. To do this, a central bank might respond to a stock market boom by keeping the money supply lower and interest rates higher than it otherwise would. The contractionary effects of higher interest rates would offset the expansionary effects of higher stock prices.

The opposite occurs when the stock market falls. Spending on consumption and investment declines, depressing aggregate demand and pushing the economy toward recession. To stabilize aggregate demand, a central bank needs to increase the money supply and lower interest rates.

While central banks keep an eye on the stock market, stock market participants also keep an eye on the central banks. Because central banks can influence interest rates and economic activity, they can alter the value of stocks. For example, when a central bank raises interest rates by reducing the money supply, it makes owning stocks less attractive for two reasons. First, a higher interest rate means that bonds, the alternative to stocks, are earning a higher return. Second, the central bank's tightening of monetary policy risks pushing the economy into a recession, which reduces profits. As a result, stock prices often fall when central banks raise interest rates. ■

Use the theory of liquidity preference to explain how a decrease in the money supply affects the equilibrium interest rate. How does this change in monetary policy affect the aggregate-demand curve?

15-2 How Fiscal Policy Influences Aggregate Demand

fiscal policy
the setting of the level of government spending and taxation by government policymakers

The government can influence the behaviour of the economy not only with monetary policy but also with fiscal policy. **Fiscal policy** refers to the government's choices regarding the overall level of government purchases or taxes. Earlier in the book we examined how fiscal policy influences saving, investment, and growth in the long run. In the short run, however, the primary effect of fiscal policy is on the aggregate demand for goods and services.

15-2a Changes in Government Purchases

When policymakers change the money supply or the level of taxes, they shift the aggregate-demand curve by influencing the spending decisions of firms or households. By contrast, when the government alters its own purchases of goods and services, it shifts the aggregate-demand curve directly.

Suppose, for example, that the federal government chooses to introduce a $5 billion job-creation program. For a given price level, the program will finance expenditures on new roads, sewers, and bridges. The program raises the demand for construction work and induces construction firms to hire more workers. The increase in demand for construction work is reflected in an increase in the aggregate demand for goods and services. As a result, the aggregate-demand curve shifts to the right.

By how much does this $5 billion government expenditure shift the aggregate-demand curve? At first, one might guess that the aggregate-demand curve shifts to the right by exactly $5 billion. It turns out, however, that this is not correct. There are two macroeconomic effects that make the size of the shift in aggregate demand differ from the change in government purchases. The first—the multiplier effect—suggests that the shift in aggregate demand could be *larger* than $5 billion. The second—the crowding-out effect—suggests that the shift in aggregate demand could be *smaller* than $5 billion. We now discuss each of these effects in turn.

15-2b The Multiplier Effect

When the government spends $5 billion on construction work, that expenditure has repercussions. For a given price level, the immediate impact of the higher demand from the government is to raise employment and profits for the construction firms involved. Then, as the workers see higher earnings and the firm owners see higher profits, they respond to this increase in income by raising their own spending on consumer goods. As a result, the government expenditure of $5 billion raises the demand for the products of many other firms in the economy. Because each dollar spent by the government can raise the aggregate demand for goods and services by more than a dollar, government purchases are said to have a **multiplier effect** on aggregate demand.

multiplier effect
the additional shifts in aggregate demand that result when expansionary fiscal policy increases income and thereby increases consumer spending

This multiplier effect continues even after this first round. When consumer spending rises, the firms that produce these consumer goods hire more people and experience higher profits. Higher earnings and profits stimulate consumer spending once again, and so on. Thus, there is positive feedback as higher demand leads to higher income, which in turn leads to even higher demand. Once all these effects are added together, the total impact on the quantity of goods and services demanded can be much larger than the initial impulse from higher government spending.

Figure 15.8 illustrates the multiplier effect. We begin at point A on aggregate-demand curve AD_1 with price level $\overline{P}$. Holding that price level constant, the increase

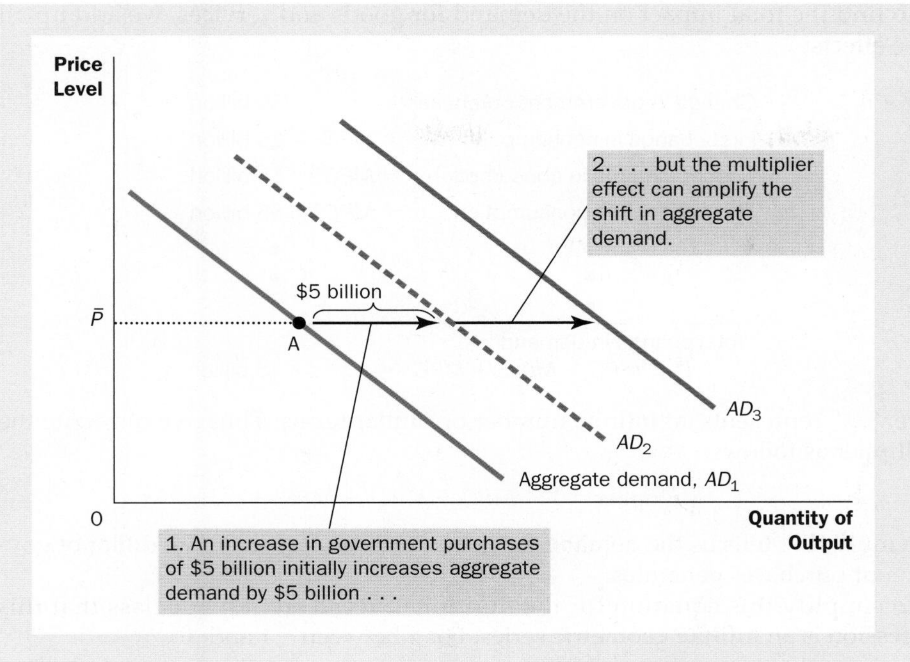

FIGURE 15.8

The Multiplier Effect
An increase in government purchases of $5 billion can shift the aggregate-demand curve to the right by more than $5 billion. This multiplier effect arises because increases in aggregate income stimulate additional spending by consumers.

in government purchases of $5 billion initially shifts the aggregate-demand curve to the right from AD_1 to AD_2 by exactly $5 billion. But when consumers respond by increasing their spending, the aggregate-demand curve shifts still further to AD_3.

This multiplier effect arising from the response of consumer spending can be strengthened by the response of investment to higher levels of demand. For instance, the construction firms might respond to the higher demand for roads and bridges by deciding to buy more paving equipment or build another cement plant. In this case, higher government demand spurs higher demand for investment goods. This positive feedback from demand to investment is sometimes called the *investment accelerator.*

15-2c A Formula for the Spending Multiplier

A little high-school algebra permits us to derive a formula for the size of the multiplier effect that arises from consumer spending. An important number in this formula is the *marginal propensity to consume* (*MPC*)—the fraction of extra income that a household consumes rather than saves. For example, suppose that the marginal propensity to consume is $\frac{3}{4}$. This means that for every extra dollar that a household earns, the household spends $0.75 ($\frac{3}{4}$ of the dollar) and saves $0.25. With an *MPC* of $\frac{3}{4}$, when the workers and owners of the construction firms earn $5 billion from the government contract, they increase their consumer spending by $\frac{3}{4} \times \$5$ billion, or $3.75 billion.

To gauge the impact on aggregate demand of a change in government purchases, we follow the effects step by step. The process begins when the government spends $5 billion, which implies that national income (earnings and profits) also rises by this amount. This increase in income in turn raises consumer spending by $MPC \times \$5$ billion, which in turn raises the income for the workers and owners of the firms that produce the consumption goods. This second increase in income again raises consumer spending, this time by $MPC \times (MPC \times \$5$ billion). These feedback effects go on and on.

To find the total impact on the demand for goods and services, we add up all these effects:

Change in government purchases	=	\$5 billion
First change in consumption	= MPC	× \$5 billion
Second change in consumption	= MPC^2	× \$5 billion
Third change in consumption	= MPC^3	× \$5 billion
•		•
•		•
•		•
Total change in demand = $(1 + MPC + MPC^2 + MPC^3 + \ldots)$		× \$5 billion

Here, "..." represents an infinite number of similar terms. Thus, we can write the multiplier as follows:

$$\text{Multiplier} = 1 + MPC + MPC^2 + MPC^3 + \ldots$$

This multiplier tells us the demand for goods and services that each dollar of government purchases generates.

To simplify this equation for the multiplier, recall from math class that this expression is an infinite geometric series. For x between -1 and $+1$,

$$1 + x + x^2 + x^3 + \ldots = 1/(1 - x)$$

In our case, $x = MPC$. Thus,

$$\text{Multiplier} = 1/(1 - MPC)$$

For example, if MPC is $\frac{3}{4}$, the multiplier is $1/(1 - \frac{3}{4})$, which is 4. In this case, the \$5 billion of government spending generates \$20 billion of demand for goods and services.

In an open economy, the formula for the multiplier looks a bit different, because many of the goods and services that people purchase are imported. Recognition of this requires that we be a little more specific about how we define the multiplier. The government-spending multiplier tells us the demand for *Canadian-produced* goods and services generated by each additional dollar of government expenditure. Suppose that the fraction of extra income that a Canadian household spends on imported goods—what we call the *marginal propensity to import* (*MPI*)—is $\frac{1}{4}$. Now for every extra dollar that a household earns, the household saves \$0.25 and spends \$0.75, as before, but only \$0.50 of that spending is on Canadian-produced goods and \$0.25 is spent on imported goods. When the construction workers and firms earn \$5 billion from the government contract, they increase their spending on all goods by $\frac{3}{4} \times \$5$ billion, or \$3.75 billion, but increase their spending on Canadian-produced goods by just $\frac{1}{2} \times \$5$ billion, or \$2.5 billion. Only this second, smaller, amount adds to the incomes of other Canadians. Because Canadians spend some of their additional income on imported goods and services, therefore, the feedback effects are smaller than in a closed economy.

The relevant formula for the government-purchases multiplier in an open economy is

$$\text{Multiplier} = 1/(1 - MPC + MPI)$$

Now, because $MPC = \frac{3}{4}$ and $MPI = \frac{1}{4}$, the multiplier is $1/\left(1 - \frac{3}{4} + \frac{1}{4}\right)$, which is 2. In this case, the \$5 billion of government spending generates \$10 billion of demand for Canadian-produced goods and services. This compares with the $20 billion of demand for goods and services generated by the $5 billion of government spending in a closed economy. The government-purchases multiplier is clearly much smaller in an open economy than in a closed economy.

These formulas for the multiplier show an important conclusion: The size of the multiplier depends on the marginal propensity to consume and, in an open economy, the marginal propensity to import. A larger *MPC* means a larger multiplier. To see why this is true, remember that the multiplier arises because higher income induces greater spending on consumption. The larger the *MPC*, the greater this induced effect on consumption and the larger the multiplier. In an open economy we also need to consider the marginal propensity to import. A larger *MPI* means a *smaller* multiplier. To see why this is true, remember that the *MPI* measures the amount of higher income that is spent on foreign-produced goods and services. The greater this amount, the smaller the amount by which spending on *Canadian-produced* goods and services increases for any increase in income. A larger *MPI*, then, means that every increase in income induces a smaller increase in spending on Canadian-produced goods and services.

An interesting implication of the role played by the marginal propensity to import in determining the size of the multiplier in Canada is the likelihood that the *MPI* has recently grown larger. We saw earlier how the implementation of free trade agreements in 1989 and 1994 has resulted in an increase in the amount of trade Canada does with the rest of the world, and with the United States in particular. As a result of this growth in trade, it seems likely that any change in income now results in a larger change in spending on imported goods than would have been the case only 20 years ago. The *MPI*, then, has likely grown larger. If so, the multiplier in Canada has grown smaller over the past 20 years.

15-2d Other Applications of the Multiplier Effect

Because of the multiplier effect, a dollar of government purchases can generate more than a dollar of aggregate demand. The logic of the multiplier effect, however, is not restricted to changes in government purchases. Instead, it applies to any event that alters spending on any component of GDP—consumption, investment, government purchases, or net exports.

For example, suppose that a recession in the United States reduces the demand for Canada's net exports by $10 billion. This reduced spending on Canadian-produced goods and services depresses Canada's national income, which reduces spending by Canadian consumers. If the marginal propensity to consume is $\frac{3}{4}$, the marginal propensity to import is $\frac{1}{4}$, and the multiplier is 2, then the $10 billion fall in net exports means a $20 billion contraction in aggregate demand.

As another example, suppose that a stock market boom increases households' wealth and stimulates their spending on goods and services by $20 billion. This extra consumer spending increases national income, which in turn generates even more consumer spending. If the marginal propensity to consume is $\frac{3}{4}$, the marginal propensity to import is $\frac{1}{4}$, and the multiplier is 2, then the initial impulse of $20 billion in consumer spending translates into a $40 billion increase in aggregate demand.

The multiplier is an important concept in macroeconomics because it shows how the economy can amplify the impact of changes in spending. A small initial change in consumption, investment, government purchases, or net exports can end up having a large effect on aggregate demand and, therefore, the economy's production of goods and services. It is because of this amplified impact of initial changes in consumption, investment, government purchases, or net exports that policymakers must pay close attention to events such as the possibility of recession among our trading partners and the possibility of stock market booms or crashes.

15-2e The Crowding-Out Effect on Investment

The multiplier effect seems to suggest that when the government spends $5 billion on construction work, the resulting expansion in aggregate demand is necessarily larger than $5 billion. Yet another effect is working in the opposite direction. While an increase in government purchases stimulates the aggregate demand for goods and services, it also causes the interest rate to rise, and a higher interest rate reduces investment spending and chokes off aggregate demand. The reduction in aggregate demand that results when a fiscal expansion raises the interest rate is called the **crowding-out effect on investment**.

crowding-out effect on investment
the offset in aggregate demand that results when expansionary fiscal policy raises the interest rate and thereby reduces investment spending

To see why crowding out occurs, let's consider what happens in the money market when the government spends $5 billion on construction work. As we have discussed, for a given price level, this increase in demand raises the incomes of the workers and owners of the construction firms (and, because of the multiplier effect, of other firms as well). As incomes rise, households plan to buy more goods and services and, as a result, choose to hold more of their wealth in liquid form. That is, the increase in income caused by the fiscal expansion raises the demand for money.

The effect of the increase in money demand is shown in panel (a) of Figure 15.9. Because the Bank of Canada has not changed the money supply, the vertical supply curve remains the same. When the higher level of income shifts the money-demand curve to the right from MD_1 to MD_2, the interest rate must rise from r_1 to r_2 to keep supply and demand in balance.

The increase in the interest rate, in turn, reduces the quantity of goods and services demanded. In particular, because borrowing is more expensive, the demand for residential and business investment goods declines. That is, as the increase in government purchases increases the demand for goods and services, it may also crowd out investment. This crowding-out effect partially offsets the impact of government purchases on aggregate demand, as illustrated in panel (b) of Figure 15.9. The initial impact of the increase in government purchases is to shift the aggregate-demand curve from AD_1 to AD_2, but once crowding out takes place, the aggregate-demand curve drops back to AD_3. For given price level $\overline{P}$, the net effect of the increase in government purchases is shown by the movement from point A on AD_1 to point B on AD_3.

To sum up: *When the government increases its purchases by $5 billion, the aggregate demand for goods and services could rise by more or less than $5 billion, depending on whether the multiplier effect or the crowding-out effect on investment is larger. The multiplier effect by itself makes the shift in aggregate demand greater than $5 billion. The crowding-out effect pushes the aggregate-demand curve in the opposite direction and, if large enough, could result in an aggregate-demand shift of less than $5 billion.*

15-2f Open-Economy Considerations

Our discussion of how fiscal policy affects aggregate demand has so far ignored open-economy considerations. Just as we found when we considered the open-economy implications for monetary policy, we will see that the story we have told so far, while correct for a closed economy, is incomplete for a small open economy like Canada.

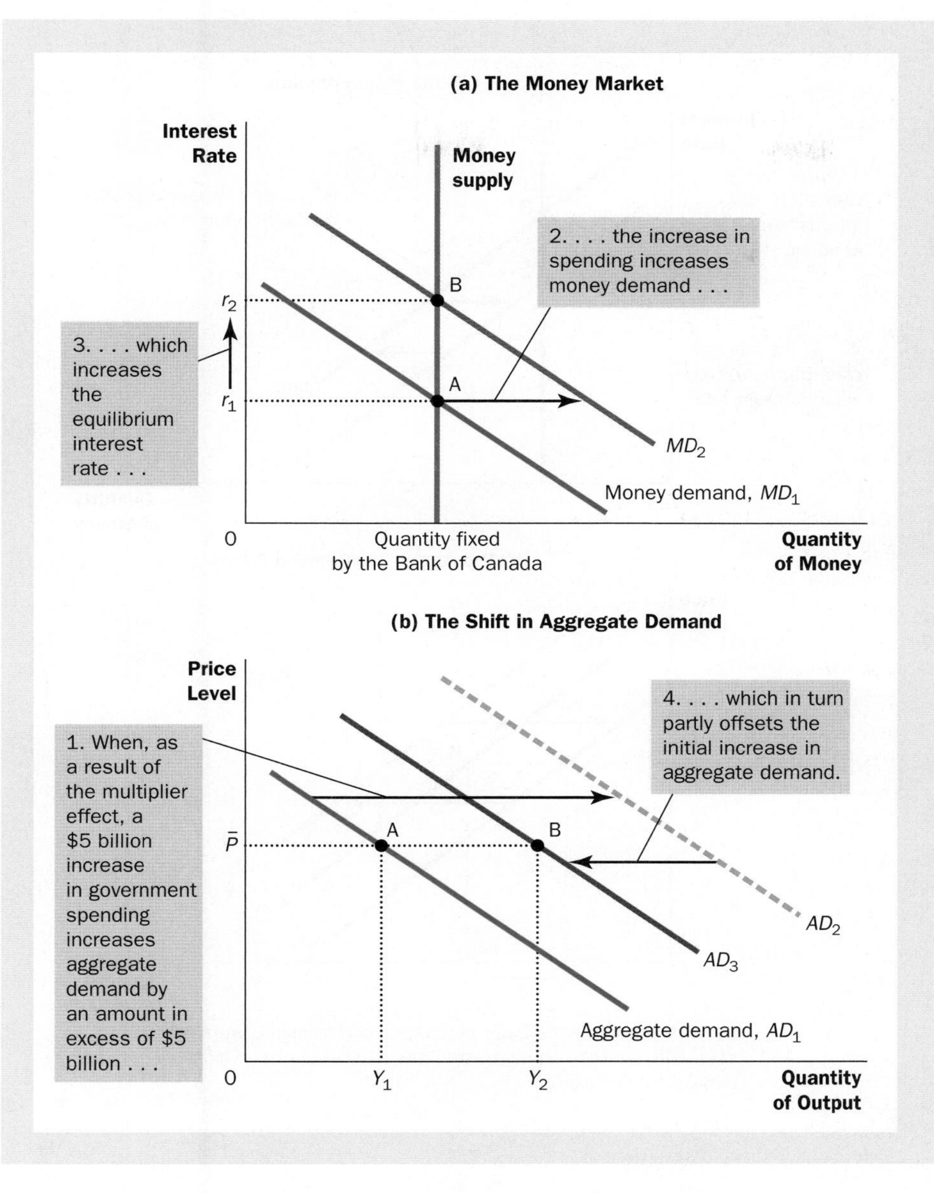

FIGURE 15.9

The Crowding-Out Effect on Investment

Panel (a) shows the money market. When the government increases its purchases of goods and services, the resulting increase in income raises the demand for money from MD_1 to MD_2, and this causes the equilibrium interest rate to rise from r_1 to r_2. Panel (b) shows the effects on aggregate demand. For given price level $\bar{P}$, the multiplier effect of the increase in government purchases shifts the aggregate-demand curve from AD_1 to AD_2. Yet, because the interest rate is the cost of borrowing, the increase in the interest rate tends to reduce the quantity of goods and services demanded, particularly for investment goods. This crowding out of investment partially offsets the impact of the fiscal expansion on aggregate demand. In the end, the aggregate-demand curve shifts only to AD_3.

Panel (a) of Figure 15.10 shows money-demand and money-supply curves intersecting at the world interest rate, r^w. Just as we did before, we begin our discussion of how fiscal policy affects aggregate demand from this point, because eventually Canada's interest rate must equal the world interest rate. To obtain a true measure of the impact of fiscal policy, we must show all of the adjustments in the economy that return Canada's interest rate to the world interest rate.

The $5 billion job-creation program raises the incomes of those directly employed and increases the incomes of workers and owners of other firms. This is the multiplier effect, and it is represented by the shift of the aggregate-demand

FIGURE 15.10

A Fiscal Expansion in an Open Economy with a Flexible Exchange Rate

In a closed economy, an increase in government purchases causes the interest rate to rise and output to increase. This is shown by the movement from point A to point B in panels (a) and (b). In a small open economy, the fact that the domestic interest rate, r_2, is greater than the world interest rate, r^w, means there must be further adjustment. Canadian and foreign savers find the Canadian interest rate more attractive than the world rate. As a result, they buy Canadian assets and sell foreign assets. This decreases the supply of Canadian dollars in the market for foreign-currency exchange and causes the exchange rate to rise. Because this increase in the interest rate decreases net exports, the demand for Canadian-produced goods and services falls from AD_2 to AD_1 in panel (b). The contraction of output from Y_2 to Y_1 requires that people hold less money to make transactions. This is shown by the decrease in the demand for money from MD_2 to MD_1 and the decrease in the Canadian interest rate from r_2 to r^w in panel (a). In the end, the economy adjusts back to point A in both panels, the interest rate returns to the world interest rate, and there is no lasting effect on aggregate demand.

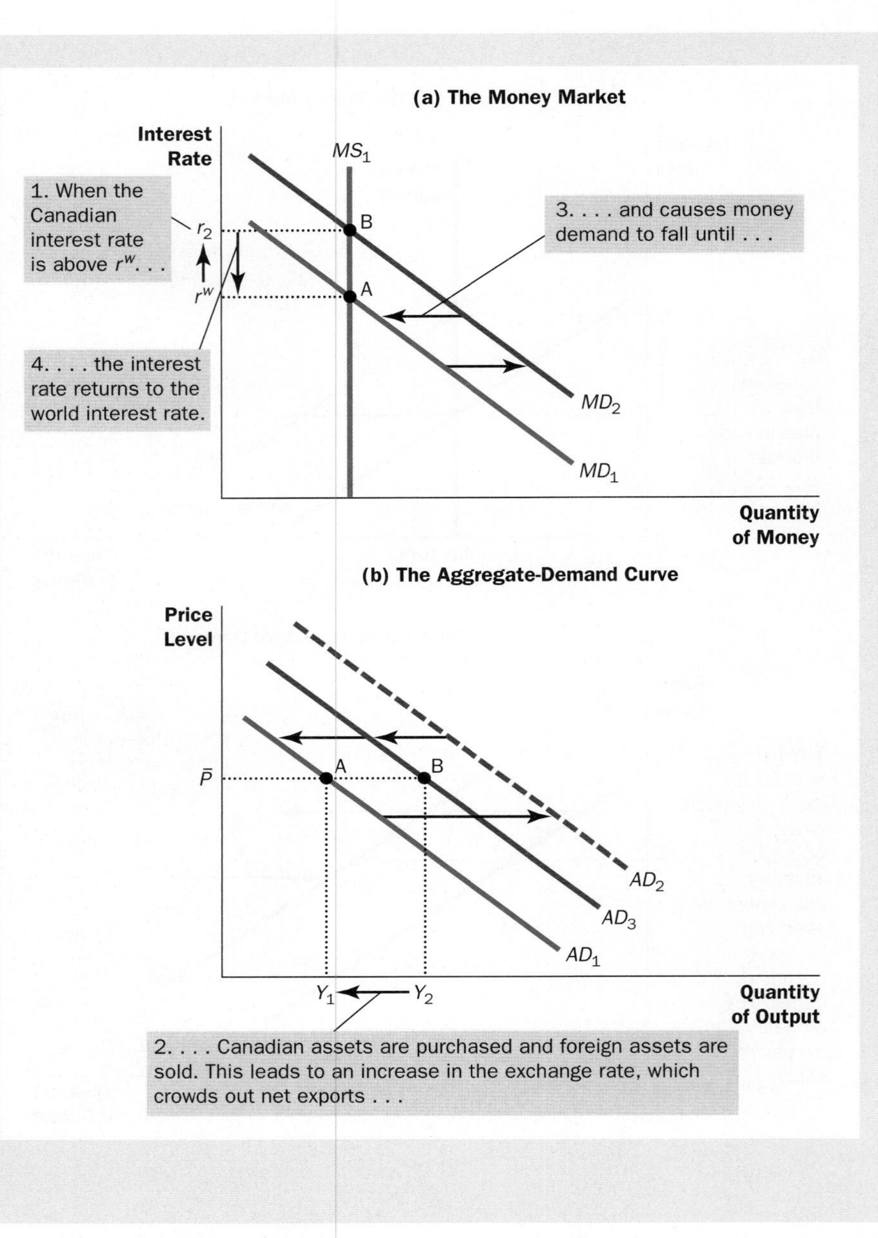

curve to the right from AD_1 to AD_2, as shown in panel (b) of Figure 15.10. The increase in demand for goods and services also increases the demand for money. In panel (a), this is shown by the shift of the demand for money curve from MD_1 to MD_2. Because the Bank of Canada has not changed the money-supply curve, the vertical money-supply curve remains the same. As a result, the interest rate must rise above the world interest rate, to r_2, in order to balance money supply and money demand.

Once again, the interest rate influences the quantity of goods and services demanded, as shown in panel (b). In particular, by increasing the cost of borrowing, the higher interest rate reduces the demand for residential and business investment. As a result, the quantity of goods and services demanded at the given price level, $\overline{P}$, falls. This is the crowding-out effect on investment, which is shown in panel (b) by the shift of the aggregate-demand curve from AD_2 to AD_3.

So far, all of this is exactly as it was previously. In a closed economy, the effect of a fiscal expansion would be summarized by the movement from point A to point B in panels (a) and (b) of Figure 15.10. In a small open economy like Canada, however, this cannot be the end of the story. We have left Canada's interest rate above the world interest rate. But, because of perfect capital mobility, Canada's interest rate must eventually adjust to equal the world interest rate. Something else must happen.

Flexible Exchange Rate We begin by assuming that the Bank of Canada has chosen to allow the exchange rate to be flexible. As we saw in our examination of the effects of a monetary injection, the assumption about whether or not the exchange rate is flexible will prove to be an important one.

When Canada's interest rate rises above the world interest rate, Canadian and foreign savers find Canadian assets, which now pay interest rate r_2, to be more attractive than foreign assets that pay the world interest rate, r^w. As a result, Canadians and foreigners sell foreign assets and buy Canadian assets. Recall, again, our discussion in Chapter 13 that while people want to trade goods, services, and financial assets with people in other countries, they want to be paid for these things in their own currency. Thus, the switch from foreign assets to Canadian assets requires a corresponding purchase of Canadian dollars and sale of foreign currencies. In the market for foreign-currency exchange, the demand for Canadian dollars therefore increases, causing the dollar to appreciate in value and the real exchange rate to rise. The rise in the real exchange rate makes Canadian-produced goods and services more expensive relative to foreign-produced goods and services. Consequently, Canada's net exports decrease.

The reduction in net exports that results when a fiscal expansion in a small open economy with a flexible exchange rate raises the real exchange rate is called the **crowding-out effect on net exports**. The decrease in net exports causes the quantity of Canadian-produced goods and services demanded at the given price level, $\overline{P}$, to decrease. This is shown in panel (b) of Figure 15.10 by the shift of the aggregate-demand curve from AD_3 to AD_1. This fall in demand for Canadian-produced goods and services also decreases the demand for money. This is shown in panel (a) by the shift of the money-demand curve from MD_2 to MD_1. This shift must be large enough to cause Canada's interest rate to fall back to the world interest rate. The end result of all of these adjustments is a decrease in the demand for money back to MD_1, a return of Canada's interest rate to the world interest rate, and a decrease in the quantity demanded of Canadian-produced goods and services, represented by a shift in the aggregate-demand curve back to AD_1.

crowding-out effect on net exports
the offset in aggregate demand that results when expansionary fiscal policy in a small open economy with a flexible exchange rate raises the real exchange rate and thereby reduces net exports

To sum up: *In a small open economy, an expansionary fiscal policy causes the dollar to appreciate. Because this appreciation of the dollar causes net exports to fall, there is an additional crowding-out effect that reduces the demand for Canadian-produced goods and services. In the end, fiscal policy has no lasting effect on aggregate demand.*

Fixed Exchange Rate Now consider the effect on aggregate demand of a fiscal policy in an open economy when the Bank of Canada chooses to prevent changes in the value of the exchange rate. Recall that the Bank of Canada can influence the value of the exchange rate by buying and selling foreign currencies in what are known as *foreign exchange market operations.* When firms and households are selling Canadian dollars in the market for foreign-currency exchange (thereby increasing the supply of dollars in that market), the Bank of Canada can prevent the value of the exchange rate from falling by increasing the demand for Canadian dollars in that market. It does this by selling foreign currencies and purchasing Canadian dollars. Similarly, when firms and households are buying Canadian dollars in the market for foreign-currency exchange (thereby increasing the demand for dollars in that market), the Bank of Canada can prevent the value of the exchange rate from rising by increasing the supply of Canadian dollars in that market. It does this by buying foreign currencies and selling Canadian dollars.

Figure 15.11 shows how expansionary fiscal policy affects aggregate demand in this case. As always, we start with the Canadian interest rate equal to the world interest rate, r^w. In panel (a), the demand for money, MD_1, is equal to the supply of money, MS_1, at r^w. An increase in government expenditures increases the quantity of goods and services demanded for given price level $\overline{P}$. As a result of the multiplier effect, the quantity of goods and services demanded increases by more than the increase in government expenditures. This is shown in panel (b) by the shift in the aggregate-demand curve from AD_1 to AD_2. As before, the increase in demand for goods and services requires that people hold more of their wealth as money. This is represented in panel (a) by the shift of the money-demand curve from MD_1 to MD_2. The increase in the demand for money increases the Canadian interest rate to r_2. As we have seen, this increase in the interest rate crowds out business and residential investment and reduces the demand for goods and services. In panel (b), this crowding-out effect on investment is shown by the shift of the aggregate-demand curve from AD_2 to AD_3.

So far, we have described the adjustment from point A to point B in panels (a) and (b) of Figure 15.11. This is how a closed economy would respond to a fiscal expansion. In an open economy, because Canada's interest rate is above the world interest rate, there is a tendency for the exchange rate to change. In particular, because Canada's interest rate is above the world interest rate, Canadian assets are preferred to foreign assets. The switch from foreign to Canadian assets requires a corresponding purchase of dollars in the market for foreign-currency exchange, and this causes the dollar to appreciate in value. We have seen that if the Bank of Canada allows the exchange rate to appreciate, net exports will fall and the economy will adjust back to point A in panels (a) and (b), so that the fiscal expansion has no lasting impact on aggregate demand. If the Bank of Canada chooses to fix the value of the exchange rate, it must increase the supply of dollars in the market for foreign-currency exchange. To do this, the Bank of Canada purchases foreign currency in exchange for dollars.

The actions taken by the Bank of Canada to fix the exchange rate also have an effect on the money supply. As we explained in Chapter 10 and reviewed earlier in this chapter, when the Bank of Canada buys something, it causes the money supply to increase. When the Bank of Canada sells something, it causes the money supply to decrease. Thus, when the Bank of Canada buys foreign currency in order to prevent the value of the dollar from changing, it expands the money supply. This is shown in panel (a) of Figure 15.11 by the shift of the money-supply

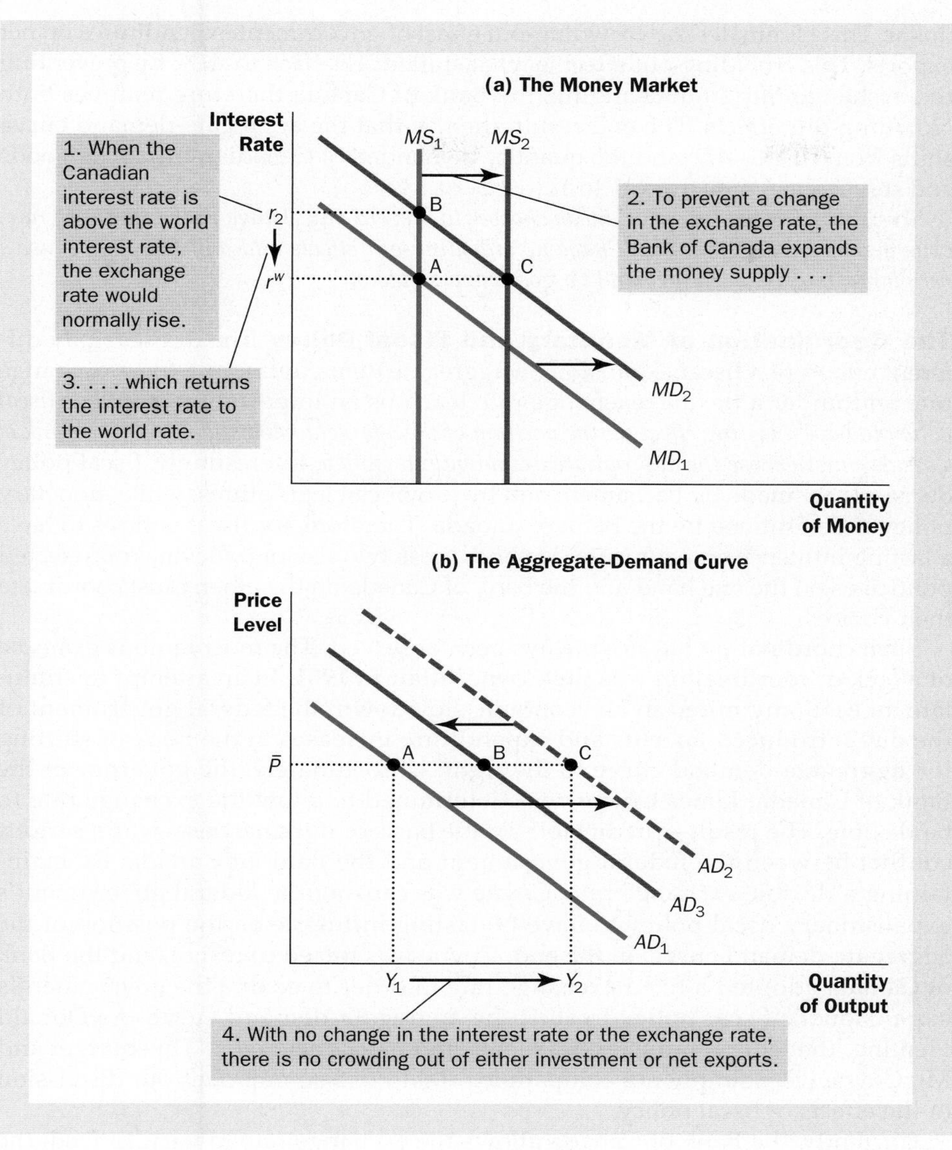

FIGURE 15.11

A Fiscal Expansion in an Open Economy with a Fixed Exchange Rate

In a closed economy, an increase in government purchases causes the interest rate to rise and output to increase. This is shown by the movements from point A to point B in panels (a) and (b). In an open economy, the fact that the Canadian interest rate is above the world interest rate would normally cause the dollar to appreciate, causing net exports to be crowded out. To prevent an increase in the value of the dollar, the Bank of Canada increases the money supply by selling dollars in the market for foreign-currency exchange. This increase in the money supply, shown by the shift of the money-supply curve from MS_1 to MS_2 in panel (a), also prevents the interest rate from changing. As a result, both forms of crowding out are avoided. In the end, the fiscal expansion has a large effect on aggregate demand, shown by the shift of AD_1 to AD_2 in panel (b) and the movement from point A to point C in both panels.

curve from MS_1 to MS_2. The shift of the money-supply curve must be sufficient to lower Canada's interest rate back to the world interest rate. Only when Canada's interest rate is equal to the world interest rate is there no reason for the exchange rate to change.

The expansion of the money supply has two effects. First, it lowers the Canadian interest rate back to the world interest rate. This eliminates the crowding-out effect of government expenditures on business and residential investment. This crowding-out effect is what shifted AD_2 back to AD_3. The second effect of the monetary expansion is that, by lowering the Canadian interest rate to the level of the world interest rate, it removes the reason for the appreciation of the dollar. This eliminates the crowding-out effect of government expenditures on net exports. This crowding-out effect is what shifted AD_3 back to AD_1. By preventing the exchange rate from changing, the Bank of Canada therefore removes both crowding-out effects. The end result, then, is that the aggregate-demand curve shifts from AD_1 to AD_2 and the quantity demanded of Canadian-produced goods and services expands from Y_1 to Y_2.

To sum up: *If the Bank of Canada chooses to prevent any change in the exchange rate, expansionary fiscal policy will have no crowding-out effects and will therefore cause a very large increase in the demand for goods and services.*

The Coordination of Monetary and Fiscal Policy The dramatically different effects of a fiscal expansion on aggregate demand under a fixed exchange rate and under a flexible exchange rate teach us an important lesson: *For fiscal policy to have a lasting effect on the position of the aggregate-demand curve, the Bank of Canada must choose the appropriate exchange rate policy.* Interestingly, fiscal policy decisions are made by Parliament and by provincial legislatures, while monetary policy is determined by the Bank of Canada. Therefore, for fiscal policies to have a lasting influence on aggregate demand, these two sets of policymakers, elected politicians on the one hand and the Bank of Canada on the other, must coordinate their choices.

Such coordination has not always been observed. The most famous example of a lack of coordination was the Coyne Affair in 1961. In an attempt to stimulate an economy mired in an economic slowdown, the federal government of the day introduced tax cuts and expenditure increases in the hope of shifting the aggregate-demand curve to the right. Unfortunately, the governor of the Bank of Canada, James Coyne, was determined to allow the exchange rate to be flexible. The result—predictable on the basis of our analysis—was a serious conflict between the federal government and the Bank of Canada. By maintaining a flexible exchange rate, Coyne was causing the federal government's expansionary fiscal policy to have no lasting influence on the position of the aggregate-demand curve. In the end, Coyne was forced to resign, and the Bank of Canada adopted a fixed exchange rate in order to enable the government's expansionary fiscal policy to shift the aggregate-demand curve. As Donald Fleming, the federal minister of Finance in 1961, concluded, "This budget and Mr. Coyne were simply not compatible." Table 15.2 summarizes our discussion of the effects of fiscal policy.

Currently, the Bank of Canada allows the exchange rate to vary. Indeed, the Canada–U.S. exchange rate garners considerable attention, and changes in its value often lead off news programs. On occasion, however, the Bank of Canada influences the value of the exchange rate by buying and selling dollars in the market for foreign-currency exchange. It does this to try to slow the rate of change in the exchange rate and thereby ensure that changes are not too abrupt. When considering what you think will be the outcome of fiscal policy choices of Canadian governments, therefore, you need to have a sense of how much the Bank of Canada will choose to try to influence the exchange rate. If the Bank of Canada is likely to allow the exchange rate to vary freely, then fiscal policy changes will have no lasting effect on the position of the aggregate-demand curve. If, however, you judge that the Bank of Canada will try to minimize changes in the exchange rate, fiscal policy changes will have a lasting influence on the position of the aggregate-demand curve.

TABLE 15.2

The Effects of Fiscal Policy: Summary

How Does Fiscal Policy Shift the Aggregate-Demand Curve in a Closed Economy?

1. An increase in government spending shifts the aggregate-demand curve to the right.
2. Increased spending increases money demand, and this increases the interest rate.
3. The rise in the interest rate crowds out investment and reduces somewhat the size of the shift in the aggregate-demand curve.

How Does Fiscal Policy Shift the Aggregate-Demand Curve in an Open Economy with a Flexible Exchange Rate?

1. Due to perfect capital mobility, and ignoring differences in default risk and taxes, Canada's interest rate must equal the world interest rate. We begin with $r = r^w$.
2. An increase in government spending shifts the aggregate-demand curve to the right.
3. Increased spending increases money demand, and this increases the interest rate.
4. The rise in the interest rate crowds out investment and reduces somewhat the size of the shift in the aggregate-demand curve. Now $r > r^w$.
5. Canadian assets now pay a higher interest rate than foreign assets. Increased demand for Canadian assets means an increased demand for dollars in the market for foreign-currency exchange. The dollar appreciates.
6. The appreciation of the dollar reduces net exports.
7. The fall in net exports means a fall in spending, a fall in money demand, and a fall in interest rates until $r = r^w$.
8. The increase in government spending has no lasting influence on the position of the aggregate-demand curve.

How Does Fiscal Policy Shift the Aggregate-Demand Curve in an Open Economy with a Fixed Exchange Rate?

1. Due to perfect capital mobility, and ignoring differences in default risk and taxes, Canada's interest rate must equal the world interest rate. We begin with $r = r^w$.
2. An increase in government spending shifts the aggregate-demand curve to the right.
3. Increased spending increases money demand, and this increases the interest rate.
4. The rise in the interest rate crowds out investment and reduces somewhat the size of the shift in the aggregate-demand curve. Now $r > r^w$.
5. Canadian assets now pay a higher interest rate than foreign assets. Increased demand for Canadian assets means an increased demand for dollars in the market for foreign-currency exchange. To fix the exchange rate, the Bank of Canada increases the supply of dollars traded in the market for foreign-currency exchange by purchasing foreign currency.
6. The purchase of foreign currency by the Bank of Canada causes the money supply to increase, and this causes the interest rate to fall until $r = r^w$.
7. The increase in the money supply shifts the aggregate-demand curve even farther to the right.

15-2g Changes in Taxes

The other important instrument of fiscal policy, besides the level of government purchases, is the level of taxation. When the government cuts personal income taxes, for instance, it increases households' take-home pay. Households will save some of this additional income, but they will also spend some of it on consumer goods. Because it increases consumer spending, the tax cut shifts the aggregate-demand curve to the right. Similarly, a tax increase depresses consumer spending and shifts the aggregate-demand curve to the left.

The size of the shift in aggregate demand resulting from a tax change is also affected by the multiplier and crowding-out effects. When the government cuts taxes and stimulates consumer spending, earnings and profits rise, which further stimulates consumer spending. This is the multiplier effect. At the same time, higher income leads to higher money demand, which tends to raise interest rates. Higher interest rates make borrowing more costly, which reduces investment spending. This is the crowding-out effect on investment. Depending on the size of the multiplier and crowding-out effects, the shift in aggregate demand could be larger or smaller than the tax change that causes it.

In a small open economy like Canada, whether the change in the position of the aggregate-demand curve that results from a change in taxes is a lasting one depends on the central bank's decision whether to allow the exchange rate to change. If the Bank of Canada chooses to allow the exchange rate to vary freely, tax changes will not have a lasting effect on the position of the aggregate-demand curve. For example, a tax cut, by pushing Canada's interest rate above the world interest rate, will cause the exchange rate to rise. Thus, the tax cut crowds out net exports just as an increase in government expenditures does. If, however, the Bank of Canada chooses to fix the value of the exchange rate, a tax cut has a large and lasting effect on the position of the aggregate-demand curve. This is so because the Bank of Canada, in order to fix the value of the exchange rate, must purchase dollars in the market for foreign-currency exchange, causing the money supply to increase. The increase in the money supply removes the crowding-out effects on investment and net exports that prevent fiscal policy from having a lasting influence on aggregate demand.

15-2h Deficit Reduction

During the 1990s and 2000s, Canadian governments at both the federal and the provincial levels took steps to reduce or eliminate their budget deficits. Some governments relied primarily on reductions in expenditures, others relied primarily on tax increases, and others relied on a combination of both approaches. Some analysts at the time suggested that efforts to reduce government deficits would be harmful to the Canadian economy because they cause a reduction in aggregate demand. Our discussion of the effects of changes in government expenditures and taxes under fixed and flexible exchange rates sheds light on this claim. As long as the Bank of Canada chooses to allow the exchange rate to vary freely, there is no reason to expect that efforts at deficit reduction will have any lasting influence on the position of the aggregate-demand curve. Once again, we see the importance of a coordinated effort between Canadian governments and the Bank of Canada. Deficit reduction can have a minimal impact on the level of aggregate demand if the central bank adopts the appropriate exchange-rate policy.

Explain how a decrease in government expenditures affects the money market and the position of the aggregate-demand curve. What is the effect for (a) a closed economy; (b) an open economy when the Bank of Canada allows the exchange rate to vary; and (c) an open economy when the Bank of Canada chooses to maintain a fixed value for the exchange rate?

FYI How Fiscal Policy Might Affect Aggregate Supply

So far our discussion of fiscal policy has stressed how changes in government purchases and changes in taxes influence the quantity of goods and services demanded. Most economists believe that the short-run macroeconomic effects of fiscal policy work primarily through aggregate demand. Yet fiscal policy can potentially also influence the quantity of goods and services supplied.

For instance, consider the effects of tax changes on aggregate supply. One of the ten principles of economics in Chapter 1 is that people respond to incentives. When government policymakers cut tax rates, workers get to keep more of each dollar they earn, so they have a greater incentive to work and produce goods and services. If they respond to this incentive, the quantity of goods and services supplied will be greater at each price level, and the aggregate-supply curve will shift to the right. Some economists, called *supply-siders*, have argued that the influence of tax cuts on aggregate supply is very large. Indeed, some supply-siders claim the influence is so large that a cut in tax rates will actually increase tax revenue by increasing worker effort. Most economists, however, doubt that the supply-side effects of cuts to tax rates are as large as this.

The fact that tax cuts cause the aggregate-supply curve to shift to the right is important because it suggests that tax cuts have a permanent effect on output. As we saw in Chapter 14, any shift in the aggregate-demand curve has only a temporary effect on output. Over time, as perceptions, wages, and prices adjust, the short-run aggregate-supply curve shifts to where the aggregate-demand curve intersects the long-run aggregate-supply curve. Unless the long-run aggregate-supply curve shifts, the shift in the aggregate-demand curve will have only a temporary effect on output. If tax cuts cause a shift to the right in the long-run aggregate-supply curve, then this represents a permanent increase in the natural level of output.

While this sounds like an exciting policy prescription—keep cutting tax rates and cause more and more permanent increases in output—we must remember that we need taxes to finance useful government programs. There would be no national defence, no social programs, and no publicly funded health care without taxes. A more sensible, although perhaps less exciting, policy prescription is to keep tax rates as low as possible given the need to finance desired government spending programs.

Like changes in taxes, changes in government purchases can also potentially affect aggregate supply. Suppose, for instance, that the government increases expenditure on a form of government-provided infrastructure, such as roads. Roads are used by private businesses to make deliveries to their customers, so an increase in the quantity of roads increases these businesses' productivity. Hence, when the government spends more on roads, it increases the quantity of goods and services supplied at any given price level and thus shifts the aggregate-supply curve to the right. The potential for causing a shift of the aggregate-supply curve to the right is why economists tend to favour increases in government spending that focus on expanding infrastructure spending.

15-3 Using Policy to Stabilize the Economy

We have seen how monetary and fiscal policy can affect the economy's aggregate demand for goods and services. These theoretical insights raise some important policy questions: Should policymakers use these instruments to control aggregate demand and stabilize the economy? If so, when? If not, why not?

15-3a The Case for Active Stabilization Policy

The Canadian economy is often subject to the effects of unexpected events. Conflicts in the Middle East, fluctuations in energy prices, exchange-rate fluctuations, and stock market booms and busts can all have serious impacts on the Canadian economy. Events such as these have often been responsible for large changes in output, employment, and income. We have seen that fiscal and monetary policy can be used to influence the position of the aggregate-demand curve and thereby cause changes in output, employment, and income. If we put these ideas together, we seem to have a strong case in favour of using policy instruments to offset the negative consequences of unexpected events. Simply put, unexpected expansions and contractions in the economy impose costs on people and firms in the form of unemployment, inflation, and uncertainty. If monetary and fiscal policy can be used to stabilize the economy, then surely these tools should be used to offset the harmful effects of economic fluctuations. This is the case in favour of using monetary and fiscal policy to stabilize the economy.

As we discussed in the preceding chapter, John Maynard Keynes's *The General Theory of Employment, Interest and Money* has been one of the most influential books ever written about economics. In it, Keynes emphasized the key role of aggregate demand in explaining short-run economic fluctuations. Keynes claimed that the government should actively stimulate aggregate demand when aggregate demand appeared insufficient to maintain production at its full-employment level. At the time Keynes wrote his book, the world's major economies were in the midst of the Great Depression. It is little wonder, then, that the Keynesian proposal to use policy instruments to lessen the severity of economic downturns proved popular. Keynes and his many followers were strong advocates of using policy instruments to stabilize the economy.

15-3b The Case against Active Stabilization Policy

Some economists argue that the government should avoid active use of monetary and fiscal policy to try to stabilize the economy. They claim that these policy instruments should be set to achieve long-run goals, such as rapid economic growth and low inflation, and that the economy should be left to deal with short-run fluctuations on its own. Although these economists may admit that monetary and fiscal policy can stabilize the economy in theory, they doubt whether it can do so in practice.

The primary argument against active monetary and fiscal policy is that these policies affect the economy with a long lag. As we have seen, monetary policy works by changing interest rates, which in turn influence investment spending. But many firms make investment plans far in advance. Thus, most economists believe that it takes at least six months for changes in monetary policy to have much effect on output and employment. Moreover, once these effects occur, they can last for several years. Critics of stabilization policy argue that because of this lag, the Bank of Canada should not try to fine-tune the economy. They claim that the Bank of Canada often reacts too late to changing economic conditions and, as a result, ends up being a cause of rather than a cure for economic fluctuations. These critics advocate a passive monetary policy, such as slow and steady growth in the money supply.

Fiscal policy also works with a lag, but unlike the lag in monetary policy, the lag in fiscal policy is largely attributable to the political process. In Canada, most changes in federal government spending and taxes must go through parliamentary committees in both the House of Commons and the Senate, and be passed by both legislative bodies. Completing this process can take months and, in some cases, years. By the time the change in fiscal policy is passed and ready to implement, the condition of the economy may well have changed.

These lags in monetary and fiscal policy are a problem in part because economic forecasting is so imprecise. If forecasters could accurately predict the condition of the economy a year in advance, then monetary and fiscal policymakers could look ahead when making policy decisions. In this case, policymakers could stabilize the economy, despite the lags they face. In practice, however, major recessions and depressions arrive without much advance warning. The best policymakers can do at any time is to respond to economic changes as they occur.

15-3c Automatic Stabilizers

All economists—both advocates and critics of stabilization policy—agree that the lags in implementation render policy less useful as a tool for short-run stabilization. The economy would be more stable, therefore, if policymakers could find a way to avoid some of these lags. In fact, they have. **Automatic stabilizers** are changes in fiscal policy that stimulate aggregate demand without policymakers having to take any deliberate action when the economy goes into a recession.

automatic stabilizers
changes in fiscal policy that stimulate aggregate demand when the economy goes into a recession, without policymakers having to take any deliberate action

The most important automatic stabilizer is the tax system. When the economy goes into a recession, the amount of taxes collected by the government falls automatically because almost all taxes are closely tied to economic activity. The personal income tax depends on households' incomes, sales taxes depend on levels of consumption, and the corporate income tax depends on firms' profits. Because incomes, consumption spending, and profits all fall in a recession, the government's tax revenue falls as well. This automatic tax cut stimulates aggregate demand, and thereby reduces the magnitude of economic fluctuations.

Government spending also acts as an automatic stabilizer. In particular, when the economy goes into a recession and workers are laid off, more people apply for Employment Insurance benefits, social assistance benefits, and other forms of income support. This automatic increase in government spending stimulates aggregate demand at exactly the time when aggregate demand is insufficient to maintain full employment. Indeed, when the unemployment insurance system was first enacted in the 1930s, economists who advocated this policy did so in part because of its power as an automatic stabilizer.

The automatic stabilizers in the Canadian economy are not sufficiently strong to prevent recessions completely. Nonetheless, without these automatic stabilizers, output and employment would probably be more volatile than they are. For evidence of this it might be useful to recall Figure 14.10. In discussing that figure, we noted that the falls in the growth rate of real output per capita associated with recessions since World War II are much smaller than the falls associated with the recessions of 1920 and the Great Depression of the 1930s. The relative smoothness of the line measuring the growth rate of real per capita GDP post–World War II compared to pre–World War II indicates that the amplitude of economic cycles in Canada has grown smaller over time. Most economists would identify the introduction of automatic stabilizers since World War II—stabilizers in the form of Employment Insurance, social assistance, and a tax system more sensitive to changes in income—as an important reason for the reduction in the size of economic cycles.

15-3d A Flexible Exchange Rate as an Automatic Stabilizer

In an open economy, policymakers can choose to make use of another type of automatic stabilizer: a flexible exchange rate. Suppose Canada's largest trading partner, the United States, slips into recession. As the incomes of American households and firms fall, they spend less and we can expect that they buy fewer Canadian-produced goods. Canada's net exports fall and the aggregate-demand curve shifts to the left.

If the Bank of Canada has chosen to allow the exchange rate to be flexible, we would expect the following to occur: The fall in net exports causes the incomes of Canadians to fall, and this reduces the demand for money. This causes Canada's interest rate to fall below the world interest rate. Both Canadians and foreigners sell Canadian assets in favour of foreign assets that pay the higher world interest rate. The switch from Canadian to foreign assets requires a corresponding sale of dollars in the market for foreign-currency exchange. The increased supply of dollars in the market for foreign-currency exchange causes the exchange rate to depreciate, and this causes net exports to increase. Canada's aggregate-demand curve now shifts back to the right, increasing the incomes of Canadians and increasing the demand for money until Canada's interest rate is again equal to the world interest rate. The recession in the United States has no lasting effects on the position of Canada's aggregate-demand curve.

This scenario demonstrates how allowing the exchange rate to be flexible enables policymakers to insulate the Canadian economy from the effects of foreign recessions. Given Canada's dependence on foreign trade, and hence Canada's exposure to the effects of foreign recessions, this would seem to be an attractive policy choice. Indeed, most economists favour flexible exchange rates, partly for this reason. Unfortunately, as economists are fond of saying, there is no such thing as a free lunch. That is, the benefits of a flexible exchange rate do not come without costs.

An important cost is the uncertainty that a flexible exchange rate introduces into the pricing decisions of exporting and importing firms. Unexpected changes in the exchange rate mean unexpected changes in the Canadian dollar prices of imported and exported goods. A firm hoping to produce goods for export might be discouraged from doing so if it cannot be sure of how many Canadian dollars it will end up receiving for goods it sells abroad.

These types of costs have sometimes led to a proposal that Canada form a monetary union with the United States. Advocates of this proposal argue that Canada should adopt the U.S. dollar as its currency and thereby avoid all uncertainty about the price importers will have to pay for U.S.-produced goods and the price exporters will receive for Canadian-produced goods sold in the United States. By eliminating this uncertainty, an important impediment to trade will be eliminated and the benefits of free trade will be maximized. At this point, the majority of economists judge that the benefit of using a flexible exchange rate as an automatic stabilizer exceeds the costs of the price uncertainty that a flexible exchange rate introduces.

How does a reduction in government spending affect the aggregate-demand curve? How does your answer differ if we consider a closed economy versus an open economy?

The Recession of 2008–09 (again)

How well did Canadian policymakers do in applying the lessons of our macroeconomic model when they responded to the recession of 2008–09? In earlier case studies, we described the origins of this recession and suggested that its major impact was felt in Canada via a fall in exports to the United States and a fall in liquidity; both influences were felt mainly via a shift to the left of the aggregate-demand curve.

In deciding how best to respond to the economic downturn, the first thing to be considered by Canada's fiscal and monetary policymakers was just how deep and prolonged the recession might be if they did nothing. This was an important consideration, because as we learned in Chapter 14, once the expectations of workers and firms caught up to the new reality of a lower level of economic output, the economy would eventually adjust back to the natural level of output. The only question was how long this would take. How long would people be left unemployed as the economy adjusted? If not very long, would it make sense to try to stabilize an economy that might soon return to full employment even without such an effort?

iStockphoto.com/cosmonaut

There is little doubt that when the magnitude of the crisis in the United States—and soon after, in the world—financial system came to light in 2007, the prevailing opinion was that without a policy response, the impact on the world economy would be very serious. Indeed, it was commonplace to hear that there was a potential for a repeat of the Great Depression of the 1930s. At the time, then, the prevailing opinion was that although policy influences the economy with a lag, the recession was not likely to be so short-lived as to cause the stimulus to take effect only after stimulus was no longer needed.

Having concluded that there was a strong case for a stabilization policy, the next question was in what form that stimulus should come. Our macroeconomic model suggests that in a small open economy, an effective response to an unexpected shift to the left of the aggregate-demand curve is to introduce an expansionary monetary policy while maintaining a flexible exchange rate. This is exactly what Canada's monetary policymaker, the Bank of Canada, did. In conjunction with central banks around the world, the Bank of Canada took steps to increase liquidity in the financial system and, in so doing, lowered interest rates and pushed the aggregate-demand curve back to the right.

What about fiscal policy? We used our macroeconomic model to suggest that fiscal policy is largely ineffective in a small open economy like Canada. Despite this, Canada's fiscal policymakers introduced a large fiscal stimulus of tax cuts and spending increases. Why? Our analysis of the effect of fiscal policy on the economy assumed a fiscal policy introduced in isolation. A feature of the fiscal expansion introduced in Canada during 2008 and 2009 is that it was introduced in coordination with other fiscal policymakers around the world and it was introduced in conjunction with an expansionary monetary policy. For both of these reasons, the crowding out of investment and net exports could be expected to be much less than otherwise and so fiscal policy more effective than otherwise.

It is also noteworthy that Canada's fiscal policymakers stressed that the fiscal stimulus should come in the form of spending on infrastructure that had been preapproved—popularly known as "shovel-ready" infrastructure spending. The reason for this was twofold. First, preapproved spending had already been through the legislative process of identifying and approving spending plans and so was more likely to expand aggregate demand very quickly and before the economy might recover on its own. Second, spending in infrastructure would not only increase aggregate demand but would also lead to a permanent increase in aggregate supply. Finally, it is worth noting that fiscal policymakers also stressed the need to rely on automatic stabilizers such as the Employment Insurance (EI) system. Changes in legislation were introduced to increase the availability of EI during the crisis.

So, how well did our policymakers do? Most economists would conclude that they implemented policies that can be supported by the conclusions drawn from the economic model we presented in this chapter. We noted in the previous chapter that at the time this case study was prepared (2015), fears of a major recession stemming from the financial crisis have largely passed and, as we saw in Figure 14.1, real GDP and investment spending continue to grow and the unemployment rate continues a gradual decline—though with some, hopefully temporary, increases in 2015. All of this suggests that the policies introduced in 2008 and 2009 were successful at stabilizing the economy. ■

15-4 A Quick Summary

We have accomplished quite a lot in this chapter. We have shown how fiscal and monetary policy can influence the position of the aggregate-demand curve in a closed economy and in a small open economy under both a fixed and a flexible exchange rate. Throughout this chapter we have made the assumption that the price level is relatively unresponsive to changing economic conditions. To emphasize the role of such price stickiness, we have assumed that the price level is fixed. This assumption characterizes the short run, the focus of this chapter. Figure 15.12

FIGURE 15.12 **The Effects of Expansionary Monetary and Fiscal Policies on the Aggregate-Demand Curve**
How fiscal and monetary policy affect the position of the aggregate-demand curve depends on whether the economy is closed or open. If the economy is open, the effect of fiscal and monetary policy depends on whether the Bank of Canada chooses to fix the value of the exchange rate or allow it to be flexible.

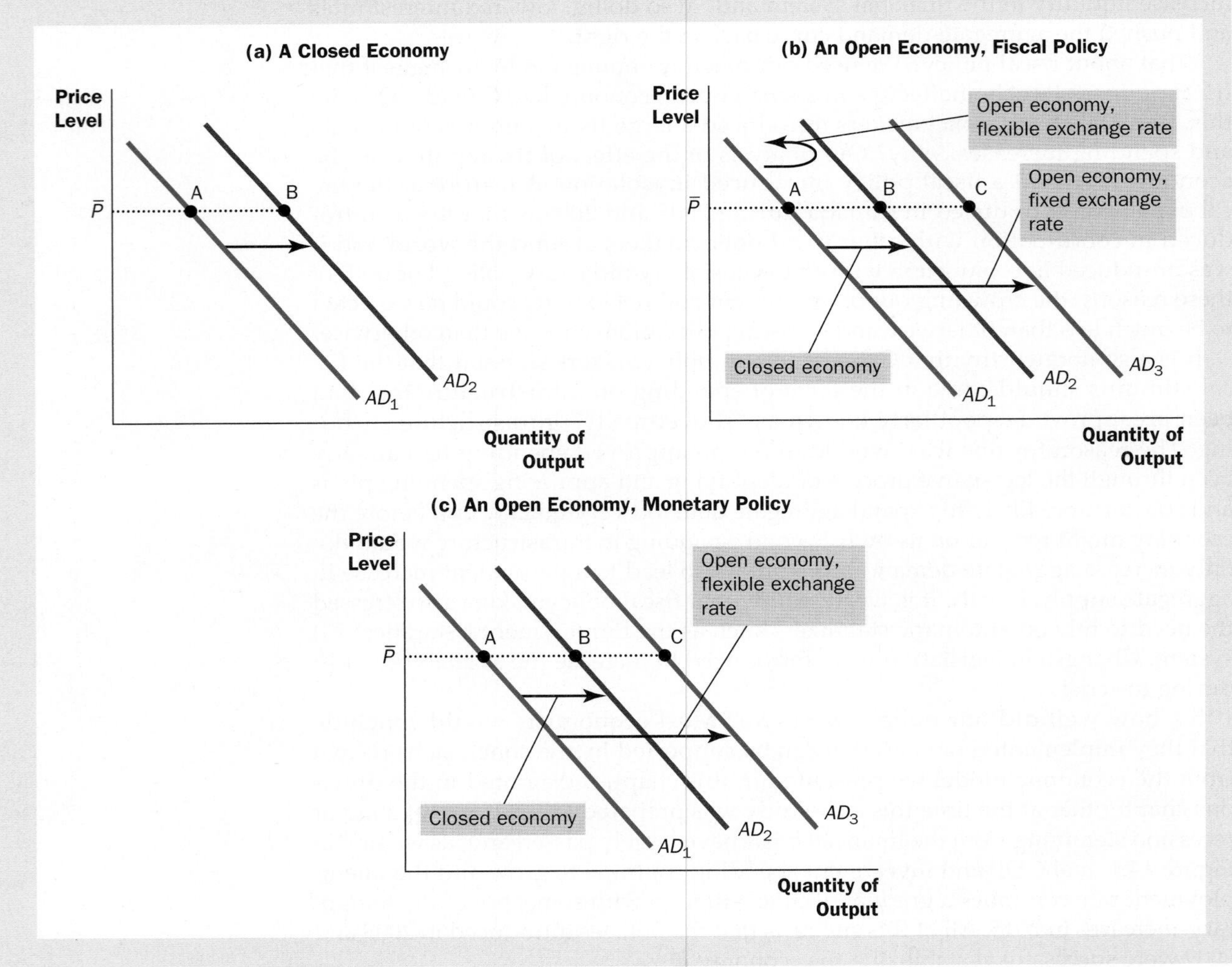

summarizes what we have discovered about how fiscal and monetary policy can be used to influence the position of the aggregate-demand curve in the short run.

Panel (a) in Figure 15.12 shows how the aggregate-demand curve shifts in response to expansionary fiscal and monetary policies in a closed economy. Our starting position is at point A on aggregate-demand curve AD_1. The price level is fixed at value $\overline{P}$. An expansionary fiscal policy (either an increase in government spending or a cut in taxes) and an expansionary monetary policy (an increase in the supply of money) both shift the aggregate-demand curve to the right (to position AD_2). In a closed economy, then, fiscal and monetary policies have the same effect on the position of the aggregate-demand curve. As we discussed in this chapter, they differ with respect to how they affect the interest rate: An expansionary fiscal policy causes the interest rate to increase because it causes the demand for money to increase; an expansionary monetary policy causes the interest rate to decrease because it involves an increase in the supply of money.

Panel (b) in Figure 15.12 shows how the aggregate-demand curve shifts in response to an expansionary fiscal policy in a small open economy. Once again, our starting position is at point A on aggregate-demand curve AD_1, with the price level fixed at value $\overline{P}$. If this was a closed economy, an expansionary fiscal policy would shift the aggregate-demand curve to position AD_2, and we would move from point A to point B at the fixed price level $\overline{P}$. In an open economy, the influence of an expansionary fiscal policy on the position of the aggregate-demand curve depends on whether the exchange rate is fixed or flexible.

Under a fixed exchange rate, the same expansionary fiscal policy that shifted AD_1 to AD_2 would shift AD_1 to AD_3, and we move from point A to point C. This occurs because the expansionary fiscal policy forces Canada's interest rate above the world interest rate and thus causes an increase in the demand for dollars traded in the market for foreign-currency exchange. To prevent the exchange rate from changing, the Bank of Canada must increase the supply of dollars in this market, something it accomplishes by buying foreign currencies. When the Bank of Canada buys something, it causes the money supply to increase, which is what gives us the second shift in the aggregate-demand curve.

Under a flexible exchange rate, the same expansionary fiscal policy that shifted AD_1 to AD_2 in a closed economy would have no lasting impact on the position of the aggregate-demand curve. The aggregate-demand curve would return to AD_1, and we would return to point A. This occurs because, while the expansionary fiscal policy once again forces Canada's interest rate above the world interest rate, this time the resulting increase in the demand for dollars traded in the market for foreign-currency exchange is not offset by the actions of the Bank of Canada. Instead, the Bank of Canada allows the exchange rate to appreciate, and this causes net exports to fall. The fall in net exports offsets the expansionary fiscal policy, with the net result that there is no lasting impact on the position of the aggregate-demand curve.

Panel (c) in Figure 15.12 shows how the aggregate-demand curve shifts in response to an expansionary monetary policy in a small open economy. Once again, our starting position is at point A on aggregate-demand curve AD_1, with the price level fixed at value $\overline{P}$. If this was a closed economy, an expansionary fiscal policy would shift the aggregate-demand curve to position AD_2, and we would move from point A to point B at the fixed price level $\overline{P}$. In an open economy, it makes sense for the Bank of Canada to pursue an expansionary monetary policy only if it allows the exchange rate to be flexible.

FYI Interest Rates in the Long Run and the Short Run

At this point, we should pause and reflect on a seemingly awkward embarrassment of riches. We appear to have many explanations of how the interest rate is determined. This embarrassment of riches is due to the fact that we have sought to explain the determination of the interest rate under a number of circumstances: in the short run and the long run, and in a closed economy and a small open economy. All of these explanations are correct, and each is useful for understanding the rest. It might be a good idea at this point to summarize their relationship to one another.

It is important to remind ourselves of the differences between the long-run and short-run behaviour of the economy. Three macroeconomic variables are of central importance: the economy's output of goods and services, the interest rate, and the price level. According to the classical macroeconomic theory that we developed in Chapters 7, 8, and 11, these variables are determined as follows:

1. *Output* is determined by the supplies of capital and labour and the available production technology for turning capital and labour into output. (We call this the natural level of output.) Changes in the price level have no influence on output.
2. In a closed economy, for any given level of output, the *interest rate* adjusts to balance the supply and demand for loanable funds. In a small open economy, the domestic interest rate is equal to the world interest rate. Net capital outflow (*NCO*) balances the supply and demand for loanable funds.
3. The *price level* adjusts to balance the supply and demand for money. Changes in the supply of money lead to proportionate changes in the price level.

These are three of the essential propositions of classical economic theory. Most economists believe that these propositions do a good job of describing how the economy works *in the long run*.

Yet these propositions do not hold in the short run. As we discussed in the preceding chapter, many prices are slow to adjust to changes in the money supply; this is reflected in a short-run aggregate-supply curve that is upward sloping rather than vertical. For issues concerning the short run, then, it is best to think about the economy as follows:

1. The *price level* is stuck at some level (based on previously formed expectations) and, in the short run, is relatively unresponsive to changing economic conditions.
2. In a closed economy, for any given price level, the *interest rate* adjusts to balance the supply and demand for money. The price level cannot adjust to balance the supply and demand for money as it does in the long run because of price stickiness. In a small open economy, the interest rate must adjust to equal the world interest rate. With a flexible exchange rate, this adjustment requires a change in the exchange rate. By affecting net exports, a change in the exchange rate affects output and thus the demand for money. In this case, then, the demand for money adjusts to balance the supply and demand for money at the world interest rate. With a fixed exchange rate, the adjustment of the domestic interest rate to the world interest rate requires the Bank of Canada to buy and sell foreign currencies, and this causes changes in the supply of money. In this case, then, the supply of money adjusts to balance the supply and demand for money at the world interest rate.
3. The level of *output* responds to net changes in the aggregate demand for goods and services that remain after the crowding-out effects induced by interest rate and exchange-rate changes are taken into account.

Thus, the different theories of the interest rate are useful for different purposes. When thinking about the long-run determinants of interest rates, it is best to keep in mind the loanable-funds theory. By contrast, when thinking about the short-run determinants of interest rates, it is best to keep in mind the liquidity-preference theory and, in a small open economy, the fact that the Canadian interest rate must equal the world interest rate.

Under a flexible exchange rate, the same expansionary monetary policy that shifted AD_1 to AD_2 would shift AD_1 to AD_3, and we would move from point A to point C. This occurs because the expansionary monetary policy forces Canada's interest rate below the world interest rate and thus causes an increase in the supply of dollars traded in the market for foreign-currency exchange. By causing the exchange rate to depreciate, the monetary expansion causes net exports to increase, giving us the second shift in the aggregate-demand curve.

Before leaving this quick summary, it is worthwhile to reiterate a point we have raised before: The predictions listed in this summary are based on an economic model characterized by a number of simplifications and assumptions. In macroeconomic courses you take in the future, some of these assumptions and simplifications will be relaxed. The result will be that some of the conclusions drawn from these models will need to be modified and restated. As we discussed in Chapter 2, constructing models based on simplifying assumptions and then observing how predictions generated by the model change with these assumptions is a part of the scientific method. Having said that, it is nonetheless true that the basic models presented in this chapter provide a very useful way of thinking about the effects of fiscal and monetary policies on aggregate demand in open and closed economies.

15-5 Conclusion

Before policymakers make any change in policy, they need to consider all the effects of their decisions. Earlier in the book we examined classical models of the economy that describe the long-run effects of monetary and fiscal policy. There we saw how fiscal policy influences saving, investment, and long-run growth, and how monetary policy influences the price level and the inflation rate.

In this chapter we examined the short-run effects of monetary and fiscal policy. We saw how these policy instruments can change the aggregate demand for goods and services and, thereby, alter the economy's production and employment in the short run. When Parliament reduces government spending in order to balance the budget, it needs to consider both the long-run effects on saving and growth and the short-run effects on aggregate demand and employment. When the Bank of Canada reduces the growth rate of the money supply, it must take into account the long-run effect on inflation as well as the short-run effect on production. In the next chapter we discuss the transition between the short run and the long run in more detail, and we see that policymakers often face a tradeoff between long-run and short-run goals.

summary

- In developing a theory of short-run economic fluctuations, Keynes proposed the theory of liquidity preference to explain the determinants of the interest rate. According to this theory, the interest rate adjusts to balance the supply and demand for money.
- An increase in the price level raises money demand and increases the interest rate that brings the money market into equilibrium. Because the interest rate represents the cost of borrowing, a higher interest rate reduces investment and, thereby, the quantity of goods and services demanded. In a small open economy, an increase in the price level also increases the real exchange rate. An increase in the real exchange rate makes Canadian-produced goods and services more expensive relative to foreign-produced goods and services. As a result, Canada's net exports fall, reducing the quantity demanded of Canadian goods and services. The downward-sloping aggregate-demand curve expresses these negative relationships between the price level and the quantity demanded.
- Policymakers can influence aggregate demand with monetary policy. An increase in the money supply reduces the equilibrium interest rate for any given price level. Because a lower interest rate stimulates investment spending, the aggregate-demand curve shifts to the right. In a small open economy, the lower interest rate also means a fall in the exchange rate. Because a lower exchange rate increases the quantity demanded of Canadian-produced goods and services, a monetary injection in a small open economy shifts the aggregate-demand curve farther to the right than it does in a closed economy. Conversely, a decrease in the money supply raises the equilibrium interest rate for any given price level and shifts the aggregate-demand curve to the left. In a small open economy, the

higher interest rate also means a rise in the exchange rate and, consequently, a fall in net exports. In a small open economy, then, a monetary contraction shifts the aggregate-demand curve farther to the left than it does in a closed economy.

- Policymakers can also influence aggregate demand with fiscal policy. An increase in government purchases or a cut in taxes shifts the aggregate-demand curve to the right. A decrease in government purchases or an increase in taxes shifts the aggregate-demand curve to the left.
- When the government alters spending or taxes, the resulting shift in aggregate demand can be larger or smaller than the fiscal change. The multiplier effect tends to amplify the effects of fiscal policy on aggregate demand. The crowding-out effect on investment tends to dampen the effects of fiscal policy on aggregate demand. The multiplier effect is much smaller in an open economy than in a closed economy.
- In a small open economy with perfect capital mobility, fiscal policy may or may not cause a lasting shift in the aggregate-demand curve. This depends on whether the Bank of Canada allows the exchange rate to vary freely. If the Bank of Canada allows the exchange rate to be flexible, fiscal policy has no lasting effect on the position of the aggregate-demand curve. This is so because the change in the exchange rate exerts an effect on net exports that is opposite to the fiscal policy in its influence on aggregate demand. If the Bank of Canada chooses to fix the value of the exchange rate, there is no such counteracting influence from net exports. In fact, by acting to fix the value of the exchange rate, the Bank of Canada causes the aggregate-demand curve to shift farther than it would in a closed economy. As a result, fiscal policy has a lasting effect on the position of the aggregate-demand curve.
- Because monetary and fiscal policy can influence aggregate demand, the government sometimes uses these policy instruments in an attempt to stabilize the economy. Economists disagree about how active the government should be in this effort. According to advocates of active stabilization policy, unexpected changes in economic conditions shift aggregate demand; if the government does not respond, the result is undesirable and unnecessary fluctuations in output and employment. According to critics of active stabilization policy, monetary and fiscal policy work with such long lags that attempts at stabilizing the economy often end up being destabilizing.

KEY **concepts**

theory of liquidity preference, *p. 352*
flexible exchange rate, *p. 362*
fixed exchange rate, *p. 363*
fiscal policy, *p. 366*
multiplier effect, *p. 366*
crowding-out effect on investment, *p. 370*
crowding-out effect on net exports, *p. 373*
automatic stabilizers, *p. 381*

QUESTIONS FOR **review**

1. What is the theory of liquidity preference? How does it help explain the downward slope of the aggregate-demand curve?
2. Use the theory of liquidity preference to explain how a decrease in the money supply affects the aggregate-demand curve. Consider the effects in both a closed economy and a small open economy.
3. The government spends $3 billion to buy police cars. Explain why aggregate demand might increase by more than $3 billion. Explain why aggregate demand might increase by less than $3 billion. Under what conditions might aggregate demand not change at all?
4. Suppose that survey measures of business confidence indicate that a wave of pessimism about Canada's economic prospects is sweeping the country. As a consequence, firms announce their intention to delay new spending on plants and equipment. If policymakers do nothing, what will happen to aggregate demand? What should the Bank of Canada do if it wants to stabilize aggregate demand? If the Bank of Canada does nothing, what might Parliament do to stabilize aggregate demand?
5. Give an example of a government policy that acts as an automatic stabilizer. Explain why this policy has this effect.

QUICK CHECK **multiple choice**

1. In a closed economy, if the central bank wants to expand aggregate demand, it can _____ the money supply, which would _____ the interest rate.
   a. increase, increase
   b. increase, decrease
   c. decrease, increase
   d. decrease, decrease
2. In a closed economy, if the government wants to contract aggregate demand, it can _____ government purchases or _____ taxes.
   a. increase, increase
   b. increase, decrease
   c. decrease, increase
   d. decrease, decrease
3. When the Bank of Canada increases the bank rate, commercial banks are ______ reserves and this in turn causes the money supply to _________ .
   a. discouraged from borrowing, contract
   b. encouraged to borrow, expand
   c. discouraged from borrowing, expand
   d. encouraged to borrow, contract.
4. In a small open economy, the increase in aggregate demand resulting from an increase in government spending is _____ if the exchange rate is _____ than if it is _____.
   a. larger, flexible, fixed
   b. larger, fixed, flexible
   c. smaller, fixed, flexible
   d. always zero
5. In a small open economy, the increase in aggregate demand resulting from an increase in the money supply is _____ if the exchange rate is _____ than if it is _____.
   a. larger, flexible, fixed
   b. larger, fixed, flexible
   c. smaller, flexible, fixed
   d. always zero
6. Which of the following is an example of an automatic stabilizer?
   a. When the economy goes into a recession, more people become eligible for employment insurance benefits.
   b. When the economy goes into a recession, stock prices decline, particularly for firms in cyclical industries.
   c. When the economy goes into a recession, Parliament begins hearings about a possible stimulus package.
   d. When the economy goes into a recession, the Bank of Canada changes its target for the overnight rate.

PROBLEMS AND **applications**

1. Explain how each of the following developments would affect the supply of money, the demand for money, and the interest rate. For each case, show what happens in a closed economy and in a small open economy. Illustrate your answers with diagrams.
   a. The Bank of Canada's bond traders buy bonds in open-market operations.
   b. An increase in credit card availability reduces the cash people hold.
   c. Households decide to hold more money to use for holiday shopping.
   d. A wave of optimism boosts business investment and expands aggregate demand.
   e. An increase in oil prices shifts the short-run aggregate-supply curve to the left.
2. Suppose banks install automated teller machines on every block and, by making cash readily available, reduce the amount of money people want to hold.
   a. Assume the Bank of Canada does not change the money supply. According to the theory of liquidity preference, what happens to the interest rate? What happens to aggregate demand? Assume a closed economy.
   b. If the Bank of Canada wants to stabilize aggregate demand, how should it respond?
3. This chapter explains that expansionary monetary policy reduces the interest rate and thus stimulates demand for investment goods. Explain how such a policy also stimulates the demand for net exports.
4. Suppose economists observe that in a closed economy an increase in government spending of $10 billion raises the total demand for goods and services by $30 billion.
   a. If these economists ignore the possibility of crowding out of investment, what would they estimate the marginal propensity to consume (*MPC*) to be?
   b. Now suppose the economists allow for crowding out. Would their new estimate of the *MPC* be larger or smaller than their initial one?

5. Suppose the government of a closed economy reduces taxes by $20 billion, that there is no crowding out of investment, and that the marginal propensity to consume is $\frac{3}{4}$.
   a. What is the initial effect of the tax reduction on aggregate demand?
   b. What additional effects follow this initial effect? What is the total effect of the tax cut on aggregate demand?
   c. How does the total effect of this $20 billion tax cut compare with the total effect of a $20 billion increase in government purchases? Why?
6. Suppose government spending increases in a closed economy. Would the effect on aggregate demand be larger (a) if the Bank of Canada took no action in response or (b) if the Bank was committed to maintaining a fixed interest rate? Explain.
7. In which of the following circumstances is expansionary fiscal policy more likely to lead to a short-run increase in investment? Explain.
   a. when the investment accelerator is large, or when it is small
   b. when the interest sensitivity of investment is large, or when it is small
   c. when the marginal propensity to import is small, or when it is large
8. Suppose the Bank of Canada contracts the money supply in an effort to reduce aggregate demand by a particular amount, say $10 billion. If Canada was a closed economy, would the amount by which the Bank of Canada would need to reduce the supply of money to accomplish this goal be greater or smaller than the amount it would need to reduce the supply of money if Canada was an open economy with a flexible exchange rate?
9. Suppose that the world interest rate rises. What happens to the position of the aggregate-demand curve in Canada? Assume that the Bank of Canada allows the exchange rate to be flexible. How does your answer change if you assume that the Bank of Canada maintains a fixed exchange rate? Illustrate your answer with diagrams.
10. Suppose that U.S. income rises. As a result, Canada's exports to the United States increase. What happens to the position of the aggregate-demand curve in Canada? Assume that the Bank of Canada allows the exchange rate to be flexible. How does your answer change if you assume that the Bank of Canada maintains a fixed exchange rate? Illustrate your answer with diagrams.
11. Suppose that the Bank of Canada decides to expand the money supply.
    a. Why would it be counterproductive for the Bank of Canada to fix the value of the exchange rate?
    b. What is the effect of this policy on the interest rate in the long run? How do you know?
12. For various reasons, fiscal policy changes automatically when output and employment fluctuate.
    a. Explain why tax revenue changes when the economy goes into a recession.
    b. Explain why government spending changes when the economy goes into a recession.
    c. If the government was to operate under a strict balanced-budget rule, what would it have to do in a recession? Would that make the recession more or less severe?

Spencer Platt/Thinkstock

CHAPTER
16

The Short-Run Tradeoff between Inflation and Unemployment

LEARNING
objectives

In this chapter, you will ...

1 Learn why policymakers face a short-run tradeoff between inflation and unemployment
2 Consider why the inflation–unemployment tradeoff disappears in the long run
3 See how supply shocks can shift the inflation–unemployment tradeoff
4 Consider the short-run cost of reducing the rate of inflation
5 See how policymakers' credibility might affect the cost of reducing inflation

Two closely watched indicators of economic performance are inflation and unemployment. When Statistics Canada releases data on these variables each month, policymakers are eager to hear the news. Some commentators have added together the inflation rate and the unemployment rate to produce a *misery index*, which purports to measure the health of the economy.

How are these two measures of economic performance related to each other? Earlier in the book we discussed the long-run determinants of unemployment and the long-run determinants of inflation. We saw that the natural rate of unemployment depends on various features of the labour market, such as minimum-wage laws, the generosity of Employment Insurance, the market power of unions, the role of efficiency wages, and the effectiveness of job search. By contrast, the inflation rate depends primarily on growth in the money supply, which a nation's central bank controls. In the long run, therefore, inflation and unemployment are largely unrelated problems.

In the short run, just the opposite is true. One of the ten principles of economics discussed in Chapter 1 is that society faces a short-run tradeoff between inflation and unemployment. If monetary and fiscal policymakers expand aggregate demand and move the economy up along the short-run aggregate-supply curve, they can lower unemployment for a while, but only at the cost of higher inflation. If policymakers contract aggregate demand and move the economy down the short-run aggregate-supply curve, they can lower inflation, but only at the cost of temporarily higher unemployment.

In this chapter we examine this tradeoff more closely. The relationship between inflation and unemployment is a topic that has attracted the attention of some of the most important economists of the last half century. The best way to understand this relationship is to see how thinking about it has evolved over time. As we will see, the history of thought regarding inflation and unemployment since the 1950s is inextricably connected to the history of the economies of North America and Western Europe. These two histories will show why the tradeoff between inflation and unemployment holds in the short run, why it does not hold in the long run, and what issues it raises for economic policymakers.

16-1 The Phillips Curve

"Probably the single most important macroeconomic relationship is the Phillips curve." These are the words of economist George Akerlof from the lecture he gave when he received the Nobel Prize in economic sciences in 2001. The **Phillips curve** shows the short-run tradeoff between inflation and unemployment. We begin our story with the discovery of the Phillips curve and its migration to North America.

Phillips curve
a curve that shows the short-run tradeoff between inflation and unemployment

16-1a Origins of the Phillips Curve

The origins and early development of the Phillips curve had an international flavour. In 1958, New Zealand economist A. W. Phillips published an article in the British journal *Economica* that would make him famous. The article was entitled "The Relationship between Unemployment and the Rate of Change of Money Wages in the United Kingdom, 1861–1957." In it, Phillips showed a negative correlation between the rate of unemployment and the rate of inflation. That is, Phillips showed that years with low unemployment tend to have high inflation, and years with high unemployment tend to have low inflation. (Phillips examined inflation in nominal wages rather than inflation in prices, but for our purposes that distinction is not important. These two measures of inflation usually move together.) Phillips concluded that two important macroeconomic variables—inflation and unemployment—were linked in a way that economists had not previously appreciated.

Two years later, Canadian economist Richard Lipsey confirmed and extended Phillips's observations. Lipsey used quantitative methods to derive a more accurate estimate of the change in inflation associated with particular rates of unemployment. In doing so, he introduced a methodology that economists would follow for many years to come.

Although the work of Phillips and Lipsey was based on data for the United Kingdom, researchers quickly confirmed their findings using data from many other countries. In the same year that Lipsey's article appeared, two American economists, Paul Samuelson and Robert Solow, entered the fray by testing the Phillips–Lipsey hypothesis using U.S. data. In their contribution, Samuelson and Solow reasoned that the negative correlation between inflation and unemployment that they found in U.S. data, and that others were finding in data from other countries, arose because low unemployment was associated with high aggregate demand and because high demand puts upward pressure on wages and prices throughout the economy. Samuelson and Solow dubbed the negative association between inflation and unemployment the *Phillips curve*. Figure 16.1 shows an example of a Phillips curve that reflects the hypothesis put forward by Samuelson and Solow.

Samuelson and Solow were interested in the Phillips curve because they believed that it held important lessons for policymakers. In particular, they suggested that the Phillips curve offers policymakers a menu of possible economic outcomes. By altering monetary and fiscal policy to influence aggregate demand, policymakers could choose any point on this curve. Point A offers high unemployment and low inflation. Point B offers low unemployment and high inflation. Policymakers might prefer both low inflation and low unemployment, but the historical data as summarized by the Phillips curve indicate that this combination

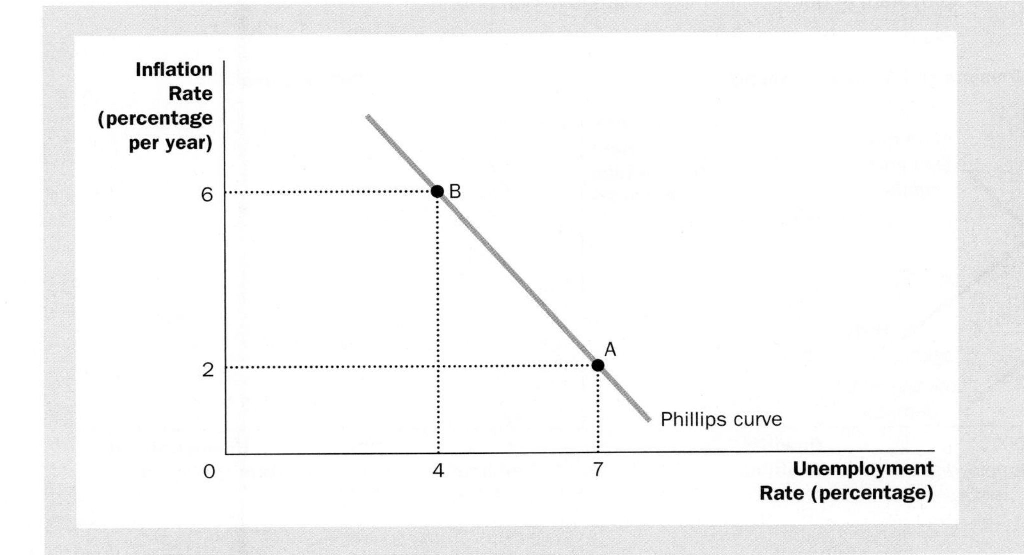

FIGURE 16.1

The Phillips Curve

The Phillips curve illustrates a negative association between the inflation rate and the unemployment rate. At point A, inflation is low and unemployment is high. At point B, inflation is high and unemployment is low.

is impossible. According to Samuelson and Solow, policymakers face a tradeoff between inflation and unemployment, and the Phillips curve illustrates that tradeoff. Thus, at this very early stage in the development of the Phillips curve, it seemed to economists that policymakers faced a permanent tradeoff between inflation and unemployment.

16-1b Aggregate Demand, Aggregate Supply, and the Phillips Curve

The model of aggregate demand and aggregate supply provides an easy explanation for the menu of possible outcomes described by the Phillips curve. *The Phillips curve simply shows the combinations of inflation and unemployment that arise in the short run as shifts in the aggregate-demand curve move the economy along the short-run aggregate-supply curve.* As we saw in Chapter 14, an increase in the aggregate demand for goods and services leads, in the short run, to a larger output of goods and services and a higher price level. Larger output means greater employment and, thus, a lower rate of unemployment. In addition, whatever the previous year's price level happens to be, the higher the price level in the current year, the higher the rate of inflation. Thus, shifts in aggregate demand push inflation and unemployment in opposite directions in the short run—a relationship illustrated by the Phillips curve.

To see more fully how this works, let's consider an example. To keep the numbers simple, imagine that the price level (as measured, for instance, by the consumer price index) equals 100 in the year 2020. Figure 16.2 shows two possible

FIGURE 16.2

How the Phillips Curve Is Related to the Model of Aggregate Demand and Aggregate Supply

This figure assumes a price level of 100 for the year 2020 and charts possible outcomes for the year 2021. Panel (a) shows the model of aggregate demand and aggregate supply. If aggregate demand is low, the economy is at point A; output is low (7500), and the price level is low (102). If aggregate demand is high, the economy is at point B; output is high (8000), and the price level is high (106). Panel (b) shows the implications for the Phillips curve. Point A, which arises when aggregate demand is low, has high unemployment (7 percent) and low inflation (2 percent). Point B, which arises when aggregate demand is high, has low unemployment (4 percent) and high inflation (6 percent).

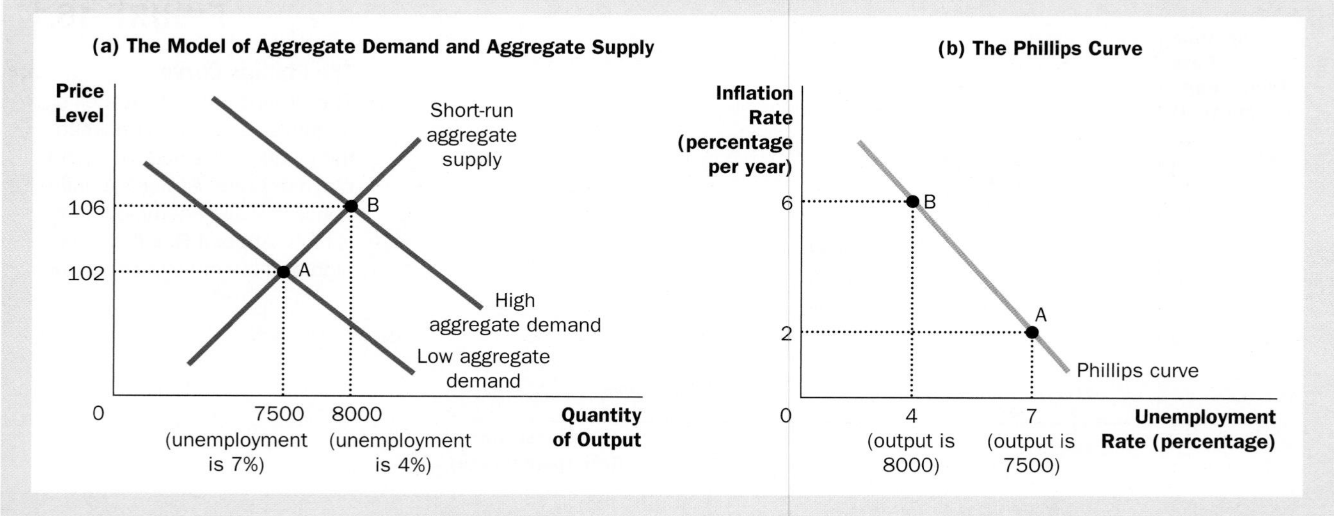

outcomes that might occur in the year 2021. Panel (a) shows the two outcomes using the model of aggregate demand and aggregate supply. Panel (b) illustrates the same two outcomes using the Phillips curve.

In panel (a) of the figure, we can see the implications for output and the price level in the year 2021. If the aggregate demand for goods and services is relatively low, the economy experiences outcome A. The economy produces output of 7500, and the price level is 102. By contrast, if aggregate demand is relatively high, the economy experiences outcome B. Output is 8000, and the price level is 106. Thus, higher aggregate demand moves the economy to an equilibrium with higher output and a higher price level.

In panel (b) of the figure, we can see what these two possible outcomes mean for unemployment and inflation. Because firms need more workers when they produce a greater output of goods and services, unemployment is lower in outcome B than in outcome A. In this example, when output rises from 7500 to 8000, unemployment falls from 7 percent to 4 percent. Moreover, because the price level is higher at outcome B than at outcome A, the inflation rate (the percentage change in the price level from the previous year) is also higher. In particular, since the price level was 100 in the year 2020, outcome A has an inflation rate of 2 percent, and outcome B has an inflation rate of 6 percent. Thus, we can compare the two possible outcomes for the economy either in terms of output and the price level (using the model of aggregate demand and aggregate supply) or in terms of unemployment and inflation (using the Phillips curve).

As we saw in the preceding chapter, monetary and fiscal policy can shift the aggregate-demand curve. Therefore, monetary and fiscal policy can move the economy along the Phillips curve. Increases in the money supply, increases in government spending, or cuts in taxes expand aggregate demand and move the economy to a point on the Phillips curve with lower unemployment and higher inflation. Decreases in the money supply, cuts in government spending, or increases in taxes contract aggregate demand and move the economy to a point on the Phillips curve with lower inflation and higher unemployment. In this sense, the Phillips curve offers policymakers a menu of combinations of inflation and unemployment.

Draw the Phillips curve. Use the model of aggregate demand and aggregate supply to show how policy can move the economy from a point on this curve with high inflation to a point with low inflation.

16-2 Shifts in the Phillips Curve: The Role of Expectations

The Phillips curve seems to offer policymakers a menu of possible inflation–unemployment outcomes. But does this menu of choices remain the same over time? Is the downward-sloping Phillips curve a stable relationship on which policymakers can rely? These are the questions that economists took up in the late 1960s.

16-2a The Long-Run Phillips Curve

In 1968, economist Milton Friedman published a paper in the *American Economic Review,* based on an address he had recently given as president of the American Economic Association. The paper, entitled "The Role of Monetary Policy," contained sections on "What Monetary Policy Can Do" and "What Monetary

Policy Cannot Do." Friedman argued that one thing monetary policy cannot do, other than for only a short time, is pick a combination of inflation and unemployment on the Phillips curve. At about the same time, another economist, Edmund Phelps, also published a paper denying the existence of a long-run tradeoff between inflation and unemployment. Based on his contributions to this debate, Phelps would win the Nobel Prize in economic sciences in 2006.

Friedman and Phelps based their conclusions on classical principles of macroeconomics, which we discussed in Chapters 7 through 13. Recall that classical theory points to growth in the money supply as the primary determinant of inflation. But classical theory also states that monetary growth does not have real effects—it merely alters all prices and nominal incomes proportionately. In particular, monetary growth does not influence those factors that determine the economy's unemployment rate, such as the market power of unions, the role of efficiency wages, or the process of job search. Friedman and Phelps concluded that there is no reason to think the rate of inflation would, *in the long run,* be related to the rate of unemployment.

Here, in his own words, is Friedman's view about what central banks can hope to accomplish in the long run:

> The monetary authority controls nominal quantities—directly, the quantity of its own liabilities [currency plus bank reserves]. In principle, it can use this control to peg a nominal quantity—an exchange rate, the price level, the nominal level of national income, the quantity of money by one definition or another—or to peg the change in a nominal quantity—the rate of inflation or deflation, the rate of growth or decline in nominal national income, the rate of growth of the quantity of money. It cannot use its control over nominal quantities to peg a real quantity—the real rate of interest, the rate of unemployment, the level of real national income, the real quantity of money, the rate of growth of real national income, or the rate of growth of the real quantity of money.

These views have important implications for the Phillips curve. In particular, they imply that monetary policymakers face a long-run Phillips curve that is vertical, as in Figure 16.3. If the Bank of Canada increases the money supply slowly,

FIGURE 16.3

The Long-Run Phillips Curve

According to Friedman and Phelps, there is no tradeoff between inflation and unemployment in the long run. Growth in the money supply determines the inflation rate. Regardless of the inflation rate, the unemployment rate gravitates toward its natural rate. As a result, the long-run Phillips curve is vertical.

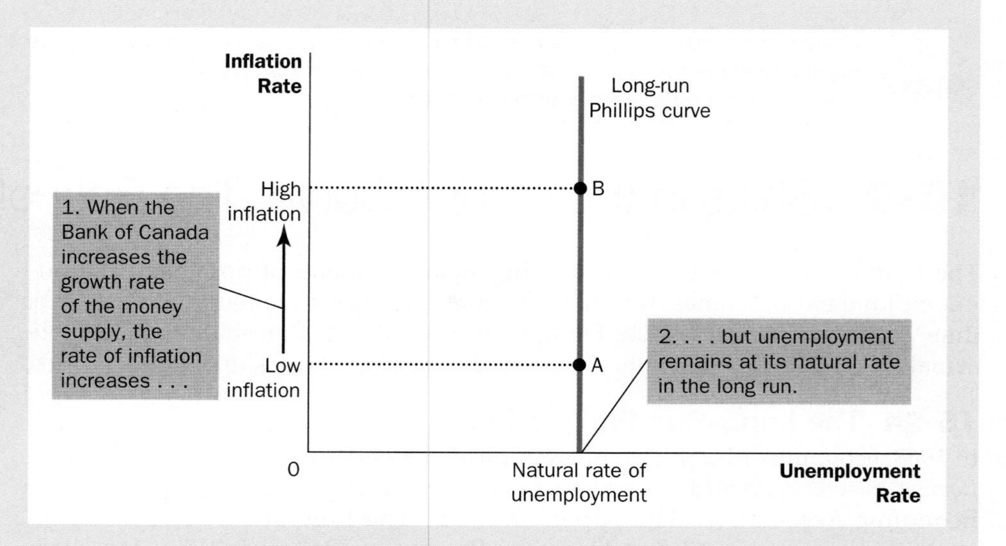

the inflation rate is low, and the economy finds itself at point A. If the Bank of Canada increases the money supply quickly, the inflation rate is high, and the economy finds itself at point B. In either case, the unemployment rate tends toward its normal level, called the *natural rate of unemployment*. The vertical long-run Phillips curve illustrates the conclusion that unemployment does not depend on money growth and inflation in the long run.

The vertical long-run Phillips curve is, in essence, one expression of the classical idea of monetary neutrality. As you may recall, we expressed this idea in Chapter 14 with a vertical long-run aggregate-supply curve. Indeed, as Figure 16.4 illustrates, the vertical long-run Phillips curve and the vertical long-run aggregate-supply curve are two sides of the same coin. In panel (a) of this figure, an increase in the money supply shifts the aggregate-demand curve to the right from AD_1 to AD_2. As a result of this shift, the long-run equilibrium moves from point A to point B. The price level rises from P_1 to P_2, but because the aggregate-supply curve is vertical, output remains the same. In panel (b), more rapid growth in the money supply raises the inflation rate by moving the economy from point A to point B. But because the Phillips curve is vertical, the rate of unemployment is the same at these two points. Thus, the vertical long-run aggregate-supply curve and the vertical long-run Phillips curve both imply that monetary policy influences nominal variables (the price level and the inflation rate) but not real variables (output and unemployment). Regardless of the monetary policy pursued by the Bank of Canada, output and unemployment are, in the long run, at their natural rates.

FIGURE 16.4

How the Long-Run Phillips Curve Is Related to the Model of Aggregate Demand and Aggregate Supply

Panel (a) shows the model of aggregate demand and aggregate supply with a vertical aggregate-supply curve. When expansionary monetary policy shifts the aggregate-demand curve to the right from AD_1 to AD_2, the equilibrium moves from point A to point B. The price level rises from P_1 to P_2, while output remains the same. Panel (b) shows the long-run Phillips curve, which is vertical at the natural rate of unemployment. Expansionary monetary policy moves the economy from lower inflation (point A) to higher inflation (point B) without changing the rate of unemployment.

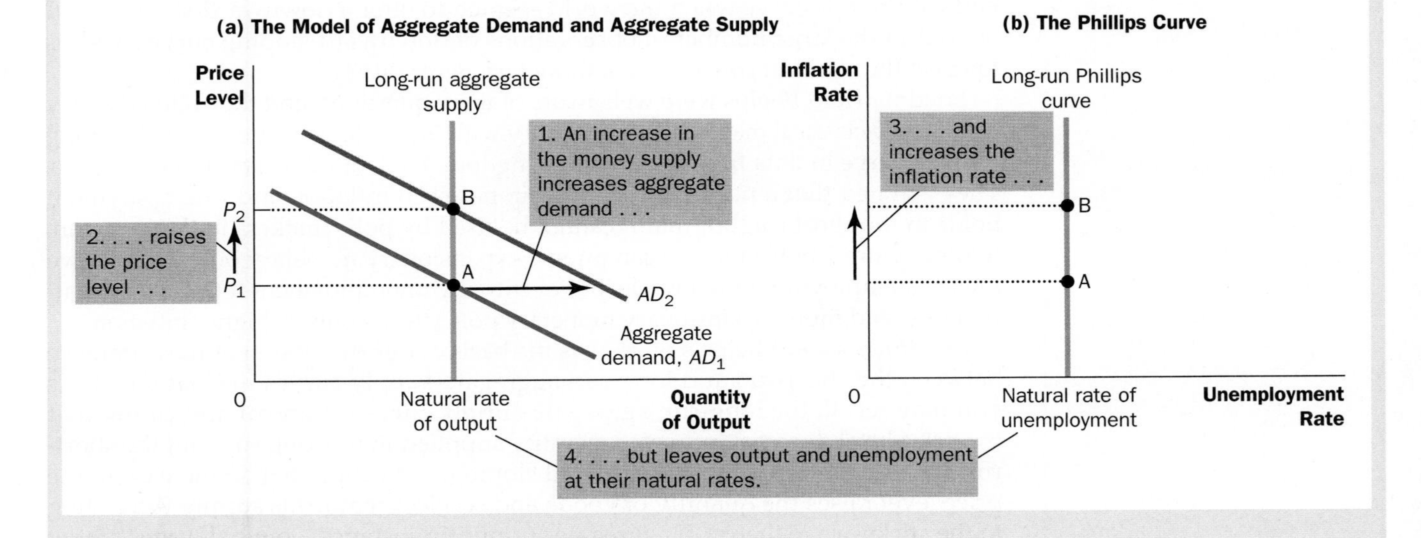

16-2b The Meaning of "Natural"

What is so "natural" about the natural rate of unemployment? Friedman and Phelps used this adjective to describe the unemployment rate toward which the economy tends to gravitate in the long run. Yet the natural rate of unemployment is not necessarily the socially desirable rate of unemployment. Nor is the natural rate of unemployment constant over time. For example, suppose that a newly formed union uses its market power to raise the real wages of some workers above the equilibrium level. The result is an excess supply of workers and, therefore, a higher natural rate of unemployment. This unemployment is "natural" not because it is good but because it is beyond the influence of monetary policy. More rapid money growth would not reduce the market power of the union or the level of unemployment; it would lead only to more inflation.

Although monetary policy cannot influence the natural rate of unemployment, other types of policy can. To reduce the natural rate of unemployment, policymakers should look to policies that improve the functioning of the labour market. Earlier in the book we discussed how various labour-market policies, such as minimum-wage laws, collective-bargaining laws, Employment Insurance, and job-training programs, affect the natural rate of unemployment. A policy change that reduced the natural rate of unemployment would shift the long-run Phillips curve to the left. In addition, because lower unemployment means more workers are producing goods and services, the quantity of goods and services supplied would be larger at any given price level, and the long-run aggregate-supply curve would shift to the right. The economy could then enjoy lower unemployment and higher output for any given rate of money growth and inflation.

16-2c Reconciling Theory and Evidence

At first, the denial by Friedman and Phelps of a long-run tradeoff between inflation and unemployment might not seem persuasive. Their argument was based on an appeal to *theory*. By contrast, the negative correlation between inflation and unemployment uncovered by Phillips and Lipsey using U.K. data, and confirmed by economists using data from many countries, was based on *observation*, not theory. Why should anyone believe that policymakers faced a vertical Phillips curve when the world seemed to offer a downward-sloping one? Shouldn't the large number of observations of downward-sloping curves lead us to reject the classical conclusion of monetary neutrality?

Friedman and Phelps were well aware of these questions, and they offered a way to reconcile classical macroeconomic theory with the finding of a downward-sloping Phillips curve in data from the United Kingdom, the United States, and elsewhere. They claimed that a negative relationship between inflation and unemployment holds in the short run but that it cannot be used by policymakers in the long run. In other words, policymakers can pursue expansionary monetary policy to achieve lower unemployment for a while, but eventually unemployment returns to its natural rate, and more expansionary monetary policy leads only to higher inflation.

Friedman's and Phelps's work was the basis of our discussion of the difference between the short-run and long-run aggregate-supply curves in Chapter 14. As you may recall, the long-run aggregate-supply curve is vertical, indicating that the price level does not influence quantity supplied in the long run. But the short-run aggregate-supply curve is upward sloping, indicating that an increase in the price level raises the quantity of goods and services that firms supply. According to the sticky-wage theory of aggregate supply, for instance, nominal wages are set in advance based on the price level that workers and firms expected to prevail. When prices come in higher than expected, firms have an incentive to increase production and employment; when prices are less than expected, firms reduce production and employment. Yet because the expected price level and nominal wages will eventually adjust, the positive relationship between the actual price level and quantity supplied applies only in the short run.

Friedman and Phelps applied this same logic to the Phillips curve. Just as the aggregate-supply curve slopes upward only in the short run, the tradeoff between inflation and unemployment holds only in the short run. And just as the long-run aggregate-supply curve is vertical, the long-run Phillips curve is also vertical. Once again, expectations are the key for understanding how the short run and the long run are related.

Friedman and Phelps introduced a new variable into the analysis of the inflation–unemployment tradeoff: *expected inflation*. Expected inflation measures how much people expect the overall price level to change. As we discussed in Chapter 14, the expected price level affects the wages and prices that people set and the perceptions of relative prices that they form. As a result, expected inflation is one factor that determines the position of the short-run aggregate-supply curve. In the short run, the Bank of Canada can take expected inflation (and thus the short-run aggregate-supply curve) as already determined. When the money supply changes, the aggregate-demand curve shifts, and the economy moves along a given short-run aggregate-supply curve. In the short run, therefore, monetary changes lead to unexpected fluctuations in output, prices, unemployment, and inflation. In this way, Friedman and Phelps explained the downward-sloping Phillips curve that had been observed in the data from so many countries.

The Bank of Canada's ability to create unexpected inflation by increasing the money supply exists only in the short run. In the long run, people come to expect whatever inflation rate the Bank of Canada chooses to produce. Because wages, prices, and perceptions will eventually adjust to the inflation rate, the long-run aggregate-supply curve is vertical. In this case, changes in aggregate demand, such as those due to changes in the money supply, do not affect the economy's output of goods and services. Thus, Friedman and Phelps concluded that unemployment returns to its natural rate in the long run.

16-2d The Short-Run Phillips Curve

The analysis of Friedman and Phelps can be summarized in the following equation (which is, in essence, another expression of the aggregate-supply equation we saw in Chapter 14):

$$\text{Unemployment rate} = \text{Natural rate of unemployment} - a\left(\text{Actual inflation} - \text{Expected inflation}\right)$$

This equation relates the unemployment rate to the natural rate of unemployment, actual inflation, and expected inflation. In the short run, expected inflation is given. As a result, higher actual inflation is associated with lower unemployment. (How much unemployment responds to unexpected inflation is determined by the size of a, a number that in turn depends on the slope of the short-run aggregate-supply curve.) In the long run, however, people come to expect whatever inflation the Bank of Canada produces. Thus, actual inflation equals expected inflation, and unemployment is at its natural rate.

This equation implies that there is no stable short-run Phillips curve. Each short-run Phillips curve reflects a particular expected rate of inflation. (To be precise, if you graph the equation, you'll find that the short-run Phillips curve intersects the long-run Phillips curve at the expected rate of inflation.) Whenever expected inflation changes, the short-run Phillips curve shifts.

According to Friedman and Phelps, it is dangerous to view the Phillips curve as a menu of options available to policymakers. To see why, imagine an economy at its natural rate of unemployment with low inflation and low expected inflation, shown in Figure 16.5 as point A. Now suppose that policymakers try to take advantage of the tradeoff between inflation and unemployment by using monetary or fiscal policy to expand aggregate demand. In the short run, when expected inflation is given, the economy goes from point A to point B. Unemployment falls below its natural rate, and inflation rises above expected inflation. As the economy moves from point A to point B, policymakers might think they have achieved permanently lower unemployment at the cost of higher inflation—a bargain that, if possible, might be worth making.

This situation, however, will not persist. Over time, people get used to this higher inflation rate, and they raise their expectations of inflation. When expected inflation rises, firms and workers start taking higher inflation into account when setting wages and prices. The short-run Phillips curve then shifts to the right, as shown in Figure 16.5. The economy ends up at point C, with higher inflation than at point A but with the same level of unemployment. Thus,

FIGURE 16.5

How Expected Inflation Shifts the Short-Run Phillips Curve

The higher the expected rate of inflation, the higher the short-run tradeoff between inflation and unemployment. At point A, expected inflation and actual inflation are both low, and unemployment is at its natural rate. If the Bank of Canada pursues an expansionary monetary policy, the economy moves from point A to point B in the short run. At point B, expected inflation is still low, but actual inflation is high. Unemployment is below its natural rate. In the long run, expected inflation rises, and the economy moves to point C. At point C, expected inflation and actual inflation are both high, and unemployment is back to its natural rate.

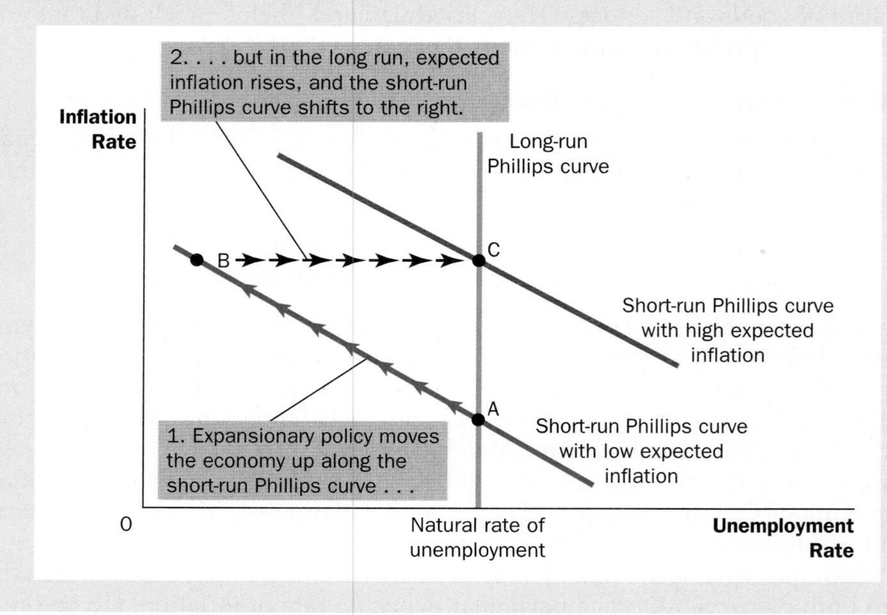

Friedman and Phelps concluded that policymakers face only a temporary tradeoff between inflation and unemployment. In the long run, expanding aggregate demand more rapidly will yield higher inflation without any reduction in unemployment.

16-2e The Natural Experiment for the Natural-Rate Hypothesis

Friedman and Phelps had made a bold prediction in 1968: If policymakers try to take advantage of the Phillips curve by choosing higher inflation in order to reduce unemployment, they will succeed at reducing unemployment only temporarily. This view—that unemployment eventually returns to its natural rate, regardless of the rate of inflation—is called the **natural-rate hypothesis**. A few years after Friedman and Phelps proposed this hypothesis, monetary and fiscal policymakers in Canada and the United States inadvertently created a natural experiment to test it. Their laboratory consisted of the Canadian and U.S. economies.

natural-rate hypothesis
the claim that unemployment eventually returns to its normal, or natural, rate, regardless of the rate of inflation

Before we see the outcome of this test, however, let's look at the data that Friedman and Phelps had when they made their prediction in 1968. Figure 16.6 shows the unemployment rate and the inflation rate in Canada for the period from 1956 to 1968. These data trace out a Phillips curve. From 1956 to 1961, inflation fell and the unemployment rate increased, while from 1961 to 1968, inflation increased and the unemployment rate fell, following virtually the same path. The economic data from this era seemed to confirm the existence of a stable tradeoff between inflation and unemployment.

The apparent success of the Phillips curve in the 1950s and 1960s made the prediction of Friedman and Phelps all the more bold. In 1958, Phillips had suggested

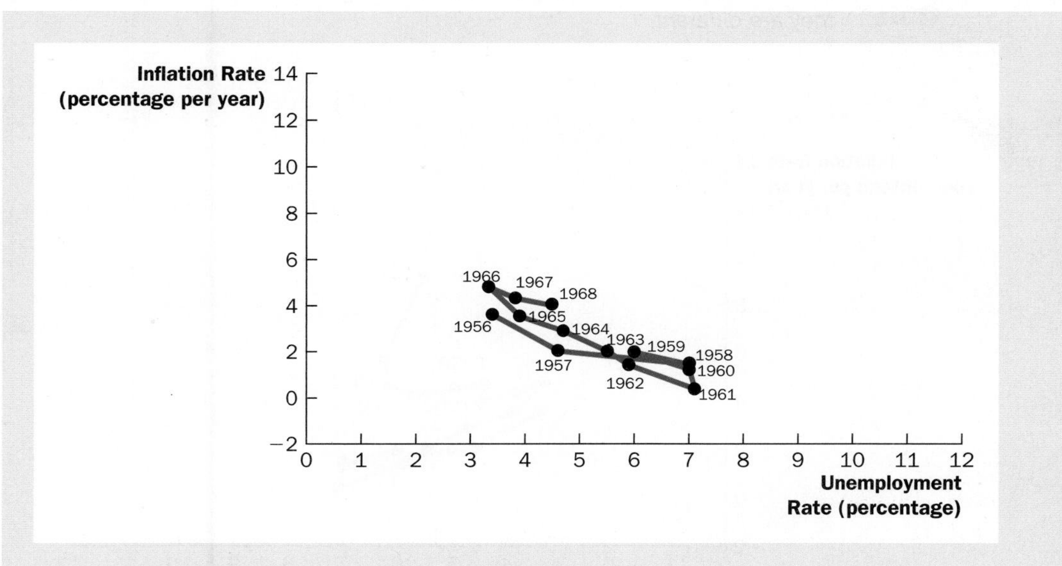

FIGURE 16.6

The Phillips Curve in the 1950s and 1960s

This figure uses annual data from 1956 to 1968 on the unemployment rate and on the inflation rate (as measured by the GDP deflator) to show the negative relationship between inflation and unemployment.

Sources: Data for 1966 to 1968 are from Statistics Canada, CANSIM, series V2062816 (unemployment rate) and V1997756 (GDP deflator). Data for 1956 to 1965 are from F.H. Leacy, ed., *Historical Statistics of Canada*, 2nd ed. (Ottawa: Statistics Canada, 1983), series D233 (unemployment rate) and series K17 (GDP deflator).

a negative association between inflation and unemployment. Another decade of data had confirmed the relationship for Canada, the United States, and many other countries. To some economists at the time, it seemed ridiculous to claim that the Phillips curve would break down once policymakers tried to take advantage of it.

But, in fact, that is exactly what happened. Beginning in the late 1960s, policies were enacted that expanded the aggregate demand for goods and services. In part, this expansion was due to fiscal policy: Federal and provincial government spending was increasing much faster than the economy. In part, it was due to monetary policy: Because the Bank of Canada was trying to hold down interest rates in the face of expansionary fiscal policy, during the period from 1969 to 1973 the quantity of money (as measured by M1) was allowed to increase at twice the annual rate it did during the period from 1956 to 1968. As a result, inflation stayed high (averaging 5.7 percent from 1969 to 1973, compared with 2.6 percent from 1956 to 1968). But, as Friedman and Phelps had predicted, unemployment did not stay low.

Figure 16.7 displays the history of inflation and unemployment from 1968 to 1973. It shows that the simple negative relationship between these two variables started to break down around 1970. In particular, as inflation remained high in the early 1970s, people's expectations of inflation caught up with reality, and the unemployment rate reverted to the 5 to 6 percent range that had prevailed in the early 1960s. Notice that the history illustrated in Figure 16.7 closely resembles the theory of a shifting short-run Phillips curve shown in Figure 16.5. By 1973, policymakers had learned that Friedman and Phelps were right: There is no tradeoff between inflation and unemployment in the long run.

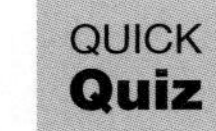

Draw the short-run Phillips curve and the long-run Phillips curve. Explain why they are different.

FIGURE 16.7

The Breakdown of the Phillips Curve

This figure highlights annual data from 1968 to 1973 on the unemployment rate and on the inflation rate (as measured by the GDP deflator). Notice that the Phillips curve of the 1960s breaks down in the early 1970s.

Sources: Data for 1968 to 1973 are from Statistics Canada, CANSIM, series V2062816 (unemployment rate) and V1997756 (GDP deflator).

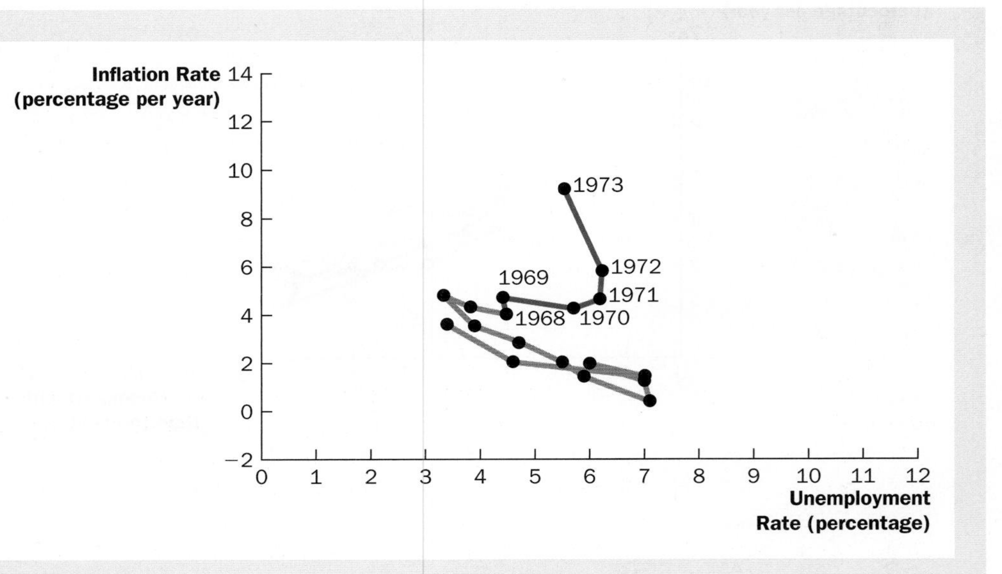

16-3 Shifts in the Phillips Curve: The Role of Supply Shocks

Friedman and Phelps had suggested in 1968 that changes in expected inflation shift the short-run Phillips curve, and the experience of the early 1970s convinced most economists that Friedman and Phelps were right. Within a few years, however, the economics profession would turn its attention to a different source of shifts in the short-run Phillips curve: shocks to aggregate supply.

This time, the shift in focus came not from two American economics professors but from events in the Middle East. The Organization of the Petroleum Exporting Countries (OPEC) was founded in 1960, but it was ineffectual at influencing oil prices until the early 1970s. Following a military takeover of the Libyan government in 1969, and following the success that country had in imposing new agreements on oil companies concerning pricing following the takeover, OPEC members began to act together to push up oil prices. At first, these efforts met with limited success. However, in the midst of the 1973 Middle East war, a war that had already caused oil prices to rise, OPEC met again and began to effectively exert its market power as a cartel in the world oil market. The countries of OPEC, such as Saudi Arabia, Kuwait, and Iraq, restricted the amount of crude oil they pumped and sold on world markets. Within a few years, this reduction in supply caused the price of oil to almost double.

A large increase in the world price of oil is an example of a supply shock. A **supply shock** is an event that directly affects firms' costs of production and thus the prices they charge; it shifts the economy's aggregate-supply curve and, as a result, the Phillips curve. For example, when an oil price increase raises the cost of producing gasoline, heating oil, tires, and many other products, it reduces the quantity of goods and services supplied at any given price level. As panel (a) of Figure 16.8 shows, this reduction in supply is represented by the leftward shift in the aggregate-supply curve from AS_1 to AS_2. The price level rises from P_1 to P_2, and output falls from Y_1 to Y_2. The combination of rising prices and falling output is sometimes called *stagflation*.

supply shock
an event that directly alters firms' costs and prices, shifting the economy's aggregate-supply curve and thus the Phillips curve

This shift in aggregate supply is associated with a similar shift in the short-run Phillips curve, shown in panel (b). Because firms need fewer workers to produce the smaller output, employment falls and unemployment rises. Because the price level is higher, the inflation rate—the percentage change in the price level from the previous year—is also higher. Thus, the shift in aggregate supply leads to higher unemployment and higher inflation. The short-run tradeoff between inflation and unemployment shifts to the right from PC_1 to PC_2.

Confronted with an adverse shift in aggregate supply, policymakers face a difficult choice between fighting inflation and fighting unemployment. If they contract aggregate demand to fight inflation, they will raise unemployment further. If they expand aggregate demand to fight unemployment, they will raise inflation further. In other words, policymakers face a less favourable tradeoff between inflation and unemployment than they did before the shift in aggregate supply: They have to live with a higher rate of inflation for a given rate of unemployment, a higher rate of unemployment for a given rate of inflation, or some combination of higher unemployment and higher inflation.

Faced with such an adverse shift in the Phillips curve, policymakers will ask whether the shift is temporary or permanent. The answer depends on how people

FIGURE 16.8

An Adverse Shock to Aggregate Supply

Panel (a) shows the model of aggregate demand and aggregate supply. When the aggregate-supply curve shifts to the left from AS_1 to AS_2, the equilibrium moves from point A to point B. Output falls from Y_1 to Y_2, and the price level rises from P_1 to P_2. Panel (b) shows the short-run tradeoff between inflation and unemployment. The adverse shift in aggregate supply moves the economy from a point with lower unemployment and lower inflation (point A) to a point with higher unemployment and higher inflation (point B). The short-run Phillips curve shifts to the right, from PC_1 to PC_2. Policymakers now face a worse tradeoff between inflation and unemployment.

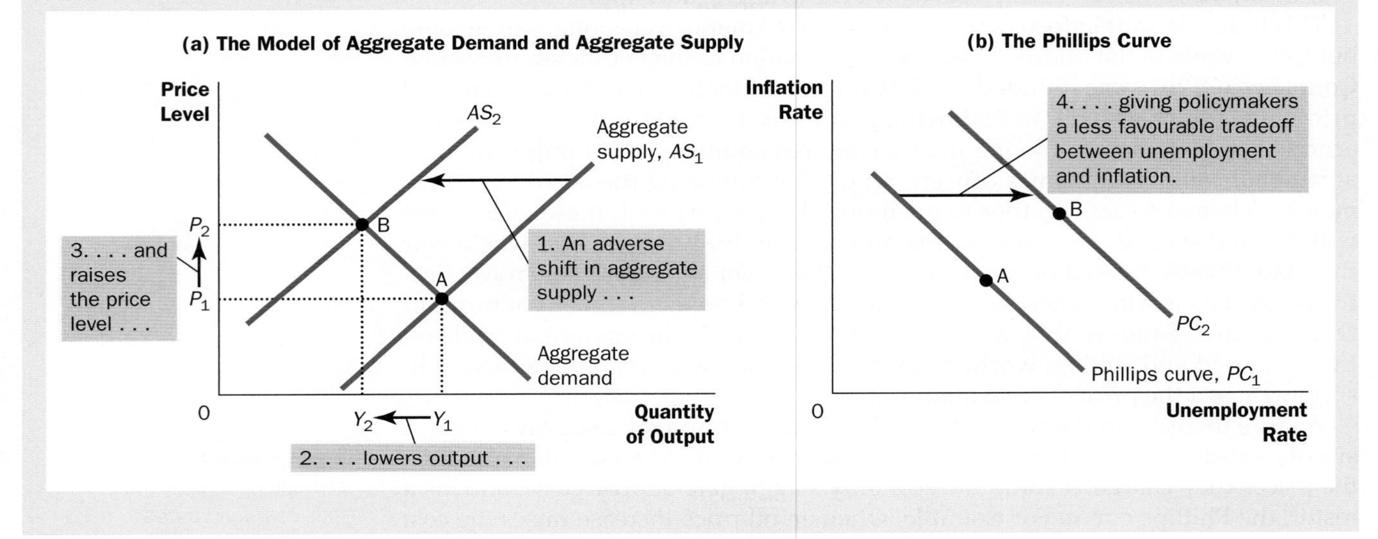

adjust their expectations of inflation. If people view the rise in inflation due to the supply shock as a temporary aberration, expected inflation does not change, and the Phillips curve will soon revert to its former position. But if people believe the shock will lead to a new era of higher inflation, then expected inflation rises, and the Phillips curve remains at its new, less desirable position.

Figure 16.9 shows inflation and unemployment in the Canadian economy during the 1970s. It shows that in the mid-1970s inflation increased dramatically as a result of the OPEC oil price shock. The increase in the price of oil meant that Canadian firms using oil as an input in their production processes would soon suffer dramatically higher costs. If nothing was done, the result would be both higher inflation and a higher unemployment rate: stagflation. Canadian policymakers were therefore faced with a difficult choice brought about by the threat of stagflation: Should they respond to the threat of stagflation by contracting aggregate demand to fight inflation but contribute to an increase in unemployment, or should they expand aggregate demand to fight unemployment but at the cost of increasing inflation and inflationary expectations even further?

Policymakers chose to attack the problem of stagflation in two ways. First, the Bank of Canada instituted a tight monetary policy. From 1974 to 1978, the money supply increased by less than 1 percent per year. Thus, during this period, the Bank of Canada was reducing aggregate demand, which would reduce prices but also contribute to a further reduction in output and an increase in the unemployment rate. The second way policymakers chose to attack inflation was to

This figure highlights annual data from 1973 to 1980 on the unemployment rate and on the inflation rate (as measured by the GDP deflator). Increases in the world price of oil in the early 1970s and again in 1979 caused large jumps in the rate of inflation and caused the short-run Phillips curve to shift to the right. In between these two oil price shocks, tight monetary policy and wage and price controls caused Canada to slide down a temporarily stable short-run curve.

FIGURE 16.9

The Supply Shocks of the 1970s

Sources: Data for 1973 to 1980 are from Statistics Canada, CANSIM, series V2062816 (unemployment rate) and V1997756 (GDP deflator).

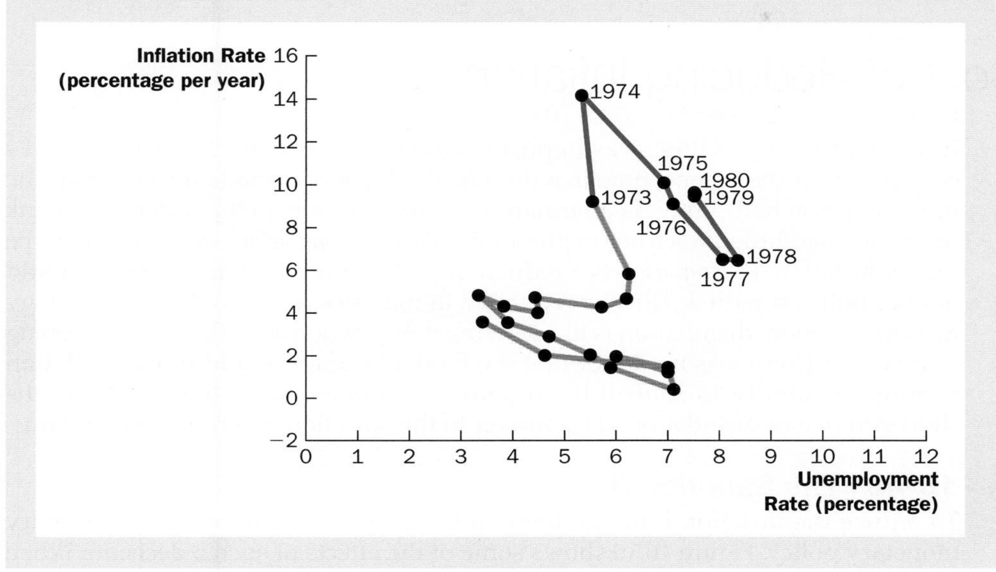

impose wage and price controls. From 1976 to 1978, federal government legislation limited increases in wages and prices to below the rate of inflation. These controls were designed to be a direct attack on both inflation and inflation expectations. The hope was that controls would signal to workers and firms that, because everyone was being made to do so, they could moderate their own demands for higher wages and prices without losing ground to other workers and firms. The result of this two-pronged attack was a dramatic reduction in the rate of inflation but also an increase in the rate of unemployment. During the 1974 to 1978 period, the Canadian economy was sliding back down the short-run Phillips curve. Unfortunately, however, the effects of the OPEC price shock had shifted the curve to the right. As a result, by the time the rate of inflation returned to 1972 levels, unemployment was 2 percentage points higher. Moreover, just as inflation had moderated and price controls had been removed, OPEC once again started to exert its market power. As a result, the price of oil more than doubled in 1979.

In the wake of the second OPEC oil price shock, the Canadian economy was faced again with a much higher rate of inflation and the threat that expectations of inflation would remain high. In 1980, after two OPEC supply shocks, Canada had an inflation rate of 10 percent and an unemployment rate of 7.5 percent. This combination of inflation and unemployment was not at all near the tradeoff that seemed possible in the 1960s. (In the 1960s, the Phillips curve suggested that an unemployment rate of 7.5 percent would be associated with an inflation rate of less than 1.0 percent. Inflation of more than 10.0 percent was unthinkable.) With the misery index in 1980 near a historic high, the public was widely dissatisfied with macroeconomic performance. Something had to be done, and soon it would be.

Give an example of a favourable shock to aggregate supply. Use the model of aggregate demand and aggregate supply to explain the effects of such a shock. How does it affect the Phillips curve?

16-4 The Cost of Reducing Inflation

In October 1979, as OPEC was imposing adverse supply shocks on the world's economies for the second time in a decade, the Bank of Canada decided that the time for action had come. As guardian of the nation's monetary system, the Bank of Canada had little choice but to pursue a policy of *disinflation*—a reduction in the rate of inflation. (*Disinflation* is a reduction in the rate of inflation, and it should not be confused with *deflation*, a reduction in the price level. To draw an analogy to a car's motion, disinflation is like slowing down, whereas deflation is like going in reverse.) There was no doubt that the Bank of Canada could reduce inflation through its ability to control the quantity of money. But what would be the short-run cost of disinflation? The answer to this question was much less certain.

16-4a The Sacrifice Ratio

To reduce the inflation rate, the Bank of Canada has to pursue contractionary monetary policy. Figure 16.10 shows some of the effects of such a decision. When the Bank of Canada slows the rate at which the money supply is growing, it

FIGURE 16.10

Disinflationary Monetary Policy in the Short Run and Long Run

When the Bank of Canada pursues contractionary monetary policy to reduce inflation, the economy moves along a short-run Phillips curve from point A to point B. Over time, expected inflation falls, and the short-run Phillips curve shifts downward. When the economy reaches point C, unemployment is back at its natural rate.

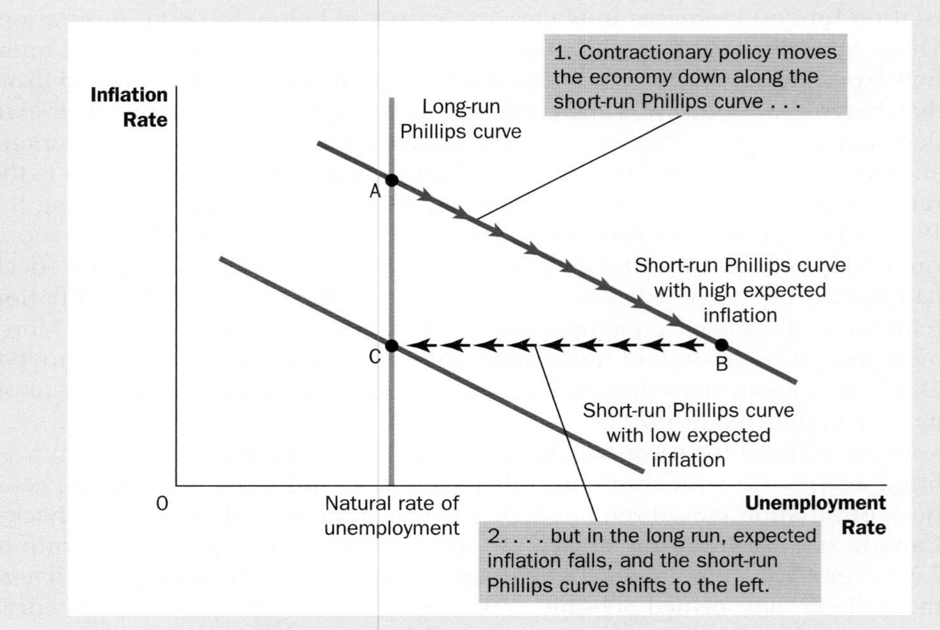

contracts aggregate demand. The fall in aggregate demand, in turn, reduces the quantity of goods and services that firms produce, and this fall in production leads to a fall in employment. The economy begins at point A in the figure and moves along the short-run Phillips curve to point B, which has lower inflation and higher unemployment. Over time, as people come to understand that prices are rising more slowly, expected inflation falls, and the short-run Phillips curve shifts downward. The economy moves from point B to point C. Inflation is lower, and unemployment is back at its natural rate.

Thus, if a nation wants to reduce inflation, it must endure a period of high unemployment and low output. In Figure 16.10, this cost is represented by the movement of the economy through point B as it travels from point A to point C. The size of this cost depends on the slope of the Phillips curve and how quickly expectations of inflation adjust to the new monetary policy.

Many studies have examined the data on inflation and unemployment in order to estimate the cost of reducing inflation. The findings of these studies are often summarized in a statistic called the **sacrifice ratio.** The sacrifice ratio is the number of percentage points of one year's output lost in the process of reducing inflation by 1 percentage point. Macroeconomists have found it difficult to obtain a precise estimate of the sacrifice ratio. Typical estimates of the sacrifice ratio for Canada fall over quite a wide range of between 2 and 5. That is, for each percentage point that inflation is reduced, between 2 and 5 percent of one year's output must be sacrificed in the transition.

sacrifice ratio
the number of percentage points of one year's output lost in the process of reducing inflation by 1 percentage point

We can also express the sacrifice ratio in terms of unemployment. For this purpose we need an estimate of how much a 1 percentage-point fall in output translates into an increase in unemployment. **Okun's law** provides such an estimate. Okun's law suggests that a change of 1 percentage point in GDP translates into a change of 0.5 percentage points of unemployment. Therefore, the range of estimates for the sacrifice ratio suggests that reducing inflation by 1 percentage point requires a sacrifice of between 1 and 2.5 percentage points of unemployment.

Okun's law
the number of percentage points the unemployment rate increases when GDP falls by 1 percentage point

Such estimates surely must have made the Bank of Canada apprehensive as it confronted the task of reducing inflation. In 1980, inflation was running at almost 10 percent per year and the unemployment rate was 7.4 percent. To reach moderate inflation of, say, 4 percent per year would mean reducing inflation by 6 percentage points. If the true size of the sacrifice ratio was at the top end of the range of estimates, so that each percentage point cost 5 percent of one year's output, then reducing inflation by 6 percentage points would require sacrificing 30 percent of one year's output. By the same token, it would cost 15 percentage points of unemployment.

According to studies of the Phillips curve and the cost of disinflation, this sacrifice could be paid in various ways. An immediate reduction in inflation would depress output by 30 percent and increase the unemployment rate by 15 percentage points in a single year. That outcome was surely too harsh even for inflation hawks. It would be better, many argued, to spread out the cost over several years. If the reduction in inflation took place over five years, for instance, then output would have to average only 6 percent below trend during that period to add up to a sacrifice of 30 percent. Similarly, reducing inflation by 6 percentage points over a five-year period would mean that the unemployment rate would need to rise by only 3 percentage points and remain at 10.4 percent for the five-year transition period. An even more gradual approach would be to reduce inflation slowly over a decade, so that output would have to be only 3 percent below trend. Whatever path was chosen, however, it seemed that reducing inflation would not be easy.

16-4b Rational Expectations and the Possibility of Costless Disinflation

Just as policymakers were pondering how costly reducing inflation might be, a group of economics professors was leading an intellectual revolution that would challenge the conventional wisdom on the sacrifice ratio. This group included such prominent economists as Robert Lucas, Thomas Sargent, and Robert Barro. Their revolution was based on a new approach to economic theory and policy called **rational expectations.** According to the theory of rational expectations, people optimally use all the information they have, including information about government policies, when forecasting the future.

rational expectations
the theory according to which people optimally use all the information they have, including information about government policies, when forecasting the future

This new approach has had profound implications for many areas of macroeconomics, but none is more important than its application to the tradeoff between inflation and unemployment. As Friedman and Phelps had first emphasized, expected inflation is an important variable that explains why there is a tradeoff between inflation and unemployment in the short run but not in the long run. How quickly the short-run tradeoff disappears depends on how quickly expectations adjust. Proponents of rational expectations built on the Friedman–Phelps analysis argue that when economic policies change, people adjust their expectations of inflation accordingly. Studies of inflation and unemployment that tried to estimate the sacrifice ratio had failed to take account of the direct effect of the policy regime on expectations. As a result, estimates of the sacrifice ratio were, according to the rational-expectations theorists, unreliable guides for policy.

In a 1981 paper entitled "The End of Four Big Inflations," Thomas Sargent described this new view as follows:

> An alternative "rational expectations" view denies that there is any inherent momentum to the present process of inflation. This view maintains that firms and workers have now come to expect high rates of inflation in the future and that they strike inflationary bargains in light of these expectations. However, it is held that people expect high rates of inflation in the future precisely because the government's current and prospective monetary and fiscal policies warrant those expectations.... An implication of this view is that inflation can be stopped much more quickly than advocates of the "momentum" view have indicated and that their estimates of the length of time and the costs of stopping inflation in terms of forgone output are erroneous.... This is not to say that it would be easy to eradicate inflation. On the contrary, it would require more than a few temporary restrictive fiscal and monetary actions. It would require a change in the policy regime.... How costly such a move would be in terms of forgone output and how long it would be in taking effect would depend partly on how resolute and evident the government's commitment was.

According to Sargent, the sacrifice ratio could be much smaller than suggested by previous estimates. Indeed, in the most extreme case, it could be zero. If the government made a credible commitment to a policy of low inflation, people would be rational enough to lower their expectations of inflation immediately. The short-run Phillips curve would shift downward, and the economy would reach low inflation quickly without the cost of temporarily high unemployment and low output.

FYI Measuring Expectations of Inflation

One reason why it is good to have an idea of what the rate of inflation will be in the future is that it enables you to understand how large a wage increase you should ask for. If the prices of goods you buy are expected to increase by 5 percent over the next year, then it makes sense for you to try to negotiate at least a 5 percent increase in your wage so that your income can keep up with the cost of living. Similarly, having an idea of what the rate of inflation will be in the future is helpful for you to understand whether signing a five-year mortgage at a 7 percent nominal interest rate is a good deal. If the rate of inflation is currently 3 percent but you believe that it is likely to jump up 6 percent in the near future, then agreeing to a five-year mortgage at a 7 percent nominal interest rate will look very attractive. This is because the real interest rate that can be expected during the course of the five-year mortgage will fall from its current rate of 4 percent to only 1 percent. In both of these examples, knowing what the rate of inflation might be in the future is a useful thing.

AlexRaths/Thinkstock

Having an idea of what households and firms believe will be the rate of inflation in the future is also of interest to Canada's central bank, the Bank of Canada. Understanding the value of the expected rate of inflation enables the Bank to determine the position of the short-run Phillips curve. If rational-expectations theorists are correct, if the position of this curve can cause people to reduce their expectations of inflation, the Bank may be able to obtain a costless disinflation. For both these reasons, it is important for the Bank of Canada to understand what people and firms believe will be the rate of inflation in the future.

But how does the Bank of Canada figure out, exactly, what those expectations are? Economists have developed a number of methods to gain insights into what are expectations of inflation. One way of doing so is to simply ask! This is what the Bank of Canada does in its regional office survey of private firms. In the survey, which is reported in the Bank of Canada's *Business Outlook Survey* and is available on its website, firms are asked which of four possible ranges of CPI inflation they expect to observe over the following two years. The Bank then reports what percentage of firms surveyed chose which option. When surveyed in the summer of 2015, 68 percent of firms surveyed indicated that they felt inflation would average 1 to 2 percent over the following two years, while 26 percent of firms predicted that the rate of inflation would average 2 to 3 percent. Only 3 percent of respondents thought inflation would average less than 1 percent and just 1 percent of respondents thought that the rate of inflation might be higher than 3 percent. The rest of those surveyed (2 percent) did not respond.

We saw in Chapter 14, and again here in this chapter, that expectations of inflation play an important role in economics. Despite the importance of this variable, its measurement is difficult and imprecise.

16-4c Disinflation in the 1980s

As we have seen, when the Bank of Canada, at the beginning of the 1980s, faced the prospect of reducing inflation, the economics profession offered two conflicting predictions. One group of economists offered estimates of the sacrifice ratio and concluded that reducing inflation would have great cost in terms of lost output and high unemployment. Another group offered the theory of rational expectations and concluded that reducing inflation could be much less costly and, perhaps, could even have no cost at all. Who was right?

Figure 16.11 highlights data on inflation and unemployment from 1980 to 1989. As you can see, the Bank of Canada did succeed at reducing inflation. Inflation came down from 10 percent in 1980 and 1981 to about 3 percent in 1985 and 1986. Credit for this reduction in inflation goes completely to monetary policy. Fiscal policy at this time was acting in the opposite direction: Increases in the budget deficits of the provinces and the federal government were expanding aggregate demand, which tends to raise inflation. The dramatic fall in inflation from 1981 to 1985 is attributable to the equally dramatic anti-inflation policies of the Bank of Canada. From 1979 to 1982, the money supply, as measured by M1, shrank by an average of almost 6 percent per year. Economists David Laidler and William

FIGURE 16.11

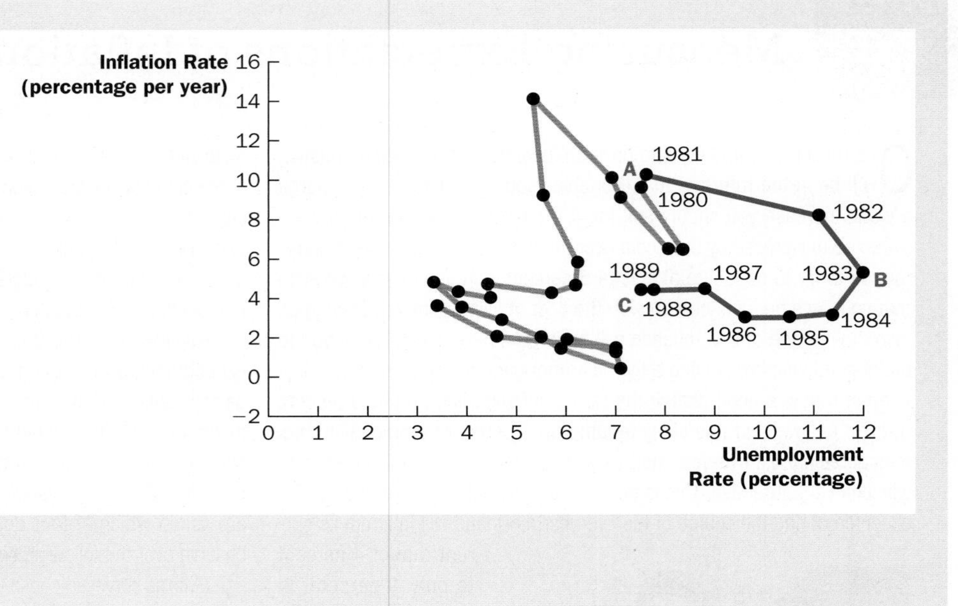

Disinflation in the 1980s
This figure highlights annual data from 1980 to 1989 on the unemployment rate and on the inflation rate (as measured by the GDP deflator). The reduction in inflation during this period came at the cost of very high unemployment from 1983 to 1986. Note that the points labelled A, B, and C in this figure correspond roughly to the points in Figure 16.10.

Sources: Data for 1980 to 1989 are from Statistics Canada, CANSIM, series V2062816 (unemployment rate) and V1997756 (GDP deflator).

Robson suggested that monetary policy during this period was "excruciatingly" contractionary. The description certainly seems appropriate.

Figure 16.11 shows that disinflation did come at the cost of high unemployment. In 1983, 1984, and 1985, the unemployment rate was more than 10 percent. At the same time, the growth rate of real GDP was well below its trend level. (See Figure 14.10 in Chapter 14.) The disinflation of the early 1980s produced the deepest recession in Canada since the Great Depression of the 1930s.

Does this experience refute the possibility of costless disinflation as suggested by the rational-expectations theorists? Some economists have argued that the answer to this question is a resounding yes. Indeed, the pattern of disinflation shown in Figure 16.11 is very similar to the pattern predicted in Figure 16.10. To make the transition from high inflation (point A in both figures) to low inflation (point C), the economy had to experience a painful period of high unemployment (point B). At the beginning of this transition period (point A), the unemployment rate was 7.5 percent, approximately equal to the natural unemployment rate. By 1989, which marked the end of the transition period (point C), unemployment was back to 7.5 percent and was again close to the natural unemployment rate. (As we showed in Figure 9.4 in Chapter 9, the natural unemployment rate is generally viewed as having increased during the 1980s; by 1988 it was roughly 8 percent. We use the estimates of the natural unemployment rate presented in Figure 9.4 in Chapter 9 in our calculations below.) If we add up the number of percentage points the unemployment rate remained above the natural rate and divide that amount by the number of percentage points inflation was reduced over this period, we arrive at an estimate of the sacrifice ratio defined in terms of sacrificed employment. The estimate we arrive at is 2.1. This indicates that during the period from 1981 to 1989, each reduction of 1.0 percentage point in inflation during this period required a sacrifice of about 2.1 percentage points of unemployment. This is at the upper end of estimates of the sacrifice ratio suggested by those economists who argued that reducing inflation could come only at great cost in terms of lost output and high unemployment. For those economists, then, the claims of rational-expectations theorists that less costly disinflation was possible seemed to carry little weight.

Despite the evidence supporting the view that inflation could be reduced only at great cost, many economists felt it was too soon to reject the notion that lower rates of inflation could be obtained at smaller cost. The main reason for this optimism was the fact that even though the Bank of Canada announced that it would aim monetary policy to lower inflation, much of the public did not believe it.

Because few people thought the Bank of Canada would reduce inflation as quickly as it did, expected inflation did not fall, and the short-run Phillips curve did not shift down as quickly as it might have. Some evidence for this hypothesis comes from the forecasts made by commercial forecasting firms: Their forecasts of inflation fell more slowly in the 1980s than did actual inflation. Thus, the disinflation of the 1980s does not necessarily refute the rational-expectations view that credible disinflation can be costless. It does show, however, that policymakers cannot count on people immediately believing them when they announce a policy of disinflation.

16-4d The Zero-Inflation Target

The latter half of the 1980s was a period of strong economic growth. By 1989, the unemployment rate had fallen by 4.5 percentage points from its high in 1983. Toward the end of the decade, however, this strong economic growth led to an increase in the rate of inflation. In 1988, the governor of the Bank of Canada, John Crow, made a speech known as the Hanson Lecture. In that speech, Crow offered a clear statement defining the future direction of monetary policy in Canada. He asserted that the sole goal of the Bank of Canada would thereafter be to achieve and maintain a stable price level and zero inflation (for technical reasons that have to do with how inflation is measured, 1 percent inflation is generally accepted as being "zero").

The purpose of the Hanson Lecture was to define a clear target for monetary policy and to announce this policy widely. Many macroeconomists believed that, because the new monetary policy target was so clearly and firmly stated by such a well-known inflation hawk as John Crow, the public ought to believe what he was saying and quickly adjust inflation expectations downward. In this way, inflation might be reduced to the targeted level with a smaller sacrifice in terms of unemployment and lost output than had been experienced previously. The Bank of Canada began contracting the money supply in 1989 and continued to do so in 1990 and 1991. Figure 16.12 shows that the unemployment rate increased from 7.5 percent in 1989 to 10.4 percent in 1994, while inflation fell from 4.5 percent to 1.1 percent. The inflation target was thus reached very quickly (the Bank of Canada's target for inflation is based on the "core" rate of CPI inflation, a rate slightly lower than that calculated here using the GDP deflator). From 1994 to 1999, the inflation rate averaged just 1.2 percent, so that the target was successfully maintained. By the end of 1999, the unemployment rate had returned to what it was in 1989, a level generally regarded as roughly equal to the natural rate.

Just as it did in response to the Bank of Canada's effort at disinflation in the early 1980s, the economy adjusted toward a lower rate of inflation from 1989 to 1999 in a way that closely corresponds to the pattern shown in Figure 16.10. If we label 1989 as point A, 1993 as point B, and 1999 as point C, the data in Figure 16.12 appear to show that inflation expectations were again slow to adjust

IN THE news

How to Keep Expected Inflation Low

The prospect of costless disinflation relies on the notion that people may lower their expectations of inflation if they can be convinced of that expectation by a credible policymaker. This news article describes how the Bank of Canada, led by former Governor Mark Carney, tried to manage peoples' expectations of inflation. We should expect that current Governor Stephen Poloz will behave in similar ways.

Inflation: Managing Expectations

By Philip DeMont

Bank of Canada Governor Mark Carney worries about what you think.

In fact, figuring out how you view the Canadian economy and whether you believe that the Bank of Canada is serious about tackling rising prices is the best tool he has for preventing this economic scourge from taking off.

The process is known as managing expectations.

And, for the past decade and a half, it has proven to be a pretty effective way of squashing inflation in Canada.

This strategy also means, however, that Carney might be very quick to react with higher interest rates if he thinks the bank's credibility as an inflation fighter is in question.

"Expectations play a big role in what the bank is trying to achieve," said Douglas Porter, an economist with BMO Capital Markets Economics.

Tough-guy Economics

Convincing Canadians that the Bank of Canada will be hard on inflation is kind of like trying to be the toughest guy in a bar. It only works if everyone else thinks you are tough as well.

In the case of the Bank of Canada, Carney has to ensure that Canadians believe he has inflation—defined as the rate of increase in the price of a basket of goods—under control.

If he is credible, workers will not go out and ask for more money, companies will not try to pass along higher prices to consumers and investors will not seek out higher returns for interest-bearing investments.

If Canadians do not think the bank is serious about battling price increases, however, they will ignore what Carney says publicly and, instead, start demanding more money for their work or their products.

Once that process begins, inflation has a tendency to spiral to very high levels.

"You get a wage–price spiral," said James Marple, an economist with TD Economics.

Back in the early 1980s, Canada saw the annual inflation rate rise above 10 per cent. A major reason was that workers kept asking for more money in order to keep pace with previous price hikes.

At that time, what the Bank of Canada did had little effect on the behaviour of Canadians.

No Spiral This Time

Carney wants to stop this self-fulfilling inflation spiral before it gets a full head of steam.

He has a few tools at his disposal in this fight, including public statements and private chats with various business leaders.

But Carney's main weapon is interest rate hikes.

Essentially, the Bank of Canada can decide to boost borrowing costs a little bit now to show people that the central bank is not afraid to hike rates to slow inflation later.

But making the correct guess at when and how hard to apply the monetary brakes to the economy is an art, not a science, according to economists.

"[Making the proper decision] is a difficult thing to do," Porter said.

So far, the bank's strategy has worked. A soft foot on Canada's interest rate pedal has kept prices from rising very fast without stopping economic growth.

According to Statistics Canada, the annual inflation rate has not topped three per cent in 16 years, a very good performance by international standards.

The question as prices rise is whether Carney will have to push up interest charges higher in order to make sure Canadians believe him.

Source: CBC News, July 29, 2008: http://www.cbc.ca/news/business/inflation-managing-expectations-1.748106. Reprinted with permission by CBC Licensing.

downward. As a result, it appears that the economy adjusted along a given short-run Phillips curve (from point A to point B) before inflation expectations adjusted, shifting the short-run curve to the left (to give us point C). If we add up the number of percentage points the unemployment rate remained above the natural rate and divide that amount by the number of percentage points inflation was reduced over the 1989–99 period, we arrive at an estimate of the sacrifice ratio equal to 6.1, an estimate almost three times as large as our estimate (2.1) for the 1981–89

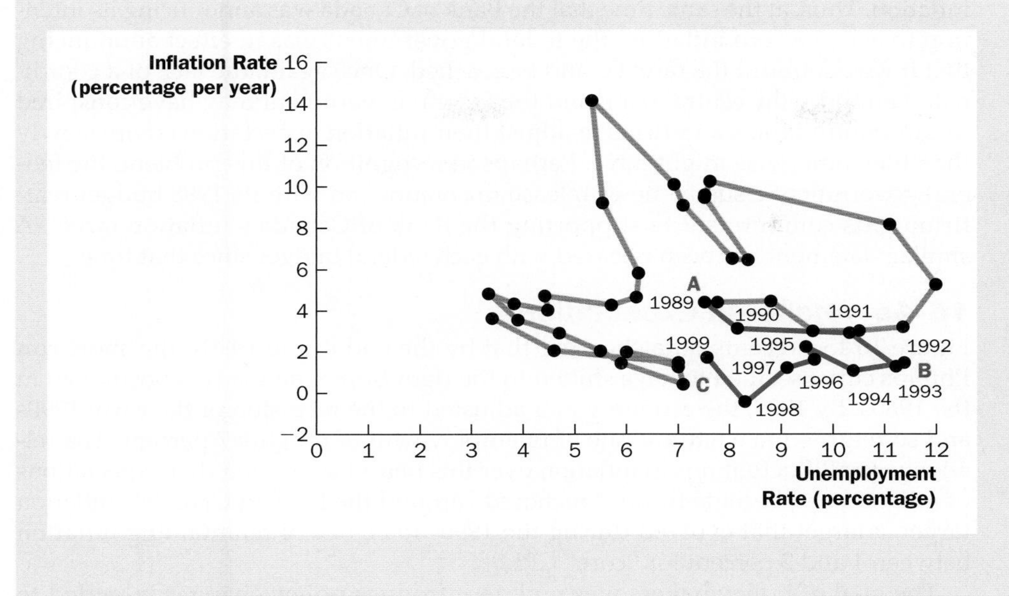

FIGURE 16.12

The Zero-Inflation Target

This figure highlights annual data from 1989 to 1999 on the unemployment rate and the inflation rate (as measured by the GDP deflator). In 1988, the Bank of Canada announced its zero-inflation target, and in 1989 monetary contraction began. The central bank's target was reached in 1994, by which time the unemployment rate exceeded 10 percent. Note that points A, B, and C in this figure correspond roughly to the points in Figure 16.10.

Sources: Data for 1989 to 1999 are from Statistics Canada, CANSIM, series V2062816 (unemployment rate) and V1997756 (GDP deflator).

period. The experience of this most recent attempt to reduce inflation has confirmed the opinion of those macroeconomists who believe that inflation can be reduced only at great cost. The Bank of Canada clearly defined and announced its intention to contract the money supply so as to reduce inflation to zero, and yet the cost of reducing inflation seemed to be larger than ever before.

Despite this evidence, many macroeconomists are still not ready to reject the notion that lower rates of inflation can be obtained at smaller cost if the central bank makes a credible statement of its intention to deflate. They maintain their optimism by pointing to a number of factors in the transition to zero inflation that may have prevented inflation expectations from falling as quickly as they otherwise might have. One such factor was that the deficits of the provinces and the federal government remained very high throughout much of this period of transition. Concern over these deficits culminated in 1995, when credit agencies lowered the rating on federal government debt. High deficits and credit downgrades may have caused people to doubt whether the Bank of Canada could reach its target of zero inflation, and thereby caused people's expectations of inflation to remain high. Critics of the Bank of Canada argue that it should have foreseen this problem because the main reason government deficits were increasing over this period was the tight monetary policy of the central bank. These critics argue that the Bank of Canada's credibility was in doubt because of its decision to launch a tight monetary policy before the federal and provincial governments reduced their deficits.

A second reason why inflation expectations may not have fallen as quickly as was hoped when the Bank of Canada announced its zero-inflation target was that the federal government, in preparing its budgets, was using a forecast of 3 percent inflation. Thus, at the same time that the Bank of Canada was announcing its intention to achieve zero inflation, the federal government was in effect announcing that it was doubtful the target could be reached. Once again, the lack of a coordinated effort by the central bank and the federal government may have conspired to cause individuals and firms to adjust their inflation expectations more slowly than they otherwise might have. Perhaps in recognition of this problem, the federal government issued a news release in conjunction with its 1998 budget reaffirming its commitment to supporting the Bank of Canada's inflation target. A similar statement has been released with each federal budget since that time.

16-4e Anchored Expectations

Figure 16.13 presents data showing that by the end of the 1990s, the short-run Phillips curve seemed to have shifted to the right from where it was positioned in the 1960s. By 1999, the economy had adjusted to the recession of the early 1990s and so returned to a natural rate of unemployment of roughly 7 percent. The relatively small fluctuations in inflation over this period suggested that expectations of inflation had become firmly "anchored" around the Bank of Canada's inflation target, a target that evolved during the 1990s to be one of maintaining inflation between 1 and 3 percent for "core" CPI.

The goal of policymakers was now to introduce policy changes intended to maintain low rates of inflation while realizing a lower rate of unemployment. The goal, in other words, was to shift the long-run Phillips curve to the left by lowering the natural rate of unemployment. In so doing, the short-run Phillips curve would also shift to the left. (Recall how earlier we explained that the short-run Phillips curve intersects the long-run curve at the expected rate of inflation and so shifts whenever the long-run Phillips curve shifts.)

Policies introduced after 2000 included reforms to the Employment Insurance program that, among other things, increased the government's investment in job retraining. New policies also included significant cuts to corporation income tax rates at both the federal and the provincial and territorial levels of government.

FIGURE 16.13

The Short-Run Phillips Curve, 1956–68 and 1989–99

This figure presents data suggesting that the position of the short-run Phillips curve shifted to the right between the 1950s and 1990s. The implication is that the natural unemployment rate increased over this time frame.

Sources: Data for 1956–1968 and 1989–1999 are from Statistics Canada, CANSIM II series v2062816 (unemployment rate) and v1997756 (GDP deflator). Data from 1956 to 1965 are from F.H. Leacy, ed. Historical Statistics of Canada, 2nd ed. (Ottawa: Statistics Canada, 1983), series D233 (unemployment rate) and K17 (GDP deflator).

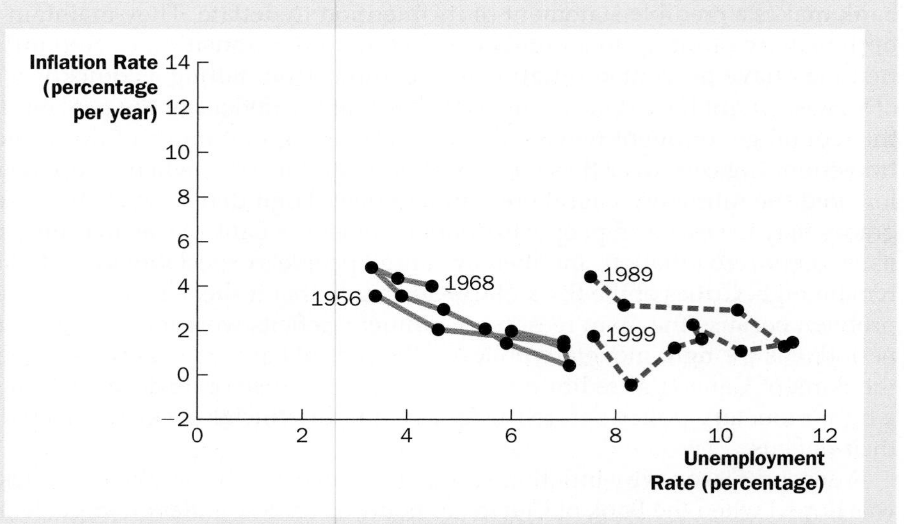

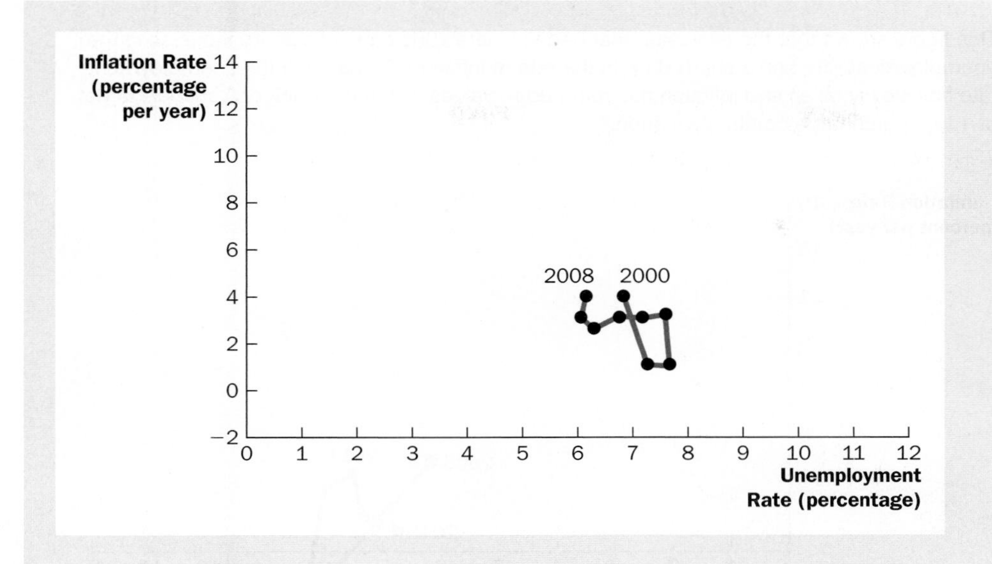

FIGURE 16.14

The Quiet before the Storm
This figure shows that between 2000 and 2008, the rate of inflation was anchored on the Bank of Canada's inflation target of 2 percent and that the natural unemployment rate was slowly falling.

Sources: Data for 2000–2008 are from Statistics Canada, CANSIM series v2062816 (unemployment rate) and v1997756 (GDP deflator).

Both sets of policies were intended to increase the supply of and demand for labour and so reduce the unemployment rate to which the economy would return in the long run. The data in Figure 16.14, showing the rate of inflation and the unemployment rate from 2000 to 2008, suggest that the effort was proving to be successful—over that period, the unemployment rate fell by 1 percentage point without much of a change in the rate of inflation.

For much of the 2000s, the Canadian economy enjoyed more or less steady rates of economic growth. The short-run Phillips curve, then, was not revealing itself in the data and would not do so again until there was an unexpected change in aggregate demand. This would occur late in 2008.

16-4f The 2008–09 Recession

We noted in previous chapters that the recession that began in Canada late in 2008 can be described as having been the result of a significant fall in aggregate demand caused by a financial crisis that began in 2007. In terms of the model of aggregate demand and aggregate supply discussed in Chapter 14, this unexpected shift to the left of the aggregate-demand curve caused the economy to slide down the short-run aggregate-supply curve to a lower price level and a level of output below the natural level of output. In terms of the Phillips curve presented in this chapter, this movement is represented by a movement down the short-run Phillips curve to a lower rate of inflation and a level of unemployment above the natural rate.

Figure 16.15 presents data describing how Canada's unemployment rate and rate of inflation changed following the onset of recession in late 2008. The recession caused a 2 percentage-point increase in the Canadian unemployment rate and a large fall in the rate of inflation, movements consistent with what our model predicts would result from a fall in aggregate demand. Since 2009, the unemployment rate has moved, albeit slowly, back toward the natural rate; a rate most economists would identify as have a value of between 6 and 7 percent. Inflation

FIGURE 16.15

The 2008–09 Recession and Its Aftermath

This figure shows that the recession that began in late 2008 caused a sharp increase in the unemployment rate and a sharp drop in the rate of inflation. Since 2009 the unemployment rate has slowly fallen and inflation has returned to values within the Bank of Canada's target of 1 to 3 percentage points of inflation.

Sources: Data for 2008–2015 are from Statistics Canada, CANSIM series v2062816 (unemployment rate) and v1997756 (GDP deflator).

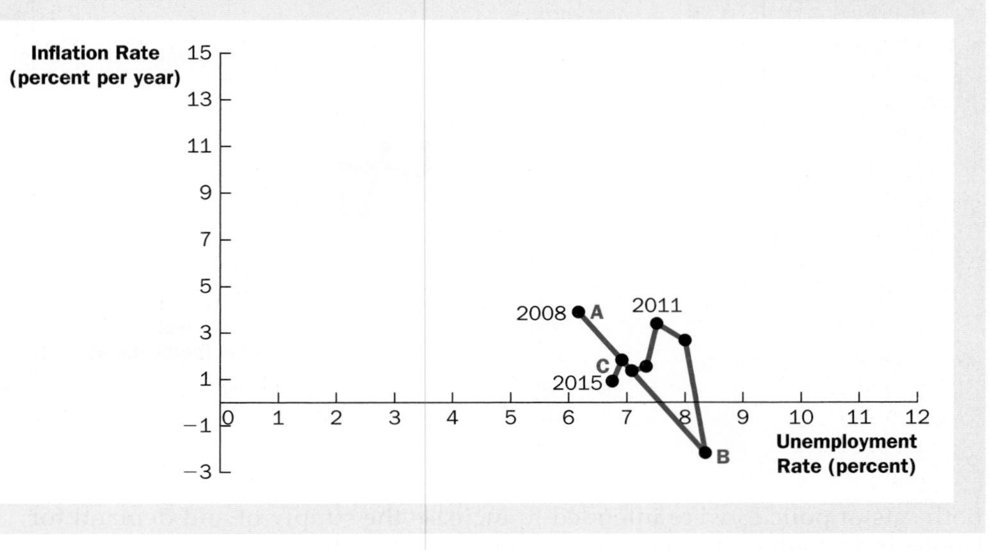

has returned to about 2 percent, showing again how solidly the expectation of inflation is anchored around the Bank of Canada's inflation target.

At the time this chapter was written in 2015, the unemployment rate was at 6.8 percent while inflation as measured by the GDP deflator was at 1 percent. Inflation and unemployment near these levels are more or less consistent with a suggestion that the economy had, by 2015, fully adjusted—at least in terms of inflation and unemployment—to the shock that precipitated the 2008–09 recession.

The apparent recovery of the economy from the recession of 2008–09 will be cheered by advocates of strong aggregate-demand policies. Advocates will emphasize that the aggregate-demand stimulus provided by the Canadian government and the Bank of Canada was a worthwhile investment because it resulted in an economic recovery and return to pre-recession rates of unemployment and inflation faster than that realized in other countries. Critics, on the other hand, will emphasize that while this recovery might not have occurred as quickly without the economic stimulus, it would nonetheless have occurred and done so without the accumulation of government debt that has also been a legacy of the stimulus effort. The debate continues.

16-5 Looking Ahead

The movements of unemployment and inflation shown in the figures presented in this chapter describe a 60-year journey of discovery during which economists have learned that the tradeoff of higher (lower) inflation for lower (higher) unemployment is only temporary and is unstable. Trying to lower unemployment below its natural rate, while possible in the short run, seems to come with a very large price tag in the long run, a price measured by the sacrifice ratio. Canadians have paid that price twice over the past 30 years and the evidence suggests that it is a price that is difficult to avoid paying. What can we expect in the future?

While some macroeconomists remain convinced that inflation can be reduced with minimal cost as long as the policy of disinflation is clear and credible, others point to the efforts at disinflation in the 1980s and the 1990s as proof that inflation can be reduced only at a substantial cost in terms of temporarily higher rates of unemployment.

Regardless of their differences of opinion about the size of the sacrifice ratio and the possibility of minimizing the costs of disinflations, all macroeconomists recognize that having achieved low rates of inflation, the Bank of Canada ought to work hard to never again allow inflation to increase to the levels observed during the 1970s and 1980s. Announcing and rigorously defending a low target for the rate of inflation is an important element of the Bank of Canada's efforts in this regard. So too is the effort of federal, provincial, and territorial governments to maintain fiscal policy discipline and so avoid inappropriately large rightward shifts in aggregate demand that must at some point require a contractionary policy and the unattractive outcomes that can entail.

The evidence provided in this chapter also sheds light on two other macroeconomic issues. The first has to do with the position of the long-run Phillips curve. The data presented in Figure 16.13 strongly suggest that the position of the Phillips curve drifted to the right during the 1970s and 1980s, so that by the 1990s the natural unemployment rate had increased by 3 to 4 percentage points. Most economists agree this increase in the natural rate of unemployment was at least partly the result of well-intended but poorly designed government policies with respect to the provision of unemployment insurance. High tax rates that discouraged hiring are also often identified as contributing to the problem. Looking ahead it seems safe to suggest that economists will be vigilant in favouring policies to reduce the natural rate of unemployment. The evidence in Figure 16.14 is suggestive that recent reforms to Employment Insurance (including an emphasis on job retraining) and cuts to tax rates are effective in meeting that goal.

Finally, the evidence presented in Figure 16.15 makes clear that external shocks such as that due to the financial crisis of 2007–09 can have a powerful effect on the Canadian economy. The large fiscal and monetary stimulus introduced in response to the crisis by the federal government and the Bank of Canada, respectively, seems at this point to have been successful at sliding the economy back up its short-run Phillips curve to a position close to where the rates of inflation and unemployment were prior to the crisis. Looking ahead, this experience might embolden policymakers to employ similar policies in the future. If so, economists will likely be ready to emphasize that policy responses like these should be used only in response to large shocks to the economy. Efforts to "fine tune" the economy should be avoided and instead the private economy should be left to respond to relatively minor shocks.

Let there be no doubt: The successful conduct of fiscal and monetary policy is difficult. It often involves consideration of tradeoffs that risk substantial sacrifices of some to benefit others. The short-run tradeoff between inflation and unemployment encapsulates this broad issue. It must have seemed like a good idea in the 1970s to stimulate the economy in the face of the stagflationary effects of OPEC oil price shocks but, in retrospect, the sacrifice—measured in percentage points of unemployment and lost output—that was required to recover from the inflationary impacts of that policy must surely have been regretted. Similarly, shooting for the goal of zero inflation was not expected to require a sacrifice in the form of the dramatically higher unemployment rates realized from 1990 to 1993.

As Canada's policymakers look ahead, the experience of the past 60 years must surely have taught them that it may take many years and a great deal of pain to recover from ill-considered responses to economic events. Getting policy right is a daunting challenge that requires careful consideration of a wide range of issues and decisions must sometimes be made with little information immediately available. More often than not, the basic principles of economics are essential guides to good policy making and that is why policymakers must be continually reminded of those basic principles. That is the job of economists like you.

What is the sacrifice ratio? How might the credibility of the Bank of Canada's commitment to reduce inflation affect the sacrifice ratio?

16-6 Conclusion

This chapter has examined how economists' thinking about inflation and unemployment has evolved over time. We have discussed the ideas of many of the best economists of the twentieth century: from the Phillips curve of Phillips, Lipsey, Samuelson, and Solow, to the natural-rate hypothesis of Friedman and Phelps, to the rational-expectations theory of Lucas, Sargent, and Barro. Five of this group have already won Nobel Prizes for their work in economics, and more are likely to be so honoured in the years to come.

Although the tradeoff between inflation and unemployment has generated much intellectual turmoil over the past half-century, certain principles have developed that today command consensus. Here is how Milton Friedman expressed the relationship between inflation and unemployment in 1968:

> There is always a temporary tradeoff between inflation and unemployment; there is no permanent tradeoff. The temporary tradeoff comes not from inflation per se, but from unanticipated inflation, which generally means, from a rising rate of inflation. The widespread belief that there is a permanent tradeoff is a sophisticated version of the confusion between "high" and "rising" that we all recognize in simpler forms. A rising rate of inflation may reduce unemployment, a high rate will not.
>
> But how long, you will say, is "temporary"?... I can at most venture a personal judgment, based on some examination of the historical evidence, that the initial effects of a higher and unanticipated rate of inflation last for something like two to five years.

Today, nearly 50 years later, this statement still summarizes the view of most macroeconomists.

summary

- The Phillips curve describes a negative relationship between inflation and unemployment. By expanding aggregate demand, policymakers can choose a point on the Phillips curve with higher inflation and lower unemployment. By contracting aggregate demand, policymakers can choose a point on the Phillips curve with lower inflation and higher unemployment.
- The tradeoff between inflation and unemployment described by the Phillips curve holds only in the short run. In the long run, expected inflation adjusts to changes in actual inflation, and the short-run Phillips curve shifts. As a result, the long-run Phillips curve is vertical at the natural rate of unemployment.
- The short-run Phillips curve also shifts because of shocks to aggregate supply. An adverse supply shock, such as the increase in world oil prices during the 1970s, gives policymakers a less favourable tradeoff between inflation and unemployment. That is, after an adverse supply shock, policymakers have to accept a higher rate of inflation for any given rate of unemployment, or a higher rate of unemployment for any given rate of inflation.
- When the Bank of Canada contracts growth in the money supply to reduce inflation, it moves the economy along the short-run Phillips curve, which results in temporarily high unemployment. The cost of disinflation depends on how quickly expectations of inflation fall. Some economists argue that a credible commitment to low inflation can reduce the cost of disinflation by inducing a quick adjustment of expectations.
- The financial crisis of 2008–09 caused a shift to the left in Canada's aggregate-demand curve and so a slide down its short-run Phillips curve. The result was a sudden increase in the unemployment rate and fall in the rate of inflation. The fiscal and monetary stimulus introduced by the federal government and the Bank of Canada in 2009–10 was designed to return the aggregate-demand curve to its pre-recession position and so slide the economy back up its short-run Phillips curve. The evidence suggests that these were successful policies.

KEY concepts

Phillips curve, *p. 392*
natural-rate hypothesis, *p. 401*
supply shock, *p. 403*
sacrifice ratio, *p. 407*
Okun's law, *p. 407*
rational expectations, *p. 408*

QUESTIONS FOR review

1. Draw the short-run tradeoff between inflation and unemployment. How might the Bank of Canada move the economy from one point on this curve to another?
2. Draw the long-run tradeoff between inflation and unemployment. Explain how the short-run and long-run tradeoffs are related.
3. What's so natural about the natural rate of unemployment? Why might the natural rate of unemployment differ across countries?
4. Suppose a drought destroys farm crops and drives up the price of food. What is the effect on the short-run tradeoff between inflation and unemployment?
5. Suppose the Bank of Canada decides to reduce inflation. Use the Phillips curve to show the short-run and long-run effects of this policy. How might the short-run costs be reduced?

QUICK CHECK multiple choice

1. When the Bank of Canada increases the money supply, it _____ aggregate demand and moves the economy along the Phillips curve to a point with _____ inflation and _____ unemployment.
   a. expands, higher, higher
   b. expands, higher, lower
   c. expands, lower, higher
   d. contracts, lower, higher
2. If the Bank of Canada increases the rate of money growth and maintains it at the new higher rate, eventually expected inflation will _____ and the short-run Phillips curve will shift _____ .
   a. decrease, downward
   b. decrease, upward
   c. increase, downward
   d. increase, upward

3. When an adverse supply shock shifts the short-run aggregate-supply curve to the left, which of the following does it also do?
   a. moves the economy along the short-run Phillips curve to a point with higher inflation and lower unemployment
   b. moves the economy along the short-run Phillips curve to a point with lower inflation and higher unemployment
   c. shifts the short-run Phillips curve to the right
   d. shifts the short-run Phillips curve to the left
4. What is believed by advocates of the theory of rational expectations?
   a. the sacrifice ratio can be much smaller if policy-makers make a credible commitment to low inflation
   b. if disinflation catches people by surprise, it will have minimal impact on unemployment
   c. wage and price setters never expect the central bank to follow through on its announcements
   d. expected inflation depends on the rates of inflation that people have recently observed
5. From one year to the next, inflation falls from 5 to 4 percent, while unemployment rises from 6 to 7 percent. Which of the following events could be responsible for this change?
   a. The central bank increases the growth rate of the money supply.
   b. The government cuts spending and raises taxes to reduce the budget deficit.
   c. Newly discovered oil reserves cause world oil prices to plummet.
   d. The appointment of a new Bank of Canada Governor increases expected inflation.
6. From one year to the next, inflation rises from 4 to 5 percent, while unemployment rises from 6 to 7 percent. Which of the following events could be responsible for this change?
   a. The central bank increases the growth rate of the money supply.
   b. The government cuts spending and raises taxes to reduce the budget deficit.
   c. Newly discovered oil reserves cause world oil prices to plummet.
   d. The appointment of a new Bank of Canada Governor increases expected inflation.

PROBLEMS AND **applications**

1. Suppose the natural rate of unemployment is 6 percent. On one graph, draw two Phillips curves that can be used to describe the four situations listed here. Label the point that shows the position of the economy in each case.
   a. Actual inflation is 5 percent and expected inflation is 3 percent.
   b. Actual inflation is 3 percent and expected inflation is 5 percent.
   c. Actual inflation is 5 percent and expected inflation is 5 percent.
   d. Actual inflation is 3 percent and expected inflation is 3 percent.
2. Illustrate the effects of the following developments on both the short-run and long-run Phillips curves. Give the economic reasoning underlying your answers.
   a. a rise in the natural rate of unemployment
   b. a decline in the price of imported oil
   c. a rise in government spending
   d. a decline in expected inflation
3. Suppose that a fall in consumer spending causes a recession.
   a. Illustrate the changes in the economy using both an aggregate-supply/aggregate-demand diagram and a Phillips curve diagram. What happens to inflation and unemployment in the short run?
   b. Now suppose that over time, expected inflation changes in the same direction that actual inflation changes. What happens to the position of the short-run Phillips curve? After the recession is over, does the economy face a better or worse set of inflation–unemployment combinations?
4. Suppose the economy is in a long-run equilibrium.
   a. Draw the economy's short-run and long-run Phillips curves.
   b. Suppose a wave of business pessimism reduces aggregate demand. Show the effect of this shock on your diagram from part (a). If the Bank of Canada undertakes expansionary monetary policy, can it return the economy to its original inflation rate and original unemployment rate?
   c. Now suppose the economy is back in long-run equilibrium, and then the price of imported oil rises. Show the effect of this shock with a new diagram like that in part (a). If the Bank of Canada undertakes expansionary monetary policy, can it return the economy to its original inflation rate and original unemployment rate? If the Bank of Canada undertakes contractionary monetary policy, can it return the economy to its original inflation rate and original unemployment rate? Explain why this situation differs from that in part (b).

5. Suppose the Bank of Canada believed that the natural rate of unemployment was 6 percent when the actual natural rate was 5.5 percent. If the Bank of Canada based its policy decisions on its belief, what would happen to the economy?
6. The price of oil fell sharply in 1986, again in 1998, and again in 2015.
   a. Show the impact of such a change in both the aggregate-demand/aggregate-supply diagram and in the Phillips curve diagram. What happens to inflation and unemployment in the short run?
   b. Do the effects of this event mean there is no short-run tradeoff between inflation and unemployment? Why or why not?
7. Suppose the Bank of Canada announced that it would pursue contractionary monetary policy in order to reduce the inflation rate. Would the following conditions make the ensuing recession more or less severe? Explain.
   a. Wage contracts have short durations.
   b. There is little confidence in the Bank of Canada's determination to reduce inflation.
   c. Expectations of inflation adjust quickly to actual inflation.
8. Some economists believe that the short-run Phillips curve is relatively steep and shifts quickly in response to changes in the economy. Would these economists be more or less likely to favour contractionary policy in order to reduce inflation than economists who had the opposite views?
9. Imagine an economy in which all wages are set in three-year contracts. In this world, the Bank of Canada announces a disinflationary change in monetary policy to begin immediately. Everyone in the economy believes the Bank of Canada's announcement. Would this disinflation be costless? Why or why not? What might the Bank of Canada do to reduce the cost of disinflation?
10. Given the unpopularity of inflation, why don't elected leaders always support efforts to reduce inflation? Economists believe that countries can reduce the cost of disinflation by letting their central banks make decisions about monetary policy without interference from politicians. Why might this be so?
11. Suppose the governor of the Bank of Canada accepts the theory of the short-run Phillips curve and the natural-rate hypothesis and wants to keep unemployment close to its natural rate. Unfortunately, because the natural rate of unemployment can change over time, the governor is unsure about the value of the natural rate. What macroeconomic variables do you think the governor should look at when conducting monetary policy?
12. The short-run Phillips curve can be represented by the following equation:

$$\text{Unemployment rate} = \text{Natural rate of unemployment} - a\left(\text{Actual inflation} - \text{Expected inflation}\right)$$

We have learned that expected inflation is well "anchored" at the Bank of Canada's target of 2 percent. Our best guess for the current value of the natural rate of unemployment is 7 percent. Finally, assume the value of variable a is 0.5.

   a. Using the numerical values provided, sketch a diagram showing the long-run and the short-run Phillips curves.
   b. If the unemployment rate is equal to the natural rate of unemployment, what is the actual rate of inflation?
   c. What is the slope of the short-run Phillips curve you have sketched? Describe in words what the measure of slope represents.
   d. Assuming that expected inflation and the value of the natural rate of unemployment are unaffected, to what level would the Bank of Canada need to increase the actual rate of inflation to lower the unemployment rate by 1 percentage point?

THE CANADIAN PRESS/POOL-Fred Thornhill

Five Debates over Macroeconomic Policy

LEARNING **objectives**

In this chapter, you will consider five topics of debate ...

1. Should policymakers try to stabilize the economy?
2. Should monetary policy be made by rule rather than by discretion?
3. Should the central bank aim for zero inflation?
4. Should governments balance their budgets?
5. Should the tax laws be reformed to encourage saving?

It is hard to open up the newspaper without finding some politician or editorial writer advocating a change in economic policy. The federal government should use the budget surplus to reduce government debt, or it should use it to finance increases in health care spending. The Bank of Canada should cut interest rates to stimulate a flagging economy, or it should avoid such a move in order not to risk higher inflation. Parliament should reform the tax system to promote faster economic growth, or it should reform the tax system to achieve a more equal distribution of income. Economic issues are central to the continuing political debate in Canada and other countries around the world.

Previous chapters have developed the tools that economists use when analyzing the behaviour of the economy as a whole and the impact of policies on the economy. This final chapter presents both sides in five leading debates over macroeconomic policy. The knowledge you have accumulated in this course provides the background with which we can discuss these important, unsettled issues. It should help you choose a side in these debates or, at least, help you see why choosing a side is so difficult.

17-1 Should Monetary and Fiscal Policymakers Try to Stabilize the Economy?

In the preceding three chapters, we saw how changes in aggregate demand and aggregate supply can lead to short-run fluctuations in production and employment. We also saw how monetary and fiscal policy can shift aggregate demand and, thereby, influence these fluctuations. But even if policymakers *can* influence short-run economic fluctuations, does that mean they *should*? Our first debate concerns whether monetary and fiscal policymakers should use the tools at their disposal in an attempt to smooth the ups and downs of the business cycle.

17-1a Pro: Policymakers Should Try to Stabilize the Economy

Left on their own, economies tend to fluctuate. When households and firms become pessimistic, for instance, they cut back on spending, and this reduces the aggregate demand for goods and services. The fall in aggregate demand in turn reduces the production of goods and services. Firms lay off workers, and the unemployment rate rises. Real GDP and other measures of income fall. Rising unemployment and falling income help confirm the pessimism that initially generated the economic downturn.

Such a recession has no benefit for society—it represents a sheer waste of resources. Workers who become unemployed because of inadequate aggregate demand would rather be working. Business owners whose factories are left idle during a recession would rather be producing valuable goods and services and selling them at a profit.

While few would suggest that policymakers should respond to every minor rise and fall in the economy, there is no reason for society to suffer through the large booms and busts of the business cycle. The development of macroeconomic theory has shown policymakers how to reduce the severity of economic fluctuations. By "leaning against the wind" of economic change, monetary and fiscal policy can stabilize aggregate demand and, thereby, production and employment. When aggregate demand is inadequate to ensure full employment, policymakers should boost government spending, cut taxes, and expand the money supply. When aggregate demand is excessive, risking higher inflation, policymakers should cut government spending, raise taxes, and reduce the money supply. Although unlikely to eliminate business cycles, such policy actions can reduce the severity of large booms and busts and lead to a more stable economy, which benefits everyone.

17-1b Con: Policymakers Should Not Try to Stabilize the Economy

Although monetary and fiscal policy can be used to stabilize the economy in theory, there are substantial obstacles to the use of such policies in practice.

One problem is that monetary and fiscal policy do not affect the economy immediately but instead work with a long lag. Monetary policy affects aggregate demand by changing interest rates, which in turn affect spending, especially residential and business investment. But many households and firms set their spending plans in advance. As a result, it takes time for changes in interest rates to alter the aggregate demand for goods and services. Many studies indicate that changes in monetary policy have little effect on aggregate demand until about six months after the change is made.

Fiscal policy works with a lag because of the long political process that governs changes in spending and taxes. To make any change in fiscal policy, a bill must go through Cabinet committees and then parliamentary committees, and then pass both the House of Commons and the Senate. It can take years to propose, pass, and implement a major change in fiscal policy.

Because of these long lags, policymakers who want to stabilize the economy need to look ahead to economic conditions that are likely to prevail when their actions will take effect. Unfortunately, economic forecasting is highly imprecise, in part because macroeconomics is such a primitive science and in part because the shocks that cause economic fluctuations are intrinsically unpredictable. Thus, when policymakers change monetary or fiscal policy, they must rely on educated guesses about future economic conditions.

All too often, policymakers trying to stabilize the economy do just the opposite. Economic conditions can easily change between the time when a policy action begins and when it takes effect. Because of this, policymakers can inadvertently exacerbate rather than mitigate the magnitude of economic fluctuations. Some economists have claimed that many of the major economic fluctuations in history, including the Great Depression of the 1930s, can be traced to destabilizing policy actions.

One of the first rules taught to physicians is "Do no harm." The human body has natural restorative powers. Confronted with a sick patient and an uncertain diagnosis, often a doctor should do nothing but leave the patient's body to its own devices. Intervening in the absence of reliable knowledge merely risks making matters worse.

The same can be said about treating an ailing economy. It might be desirable if policymakers could eliminate all economic fluctuations, but that is not a realistic goal given the limits of macroeconomic knowledge and the inherent unpredictability of world events. Economic policymakers should refrain from intervening often with monetary and fiscal policy and be content if they do no harm.

Explain why monetary and fiscal policy work with a lag. Why do these lags matter in the choice between active and passive policy?

17-2 Should Monetary Policy Be Made by an Independent Central Bank?

As we first discussed in Chapter 10, the Bank of Canada determines the rate of monetary growth in Canada. On the basis of an evaluation of current economic conditions and forecasts of future conditions, the Bank of Canada chooses whether to raise, lower, or leave unchanged the supply of money in Canada. The rate of monetary growth is set so as to meet a monetary policy goal. Since 1988, the Bank of Canada has asserted that its goal would be to achieve and maintain a stable price level. In 1991, the Bank made this goal more specific by announcing its intention to conduct monetary policy in such a way as to hold inflation, as measured by the rate of change in the consumer price index, between 1 and 3 percent. In November 2011, the Bank announced its intention to extend this target band for inflation to the end of 2016. At that time the federal government and the Bank will determine whether this will remain the long-run target for monetary policy or whether a new target needs to be announced.

The relationship between the Bank of Canada and the federal government has evolved in such a way that the Bank has almost complete discretion over the conduct of monetary policy. The laws that created the Bank gave the institution vague recommendations about what goals it should pursue. However, these laws did not tell the Bank how to pursue these goals, nor did they indicate whether some of these goals might be more important than others. These choices have largely been left in the hands of the governor of the Bank. The Bank has used this independence to adopt a monetary policy rule: The rate of growth in the money supply will be sufficient to maintain a rate of inflation between 1 and 3 percent. This target rate of inflation was achieved in 1994 following a number of years of monetary contraction that caused considerable economic pain in the form of high unemployment.

Some economists are critical of the Bank of Canada's independence. Our second debate over macroeconomic policy, therefore, focuses on whether the Bank should be allowed to conduct monetary policy without being directly answerable to the electorate or to elected officials.

17-2a Pro: Monetary Policy Should Be Made by an Independent Central Bank

Allowing elected officials to have influence in conducting monetary policy has two problems. First, when given this power, politicians are sometimes tempted to use monetary policy to affect the outcome of elections. Suppose that the vote in an upcoming federal election is based on economic conditions at the time of the election. Politicians who are able to influence monetary policy might be tempted to pursue expansionary monetary policies just before the election in order to stimulate production and employment, knowing that the resulting inflation will not show up until after the election. In a small open economy with a flexible exchange rate, like Canada, monetary policy has very large effects on aggregate demand. As a result, the temptation to use monetary policy for political ends is even stronger. Thus, to the extent that politicians influence monetary policy, economic fluctuations may come to reflect the electoral calendar. Economists call such fluctuations the *political business cycle*.

The second, more subtle, problem with allowing elected officials a say in conducting monetary policy is that such influence might lead to more inflation than is desirable. Suppose that policymakers, knowing there is no long-run tradeoff between inflation and unemployment, announce that their goal is zero inflation. Economists believe that zero inflation is more likely to be achieved if the central bank is independent of political influence. Why? Economists believe that, once the public forms expectations of inflation, policymakers face a short-run tradeoff between inflation and unemployment. They are tempted to renege on their announcement of price stability in order to achieve lower unemployment.

This discrepancy between announcements (what policymakers say they are going to do) and actions (what they subsequently do) is called the *time inconsistency of policy*. When policymakers act in a time-inconsistent manner, people become skeptical about policy announcements. As a result, people always expect more inflation than policymakers claim they are trying to achieve. Higher expectations of inflation, in turn, shift the short-run Phillips curve upward. This not only causes the rate of inflation realized in the long run to be higher than it would otherwise be, but also causes a less favourable short-run tradeoff between inflation and unemployment. Since elected officials face a greater incentive to try to exploit the short-run tradeoff in order to curry favour with voters, the rate of inflation realized in the long run and the sacrifice ratio measuring the short-run costs of disinflation will always be higher than they would be if monetary policy were conducted by an independent central bank.

One way to avoid these difficulties is to conduct monetary policy independent of political influence. Because the governor of the Bank of Canada is not elected, the governor faces little incentive to try to exploit the short-run tradeoff between inflation and unemployment for political gain. In addition, because people know that the governor faces little incentive to exploit the short-run tradeoff, they are more likely to believe the Bank of Canada's announcements of low- or zero-inflation targets. In the long run, therefore, the rate of inflation will be lower. Empirical evidence seems to support this conjecture: When economists have compared average rates of inflation across countries, those countries with the most independent central banks tend to have the lowest rates of inflation.

17-2b Con: Monetary Policy Should Not Be Made by an Independent Central Bank

Although there are pitfalls in allowing elected policymakers a say in conducting monetary policy, there is also an important advantage: accountability. Giving central banks complete independence in conducting monetary policy is a problem because it does not limit incompetence and abuse of power. When the government sends police into a community to maintain civic order, it gives them strict guidelines about how to carry out their job. Because police have great power, allowing them to exercise that power in whatever way they want would be dangerous. When the government gives central bankers the sole authority to maintain economic order, it gives them no guidelines. Instead, it gives monetary policymakers undisciplined discretion and does not make them answerable for mistakes. In a small open economy with a flexible exchange rate, monetary policy has a large and lasting influence on aggregate demand. Since changes in aggregate demand translate into changes in employment and income, it is important that someone be accountable for monetary policy choices.

Moreover, the practical importance of time inconsistency is far from clear. Despite clear and forceful statements by the Bank of Canada, it is not obvious that enhancing the credibility of inflation targets has reduced the short-run cost of achieving lower inflation. The sacrifice ratio associated with the Bank of Canada's effort at disinflation in the early 1990s was not made obviously smaller by repeated announcements of a zero-inflation target. In fact, evidence suggests that the sacrifice ratio involved with this effort at disinflation was *larger* than that associated with earlier efforts. The supposedly enhanced credibility of monetary policy announcements that comes from central bank independence therefore seems to yield few dividends.

Finally, the idea that elected policymakers might use monetary policy to generate political business cycles seems at odds with the concept of rational expectations and the incentive that people have to understand the implications of policy announcements. If people understand that reductions in unemployment before an election are temporary and will be followed by increases in unemployment following the election, it seems difficult to understand how elected policymakers can benefit from manipulating monetary policy.

What's more, monetary policy influences inflation and nominal interest rates. It is difficult to direct the benefits of changes in inflation and interest rates to any but very broad interest groups (for example, unexpectedly higher inflation benefits borrowers at the expense of savers). Thus, elected policymakers would not find monetary policy to be a very useful way of trying to influence voters. Fiscal policy seems much better suited for this purpose. Changes in government spending and tax laws can be more easily targeted to very specific interest groups with which a policymaker might want to curry favour. Despite this, the fact that fiscal policy decisions are determined by elected policymakers has not been deemed a serious problem. On the contrary, political accountability with respect to fiscal policy decisions ("no taxation without representation") is a cornerstone of democracy. Why should this not also be true of monetary policy? Economists Lars Osberg and Pierre Fortin, editors of the book *Hard Money, Hard Times,* argue forcefully that it is inappropriate that major economic decisions, with implications for many aspects of Canadian life, are outside the influence of the democratic political process. As the legal mandate of the Bank of Canada recognizes, a complex market economy has a real need for macroeconomic stability. The Bank of Canada is rightly assigned the duty to "mitigate by its influence fluctuations in the general level of production, trade, prices and unemployment, so far as may be possible in the scope of monetary action, and generally to promote the economic and financial welfare of Canada." The citizens of a democracy also have a right to expect that their views will matter in major issues of public policy, such as the balance which is struck among these objectives.

Should the governor of the Bank of Canada be elected? Explain.

17-3 Should the Central Bank Aim for Zero Inflation?

One of the ten principles of economics discussed in Chapter 1, and developed more fully in Chapter 11, is that prices rise when the government prints too much money. Another of the ten principles of economics discussed in Chapter 1, and developed in more detail in Chapter 16, is that society faces a short-run tradeoff between inflation and unemployment. Put together, these two principles raise a question for policymakers: How much inflation should the central bank be willing to tolerate? Our third debate is whether zero is the right target for the inflation rate.

17-3a Pro: The Central Bank Should Aim for Zero Inflation

Inflation confers no benefit on society, but it imposes several real costs. As we discussed in Chapter 11, economists have identified six costs of inflation:

1. Shoeleather costs associated with reduced money holdings
2. Menu costs associated with more frequent adjustment of prices
3. Increased variability of relative prices
4. Unintended changes in tax liabilities due to nonindexation of the tax laws
5. Confusion and inconvenience resulting from a changing unit of account
6. Arbitrary redistributions of wealth associated with dollar-denominated debts

Some economists argue that these costs are small, at least for moderate rates of inflation, such as the 2 percent average rate of inflation experienced in Canada since 1990. But other economists claim these costs can be substantial, even for moderate inflation. Moreover, there is no doubt that the public dislikes inflation. When inflation heats up, opinion polls identify inflation as one of the nation's leading problems.

Of course, the benefits of zero inflation have to be weighed against the costs of achieving it. Reducing inflation usually requires a period of high unemployment and low output, as illustrated by the short-run Phillips curve. But this disinflationary recession is only temporary. Once people come to understand that policymakers are aiming for zero inflation, expectations of inflation will fall, and the short-run tradeoff will improve. Because expectations adjust, there is no tradeoff between inflation and unemployment in the long run.

Reducing inflation is, therefore, a policy with temporary costs and permanent benefits. That is, once the disinflationary recession is over, the benefits of zero inflation would persist into the future. If policymakers are farsighted, they should be willing to incur the temporary costs for the permanent benefits. This is precisely the calculation made by the Bank of Canada in the early 1980s and again in the early 1990s when it introduced monetary contractions designed to reduce the rate of inflation.

Moreover, the costs of reducing inflation need not be as large as some economists claim. If the Bank of Canada announces a credible commitment to zero inflation, it can directly influence expectations of inflation. Such a change in expectations can improve the short-run tradeoff between inflation and unemployment, allowing the economy to reach lower inflation at a reduced cost. The key to this strategy is credibility: People must believe that the Bank of Canada is actually going to carry through on its announced policy. Parliament could help in this regard by passing legislation that made price stability the Bank of Canada's primary goal. Such a law would make it less costly to achieve zero inflation without reducing any of the resulting benefits.

One advantage of a zero-inflation target is that zero provides a more natural focal point for policymakers than any other number. Suppose, for instance, that the Bank of Canada were to announce that it would keep inflation at 2 percent—the average rate experienced since 1990. Would the Bank of Canada really stick to that 2 percent target? If events inadvertently pushed inflation up to 4 or 5 percent, why wouldn't the Bank just raise the target? There is, after all, nothing special about the number 2. By contrast, zero is the only number for the inflation rate at which the Bank of Canada can claim that it achieved price stability and fully eliminated the costs of inflation.

17-3b Con: The Central Bank Should Not Aim for Zero Inflation

Although price stability may be desirable, the benefits of zero inflation compared to moderate inflation are small, whereas the costs of reaching zero inflation are large. Estimates of the sacrifice ratio suggest that reducing inflation by 1 percentage point requires giving up between 2 and 5 percent of one year's output. Using the midpoint of this range of estimates, to reduce inflation from, say, 4 percent to zero requires a loss of 14 percent of a year's output. Although people might dislike inflation of 4 percent, it is not at all clear that they would (or should) be willing to pay this much to get rid of it.

The social costs of disinflation are even larger than this 14 percent figure suggests, because the lost income is not spread equitably over the population. When the economy goes into recession, all incomes do not fall proportionately. Instead, the fall in aggregate income is concentrated on those workers who lose their jobs. The vulnerable workers are often those with the least skills and experience. Hence, much of the cost of reducing inflation is borne by those who can least afford to pay it.

Although economists can list several costs of inflation, there is no professional consensus that these costs are substantial. The shoeleather costs, menu costs, and others that economists have identified do not seem great, at least for moderate rates of inflation. It is true that the public dislikes inflation, but the public may be misled into believing the inflation fallacy—the view that inflation erodes living standards. Economists understand that living standards depend on productivity, not monetary policy. Because inflation in nominal incomes goes hand in hand with inflation in prices, reducing inflation would not cause real incomes to rise more rapidly.

Moreover, policymakers have taken steps to reduce many of the costs of inflation. In the fall of 2000, the federal government indexed income tax brackets to prevent inflation from pushing taxpayers into higher tax brackets. They can also reduce the arbitrary redistributions of wealth between creditors and debtors caused by unexpected inflation by issuing indexed government bonds, as in fact the Bank of Canada did in 1991. Such an act insulates holders of government debt from inflation. In addition, by setting an example, it might encourage private borrowers and lenders to write debt contracts indexed for inflation.

Reducing inflation might be desirable if it could be done at no cost, as some economists argue is possible. Yet this trick seems hard to carry out in practice. When economies reduce their rate of inflation, they almost always experience a period of high unemployment and low output. It is risky to believe that the central bank could achieve credibility so quickly as to make disinflation painless.

Indeed, a disinflationary recession can potentially leave permanent scars on the economy. Firms in all industries reduce their spending on new plants and equipment substantially during recessions, making investment the most volatile component of GDP. Even after the recession is over, the smaller stock of capital reduces productivity, incomes, and living standards below the levels they otherwise would have achieved. In addition, when workers become unemployed in recessions, they lose valuable job skills, permanently reducing their value as workers. Some economists have argued that the slow speed at which Canada's unemployment rate falls following recessions is the result of workers losing job skills while they are unemployed and thus finding re-employment difficult.

A little bit of inflation may even be a good thing. Some economists believe that inflation "greases the wheels" of the labour market. Because workers resist cuts in nominal wages, a fall in real wages is more easily accomplished with a rising price level. Inflation thus makes it easier for real wages to adjust to changes in labour market conditions.

In addition, inflation allows for the possibility of negative real interest rates. Nominal interest rates can never fall below zero, because lenders can always hold on to their money rather than lending it out at a negative return. If inflation is zero, real interest rates can never be negative as well. However, if inflation is positive, then a cut in nominal interest rates below the inflation rate produces negative real interest rates. Sometimes the economy may need negative real interest rates to provide sufficient stimulus to aggregate demand—an option ruled out by zero inflation.

FYI Price-Level Targeting

Like many central banks, the Bank of Canada maintains a target for the rate of inflation. Since 1989, when its target was first announced, the Bank has endeavoured to keep the rate of inflation as close as possible to 2 percent per year. The fact that the rate of inflation in Canada as measured by the CPI has averaged just slightly over 2 percent over this period suggests that the Bank of Canada has enjoyed great success with inflation targeting. The debate we have just described concerns the question of whether it is appropriate to lower the inflation target from 2 to zero percent. The debate, then, is about the appropriate level of the inflation target, not about whether targeting inflation is the best approach for guiding monetary policy.

But is it? The Bank of Canada has asked, and has been busy trying to answer, that question for a number of years.

An alternative to inflation targeting is price-level targeting. That is, rather than target the rate of change in the price level (i.e., the rate of inflation), why not set targets for the price level itself? Let's see how this might work.

The Bank of Canada's inflation target is to maintain the actual rate of inflation as close as possible to the middle of a band between 1 and 3 percent. When actual inflation creeps up close to the upper limit of 3 percent, the Bank tightens monetary policy to lower the rate of inflation back closer to the 2 percent target. Similarly, when actual inflation creeps down toward the lower limit of 1 percent, the Bank loosens monetary policy to allow the rate of inflation to increase back closer to the 2 percent target.

The variability in the actual rate of inflation that is allowed by the Bank's inflation target means that someone making a 25-year investment—in a mortgage, long-term bond, or direct investment in a new factory—must plan for cumulative inflation of as much as 109 percent (if the actual rate of inflation is always at the upper end of the range) or as little as 28 percent (if actual inflation is always at the lower end of the range). In this example, a price level starting from a value of 100 in the first year will increase to a value of anywhere between 128 or 209 by year 25. A lot of uncertainty exists about where prices will be 25 years from now.

Let's continue to assume that the Bank judges 2 percent inflation, on average, to be ideal but now suppose the Bank chooses to target the price level instead of the rate of inflation. In this case, if the price level is 100 in 2010, the Bank will target for it to be 102 in 2011, 104.04 in 2012, 106.12 in 2013, and so on. After 25 years, the price level will be 164.06 with certainty.

Of course, the Bank is unlikely to hit its price-level target every year. Suppose that during 2011, the price level increases from 100 to 101. The Bank would note that the price level is below its target of 102 for 2011. It would also note that since its target for the price level in 2012 is supposed to equal 104.04, it needs to speed up the rate of growth in prices. During 2012, then, it needs to cause the price index to increase from 101 to 104.04 to get back on track for hitting its price-level target. This requires a rate of inflation equal to 3 percent.

What this example shows is that gaining certainty in the price level requires uncertainty with respect to the rate of inflation. With a price-level target, inflation will need to speed up or slow down as necessary to maintain the long-term target for the price level.

What is to be gained if all we are doing is trading uncertainty in the price level for uncertainty in the rate of inflation? One thing that switching to a target for the price level gains the Bank of Canada is flexibility in the conduct of monetary policy. Suppose, for example, there is a housing boom that is encouraging excessive mortgage borrowing. The Bank of Canada might be hesitant to raise interest rates (to dampen excessive mortgage borrowing) if doing so also caused the rate of inflation to fall below its target. Under price-level targeting, the central bank could raise interest rates and so lower inflation as long as it committed to speed inflation at a later date and so make up for lost ground on the long-term price-level target.

The relative merit of price-level as opposed to inflation targeting is by no means settled. An important issue is whether households and firms will fully understand what the Bank is trying to do if it adopts price-level targets. That is, households and firms will need to understand that although the Bank may allow the rate of inflation to vary, it nonetheless remains committed to hitting a price-level target down the road. They will, in other words, need to understand that higher than normal rates of inflation now mean lower than normal rates later.

The Bank of Canada seems, for now, to be committed to inflation targeting. It continues, however, to study the question of whether it should abandon inflation targets for a price-level target.

In light of these arguments, why should policymakers put the economy through a costly, inequitable disinflationary recession to achieve zero inflation, which may have only modest benefits? Economist Alan Blinder, a former vice-chairman of the U.S. Federal Reserve, argued forcefully in his book *Hard Heads, Soft Hearts* that policymakers in countries like Canada and the United States—countries that typically experience moderate rates of inflation—should not make this choice:

> The costs that attend the low and moderate inflation rates experienced in the United States and in other industrial countries appear to be quite modest—more like a bad cold than a cancer on society.... As rational individuals, we do not volunteer for a lobotomy to cure a head cold. Yet, as a collectivity, we routinely prescribe the economic equivalent of lobotomy (high unemployment) as a cure for the inflationary cold. Blinder concludes that it is better to learn to live with moderate inflation.

Explain the costs and benefits of reducing inflation to zero. Which are temporary and which are permanent?

17-4 Should Governments Balance Their Budgets?

A persistent macroeconomic debate concerns government finances. Throughout most of the 1970s, 1980s, and 1990s, Canadian federal and provincial governments spent more than they collected in tax revenue and financed the resulting budget deficits by issuing government debt. As we discussed in Chapter 8, the result was an accumulation of a startling amount of government debt. In that chapter we saw how budget deficits affect saving, investment, and interest rates. Recently, however, most governments in Canada have taken measures to reduce and even eliminate their deficits. In February 1998, the federal government announced its first balanced budget since 1970. For the next ten years, budget surpluses—an excess of tax revenue over government spending—were the norm and the federal government managed to reduce its debt by almost $100 billion. A serious recession in 2009 resulted in a return to deficits and debt accumulation for a few years at least, but political parties of all stripes stated publicly that they were determined to return to balanced budgets. Provincial governments have been less successful at debt reduction but all seem determined to avoid, or at least keep short, those periods of time during which they run budget deficits and so add to their debts.

Our fourth debate concerns whether fiscal policymakers should make balancing the government's budget a high priority.

17-4a Pro: Governments Should Balance Their Budgets

From the mid-1970s to the mid-1990s, governments in Canada spent substantially more than they received in tax revenue. At the federal level, the resulting budget deficits caused the federal debt to rise from $25 billion in 1975 to $609 billion in 1997. Despite some success at debt reduction in the 2000s, a recession in 2008–09 and a slow recovery since then pushed the federal government's debt back up to $687 billion by 2015. Provincial and territorial governments also carry a lot of debt. In 1997, they owed $234 billion in aggregate, an amount that has grown to $566 billion by 2015. If we sum the amount of federal government debt plus the amount of provincial and territorial government debt and divide by the population of Canada, we find that each Canadian owed about $35 037 in 2015.

© Courtesy of Ronald Kneebone

"Our share of the government debt is $35 037 each."

The most direct effect of the government debt is to place a burden on future generations of taxpayers. When these debts and accumulated interest come due, future taxpayers will face a difficult choice. They can pay higher taxes, enjoy less government spending, or both, in order to make resources available to pay off the debt and accumulated interest. Or they can delay the day of reckoning and put the government into even deeper debt by borrowing once again to pay off the old debt and interest. In essence, when the government runs a budget deficit and issues government debt, it allows current taxpayers to pass the bill for some of their government spending on to future taxpayers. Inheriting such a large debt cannot help but lower the living standard of future generations.

In addition to this direct effect, budget deficits also have various macroeconomic effects. Because budget deficits represent *negative* public saving, they lower national saving (the sum of private and public saving). Reduced national saving causes the real exchange rate to rise and net exports to fall. Large and persistent budget deficits, and the accumulation of debt, also increase the default risk that lenders perceive when they consider buying Canadian debt. This causes the real interest rate in Canada to remain above the real interest rate in the rest of the world. Because higher real interest rates cause investment to fall, the capital stock grows smaller over time. A lower capital stock reduces labour productivity, real wages, and the economy's production of goods and services. Thus, when the government increases its debt, future generations are born into an economy with lower incomes as well as higher taxes.

There are, nevertheless, situations in which running a budget deficit is justifiable. Throughout history, the most common cause of increased government debt is war. When a military conflict raises government spending temporarily, it is reasonable to finance this extra spending by borrowing. Otherwise, taxes during wartime would have to rise precipitously. Such high tax rates would greatly distort the incentives faced by those who are taxed, leading to large deadweight losses. In addition, such high tax rates would be unfair to current generations of taxpayers, who already have to make the sacrifice of fighting the war. For a similar reason, we would prefer that governments finance the purchase of infrastructure—roads, bridges, sewers, etc.—by borrowing. Infrastructure benefits not only current but also future generations of taxpayers. Requiring current taxpayers to pay the full cost of new infrastructure puts an unfair burden on them.

It is also reasonable to allow a budget deficit during a temporary downturn in economic activity. When the economy goes into a recession, incomes and consumption expenditures fall and this causes income tax and sales tax revenues to fall. A recession also results in more unemployment and hence larger expenditures on Employment Insurance. If the government tried to balance its budget during a recession, it would need to offset the budgetary implications of these automatic tax and spending changes by increasing tax rates and chopping spending programs. Such a policy would tend to depress aggregate demand at precisely the time it needed to be stimulated and, therefore, would tend to increase the magnitude of economic fluctuations.

The massive accumulation of debt incurred by the federal and provincial governments since the mid-1970s is difficult to justify. The major culprit seems to be the failure of fiscal policymakers to take advantage of periods of strong economic growth to pay down the debt incurred during recessions. For example, the federal government's debt increased quite substantially as a result of the 1980–81 recession. This recession, at that point the worst experienced in Canada since the Great Depression, caused a large fall in tax revenue and necessitated a large increase in spending on programs such as Employment Insurance.

Not surprisingly, the federal government's deficit was large during this period and its debt grew. From 1983 to 1988, however, real output grew by an average of 4.5 percent per year. During this period, the rapid growth in incomes caused tax revenue to grow quickly and expenditures on programs such as Employment Insurance to fall. This was the federal government's opportunity to run budget surpluses and pay down the debt incurred as a result of the recession. Instead, the federal government continued to run large deficits and to add to its debt. Indeed, in 1985, despite real output growth of 5.3 percent, the federal government announced a deficit in excess of $38 billion (equivalent to $76 billion in 2015 dollars).

It is hard to see any rationale for this policy. Although governments need not commit themselves to a balanced budget as an inflexible rule, after allowing for borrowing to finance new infrastructure, the budget should be balanced over the course of a business cycle. This requires budget surpluses during good times to offset the budget deficits that naturally arise during bad times. If the federal government had been consistently operating with such a plan in place since 1975, today's university and college graduates would be entering an economy that promised them greater economic prosperity.

It is time to reverse the effects of this policy mistake. When next a combination of fiscal prudence and good luck leaves our governments with budget surpluses, we should use these surpluses to repay some of the debt that our governments have accumulated. This was the policy followed from 1998 to 2008, a period during which the federal government reduced its debt by $93 billion. Once the economy fully recovers from the 2008–09 recession, it is a policy to which the federal government, and all provincial governments, should return as quickly as possible.

Compared to the alternative of ongoing budget deficits, a balanced budget means greater national saving, investment, and economic growth. It means that future college and university graduates will enter a more prosperous economy.

17-4b Con: Governments Should Not Balance Their Budgets

The problem of government debt is often exaggerated. Although the government debt does represent a tax burden on younger generations, it is not large compared to the average person's lifetime income. The combined debt of all Canadian governments is about $35 037 per person. A person who works 40 years for $40 000 a year will earn $1.6 million over his lifetime. His share of the government debt represents just 2.1 percent of his lifetime resources.

Moreover, it is misleading to view the effects of budget deficits in isolation. The budget deficit is just one piece of a large picture of how the government chooses to raise and spend money. In making these decisions over fiscal policy, policymakers affect different generations of taxpayers in many ways. The government's budget deficit or surplus should be considered together with these other policies.

For example, suppose governments use their budget surpluses to pay off government debt instead of using it to pay for increased spending on education. Does this policy make young generations better off? The government debt will be smaller when they enter the labour force, which means a smaller tax burden. Yet if they are less well educated than they could be, their productivity and incomes will be lower. Many estimates of the return to schooling (the increase in a worker's wage that results from an additional year in school) find that it is quite large. Reducing the budget deficit rather than funding more education spending could, all things considered, make future generations worse off.

Single-minded concern about government debt is also dangerous because it draws attention away from various other policies that redistribute income across generations. For example, the federal government has for a number of years discussed the question of whether to increase the payroll tax used to finance Canada Pension Plan (CPP) payments to elderly people. If implemented, this change would redistribute income away from younger generations (who would pay the higher payroll tax) toward older generations (who would receive the additional CPP payments), even though it does not affect the federal debt. Thus, government debt is only a small piece of the larger issue of how government policy affects the welfare of different generations.

To some extent, the adverse effects of government debt can be reversed by forward-looking parents. Suppose parents are enjoying the benefits of low taxes and high government spending on social programs but are worried about the impact of the resulting government debt on their children. Parents can offset the impact by using the income they are saving as a result of low taxes to leave their children a larger bequest. The bequest would enhance the children's ability to bear the burden of future taxes. Some economists claim that people do, in fact, behave this way. If this were true, higher private saving by parents would offset the public dissaving of budget deficits, and deficits would not affect the economy. Most economists doubt that parents are so farsighted, but some people probably do act this way, and anyone could. Deficits give people the opportunity to consume at the expense of their children, but deficits do not require them to do so. If the government debt were actually a great problem facing future generations, some parents would help to solve it.

Critics of budget deficits sometimes assert that the government debt cannot continue to rise forever, but in fact it can. Just as a bank evaluating a loan application would compare a person's debts to his income, we should judge the burden of the government debt relative to the size of the nation's income. Population growth and technological progress cause the total income of the Canadian economy to grow over time. As a result, the nation's ability to pay the interest on the government debt grows over time as well. As long as the government debt grows more slowly than the nation's income, there is nothing to prevent the government debt from growing forever.

Some numbers can put this into perspective. The real output of the Canadian economy grows on average about 3 percent per year. If the inflation rate is 2 percent per year, then nominal income grows at a rate of 5 percent per year. The government debt, therefore, can rise by 5 percent per year without increasing the ratio of debt to income. In 2015, the federal government debt was \$687 billion; 5 percent of this figure is \$34.3 billion. As long as the federal budget deficit is smaller than \$34.3 billion, the policy is sustainable. There will never be any day of reckoning that forces the budget deficits to end or the economy to collapse.

If moderate budget deficits are sustainable, there is no need for the government to raise tax rates or cut spending to achieve budget balance. Let's instead recognize that moderate deficits are not a problem and so maintain lower tax rates and higher government spending than would be the case if we balanced the budget.

Explain how reducing the government debt makes future generations better off. What fiscal policy might improve the lives of future generations more than reducing the government debt?

FYI Progress on Debt Reduction?

In Chapter 8 (FYI: How Large Is Government Debt?), we learned that a lot of considerations are involved in determining just how indebted a government might be. Whether the total amount of government debt is large or small depends, for example, on whether we include unfunded liabilities and whether we worry about what the future holds for later generations of taxpayers. Even if we cannot nail down a single measure of the size of government debt, can we at least determine if it is getting bigger or smaller?

As you have probably guessed, this is not as simple as one might think. It depends on how you look at it.

In 1997, the net debt of the federal government was equal to $609 billion. (Data on government debt are available from the *Fiscal Reference Tables* published by the federal government's Department of Finance Canada at www.fin.gc.ca). By 2015, that debt stood at $687 billion. That was easy: The federal government's debt increased by $78 billion, or a little less than 13 percent. Right?

Well, maybe, but three things other than the debt increased between 1997 and 2015 that might cause you to reevaluate.

One of these things was inflation. Between 1997 and 2015, the prices of goods and services in the economy increased by 47 percent, as measured by the GDP deflator. If you owe money in the form of a loan or a mortgage or a car loan, inflation is your friend because it reduces the real value of your debt. The same is true for the federal government: Inflation reduces the real value of its debt. If we take inflation into account, the net debt of the federal government fell from $609 billion to $467 billion when measured in terms of what a dollar could buy in 1997. From this perspective, once we take inflation into account, the federal government's debt has *fallen* by 23 percent since 1997.

SurangaSL/Shutterstock.com

Something else happened between 1997 and 2015: Canada's population increased by 5.9 million people. Since one of the reasons governments borrow is to provide government services, then even if nothing else changed, we might expect debt to grow with population. What's more, since the government's debt is the debt of all Canadians, if there are more Canadians the burden of that debt is spread more thinly across us all. If we now calculate the amount of debt, measured in real dollars, that is owed by each Canadian, we find that it has fallen from $20 390 in 1997 to $13 062 in 2015. From this perspective, then, the size of the federal government's debt has fallen by 36 percent since 1997.

The third relevant thing that happened between 1997 and 2015 is that our collective income—gross domestic product (GDP)—increased by 60 percent. This is an important consideration because our ability to pay off our debts depends on our income. This is as true for the nation as a whole as it is for individuals. If we now compare the size of the federal government's debt relative to our collective income (GDP), we arrive at the conclusion that the ratio of debt to income has fallen from 69 percent in 1997 to 33 percent in 2015. From this perspective, then, the federal government's debt has fallen by over 50 percent.

So, which is it? Between 1997 and 2015, did the federal government's debt increase by 13 percent, fall by 23 percent, fall by 36 percent, or fall by over 50 percent? It depends on how you look at it.

17-5 Should the Tax Laws Be Reformed to Encourage Saving?

A nation's standard of living depends on its ability to produce goods and services. This was one of the ten principles of economics in Chapter 1. As we saw in Chapter 1, a nation's productive capability, in turn, is determined largely by how much it saves and invests for the future. Our fifth debate is whether policymakers should reform the tax laws to encourage greater saving and investment.

17-5a Pro: The Tax Laws Should Be Reformed to Encourage Saving

A nation's saving rate is a key determinant of its long-run economic prosperity. When the saving rate is higher, more resources are available for investment in new plant and equipment. A larger stock of plant and equipment, in turn, raises labour productivity, wages, and incomes. It is therefore no surprise that international data show a strong correlation between national saving rates and measures of economic well-being.

Another of the ten principles of economics presented in Chapter 1 is that people respond to incentives. This lesson should apply to people's decisions about how much to save. If a nation's laws make saving attractive, people will save a higher fraction of their incomes, and this higher saving will lead to a more prosperous future.

Unfortunately, the Canadian tax system discourages saving by taxing the return to saving quite heavily. For example, consider a 25-year-old worker who saves $1000 of her income to have a more comfortable retirement at the age of 70. If she buys a bond that pays an interest rate of 10 percent, the $1000 will accumulate at the end of 45 years to $72 900 in the absence of taxes on interest. But suppose she faces a marginal tax rate on interest income of 40 percent, which is typical of many workers once federal and provincial or territorial income taxes are added together. In this case, her after-tax interest rate is only 6 percent, and the $1000 will accumulate at the end of 45 years to only $13 800. That is, accumulated over this long span of time, the tax rate on interest income reduces the benefit of saving $1000 from $72 900 to $13 800—or by about 80 percent.

The tax laws further discourage saving by taxing some forms of capital income twice. Suppose a person uses some of his saving to buy shares in a corporation. When the corporation earns a profit from its capital investments, it first pays tax on this profit in the form of the corporate income tax. If the corporation pays out the rest of the profit to the shareholder in the form of dividends, the shareholder pays tax on this income a second time in the form of the individual income tax. This double taxation substantially reduces the return to the shareholder, thereby reducing the incentive to save.

In addition to the tax laws, many other policies and institutions in our society reduce the incentive for households to save. Some government benefits, such as Old Age Security pension payments, are means-tested; that is, the benefits are reduced for those who in the past have been prudent enough to save some of their income. Colleges and universities grant financial aid as a function of the wealth of the students and their parents. Such a policy is like a tax on wealth and, as such, discourages students and parents from saving.

There are various ways in which the tax laws can provide an incentive to save, or at least reduce the disincentive that households now face. Already the tax laws give preferential treatment to some types of retirement saving. Tax-Free Savings Accounts (TFSAs) were introduced in 2009 as a way of allowing individuals to save without having to pay taxes on the income earned by those savings. Thus, eligible individuals can contribute to a special tax account and never have to pay taxes on the interest earned on those savings. Another way the government encourages savings is via a registered retirement savings plan (RRSP). When taxpayers put income into RRSPs, they receive a tax deduction equal to the amount of their contribution and so reduce their tax bill. What's more, the interest earned on savings placed in RRSPs is not taxed until the funds are withdrawn at retirement. In both ways, RRSPs encourage people to save. There are, however, limits on the amounts that can be put into a TFSA and into an RRSP. Only $5000 can be contributed to a TFSA each year and, as of 2015, a maximum of $24 930 can be contributed to an RRSP each year. These recent changes are encouraging signs that the federal government understands the importance of using tax policy to encourage saving.

An important step the federal government took to encourage greater saving was to introduce the Goods and Services Tax (GST) in 1991. The great majority of federal tax revenue is collected through the personal income tax. Under an income tax, a dollar earned is taxed the same whether it is spent or saved. The GST is a consumption tax, meaning that a household pays tax only on the basis of what it spends. Income that is saved is exempt from consumption taxation until the saving is later withdrawn and spent on consumption goods. For this reason, a consumption tax increases the incentive to save. Because of this, economists were generally in favour of adding the GST to the federal government's tax mix, and many would favour an increased emphasis on consumption taxation, as opposed to income taxation. A switch from income to consumption taxation would increase the incentive to save.

Despite the general preference of economists for a greater emphasis on consumption taxation, in 2006 the federal government did the opposite and reduced the GST tax rate from 7 percent to 6 percent. In 2008, it went one step further and reduced the GST rate from 6 percent to 5 percent. By increasing, rather than reducing, its reliance on income taxation, the federal government is moving in a direction that the great majority of economists does not support.

17-5b Con: The Tax Laws Should Not Be Reformed to Encourage Saving

Increasing saving may be desirable, but it is not the only goal of tax policy. Policymakers also must be sure to distribute the tax burden fairly. The problem with proposals to increase the incentive to save is that they increase the tax burden on those who can least afford it.

It is an undeniable fact that high-income households save a greater fraction of their income than low-income households. As a result, any tax change that favours people who save will also tend to favour people with high income. Policies such as RRSPs may seem appealing, but they lead to a less egalitarian society. By reducing the tax burden on the wealthy who can take advantage of these plans, they force the government to raise the tax burden on the poor.

Moreover, tax policies designed to encourage saving may not be effective at achieving that goal. Many studies have found that saving is relatively inelastic—that is, the amount of saving is not very sensitive to the rate of return on saving. If this is indeed the case, then tax provisions that raise the effective return by reducing the taxation of capital income will further enrich the wealthy without inducing them to save more than they otherwise would.

Economic theory does not give a clear prediction about whether a higher rate of return would increase saving. The outcome depends on the relative size of two conflicting effects, called the *substitution effect* and the *income effect*. On one hand, a higher rate of return raises the benefit of saving: Each dollar saved today produces more consumption in the future. This substitution effect tends to raise saving. On the other hand, a higher rate of return lowers the need for saving: A household has to save less to achieve any target level of consumption in the future. This income effect tends to reduce saving. If the substitution and income effects approximately cancel each other, as some studies suggest, then saving will not change when lower taxation of capital income raises the rate of return.

There are other ways to raise national saving than by giving tax breaks to the rich. National saving is the sum of private and public saving. Instead of trying to alter the tax laws to encourage greater private saving, policymakers can simply raise public saving by increasing the budget surplus, perhaps by raising taxes on the wealthy or by restraining government spending. This offers a direct way of raising national saving and increasing prosperity for future generations.

Indeed, once public saving is taken into account, tax provisions to encourage saving might backfire. Tax changes that reduce the taxation of capital income reduce government revenue and, thereby, lead to a budget deficit. To increase national saving, such a change in the tax laws must stimulate private saving by more than the decline in public saving. If this is not the case, so-called saving incentives can potentially make matters worse.

Give three examples of how our society discourages saving. What are the drawbacks of eliminating these disincentives?

17-6 Conclusion

This chapter has considered five debates over macroeconomic policy. For each, it began with a controversial proposition and then offered the arguments pro and con. If you find it hard to choose a side in these debates, you may find some comfort in the fact that you are not alone. The study of economics does not always make it easy to choose among alternative policies. Indeed, by clarifying the inevitable tradeoffs that policymakers face, it can make the choice more difficult.

Difficult choices, however, have no right to seem easy. When you hear politicians or commentators proposing something that sounds too good to be true, it probably is. If they sound like they are offering you a free lunch, you should look for the hidden price tag. Few if any policies come with benefits but no costs. By helping you see through the fog of rhetoric so common in political discourse, the study of economics should make you a better participant in our national debates.

summary

- Advocates of active monetary and fiscal policy view the economy as inherently unstable and believe that policy can manage aggregate demand to offset the inherent instability. Critics of active monetary and fiscal policy emphasize that policy affects the economy with a lag and that our ability to forecast future economic conditions is poor. As a result, attempts to stabilize the economy can end up being destabilizing.
- Advocates of an independent central bank argue that such independence guards against politicians using monetary policy in an attempt to influence voters. They also assert that a lower rate of inflation and a more favourable short-run tradeoff between inflation and unemployment are possible when the central bank is independent of political influence. Critics of central bank independence argue that because monetary policy has large and lasting influences on aggregate demand, and hence on output and employment, citizens should have a say on the conduct of monetary policy, just as they do on the conduct of fiscal policy.
- Advocates of a zero-inflation target emphasize that inflation has many costs and few if any benefits. Moreover, the cost of eliminating inflation—depressed output and employment—is only temporary. Even this cost can be reduced if the central bank announces a credible plan to reduce inflation, thereby directly lowering expectations of inflation. Critics of a zero-inflation target claim that moderate inflation imposes only small costs on society, whereas the recession necessary to reduce inflation is quite costly.
- Advocates of balancing government budgets argue that budget deficits impose a burden on future generations by raising their taxes and lowering their incomes.

Critics of balanced government budgets argue that the deficit is only one small piece of fiscal policy. Single-minded concern about budget deficits can obscure the many ways in which the government's tax and spending decisions affect different generations.

- Advocates of tax incentives for saving point out that our society discourages saving in many ways, such as by heavily taxing the income from capital and by reducing benefits for those who have accumulated wealth. They endorse reforming the tax laws to encourage saving, perhaps by switching from an income tax to a consumption tax. Critics of tax incentives for saving argue that many proposed changes to stimulate saving would primarily benefit the wealthy, who do not need a tax break. They also argue that such changes might have only a small effect on private saving. Raising public saving by increasing the government's budget surplus would provide a more direct and equitable way to increase national saving.

QUESTIONS FOR **review**

1. What causes the lags in the effect of monetary and fiscal policy on aggregate demand? What are the implications of these lags for the debate over active versus passive policy?
2. What might motivate a central banker to cause a political business cycle? What does the possibility of a political business cycle imply for the debate over whether monetary policy should be conducted by an independent central bank?
3. Explain how credibility might affect the cost of reducing inflation.
4. Why are some economists against a target of zero inflation?
5. Explain two ways in which a government budget deficit hurts a future worker.
6. What are two situations in which most economists view a budget deficit as justifiable?
7. Give an example of how the government might hurt young generations, even while reducing the government debt they inherit.
8. Some economists say that the government can continue running a budget deficit forever. How is that possible?
9. Some income from capital is taxed twice. Explain.
10. Give an example, other than tax policy, of how our society discourages saving.
11. What adverse effect might be caused by tax incentives to raise saving?

QUICK CHECK **multiple choice**

1. Approximately how long does it take a change in monetary policy to influence aggregate demand?
   a. one month
   b. six months
   c. two years
   d. five years
2. Which of the following is a frequent argument made by advocates for setting monetary policy by rule rather than discretion?
   a. central bankers with discretion are tempted to renege on their announced commitments to low inflation
   b. central bankers following a rule will be more responsive to the needs of the political process
   c. fiscal policy is a much better tool for economic stabilization than is monetary policy
   d. it is sometimes useful to give the economy a burst of surprise inflation
3. Which of the following is NOT an argument for maintaining a positive rate of inflation?
   a. It permits real interest rates to be negative.
   b. It allows real wages to fall without cuts in nominal wages.
   c. It increases the variability of relative prices.
   d. It would be costly to reduce inflation to zero.
4. Which of the following is an argument made by advocates of taxing consumption rather than income?
   a. a consumption tax is a better automatic stabilizer
   b. taxing consumption does not cause any deadweight losses
   c. the rich consume a higher fraction of income than the poor
   d. the current tax code discourages people from saving

PROBLEMS AND **applications**

1. The chapter suggests that the economy, like the human body, has "natural restorative powers."
   a. Illustrate the short-run effect of a fall in aggregate demand using an aggregate-demand/aggregate-supply diagram. What happens to total output, income, and employment?
   b. If the government does not use stabilization policy, what happens to the economy over time? Illustrate this on your diagram. Does this adjustment generally occur in a matter of months or a matter of years?
   c. Do you think the "natural restorative powers" of the economy mean that policymakers should be passive in response to the business cycle?
2. In Chapter 15, we learned that the multiplier effect associated with a change in government purchases could be expressed as $1/(1 - MPC + MPI)$, where *MPC* is the marginal propensity to consume and *MPI* is the marginal propensity to import. If $MPC = 0.90$ and $MPI = 0.10$, then we can use this formula to calculate that the multiplier effect associated with a change in government purchases is equal to 5. A problem with which fiscal policymakers must deal is the fact they are not absolutely certain what the true magnitudes of the *MPC* and *MPI* are. Suppose these values were actually 0.95 and 0.05, respectively. How would this affect the size of the multiplier effect? How does uncertainty about the size of the values of *MPC* and *MPI* affect your position on the debate over whether policymakers should try to stabilize the economy?
3. Suppose that people suddenly wanted to hold more money balances. For simplicity, assume Canada is a closed economy.
   a. What would be the effect of this change on the economy if the Bank of Canada followed a rule of increasing the money supply by 3 percent per year? Illustrate your answer with a money-market diagram and an aggregate-demand/aggregate-supply diagram.
   b. What would be the effect of this change on the economy if the Bank of Canada followed a rule of increasing the money supply by 3 percent per year *plus* 1 percentage point for every percentage point that unemployment rises above its normal level? Illustrate your answer.
   c. Which of the foregoing rules better stabilizes the economy? Would it help to allow the Bank of Canada to respond to predicted unemployment instead of current unemployment? Explain.
4. In earlier chapters, we learned about automatic stabilizers in the tax system and government spending programs.
   a. Provide an example of an automatic stabilizer that works via the tax system in Canada and another of an automatic stabilizer that works via a government spending program.
   b. How does the existence of automatic stabilizers affect your position on the debate over whether policymakers should try to stabilize the economy?
5. The problem of time inconsistency applies to fiscal policy as well as to monetary policy. Suppose the government announced a reduction in taxes on income from capital investments, like new factories.
   a. If investors believed that capital taxes would remain low, how would the government's action affect the level of investment?
   b. After investors have responded to the announced tax reduction, does the government have an incentive to renege on its policy? Explain.
   c. Given your answer to part (b), would investors believe the government's announcement? What can the government do to increase the credibility of announced policy changes?
   d. Explain why this situation is similar to the time-inconsistency problem faced by monetary policymakers.
6. Chapter 2 explains the difference between positive analysis and normative analysis. In the debate about whether the central bank should aim for zero inflation, which areas of disagreement involve positive statements and which involve normative judgments?
7. Why are the benefits of reducing inflation permanent and the costs temporary? Why are the costs of increasing inflation permanent and the benefits temporary? Use Phillips curve diagrams in your answer.
8. Suppose the federal government cuts taxes and increases spending, raising the budget deficit to 12 percent of GDP. If nominal GDP is rising 7 percent per year, are such budget deficits sustainable forever? Explain. If budget deficits of this size are maintained for 20 years, what is likely to happen to your taxes and your children's taxes in the future? Can you do something today to offset this future effect?
9. Explain how each of the following policies redistributes income across generations. Is the redistribution from young to old, or from old to young?
   a. an increase in the budget deficit
   b. more generous subsidies for education loans
   c. greater investments in highways and bridges
   d. indexation of Old Age Security benefits to inflation
10. Surveys suggest that most people are opposed to budget deficits, but these same people elected

representatives who in the 1970s and 1980s passed budgets with significant deficits. Why might the opposition to budget deficits be stronger in principle than in practice?

11. In 1991, the federal government simultaneously reduced the income tax rate and introduced the Goods and Services Tax (GST). Explain why economists applauded this switch from taxing incomes to taxing spending.

12. The following table presents data taken from Finance Canada's *Economic and Fiscal Update, November 2003*. It shows borrowing in the market for loanable funds by Canadian governments and Canadian businesses in fiscal years 1992–93 and 2001–02.

	1992–93	2001–02 (billions of dollars)	Change
Government	+\$45.1	−\$10.3	−\$55.4
Business	+\$22.0	+\$59.1	+\$37.1

Source: The Economic and Fiscal Update, http://www.fin.gc.ca/ec2003/ec03e.pdf, Department of Finance Canada, 2003.

In the earlier period, Canadian governments were running large deficits. As a result, they borrowed \$45.1 billion in capital markets. In the later period, Canadian governments were realizing budget surpluses and as a result provided \$10.3 billion in funds to capital markets. The table shows how the change in government borrowing enabled the private sector greater access to loanable funds. How do you think this change in government policy affected interest rates? How do you think this change affected the ability of Canadian businesses to expand and create new employment?

13. The following table presents data taken from Finance Canada's *Economic and Fiscal Update, November 2003*. It shows federal government spending, after removing spending on interest payments on the debt, in fiscal years 1992–93 and 2001–02. The spending measured here is on health care, defence, pensions, Employment Insurance, and other goods and services.

	1992–93	2001–02 (percentage of GDP)	Change
Federal government program spending	16.8%	11.3%	−5.5%

Source: The Economic and Fiscal Update, http://www.fin.gc.ca/ec2003/ec03e.pdf, Department of Finance Canada, 2003.

In the earlier period, the federal government spent an amount equal to 16.8 percent of GDP on such programs. In the later period, federal spending on these programs amounted to only 11.3 percent of GDP. How do you think this change in government spending policy affected Canadians receiving health care, pensions, and Employment Insurance?

A

absolute advantage the comparison among producers of a good according to their productivity (p. 52)

aggregate-demand curve a curve that shows the quantity of goods and services that households, firms, and the government want to buy at each price level (p. 317)

aggregate-supply curve a curve that shows the quantity of goods and services that firms choose to produce and sell at each price level (p. 317)

appreciation an increase in the value of a currency as measured by the amount of foreign currency it can buy (p. 269)

automatic stabilizers changes in fiscal policy that stimulate aggregate demand when the economy goes into a recession, without policymakers having to take any deliberate action (p. 381)

B

balanced trade a situation in which exports equal imports (p. 258)

bank capital the resources a bank's owners have put into the institution (p. 218)

Bank of Canada the central bank of Canada (p. 213)

bank rate the interest rate charged by the Bank of Canada on loans to the commercial banks (p. 221)

bond a certificate of indebtedness (p. 155)

budget deficit a shortfall of tax revenue from government spending (p. 162)

budget surplus an excess of tax revenue over government spending (p. 162)

business cycle fluctuations in economic activity, such as employment and production (p. 14)

C

capital flight a large and sudden reduction in the demand for assets located in a country (p. 301)

capital requirement a government regulation specifying a minimum amount of bank capital (p. 219)

catch-up effect the property whereby countries that start off poor tend to grow more rapidly than countries that start off rich (p. 138)

central bank an institution designed to regulate the quantity of money in the economy (p. 213)

circular-flow diagram a visual model of the economy that shows how dollars flow through markets among households and firms (p. 21)

classical dichotomy the theoretical separation of nominal and real variables (p. 236)

closed economy an economy that does not interact with other economies in the world (p. 257)

collective bargaining the process by which unions and firms agree on the terms of employment (p. 195)

commodity money money that takes the form of a commodity with intrinsic value (p. 209)

comparative advantage the comparison among producers of a good according to their opportunity cost (p. 53)

competitive market a market in which there are many buyers and many sellers so that each has a negligible impact on the market price (p. 64)

complements two goods for which an increase in the price of one leads to a decrease in the demand for the other (p. 68)

consumer price index (CPI) a measure of the overall cost of the goods and services bought by a typical consumer (p. 113)

consumption spending by households on goods and services, with the exception of purchases of new housing (p. 96)

core inflation a measure of the underlying trend of inflation (p. 115)

crowding out a decrease in investment that results from government borrowing (p. 169)

crowding-out effect on investment the offset in aggregate demand that results when expansionary fiscal policy raises the interest rate and thereby reduces investment spending (p. 370)

crowding-out effect on net exports the offset in aggregate demand that results when expansionary fiscal policy in a small open economy with a flexible exchange rate raises the real exchange rate and thereby reduces net exports (p. 373)

currency the paper bills and coins in the hands of the public (p. 209)

cyclical unemployment the deviation of unemployment from its natural rate (p. 187)

D

demand curve a graph of the relationship between the price of a good and the quantity demanded (p. 65)

demand deposits balances in bank accounts that depositors can access on demand by writing a cheque or using a debit card (p. 211)

demand schedule a table that shows the relationship between the price of a good and the quantity demanded (p. 65)

depreciation a decrease in the value of a currency as measured by the amount of foreign currency it can buy (p. 269)

depression a severe recession (p. 311)

diminishing returns the property whereby the benefit from an extra unit of an input declines as the quantity of the input increases (p. 137)

discouraged searchers individuals who would like to work but have given up looking for a job (p. 185)

E

economics the study of how society manages its scarce resources (p. 2)

efficiency the property of society getting the most it can from its scarce resources (p. 3)

efficiency wages above-equilibrium wages paid by firms in order to increase worker productivity (p. 198)

Employment Insurance (EI) a government program that partially protects workers' incomes when they become unemployed (p. 192)

equilibrium a situation in which the price has reached the level where quantity supplied equals quantity demanded (p. 74)

equilibrium price the price that balances quantity supplied and quantity demanded (p. 74)

equilibrium quantity the quantity supplied and the quantity demanded at the equilibrium price (p. 74)

equity the property of distributing economic prosperity fairly among the members of society (p. 3)

exports goods and services produced domestically and sold abroad (pp. 57, 257)

externality the impact of one person's actions on the well-being of a bystander (p. 11)

F

fiat money money without intrinsic value that is used as money because of government decree (p. 209)

financial intermediaries financial institutions through which savers can indirectly provide funds to borrowers (p. 158)

financial markets financial institutions through which savers can directly provide funds to borrowers (p. 155)

financial system the group of institutions in the economy that help to match one person's saving with another person's investment (p. 154)

fiscal policy the setting of the level of government spending and taxation by government policymakers (p. 366)

Fisher effect the one-for-one adjustment of the nominal interest rate to the inflation rate (p. 242)

fixed exchange rate a policy by which the value of the exchange rate is held fixed by the central bank (p. 363)

flexible exchange rate a policy by which the value of the exchange rate is allowed to vary without interference by the central bank (p. 362)

foreign exchange market operations the purchase or sale of foreign money by the Bank of Canada (p. 223)

fractional-reserve banking a banking system in which banks hold only a fraction of deposits as reserves (p. 216)

frictional unemployment unemployment that results because it takes time for workers to search for the jobs that best suit their tastes and skills (p. 188)

G

GDP deflator a measure of the price level calculated as the ratio of nominal GDP to real GDP times 100 (p. 100)

government debt the sum of all past budget deficits and surpluses (p. 168)

government net debt the difference between the value of government financial liabilities and financial assets (p. 171)

government purchases spending on goods and services by local, territorial, provincial, and federal governments (p. 96)

gross domestic product (GDP) the market value of all final goods and services produced within a country in a given period of time (p. 93)

H

human capital the knowledge and skills that workers acquire through education, training, and experience (p. 133)

I

import quota a limit on the quantity of a good that is produced abroad and sold domestically (p. 299)

imports goods and services produced abroad and sold domestically (pp. 57, 257)

incentive something that induces a person to act (p. 6)

indexation the automatic correction of a dollar amount for the effects of inflation by law or contract (p. 121)

inferior good a good for which, other things equal, an increase in income leads to a decrease in demand (p. 67)

inflation an increase in the overall level of prices in the economy (p. 13)

inflation rate the percentage change in the price index from the preceding period (p. 115)

inflation tax the revenue the government raises by creating money (p. 241)

interest rate parity a theory of interest rate determination whereby the real interest rate on comparable financial assets should be the same in all economies with full access to world financial markets (p. 279)

investment spending on capital equipment, inventories, and structures, including household purchases of new housing (p. 96)

J

job search the process by which workers find appropriate jobs given their tastes and skills (p. 189)

L

labour force the total number of workers, including both the employed and the unemployed (p. 180)

labour-force participation rate the percentage of the adult population that is in the labour force (p. 181)

law of demand the claim that, other things equal, the quantity demanded of a good falls when the price of the good rises (p. 65)

law of supply the claim that, other things equal, the quantity supplied of a good rises when the price of the good rises (p. 70)

law of supply and demand the claim that the price of any good adjusts to bring the quantity supplied and the quantity demanded for that good into balance (p. 76)

leverage the use of borrowed money to supplement existing funds for purposes of investment (p. 219)

leverage ratio the ratio of assets to bank capital (p. 219)

liquidity the ease with which an asset can be converted into the economy's medium of exchange (p. 208)

M

macroeconomics the study of economy-wide phenomena, including inflation, unemployment, and economic growth (pp. 26, 91)

marginal changes small incremental adjustments to a plan of action (p. 4)

market a group of buyers and sellers of a particular good or service (p. 63)

market economy an economy that allocates resources through the decentralized decisions of many firms and households as they interact in markets for goods and services (p. 9)

market failure a situation in which a market left on its own fails to allocate resources efficiently (p. 11)

market for loanable funds the market in which those who want to save supply funds and those who want to borrow to invest demand funds (p. 163)

market power the ability of a single economic actor (or small group of actors) to have a substantial influence on market prices (p. 11)

medium of exchange an item that buyers give to sellers when they want to purchase goods or services (p. 208)

menu costs the costs of changing prices (p. 246)

microeconomics the study of how households and firms make decisions and how they interact in markets (pp. 26, 91)

model of aggregate demand and aggregate supply the model that most economists use to explain short-run fluctuations in economic activity around its long-run trend (p. 317)

monetary neutrality the proposition that changes in the money supply do not affect real variables (p. 237)

monetary policy the setting of the money supply by policymakers in the central bank (p. 214)

money the set of assets in an economy that people regularly use to buy goods and services from other people (p. 208)

money multiplier the amount of money the banking system generates with each dollar of reserves (p. 218)

money supply the quantity of money available in the economy (p. 214)

multiplier effect the additional shifts in aggregate demand that result when expansionary fiscal policy increases income and thereby increases consumer spending (p. 366)

mutual fund an institution that sells shares to the public and uses the proceeds to buy a portfolio of stocks and bonds (p. 158)

N

national saving (saving) the total income in the economy that remains after paying for consumption and government purchases (p. 162)

natural level of output the production of goods and services that an economy achieves in the long run when unemployment is at its normal rate (p. 326)

natural-rate hypothesis the claim that unemployment eventually returns to its normal, or natural, rate, regardless of the rate of inflation (p. 401)

natural rate of unemployment the rate of unemployment to which the economy tends to return in the long run (p. 187)

natural resources the inputs into the production of goods and services that are provided by nature, such as land, rivers, and mineral deposits (p. 133)

net capital outflow the purchase of foreign assets by domestic residents minus the purchase of domestic assets by foreigners (p. 262)

net exports the value of a nation's exports minus the value of its imports; also called the *trade balance* (pp. 97, 258)

nominal exchange rate the rate at which a person can trade the currency of one country for the currency of another (p. 268)

nominal GDP the production of goods and services valued at current prices (p. 100)

nominal interest rate the interest rate as usually reported without a correction for the effects of inflation (p. 122)

nominal variables variables measured in monetary units (p. 236)

normal good a good for which, other things equal, an increase in income leads to an increase in demand (p. 67)

normative statements claims that attempt to prescribe how the world should be (p. 27)

O

Okun's law the number of percentage points the unemployment rate increases when GDP falls by 1 percentage point (p. 407)

open economy an economy that interacts freely with other economies around the world (p. 257)

open-market operations the purchase or sale of Government of Canada bonds by the Bank of Canada (p. 222)

opportunity cost whatever must be given up to obtain some item (pp. 4, 52)

overnight rate the interest rate on very short-term loans between commercial banks (p. 221)

P

perfect capital mobility full access to world financial markets (p. 279)

Phillips curve a curve that shows the short-run tradeoff between inflation and unemployment (p. 392)

physical capital the stock of equipment and structures that are used to produce goods and services (p. 133)

positive statements claims that attempt to describe the world as it is (p. 27)

private saving the income that households have left after paying for taxes and consumption (p. 162)

production possibilities frontier a graph that shows the combinations of output that the economy can possibly produce given the available factors of production and the available production technology (p. 23)

productivity the quantity of goods and services produced from each hour of a worker's time (pp. 12, 132)

property rights the ability of an individual to own and exercise control over scarce resources (p. 10)

public saving the tax revenue that the government has left after paying for its spending (p. 162)

purchasing-power parity a theory of exchange rates whereby a unit of any given currency should be able to buy the same quantity of goods in all countries (p. 274)

Q

quantitative easing the purchase and sale by the central bank of non-government securities or government securities with long maturity terms (p. 223)

quantity demanded the amount of a good that buyers are willing and able to purchase (p. 64)

quantity equation the equation $M \times V = P \times Y$, which relates the quantity of money, the velocity of money, and the dollar value of the economy's output of goods and services (p. 238)

quantity supplied the amount of a good that sellers are willing and able to sell (p. 70)

quantity theory of money a theory asserting that the quantity of money available determines the price level and that the growth rate in the quantity of money available determines the inflation rate (p. 235)

R

rational expectations the theory according to which people optimally use all the information they have, including information about government policies, when forecasting the future (p. 408)

rational people those who systematically and purposefully do the best they can to achieve their objectives (p. 4)

real exchange rate the rate at which a person can trade the goods and services of one country for the goods and services of another (p. 270)

real GDP the production of goods and services valued at constant prices (p. 100)

real interest rate the interest rate corrected for the effects of inflation (p. 122)

real variables variables measured in physical units (p. 236)

recession a period of declining real incomes and rising unemployment (p. 311)

reserve ratio the fraction of deposits that banks hold as reserves (p. 216)

reserve requirements regulations on the minimum amount of reserves that banks must hold against deposits (p. 223)

reserves deposits that banks have received but have not loaned out (p. 215)

S

sacrifice ratio the number of percentage points of one year's output lost in the process of reducing inflation by 1 percentage point (p. 407)

scarcity the limited nature of society's resources (p. 2)

shoeleather costs the resources wasted when inflation encourages people to reduce their money holdings (p. 245)

shortage a situation in which quantity demanded is greater than quantity supplied (p. 75)

small open economy an economy that trades goods and services with other economies and, by itself, has a negligible effect on world prices and interest rates (p. 279)

stagflation a period of falling output and rising prices (p. 341)

sterilization the process of offsetting foreign exchange market operations with open-market operations, so that the effect on the money supply is cancelled out (p. 223)

stock a claim to partial ownership in a firm (p. 156)

store of value an item that people can use to transfer purchasing power from the present to the future (p. 208)

strike the organized withdrawal of labour from a firm by a union (p. 196)

structural unemployment unemployment that results because the number of jobs available in some labour markets is insufficient to provide a job for everyone who wants one (p. 188)

substitutes two goods for which an increase in the price of one leads to an increase in the demand for the other (p. 68)

supply curve a graph of the relationship between the price of a good and the quantity supplied (p. 71)

supply schedule a table that shows the relationship between the price of a good and the quantity supplied (p. 70)

supply shock an event that directly alters firms' costs and prices, shifting the economy's aggregate-supply curve and thus the Phillips curve (p. 403)

surplus a situation in which quantity supplied is greater than quantity demanded (p. 75)

T

tariff a tax on goods produced abroad and sold domestically (p. 299)

technological knowledge society's understanding of the best ways to produce goods and services (p. 134)

theory of liquidity preference Keynes's theory that the interest rate adjusts to bring money supply and money demand into balance (p. 352)

trade balance the value of a nation's exports minus the value of its imports; also called *net exports* (p. 258)

trade deficit an excess of imports over exports (p. 258)

trade policy a government policy that directly influences the quantity of goods and services that a country imports or exports (p. 299)

trade surplus an excess of exports over imports (p. 258)

U

unemployment rate the percentage of the labour force that is unemployed (p. 181)

union a worker association that bargains with employers over wages and working conditions (p. 195)

unit of account the yardstick people use to post prices and record debts (p. 208)

V

velocity of money the rate at which money changes hands (p. 238)

vicious circle the cycle that results when deficits reduce the supply of loanable funds, increase interest rates, discourage investment, and result in slower economic growth; slower growth leads to lower tax revenue and higher spending on income-support programs, and the result can be even higher budget deficits (p. 170)

virtuous circle the cycle that results when surpluses increase the supply of loanable funds, reduce interest rates, stimulate investment, and result in faster economic growth; faster growth leads to higher tax revenue and lower spending on income-support programs, and the result can be even higher budget surpluses (p. 170)

INDEX

Note: Following a page number, "f" denotes a figure; "n" denotes a note; "t" denotes a table. Boldface page numbers denote defined terms.

D

E

F

G

H

I

N

O

P

Q

R